This is a volume in

THE UNIVERSITY OF MICHIGAN HISTORY OF THE MODERN WORLD

Upon completion, the series will consist of the following volumes:

The United States to 1865 *by Michael Kraus*

The United States since 1865 *by Foster Rhea Dulles*

Canada: A Modern History *by John Bartlet Brebner*

Latin America: A Modern History *by J. Fred Rippy*

Great Britain to 1688: A Modern History *by Maurice Ashley*

Great Britain since 1688: A Modern History *by K. B. Smellie*

France: A Modern History *by Albert Guérard*

Germany: A Modern History *by Marshall Dill, Jr.*

Italy: A Modern History *by Denis Mack Smith*

Russia and the Soviet Union: A Modern History *by Warren B. Walsh*

The Near East: A Modern History *by William Yale*

The Far East: A Modern History *by Nathaniel Peffer*

India: A Modern History *by Percival Spear*

The Southwest Pacific to 1900: A Modern History *by C. Hartley Grattan*

The Southwest Pacific since 1900: A Modern History *by C. Hartley Grattan*

Spain: A Modern History *by Rhea Marsh Smith*

Africa to 1875: A Modern History *by Robin Hallett*

Africa since 1875: A Modern History *by Robin Hallett*

Eastern Europe: A Modern History *by John Erickson*

CANADA

A Modern History

The University of Michigan History of the Modern World

Edited by Allan Nevins and Howard M. Ehrmann

CANADA

A Modern History

BY J. BARTLET BREBNER

NEW EDITION
REVISED AND ENLARGED BY DONALD C. MASTERS

Ann Arbor: The University of Michigan Press

Copyright © by The University of Michigan 1960, 1970
All rights reserved
SBN 472-07091-6
Library of Congress Catalog Card No. 72-107983
Published in the United States of America by
The University of Michigan Press and simultaneously
in Don Mills, Canada, by Longmans Canada Limited
Printed in the United States of America
by Vail-Ballou Press, Inc., Binghamton, N. Y.

FOR
ELLIOT

Preface

This story of Canada's development, independent of the expansive United States, has been written chiefly in the hope that it might interest and inform non-Canadians who have wondered how it happened and where Canada's strength came from. Canadian readers, also, may be curious enough about what their country's history looks like from the outside to consider the explanations that are offered here.

Nearly all of the immense amount of published Canadian history has been written primarily with Canadian readers in mind, which explains in part why so little of it is known abroad. Born in Canada, I had my interest first aroused by Canadian achievement during World War I and, although I have lived outside Canada for the most part since then, I have been active in investigating and writing its history. Naturally this book depends largely on the researches of hundreds of Canadian and other scholars. Although it is impossible in a volume of this sort to acknowledge those debts in detail, it is hoped that the Suggested Readings may serve as a guide to more intimate and immediate accounts of persons and performances than are practicable in a general history.

I have been especially fortunate in that Professors D. C. Masters of Bishop's University and Allan Nevins formerly of Columbia University read the first version of this book, bringing their knowledge and critical skill to bear upon it in most helpful ways. Their generosity was paralleled by Professor Mason Wade, who allowed me to read and borrow from *The French Canadians, 1760–1945* before its publication.

Foreword

Perhaps the most striking thing about Canada is that it is not part of the United States. Somehow more than half of North America has escaped being engulfed by its immensely more powerful neighbor although that neighbor has expanded fairly continuously in North America and elsewhere from 1776 to the present day. It might be thought that the United States never wanted Canada, but the record reveals two American attempts to conquer it by war, two quite threatening and prolonged encouragements of filibustering against Canada, and an intermittent barrage of annexationist invitations, threats, and other devices lasting almost two hundred years.

Perhaps, then, the answer has been that Great Britain prevented the United States from taking Canada? The Canadian would be quick to concede that most of his land had been defended, largely by Great Britain, during the War of American Independence and the War of 1812, but he would be likely to recall that, during and immediately after the American Civil War, British Conservatives and Liberals alike had lost their belief in the usefulness of defending Canada and were prepared to see it enter the United States if the Canadians wanted to go. When they made it plain that they did not, their action helped to revive an imperial sentiment in Great Britain which made Canada seem valuable and important again after a generation of obviously impatient British distaste.

Ever since Great Britain, the United States, and Canada settled their outstanding differences and attained their fundamental understanding at Washington in 1871, Canadian disinclination to enter the United States has been enough to puncture the various trial balloons of American annexationism which have been sent up from time to time. The three countries have been bound together by common economic advantage and common political ends. They have also been open to penetration by each others' investment, goods, and persons.

Men and women, money and goods, ideas and beliefs, have moved from one country to another with astonishing freedom in spite of tariffs, immigration quotas, and wars. Canadians have been willing to pay, in the form of a slightly lower standard of living, for the privilege of not being Americans, and Americans have shown that they respect that decision.

In general, however, since 1871 Canadian confidence must have been founded largely on Canadian strength, and the map of North America seems to indicate that Canadian strength rests on Canada's size. Nothing could be more misleading. Canada's size in relation to her population is one of her most serious problems. Her sixteen million people amount to about a tenth of the population of the slightly smaller United States. Practically all of them live within a hundred miles or so of the United States; in fact, thanks to the southward dip of the Great Lakes and the St. Lawrence River, about three-quarters live south of the forty-ninth parallel which forms the northern boundary of the United States from the Lake of the Woods to the Pacific.

In other words, most of Canada is almost uninhabited, or, to put it in another way, Canada has attracted and held a share of the population of North America roughly corresponding to her capacity to maintain for them a North American standard of life. Canada's thickly populated regions are rather more sharply separated from each other than they are from corresponding areas in the United States. The four Maritime Provinces are divided from each other by water and from Quebec by rough, low mountains. Quebec is divided from Ontario by language, cultural heritage, and religion. The Canadian Shield, a low rocky plateau of countless lakes, streams, and swamps, interposes over a thousand miles of wilderness between fertile southern Ontario and the high, short-grass plains west of Lake Winnipeg. Range after range of soaring, jagged cordilleran mountains pre-empt all except a few fertile valleys and a meager coastal shelf between the high plains and the Pacific. North of the separated fertile areas near the international boundary lie about three million almost uninhabited square miles of dwindling forest, arctic tundra, and the rock, snow, and ice of the Arctic Archipelago, crisscrossed with a faint web of communications by rail, water, and air.

Yet these sixteen million people and these millions of square miles have combined to make Canada an enormous producer for the world's markets, the sixth greatest trading nation in 1939 and the third or fourth during and since World War II. This abundant economy was founded upon prodigious production of staples like fish, fur, timber, and wheat, but since the first decade of the twentieth century manufacturing production has exceeded agriculture, and recently mining has also passed it. By 1940 the net value of manufactures alone exceeded the net value of all primary production. That is, during the generation since 1910 Canada has become one of the leading industrialized nations of the world as well as one of its mightiest primary producers. Canadians live well because they export about a third of what they produce, and import in proportion.

Who are the Canadians? Six out of seven are Canadian-born, but their origins are interesting and significant. The French stock is the oldest and amounts to about 31 per cent. The British Isles, either directly or through the United States, furnished about 48 per cent. Continental Europe provides practically all the rest, and these "New Canadians" move gradually into the English- rather than the French-speaking culture. Nonetheless the existence of a minority of three in ten, concentrated for the most part in one area of Canada, constitutes a test of national existence and action which groups Canada with Belgium and South Africa in the society of nations. In addition to formidable geographical divisions, Canada must accommodate herself to a profound cultural split. The French Canadians, menaced as they feel themselves to be not only by their English-speaking compatriots but by the much more powerful and pervasive civilization of the United States, cannot help being driven in on themselves to some extent. In their passionate desire to remain themselves they are capable of clinging to the traditional and the introspective at the cost of ignoring the very steps needed to meet changes in their environment.

Clearly Canada is an extraordinary country, a standing rebuke to the habit in Americans and Britons, her close partners, of taking her for granted. Many observers from outside have been trying to tell the world this for generations, but nearly all of them, for instance Walt Whitman and Rupert Brooke, have tried to do it on the basis of some travel, some conversation, and some contemporary analysis of cross sections. Canada will not yield her character to that kind of diagnosis. She has been a hard land to master, and has provided a generous way of living only at the price of centuries of adventure, originality, and hard work. The Canadian tradition and the aspirations that infuse modern Canadian literature and art can be understood only in the knowledge of how ten generations of European invaders (and their Indian predecessors) translated endless trial and error into health and strength.

Contents

MAPS

BOOK 1
THE FOUNDATIONS

CHAPTER I

Land and Aborigines

According to some highly tentative approximations made by geologists, sometime between two billion and five hundred million years ago Canada got her first enduring foundations, so to speak, when the Pre-Cambrian mountain-folding revolution heaved up from the earth's depths a huge mass to anchor northern and northeastern North America. Its remnants form the Canadian Shield of today. About three hundred million years ago the Caledonian revolution and about a hundred and fifty million years ago the Appalachian revolution reared up another series of great folds to form the eastern rim of the continent from Georgia to Newfoundland. About four million years ago the earth's last observable mountain-folding exploit, the Cainozoic revolution, raised a forbidding western rampart along the Americas almost from pole to pole.

At intervals of a little less than a hundred thousand years from the time that the mountains were thrown up, ice came down from the north to cover and scour the land before melting and retreating again. The expanse and thickness of the glaciers were great enough to push in the earth's skin so as to form inland seas, and the glaciers lowered the oceans by locking up much of their moisture in ice. Canada went through this process at least four times and probably more, the last visitation being about twenty-five thousand years ago. During the intervals between glaciations, when Canada was much warmer than now, rich subtropical vegetation and corresponding animal life extended northward well into what is now mainland Canada and their temperate equivalents invaded the Arctic Archipelago and Greenland.

It stands to reason that nature's sculpturing of Canada's torso vastly transcends anything that man has been able to do to it since. Instead, he has had to adjust himself and his ways to a variety of powerful environments, and naturally he has clustered more thickly in the various areas, amounting in all to less than a tenth of the whole, which he has found most congenial to settlement. Yet, since he has learned how to extract sustenance and even surpluses of various sorts from nearly all the other parts, it should be useful to have a general idea of the whole land as it was when he found it.

🍁 THE CANADIAN SHIELD

Its largest single feature was the Canadian (or Pre-Cambrian) Shield, for it comprised the northern and eastern two-thirds of Canada. Its backbone was a range of mountains along the Atlantic margin from Newfoundland to the northern end of Baffin Island. It included the Arctic Archipelago, and its outer boundary appeared on the Arctic mainland not far east of the Mackenzie Delta and swung in a southeastern curve to western Lake Superior. From Sault Ste Marie it skirted the northern shore of Lake Huron, cupped Georgian Bay to its southeastern corner, cut east to the St. Lawrence east of Kingston, and withdrew again to a point about a third of the way up the Ottawa River. From there it ran northeast to the St. Lawrence below Quebec and extended above the broadening river and gulf until it joined the mountain backbone again at the Strait of Belle Isle.

As was natural for the oldest and most battered portion of the earth's crust, the Shield was wrinkled and worn—a low, scarred plateau where all except a few of the ancient mountains had been ground down to rounded stumps, and where thousands of square miles were unmarked by elevations of as little as a hundred feet above prevailing levels. Soil was thin or lacking except in the enormous soggy lowlands on the western and southern sides of the Hudson and James bays and in the Clay Belt which ran east and west through the forest a little farther south. All the wrinkles and hollows of the Shield were filled with water —thousands of lakes, countless rivers and streams, and huge areas of muskeg swamp and soaking beaver meadows.

Except in winter, travel across it must be by canoe or light boat. The eastern and northern margin was girdled by the Atlantic and the Arctic; the western and southern by the earth's greatest series of enormous inland lakes. The vegetation varied, ranging from magnificent conifers along the southern margins to sparse evergreen forests and then to the clinging ground vegetation of the northern tundra, which flowered and fruited miraculously quickly during the brief summers of almost nightless days. The oceans yielded whales, seals, and fish. The fresh waters teemed with fish. Wild fowl were numerous. Across the land, animals from moose to mink and caribou to weasels grew winter furs of superb quality.

❧ ENTRIES FROM THE OCEANS

South and east of the Shield, the combined Caledonian and Appalachian ranges stretched northeast towards Newfoundland, forming a barrier between the Atlantic and the interior. These ranges contained many narrow valleys parallel to their trend until they reached a former sea fiord that served as valley for the Hudson River. Here the mass of the Adirondacks effected a kind of interruption, with the Mohawk Valley providing a corridor between it and the Appalachians from the Hudson to the Great Lakes Basin, and the Champlain Valley another to the St. Lawrence. Indeed, the great northeastern sweep of the St. Lawrence River into the Gulf seemed a kind of extension of the internal Appalachian trenches. The Gaspé Peninsula was a mountain finger pointing out into the Gulf towards Newfoundland, and the Maritime Provinces were like mountain plateaus and peaks with the seas lapping their sides and reaching into their valleys.

The St. Lawrence, in its trench between the Shield and the Appalachian barrier, was the great corridor from the Atlantic to the Great Lakes in the interior. Its western tributary, the Ottawa, reached up into the Shield to a point from which other streams and lakes provided a short cut to upper Lake Huron and Lake Superior. Actually the heights of land which divided the great basins of the interior—the Great Lakes, the Hudson Bay in the heart of the Shield, the Mississippi Valley, and the Mackenzie Valley—were so low that the St. Lawrence provided an avenue to almost any part of the continent if a man knew how to travel the waterways and was willing to carry his canoe and goods across the portages or could get others to do so. Much of the history of Canada was dominated by the St. Lawrence.

Yet it must be remembered that Canada's waterways were locked, or at best undependable, because of the winter's ice. The northern entry by Hudson Bay into the heart of the continent was closed for about eight months or so a year. The St. Lawrence was closed for about five months. The smaller lakes and rivers froze over fairly dependably, but the larger areas and more powerful currents broke up their covering in ways which made travel and transport difficult and dangerous. Canada's ice-free Atlantic ports were to be built at Saint John and Halifax, available to the rest of the country during the winter only after the railroad had conquered the intermediate mountainous wilderness.

The abrupt, glistening, eastern rampart of the Rocky Mountains that confronted the westward traveler up the Saskatchewan or the Peace, and the equally abrupt but wooded mountains that rose directly from the Pacific formed the last great land barriers of Canada to greet the European invaders. At their southern Canadian boundary they spread out for about six hundred miles in seven or eight ranges with narrow valleys and an ocean channel between them, but a little farther north a rough mountainous plateau or trough three to four hundred miles broad opened out between the soaring walls along the ocean and on the margin of the interior plain and extended all the way into Alaska. One swift, unnavigable river, the Fraser, drained the southern part of the plateau and the mountain walls through deep canyons; short, roaring streams drained the middle region through breaches eastward to the Mackenzie Basin or westward to the Pacific; and the Yukon flowed north through the center of Alaska into the Bering Sea.

Good soils, good climate, and good transportation were to decide where most men would live on this half-continent, but the surrounding oceans exerted two powerful influences as well. The gentle Atlantic slope projected out to sea in the form of a submerged continental shelf, marked by shallows or "banks," from New Jersey to the area southeast of Newfoundland. This shelf, combined with favorable conditions of temperature, salinity, and so forth, made the waters around Nova Scotia and Newfoundland and in the Gulf of St. Lawrence perhaps the greatest reservoir of edible fish in the world.

On the Pacific coast the abruptness of the mountains made the shelf narrower and its shallows smaller and fewer, but here again special conditions of temperature and current resulted in great concentrations of such sea fish as halibut, cod, and herring, and the salmon which migrate between fresh water and salt. There were Atlantic salmon in great abundance, but nothing to compare with the "silver hordes" which seemed almost to fill the Pacific rivers from bank to bank during their runs, sometimes of hundreds of miles, to spawning grounds in the interior.

🍁 FARMING REGIONS

The invaders from Europe found that there was little farming land in Newfoundland, but that Cape Breton would yield some crops and that Nova Scotia around the Bay of Fundy and along the Gulf coast provided fine arable land. Prince Edward Island was warm and generally fertile. New Brunswick contained the rich valley of the St. John, leading down to the Bay of Fundy, and the margin of the Gulf was also attractive. Westward of Chaleur Bay, the farming grew very thin indeed, little more than a modest adjunct to the fisheries, until broadening shelves of fertile lowlands opened up on both sides of the St. Lawrence near Quebec and up the Ottawa Valley to the Shield. A rocky bridge across the St. Lawrence almost joined the Shield to the Adirondacks near the outlet of Lake Ontario, but beyond it the large southern prong of Ontario was one of the most fertile and salubrious areas on earth. It still provides about half of Canada's agricultural wealth.

Yet there the promises seemed to end, for Canada had no counterpart to the American Middle West. The next great expanse of agricultural lands lay well to the west of Lake Superior. Some Canadians reached it by swinging south of the Lakes through the United States; others waited until a railway was daringly built across the Shield. All of them reached what was to become one of the earth's greatest granaries.

As might be expected, the first settlers came into the Pacific region from the west rather than from the east. They huddled on tiny shelves along the ocean and its fiords until the pursuit of minerals led them into the interior and to the discovery of mountain valleys, where they could raise marvelous fruit, and broader expanses of plateau, where they could grow grain and breed livestock. Yet even then the great apparatus of sea and river fisheries, of forest operations, of mining, and of farming assumed the form of thin, far-flung enterprises in an empty, mountainous land, and most of the inhabitants were concentrated at the warm southwest corner on the Pacific.

🍁 CLIMATIC FACTORS

In fact, climate plays such an enormous part everywhere in Canada, and Kipling's title, "Our Lady of the Snows," echoes in so many memories, that some corrective is needed for guesses which are based upon the mere arithmetic of high latitudes.

Most of inhabited Canada, except southernmost Ontario and the Pacific coast, has very cold winters, very hot summers, and rather long mixed periods in between. The coasts are much more moderate in their variations than the interior, but the Atlantic is cooled by its broad, open, northern margins, whereas the Pacific, almost closed at its northern end, is warmed by currents from the tropics. Thus the climate is harsh and unfriendly along the Atlantic shores of Newfoundland and Labrador, but soft and warm (and excessively rainy) along the Pacific coast.

It is the mid-continent which is the battleground between the hot and the cold, between the icebox of Hudson Bay and the Arctic and the humid kettle which simmers in the Gulf of Mexico and the tropics. The cordilleran ranges are so high that they dry out the warm, moist, west winds from the Pacific and deflect them towards the northwest in winter and towards the southwest in summer. The occasional warm mass of air which finds its way directly eastward over the ranges is known as a Chinook. The speed with which it can remove the snows has produced in Alberta folklore such tall tales as that of the man who raced his team and sleigh east from the foothills toward Calgary with the horses on snow and his rear sleigh-runners barely ahead of the emerging mud.

The main consideration in the western plainsmen's lives, however, is that the winds from over the mountains carry very little moisture. Contrary to general belief, the snows are seldom deep on the wind-swept prairie. The high plains in Canada are dry until they merge with the Shield and reach the central trough of the continent, where winds bring rain clouds from north and south into airy conflicts that water the lands. On the plains grows short grass; on the Shield, trees; and between them lies the park land with its mixture of meadows and forest.

Over the eastern half of the continent the Arctic wins in winter, sending winds circling south and east, but in summer winds fan out from the Gulf of Mexico almost to Hudson Bay to build up a vengeful trend towards the ice plateau of Greenland. Spring and fall yield now to the northern forces, now to the southern. The net result for Canada is that zones of equal temperatures east of the Rockies do not correspond to the parallels of latitude, but during the winter occur as a series of rough semicircles from the northeast and northwest around Hudson Bay. In summer the belts of equal temperature swing down southwest from Newfoundland, across New England to the Great Lakes, and then northwest across the plains to the Mackenzie Valley and down it to central Alaska. Along the Pacific coast from northern California to Alaska the relatively high mean temperatures fall only about one degree to each increasing degree of latitude.

🍁 THE ABORIGINES

Long before the Europeans reached North America, and still longer before they began to occupy Canada, it was peopled by aborigines whose skills in living in its various environments evidenced thousands of years of successes, successes from which the Europeans were to learn a great deal. Anthropologists are by no means yet in agreement about how many years the land had been inhabited, but studies of aboriginal languages from the Arctic to Tierra del Fuego have indicated extraordinary migrations and dispersions of distinct linguistic groups which must have taken ages to perform. Two things seemed clear. These people had come from Asia, and they had adapted themselves completely to scores of different American environments.

Even by studying their languages, we can only faintly reconstruct the uneasy adjustments of the aboriginal groups to each other before the coming of the white man. The picture which emerges is of a Canada for the most part sparsely peopled—less than a quarter of a million persons were scattered roughly in proportion to the wild life available for food, except along the St. Lawrence and in southern Ontario where a modest agriculture was practiced. Probably the greatest concentration of population was along the coasts and salmon rivers of British Columbia. Everywhere seasonal opportunities and needs for food brought different groups together, usually in conflict, but occasionally in intricately ceremonialized trade. Sometimes the strong overcame and enslaved the weak; sometimes the privileged grew slothful and soft enough to be conquered by hungrier neighbors.

The treeless tundra, for instance, was contested by Eskimos along the salt water and hunting Indians from the dwindling forests. The Eskimos based their seaside lives chiefly on fish, waterfowl, and sea mammals, using driftwood and bones for the frames of houses, sleds and boats, and for some tools; blubber and oil for winter fuel; and skins for clothing, shelter, and boats. Some of them built domed snow-houses in winter. The Indians of the marginal woods lived on fish, birds, and land animals, using wood for their wigwams, fuel, and some tools, and skins for clothing and shelter. They acquired from more southern regions the tiny light canoes which they sometimes navigated and sometimes carried on their backs. The chief prize in contests between them and the Eskimos was the chance to slaughter caribou, usually at fording places on the rivers where those animals packed together in helpless thousands during their annual, if somewhat unpredictable, migrations across the barrens.

Within the northern conifer forest, a broad belt circling the Canadian north from the mouth of the St. Lawrence to the mouth of the Mackenzie, the Indian groups seem to have centered upon desirable river valleys or lake basins that provided easily defined fishing and hunting regions. This was the world of skillfully built birch-bark canoes, of bark wigwams, and of snowshoes and toboggans. If there was plenty of game, it was widely scattered, hard to kill with wooden bows and traps, and subject both to seasonal fluctuations and to unaccountable cycles of abundance and scarcity. Even when surpluses could be accumulated, it was almost impossible to cure and cache them securely from equally hungry foxes and powerful bears and wolverines.

All in all, it was a land where life was fitfully nomadic and hard. Barter of an involved sort went on, and war was a curiously formalized game for status and prestige in which the greatest bravery was displayed after capture in a grim, but almost stately, progress through the most ingenious tortures to death.

It was not until the conifers made way for the deciduous trees of the park lands along the southern margin of the Shield that the forest was supplemented by the farm. The transition was from the soft, small berries of the tundra and the Shield to wild rice and nuts, and from them to small clearings where corn, beans, sunflowers, gourds, and tobacco were grown until the soil was exhausted, or sanitary considerations or dearth of firewood dictated the removal of a village. Such semisedentary settlements could be found in Nova Scotia, Prince Edward Island, and New Brunswick, along the upper St. Lawrence and lower Ottawa, and in southern Ontario.

Yet even they were not large assemblages, for these Indians were not good farmers and their lives were interrupted by hunting animals and wild fowl, by seasonal fishing, and by wars. They built semipermanent houses of wood and bark; they could weave bags and baskets and make rough pottery. The best-situated groups, like the Hurons, even organized exchanges of commodities among other tribes; the Hurons as middlemen became "rich" while others slaved to acquire trading surpluses of products such as furs, skins, tobacco, or wampum.

In the West the park lands lay between the conifers and the short-grass plains, those dry steppes across which thousands of buffalo migrated. Here the semisedentary marginal agriculture seems to have been almost lacking and the transition from forest to plains life relatively sudden. Here snows and rains were light and winds were unimpeded.

We know almost nothing about the plains before the advent of the horse. Most of life depended on the buffalo which, with modest supplements from other animals and birds, fed, clothed, housed, and even, by its dried dung, provided fuel for man. There was little or no attempt to cultivate food plants, but meat was dried and pounded, mixed with fat and berries, and stored in skin bags (pemmican). Shortly after 1700, when horses were introduced from the Spanish settlements, life became so much easier that during the winter of 1754–55, when Anthony Henday first reached the Blackfeet and tried to induce them to go down to Hudson Bay to trade, they (and he) could see no reason whatever for changing their ways.

Yet here, too, life was uneasy and violent, and the number of inhabitants was small. The plains tribes tried to keep control over definable areas of advantage—ponds and constant streams, patches of trees, good pasturage, sheltered coulees, buffalo wallows, fords and watering places to which animals resorted, and so on. In order to hold these places and their valuable bands of horses against other plains tribes they had to be ready to fight. In addition, raiding groups from the mountains and the forests, who were driven by need and greed to try to share in nature's bounty on the plains, could not always be satisfied merely by barter or by an occasionally conceded chance at the buffalo herds.

West of the Rockies lay the great inner cordilleran plateau, relatively dry and walled in by lofty mountains east and west. The passes to the east were high (3700 to 7100 feet) and difficult, except in the most favorable seasons; those to the coast were lower, but precipitous. Yet two great rivers, the Columbia and the Fraser, with their tributaries each year brought into this mountain-locked area a harvest from the ocean in the form of the massive runs of salmon on their way to lakes and shallows where they might spawn. These fish could be easily taken in vast quantities by spear, net, or trap, and their flesh, when dried and pounded, could be stored as reserves for the rest of the year.

When one adds abundant game and wild fowl and large supplies of edible roots, it can be seen that the plateau could maintain relatively great numbers of Indians in superior comfort. They built permanent, large, *A*-shaped, multifamily residences constructed of pole framework and covered by bark or mats; these were clustered at jealously guarded vantage points along the rivers. Their wars were in the long run largely due to the pressure on the lower valleys of the great rivers from the less privileged tribes deeper in the interior and farther off in the colder north.

The coast provided the richest, most dependable life for Indians in all Canada. Large fish like halibut and cod, great schools of oolakan from which oil could be made, sea lions, seals, and whales, and above all the salmon encouraged human life. Fittingly enough, the rainy, lowering Pacific coast reared the most accomplished, stratified, and sophisticated societies, the most subtle artists and accomplished craftsmen, and the gloomiest religion. Since the area was so desirable, pressures on it from the less privileged seem to have been continuous. Because the solidly wooded coasts were so precipitous and the salmon streams so valuable, the tribal villages were scattered. Yet each individual village was tightly knit, usually huddled in the narrow confines where the rivers entered the ocean but occasionally extended along low stretches of shore or on islands which afforded some protection from surprise. The natives raided and fought each other and made slavery an important institution in their societies. Their poetry mirrored the pessimism, the rank violence, the sharp social gradations, and the cruel glory of their lives.

Next to the salmon in importance was the cedar. It towered tall and straight, was light and fine grained, and was easy to split and work. Its bark could be shredded, spun, and woven. From it the Indians built magnificent community houses of large timbers, fitted beams, plank walls, and board roofs, sometimes several hundred feet long, twenty or twenty-five feet high, and fifty to sixty feet wide. They also built beautiful sea-going dugouts up to seventy feet long which they paddled on war forays, on whale, otter, sea lion, and seal hunts, and on fishing expeditions for halibut and other food fish.

The Indians possessed elaborate garments and headgear. In addition to such fine furs as sea otter and seal, they wove bark, dog's hair, and wild sheep or goat hair into cloth which was decorated with conventionalized representations of animals. Their baskets, boxes, ceremonial masks, and houses were carved and painted in the same way. Their most spectacular ceremony was the potlatch, the distribution by an individual of the largest possible amount of property for the sake of status. Since it obligated the recipients very precisely, the potlatch system amounted to loans and exchanges which taxed memories and strained relationships.

Perhaps the greatest of these coast-dwellers were the Haidas of the Queen Charlotte Islands, arrogant seafarers who lorded it in long raids to Vancouver Island or the mainland and who exulted in their mastery of island fortresses out in the Pacific in the center of the halibut fisheries. Their precise, fluent stone-carving in argillite challenges comparison today.

The European penetration of Canada would have been a slow, faltering business without the aborigines, for they knew how to live off the country and the white man emphatically did not. They guided and maintained him, showing him the waterways and trails and teaching him what he could learn of their arts of fishing and hunting. Their canoes, of birch and spruce and elm bark, carried him, as did their snowshoes and toboggans. Their garments and moccasins clothed him. He took over their corn, beans, edible gourds, and tobacco. Their pemmican and dried fish made possible his longest journeys and his most extended lines of trade.

In return he brought them axes and knives, metal pots, guns, powder, and lead, but these miraculous substitutes for their own equipment enslaved them by dependence. Moreover, the new tools and weapons were devoted to satisfying a foreign appetite for furs which far outran natural reproduction. Alcoholic drinks proved practically irresistible and wrought fearful havoc. Even more devastating were the white man's diseases—smallpox, measles, typhus, tuberculosis, influenza, and venereal diseases. Worst of all, the European culture destroyed the aboriginal, casting the Indians adrift, robbing them of their standards and codes, stripping them of all dignity and sense of worth. And not even the most devoted Christian missionaries could build a bridge between the Indians' lost world and the new one. The first inhabitants of Canada paid a high price for their so-called backwardness.

CHAPTER II

Europe Repelled (900-1600)

It has always been a difficult business to get from Europe to North America, even in days of travel by air. The North Atlantic is broad and open to the ice and cold of the Arctic, and the prevailing winds are from west to east. The Arctic ice pack advances and retreats, the Greenland glaciers and others calve icebergs, and the Labrador current brings icy waters and islands of ice down the North American coast from the mouths of the northern straits. Navigation meets perils also in the submarine Continental Shelf projecting from Iceland, Greenland, and North America, particularly off Labrador, Newfoundland, and Nova Scotia, where islets and shoals loom up from the depths. Sable Island, a graveyard for ships ninety miles off Nova Scotia, is the dry top of a long undersea ridge. The Atlantic shores from Iceland to Cape Cod are for the most part rough and rocky, and often scantily clothed with vegetation.

THE SCANDINAVIANS

Naturally enough, the Scandinavians were the first to work their way across. We know from their sagas that they were bold sailors, fishermen, and hunters along the margins of the ice pack. Pushed outwards from their own lands by various forces, they planted themselves in the British Isles, the Shetlands, the Orkneys, Iceland, and Greenland. In southwest Greenland they managed to maintain themselves for about five hundred years (approximately 990–1500), and from that base they launched expeditions to the North American mainland.

They left no abiding impression on the development of Canada, but the failure of their enterprises indicates the basic problem to be solved. It was possible for determined Europeans to reach Canada, but if they were to remain, they must be resolutely sustained by Europe until they could produce surpluses of goods which would make the continuing adventure mutually profitable. The Scandinavians failed in this, and the record of their North American enterprises did not find its way into the body of general European knowledge.

THE MAGNET OF THE FAR EAST

The truth was that the rest of Europe was much more interested in the Far East, because it was from that little-known region that there came trickles of luxuries by long and involved sea and land routes out of China, the East Indies, India, and Persia. While it could hardly be argued that the West *needed* the gold and jewels, silks and spices of the East, yet spices were more agreeable than mere salt in the preservation and preparation of foods, jewels and silks were coveted, and a Europe which produced little gold and silver itself tended to be drained of bullion by its very greed for the rarities which were for sale in the Levant. The few bold and lucky Europeans who had reached the East by overland routes spoke of its opulence in paradisal terms (which grew in the telling), partly because the travelers were taken to courts and capitals and partly because they journeyed only in imagination to farthest Japan, where "the roofs were made of gold."

In the European merchant's view there were two basic problems to be solved. In the first place, if he could somehow establish direct contact with the sources of these goods, he knew that he could obtain them for a fraction of their Levantine price. He was less urgently aware of the second problem—Europe's dearth of bullion—but in a practical way he knew that he could make money on both sides of the transaction if he could sell European goods where he bought Eastern. Unfortunately Europe produced little that the tropical East wanted. Until Europe could find either more bullion or markets where her homely staple products could be sold for bullion, her supply of Eastern products must be limited. It could be increased somewhat by any man who could find a direct route to the East and thereby reduce costs.

Most of the energy and enterprise which Europe had to spare for trading adventure beyond the Mediterranean and the Atlantic coast during the thirteenth, fourteenth, and fifteenth centuries went into daring efforts to cross the land barrier of the Middle East through the Black Sea, or the Red Sea (by way of Egypt and Abyssinia), or to find a route through or round Africa by feeling out the way down its west coast. The latter enterprise, promoted by the Portuguese, an Atlantic people, may be said to have opened a great chapter in the earth's history during which mastery of ocean navigation exposed the whole globe to European exploitation. At last the Atlantic peoples were to move from the back of the top gallery in the world theater to occupy the center of the stage.

We do not know much about the kind of mariners' gossip which went on in the taverns of Europe's ports during the fifteenth century, but we know enough to be sure that a new idea was working like yeast in about 1475. Since no one had managed to locate and maintain an inexpensive route to the East across the Middle East, and since the Portuguese had spent fifty years in almost unremunerative efforts to reach the bottom of Africa, why not sail westward out into the Atlantic on the latitude of Japan? Or, if that was too daring, because of the possible space of open sea, why not build upon the knowledge which the Portuguese and the English had accumulated in their Azores-Lisbon-Bristol-Iceland trade and strike west from Iceland? The Italians, the most skillful navigators in Europe, thought enough of these ideas to try to promote them in Portugal, Spain, and England. One Genoese, whom we know as Christopher Columbus, got Spanish backing for the first plan in 1492; another, whom we know as John Cabot, got English backing for the second plan in 1497.

Columbus came upon the Bahamas lying athwart his ocean line for Japan, turned southwest, and entered the garden region of the West Indies, the Gulf of Mexico, and the Caribbean Sea. "Always the land was of the same beauty," he wrote, "and the fields very green and full of an infinity of fruits, red as scarlet, and everywhere there was the perfume of flowers and the singing of birds, very sweet." He and the swarms of adventurers who followed him were lucky enough to find at once both gold and pearls in sufficient abundance to make transatlantic voyaging and settlement profitable.

And then in Central America, Mexico, and Peru, the Spaniards came upon and conquered opulent urban civilizations whose treasures of silver and gold they seized. Finally, they forced the American natives to work the mines and produce a huge flow of bullion. The rest of Europe either envied, with Christopher Marlowe:

> . . . the golden fleece
> That yearly stuffs old Philip's treasury

or did its best to intercept some of it by raids, by trade, or by piracy.

Far different was the luck of John Cabot and his successors in the north. The Bristol merchants outfitted him with a tiny bark, named the "Matthew," and a company of seventeen; King Henry VII gave him letters patent for the discovery of "whatsoever islands . . . which before this time were unknown to all Christians." The expedition, which set sail on May 2, 1497, reached North America (probably near the southwest corner of Newfoundland, possibly near the northern tip of Cape Breton Island, or less possibly on the Labrador coast), on

June 24. After a little coasting along those forbidding shores, they hurried home with the news that they had reached northeastern Asia, with Japan awaiting them to the south and west. They had found no gold, no inviting lands, no imperial cities. The rare natives whom they encountered were primitive folk, useful only as slaves.

Now the English had their "Great Admiral" to rival Columbus, "the Admiral of the Ocean Sea." "Vast honour is paid to him and he goes dressed in silk, and these English run after him like mad." That cautious king, Henry VII, gave him £10 and an annuity of £20 from the customs receipts of Bristol. Six ships loaded with merchandise set out for new-found Asia the following May.

🍁 A CENTURY OF DISAPPOINTMENTS

At this point the inquirer enters on uncertainty about what Europeans were doing for over a century along the North Atlantic coast of North America—a startling contrast to the abundance that is known about Spanish activities farther south. The situation was neatly explained by Peter Martyr of Anghiera, an Italian at the Court of Spain who had been considering reports received about how similar to Europe the regions north of Florida were. "But what need have we of what is found everywhere in Europe? It is towards the south, not towards the frozen north, that those who seek fortune should bend their way; for everything at the equator is rich."

Why then did Europeans keep pegging away at the northern regions? No one knew positively whether the Americas formed a single land mass from the Antarctic to the Arctic or were a group of islands. No one knew how broad they were. The voyage round Cape Horn and across the Pacific begun by Magellan in 1519 made it seem likely that the broad Pacific lay between North America and Asia; but perhaps North America was a kind of appendage of northeastern Asia, a region which no European had seen or even heard about.

The three possibilities of the northern American regions which led hardheaded European merchants and monarchs during the sixteenth century to spend the great sums which exploration required were: (a) the hope that there was a passage to the Pacific through northern North America; (b) the possibility that it contained rich kingdoms like Mexico and Peru; and (c) the hope that there was a northern passage around it. The pope had awarded the southern passage around Africa to Portugal, and the southern American passage to Spain.

One must have voyaged along the American shores of the North Atlantic to be able to grasp even faintly the endless labors and endurance which went into the revelation of their character. The marvel is that men could be found to keep at it for a century and a half, until men's hopes of a North American passage to Asia were dashed.

The records of failure have a way of being lost and forgotten, and in addition this was a period when European nations jealously guarded their special knowledge. We know little or nothing for certain about John Cabot's second voyage, partly for these reasons and partly because later his son Sebastian had a way of blending what he knew and what he wanted others to believe in order to further ends of his own. At any rate, England's hopes were temporarily crushed.

It is certain, however, that Portugal took up the work in 1499, using the Azorians who had been in the Bristol-Iceland trade, and sometimes in co-operation with the Bristol merchants. They seem to have probed the coast from Greenland to Maine and to have entered both the Gulf of St. Lawrence and the Bay of Fundy, but much of their knowledge died with them since the losses of men and ships were appalling. Fifty years later the king of Portugal reported that he and his father had each lost two fleets in the region and that it promised nothing. Sebastian Cabot almost certainly made a voyage for England in 1509, but his report aroused so little response that he went over to Spain in 1512, during the obsession with Central America and Mexico.

Active interest in the north apparently revived about 1520. Portugal sent out Fagundes to explore the vicinity of Cape Breton and Nova Scotia. France sent out Verrazano in 1523 and 1524. He reported that he had, in 1524, explored the coast between latitude 34° (Cape Fear) and latitude 50° (possibly 54°, Labrador), beyond which he said the Portuguese had established continuous mainland. He found New York harbor and Narragansett Bay, and thought he saw the Pacific across a narrow sandy spit of land somewhere south of the Hudson, about 37°. Next year Gómez, a Portuguese in the service of Spain, surveyed the whole coast from Nova Scotia to the Caribbean so much more thoroughly that he disposed of Verrazano's Pacific, indeed of any territorial interest north of the West Indies, so far as Spain was concerned. Yet France, England, the Low Countries, and Scandinavia cherished Verrazano's Pacific myth for another eighty years because they wanted so much to believe in it.

At this time, however, we begin to find substantial hints of interest in an area that was at last rewarding adventurers from Europe—the great fisheries on the Atlantic banks and inside the Gulf of St. Lawrence. Fishermen are such close-mouthed men about their fishing grounds that no explicit record can be put together, but there are records of northern explorers happening on fishing vessels or being rescued by them. John Cabot had reported that the sea was "swarming with fish, which can be taken not only with the net, but in baskets let down with a stone." Sebastian Cabot, who was with reason suspected of being a decorative liar on occasion, told Peter Martyr that "great fish like tunnies" were packed so thickly "that at times they even stayed the passage of his ships."

Perhaps before the Cabots, therefore, and certainly thereafter, European fishermen began to make the voyages to the banks and shores of the North Atlantic which they have been making ever since. They were not settlers or invaders, but, ironically enough, they were soon to be harvesting greater wealth each year than came from the mines of precious metals in Spanish America.

THE FAILURES OF CARTIER

It seems practically certain that one of Verrazano's company in 1524 was a skilled navigator and remarkable pilot from St. Malo named Jacques Cartier. Ten years later he moved to the center of the Canadian stage for eight or nine years, during which he lost a very expensive gamble for France.

On April 20, 1534, Cartier set out from his home port in behalf of Francis I with two sixty-ton ships and sixty-one men "to the New lands to discover certain islands and countries where it is said that he should find great quantity of gold and other valuable things." His clear and detailed account of this voyage indicates that he hoped to find a passage either through or around North America, or, if the new land was Asia, deep enough into its interior to furnish access to Cathay. It also seemed possible that what he knew as the Great Bay inside the Straits of Belle Isle might lead him by a back door, as it were, to unspoiled American kingdoms like Mexico or Peru before the Spaniards got there from the Caribbean or the Gulf of Mexico.

The abundance of excellent evidence about Cartier's activities from 1534 to 1542, following the mere fragments concerning earlier men, is an almost irresistible temptation to exaggerate the value of what he did. The fact is, however, that he failed so completely that it was not until 1608 that France found dubious, but completely new, justification for attempting to occupy the region which he explored and claimed for Francis I. Yet the nature of his failure should be indicated.

He sailed confidently and quickly across the Atlantic and into the Straits of Belle Isle between Newfoundland and Labrador. Turning south at the end of May, 1534, from the forbidding region that he believed must be "the land God gave to Cain," he skirted western Newfoundland and the Magdalen Islands on a course which took him past Prince Edward Island to the western shore of the Gulf of St.

Lawrence. He was delighted with the fruitfulness of the land and the hot summer climate, but his hopes were dashed when the shores of Chaleur Bay narrowed to a close.

Sailing east and north, he somehow missed the main channel of the St. Lawrence River, swung round the eastern end of Anticosti Island, and worked his way against adverse currents to its western end. It was now August. He went back to France the way he came, apparently not knowing Newfoundland to be an island. He could report rich fisheries; abundance of seafowl, whales, seals, and walruses; fertile lands; and fine timber; all in an attractive temperate climate inside the weather-bulwark of Newfoundland. But he had clearly entered a river mouth instead of a sea strait to Asia.

When Francis I sent him back next year, there seemed to be three profitable possibilities. First, there might be a sea strait to Asia somewhere along the north shore of the Gulf. Cartier spent the first part of his voyage in a most laborious, if vain, investigation of that hope. Second, the great river west of Anticosti might lead deep into Asia, if this was a projection of Asia, or nearly across America, if an America lay between Europe and Asia. Third, the friendly Huron-Iroquois Indians who had clamored for European goods when his ship had been in Miramichi and Chaleur bays in 1534, and two of whom Cartier had taken back to France, were summer visitors from the great river. They reported the existence of three kingdoms in the interior: Saguenay, north of the river of that name; Stadacona (from which they came), near modern Quebec; and Hochelaga, near modern Montreal. All Europe was afire with reports of the American kingdoms which Spain was then looting. It seemed that France's turn had come in the north.

Cartier got into the river during the rich harvest of September, found Stadacona merely a Huron-Iroquois village below the natural fortress at Quebec, and with difficulty broke through the determined efforts of its inhabitants to monopolize European bounty for themselves. In the bark "Emérillon" and two longboats, the Frenchmen pushed on south-westerly to reach Hochelaga on October 2nd. This triple-palisaded town, set among cultivated fields, was distinctly impressive with its fifty Iroquois long houses, each well over a hundred feet long and thirty or more wide. Its inhabitants received them as healing gods. Behind it rose Mont Royal and the promise of viewing the country beyond.

The view, however, flatly discouraged their immediate hopes. The great river extended southwest as far as they could see, but it was barred by impassable rapids. Another great river, the Ottawa, joined it from the west, but besides swelling the neighboring rapids, it had others of its own. At Hochelaga, a thousand miles from the Atlantic, there was no "passage to the other southern ocean." The baffled Cartier hurried back to set up winter quarters at the "capital" of the "kingdom" of Stadacona.

The first European wintering was, of course, an appalling experience in that climate, and the Indians in their greed seemed unpredictable, dangerous neighbors. Some of them wanted to capture the Frenchmen for the sake of their miraculous goods and skills. Yet Cartier's previous success in taking two Stadacona Indians to Europe and back stood him in good stead. For one thing, they taught him how to cure scurvy by infusing conifer leaves and bark, and for another they gave him some idea of what was going on in the Indians' minds. At any rate, the Frenchmen came through the winter, launched and prepared their ships, and sailed for France early in May carrying with them Donnacona, the local chief whom they had kidnapped instead of being kidnapped by him. This time they knew enough to go home through the Cabot Strait south of Newfoundland.

Five years later Cartier came back again, as second in command of a much more imposing and expensive expedition. Considering his now extensive knowledge of the St. Lawrence region and its lack of any quickly realizable wealth, what can he and his debt-ridden king have expected to find which would justify such extraordinary expenditures?

The Frenchmen came back to find the mythical kingdom of Saguenay, created in glowing colors by the interplay between their own eager imaginations and the shrewd responses of a homesick Donnacona. Before he died in France, that Indian had adorned Saguenay with everything which Frenchmen coveted or Spaniards had looted from Mexico and Peru. Indeed his picture of towns crowded with woolen-clad, white-complexioned citizens who possessed "great store of gold and copper" and "immense quantities of gold, rubies and other rich things" sounded more like fabled Asia than new-found America. A month's travel by canoe from Canada, he said, he had found oranges, cinnamon, and cloves growing. In spite of his tales of pygmies, "men who fly," men who "have only one leg," and others who "never eat nor digest," Francis I and Cartier decided that he had "never ceased travelling about the country by river, stream and trail since his earliest recollections."

Their conviction that Saguenay must be the "outer limit of Asia" leaked out and so greatly agitated Emperor Charles V that he would have combined the Spanish and Portuguese fleets to smash the French enterprise had he been able to rally them in defense of the monopoly in the Western Hemisphere which the pope had awarded to Spain. Francis I laughed at the emperor's ambassadors and said "he much desired to see Adam's will to learn how he had partitioned the world."

The expedition was to consist of ten ships provisioned for two years,

400 sailors, 300 soldiers, materials for eighteen or twenty small gun-boats, and a company of artisans, women, and livestock calculated to colonize Canada (Stadacona). The colony was to serve as a base for the conquest of Saguenay. Cartier went off with five ships and set up his headquarters at Cap Rouge, nine miles up river from Quebec, in the autumn of 1541. The Sieur de Roberval, his superior, was de-layed by indulging in some privateering or piracy in the Channel and did not reach Canada until the summer of 1542. The surviving records of this venture are scanty, doubtless because it came to nothing.

Cartier had actually set out for home in the spring of 1542 before Roberval arrived. He had gone up to Hochelaga again only to find that it had been moved, Indian-fashion, to a new site. Investigation of the St. Lawrence and Ottawa rapids seems to have convinced him that it was impracticable to carry the materials and armaments for the gunboats for assembly beyond them.

Perhaps, belatedly, he realized that he had been hoodwinked by Donnacona, and in any case he had become greatly excited over what appeared to be the incalculable riches of the mineral formations in the Canadian Shield at Cap Rouge. Certainly that mixture of ancient rocks provided dazzling variety in its quartzes, micas, "fool's gold" (iron pyrites), and corundum crystals. The Frenchmen's wishful imagina-tions did the rest. They believed they had discovered (to quote an English report on their finds) "a goodly Myne of the best yron in the world," "certaine leaves of fine gold as thick as a man's nayle," "veines of mynerall matter, which shewe like gold and silver," and "stones like Diamants, the most faire, pollished and excellently cut that it is pos-sible for a man to see."

Loaded with many barrels of worthless Pre-Cambrian rock, Cartier's ships met Roberval's at what is now St. John's, Newfoundland, in June. Some of the ore was tried in a furnace and seemed to yield gold. When Cartier reported that he was leaving the St. Lawrence because the Indians had become dangerously menacing, Roberval commanded him to return and fight it out, but Cartier's company sneaked away the next night to report their marvelous discovery to the king. Roberval went on to winter at Cap Rouge, explored the Saguenay River gorge, and at least planned to push on beyond the Lachine Rapids of the St. Lawrence in 1543, but all we know is that after some trouble with mutinous colonists he and they were back in France that autumn.

Interestingly enough, Spain too had just then become disillusioned about the interior of North America. During the previous five years three very costly expeditions had ranged the southern part of the continent as far north as the Ohio and the Missouri rivers in vain searches for

kingdoms, gold, and jewels, and the Pacific coast up to latitude 42°
or 43° in an equally vain quest of a strait leading to the Atlantic.

On his return to France, Roberval's chief pilot, Jean Fonteneau (also
called Alfonse de Saintonge), who knew something of Spain's past
triumphs and continuing dreams, tried in vain to rouse France to
further action by linking New France to New Spain and both to Asia.
"The lands running towards Hochelaga are much better and warmer
than those of Canada," he wrote, "and this land of Hochelaga extends
to Figuier [Yucatán] and to Peru, where gold and silver abound. Mark,
too, that the inhabitants say that in a city called Cebola [somewhere in
the Southwest] . . . the houses are all covered with gold and silver
and equipped with vessels of gold and silver. These lands are attached
to Tartary, and I think that they form the outer limit of Asia, reckoning
from the roundness of the earth."

Despite that plea, the curtain had fallen for a long entr'acte in the
drama of French colonization and conquest in the St. Lawrence area.
Cartier and Roberval had failed to plant Europe in northern North
America as utterly as the Scandinavians had failed five hundred years
before. Until northern North America could be made to yield profits,
indeed larger profits for equal effort than at home, the region would
be left to its aboriginal inhabitants. Thus almost fifty years of daring
enterprise, 1497–1543, were to be followed by over sixty years, two
full generations, of abandonment before France felt impelled to occupy
the great avenue into North America which Cartier had explored and
claimed for his king.

🍁 PROBINGS FOR A NORTHWEST PASSAGE

One activity that continued to bring Europeans at least to the shores
of North America was the search for a northwest passage which went
on intermittently from 1576 to 1632. These astounding enterprises, in
which men gambled tiny, if sturdy, ships against ice floes and icebergs,
roaring winds and racing currents, treacherous shores and shrouding
fogs, were carried on chiefly by Englishmen, with occasional ventures
by the Danes. Meanwhile the Dutch and the English were also trying
to locate a northeast passage. These northern routes to potential northern
markets in Asia were attractive to the English partly because of their
shortness, but largely because, as their great promoter of overseas enterprise, Richard Hakluyt, explained: "Our chiefe desire is to find out
ample vent of our wollen cloth (the naturall commoditie of this our
realme)."

The idea of a northern passage was an old one. In 1527 Robert
Thorne had written: "If I had faculty to my will, it should be the first

thing that I would understand, even to attempt, if our seas northward be navigable to the Pole, or no." No shorter route to Tartary could be imagined. Sebastian Cabot claimed that in 1509 he had sailed west about latitude 67° (which would be halfway up Baffin Island), "and finding the sea open and without any obstacle, he firmly believed that by that way he could pass towards Eastern Cathay," but was compelled by mutiny to turn back. Contemporary Portuguese maps indicate the same belief. Sir Humphrey Gilbert, a shareholder in the English Muscovy Company, systematically agitated the idea in a *Discourse* which he published in 1566, and ten years later Martin Frobisher took up the task in behalf of Michael Lok, a London merchant.

Frobisher's three daring expeditions of 1576, 1577, and 1578 yielded little knowledge because, in the first place, he landed in the dead end of the bay named after him instead of in Hudson Strait, just to the south, and in the second, he happened on some worthless mineral there (probably iron pyrites) which his backers insisted on having mined for the gold which they expected to smelt from it in England.

During the years just before the Armada, John Davis made another series of three voyages between Greenland and the Arctic Archipelago without finding a break to the westward, but he did notice what he named the "Furious Overfall" at the mouth of Hudson Strait where the mighty currents out of the Western Arctic clashed with the Atlantic. The English East India Company picked up that tip in 1602 and sent out George Waymouth in the "Discovery" to investigate it, but his company mutinied in those eerie waters and he had to turn back after penetrating for a hundred leagues.

The man who apparently found the passage at the cost of his life was Henry Hudson, a Londoner who served Dutch and English interests and who made an undying reputation during four years (1607–11) in spite of quite marked incapacities in his chosen career. He failed to sail across the Pole to the East in 1607, and to make the Northeast Passage in 1608. In 1609, when his men mutinied near Novaya Zemlya, they agreed to cross the Atlantic to look for "a sea leading to the western ocean" which Captain John Smith of Virginia, echoing Verrazano's report of 1524, believed to be about latitude 40°. This expedition happened upon the fiord of the Hudson River and explored it.

In 1609, Hudson's men had declined a second alternative which he offered them, but an English merchant syndicate thought otherwise and in April, 1610, sent him off in Waymouth's "Discovery" to "try if, through any of these inlets which Davis saw, but durst not enter, any passage might be found to the other ocean called the South Sea."

He entered his Strait on June 25, 1610, and somehow drove his mutinous crew for almost seven weeks of terrifying navigation until August 3, when his surviving journal breaks off with the words: "Then I observed and found the ship at noone in 61 degrees, 20 minutes, and a sea to the westwards." He had reached the bay that commemorates him. Turning south past the rocky, forbidding islands along the eastern shore, he ended up in the bottle of James Bay, where he beached the "Discovery" and spent a dreadful winter.

Apparently his determination to explore westwards in 1611 sealed his fate. His men mutinied, cast off him, his son, and six others in a shallop, and sailed the "Discovery" towards home. The ship and eight survivors were rescued off Ireland and the news they brought was valuable enough to save their lives. No one knows what happened to Hudson and his loyal companions.

During the next twenty years a series of bold and costly attempts was made to sail westward from Hudson Bay. The record of these amazing adventures was carefully compiled in euphuistic prose by the literary mariner, Luke "Northwest" Foxe. One of the narratives furnished the raw material for Coleridge's *Rime of the Ancient Mariner*. One expedition, that of Jens Munck and a mixed Danish and English group of sixty-five men and two ships, after wintering, 1619–20, at the mouth of the Churchill, had only three survivors. Yet when the effort died away in 1632, and Hudson Bay was abandoned for another thirty-six years, it was because the most thorough searching, even into Roe's Welcome beyond Southampton Island and through Foxe Channel into Foxe Basin, revealed no passage to the West.

In the meantime the oldest successful European enterprise in northern North America, the fisheries which went on so quietly and inconspicuously, growing from year to year, had gradually generated a secondary enterprise which was at last to plant Europeans in the regions which had repelled them for seven hundred years.

CHAPTER III

Europe Strikes Roots (1600-1663)

The progression from fishing to fur trading to settlement was a direct
one, although rather long drawn out, and the most powerful force contributing to it came from the Indians, who thereby sealed their fate.
They had only to see European articles of everyday use to become
passionately determined to obtain them. In 1534 Cartier reported that
"they offered us everything they owned, which was, all told, of little
value"; and, during the winters they spent at Quebec, the Frenchmen's
possessions endangered their lives.

🍁 INDIAN VULNERABILITY

The Indians' greed is easily explained by comparing their poor tools
and utensils, made as they were of wood, bark, bone, skin, stone, and
occasionally of fragile pottery, with iron or steel axes, knives, awls,
needles, nails, and iron or brass kettles. The last, in particular, could
revolutionize daily living. "The Hurons," says an early report, "think
the greatest rulers in France are endowed with the greatest powers and
. . . can make the most difficult things such as hatchets, knives, and
kettles. They infer from this that the King makes the largest kettles."
The ultimate in desirability for the Indians was, of course, firearms, at
first for their shocking effectiveness in war and later for their usefulness
in hunting.

Possession of these goods would give any group of Indians incalculable advantages over the past in ordinary living, and similar advantages in competition, trade, or war over Indians who had not made
contact with Europeans. The Stadacona people had done everything
they could think of to prevent Cartier from going on to Hochelaga in
1535, and this anxiety to become monopolists or middlemen of European goods, arising as it did from similar patterns in pre-European
trade, was to deepen into a striking characteristic in the future. The

most fateful characteristic of the future, however, was that once the Indians supplanted their old utensils and tools by the new ones, they rapidly lost many of their intricate, laborious skills and became almost literally dependent for their lives on the newcomers and their goods.

The first problem, however, was that, as Cartier disdainfully observed, the Indians had nothing valuable to offer in exchange to the Europeans—"not anything above the value of five sous, their canoes and fishing nets excepted." Gradually, during the sixteenth century, as the fisheries of Newfoundland and Nova Scotia and inside the Gulf of St. Lawrence became ever more substantial, and particularly when, in order to save salt, the fishermen began to resort regularly to harbors and beaches where they could dry-cure their catch, the Indians began to trade furs for metalware. At first luxurious furs like marten were most in demand, but the hat-makers of Europe soon discovered that the downy fur below the guardhairs of the plentiful beaver made the best and most durable felt hats in the world.

"In the time of Jacques Cartier," wrote Lescarbot, "beavers were held in no esteem"; but now the Indians were quick to respond, for, as one of them said: "In truth, my brother, the beaver, does everything to perfection. He makes for us kettles, axes, swords, knives, and gives us drink and food without the trouble of cultivating the ground." Thus a European fashion created an immense and continuous market for North America, and, since the very axes which the Indians acquired put the beaver lodges at their mercy, there ensued in the next two hundred years a pursuit and near-extermination of the beaver across North America.

Towards the end of the sixteenth century, indications multiplied that the fisheries and their attendant fur trade had reached such large proportions that they encouraged individuals and groups to ask their kings for charters of monopoly. Naturally enough, the earliest monopolists found that their kings expected them to defend their monopolies themselves. These monarchs also insisted that the only effective way to do that was to plant colonists as resident guardians.

Cartier's nephews got a St. Lawrence fur monopoly from Henry III in 1588 as compensation for their uncle's unpaid accounts, but other traders soon forced its withdrawal. Finally, however, Pierre Chauvin and his associate, François du Pontgravé, secured a monopoly which they planned to base on Tadoussac at the mouth of the Saguenay, a spot, like Ile Percée and the Gut of Canso, where far-flung Indian commerce had gone on every summer, long before the white man came. Not only fishermen-traders came there, but French and Spanish Biscayan whalers as well. Tadoussac in winter was another matter—"if there is an ounce of cold forty leagues up the river, there will be a pound of it here," said Champlain—and only a few colonists survived the winter of 1600–1601 to be taken away in the spring. A reorganization of the St. Lawrence trade in 1602 brought about the entry of Samuel Champlain of Brouage next year. Champlain was to be the true founder of Canada.

🍁 CHAMPLAIN

The subtitle of Morris Bishop's fine biography of Champlain is "The Life of Fortitude," a reminder that the character of the great Frenchman must not be eclipsed by his remarkable technical accomplishments. He was an essentially good man whose goodness was appreciated by the Indians. He was an idealist who aimed to found Canada on justice and mercy and whose passion for discovery was never satisfied. Tough and determined, he survived what would have destroyed or thwarted others, and thereby laid the enduring foundations of a nation. He was, however, a little too easily dissuaded from insisting on the execution of some policies which his own good sense told him were the best.

The great technical skills which he possessed were combined with an extraordinary geographical imagination. He had been lucky enough to spend 1599 and 1600 in the West Indies, Mexico, and the Caribbean; and he devoted three months of the summer of 1603 to a most careful and thoughtful investigation of the Gulf of St. Lawrence and the river below Lachine.

Putting together what he saw and heard, he constructed a remarkable hypothetical picture of the northeastern quarter of North America, including the Saguenay-Mistassini traverse to the Rupert River and Hudson Bay and the Richelieu–Lake Champlain traverse to the Hudson River and the Atlantic, both years before Hudson made his discoveries. His conception of the Great Lakes was complicated by the fact that the Indians told him that Lake Huron was salt water (to him, therefore, the Pacific), but he knew that it could be reached from Lachine by a westerly route up the Ottawa and across to Georgian Bay and also by two more southerly routes along intervening lakes. Since his original ambition was "to find a route to China by the north," he apparently allowed this aim and his associates' wishes to divert him to a search along the Atlantic coast for an ice-free port, a more salubrious site for a colony, and a river which would provide a shorter and better route to the Pacific than the St. Lawrence.

From 1604 to 1607, therefore, he and his associates based their operations at the mouth of the Bay of Fundy, first, and very disastrously (thirty-five out of seventy-nine died), on Dochet (Sainte Croix) Island at the mouth of the St. Croix, and second, in comfortable quarters on good land among friendly Indians near the head of the Annapolis Basin in Acadia (Nova Scotia). Here was established the first abiding French settlement in North America by a well-regulated group which included the chartered monopolist, Pierre du Gua de Monts; Marc Lescarbot, the gay recorder of their doings; Jean de Biencourt, Seigneur de Poutrincourt, who aimed to establish himself and his family on a new estate in these lands; Louis Hébert, master of pharmacy of Paris and son of Catherine de Medici's apothecary; and, as a "paying guest," the delighted sagamore of the local Indians, Membertou.

From the beginning in 1604 until word arrived in 1607 that De Monts' monopoly had been annulled, the settlers' work of building and planting and digging fishponds had been paralleled by the most searching examination of the coasts from Cape Breton down almost to Buzzards Bay beyond Cape Cod. Champlain's cartographical skill converted these findings into magnificent, detailed, and surprisingly accurate charts.

Yet Champlain failed to find his river leading to the Pacific. Farther west, the Connecticut would certainly have tempted him and the Hudson might well have dictated French settlement, as it did Dutch after Hudson reported on it. Failing these discoveries, however, the hostility of the New England Indians, corrupted by a century of dubious contacts with irresponsible European visitors, and the scattered thinness of the coastal fur supply as compared with the abundant concentration in the funnel of St. Lawrence, determined that Champlain and the merchants whose trade supported him would return to Canada. If they had not gone there, someone else would have, for the prospect of furs was irresistible.

After harvesting their wheat and other grains in August, 1607, the colonists quitted temperate Acadia, where they had picnicked in mid-January and where Lescarbot had written his rhymes and directed his pageant, *The Theatre of Neptune*. There Champlain had practically eliminated winter scurvy by keeping the men active, feeding them fresh game, fish, and shellfish, and celebrating each day's fare by making it the chef-d'oeuvre, in rotation, of a benapkinned, bestaffed, and becollared Governor of the Order of Good Cheer. Frenchmen did not completely abandon the area. Although northern North America was to be contested for a century and three-quarters by Frenchmen, Englishmen, Scots, Hollanders, and finally rebellious Americans, it had won forever the heirs and emulators of the first colonists of 1604.

The St. Lawrence adventure was to be a very different matter, the beginning of a plunge into the heart of the continent and a fanning out over the interior which would take Frenchmen to Hudson Bay, the forks of the Saskatchewan, the headwaters of the Rio Grande, and the mouth of the Mississippi during the next century and a half. From the beginning it was an attempt to gather the furs from as much as possible of the continent to the strategic cliff where the St. Lawrence narrows just above the Ile d'Orléans.

Here, on July 3, 1608, Champlain founded Quebec and Canada. Here he built his fourth North American *habitation* of three small two-storied buildings and a warehouse below the cliffs where the tiny church, Notre Dame des Victoires, stands today. Here eight men out of twenty-four survived the first forbidding winter.

🍁 THE INDIAN PROBLEM

The Quebec settlement involved the French irrevocably in a lasting contest among the Indians. South of the upper St. Lawrence and Lake Ontario lived the Iroquois in their remarkable confederacy of five (later six) tribes. They were an agricultural people who, particularly in the Mohawk Valley, occupied a strategic position between the Indians of the Atlantic coast and those of the Great Lakes. The Huron branch of their family, whom Cartier had found occupying the shores of the St. Lawrence but who had been driven away by 1603, had long been enemies of the confederacy. They were now settled south and southeast of Georgian Bay where their agriculture and great trading skill made them the middlemen in intricate exchanges between the northern Indians and those to the west and south.

Their hostility to the Iroquois Confederacy and their immense interest in the European goods which entered the St. Lawrence during the sixteenth century made them align themselves with the Algonquins of the Ottawa Valley, of the region along and north of the St. Lawrence (Champlain's "Montagnais"), and of Maine (Etchemins). At Tadoussac in 1603, François du Pontgravé and Champlain had assured the leaders of an alliance of these three Algonquin groups, who were celebrating a recent victory over the Iroquois on the Richelieu River, that Henry IV had promised to support them. The foundation of Quebec would necessitate fulfillment of that promise.

By subtle, critical examination of the various kinds of records which have come down to us, anthropologists have been able to demonstrate that the war between the Iroquois and their northern foes may well have begun as a characteristic struggle to retain the desirable territory along the lower Great Lakes and the St. Lawrence. By the beginning of the sixteenth century the war had become intricately formalized and accompanied by strong rituals of preparation, of battle behavior, and of treatment of prisoners. It was inextricably interwoven with the culture and religion, rather than the economy and polity, of the tribes. Although terrible to the white man because its rules, particularly of ceremonial torture and stoical endurance, were different from his own, it seems originally to have involved relatively few deaths.

In many ways it was a ceremonialized, aristocratic sport, as full of conventions of behavior as were the contests of Arthurian chivalry. And then, gradually but cumulatively, it became tainted by greed for and dependence on European goods as they became available along the Atlantic coast and up the St. Lawrence and began to filter into the interior. We can never know how this or that capricious contact and trade upset the precarious balances of forces among the Indians during the sixteenth century, but it is perfectly obvious how competitive European settlement after 1604 built up demands for fur which sent out reverberations hundreds of miles ahead of the Europeans, exterminating game, revolutionizing life, and converting the Iroquois, for instance, into professional warriors or mercenaries.

The annals of the first two generations in New France are intricate, particularly in their business aspects, but the general trends, the contradictory elements of which Champlain spent his life trying to reconcile, stand out clearly. He aimed to find a water route to the Pacific and China, but knew that he must make money from the fur trade in order to explore. He also aimed to colonize New France, but knew that the principal obstacle to this "was on the part of the gentlemen of the Company, who, to monopolize trade, did not wish the country to be settled, and did not even wish to make the Indians sedentary." He wanted to Christianize the Indians and also to have the French intermarry with them, but he knew from the beginning that contact with Europeans debauched both the Indians and the Frenchmen who lived among them, and that the success of the fur trade meant war. In all this, it was his one good fortune to have the understanding if not always decisive support in France of De Monts, who deserves far greater recognition in Canada than he has had.

The French understanding of 1603 with the Algonquin-Huron alliance involved Champlain in war with the Iroquois at once. In July, 1609, he and two Frenchmen accompanied a band of sixty warriors up the Richelieu and Lake Champlain to Ticonderoga, where, in a highly formal contest begun in Indian style, the three Frenchmen in half-armor supported their Indians with arquebuses to defeat over three times as many Iroquois who were on their way to raid the Montreal trading region. A year later, he and a larger group of Frenchmen employed their wonder-working weapons in the conquest of an Iroquois barricade at the mouth of the Richelieu. The defenders were exterminated instead of being allowed to retreat, as had been customary in the past. These two revolutionary victories established Champlain as the great ally of the Algonquins and Hurons and in their eyes diminished his French trading competitors at Lachine to "women, who wish to make war only on our beavers."

In order to improve his trading position and at the same time to learn about the interior, Champlain began in 1610 to persuade the Indians to take French youths to live with them. The most notable, Étienne Brulé, spent the succeeding winter with the Ottawa Algonquins and went inland with the Hurons in 1611. Another, Nicholas du Vignau, who went up the Ottawa with the Algonquins that autumn, subsequently did some very silly, stubborn lying about having gone on to Hudson Bay where he had seen the scalps of an English expedition exterminated by the Indians (a guess at the fate of Hudson's company). He thereby not only led Champlain to undertake an exhausting expedition up the Ottawa as far as the Algonquin "toll gate" at Allumette Lake, but also severely damaged French prestige.

These youngsters were the first of the *coureurs de bois,* or *voyageurs,* the spearheads of French penetration of the continent, most of them unnamed and unrecorded. They gladly exchanged the poverty, squalor, subordination, and social discrimination which had been their lot in Europe for an adventurous, free life of prestige and advantage among the Indians. Materially they were better off, their chances of a long life may well have been greater, and their personal satisfactions were incomparably more abundant. They could hunt, as only aristocrats could at home; they could gorge themselves frequently and idle for considerable periods; a different set of sexual morals invited their endless indulgence; and their knowledge of lands and languages made them courted by both Indians and Europeans. After all, even Champlain had finally decided that, "with all their wretchedness," he considered the Indians themselves happy.

To make them happier, he brought in missionaries. In 1615, four Recollects (extremely strict Franciscans) went plunging into the wilderness, delighted to combine their self-abasement with the salvation of souls, but the poverty of their order led them to invite the rich Jesuits to help them in 1624. The Jesuits, having been ejected from Acadia (1611–13) by the Virginian English, were more than happy to make a Canadian start in 1625. They began at once to try to cleanse the colony of Huguenots, and within seven years managed to exclude from New France not only those French Protestants but the Recollects as well. (The latter, it is often forgotten, furnished the first Canadian Christian martyr, Nicolas Viel, in 1625.) The Jesuits seem to have hoped to do in Huronia, south of Georgian Bay, what their order did later with greater success in Paraguay, that is, insulate the Indians as much as possible while transforming them into a Christian community.

This enterprise failed; indeed missionary enterprise had very little enduring effect until generations had passed. As one critical missionary observed, the Indians "would be baptized ten times a day for a glass of brandy." History affords few nobler passages than those provided by the fervor, the endurance, and the martyrdoms of the seventeenth century. Catholic Europe, moved by the Counter-Reformation, responded to such skillful appeals as the *Jesuit Relations* with an immense outpouring of material aid. And yet the number of practicing Christian converts was nearly negligible. Real spiritual communion between Christian and pagan was next to impossible and deep conversion must await a long, slow process of education, observation, and choice.

Champlain thought the Hurons showed "natural good sense" when they told him that "if you would do well, you should dwell in our country, and bring women and children, and when they come to these regions we shall see how you serve this God whom you worship." The main impact of Europe, on the contrary, was of *coureurs de bois* and traders, whose lives contradicted Christian teachings, who tried to thwart the missionaries in every possible way, and whose rivalries, national and international, bred devastating disturbances and wars in which the Indians were the principal actors and overwhelmingly the principal victims.

INTERNATIONAL RIVALRIES

The French, by a slight margin in Acadia, had been merely the first European people to colonize northern North America. The English began to establish themselves on Chesapeake Bay in 1607. The Bermuda settlement began in 1609. The Dutch followed on Hudson's heels to his great river in 1610. After several failures, the English set up the core of an enduring colony in New England in 1620. The English and the French began to strike roots in the West Indies about 1625. In 1638 the Swedes set up a colony on the Delaware. By 1650 the Atlantic coast was beaded with settlements where Europeans were becoming Americans.

In their beginnings, these colonies, each of which had to be an immensely expensive venture, were forced to base their survival on the salable surpluses which they could produce. There were only two

American commodities quickly available. As Captain John Smith reported in 1614, "Fish and Furres was then our refuge." Fortunately for the coastal colonies, and unfortunately for New France, the people in the former slowly learned how to extract sustenance and surpluses from timber, tobacco, grain crops, and other rewards for enterprise. While these forms of production swelled, the fisheries and the fur trade continued, the one on the coasts and banks and the other along the land frontier, both engendering conflicts because of their inborn tendencies toward greater profits from monopoly.

Champlain faced European international rivalry almost at once. As early as 1611, he caught echoes of Indian movement generated by the Dutch on the Hudson or Susquehanna. By 1615 events in the interior made it perfectly clear that Dutch appetite for furs was likely to convert the Iroquois into an immensely dangerous menace to the Algonquins and Hurons and therefore to the fur trade of New France. The only thing to do was to yield to Indian urgings and try to blunt the menace immediately.

Champlain set off hurriedly early in July, 1615, with a dozen of his men to make for the first time the hard canoe journey up the Ottawa, across the Mattawa-French River traverse to Georgian Bay, and down to the home of the Hurons on fertile lands southeast of it. After tedious preparations there, thirteen Frenchmen and about five hundred Indians moved east, picked up an Algonquin detachment en route, and crossed Lake Ontario at its eastern end.

Meanwhile Brulé went off with a dozen Hurons to recruit the Andastes who lived south of the Iroquois on the upper Susquehanna (near Elmira, New York) in order to conduct their war party to a combined attack with Champlain's Huron-Algonquin force on a great Iroquois stronghold at the southern end of Onondaga Lake (near Syracuse, New York). Brulé arrived late, but Champlain's party had departed anyway after having got badly out of hand and mishandled the assault.

This failure greatly injured French prestige, for the arquebus had proved less effective than the bow in North American siege warfare, and the defenders had instinctively organized themselves better than the attackers. Champlain was painfully wounded during his nine-day siege and had to winter with the Hurons. Brulé improved the occasion by traveling down the Susquehanna to Chesapeake Bay and back that winter. The Iroquois quickly made the upper St. Lawrence impassable for the French and their allies, and the lower Ottawa supremely dangerous.

Quebec got its first real settlers in 1617 in the persons of Louis

Hébert, his wife, and three children, for they had seen and lived in Acadia between 1606 and 1614 and had been spoiled for life in Paris. Hébert was determined to farm at Quebec, in spite of the sterner climate and the lack of either a plow or an animal to draw it.

Meanwhile Champlain was in Paris, trying in vain to arouse the king to the salvation and development of New France, whose present commercial importance and future as "the means of reaching easily to the Kingdom of China and the East Indies" he painted in glowing colors. The immediate problem, he pointed out, was the nearness of the Dutch and the English. They kept others out of their own preserves and obviously coveted Acadia and New France. The French fur trade handled fifteen to twenty thousand beaver skins a year, but the settlement at Quebec counted less than fifty persons.

The English had designs on the St. Lawrence region for a generation, chiefly on account of its Gulf fisheries and the oil ("train") obtainable from whales, walruses, and seals, "which if it will make sope, the King of Spaine may burne some of his Olive trees." They had also so thoroughly harried Acadia that the few French there had pretty much taken to the woods. On September 29, 1621, following negotiations with Captain John Mason (Governor of Newfoundland 1615–21) and Ferdinando Gorges (Treasurer of the Council for New England), James I by charter endowed his Scottish friend and courtier, Sir William Alexander, with the whole region from Gaspé to the St. Croix to stand as Nova Scotia between New England and New France.

This enterprise rapidly degenerated into a shady device for selling baronetcies, but about 1627 it came to active life as part of a grand design to eliminate the French from North America. War had just then broken out between England and France. An English Canada Company was organized in collaboration with the feeble Nova Scotian project as a counterbalance to Cardinal Richelieu's impressive Company of New France, and with three dashing, highly competent, Anglo-French brothers from Dieppe—David, Louis, and Thomas Kirke—as its active agents in North America.

The whole enterprise was excellently planned and executed. In 1628 Tadoussac was occupied as a base and Champlain was courteously warned of his fate—blockade and starvation or surrender. The same year some seventy Scotsmen ("and tua weemen") were planted close to the site of Champlain's former *habitation* on the upper Annapolis Basin. An attempt to do the same thing on Cape Breton Island, however, was destroyed by one of the first efforts of the Company of New France.

A fleet of the French Company's ships, loaded with two hundred settlers and their equipment, tried to break through the Tadoussac-based blockade to reinforce Champlain at Quebec, but the Kirkes met them and captured all but one in a fourteen-hour naval battle. Champlain's little company of seventy-five persons, now hungry, sick, and despairing, accepted the inevitable when three English ships came round the western end of Ile d'Orléans on July 19, 1629. The surrender took place very politely the next day and most of the Frenchmen were taken back to Europe.

It looked as if the French had been ousted from North America for good, but a curious combination of events restored them three years later. The Nova Scotian enterprise had been supported so half-heartedly in Scotland that the area was handed back to the management of two resourceful Acadians, Claude de la Tour and his son Charles, who were made baronets of Nova Scotia during the winter of 1629–30 in order to preserve appearances. Charles I of England had just embarked on government without Parliament and needed money. His French queen's dowry was in arrears. The treaty of St. Germain-en-Laye of March 29, 1632, therefore, awarded Charles I the payment of 400,000 crowns and returned Acadia and Canada to France. Champlain, who was publishing his revised *Voyages* in Paris that year, put it through the press, settled estates with his wife, and returned to rebuild his Quebec in 1633.

He was now the king's commander, supported from home and re-spected and loved in Canada. The powerful Jesuits were solidly estab-lished at Quebec and preparing for enterprise in Huronia and else-where. A party of real colonists came out in 1634, a herd of cattle was established, and the first settlement was founded at Three Rivers. And then, in October, 1635, the tired old man of sixty-eight was stricken by paralysis. He lingered to say his farewells and will his per-sonal property to the Church, and died on Christmas Day. As a Jesuit said fittingly: "Would to God that all the French who first came to this country had been like him: we should not so often have to blush for them before our savages."

During the next thirty years, both Acadia and New France grew in numbers and strength, but remained relatively as unable as before to surmount fundamental weaknesses. Acadia, in particular, was be-coming a sort of international football. Its bastion-like position, project-ing northeast into the Atlantic, could menace St. Lawrence traffic from the south and New England traffic from the north and east. Its fisheries, proximity to other fisheries, and modest fur trade, particularly from the St. John Valley, gave it considerable importance in itself. And finally, its settlers had imported from Europe the techniques which were to equip it with an agriculture capable of sustaining considerable population and even of producing surpluses, particularly of livestock.

Owing to the shape and position of the Bay of Fundy, its tides were extraordinarily high. Consequently they not only inundated the shores of the bays, but drove far up the little rivers. These conditions clearly invited men to dike and drain the marshes and thereby secure fertile lands, treeless and stoneless and level. The process began on the Annapolis Basin (Port Royal) and spread to the Minas Basin and the Fundy side of the Isthmus of Chignecto. Dikes were raised against the tides, and the deep little creeks and drainage ditches emerging from the reclaimed area were protected by simple clapper valves or sluices set in timber frames.

This agriculture kept both humble folk and their "betters" alive, but money was to be made from fish and fur. The consequence was that our principal early Acadian records are of international contests for strategic and exploitative purposes, and of domestic struggles among fishery promoters and fur traders for monopolistic privileges and posts of vantage, while unrecorded farmers were making the land their own. During four active years (1632–36) under Governor Isaac de Razilly, the Company of New France planted perhaps two hundred settlers who, with very slight subsequent additions, were the ancestors of the Acadian people.

From 1636 to 1653 there was a spectacular contest on both sides of the Bay of Fundy between two fur barons, Charles de la Tour and Charles de Menou, Seigneur d'Aulnay de Charnisay. Aulnay captured Madame de la Tour, who died while his prisoner, and, after Aulnay was drowned in 1650, La Tour married his widow so as to unite the conflicting claims. What was indicative of the future, however, was that both men had turned to Boston for help and La Tour had even mortgaged all his property there.

A natural consequence was that in 1654, when a Cromwellian expedition for the conquest of Dutch New York was halted in Boston by news of a peace, "it was conseaved that to spend a lytle tyme upon ye coast in lookeinge after ye ffrench might torne to some accompt." Penobscot, Saint John, and Port Royal quickly fell, but La Tour, having conveniently recalled that he was a baronet of Nova Scotia, managed to secure Cromwell's approval in 1656 for a triangular deal embracing Acadian, London, and Boston interests.

There followed fifteen years of incredibly tangled claims and counterclaims, not unmarked by actual confiscatory raids, during which Sir Thomas Temple, an Englishman become a Bostonian, emerged as the dominant figure, only to lose out after all. Charles II forced him to hand Acadia back to France early in 1671 as a pawn in the intricate game which the king was playing with Louis XIV. Acadia was conquered by the Dutch three years later, but they were unable to make anything of it. Meanwhile the real Acadians had increased to number about 450 persons.

New France was a good deal less accessible to its rivals, but its dependence on the fur trade committed it to almost unceasing contest with the Iroquois over control of the waterways from the west. As the fur supply dwindled in the earlier exploited regions, the "beaver frontier" moved deeper into the continent while Dutch and French, Iroquois and Algonquins, tried to attract its harvest to the Hudson or the St. Lawrence. The battleground was the "island" or triangle of what is now southern Ontario. By this time a good many of the Indians on both sides used firearms. They did little or no trapping or hunting for furs themselves; they had become middlemen for less sophisticated tribes, and fighters for the trade which had become as much their own sustenance as that of their European masters.

After the restoration of Quebec in 1632, royal interest rapidly diminished because there were bigger fish to fry in the European Thirty Years' War, but thanks to the popular religious and missionary fervor of the time, very ably attracted towards Canada by the *Jesuit Relations,* private philanthropy was great. In the spring of 1639 Madame de la Pelterie brought to Quebec three Ursuline nuns (including the great Marie de l'Incarnation) to found a school, and three nuns sent by the Archbishop of Rouen to found a hospital. "The news seemed at first almost a dream. . . . From a floating prison were seen issuing these virgins consecrated to God, as fresh and rosy as when they left their homes." They got to work at once and by November, 1642, the Ursulines had entered their new stone convent, ninety-two feet long by twenty-eight feet wide.

That same year Montreal was founded to be at once the fur trade's bastion at the mouth of the Ottawa and the St. Lawrence rapids and an outpost of Christian and missionary endeavor—Ville Marie de Montréal. While it must be admitted that its mixture of merchants, dramsellers, *coureurs de bois,* half-breeds, and friendly Indians quickly made it a roistering frontier town, yet it was also a garrison of dedicated Christian warriors like Paul de Chomédy, Sieur de Maisonneuve, and the stout-hearted saintly nurse, Jeanne Mance.

Much of the money for founding the city came from a devout Angevin tax collector, Jerome de Royer, Sieur de la Dauversière, and the hospital was endowed by the wealthy Madame de Bullion. In 1657 Marguerite Bourgeois began teaching Christianity in a stone stable which she followed up two years later by founding the educational Congregation of the Sisters of Notre Dame. In 1657, also, the Sulpicians of Paris, who had been especially interested in Montreal since before it was founded, set up a daughter seminary there which was soon to receive the island of Montreal in seigneury from the five surviving members of the original promotional company.

Thanks largely to the money and energy which were poured into the founding of Montreal on its fertile, pleasant island, the population of New France had grown to about 2500 by 1663, not a great number compared to Virginia or Massachusetts Bay, but an improvement on less than a tenth as many when Champlain died. The wealth and endeavors of the faithful, in France and New France, had been poured for a generation into the establishment of three little towns on the St. Lawrence—Quebec, Three Rivers, and Montreal. Around them the fields were being tilled and livestock tended. These new Americans were now settled for good, but they were still dependent on Europe for many necessities which they could pay for only as long as the Indians brought furs or their own situation evoked support from the Crown or from the charitable in France.

The keystone of the arch was the fur trade. During the 1620's and 1630's the Ontario triangle had been thoroughly investigated by traders and missionaries, but the rapid decline in its production, combined with the constant menace of the Iroquois, had sent Brulé westward along the north shore of Lake Huron toward Sault Ste Marie, perhaps even to Lake Superior, about 1623. The Nipissing Algonquins traded there with western Indians.

Ten or fifteen years later Jean Nicolet followed the same route, but swung south to Green Bay off Lake Michigan and up the Fox River far enough to hear about the portage route to the Mississippi. Both these men brought back stories of civilized men still farther west which kept alive the French hope for a route to China. Nicolet even carried with him a ceremonial robe "of China damask, all strewn with flowers and birds of many colours."

THROTTLED BY THE IROQUOIS

Meanwhile, after some disappointing experiments elsewhere, the Jesuits had embarked wholeheartedly on their great and tragic adventure of the Huron missions. They lived in the squalid villages, taught all who would listen, and strove by example and argument to demonstrate the Christian life amidst people almost incapable of grasping it, or indifferent, or scornful, or bitterly hostile. Rarely indeed did they make a convert by systematic instruction; usually it was a matter of baptizing the dying. And always the Iroquois menace was present, at first in raids on outlying areas or communications and then in an encroachment the pressure of which increased as the prospective victims were weakened by the interruptions in their connection with Montreal. One great Jesuit, Isaac Jogues, had made an attempt to check the evil at its source by converting the Iroquois, returning to the Mohawk Valley twice in 1645 after having been a grimly abused prisoner there during the winter of 1642–43. He had barely arrived in the autumn of 1645 when his head was split open by a tomahawk.

The final blows fell in 1648 and 1649 when the Iroquois rapidly stormed and destroyed the Huronian villages, killing most of the Hurons and their priests and scattering the remnants. The hideous deaths of the Jesuits constitute one of the great epics of Christendom. The Canadian poet, E. J. Pratt, has commemorated them unforgettably in *Brébeuf and His Brethren* (1943) by telling how the Iroquois:

> . . . multiplied the living martyrdoms
> Before the casual incident of death.

The Iroquois triumphed over the other Indians from Michigan to Tadoussac and from the Delaware and the Ohio almost to Hudson Bay. The terror of their name reached farther. It is true that they over-reached themselves west of Lake Michigan in 1653 and that they had used up so many of their warriors by then that they had to recruit others by adoption, even from the fugitive Hurons at Quebec. From 1653 to 1658 they were at comparative peace with the French and allowed the heroic Jesuits to maintain a mission among the Onondagas from 1656 to 1658. Yet this was a mere truce while the Confederacy digested its triumphs and reorganized itself in the midst of the chaos which those triumphs had created.

Except for this uneasy interlude, the thirty years after the restoration of New France in 1632 were years of mounting terror for the French and their Indian allies, and years of joyful bravado for the Iroquois. "They approach like foxes, fight like lions, and fly away like birds," reported the Jesuits. Their war bands raided the St. Lawrence down as far as Tadoussac, yelled insults at the huddled fugitives in Quebec, and conducted a mock funeral and mass clad in the garments of a murdered Sulpician in front of the palisades of Montreal. Farmers were killed in their fields; cattle were slain; and outlying buildings put to the torch. The annual death toll from 1658 to 1663 was between fifty and a hundred persons. And, worst of all, the Hurons and the Ottawa Algonquins, the managers of the life-giving flow of furs from the interior, were dead or dispersed.

The new Indian center for fur collection was now at Sault Ste Marie, between Lake Superior and Lake Huron, the point at which the over-extended Iroquois had been halted in 1653. It had become the meeting place for fragments of the dispersed tribes with their former northern and western customers, a center of grim determination to find a way out of dislocations, despair, and deprivation of European goods.

In 1653 a fur brigade had got through to the St. Lawrence below Montreal by using the incredibly laborious route from the upper Ottawa to the upper St. Maurice, and in 1654 some Hurons had run the gauntlet of the Ottawa. Yet an occasional breakthrough was not enough. Economic salvation still depended on somehow breaking the Iroquois' grip on the lower Ottawa. New France could not summon the energies for this task. Would the unremitting stream of appeals to Old France call forth aid before it was too late?

CHAPTER IV

French North America (1663-1760)

By 1660 the St. Lawrence, with its tributary lakes and rivers, had established itself as dictator of future European enterprise in northern North America, but it was by no means certain what nation would benefit by that enterprise. If France could be induced to rescue New France from foreign threats to her existence, it would be Frenchmen or French Canadians who would hold the great river and fan out over the interior.

No other nation commanded such a magnificent, alluring avenue into North America. The Spanish Mississippi was too difficult and dangerous to ascend. The English Hudson Bay carried Europeans most deeply and most cheaply into the mid-continent, but access to it was closed by ice for at least eight months of the year. The Dutch Hudson and the Iroquois Mohawk combined to provide the one real competition, for the portage to Lake Ontario was a less serious obstacle than the rapids between Lake Ontario and Montreal, but perhaps France would make the capture of New Amsterdam part of her mounting rivalry and conflict with the Dutch. Or perhaps the Iroquois could be curbed.

On his return to Canada in 1633, Champlain had written to Cardinal Richelieu: "Possessing the interior of the country we shall be able to expel our enemies . . . and compel them to retire to the coast, and if we deprive them of trade with the . . . Iroquois, they will be forced to abandon the whole country." He was a little naïve in believing that an end to the fur trade would mean an end to New Amsterdam, but thirty years later, when New France was on the brink of extinction, the retiring Governor, Baron Dubois d'Avaugour, again besought the king to act against the Dutch at once.

With 4000 men, 10 warships, and 400,000 francs a year for ten years, he offered to conquer New England and the Dutch colony and make New France, with Newfoundland and Acadia, into a self-sustaining, interdependent empire unrivaled in the world. It was now too late, however, for in 1664 the English, who had been contesting Dutch claims to the Hudson area for some time, sent out an expedition which secured the surrender of New Amsterdam without a fight.

🍁 FRANCE TAKES OVER

Yet, in a larger sense, D'Avaugour's memorandum had been well calculated, for his previous three years in Canada had coincided with young Louis XIV's assumption of personal power in France, and the governor's report was bound to enter into the policy-making for North America. Basically that policy, as Louis XIV and his great minister, Jean-Baptiste Colbert, formulated it in the spring of 1663, was to end the rule of the Company of New France, to convert the colony into a royal province of France, to render its core secure in a military sense, and then to build up the St. Lawrence settlements and throw out a network of trading monopolies over the interior.

These decisions ended a period of about twenty years during which the little body of Canadians had been given responsibilities in the conduct of the fur trade and their own government. The Sun King put an end to this modest degree of autonomy. Canada was to be told what its part would be in the great world design, political and mercantilistic, which became possible now that France had humbled both branches of the Hapsburgs.

The obvious initial step was to smash the Iroquois, but the available forces had first to be used in the more important Caribbean and West Indies areas. It was not until the summer of 1665, therefore, that the Marquis de Tracy arrived at Quebec with the Carignan-Salières Regiment and posted 800 of them in three forts along the Richelieu. Having waited until the crops were ripe in September, 1666, he marched his army into the Mohawk Valley, burned the villages and their winter's stores, and destroyed what remained of the harvest in the fields around them. The lesson was an unmistakable one. Two years later it seemed safe to recall the regiment. About 400 of them accepted the offer of land and assistance in money and supplies to enable them to settle in Canada.

Clearly affairs in New France were looking up. As a royal province of the new authoritarian type, its administration was now nominally in the hands of a governor, an intendant, a bishop, and a Superior Council, but the absolutist king and his chief minister had no idea of relinquishing control. The governor, as personal representative of the king, had great dignity and great responsibility in military and diplomatic

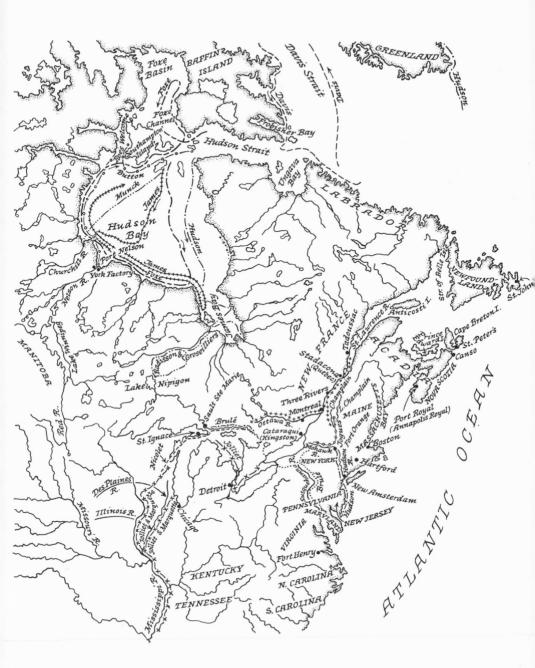

EXPLORERS of NORTH AMERICA

affairs. The intendant ("of Justice, Police, and Finance") was expected to superintend the whole colony, stimulating approved activities, initiating new ones, and curbing injurious ones, all in accordance with the over-all plan worked out in France and only modified in the light of Canadian circumstances after the most elaborate representations and deliberate consideration.

The sheer immensity of the correspondence between the two Canadian officials and "the Minister" in France inspires today's inquirer with awe, not unmixed with skepticism about the efficiency of a transatlantic give-and-take which often necessitated the passage of three or four years before a decision could be reached. There is a classic fable of a lonely Negro hangman at Quebec who died of ennui long before a double to-and-fro correspondence brought a West Indian Negress to Quebec via France to marry him. The only thing to do then was to sell her to pay the expenses.

The bishop, who since 1659 had been the nobleman François de Montmorency-Laval, was also a power. Like the Jesuits whom he admired, he was a sturdy supporter of papal supreme power, whereas Louis XIV in these early years was a Gallican who insisted on a national Church of France. Conflict between Laval and the king's governors and intendants in this and many other matters was inevitable. When it is added that from 1675 on these three sat with fourteen royally appointed members to form the Superior Council, it can be surmised that the frictions of government were very great.

The Council was like a modified French provincial parlement in that it registered royal decrees. Its own ordinances had to be approved in France. It enforced decrees and ordinances and could act as a Canadian court of appeal. When, in 1672, the governor, Louis de Buade, Count Frontenac, summoned representatives of the three estates in the manner of the ancient pays d'états at home, he was sharply reprimanded by Colbert. "Since our Kings have long regarded it as good for their service not to convoke the Estates-General of the kingdom, in order perhaps to abolish insensibly this ancient usage," Colbert asserted, "you, on your part, should very rarely, or, to speak correctly, never, give a corporate form to the inhabitants of Canada. You should even, as the colony strengthens, suppress gradually the office of Syndic [of towns], who presents petitions in the name of the inhabitants, for it is well that each should speak for himself and no one for all."

The law of the new province was rather complicated in theory, but achieved greater simplicity in practice among a people who positively enjoyed litigation. Its base, from 1637 on, was the most developed of the old regional collections of legal tradition in France, the Custom of

Paris. To this were added overriding new elements—certain principles of Roman law, royal edicts and decrees, approved ordinances and decisions of the Superior Council, and instructions of the intendant. In its more serious aspects this great mixture of law was administered in royal courts of criminal and civil jurisdiction sitting twice a week at Quebec, Three Rivers, and Montreal, with appeal to the weekly sessions of the Superior Council. In addition, the intendant, as chief law officer, could take cases from the courts for decision before him.

But all of this political apparatus, with its functionaries involving about two hundred persons, was rather remote from the lives of the people, and the great new circumstance after 1663 was that New France was to be systematically peopled. Louis XIV, Colbert, and Jean-Baptiste Talon, the great intendant (1665–72), collaborated vigorously and ingeniously in building up numbers. A systematic census taken in 1666 revealed 3,215 resident inhabitants, a total which reflected the arrival of a few hundred apprenticed laborers sent out each year from 1664 on. To these were added about 400 retired soldiers in 1668 and, that bounty to the lonely male majority, the successive brigades of "the King's Daughters," perhaps a thousand in all, who were brought out with a royal dowry of household goods and provisions.

The quizzical Baron de Lahontan described the hasty marriage market among these persons of mixed character and accomplishment:

> The Vestal Virgins were heaped up, (if I may so speak) one above another, in three different Apartments, where the Bridegrooms singled out their Brides, just as a Butcher does an Ewe from amongst a Flock of Sheep . . . And indeed the market had such a run, that in fifteen days' time, they were all disposed of. I am told the fattest went off best, upon the apprehension that these being less active, would keep truer to their Ingagements, and hold out better against the nipping cold of the Winter.

All this came on top of a royal edict of April 12, 1660, which penalized fathers whose sons were not married at twenty or daughters at sixteen, awarded the dutiful young people twenty livres each as a wedding present, and gave pensions of 300 livres to parents of ten living legitimate children and of 400 to parents of twelve.

As a result of these measures, the census of 1673 showed 6,705 inhabitants, more than double the population in 1666. Thereafter, with relatively small and intermittent migration from France, the numbers of French North Americans were to grow towards the four or five millions of today. And for over two centuries they were to grow chiefly through the natural, if ruthlessly selective, fertility of an agricultural people, for every policy was designed to plant them on the forested, unpopulated lands which they were to subdue for their own and others' sustenance.

The pattern of pioneering settlement in seventeenth-century Canada was not unlike that in ninth-century France or in seventeenth-century New England, since the problem in each case was to create self-reliant and co-operative group settlements. The seigneurial system used in Canada was feudal in theory, but more like the New England township in fact. It began afresh after 1660 with the cancellation of old unimproved seigneuries and the creation of new ones. Since the church in its various forms had both great influence and the best record in land management, it ultimately came to possess about one quarter of the grants.

Ordinarily, however, an individual of decent social standing received from the Crown a large grant on condition of developing it by the introduction of settlers. He himself was expected to provide military service when called upon, but his tenants (habitants), who had the same obligation, served under a captain of militia, one of their own number whose appointment had to be formally accepted by them. Both seigneur and habitant were under specific, if loosely enforced, requirements as to land improvement, and in 1711 the two *arrêts,* or royal decrees, of Marly at least potentially tightened up these requirements.

The whole system was accompanied by obligatory services and payments such as those for mill-building by the seigneur, payments on inheritance or alienation of holdings, and annual dues, but these did not amount to much; when some seigneurs attempted to exploit their control of especially desirable lands they could be curbed under the *arrêts* of Marly. The *corvée,* the habitant's labor service to the seigneur which was so intolerable a feature of feudalism in France, was soon either commuted for a small payment or became synonymous with what was called a "bee" among English-speaking frontiersmen, that is, a joint effort, picnic, and frolic for such things as harvests, barn-raisings, or threshings.

In Canadian circumstances, there could seldom be much difference between the average seigneur and the average habitant, certainly nothing approaching the relation of noble and peasant. It was absurd to think of enforcing hunting, fishing, or forest privileges, and the seigneur's rights of *haute, moyenne, et basse justice* boiled down to little more than informal arbitration of petty local disputes. The outcome was that a very few Canadian seigneurs, for extraordinary distinction, received patents of nobility, a few others were by birth or by service ranked as gentlemen, and the majority (aside from the Church) were ordinary untitled burghers and farmers who had risen a little in their world.

Normally the seigneury coincided with the parish and the seigneur who built a church was in theory entitled to select the priest to fill its pulpit. The curé, in turn, was to collect for the general church one twenty-sixth of the grain harvest as tithe. Practically, however, it proved a long, slow task to furnish even temporary places of worship outside the towns and to provide them with even occasional clergy. There were thirty-six parishes in all in 1685, and only eighty-two by 1721. Laval met this situation by a device which frontier Methodists were to employ a century later. Instead of placing a priest on a seigneury for life as possessor of its ecclesiastical benefice, he moved his little force about and made each of them serve several parishes and missionary stations. His system of removable priests persists to the present day.

Meanwhile the religious orders were busy with education, hospitals, and missions. The Jesuit College founded at Quebec in 1635 was a primary school which grew into what would now be called a classical college. The Sulpician Seminary of 1657 in Montreal developed in much the same way. Gradually, after the founding of Laval's Great Seminary in 1663 and the Lesser Seminary in 1668, Canadians began to supply an increasing proportion of the priesthood. The Great Seminary, the recipient of all tithe and other substantial revenues, was Laval's head-quarters for tight ecclesiastical control of the province. About 1700 the permanence of France in America began to be symbolized by stone churches and other religious buildings, unpretentious, but well proportioned and tastefully, sparsely decorated.

The common term for a seigneury in New France was *côte,* or shore. Each early habitant received a narrow water frontage on the river that provided transportation, and a long ribbon of land stretching inland. The houses were built near the shore. When holdings were divided after death, the estates grew so narrow that their reduction had to be limited by law. Gradually, therefore, the St. Lawrence, St. Maurice, and Richelieu assumed the appearance of a broken series of ribbon villages. Much later, the whole performance was repeated in successive "ranges" along roads inland which roughly paralleled the rivers.

During his endlessly busy term as intendant, Talon did what he could to stimulate production on the lower St. Lawrence in the hope of establishing trade with the West Indies as well as with France. He put money and energy into the fisheries, into oil-rendering from seals and walruses, and into the preparation of boards, staves, and ship timber. He established a shipyard at the mouth of the St. Charles which progressed from small craft suitable for river and gulf to the building of seagoing vessels. He failed to build up the production of potash, pitch, and tar from the forests to surpluses for export, and did little more than indicate the possibility of iron production on the St. Maurice northwest of Three Rivers.

That town, however, was more interested in building canoes; that is, it keyed its life to the activity which Talon and his masters knew basically maintained New France. The birch-bark canoe, which had entranced Champlain in 1603 with a vision of swift travel and of seeing "all that is to be seen, good and bad, within the space of a year or two," had undergone considerable transformation since then. The Indians' marvelous, graceful creation of bark, light framework, fibers, and gum had followed no standard specifications, but the fur trade began to dictate them and to provide the tools which made manufacture easier and more precise. The larger craft (thirty to thirty-six feet long) still possessed the advantages of lightness, shallow draft, and easy repair, but could carry great loads—six paddlers and five to six tons of goods—not only on the rivers, but along the shores of the Great Lakes.

Before he left New France in 1672, Talon arranged and partially carried out a series of symbolic declarations of French sovereignty in North America which demonstrated what France hoped to do. In Acadia, on the Rupert River leading into James Bay, at Sault Ste Marie, and elsewhere the arms of France and the Cross were raised with great ceremony and the entire tributary areas claimed for Louis XIV and his successors. Something new was happening in the interior to the north and west of the St. Lawrence.

ᘓ FUR TRADE BEYOND THE LAKES

The principal known agents in opening up new possibilities were two inhabitants of Three Rivers, Médard Chouart des Groseilliers and Pierre Esprit Radisson. Their thrilling adventures (real and imaginary), recorded for the most part by the self-advertising Radisson, have been untangled in Miss G. L. Nute's *Caesars of the Wilderness*. Picturesque and fantastic though these adventures were, their hard core amounted to the discovery of how to develop a new and vastly greater fur trade.

What had happened was that Groseilliers, accompanied probably by a half-breed named Jean Péré, had in 1654 gone back to the Michigan-Wisconsin area with the Indians who had come down to the St. Lawrence after the Iroquois overreached themselves near the Sault. The two Frenchmen returned to Quebec in 1656, not only escorting fifty canoes "laden with goods which the French came to this end of the world to procure" but with some encouraging ideas about how to profit by the passionate desire of the western Indians for European goods.

Groseilliers and Radisson believed that a trade which would now require two years instead of one could be sustained by systematic cultivation of corn near trading posts in the interior. On a second journey, they explored the Lake Superior region, discovering even greater possibilities. Their return down the Ottawa in 1660 was made possible by the epic eight-day fight against hundreds of Iroquois beside the Long Sault Rapids in which Adam Dollard des Ormeaux and sixteen other Montrealers fought until they died in a superb demonstration of the indomitability of New France.

Rich in furs and eager Indians as the Michigan-Wisconsin area was, the two Frenchmen looked beyond it to the great river (Mississippi) leading to the south, to the Siouan tribes westward beyond Lake Superior, and to the filigree of lakes, rivers, and beaver ponds dominated by the Crees between Lake Superior and James Bay. The last, they decided, was the richest prize, not only because northern furs were superior, but because Hudson Bay provided access to the mouths of the rivers that drained it. Trade goods could be brought in directly by sea at much lower cost than by ship to Quebec, by boat to Montreal, and by canoe from there on.

Instead of seizing upon this idea, the governor of a tottering New France, Pierre de Voyer, Vicomte d'Argenson, used the excuse of their unauthorized departure in 1659 to plunder them by fines "that he might the better maintain his coach & horses at Paris." When Groseilliers went to Paris with his plan and pleas for redress, he got nowhere. Recourse to the New Englanders who were exploiting Cromwellian Nova Scotia ("inhabited by the French under the English Government") secured a New England ship in 1663, captained by Zachariah Gillam, but it turned back before the icebergs of Hudson Strait because of the fears of "our master, that onely were accustomed to see some Barbadoes Sugers, and not mountains of suger candy."

Next year, however, the two Canadian adventurers were picked up in New England by Colonel George Cartwright, who took them to the Court of Charles II. The old English dream of Hudson Bay promptly revived in new form. One ship got through in 1668, wintered at the mouth of the Rupert, and brought back a promising cargo. Thereupon, in 1670, the inspiration of two French Canadians flowered into "The Governor and Company of Adventurers of England trading into Hudson's Bay" which survives to this day. It followed the tradition, practiced by the English in India, of setting up "factories" near the mouths of the rivers which drained the huge basin and encouraging the Indians to bring their furs down to tidewater.

It was in a vain attempt to counteract England's disconcerting success that Talon sent Paul Denis de St. Simon and Father Charles Albanel in 1671 to make the Saguenay-Mistassini-Rupert traverse to Hudson Bay for the first time and proclaim French sovereignty. It took them two years to do it, but they naturally failed to persuade the Indians of that basin to struggle upstream and across the height of land to trade at Tadoussac.

🍁 THE MISSISSIPPI VALLEY

In the meantime, the Jesuits, who gathered up and pieced together all the geographical lore of the day, decided that the situation south of Lake Superior invited an attempt to make up for the loss of Huronia. The new West was attracting the *coureurs de bois* as honey attracts bees—"it was a Peru for them"—and where fur traders went, missionaries went too. Father Ménard, formerly of Huronia, went back with the Indians in 1660, only to lose his life in the interior near the Mississippi next year. Father Claude Allouez went out in 1665, but by now it was clear that Lake Superior must wait, for, although the Sault was a great trading center, enterprise had on the whole turned southwest into Lake Michigan, to Nicolet's Green Bay, and to the easy Fox River route towards the Mississippi.

In fact, once the Iroquois were cowed in 1666, a host of circumstances and of known and unknown men converged on the linking up of the St. Lawrence across the low height of land south of the Great Lakes with the great valley leading to the Gulf of Mexico. The Spaniards had known of the Mississippi for a century and a half, but they had occupied none of it. Florida they occupied only in order to protect the Bahama Channel. In New Spain they remained west of the Rio Grande. The English along the Atlantic coast were the likeliest rivals of France, for their frontier fur traders were probing through the Appalachian barrier and launching pack trains and "long traders" on horseback west of Virginia and the newly founded Carolinas. It was to be a race for control of the Mississippi before Spain should awaken to her loss.

The Mississippi enterprise was merely one part of a great pattern of enterprise woven by Talon. As he said, "We must shut against them [the English] the road to the river [St. Lawrence] and secure for his Majesty all the outlets of the Lakes and of the Rivers commencing therewith, in order that the Europeans may lose all desire they may feel to share with his Majesty so beautiful and so vast a country."

Jean Péré and Louis Jolliet, for instance, demonstrated the usefulness of the continuous Great Lakes route in 1668, an idea taken up by the Sulpicians of Montreal at once. More important, however, were the activities of a friend of the Sulpicians, Robert Cavelier de La Salle, who had received from them a seigneury by the St. Lawrence rapids, mockingly called La Chine because of his talk of a route to Asia.

🍁 LA SALLE

La Salle's task was to examine the country south of the lower lakes in the hope of finding an easy portage to the Ohio and Mississippi. He ranged that country far and wide by canoe and on foot, for Talon proposed to confine the English "within very narrow limits" by building a fort at Cataraqui (the outlet of Lake Ontario) as the hinge of a door which should keep them east of the Appalachians and shut them out of the Mississippi Valley. In 1671 the western Iroquois were given a warning of French capacities when a trial military expedition, traveling in bateaux, or flatboats, worked its way up the hitherto unconquered St. Lawrence from Montreal to Cataraqui.

Our knowledge of La Salle's movements between the lakes and the Ohio from 1669 to 1673 is slight and obscure and so also, apparently, was Talon's. In any case he had to act quickly, for word had come from France that a renegade Spaniard, Diego de Penalosa, lately governor of New Mexico, had fired Louis XIV and Colbert with the idea of using the Mississippi as an avenue to "the Spanish mines" and the Pacific. Late in the autumn of 1672, therefore, Louis Jolliet was sent off posthaste to St. Ignace on Mackinac Strait to recruit Father Marquette and an expedition to explore the Mississippi from Green Bay, "either that they might seek a passage from here [Quebec] to the Sea of China by the river that discharges into the Vermilion, or California Sea; or because they desired to verify what has for some time been said concerning the two kingdoms of Theguaio and Quivira, which border on Canada, and in which numerous gold mines are reported to exist."

During the summer of 1673, Jolliet and Marquette crossed to the Mississippi by the Fox and the Wisconsin; followed it as far as the mouth of the Arkansas, by which time they were sure that it flowed into the Gulf of Mexico instead of into the Atlantic or the Gulf of California. They returned by the Illinois and the easy Chicago portage to Lake Michigan. By that time Talon had been recalled to France. Moreover, Louis XIV had begun in 1672 the series of great wars by which he hoped to become master of Europe and New France was to be left pretty much to its own enlarged resources. La Salle now took up the work of exploiting the Mississippi Valley. He planned to do it on a large scale, employing boats instead of canoes on the Great Lakes and the great river, with a narrow land bridge between them at the lower end of Lake Michigan.

Plagued by meager responses to his plans, by the disastrous loss of his ship "Le Griffon" on the Lakes, and by jealous rivalries in North America and Europe, the remainder of La Salle's career was tragic. He descended the Mississippi to its mouth in 1682. He was murdered in March, 1687, while attempting to make his way overland to the Illinois country from a settlement which he had established in 1684 on the Gulf of Mexico near Matagorda Bay in western Texas. That ill-starred venture had been an attempt to win Louis XIV's favor by capturing the silver mines of northern New Spain while at the same time maintaining control of the lower Mississippi.

🍁 SOUTHWEST AND NORTHWEST

Yet the Mississippi adventure was not lost, and, while its achievements did not ultimately accrue to Canada, they should be remembered as part of the amazing French enterprise launched from the St. Lawrence. To begin at the headwaters, the triangle formed by the river and Lakes Michigan and Superior was explored in 1678–80 by Daniel Greysolon, Sieur Dulhut (Duluth), but in spite of his bright pageantry of French sovereignty on Lake Mille Lacs, it became a dangerous area of persistent ferments because the middlemen Fox Indians fought the French until those Indians were wiped out (approximately 1700–1740). The Sioux, secure in the possession of Spanish horses which put the all-bountiful buffalo at their mercy, were implacably opposed to the French and their Cree allies.

Midway down the Mississippi, where it was joined by the Chicago-Illinois route and the Missouri, a great trading center and settlement grew up, holding off the English advance from the east by the Ohio, the Cumberland, and the Tennessee, and reaching out to win the Indian trade of the west and southwest from New Spain. And finally in 1699, at the mouth of the great river, a remarkable Canadian warrior, Pierre le Moyne, Sieur d'Iberville, made good the claim to "Louisiana" which La Salle had asserted for his king seventeen years before.

The race with England had been very close, for the Carolinians arrived by land and sea at the same time, but they were evicted by Iberville. Spain could maintain herself no nearer than Pensacola. For the next fifty years, from the Illinois country and from Louisiana, French enterprise was triumphant in the Southwest as far as the Rio Grande and the Pecos. The most dramatic example was the great journey of the Mallet brothers, 1739–41. They traveled up the Missouri and the Platte, penetrated the Rocky Mountains to Spanish Taos and Santa Fé on the upper Rio Grande, and made their way down the Canadian and Arkansas rivers to the Mississippi and New Orleans. Thus, while French Americans never fulfilled the dream of Jean Alfonse at Lachine in 1543 by finding the Spanish North America "where gold and silver abound," they did make themselves masters of the fur and Indian trades between the Appalachians and the Rockies.

Moreover, New France added other plumes to its bonnet by pulling much of the North and Northwest into economic connection with Montreal. The English success on Hudson Bay and the drainage of that basin's furs were not only damaging to French prestige, but, in French-Canadian eyes, unnecessary limitations on profits which could be realized on the St. Lawrence. From 1673 onwards, therefore, an intermittent series of French-Canadian expeditions, overland and around by sea, harassed the English on the bay, practically eliminating their hold in 1683, in 1686, and in 1697. Yet these remarkable successes could somehow never be converted into diplomatic recognition of French sovereignty.

The next best thing, therefore, was to work around the bay inland in a clockwise movement, erecting trading posts where the Indians might be intercepted on their way down the rivers to the English factories. That movement began in 1684 when Dulhut and his brother, La Tourette, occupied both the beginning of the Grand Portage from Lake Superior and the head of Lake Nipigon. In 1688 and 1689 Jacques de Noyon worked in from the Grand Portage to Rainy Lake and Lake of the Woods, but further efforts were delayed by wars. The diminishing fur supply in the Lake Superior region and the drain from the west and north to Hudson Bay led to a revival of the encircling effort in 1728 by Pierre Gaultier de Varennes, Sieur de La Vérendrye, a fur trader of Three Rivers.

Assisted by his remarkable family, he moved in from Nipigon and the Grand Portage, swinging north of the Sioux, to establish himself firmly in control of the Manitoba Basin in 1731–34, thereby intercepting the flow of furs down to York Factory at the mouth of the Nelson River on Hudson Bay. In the autumn of 1738 he crossed on foot from Portage-la-Prairie on the Assiniboine to visit the impressive sod-house village of the Mandans at the great westward bend of the Missouri. From that point two of his sons made a great circuit on foot and horseback during the winter of 1742–43 which took them as far west and south as the Black Hills.

By 1749 the Vérendryes had demonstrated the practicability of cutting off the fur flow down the Saskatchewan, which they had ascended as far as the forks. Their successors in the Winnipeg monopoly claimed to have gone up the river to the Rockies in 1750–51, but the surviving evidence serves rather to indicate that they felt no need to go beyond The Pas except perhaps for some exploration of the portage route between it and the Churchill River, at the mouth of which the English had built a fort and factory in 1731.

By any standards this pre-emption of most of a continent by a population that never exceeded, all told, a hundred thousand French Americans in Newfoundland, Acadia, Canada, the Illinois country, and Louisiana, was an astounding achievement. Increasingly, however, it was an achievement on sufferance. From the days of the Virginians' raids on Acadia at the beginning of the seventeenth century there had been building up along the Atlantic coast a far more substantial aggregation of American population and resources. Unlike the French possessions, the English settlements were divided and discordant. Yet if they ever came to see conquest of the French as a desirable common end and could rally to their support the naval, military, and economic powers of their mother country, it would be next to impossible to prevent their success.

CHAPTER V

Great Britain Closes In (1689-1760)

Modern Americans ordinarily speak of King William's War (1689–97), Queen Anne's War (1702–13), King George's War (1744–48), and the French and Indian War (1754–63). Modern Canadians give these clashes their European titles: the War of the League of Augsburg, the War of the Spanish Succession, the War of the Austrian Succession, and the Seven Years' War.

Natural though it is for North Americans of today to try to slough off any feeling of responsibility for those many years of violence, the fact is that the bitter rivalries of their ancestors for mastery of the continent were every bit as war-provoking as the dynastic, economic, and strategic conflicts in Europe and elsewhere which Voltaire portrayed piercingly in *Candide*. It is worth recalling that to Voltaire New France was a mere few acres of snow and that he wrote to the king's chief minister that he very much preferred peace to Canada.

✲ EUROPEAN RIVALRIES

More important towards understanding the evolution of Canada than the detailed circumstances which set off European wars and provided excuses for their American accompaniments is some recollection of the change in the general European balance of forces. The great sway and prestige of the Austrian and Spanish Hapsburgs had been broken during the first half of the seventeenth century and France had stepped forward to take their place, only to find that two minor (but maritime) powers, the Hollanders and the English, could prove somewhat troublesome.

Fortunately for France, they at first troubled chiefly each other in a series of wars for maritime mastery between 1652 and 1674, but France's hand in nourishing that struggle became obvious at last and both parties were glad to stop, particularly when France also made it evident that she herself intended to subjugate the Low Countries.

Largely because the Dutch had land frontiers which were very expensive to defend, while the English did not, the total effect was almost to eliminate the Hollanders as a threat to English enterprise. In fact, in 1688, when the English found their Stuart king intolerable, they called in as a substitute William of Orange, the Dutch Stadholder who had successfully defied Louis XIV since 1672. "Dutch William" was glad to recruit the resources of his new kingdom into a grand, if somewhat inharmonious, alliance of European states against the French bid for European hegemony.

For about half of the next century and a quarter France and England were at war, war which from the beginning was more and more a contest for world empire. Clearly a struggle lasting four generations betokened reasonably equal strength. France enjoyed truly great advantages in natural wealth, population, and advancement in learning and culture, but she had land frontiers which inevitably involved her in the costly business of disciplining and defending her own borders and countering the ambition or presumption of neighbors who could and did league against her. England was a rather lethargic, primitive country by Continental standards during the first half of the eighteenth century, but was amassing, in a curiously obscure way, remarkable productive strength from her improvements in agriculture and manufactures. The conquest of Canada and mastery of India were to be the first great manifestations of this strength, when a Great Britain, only half-awakened to her potentialities, surprised herself by a complete triumph over France in a war which had begun about as disastrously as possible.

Thus Britain was making up for her small population and relative backwardness by domestic production of such homely staples as woolens, hardware, rum, and cottons; by maritime enterprise which made her a considerable supplier of fish, furs, tobacco, sugar, and Far Eastern products; and by spending a modest proportion of the national income on a navy. She had brought Scotland into the United Kingdom in 1707, thus eliminating her only land frontier, and repression of Scottish and Irish rebellions was thereafter not unduly costly.

NORTH AMERICAN RIVALRIES

When one turns to North American rivalries, it comes as a shock to realize that possession of a single West Indian sugar island, in itself and as a breach in Spanish mercantile control of Central and South America, could be thought more valuable and important to Britain and France than the whole of Canada. The Asiento, or monopoly of trade and of supplying slaves to Spanish America, was regarded as the really great prize won from France after Queen Anne's War in 1713;

indeed much of Britain's liquid capital was gambled on exploiting it in the famous South Sea Bubble. Britain's trade with Jamaica, inside the island barrier of the West Indies and therefore inside Spanish controls, was greater than with Virginia and Maryland, or with Pennsylvania and New York, or with all New England. In other words, the long Anglo-French contest for Canada was thought of in Europe as a troublesome side show. What kept it alive?

Recall the great Y of French North America—St. Lawrence and the lower Great Lakes, Mississippi, the upper Great Lakes and Manitoba Basin. Spain was no threat to this thinly held structure, either from the southwest or from Florida, but the English had found ways both around the bottom and through the passes of the Appalachians all the way north from the Gulf of Mexico to the Mohawk and Richelieu; they had been badgering or dominating Acadia since its foundation; their grip on the Avalon Peninsula and the east coast of Newfoundland was evidence that they would not be ousted from the fisheries; and their dogged persistence in Hudson Bay rewarded them with supplies of furs which New France both coveted and had proved capable of securing. The conflict-breeding urge to monopoly, natural enough in itself, was moderately aggravated by the need for shore stations near the fisheries and became immoderately intense in the conduct of the fur trade.

In normal human fashion, each side felt that it was being "encircled" by the other. La Salle feared that the English would "complete the ruin of New France, which they already hem in by their establishments in Virginia, Pennsylvania, New England, and Hudson's Bay." Fiery Governor Thomas Dongan of New York, who objected to the French extending themselves "so far to the Southward and Westward on the Back side of his Matys Plantacons," wrote to them to say: "I hear that you maintain that the French king might have a title to this province, Virginia, Maryland, and Carolina, because some rivers that run through them rise in the Canadian lakes. He might as well pretend to all the countries that drink clarett and brandy."

A glance at a map of North America brings out the basic strategic considerations in bold relief. The British colonies, stretching from French Acadia to Spanish Florida, were populous and prosperous, exploiting the resources of land and sea so successfully in so many ways that most of them could get along quite well without help from Great Britain. No existing navy could blockade all their ports; no existing army could subjugate and garrison their area or round up their inhabitants. They could only be conquered piecemeal by a sustained campaign of a sort never yet undertaken.

The French colonies, stretching from Newfoundland to New Orleans, were thinly peopled and less than self-sustaining, requiring even some of their foodstuffs from abroad. Whereas the British colonies could trade with each other and the West Indies practically all year round, ice locked New France within the St. Lawrence and cut her off from Acadia, Newfoundland, and the rest of the world for five months of the year. During the winter, communication between the interior and the coast was at best barely possible for men who knew how to travel light. A New Englander could make up a mixed cargo of fish, farm produce, and lumber for the West Indies after the September storms or even after Thanksgiving and be home before Christmas. A Canadian who waited for his harvest knew that he had better stay home.

Moreover, the two stoppers to the Canadian bottle, Newfoundland and Acadia, were by no means impregnable, and, if they were conquered, New France could relatively easily be blockaded into submission. Additional strangling pressure could be exerted up the Hudson-Champlain trough and across the Mohawk-Oswego traverse which would compel costly defenses and threaten diversion of the fur trade, the economic lifeblood of the colony. Farther south, increasingly well-known pack train routes led from the Atlantic coast into the Ohio and Tennessee valleys. Hundreds of "long traders," often in association with renegade *coureurs,* weakened the link between Quebec and New Orleans, not so much in a military sense as by diminishing the returns of both from the Indian trade. During the third quarter of the seventeenth century the desertion of French *coureurs* to the English side showed the superiority of the island kingdom's production and distribution for the Indian market. Rum was cheaper than brandy, and British woolens, hardware, and cured tobacco suited the natives' tastes and values better than French.

APPETITES FOR LAND

British penetration of the Mississippi Valley opened up a great medley of half-felt anticipations of the future. The claims of some coastal colonies to transcontinental extension westward proved to be mere diplomatic pawns unless reinforced by effective enterprise. Fur trading, now a distinctly secondary consideration in the maturing British communities, was too sparse and diffuse an activity to excite the home and colonial governments to conquest for its sake alone. The appetite for land as land, however, was constantly growing, not only among the influential in Great Britain and the colonies, but among the general population as well.

The eighteenth century was notable in Europe for its gambling and large speculations. It was also a time when most wealth was in land

and when great profits were made by its improvement and by its growth in value as population increased. In the colonies, the easiest and most "natural" road to wealth had manifestly proved to be landowning, in fact, the classic colonial scandals grew from the exploitation of official privilege in securing land grants. With immigrants pouring in to reinforce the large natural increase of the established Americans, any man could see where his economic advantage lay.

If this greed seems greatly out of line with the actual needs of the existing colonial populations, one has only to remember how land values grew. Every swell in population pushed them up in nearly every category from the docks and warehouses on tidewater to the unbroken lands on the frontier. Booms and depressions provided a short-run "speculative" element, but the long-run "investment" trend was up except where soils were exhausted. However, soil-exhaustion itself stimulated expansion.

This was becoming evident on the tidewater shelf south of Pennsylvania where clearing and continuous cropping had exhausted the light soils of the great plantations. When their proprietors sought to expand into the heavier soils of the Piedmont, they found that small farmers were ahead of them. It was the great southern proprietors, therefore, who became curious about the Ohio country beyond the Appalachians. New Englanders, pressing against the confines of a much narrower and less fertile Atlantic slope, embarked on township promotions up their long, forested river-valleys and cast envious eyes on the clear, level marshlands on the Bay of Fundy which made Acadia something more to them than merely a strategic area and a base for trade and fisheries.

🍁 THE WARS BEGIN

Thanks to the copious records which have come down to us concerning the tragic woes of the frontiersmen during the Anglo-French wars, we are apt to think of them as the principal victims. Actually, of course, the chief sufferers were the Indians. Living between the contestants, they became pensionaries and agents of terror for whom there was no escape from vassalage. Torn from their own cultural moorings, debauched by alcohol, and decimated by European diseases, whole tribes dwindled away to fragments of little account to others or themselves.

Governor Frontenac's greatest claim to distinction lay in his theatrical, confident, forceful handling of the Iroquois, but after his recall in 1682 those tribes, backed by the English, began to make trouble in the Middle West. Frontenac's successor failed dismally to check their resurgence by invading their homeland from Oswego. The Marquis de Denonville, sent out in 1685 to retrieve the situation, attempted to

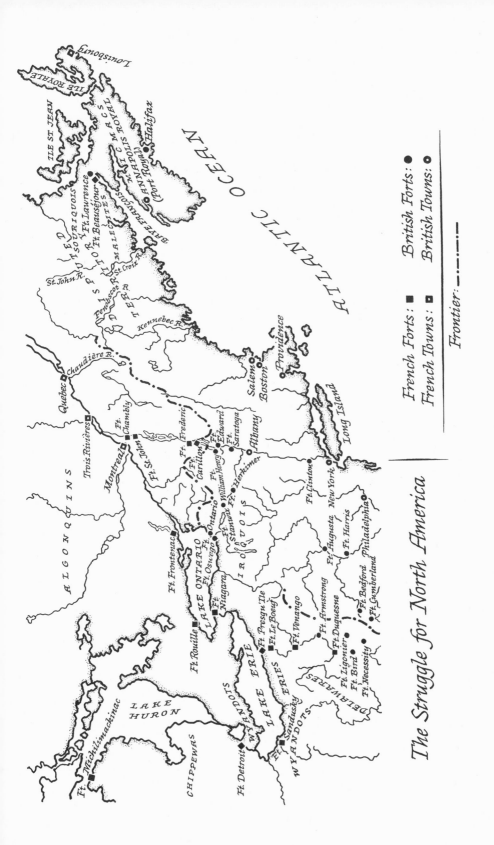

The Struggle for North America

dominate the Great Lakes route by building a fort at Niagara in 1687 and bringing down friendly Indian warriors from the upper Lakes to join a huge French force in cowing the western Senecas.

That was done in the fashion of De Tracy in 1666, but the fort itself could not be maintained and a piece of rank French treachery during some peace negotiations at Fort Frontenac (Cataraqui) so enraged the eastern Iroquois that 1400 of them descended by night on Lachine in August, 1689, and butchered its men, women, and children with appalling cruelties. Now even Fort Frontenac had to be abandoned and the whole colony was in such jeopardy that the aged Governor Frontenac was sent out again to stop the rot and drive the English traders from the Lakes.

The war which began in Europe that year, therefore, was easily grafted onto the war in North America. New France struck at New York. New England struck at Acadia. Superficially 100,000 English colonists were opposed to less than 15,000 French, but the recent revolutionary events in England had upset the colonies and made them less capable than ever of combining. Frontenac terrorized New York into inaction by a night surprise and massacre of about sixty persons at Schenectady early in 1690 and launched similar terroristic raids on the frontiers of New England. New York proved unable or unwilling to counterattack. Maritime New England responded the same year by assaulting and ravaging neglected Acadia, but when the expedition sailed on up the St. Lawrence to Quebec, Frontenac boldly relied on his defenses and the lateness of the season to thwart them.

With the threat to the heart of New France disposed of, the French carried the war to the enemy until its close in 1697. Frontenac destroyed the Mohawk villages in 1693, re-established Fort Frontenac in 1694, and laid waste the Onondagas and Oneidas in 1696. The Iroquois were removed as a menace for sixty years. Bloody raids cowed and drove in the frontiers of New York and New England by land and sea. Secure in Acadia, the French became masters of Newfoundland and triumphed on Hudson Bay. Frontenac died in 1698, just a year before his Canadian war hawk, Iberville, crowned the achievement by establishing control of the lower Mississippi.

Half-submerged in the dubious behavior of New York during this and later wars was the knowledge of the Albany traders that they possessed advantages in the Indian trade which Montreal could not equal. For about a generation the Albany market had proved so advantageous that a smuggling trade had grown up, not only by Indians and *coureurs* threading the inland forests and waterways, but directly from Montreal by the Richelieu and Lake Champlain. The Canadian authorities estimated that this contraband amounted to about 50,000 pounds of beaver a year, that is, it was equal to a quarter or possibly a third of the annual legitimate export of furs from New France. They tried to stop it by fines, imprisonments, and even military garrisons, but could not stamp out skilled groups of Indian smugglers backed by astute and defiant "waterfront rascals" in the merchant community of Montreal. All of the parties concerned in the trade would have been best pleased by a state of peace or, if war broke out, of local neutrality.

A quite similar state of affairs existed between New England and Acadia, reaching round to the Gulf and even into the St. Lawrence River, again because of the superiority of British production and distribution over French. New England merchants actually maintained small warehouses in French Port Royal during times of peace in spite of mercantilistic prohibitions. A Boston group, with connections and influence in official circles, was building up a highly profitable trade, even in contraband during war.

King William's War pretty well convinced Albany and Boston that peace or neutrality was out of the question, and at this point a new actor appeared on the scene. This was Samuel Vetch, a professional soldier who brought to New York in 1699 what could be salvaged from the disastrous failure of the Scottish colony at Darien on the Isthmus of Panama. His marriage in 1700 to Robert Livingston's daughter Margaret allied him with the Albany Scottish and Dutch merchants and their designs. About 1702 he moved to Boston, where he plunged quickly into the dubious Massachusetts trade with Acadia and New France.

After some serious clashes with colonial opinion and British authority he became persuaded that the only solution lay in conquest. From 1706 or 1707 on, he devoted his energies to rousing Great Britain and her colonies to undertaking the joint enterprise, the blending of Albany's and Boston's ambitions, which could so relatively easily deliver North America into their hands—so easily, he felt, that Spain might subsequently be evicted. In memorial after memorial he demonstrated in detail the practicability of his amplification of the so-called Albany Plan—the combination of a land attack from the Hudson on Montreal with a water-borne assault from Boston on Acadia and Quebec. This was to become a strategical commonplace in North America for a century and a quarter.

THE OUTPOSTS FALL

The Treaty of Ryswick in 1697 marked a halt for financial recuperation in Louis XIV's ambitions. His situation in Europe was so uncertain that he agreed to a mutual restitution of conquests, a solution singularly out of keeping with French achievements in North America. Five years later, however, succumbing to a prospect of glory and power, he planted a Bourbon on the throne of Spain, and the duel with "Dutch William's" England was on again for eleven years.

This time the English produced a military genius and artist in the management of allies—John Churchill, Duke of Marlborough, who won a series of smashing victories over the French armies which put France herself at his mercy and started her decline. French weakness in Europe was naturally reflected in North America. Canada and Acadia were thrown on the defensive for the most part. Only one considerable raid was made against New England, at Deerfield on the Connecticut in 1704. In order to protect the precarious St. Lawrence entry with almost no help from home, the French commanders of Placentia (Newfoundland) and Port Royal embarked on brilliant, dashing, self-supporting privateering against the British and colonial shipping which followed the Great Circle past Acadia and Newfoundland.

Obviously this was the occasion for Vetch's plan to become public policy, and so it did. In 1709, Pennsylvania, New Jersey, and New York were to combine in the land attack by Lake Champlain and the Richelieu on Montreal. New England was to assemble men and transports at Boston to join a British naval and military assault on Quebec. In spite of sad controversies among the colonists and unfulfilled obligations on the part of New Jersey and Pennsylvania, a remarkably good job was done in America, but British aid was diverted to Portugal.

A second attempt in 1710 was co-ordinated so late in the year that the land attack on Montreal had to be put off and the great Boston assemblage could be used only to overwhelm little Port Royal (henceforth Annapolis Royal) in Acadia. The new Tory Government in Great Britain decided to finish things off in 1711 with 6000 of Marlborough's veterans, but they entrusted the commands to political favorites—General "Jack" Hill and Admiral Sir Hovenden Walker. These misfits quarreled with the colonists and the sea captains, failed to use Vetch's advice and knowledge of the St. Lawrence, and ended up by piling ten ships on Egg Island in the St. Lawrence with the loss of about 750 men. They refused to go on to Quebec or even to attack Placentia and the land expedition towards Montreal had to retreat in a hurry.

In all of this New France had been lucky, and France itself was lucky too, for the British Tories used their influence on Queen Anne to dismiss Marlborough and force a conclusion of the long war in 1713. Yet the Treaty of Utrecht of that year had to reflect in some degree the defeat of France. In Europe the transfer of the Asiento to Great Britain was the great reward; indeed the subsequent profits from trade in slaves and goods with the Spanish colonies amounted to an enormous accretion of strength during the next generation.

In America, France surrendered her territorial claims to "the outposts of the Canadian citadel"—Hudson Bay, Newfoundland, and Acadia—but managed to qualify these surrenders. The boundaries of Hudson Bay and Acadia were not specified. Fishing rights were retained on "the French Shore," i.e. most of the east and west coasts of Newfoundland. The islands of the Gulf of St. Lawrence remained French, most notably Cape Breton and Ile St. Jean (later Prince Edward Island).

THE BENEFITS OF PEACE: ACADIA

Thanks largely to Sir Robert Walpole's refusal to embroil Great Britain in war, North America now enjoyed peace for a generation, and both Acadia and New France benefited greatly. Most of the Acadians, who had permission to emigrate, found that they preferred their own land under lackadaisical British masters to the rigors of life on Cape Breton, which France was converting into a Gibraltar for the St. Lawrence by building a great fortress at Louisbourg. Since neither Great Britain nor New England was prepared to colonize Nova Scotia, British sovereignty there was represented by a puny garrison, coasting merchants from New England, and a vigorous summer fishery up at Canso.

In these circumstances, the Acadians stubbornly insisted that they must be treated as neutrals in any Anglo-French war or conflict with the Indians, and by 1730 they succeeded in extracting from Governor Richard Philipps this qualification to their oath of allegiance, verbally and recorded by their priests. They then settled down to the happiest period of their existence. They had their priests as leaders and self-chosen deputies from their own number to speak for them in dealings with the British administration. They followed their own law and custom, while their tiny company of military masters tried to regulate their own shadowy administration and law by obeying British orders to follow the procedures of Virginia.

The best evidence that the Acadians (known commonly as "the French Neutrals") were well off was their expansion in population and settlement. Having passed the thousand mark about 1693, they numbered about 1600 at the time of their conquest in 1710. From then on their numbers swelled so rapidly that there may have been as many as 10,000 of them by the middle of the century. The Annapolis region was like a beehive which produced swarms to settle elsewhere. Young men aiming to set up for themselves traveled up the Annapolis Valley, across the barrens at its head, and down into the fertile Minas Basin

From it, in turn, they pushed on to Beaubassin and the Isthmus of Chignecto, using their dyking technique to reclaim their lands.

They built modest but substantial homes; set out gardens and orchards; and practiced for the most part an easy, careless agriculture which produced more hay, feed, and livestock than grain. Hunting and fishing provided fun as well as sustenance. Their local and New England markets were supplemented by their ability to transport livestock on its own feet across the isthmus to ships which carried it to Louisbourg. They had little shipping of their own beyond rowboats and small fishing craft, but coasting ships from New England came almost to their doors to carry on the most variegated barter.

🍁 NEW FRANCE

Guy Frégault has painted in *La civilisation de la Nouvelle-France* (1944) a glowing but critical picture of what was happening during the same years along the St. Lawrence. It was, as he points out, an armed peace, and of all the problems which New France had to face, the most basic was the lack of manpower. Attempts to remedy this brought possibly 4000 recruits from overseas between 1713 and 1744, but natural increase was more rewarding, for the population rose from 18,119 in 1713 to 33,682 in 1730, and to about 45,000 in 1744, in spite of the inroads of epidemics and the climatic and other risks of somewhat marginal existence.

In the face of quite astonishing ecclesiastical commands and inquisitions, calculated to secure the ascetic behavior of the governor and his circle, Quebec was acquiring the elegance and learning which led the Swedish traveler, Peter Kalm, to regard its core in 1749 as the most cultivated, polished little society in North America. Montreal was more like Albany, a hard and somewhat unsavory assemblage of merchants on the make which became a brawling frontier town when the fur brigades arrived or departed. Fortunately or unfortunately, France rather than New France controlled the fur trade and reaped its basic profits, so that the Montreal burghers did not acquire enough wealth from their undertakings to rival the comfortable townsmen's pretensions of their counterparts in Boston or Philadelphia. Thanks, therefore, to the almost identical social effects of the colony's political, ecclesiastical, and economic patterns, its high culture was a transplanted European culture with shallow roots in North America. It was no accident that New France never had a printing press.

Urban and rural society were becoming increasingly differentiated and divided—a schism which was to broaden in the future. There was an absurd, disproportionate emphasis on status which had much to do with the numerous, endless quarrels about rank and often empty privilege. Seigneurs and captains of militia were frequently at odds because the latter represented in part habitant attitudes and in part the wishes of central authority. The chronic conflicts between churchmen and administrations, on the other hand, laid the foundations of an alliance between ecclesiastics and seigneurs.

The seigneurs provided little or no aristocracy; their livelier sons and the livelier young habitants frequently took to the woods as licensed or unlicensed *coureurs de bois,* and four-fifths of the people wrestled with the endless tasks of frontier agriculture on the margins of the forest. By 1760, the majority of the lay seigneurs were the sons of habitants. The habitants felt the benefits of good and thoughtful administrations and suffered in remote, mysterious ways from the operations of looting officialdom. Their gnawing, unsatisfied need was for manpower to open up the lands.

Like the other American colonies, New France was chronically subject to the drain of hard money into the hands of the outsiders, French and English, who exploited it. As early as 1685, resort had been had to paper money in the form of playing cards cut into four pieces each, signed and denominated by the intendant. Similar practices continued. Bitter experience with the accompanying inflation, culminating as it did in gross corruption during the Seven Years' War, bred lasting suspicions of public taxes, but the habitants were milked dry in indirect ways.

"Extreme poverty is the rule in Canada," reported the governor and the intendant in 1737. The Canadians' only effective response was intractability. In 1720, Governor Vaudreuil castigated their intractable and mutinous disposition, and ten years later Intendant Hocquart reported flatly: "They are naturally perverse." Lacking money, they quietly built up a gay, neighborly existence based on the homes they built for themselves and the rude plenty they extracted from the land and denied to officialdom.

Fundamentally, then, theirs was a marginal economy, exploited by individual French officials and merchants, but intermittently supported by France through state and church and philanthropy because it represented a great French commitment which ought to be maintained against Britain and her imposing colonies and against protestantism and its ways. Yet the main burden of the grossly unequal economic contest with the British in America fell on the French in America and their Indian allies. In a military sense, the burden also fell chiefly on the Indians and the local militia.

Frégault's summary is to the point: "Here are men who have

mastered a homeland for themselves; when it has had to be defended and then reconstructed, they have had to depend in effect on their resources alone. Today their land is their achievement. It belongs to them. They belong to it. This is the profound justification of their national feeling." As early as 1730 that feeling was so strong that the Bishop proposed to put a French priest between any two parishes served by Canadians, and Canadian officers took pride in distinguishing themselves from French.

❧ WAR AGAIN

Wounded at its tenderest point, the legal and illegal trade with the Spanish Empire in the Americas, Great Britain went to war with Spain in 1739 in spite of Walpole. That war became the general European War of the Austrian Succession in 1744 and evoked in North America open manifestations of the contests which had been going on below the surface during the armed peace.

During that interval, threatened France and New France had taken many precautionary steps. At Louisbourg on Cape Breton a great stone fortress had been built. Its own defensive strength and protected anchorage were designed to be guarantees of sure access to the St. Lawrence and a menace to British sovereignty, trade, and fisheries in Acadia and Newfoundland. In the interior, forts and trading posts staked out four defense lines. Across the St. Lawrence from Quebec the Chaudière Valley, leading towards the Kennebec, had been systematically settled on semimilitary lines. Montreal was similarly served along the Richelieu, with Fort Fréderic (Crown Point), almost at the head of Lake Champlain, as a strong outpost. A third line, defended by Fort Frontenac and Fort Niagara, was to secure control of the Lakes and the Presque Isle portage from Lake Erie to the Allegheny and the Ohio. The posts at Detroit and Michilimackinac, the fourth line, were to cover the Chicago portage and also Lake Superior, beyond which La Vérendrye was establishing control of the Manitoba Basin.

To all this Britain and her colonies had made almost no substantial response. The fort at Annapolis Royal was rotting and washing away. Canso was defended by little more than ramshackle barracks. Oswego was far more a successful trading and smuggling center than a military stronghold. In fact the one really substantial new defense was a huge stone fortress at Churchill on the west side of Hudson Bay, where homesick stone masons struggled with Arctic frosts from 1732 to 1771 without ever really completing their job. Perhaps fittingly, it was surrendered to the French in 1782 without firing a shot.

It was a good thing for Great Britain that the navy had been built up during the previous five years of war with Spain, for when the Anglo-French war broke out the French promptly snuffed out Canso and bottled up the garrison at Annapolis until New England came to the rescue. Then under the inspired leadership of Governor William Shirley, New England promptly did even more. With the aid of ten cannon from New York and a highly efficient naval flotilla brought up from the West Indies, four thousand Puritans, led by the merchant, William Pepperell, surprised themselves and everyone else by overwhelming Louisbourg in about six weeks of the summer of 1745. The defending regulars were aggrieved, the militia was untrained, stores and munitions were deficient, and the British navy fought off relief by sea.

And then, in a curious series of deflations, the war which had begun so vigorously as to presage a decisive assault on Quebec came to an inconclusive end. In 1746 half the naval force of France was committed to an expedition for the reconquest of Nova Scotia and an attack on Boston only to be dissipated by storms, disease, and despair, at sea and in a ghastly encampment at Chebucto (Halifax and the Bedford Basin). Not only did the co-operating Canadian land force have to disperse, but, with the threat miraculously lifted, a huge American contingent designed for an attack on Quebec was ordered to disband. In 1747 France tried again, only to lose most of her navy and much of her merchant marine in two smashing British victories off the European coast. The prospective Canadian land force had performed a remarkable, if bloody, feat that February by a snowshoe attack, surprise, and massacre of a New England garrison at Grand Pré on the Minas Basin.

INSINCERE TRUCE

In Europe Marshal de Saxe was winning the Low Countries for France, as Marlborough once had for England. Both countries, however, were on the edge of financial collapse. Peace that meant only a truce was made at Aix-la-Chapelle in April, 1748. London got the French out of Madras and the Low Countries at the price of handing back Louisbourg, a blow to New England which £235,000 for expenses could not assuage. Next year Britain made more welcome amends by embarking on the prodigiously expensive business of founding Halifax and trying to make a British colony out of Acadian Nova Scotia.

In North America, the peace was a pretense. A self-conscious, vigorous, and expansive New England took Nova Scotia under its wing, pretty well submerged the British and Continental Protestant colonists brought out to Halifax, and planned unceasingly the anglicization of Nova Scotia and a new assault on Canada. The French, in reply, operating from Cape Breton and Ile St. Jean (Prince Edward Island), gave remarkably free rein to a fanatical priest, Jean Louis Le Loutre, in his efforts to create a belligerent "French Acadia" on the Isthmus of Chignecto under the protection of Fort Beauséjour. The Acadians wanted to be neutral, but he forced the withdrawal of some of them by burning their nearest settlement and by using his Indians to overawe them. Many of the rest of the Acadians, whose homes had not been burnt, also withdrew in fear. A temporary stalemate was established by the building of Fort Lawrence just east of Beauséjour in 1750, after which increasing pressure was exerted on the Acadian majority within the British sphere.

🍁 A NORTH AMERICAN WAR

Not much happened immediately on the New York frontier, for the New Yorkers were diffident and divided. The great inland focus of attention was now the Ohio country, for not only were British traders increasingly active in the area, but the Virginia and Maryland Ohio Company announced in 1748 its extensive and rather flimsy territorial claims. Here it was that North American war broke out in 1754 between Virginian aggressors and French-Canadian defenders two years before the nations became embroiled in Europe. Very swiftly, from the West Indies and Louisiana to Hudson Bay, all Americans were involved willy-nilly. This time over a million British colonists were to bring their energies to bear upon about 10,000 Acadians and 55,000 French Canadians.

It took six years to finish the job. From 1754 to 1758 almost everything went disastrously for Britain and her colonists, while Louisbourg still menaced Nova Scotia and New England and protected Quebec. One tragic consequence of this, and of the galloping fear which followed the destruction of Braddock's great expedition to the Ohio in 1755, was that Beauséjour was captured and the Acadians were told that they must accept the full obligations of British subjects. When they insisted once more on the neutral status which had been tolerated and to which they had on the whole been faithful for forty-five years, the consequences of their unfortunate geographical position overwhelmed them. They were rounded up in their settlements and distributed in small batches amongst the coastal colonies.

The turn of the tide towards Great Britain came at the end of 1757 when the dynamic William Pitt began to pour energy and inspiration into the now classical plan for the conquest of Canada. Here he would defeat France while his subsidized allies fought the land war in Europe. Seldom has there been so overwhelming a superiority in men and ships and arms so deftly and daringly resisted by its predestined victim, for in the Marquis de Montcalm New France enjoyed a superb defender, and the French navy distinguished itself greatly in getting supplies and reinforcements through to the besieged colonies. Montcalm fought so brilliantly against attacks in the crucial Lake George–Lake Champlain and Oswego areas that he practically dictated diversion of the British menace to Louisbourg and Quebec, both of which might be aided from France by sea.

The men who won the British victory have received too much acclaim, for students of warfare have demonstrated that their talents were moderate. Once the overpowering British and colonial forces were set in motion with assurance of sustained support, they could scarcely have failed.

In 1758 Admiral Boscawen, General Amherst, and Colonel Wolfe subjugated Louisbourg in an eight weeks' siege by land and sea, but an attack at Ticonderoga on Lake Champlain, though the attackers were in a majority of three to one, failed with appalling casualties. The captures of Fort Frontenac and Fort Duquesne (Pittsburgh) were small compensation. In 1759 navy and army under Admiral Saunders and the now General Wolfe moved up the unprotected St. Lawrence to besiege Quebec. Montcalm held them off brilliantly in clash after clash from June 26 to the beginning of September. With winter threatening to force withdrawal of the life-giving fleet, Wolfe decided on a last gamble by landing upriver from Quebec. After a brisk battle on September 13, in which both commanders were mortally wounded, beleaguered Quebec surrendered five days later.

The cautious Amherst was to have come up the Champlain trough and down the river to join the seaborne expedition at or above Quebec, but he never got there. The French forces at Montreal were therefore able to attempt the recapture of Quebec in the spring of 1760. They too won a battle just to the west of Quebec and drove General Murray into the fortress, but they had not the artillery with which to besiege it. The fate of Canada was settled, however, when the British navy got into the St. Lawrence before the French and reached Quebec early in May.

The French army retreated with Murray in pursuit. At Montreal the converging forces from Quebec, from Lake Champlain, and from Lake Ontario at last came together in the first week of September. There was nothing for Governor Vaudreuil to do but surrender. The far-flung empire of France in North America was at Britain's mercy. After very serious discussion as to whether it would be more advantageous to Great Britain to obtain the West Indian island of Guadeloupe instead of Canada at the peace conference in 1763, all French North America east of the Mississippi except two tiny unfortified islands south of New-foundland passed into the British hands, which conceivably might have grasped it long before.

CHAPTER VI

British North America (1760-75)

🍁 IMPERIAL DISCORDS

By her great victory over France, Great Britain acquired more than she had the political wit to handle. Grenada was added to her West Indian possessions. East and West Florida, with the Bahamas, gave her control of the vital channel which Spain had successfully defended for 250 years. Nova Scotia's boundaries might now be whatever Britain chose to make them. The islands in the Gulf of St. Lawrence and the shores of Gaspé, Newfoundland, and Labrador conferred command of the richest bank and boat fisheries in the world, not to speak of a great salmon fishery and abundance of whales, walruses, and seals. The St. Lawrence and Hudson Bay were both centers for the prosperous great fur trade, and a lethargic Spain promised little effective resistance if the eastern half of the Mississippi Basin set out to exploit the western.

Nothing could have been more inviting to co-ordinated enterprise if the managers of empire in London had been able to marshal their counters like chessmen, but the plain fact was that each piece on the board possessed energies and ambitions of its own, occasionally harmonizing neatly with British mercantilistic designs, but for the most part at odds with Britain, or with some other counters, or with both. Many of the older colonies were even sharply at odds within themselves, most frequently in the form of enmity between the privileged oligarchical owners of property and capital along the coast and the robust, money-poor frontiersmen who were systematically deprived of an equitable share in government and "milked" by merchants and lenders.

Conquest had not erased local particularisms. Few of the transplanted Acadians, for instance, struck roots in the British colonies. Their consuming ambition was to escape. Hundreds died in the French

West Indies; a few formed a refuge in Spanish Louisiana; others gathered in British Quebec and French St. Pierre. Most of the survivors, however, made for home, even one large and especially privileged group who were wards of the king in France. By 1767, when France evicted about 1200 of them from St. Pierre and Miquelon, timorous Nova Scotia at last was brought to agree that they were harmless and they were allowed to become legal settlers in some of the less desirable parts of the province. A good many thought it safer to move quietly into areas beyond the ordinary operation of authority.

In other words, most of the Europeans in North America had become so American as to be unhappy in Europe and so attached to their own localities and cultures as to feel both defensive and hostile towards others.

Most of settled North America might now be under one flag, but there was little corresponding sense of solidarity among the North Americans thus embraced. The old hostilities between colonists of French, British, and Spanish stocks could not be expected to vanish overnight, and added to these were strangeness and distrust involving Acadians, Canadians, Illinoians, and Louisianans, and analogous sentiments separating the colonists of predominantly British blood. Even within colonies there were harsh and rending regional, economic, and social schisms. Some of the older British colonies had tried at Albany in 1754 to form a plan of union and had failed utterly. Even during the wars, colony had abused colony for its real or imagined failings, and frontiersmen had flamed with grief-stricken anger against lethargic, comfortable townsmen. The deepest dividing chasm, of course, was that between Protestant New England and the Catholics of the Maritime region and Quebec, for in almost every facet of existence they were diametrically opposed—religion, language, government, law, economic philosophy, and social organization.

Moreover, a change of masters could not change the regional activities which the resources of North America had dictated to its exploiters during the past century and a half. The Maritime region, where the St. Lawrence reached the Atlantic, would breed the same rivalries among British subjects as it had bred between British and French. British masters of the St. Lawrence would continue to use their monopoly of the avenue to the Great Lakes, the Ohio country, and the Mississippi Valley against New York and the colonies farther south, and their capacity to divert the furs of North and Far West to Montreal against the Hudson Bay region.

Finally, the area from the crest of the Appalachians to the Atlantic, by its resources and its very proximity to the ocean, had called into being a complex trading economy whose growth flatly contradicted Great Britain's own mercantilistic design. New England had become as maritime-minded as Old England, and the other older colonies, being coastal too, were voluntarily or involuntarily contributing to an ever more imposing American apparatus of trade and transportation. American ships were carrying American products to Europe and the West Indies in a singularly efficient way. They were also carrying European products to Africa and America, slaves to the West Indies, and sugar, tobacco, and molasses to American consumers and distillers and traders, regardless of whether these products came from British or French islands. They were increasingly defiant of British attempts at regulation, increasingly prosperous from illegal trade with French and Spanish possessions, and increasingly confident that they could get along best if operating on their own.

BRITISH POLITICAL ENGROSSMENTS

Conceivably no power on earth was capable of unifying and managing so heterogeneous an American empire, not to speak of African and Asiatic possessions as well. In any case, however, the course of domestic politics in Great Britain almost guaranteed that imperial affairs would not get adequate attention. In 1760 the new king, George III, supported by a substantial part of the governing class, began a twenty-five year campaign to break the quasi monopoly of political power which the Whigs had built up after 1688 and had operated in an increasingly arrogant way for the past forty years. It is unnecessary to pursue the clashes of interest and faction. One has only to recall how home politics characteristically eclipse foreign or imperial in almost any society to understand why British affairs overseas received less than enlightened attention precisely during the years when they demanded it in unprecedented degree.

PONTIAC'S WAR

Canada surrendered in September, 1760, and the treaty confirming the surrender was signed in February, 1763. While a recently shuffled British government was working out arrangements for the future based upon the capitulations of Quebec and Montreal and the treaty, an American event made action urgent. Out in the region between Lake Erie and Lake Michigan the Indians had risen against their new British masters. A very few experienced men had known that this was almost bound to happen when peace came and the Indians' "value" collapsed because Britain and France ceased competing for their services.

In the Lakes region and the Ohio country both soldiers and traders were contemptuous of the Indians in spite of the warnings of experts like Sir William Johnson of the Mohawk and George Croghan of Pennsylvania. Jeffrey Amherst, with fatal shortsightedness, prohibited the allowance of "any presents by way of *Bribes,* for, if they do not behave properly, they are to be punished." The traders, instead of humoring the natives, made it obvious that they intended to stand for no nonsense from them. British colonial frontiersmen were convinced that "the only good Indian is a dead Indian." These abrupt deflations of the Indians' economic and personal status were beyond bearing.

The revolt, under the leadership of Pontiac, was a wily and hideous affair; it was full of such stratagems as the lacrosse game outside the fort at Michilimackinac where the ball led players, turned warriors, inside to capture the fort. Pontiac's theme, in the form of a communication from the Great Spirit, was a fundamental one.

Why do you suffer the white men to dwell among you? . . . Why do you not clothe yourselves in skins, as [your ancestors] did, and use the bows and arrows, and the stone-pointed lances, which they used? . . . You have bought guns, knives, kettles, and blankets, from the white men, until you can no longer do without them; and, what is worse, you have drunk the poison firewater, which turns you into fools. Fling all these things away. . . . And as for these English . . . you must lift the hatchet against them . . . The children of your great father, the King of France, are not like the English. . . . They are very dear to me, for they love the red men, and understand the true mode of worshipping me.

One after another eight forts and trading posts west of Niagara fell to the Indians before the lethargic Amherst came to life. His belated relief expeditions, however, coincided with the exhaustion of the Indians' supplies of food and munitions, so that at Niagara, in July, 1764, Sir William Johnson was able to convince the Indians that they must henceforth depend on Great Britain alone. George Croghan, mopping up from the Ohio country a year later, imposed the same conclusion upon Pontiac himself at Detroit, the only western post which had held out. Four years later a British trader bribed an Illinois Indian to tomahawk the once-great leader in the woods.

❧ THE PROCLAMATION OF 1763

Pontiac's rising was to haunt the memories and affect the thinking of experts in the affairs of the interior for another thirty years or more, but in 1763 it added urgency to the issuance of the king's proclamation (of October 7, 1763) for the governance of his recent conquests. That proclamation (supplemented by governors' commissions and instructions) was one of the most ingenious and yet wrongheaded instruments in the history of British colonial policy. Its basic aim was to attract "old subjects" to settle in Quebec, East Florida, and West Florida. It therefore offered vacant lands free to ex-soldiers and on easy terms to others.

To make these areas congenial, intending settlers were promised general assemblies as soon as circumstances would permit, and in the meantime, under a governor, four officials, and a council of local residents, they might "confide in our Royal Protection for the Enjoyment of the Benefit of the Laws of our Realm of England." And then, in an attempt to kill two birds with one stone, to divert the expanding population of the coastal colonies into the new provinces and at the same time to follow the French example and tranquilize the interior of the continent as the Indians' hunting ground, settlement was forbidden west of "the Heads or Sources of any of the rivers which fall into the Atlantic Ocean."

The new province of Quebec was to be a relatively small area, a rough parallelogram enclosing the St. Lawrence from its opening into the Gulf to a southwestern boundary made up of the forty-fifth parallel from the Connecticut to the St. Lawrence and a line from there to Lake Nipissing. The southeastern boundary along the height of land from Chaleur Bay to the Connecticut was to keep the French Canadians off the Atlantic coast. Labrador was attached to Newfoundland so that the naval stations on the island could prevent smuggling. The northwestern boundary was designed to keep Quebec outside the preserves of the Hudson's Bay Company.

Why was all this ingenuity wrongheaded? Because it contradicted inexorable facts. Pioneering British Americans had little inclination to move to French Quebec, but many of them and many land speculators were determined to get into the now fabled Ohio lands in spite of George III and the Indians. Sixty-five thousand French Canadians, with generations of their own law and custom ingrained in all their ways, were sure to be utterly dismayed by, rather than enjoy, "the Benefit of the Laws of our Realm of England." On the other hand, two or three hundred "old subjects," mostly merchants, who did follow their business-seeking noses into Quebec, were bound to rave with frustration if denied "the rights of Englishmen" and the customary processes of English commercial law. The French, being Roman Catholics, could neither vote for, nor sit in, a British colonial assembly. If the few Britons were allowed to have one, it would be about as unrepresentative a body as could be invented. Finally, Quebec was denied control of the hinterland which had always been its nourishment.

THE OLD PROVINCE
OF QUEBEC

Boundary, 1763
Boundary Extension, 1774

🍁 THE CANADIAN FACT

Many books have been written about Britain's efforts from 1760 to 1774 to solve the problem of government in Quebec, for the intricacies and complexities of that experiment were to have consequences of the greatest importance. Yet an enquirer comes back always to "the Canadian fact," that is, to the ordered and resourceful existence in a particular part of North America of 65,000 persons who had made it their own. Even if the obloquy and shame attached to the expulsion of the Acadians had not been present in British minds, there could be no practical possibility of expelling that number of Canadians.

In fact, just as the prospect of losing Acadian settlers to French Cape Breton and Ile St. Jean had clouded Nova Scotian policy after 1710, so did the usefulness of Canadians as a potential threat to wayward spirits in the coastal colonies color British policy towards Quebec. In November, 1759, while he was locked up in Quebec and the fate of Canada still unsettled, General James Murray wrote to General Amherst:

> Every Body will inform you how powerful and how flourishing this Colony was, and how formidable it might be under any other Government than that of Monsʳ Vaudreuil; En bonne Politique it should perhaps be destroyed, but there may be Reasons why it should remain, as it is a Guarantee for the good Behaviour of its neighboring Colonies.

Even such strategic ideas as these, however, were less than the Canadian fact. Great Britain and the future Canada were going to be forced to adapt themselves to it rather than manipulate it to their ends. The original Canadians were the tenacious survivors of a long struggle for existence. They had learned successful American ways and they had modified European ones. They had made a good life for themselves.

They were also a conquered people, thrown back on their inner, spiritual resources for defense of their individual and collective sense of distinct being. Like subject and minority peoples throughout history, they were impelled to reassure themselves of their separate entity with such mottoes as *"Je me souviens," "Soyons nous mêmes,"* and *"Je suis canadien."* And, tragically, if understandably, practically any action, look, or phrase of their conquerors would be interpreted as contempt, superiority, or malice towards them. This terrible heritage of sheer inability in two kinds of Canadians to understand each other has been the heaviest cross that Canada has had to bear. Physical nature made Canada a tough country to master. Human nature proved unmasterable.

⚜ GOVERNMENT UNDER THE PROCLAMATION

The period of military government before the Proclamation of 1763 came into force on August 10, 1764, was much pleasanter for the Canadians than what had gone before. During the winter of 1759–60, the troops stinted themselves to feed the Canadians and Quebec women knitted stockings for bare-legged Highlanders. Governor Murray liked the Canadians for their apparent docility and treated them very well. They were, he said, "perhaps the bravest and best race upon the globe" and if relieved of some political disabilities (as Catholics) would soon "become the most faithful and useful set of men in this American empire." British soldiers were better masters than the last corrupt group of French officials. They could be stern on occasion, but they were quite prepared to take advice from the captains of militia and to adapt their own ideas of law and justice to what they could learn about Canadian law and custom.

Real trouble naturally developed under the inappropriate proclamation, and for ten years there was a continuous series of investigations and reports into how some substitute for that silly edict could be fashioned. The habitants apparently rather enjoyed the confusion, for they could if they wished evade or delay payment of dues to seigneurs and tithes to the church, and there was quite a lot of fun to be had from their old entertainment of litigation. Advantage could be taken of the Britons who had bought seigneuries when the French army and officials moved out. Moreover, the farmer was paid for his goods and services in hard cash instead of almost worthless paper.

To the little British mercantile communities at Quebec and Montreal, however, the situation was infuriating. They naturally wanted a substantial voice in government. They could point to the unfulfilled promises of the proclamation, but knew quite well that these could not be fulfilled in the circumstances. They could and did get Governor Murray recalled for real or fancied offenses against their group, but they received Governor Guy Carleton in his place.

Carleton was another soldier who soon liked peasants infinitely better than merchants, and who quite naturally thought in terms of allying government with the "gentry," that is, with the seigneurs and clergy, so that the latter might control and direct the general population towards approved ends. A tacit subterfuge gave Quebec a Roman Catholic bishop as early as 1766. Carleton carried Murray's idea of 1759 to an extreme conclusion, for he believed that the Canadians might be organized and armed to form a force which would keep the unruly coastal colonies subject to British authority.

🍁 THE QUEBEC ACT

Yet, although we shall see that these colonies were rapidly moving towards overt rebellion, it must be asserted that it was the Canadian fact which dictated the settlement of 1774 in Quebec. The Quebec Act of that year, to all intents and purposes, gave the French Canadians what they had had before the conquest, with London substituted for Versailles. Fifteen years of reports and suggestions from Canada, set over against fifteen years of hectic domestic politics in Great Britain, could produce nothing better.

The act committed the government of Quebec to a governor and a nominated council of from seventeen to twenty-three members, English and French. It established the old French feudal system and civil law, and introduced the more open, if not necessarily more humane, English criminal law. It gave the church its tithes and the seigneurs their dues. By alteration of the forms of British antipapal oaths, it admitted Roman Catholics to office and citizenship.

The instructions to Carleton which followed the act explained how he and the council might use their legislative power to modify or amplify the law so as partially to satisfy the merchants. They recommended the introduction of habeas corpus and of English law for "personal actions grounded upon debts, promises, contracts and agreements, whether of a mercantile or other nature, and also of wrongs proper to be compensated in damages." The imminence of rebellion elsewhere in North America strengthened Carleton's disinclination to make even this attempt to adjust to the practices of a particularly aggressive group. He therefore concealed those instructions.

One great concession had been made to the merchants in the act by the enormous extension of the boundaries of Quebec. Not only was Labrador taken from Newfoundland, but Montreal was confirmed in its advantage over Albany and Philadelphia by extension of the boundary to the height of land between the St. Lawrence–Great Lakes Basin and Hudson Bay. The boundary followed the height of land to the headwaters of the Mississippi, and embraced practically the whole area north of a line made by the upper Mississippi and the Ohio. This was recognition of a situation which had crystallized in practice about 1768, and it was accompanied by an express proviso that it would not prejudice the western claims of the older colonies, but it added fuel to the flames of rebellion. Many "old subjects" saw in it and the rest of the Quebec Act a reconstruction of the menace of New France as it had taken form in Talon's mind a hundred years before.

⚜ A NEW NEW ENGLAND

"Down east" from Massachusetts, where the frontier was the ocean instead of the interior of North America, circumstances dictated a different solution. The resolute, mounting aggressiveness against French America displayed since 1690 by Massachusetts was part of an expansive energy, an imperialism if you will, which could occupy territory as well as advance commerce. Nova Scotia, which had been a protectorate from 1710 to 1760, was now an empty region to colonize, and once the French and Indian menaces were removed, New Englanders poured in, using the old techniques of township promotion which had served them well in opening up their own areas. They carried with them the maturity and assurance in social, economic, and political matters which they had been consolidating during the past hundred and thirty years.

Even before the war was over and the new townships were laid out, they had imposed their will on the authoritarian governor at Halifax, Charles Lawrence, a soldier in charge of a vitally strategic area who had little love for New England "republicanism." "I know nothing so likely to obstruct and disconcert all measures for the publick Good," he reported to London late in 1755, "as the foolish squabbles that are attendant upon Elections and the impertinent opinions that will be propagated afterwards amongst the multitude by Persons qualified in their imaginations only as able Politicians." He fought and evaded the establishment of an assembly from 1753 to 1758 with a stubbornness bordering on insubordination in the face of a lively New England lobby in London and the official conviction there that Nova Scotia was legally obligated to establish representative government.

The fall of Louisbourg and inescapable orders from the British government were followed by the meeting of the first representative assembly in what is now Canada on October 2, 1758. On December 26, Lawrence expressed his surprised relief: "I have reason to hope from their proceedings hitherto, that we shall get through the whole business in good time, and with less altercation than (from the seeming disposition of the people) I was heretofore apprehensive of."

⚜ MIGRATION TO NOVA SCOTIA

Yet even an assembly was not enough to stimulate mass migration from New England. In January, 1759, therefore, Lawrence issued and circulated in New England what T. C. Haliburton called "The Charter of Nova Scotia." This promised that the New England township system would be adopted to supplement the normal colonial administration by governor, council, and assembly, and the establishment of courts of justice "in like manner with those of the Massachusetts, Connecticut and other Northern colonies."

That did the trick. Township managers flocked to Halifax for inspections and grants, and once Canada capitulated, their settlers poured in. From about 2500 inhabitants after the expulsion of the Acadians in 1755, the population rose to about 8200 by the autumn of 1763, and to about 13,500 in 1767. Next year the Treaty of Fort Stanwix in New York opened up for the first time former Indian lands in the West that far outweighed Nova Scotia's appeal to American frontiersmen. Nonetheless, by 1775 Nova Scotia had between 17,000 and 18,000 inhabitants, chiefly New Englanders, or nearly twice as many as the unfortunate Acadians whom they had dispossessed.

These people not only took over and extended the Acadians' farmlands (with the assistance of Acadian prisoners), but some of them, possessing ships, capital, and commercial connections, established enterprising "fishing townships" along the Atlantic coast. Except at Canso and Cape Breton, the inshore boat fishery was not remarkably good, but greater proximity to the banks reduced the risk of spoilage during the run from them to drying and curing stations ashore. Even so, few of the so-called outports could have survived if they had been dependent on this single staple.

What broadened their economic base was the combination of forests and swift rivers. During the winter they cut and hauled the great conifers to the waterside and in the spring floated them to sawmills driven by those waters. Oak and other hardwoods which did not float so easily were valuable enough to justify carriage on sleds or, rarely, wagons. Then a man who had capital or credit could barter and traffic in fish, furs, and lumber; could build or charter small ships; and occasionally organize trading ventures to Europe or the West Indies. The New Englanders of Nova Scotia were painfully repeating the pattern laid down by their ancestors a century before.

The blight on their lives was what withered frontiersmen everywhere in North America—a lack of capital which seemed to enslave them to the merchants and money-handlers of Halifax, Boston, and London. Generally speaking, the Nova Scotians produced goods which wealthier folk converted into still greater accumulation of capital. The pioneers' own precarious progress from bare sustenance to rough comfort and abundance seemed to be unfairly gradual by contrast.

Moreover, the "haves" were very adroit in protecting their advantages. In Nova Scotia they rigged and managed the legislature in such ways that official Halifax outweighed the rest of the colony and monopolized the outpourings from the British Exchequer. Burke chose Nova Scotia as a horrible example when he thundered his demands for economical reform. "Good God! What sum the nursing of that ill-thriven, hard-visaged, and ill-favored brat, has cost to this wittol nation!" He calculated the direct expenditures, 1749–80, "not less than seven hundred thousand pounds," and the indirect receipts, particularly during wars, of course amounted to much more. This largesse to what he called "overflowings from the exuberant population of New England" reached the ordinary settlers in mere trickles, nourished the Haligonians well, and somehow most of it seemed to find its way ultimately either to Boston or back to London.

Halifax was not content merely to thwart the settlers through the central government, it repudiated its promises in local government as well. By means of an obscure, now apparently undecipherable series of maneuvers of the council, the legislature, and the courts from 1758 to 1765, the townships were neatly and completely overborne when they claimed the usual forms of self-government.

The men of Liverpool appealed in vain to their status as "freemen and under the same Constitution as the rest of His Majesty's King George's other Subjects not only by His Majesty's Proclamation, but because we are born in a country of Liberty in the Land that belongs to the Crown of England . . . we conceive we have Right and Authority invested in ourselves (or at least we pray we may) to nominate and appoint men amongst us to be our Committee & to do other offices that the Town may want." Deprivation by governor and council of this privilege "to rule ourselves as we think ourselves capable . . . is encroaching on our Freedom and Liberty."

New Englanders on the Minas Basin tried unsuccessfully to reach London authorities with a reminder of Lawrence's "Assurance of the Protection of the Government and all our civil and Religious Rights and Liberties, as we enjoyed them in the Governments from whence we Came," and with their assertion that "the Inhabitants are prevented from transacting the necessary Affairs of the Townships, though we were promised the [same] shou'd be by the late Governor Lawrence, in the same manner as they are in Other Colonies."

This dehorning of frontier democracy, appearing for the first time in the future Canada, was already an old story farther down the Atlantic coast. Congenial as it was to colonial oligarchies along the tidewater, it was just as congenial to the oligarchy which ruled Great Britain (and succeeded in postponing democracy there until 1884) because it seemed to promise that the hand of authority would suppress criticism of, and resistance to, the mandates of British policy.

🍁 THE GULF OF ST. LAWRENCE

Beyond Nova Scotia, New England's expansive energies became diffused. It was notable, for instance, that the American mariners who now began to operate in the Gulf of St. Lawrence off Newfoundland and even off Labrador were more properly traders in fish than fishermen and usually smugglers of foreign merchandise on the side. Inside the Gulf there was a strenuous competition for fish and sea mammals among adventurers from New England, Quebec, the English west country, the Channel Islands, and France. Already Isle St. John (later Prince Edward Island) was a fruitful agricultural region in the midst of fisheries and a center of illegal trade. Most of its French inhabitants had been dispersed in 1755 and later, and those who returned did so as inconspicuously as possible, for in 1767 their island had been partitioned in a grand British lottery. Some sixty-seven persons became proprietors on condition of planting settlers. Since most of them were absentees who evaded their own obligations but insisted on those of their tenants, the settlers were plagued and burdened for over a century.

🍁 NEWFOUNDLAND AND ITS FISHERIES

Newfoundland (with Labrador) was *sui generis,* largely because of certain technicalities in the fisheries. The cod and other fish were taken, for the most part from boats, by hand-lines or setlines whose hooks were baited with pieces of herring or other small fish caught inshore. Large, fine fish taken on the banks could be cleaned on the ships and taken to Europe "green," that is, in strong brine. This fishing involved fairly large ships, an abundance of salt, and only occasional contact with the land. Expensive salt might be saved and an almost imperishable product obtained if the fish were cleaned at sea, or on the way to shore, for salting and drying on racks on the beaches.

When cured, they looked and were handled like shingles, and naturally some fish came out better than others. The large, "bright," unscarred variety were kept for the omnivorous European market, while the poorer "Tal Qual" or "Jamaica" grades were consigned to feed the slaves or "poor whites" of the tropical and semitropical plantations. As time went on, there was an inevitable tendency toward division of labor between fishermen and curers on the one hand and traders and carriers on the other, involving large "sack ships" from Europe and smaller, faster schooners from New England.

The original ambition of the English fishermen (from the west country), as they gradually improved their standing in this international fishery during the sixteenth century, had been to treat Newfoundland merely as a summer base and to prevent settlement. This was because the resident fishermen would have advantages over the summer visitors in pre-empting the best beaches and harbors for curing and in starting earlier in the year; because London and Bristol merchant-capitalists, using sack ships, might organize the settlers to outdo the single-vessel ventures of the small western ports; and because chartered territorial monopolists might levy shore dues of various sorts.

Anthony Parkhurst demonstrated as early as 1578 that settlement and agriculture (and therefore monopoly) were possible, but the west country lobby at Westminster fought the idea stubbornly. Their most potent argument, to the managers of a country needing a navy, was that the nonsedentary fisheries formed an incomparable "nursery for seamen." The battle between would-be landed proprietors and the west country to become "lords of the whole fishing" went on in various forms until the eighteenth century.

Well before that time, however, it was clear that settlement must be tolerated in any case, if only to balance at St. John's and the Avalon Peninsula what the French were doing at Placentia and along the south shore. The resident population did, in fact, increase, and the anticipated disadvantages to the annual visitors materialized and grew.

By the middle of the seventeenth century, Newfoundland was obviously an *entrepôt,* not only in the fisheries but in migration from the British Isles to New England. Its resident population of about five hundred took one-third of the catch and was half as large as the annual visitation of "boatmen and servants," and ambitious members of both groups contrived to push on to the mainland. About this time also Newfoundland's strategic importance in Anglo-French rivalry in North America began to affect British policy, and during the Dutch wars the Hollanders wrought havoc in the English settlements. The firm decision to retain and fortify eastern Newfoundland as a base was taken on April 14, 1678.

The raids and counterraids during the Anglo-French wars were innumerable and need not be recounted here. In general, the French held the upper hand, just as they did on the mainland until Great Britain organized overpowering force. Yet neither France nor Great Britain could maintain complete sovereignty. Even the so-called surrender of Newfoundland by the Treaty of Utrecht in 1713 was counterbalanced by the concession to Frenchmen of the right "to take and dry fish" from Bonavista around the northern and western coasts to Point Riche.

In the long view, however, it was significant that settlement was legalized in 1698 and a rough form of all-year-round government established in 1728–29. Previous to that time, the most ancient practice of government had been to make the skipper of the first ship to arrive at each harbor in the spring "fishing admiral" and let him dispense authority, but this practice had been corroded during the war-ridden last quarter of the seventeenth century when the captains of the protective naval convoy received authority over the fishing admirals and the military commander.

During "Walpole's Peace," Newfoundland slipped out of tutelage. The west country ports had to yield the shore fisheries to the Newfoundlanders and themselves retreat to the banks. The islanders, a self-reliant and thoroughly unruly lot, subdivided their enterprise. A few merchants in St. John's established an economic overlordship which has persisted in large degree to the present day. They traded wherever they could to most advantage almost regardless of British mercantilistic regulation. French Louisbourg could hardly have been built and victualed without Newfoundland aid. Newfoundland fish was a principal component in the legal and illegal New England trade with the West Indies.

The tragedy of the island was that it contained only two classes— merchants and helots. Fortunes made there migrated with their possessors, usually to Britain, instead of contributing to the growth of resident wealth and amenities. Small wonder, then, that there was a constant emigration to the North American mainland from a hardworking but neglected populace, scattered in tiny ports along the coasts, idle and on the margin of survival during the winter, with practically no educational or religious facilities, and all dependent on a single "crop" whose fluctuations in supply and price were quickly reflected in the uproarious grogshops. Even so, in 1765 the 15,000 colonists or "livyeres" comfortably outnumbered the 9000 visiting fishermen.

LABRADOR

The coast of Labrador, administratively attached to Newfoundland from 1763 to 1774, was as yet an unconquered shore indented by bays and coves, or "tickles," where vegetation was, as it were, blown or washed off the underlying rock. Trees could be found inland, but dwindled into tundra vegetation towards Hudson Strait. Hamilton Inlet and the large fishing bank outside it invited settlement, as did a few salmon rivers, but this must be a precarious, interrupted affair until Labrador became an outpost of a more secure economy in Newfoundland itself.

HUDSON BAY

Finally there was Hudson Bay. Since it will be more revealing to consider its history in connection with general North American enterprise in the western half of the continent, it is sufficient to notice here that the resident agents of the company could be little more than simply agents. They represented a projection of mercantile London, and in the sense of controlling or decisively directing their own course, they had relatively little entity of their own. Geography and a century or more of past fur trading made it clear that the contest between Montreal and the Bay had not yet been resolved. It was to go on with mounting friction and violence between British Montrealers and the company's Orcadians (Orkney men) almost as it had in the days of New France.

CHAPTER VII

Partition Again (1765-83)

The aptest analogy for Britain and her American empire of 1763 is the family, with the colonies regarded as a large group of children by birth or adoption. Some of them were mature and self-reliant, others young and dependent, and a number in between. A few had learned the family business well enough to set up on their own, and had, in fact, for some time been running self-profiting side lines which cut into expected parental profits. Others had built up the production of specialties which the home firm handled monopolistically with varying degrees of mutual benefit. A small number depended for their continued existence on remittances from home.

If George III and his Parliament are regarded as the parents, the former was a well-intentioned but stubborn father of limited intelligence, and the latter like The Old Woman Who Lived in a Shoe. To make matters worse, husband and spouse were deeply involved in a twenty-five-year-long wrangle over their powers which left little thought or energy for their offspring. Yet defiance of parental authority or insistence on adult status were alike insupportable.

🍁 TRADITIONAL IMPERIALISM

After the peace in 1763, it became clear that Great Britain intended to pursue traditional imperial policies. The colonies were, in general, to produce raw materials, sometimes under subsidies, most of which were to be carried in British or colonial ships to British or colonial markets, where preferences were extended to them. In turn, the colonial markets were to be closed for the most part to all except British and colonial goods. With minor exceptions, the colonists must not manufacture articles which were being manufactured in Great Britain. And since, as Adam Smith said, defense was more important than opulence, special care and regulation must ensure the health and growth of the fisheries and the mercantile marine as adjuncts to the navy.

If this apparatus had been operated either loosely or adaptably, perhaps crises might have been avoided and compromises worked out, but two circumstances tended to tighten it into rigidity. In the first place, the easy success of colonial coasters in manifold trade with the West Indies, French as well as British, gave the West Indies sugar lobby in London abundant excuse for demanding restrictive legislation and its enforcement. The shipping lobby and the fisheries lobby had axes to grind as well, particularly in the light of the flagrant disregard of imperial regulations in and around Newfoundland.

In the second place, the recent war had been appallingly costly. What more likely, then, than that Britons who had never bothered really to acquaint themselves with their colonial offspring should decide that they should help to pay for the removal of the French menace? This could be done and at the same time the whole mercantile empire be "tuned up" by strict collection of customs duties and strict enforcement of the acts of trade and navigation. This may have been logical from the British point of view, but it was unwise from the imperial, if only because removal of the French menace made association with Great Britain seem much less necessary to some American colonists.

In fact, the attempts to enforce mercantilist authority sorted out the American colonies. A core of resistance rapidly hardened in New England and the Middle Colonies. Maryland and Virginia were highly sympathetic, partly because they resented the ruthless way in which their need for credit had been exploited in Great Britain, but largely because the Proclamation of 1763 flatly contradicted their ambitions beyond the Appalachians.

Outside that core, however, attitudes about resistance grew more dubious with distance. Georgia, for instance, although now freed from the Spaniards in Florida, was accustomed to depend heavily on the British grants which her frontier position had justified. Nova Scotia, at the other end of the line, had been a military pensionary for still longer. Massachusetts' District of Maine was a debatable land, but more manageable from Massachusetts than from Nova Scotia. The upland later to be Vermont was not disposed to resistance, for it was at odds with New England and New York because of the usual conflicts between the frontier and tidewater, and a great part of it was tributary, by Lake Champlain and the Richelieu, to the St. Lawrence. Since the British West Indies were being outdone by French islands in the sugar economy, they needed the privileged British market. Bermuda was still a way-station, uncertain of her affiliation. Newfoundland was incapable of standing alone. Quebec was still engaged in finding herself after conquest. Hudson Bay was a set of London outposts like those of the East India Company.

🍁 THE STAMP ACT

Out of the long to-and-fro of provocation and appeasement between Britain and America, 1763–75, two episodes differentiated Nova Scotia and Quebec from the rebellious core—the Stamp Act and the Quebec Act. The Stamp Act—taxation without representation—and an accompanying act for colonial assistance in billeting and associated services were designed to make the colonies pay one-third of the cost of maintaining 10,000 regular troops in North America. This tax on newsprint and legal and commercial paper produced an outburst of popular agitation and riotous violence from North Carolina to Massachusetts which was adroitly nourished by the merchants until it frightened them. Many colonial legislatures protested the act and proposed to combine against it.

In Halifax, the popular agitation was present, but the government was submissive. From November 7, 1765, to February 13, 1766, the weekly Halifax *Gazette* carried on a campaign against the act by reporting resistance elsewhere, by coming out printed in mourning, and finally either by substituting a black skull and crossbones for the stamp or by enclosing the reversed stamp in a block print of a devil with a pitchfork exclaiming "Behold me the Scorn and contempt of AMERICA, pitching down to Destruction, D—ils clear the Way for B——s and STAMPS." A gallows on Citadel Hill was hung with effigies of a stamp collector and a devil, a boot, a picture of Satan directing Lord Bute, and rhymed "confessions" from the collectors and Bute.

Yet the proprietor, Anthony Henry, and his lively young assistant, Isaiah Thomas (later historian of American printing and founder of the American Antiquarian Society), were discharged by the government, and the legislature, which had not been in session, submissively acknowledged repeal of the act without critical comment early in July. Liverpool, on the other hand, celebrated. "Day of rejoicing over the repeal of the Stamp Act. Cannon at Point Lawrence fired, colors flown on shipping. . . . People made a bonfire out of the old house of Capt. Mayhew, a settler here, and continued all night, and part of next, carousing."

The behavior of Quebec in this matter was distinctly apathetic. In its first number, June 21, 1764, the *Quebec Gazette* reported with approval the efforts of agents for Connecticut and Pennsylvania to hold up the Stamp Act in the British Parliament because of "the illegality of an internal tax," but thereafter this matter practically disappeared from sight in the midst of the furious campaign of the merchants for the withdrawal of Governor Murray and their confused realignment when Carleton came out to replace him in 1766.

Neither province responded to subsequent invitations from the older colonies to join in nonimportation agreements, but some Halifax merchants made a strong, if unsuccessful, attempt during the summer of 1774 to boycott the East India Company's tea which was being sent to Halifax when rejected elsewhere. "Many people complained against the landing of it." "Were it the property of the East India Company the people would be prejudiced against it."

Two merchant leaders of the opposition were removed from all their public offices and the governor issued a proclamation against "Meetings & Assemblies of the People at different times, in several of the Townships in the Province . . . held . . . contrary to the Public Good." Official Halifax was determined to portray Nova Scotia to London as a loyal and submissive colony and the inhabitants outside the oligarchy were too weak and divided to prevent this.

🍁 THE QUEBEC ACT

Neither Nova Scotia nor New England was much interested in the Quebec Act per se, but the company in which it appeared, four harsh acts designed to dragoon Massachusetts into submission, meant that its basic foundation in terms of the Canadian fact was completely overlooked. The clause which protected the western claims of the old colonies was so completely ignored that many historians of the United States today write in ignorance of its existence. To Americans who were so inflamed by the "Five Intolerable Acts" of 1774 as to gather in the First Continental Congress at Philadelphia in September, the Quebec Act could be nothing but a re-creation of the threat of New France.

That Congress invited the Canadians to choose delegates for the Second Congress in May, 1775, but its letter, citing "the rights of Englishmen," was inept and disingenuous. "What would your countryman, the immortal *Montesquieu,* have said to such a plan of domination, as has been framed for you?" "We are too well acquainted with the liberality of sentiment distinguishing your nation, to imagine, that difference of religion will prejudice you against a hearty amity with us. You know, that the transcendent nature of freedom elevates those, who unite in her cause, above all such low-minded infirmities."

When this appeal was followed up by a mission to Montreal early in 1775 under John Brown, the efforts of American sympathizers, while apparently infecting some French Canadians, were thwarted by the utter inability of the mercantile community to survive adherence to the Congressional nonimportation agreement. They did send James Price as an unofficial delegate to the Second Congress, however.

In general, the prevailing mood of the Canadians was "a plague on both your houses." In Montreal on the morning when the Quebec Act came into force, the king's bust on the Place d'Armes was desecrated by a blackened face, a rosary of potatoes, and an inscription: *Voilà le Pape du Canada ou le sot Anglois*. Carleton had believed that practically the whole population would burst into acclaim and that thousands would enlist in the British disciplining of their old enemies along the Atlantic. "A Canadian Regiment would compleat their Happiness, which in Time of Need might be augmented to two, three, or more Battallions."

Only the clergy and the seigneurs welcomed the Quebec Act. The habitants saw nothing in it for them, indeed now, after fifteen years of freedom, they were again legally obligated for tithe and seigneurial dues. "An act passed for the express purpose of gratifying the Canadians, and which was supposed to comprehend all that they either wished or wanted," wrote Chief Justice Hey, "is to become the first object of their discontent and dislike." Carleton was very sad. "Though the gentlemen testified great zeal, neither their entreaties or their example could prevail upon the people. . . . I think there is nothing to fear from them, while we are in a state of prosperity, and nothing to hope for when in distress."

REPULSE OF THE THIRTEEN COLONIES

Once American rebellion became overt at Concord in April, 1775, any American Congress would feel bound by necessity to attack Canada, for this was the oldest strategic dictate in North America. The Second Continental Congress authorized invasion in June, 1775, with full knowledge that, lacking a navy, the job must be done before Great Britain could reinforce. Carleton had almost stripped the colony of troops to help Gage at Boston.

Already, however, fourteen months before the Declaration of Independence, less than a hundred unauthorized New England backwoodsmen under Ethan Allen and Benedict Arnold had seized, without resistance, the key forts at Ticonderoga and Crown Point with their armament. Arnold then surprised and took the only armed sloop on Lake Champlain, but some British regulars managed to establish themselves in the fort at St. John on the Richelieu. When the overconfident Allen bypassed St. John to attack what he expected to be a sympathetic

Montreal in September, he was defeated and captured by a curious mixed force of French and English militia. Meanwhile, however, the great Congressional invasion had got under way.

This enterprise was one of the boldest gambles in North American history, but it failed, chiefly because the Americans had no adequate navy. Down the Richelieu came about 4000 Americans under Richard Montgomery, an Irish baronet's son who had married into the Livingston clan of New York and who had fought the French over the same territory. They overwhelmed the fort at Chambly, starved out the fort at St. John, and then, having eliminated most of the regular troops in the province, received the surrender of Montreal on November 12, almost capturing Carleton in the process.

During this invasion, the behavior of the Canadians had been ominous. When Carleton had tried to enroll the militia, many of the inhabitants had assembled with farm tools and muskets to resist. Some hundreds enlisted with the Americans. In general the imposing invaders were treated as visitors to be placated.

Then, just as Montgomery was settling his smallpox-ridden army into winter quarters, news arrived that Benedict Arnold had succeeded in a daring substitute for the classical naval invasion of the St. Lawrence. By some wizardry of masterful determination he had brought 675 men to Quebec overland by the appallingly difficult Kennebec-Chaudière traverse which no one hitherto had exploited. They owed their survival to French-Canadian help. Montgomery scraped up about 300 men to join Arnold, and the two commanders embarked on the unparalleled adventure of a winter siege of Quebec, without artillery capable of breaching its walls.

Carleton had rallied about twice as many defenders, silenced the disloyal by expelling them, and patched up the weakest points in the defenses. When the attackers resorted to an attempted surprise during a howling snowstorm on New Year's Eve, 1775, it failed, bravely but disastrously. Montgomery was killed and Arnold seriously wounded. The survivors (the killed and captured numbered about 550 to the defenders' losses of about 30) had the nerve to maintain the siege; indeed they were reinforced to number 3000, but in May, 1776, just as in May, 1760, the British navy arrived, this time with a fully equipped army of 10,000.

John Adams was a good deal less than candid when he attributed the American retreat to smallpox "which infected every man we sent there." It is a comment on Carleton as a soldier that he muffed two easy chances to capture the main American army and left the Americans in command of Crown Point and Ticonderoga.

That meant that the command of the counterinvasion of 1777 went to "Gentleman Johnny" Burgoyne, who proved little, if any, better. In fact, those who have studied in detail Great Britain's conduct of war against the Americans from 1775 to 1778 are pretty well agreed that the naval and military high command hoped to overawe their blood brothers rather than shed so much blood that reconciliation would be impossible. Carleton's refusals to grasp obvious military advantage and his wholesale freeing of American prisoners could be paralleled in many ways elsewhere. Nonetheless, it was Burgoyne's surrender of October 17, 1777, at Saratoga, where he had at last really entered the Hudson Valley, which brought a revengeful France into the war on the side of the Americans.

FRANCO-AMERICAN ALLIANCE

This alliance proved to be a great defense for Canada, since Washington and other American leaders had no liking for the re-establishment of France in North America. Lafayette's plan of 1778–79 to bring the French navy and army to the conquest of Canada was debated and shelved by Congress. Later, in 1780 and 1781, when the American cause was obviously triumphant, the French vetoed Washington's plans to make another assault because a British Canada would keep an independent United States more dependent on France.

The great unknown in this first American attempt to incorporate Canada, an unknown which persists substantially to the present day because of incomplete, uncandid, and conflicting records, was the behavior of the French Canadians. Had they sided wholeheartedly with the Americans, the Province of Quebec would have been conquered. Had they been loyal to Great Britain, Quebec could not have been invaded as it was.

Carleton's "nothing to fear from them while . . . in . . . prosperity, and nothing to hope for when in distress" might well have been echoed by the American commanders. When the Americans marched in, meeting little organized British resistance and paying for services and enlistment in hard cash, the Canadians could do little but assent and be grateful for the added bounty. But soon the Americans were resorting to paper money, "the Congress having tried every method to collect hard money for the Army in *Canada,* without success." The habitants, who could look back almost a century to disasters connected with paper promises to pay, became less friendly. The funds of the pro-American merchants in Montreal were borrowed and exhausted. Requisitioning officers and men began to take what they needed, partly by force, partly by threats, and partly by paper promises which they did not always bother to sign.

And then the traditional antipathies of almost two centuries in North America began to crop up again as tempers shortened and the American position became more precarious. Particularly was this true in religious matters. Most of the Americans habitually despised Catholics and "Canucks" and, under strain, revealed this by unforgettable insults to the habitants and their faith.

Congress sent Benjamin Franklin, Samuel Chase, and Charles Carroll to Montreal on the very margin of the spring breakup in 1776 in order to remedy this situation. They took with them Carroll's elder brother, the Maryland Jesuit who was to be first archbishop of Baltimore, and the French printer, Fleury Mesplet, and his press, but all they achieved was the recall of the foolish and provocative American commander, David Wooster. The French-speaking Canadians who felt that they had committed themselves to the American cause too conspicuously for subsequent absolution accompanied the pro-American English-speaking Canadians in the retreat of the American armies. Congress ultimately rewarded them with grants of land in the trans-Appalachian wilderness.

THE NEUTRAL YANKEES OF NOVA SCOTIA

The behavior of Nova Scotia during the American War of Independence was even more discouraging to the Americans than that of Quebec, again because the Americans lacked a navy. To the more fervid apostles of rebellion, Nova Scotian lack of initiative was almost incredible because most of the inhabitants had left New England within the past fifteen years. Why did they not instantly join their brothers in arms? Were they, as John Adams growled, merely "a set of fugitives and vagabonds who are also kept in fear by a fleet and an army"? Were they, as an address of their Assembly to the Crown claimed, "fully sensible, that we have no right to pray for redress of Grievances to request privileges or Regulations unless we Acknowledge your right over us . . . and that it is our indispensable duty to pay a due proportion to the Expence of this great Empire"?

There is no simple answer to those questions, for Nova Scotia was anything but simple. Moreover, its affairs were made additionally complicated from October, 1773, to April, 1776, by a most tortuous (and successful) campaign to get rid of a governor, Francis Legge, who had dared to uncover the local spoils system, "the *third* Governor, *Mauger's* interest has turned out." By 1777, it was the merchant John Butler, Halifax agent of Joshua Mauger, the adventurer in London who had made himself overlord of Nova Scotia, "who calls himself lord, king, governor of Halifax."

These politico-economic maneuverings were much too labyrinthine to be recounted in detail here. Suffice it to say that Mauger and his British and Nova Scotian associates had gradually insinuated themselves into control of Nova Scotia while the New Englanders, its former masters, were becoming increasingly engrossed in their conflict with Great Britain. Mauger's basic power rested on his control of the largest block of the provincial public debt as well as on many private obligations. He used this power to promote his trading enterprises and his near monopoly of distilling in Nova Scotia. Since this necessitated control of tariff policies, he had occasional temporary setbacks from governors and assemblies, but his force and skill were normally great enough to triumph over them.

In 1774 some assemblymen and a young lawyer, Richard Gibbons, managed (too late) to describe the whole apparatus in detail to London —"a plan of Dominion for himself and Dependants." "The power exercised by Mr. Mauger's Agent in this Province, is so notorious, that even the Officers of Government, and of the Courts of Law, are Sub-jected to his will, and he has publicly insulted and threatened the House of Assembly." Mauger was able, however, both to undermine New England influence and to make himself the authority on Nova Scotian affairs in London by stressing the pretended dutiful behavior of the Nova Scotians as compared to unruly other Americans. The successive Halifax administrations were with him in that, for they were dependents on the imperial bounty.

Obviously, however, no one man could dictate to 18,000 others across the Atlantic; the "great man theory" of history cannot simply cancel out the sum of so many tough North American frontiersmen. What mastered them was the isolation, the poverty, and the lack of solidarity which Nova Scotia imposed on them. Their struggling settle-ments were scattered widely over a rough terrain which had practically no roads. Since the salable products which they extracted were handled chiefly by others, they were abnormally affected by general contractions and disturbances in outside commerce.

They faced depression when the Treaty of Fort Stanwix opened up Ohio lands in 1768, recovered in 1769 and 1770, and then declined steadily until 1775. Simeon Perkins, the leader of Liverpool, wrote in January, 1773: "The outlook is bad. I think Liverpool is going to decay and it may be many years ere it is more than a fishing village." The greatest merchants in Halifax were trying, from 1770 to 1775, to collect accounts due, sell out, and get away. In March, 1773, even John Butler advertised that he was "closing all Mr. Mauger's and his own Mercantile affairs in this Province." Two able Yorkshire farmers who were prospecting the farming townships in 1774 found that many of the agricultural settlers were also trying to sell out and leave.

The political consequence was that the outsettlements might elect representatives to the assembly, but if they chose from among their own numbers, their men could seldom afford to attend for more than a day or two or, more frequently, attend at all. Halifax, which had heavily weighted the constituency system in its favor from the beginning anyway, was only too glad to provide assemblymen for other constituencies. Its 1800 inhabitants were about one-tenth of the total population, but by 1775, as Liverpool learned, its political bosses were strong enough to force Haligonians on unwilling townships. Liverpool thereupon raised twenty dollars so that Simeon Perkins might attend assembly for the first time, and keep an eye on Thomas Cochran, the Halifax merchant who had commandeered the other seat.

An anonymous member of the Assembly published in 1774 *An Essay on the Present State of Nova Scotia,* which contradicted the myth created and nourished by the official correspondence. Two extracts sum up the political situation with some venom, but with substantial accuracy:

GOVERNMENT is considered not as the parental Protector of the Rights of Individuals and the faithful Steward of the Public Property: But rather as a Junto of cunning and wicked Men, whose Views extend no further than their own private Emolument, and who further the Distresses of the Community in order to promote a slavish Dependance on themselves.

THE HOUSE OF ASSEMBLY under the present Mode of Election, and other Disadvantages, which they labor under cannot be called the Delegates of the People, hitherto the Majority have been chose and managed by the Council, by Excise Officers, and other Placemen, thus circumstanced it is not to be wondered at, that the real Good of the Province has never been attended to.

All this has a characteristic sound to those familiar with British politics of the eighteenth century, and even pensionary Halifax had its schisms and factions. Anthony Henry, supplanted on the *Gazette* over the Stamp Act, set up a rival paper and drove his government-supported rival out of business in less than two years (1769–70) by amply presenting the American cause against Great Britain. The tea troubles of 1774 were followed by arson at the navy yard and of some hay collected for the Boston garrison, as well as by meetings in the townships.

Yet 1774 and 1775 smelled of war, and war had always meant wealth for Halifax. Gage not only called the troops in Nova Scotia to Boston, but he initiated the provision trade from Nova Scotia to support them.

If the continental colonies adopted nonimportation agreements, Halifax could profit. If they rebelled, Nova Scotian merchants thought they could seize the opportunity created in the West Indian trade. Pro-American sentiment in the provincial capital was all but completely submerged.

It was far otherwise in the townships, where the majority of the inhabitants favored the American cause and where Halifax was incapable of exercising continuous authority. But what could these New Englanders do when the sea separated them from home and the Continental Congress had no navy? When they begged George Washington to support an invasion by way of the Minas Basin for the destruction of Halifax, he admitted the possibility and the advantage in cutting off his enemy's supply of provisions, but pointed out that such a force could not maintain itself against a naval power and would therefore quickly call down disaster on itself and on sympathizers in Nova Scotia.

In the autumn and winter of 1775–76, therefore, the long-suffering Nova Scotian settlers did two things. They made it plain to the authorities that they would not serve in militia or regular army against the Americans, and they demanded the status of neutrals. In parallel circumstances, the supplanters of "the neutral French" became "the neutral Yankees."

We have their sturdy, dignified, and touching memorials from all parts of the outsettlements. We know that they refused to give even minor assistance to the regular troops at the time of an absurdly rash, unsuccessful raid led by Jonathan Eddy of Cumberland Township against Fort Cumberland in the late autumn of 1776. Let the words of the inhabitants of Yarmouth speak for all the neutral Yankees:

WE DO all of us profess to be true Friends & Loyal Subjects to George our King. We were almost all of us born in New England, we have Fathers, Brothers & Sisters in that Country, divided betwixt natural affection to our nearest relations, and good Faith and Friendship to our King and Country, we want to know, if we may be permitted at this time to live in a peaceable State, as we look on that to be the only situation in which we with our Wives and Children, can be in any tolerable degree safe.

But it was a long war, 1775 to 1783, and Nova Scotia was one part of Great Britain's dominions which seafaring Americans, equipped with fast little vessels and empowered to engage in privateering, could attack and damage. Halifax was dilatory and dubious about arming the settlements and incapable of defending them. During the Revolution, therefore, Nova Scotia made its enduring, if never more than partial, separation from New England because of four somewhat contradictory sets of circumstances. British money was pouring into Halifax and some of it inevitably trickled out to the townships. American privateers not only ravaged Nova Scotian shipping, but landed at many towns and looted with an excruciating thoroughness which evoked an unneutral resistance at several points. A large, though devious and precarious, trade grew up between Nova Scotia and the rebels. The latter were so desperately in need of some manufactured goods that, for instance, John Allan, the American agent for using the Indians of Maine against Nova Scotia, complained bitterly because Massachusetts would not allow him to buy gifts and supplies for his Indian allies from Nova Scotian traders! On the other hand, the London-Halifax mercantile combination excluded Boston from legitimate Nova Scotian trade. Simeon Perkins had the galling experience of having to break his old credit and family affiliations with New England and come to business agreement with the very Thomas Cochran whom he had tried to prevent from securing a Liverpool seat in the Assembly.

🍁 AMERICAN INDEPENDENCE

Fittingly enough, it was the French and Spanish navies which created the opportunity for American and French forces to end an apparently interminable war by forcing Cornwallis to surrender at Yorktown, Virginia, in October, 1781. Even George III had to give up after that and concede American independence. And then, as has so often happened, peacemaking dislocated former alignments in a realignment of forces. Great Britain had greatly enhanced her position after Yorktown, at least in French and Spanish eyes, by a resounding naval victory over them in the West Indies and by thwarting their siege of Gibraltar. In the peace negotiations of 1782–83, it was every country for itself.

The principal clue to British policy was determination to re-create understanding and, if possible, friendship with the Americans on grounds partly of sentiment, partly of politics, and partly of economics. Many Britons had sympathized with the rebels throughout, and even enlisted, with other enlightened Europeans, in the cause of liberty against despotism. Then, although very few men in Europe or America conceded to the new American nation much chance of survival, it seemed important to wean whatever state did take form from alliance with Britain's enemies, France and Spain. And finally, the British trading interest was vitally interested in recapturing the American market, a sanguine prospect which was justified by Britain's unassailable superiority in capital and industrial production.

In the light of all this, the surviving British North American colonies could be of little more than minor importance. Britain would, of course, insist on control of Nova Scotia and Newfoundland for the sake of their demonstrated strategic importance and their relation to the fisheries and the "nursery for seamen." Quebec, too, was far too important strategically to be given away. But the new ideas of freer international commerce to which Adam Smith had given classical (and political) utterance in *The Wealth of Nations* in 1776, and which directly influenced Great Britain's peacemakers, made mere territory seem relatively unimportant.

If Great Britain could manufacture and deliver goods more economically than any other country, she could buy and sell with less and less concern about conventional mercantilistic principles. While European countries, always her greatest market, might be hard to convince that freer trade was advantageous, the new United States, an established and rapidly growing market and a large supplier of non-British commodities, was almost sure to see the point. In fact, it was hard to conceive how Americans could get along without British markets, goods, and capital. Only France seemed a possible competitor, and France had not only shown signs of productive inferiority in staple lines for almost a century, but seemed on the brink of bankruptcy.

The territorial provisions of the peace treaty reflected both these new British ideas and American ingenuity in taking advantage of them. The Floridas were restored to Spain, certainly no industrial competitor, along with sovereignty over Louisiana and the trans-Mississippi west. France was as completely excluded from North America as in 1763. She did not even get the Hudson Bay area which she had once again mastered, including the great stone fortress at Churchill. Territorially the United States extended eastward only to the St. Croix boundary which Massachusetts had succeeded in getting for herself in 1763, but New England's ancient claims and ambitions in the North Atlantic fisheries were appeased by the "liberty" to take fish, even in British territorial waters, and to dry and cure fish on uninhabited shores. This of course meant continuance of the New England habit of trading in fish and illegal goods.

❧ THE INTERNATIONAL BOUNDARY

From the mouth of the St. Croix, the boundary for the repartitioning of North America began in tradition and ended in shocking novelty. A line drawn from the as yet unknown source of the St. Croix to meet the old line drawn from the head of Chaleur Bay along the height of land between the St. Lawrence and the Atlantic was understandable enough as maintaining the decision of 1763 to keep the French Canadians off the Atlantic coast. Reaffirmation of the 1763 boundary from the headwaters of the Connecticut westward along the forty-fifth parallel was harder for Quebec to swallow because the Champlain Basin was, after all, tributary to the St. Lawrence, but in that area the honors of war were certainly American. The unbelievable blow to Quebec came after the boundary along the forty-fifth parallel met the St. Lawrence, for it then followed the middle of the river and the Great Lakes to a point on Lake Superior which gave the Grand Portage (into the Manitoba Basin) to the United States. The boundary then ran along the Rainy River to the northwest corner of Lake of the Woods, from which a line was supposed to run due west to the Mississippi (its headwaters were actually much farther south), and down it to the Spanish boundary near its mouth.

The Montreal merchants were aghast, for they had been bombarding London with explanations of their aims and proofs of their mastery of the fur trade of the interior and the Far West. They recalled how "the French, on this very ground, had formed a plan of Empire perhaps as grand as was ever devised by man." They indicated the value of the Champlain Basin; recalled the Lake Erie–Ohio traverse established by the French and used as the boundary in the Quebec Act; pointed to the usefulness of traverses to the Ohio or Mississippi from western Lake Erie, Chicago, Green Bay, and Lake Superior; and emphasized the crucial importance of the Grand Portage. Word of the treaty's *fait accompli* left them dumfounded. Every important trading post from Montreal to Superior was now in American territory.

By the Treaty as it is, The Trade is supposed to be the property of this Country, but on examining into that more particularly it will be found that the means of carrying it on, are given away. . . . We have gone progressively on from Step to Step [of the peace negotiations], with anxious hearts and hopes, that a stand may be made at each intermediate line we have pointed out, so that as little of the Country and its consequences be thrown into the scale of our rivals as possible— We cannot bring our mind to conceive that a surrender of the Posts is meditated by Great Britain.

Yet this and its like had meant little or nothing to a Great Britain which had never had an inland colony before, did not think it much wanted one, and calculated that both the supply and the market of the interior would be largely British. The total value of the fur trade of Quebec would be less than the cost of maintaining the fortified posts at which it was carried on.

No one concerned, perhaps least of all Montrealers whose trade contradicted settlement, imagined a future North America divided between two indigenous nations. One new and very shaky nation had set itself up and had won practically everything that it demanded, indeed much more than it could presently manage. The rest of North America, British and Spanish, was practically empty. Its little clots of settlement, puny by comparison with those of the United States, held no apparent promise of more than uneasy survival.

A very few Americans believed in a successful and expanding United States. Almost no one else did. No man seems to have had the faintest idea of a future Canada except perhaps some French Canadians. Having survived so much, having been callously, as they thought, abandoned by France, and having nonetheless increased and prospered, "the meek" were entitled to dream of expanding to inherit at least the Canadian earth.

CHAPTER VIII

The Partition Confirmed (1783-1823)

⚜ BRITISH NORTH AMERICA SUBORDINATED

For a generation and more after the recognition of American independence, the development of British North America was very largely conditioned by the bitter business of accommodation between Great Britain and the United States. Time's perspective reveals the forces that compelled them to adjust to each other. We can also see the legacies from the past, the areas of sheer conflict, and the outside events that made them hate and despise each other and resort to a second war.

It is less easy to give these overriding occurrences their proper proportions in relation to British North America. Certainly the British North Americans found it hard to accept them when they contradicted what members of an empire felt entitled to receive from the mother country. And it must be remembered that the colonies were still colonies, for the American, French, and Irish revolutions had the effect of making Great Britain less rather than more inclined to concede to them any substantial degree of autonomy.

In British eyes, although there was the expectation of resuming profitable economic intercourse with the United States, America could be construed as a double threat: a maritime mercantile rival and a territorial one. It was, however, considered far more ominous as a maritime rival owing to the British habit of thinking in terms of the seas and their commerce rather than in terms of land masses.

Some British-American colonies were also maritime, and therefore presumably capable of aiding in the Anglo-American mercantile contest. Another colony was in the interior, involved willy-nilly and expensively in a territorial rivalry of no great interest to Britain. The sum total of these equations was that the maritime colonies received thoughtful British attention, the St. Lawrence to the end of tidewater at Montreal a good deal less, and the region beyond Lachine least of all.

When one says "thoughtful attention," it must be with some substantial reservations. In the first mood of disillusionment over the loss of the thirteen central colonies, Parliament abolished the department responsible for American affairs. Colonial experts remained, but they knew that governments had much more absorbing concerns, even during the peace of the 1780's, not to speak of the grim days of the French wars, from 1792 to 1815. The new free-trade, anti-imperialistic ideas, while making headway with such influential persons as Lord Shelburne, Richard Oswald, and the younger Pitt, were stubbornly fought by vested interests such as the West Indian planters, the merchant marine, and the fisheries. The old mercantilistic ideas had become habitual, interlocked with ramifications on domestic production, finance, and so on.

This was a period, therefore, when the British North Americans had to develop aptness in defining their interests, enterprise in pursuing them on their own, and various qualities of promotion and resistance in order to get their way. A great deal of the tough, politically artful, local particularism that persists in federated Canada has its deep, nourishing roots in the dubious days after the American Revolution.

THE LOYALISTS AND THEIR LOT

The striking new circumstance in British North America, a factor of great, if incalculable, weight, was the migration from the United States of thousands of loyalists, "Tories" to the Americans, "United Empire" loyalists on the British side. These people were a very mixed lot, characteristic victims of the first American civil war. The most conspicuous among them were former members of colonial oligarchies and senior officers of loyalist military forces. Most of these had consciously chosen their side in the quarrel and were suffering the consequences of defeat. Below their ranks, however, were humbler men, some of whom were loyalists by conviction and others by the kinds of accident that accompany a civil war.

All had reason to hate the United States and to emphasize their faithfulness to Great Britain. "Canadians," A. R. M. Lower has said, "are the children of divorced parents and they know the bitterness that comes of a broken home. . . . Neither Englishmen nor Canadians, especially Canadians, have realized to this day what Revolution really means, how wide and enduring is the gulf that it opens between the winning and the losing sides."

The loyalists had been divested of their property and their station. Some had been tarred and feathered, ridden on rails, or otherwise violently used. And in the Anglo-American peace treaty, all that the British negotiators had been able to extract in their behalf was that the almost powerless Congress would "earnestly recommend" to the states that they restore the confiscated property of "real British subjects" and of those who were within the British lines but had not borne arms against the United States. Others (i.e. fighting loyalists) were to be free to return and spend a year unmolested endeavoring to recover their property under cover of two other "earnest recommendations" by Congress: one that the states revise their confiscatory legislation to make it "perfectly consistent, not only with justice and equity, but with that spirit of conciliation, which, on the return of the blessings of peace, should universally prevail"; and the other that, while property was to be restored, the loyalist must repurchase it at the price paid if it had meanwhile been sold by public authority to private purchasers.

This was almost sheer nonsense, as British negotiators with any knowledge of what had happened in their own civil war, or in any other, must have known. They also knew that it was literally all that could be done by the Congress. The states, except South Carolina, ignored it, and loyalists who went back under cover of it were about as badly abused as before, even to the point of murder. Since Great Britain could hardly go to war again for the victims, she used their plight as a diplomatic counter (to be discussed later) and undertook to compensate them herself by grants of land, aid in supplies and equipment, and payments in money proportionate to what they claimed to have lost.

Since an elaborate mythology has grown (and been built up) around the loyalists who came to British North America, it is well to recall some salient facts about their migration. To begin with, they were a distinctly small minority of the whole body of Americans who had fought in the British forces or had sheltered under British guns. This was partly because most of the loyalists found compromises that permitted them to stay in the United States, and partly because life in Great Britain appealed to the wealthiest and most influential, and life in Bermuda, Florida, or the West Indies appealed to southern planters, far more than frontier life in Nova Scotia or Quebec. Also, a large number of those who emigrated went back to the United States as soon as they judged it safe to do so, frequently on invitation from Americans who wanted their knowledge, abilities, or useful affiliations in Great Britain.

M. L. Hansen, the historian of the mingling of the Canadian and American peoples, has stated another circumstance very well. "The net result [of refugee concentration at New York, on the New York frontier, and in eastern Maine, and of the proximity of undeveloped lands] was that the involuntary Loyalist migrations followed and broadened North American routes which had been established by voluntary land seekers long before their day. Pre-Loyalists or Loyalists, they were all North Americans bent upon doing the best they could for themselves on the continent which they were making their own."

Hence it was that the largest group, about twenty-eight thousand, went to Nova Scotia. Since most of the advantageous parts of the peninsula were pre-empted, the persistent gradually dispersed, for the most part to emptier lands in the St. John Valley, Cape Breton, and St. John Island. Two other groups, perhaps amounting to seven thousand in all, moved out of New York, as one might expect, by the Hudson-Champlain route into the St. Lawrence Valley and by the Mohawk Valley to Lake Ontario or the Niagara region. The Nova Scotian group contained a large proportion of tidewater town-dwellers, often of superior social and economic station, many of whom could not stand Nova Scotian conditions. The Quebec groups were "mostly farmers from the back parts of New York Province." A conservative lot of Dutch, Scottish, and German stock for the most part, they made a timely contribution of pioneering skill for opening up the Lake Ontario lands.

The interaction of the loyalists' own conservatism with the British Toryism of the day, aggravated as both were by hostility to American republicanism, left its mark on the future Canada, particularly since the French Revolution and the unsuccessful Irish Revolution soon deepened British authoritarianism. This British and colonial conservatism and anti-Americanism deeply affected, not only the St. John Valley where the loyalists were a majority, but other regions where they were a minority from the beginning or quickly became one. It interlocked neatly with the prevalent conceptions of oligarchy and privilege, thus consolidating an antirepublican, antidemocratic, politico-economic system in Britain and America which was repugnant to the great majority of the colonists, but which proved stronger than they for a long time. Something quite similar prevailed in the United States from 1787 until about 1820.

The arrival of the loyalists in Nova Scotia precipitated the division of the Maritime area into four colonies, one of which, Cape Breton Island, was a sort of subcolony under a lieutenant governor. It persisted only until 1820, when it was reabsorbed in Nova Scotia. During the Revolution, the creation of a colony called New Ireland out of eastern Maine and the north shore of the Bay of Fundy was seriously considered. The creation of New Brunswick was partly the residue of those proposals and partly one piece in a policy of multiplying colonial units in order to heighten British authority over them. The new province extended from the St. Croix to the Quebec line and met Nova Scotia at the old Anglo-French dividing line on the Isthmus of Chignecto. Across the Northumberland Strait lay the fourth colony, St. John Island.

Newfoundland did not properly belong with this group, for it was deep in troubles peculiar to itself. The accommodation of a basically Protestant society to the Roman Catholic Irish who were coming out in large numbers as settlers and as "servants" in the fisheries was a violent process, made more so by Anglo-Irish troubles at home. An expectation, corroborated by the peace treaty, that the French would be deprived of their fishing rights was contradicted by a secret Anglo-French agreement of September 3, 1783, which forbade, under pain of "the most positive measures," British subjects from interfering with French fishing operations from Cape St. John on the east shore around to, and down, the west shore to its terminus at Cape Ray.

This shocking betrayal, a vestige of the old conception of Newfoundland as a mere mooring near the banks, actually involved the removal of some British settlements, but was soon submerged by the hostilities of the Anglo-French wars of 1792–1815. The wars had the effect of making Newfoundland prosperous, but its settled government amounted to little more than a permanent court structure, for its governors were still visiting admirals and it had no legislature. Its real masters were the merchants and shipowners who held the population in their debt.

Naturally the governments of what came to be called "the Maritimes" were of the old authoritarian "Royal Government" model—nominated governors and legislative and executive councils holding the whip hand over elected assemblies. And now the arrival of the loyalists in Quebec raised the question of extending the same system to that colony. The Quebec Act had never truly operated because of Carleton's concealment of his instructions, the confusion of the Revolution, and the contradictions between the act and what was practicable. In 1786, Carleton, now created Lord Dorchester, was sent out as governor to find a new formula. He had none himself, but he had, as his chief collaborator, William Smith, a Tory lately Chief Justice of New York, who credited the American Revolution to the colonies having been "abandoned to Democracy."

During the Revolution most of the Quebec loyalists had congregated near Sorel, at the mouth of the Richelieu. After it, they were settled in a studied spectrum of ethnic and religious groups along the St. Lawrence and Lake Ontario between the Ottawa and the Bay of Quinte—Catholic Scottish Highlanders, Scottish Presbyterians, German Lutherans, and Anglo-Dutch Calvinists or Anglicans. From these little ribbons of settlement it was a far cry to the New York and Pennsylvania frontiersmen settled at Niagara and still farther to the mixed fur-trading community around and opposite Detroit. In 1784 it looked as if the region west of the Ottawa was to be a loyalists' preserve like the valley of the St. John in New Brunswick.

The area, however, lay across a natural migration route for the expanding population of coastal North America. The famous Northwest Ordinance of 1787, by which the American Congress laid down a policy for its new lands, was politically imaginative in its provisions for steps towards statehood and federal incorporation in the republic, but economically severe in its requirement that a settler take up 640 acres at a minimum price of $1.00 an acre. British North America was much less exacting, indeed lands were often free.

Some New Englanders, who were at first systematically excluded from the strategic Lake Champlain–St. Lawrence area by soldier governors, were allowed to take up those desirable lands after 1791. Others, along with restless "Yorkers," discouraged by the new land companies in upper New York, crossed the lake from Oswego into cheaper British lands. Up from the Susquehanna and across the Niagara came land seekers from New York and New Jersey, and sectaries (largely German) from Pennsylvania who were disquieted by revolutionary changes. Other forces which tended to herd the northern streams of migrants into British territory were the highlands of Pennsylvania which jutted up to the eastern end of Lake Erie, the malarial swamplands between the Ohio and that lake, and the fact that the British got along well with the Indians while the Americans were at constant war with them.

It is unlikely that Dorchester and Smith consciously took this migration into their calculations. Some of the migrants pretended to be delayed loyalists, among them the American executioner of the British spy André. These were half-derisively called "late loyalists." Many others came in without any one knowing much about them. In any case, they rapidly outnumbered the loyalists, who were hard put to perpetuate the impression that the inland settlements were true-blue "United Empire." Precise statistics are lacking, but a well-informed estimate of about 1812 held that 60 per cent of the population was nonloyalist American, 20 per cent loyalist, and 20 per cent of other origin.

⚜ THE CONSTITUTION OF 1791

The political decision arrived at in 1791, embraced in the Constitutional or Canada Act, was to authorize the division of Quebec into two colonies, with the dividing line running from a little west of Montreal island to the Ottawa and up it to Hudson's Bay Company territory, and to impose on both an especially refined version of royal colonial government. This was hard on the hapless little English-speaking minority, now locked-up in French-speaking Lower Canada, which was in turn alarmed lest an assembly be a taxing-machine, but it gave what the British government considered the appropriate "rights of Englishmen" to the colonists of Upper Canada beyond the Montreal rapids.

The most revealing refinements of the now classical colonial model were that the Legislative Council was to emulate the House of Lords by being composed of a colonial nobility and the Canadian Church was to emulate the Church of England under the stipulation that an amount of land equal to one-seventh of future land grants in both provinces should be reserved for the benefit of a Protestant clergy. The ridiculousness of the former made it a nullity, but the substance of the latter was to constitute a serious obstacle to pioneer settlement.

Beyond these provisions, since the Quebec Act was not specifically repealed, the clear intention was to empower the majorities of the people of the two areas to regulate their lives and tax themselves according to their own habits and inclinations, subject to the powers of veto and delay of governors and councils in the colonies and overriding authority in Great Britain.

By 1792, therefore, seven little British North American colonies, restricted from straying by neat constitutional hobbles, lay alongside an expansive American republic whose states had also been bridled and curbed by the brilliantly original federal Constitution of 1787. National independence, substantial state sovereignties, and ingenious provisions for growth and change meant that Americans would enjoy freedom of action denied to British North Americans for over a hundred years. At the moment, however, the constitutional criterion seemed less important than the abounding energies of 4,000,000 people as they might affect, not only their less than 250,000 neighbors, but the course of Great Britain.

⚜ MERCANTILE INADEQUACY OF THE MARITIMES

As early as 1774, it had occurred to British and Nova Scotian authorities that the Maritime region might assume the role in the fisheries and in the West Indian and other trades that had hitherto been enjoyed by New England; indeed one of the hoped-for effects of the "Intolerable Acts" was "to give a Spur to the Industry & Activity of [Nova Scotia's] Inhabitants, in a Vigorous Prosecution both of the Lumber Trade and the Fishery."

Yet, even when Nova Scotia, herself incapable of producing agricultural surpluses, was linked with Quebec in this matter, the dream was capable of only very modest and slow realization. Seasonal influences made it difficult to combine Quebec farm products with Nova Scotian fish and wood products for trading voyages, and Nova Scotia's accumulation of capital, liquid or in the form of ships and equipment, was far behind the aggressive New Englanders'. The result was that the West Indians themselves repudiated the substitution as early as 1784. As one of them said:

> Whatever your North American has predicted of the eventual grandeur, population and ability of Canada and N.S., he must certainly be aware that the inhabitants of our West India Islands . . . will not bear to be kept upon rations of refuse, cod-fish and a short allowance of musty bread for years to come. . . . A hundred years is an inconsiderable time to wait for a Bellyful.

Yet Great Britain's creed might still be summed up in William Knox's statement that "it was better to have no colonies at all, than not to have them subservient to the maritime strength and commercial interest of Great Britain." The next effort, therefore, was to keep the Americans out of the West Indies, but induce them to export either to Nova Scotia or New Brunswick for transshipment, or by means of the British ships which brought British manufactures to the United States. The Americans, quite as wise in the ways of mercantilism as Britons, refused, and persisted in the West Indian trade, using their small vessels on frequent trips to outdo the infrequent big British ones.

ANGLO-AMERICAN MERCANTILE RELATIONS

The Anglo-French wars of 1792–1815 greatly confused the course of this Anglo-American contest. In 1798–99, for instance, when Franco-American relations were so tense that unfortified Charleston feared that it might be overwhelmed, George III responded to urgent American pleadings by first lending and then giving to the United States "a parcel [24] of iron 24-pounders" (and their munitions) that George II had once given to South Carolina, only to have them carried off during the Revolution and stored at Halifax.

This anticipation of "lend-lease" was one part of broad assistance to the United States, involving actual armaments, technical information, military and naval intelligence, and permission for surplus British naval officers to accept temporary commissions in the American navy. It fell short of an alliance because of President Adams' determination to make peace with France and because of British naval interference with American seamen.

Yet the underlying mercantile contest continued, with significant effects on Great Britain and the Maritimes. The former may be summarized by saying that Great Britain failed to keep the Americans out of the West Indies and failed to discriminate effectively against American trade. By about 1822, the economic importance of the United States to Great Britain had become an enormous influence in Britain's progression from mercantilism to free trade. In fact, what had been since 1778 an unsuccessful British effort to win back American friendship had been transformed into a rather cool mutual understanding as to economic benefit. This had been particularly noticeable in the efforts of both to benefit by the breakup of the Spanish Empire after 1800. It was brilliantly signalized by the Monroe Doctrine of December 2, 1823, which may not unfairly be described as Canning's invention, seized upon and strikingly amplified for American ambitions, and enforced by the British navy.

The effects on British North America of the Anglo-American and Anglo-French contests were enormous. Napoleon's "Continental System" exposed Great Britain's need of North American products, particularly the timber and naval stores which had hitherto come from the Baltic. Not only did the declining enterprises of the Maritimes spring to life in response, but American fishermen, lumbermen, and farmers moved in, and American products streamed in enormous quantities across the boundary. When the United States, under Jefferson's leadership, tried to keep out of the European war by self-denying embargoes, enterprising Americans refused to be bound. Smuggling was rampant, and official interference was overcome by force. The constrained merchants of Philadelphia suggested bitterly that the Maritimers ought to send Jefferson a testimonial gift of plate.

Thus the Maritimes, favored in an empire where national power was calculated in terms of sea power, received a tremendous economic fillip which matured their economies and provided them with the capital, the leadership, the equipment, and the skills necessary for independent enterprise. Lacking the contiguous internal market which New England enjoyed, they never caught up with that enterprising region, but they moved into its former place at Newfoundland and the ships they built and manned had to be most shrewdly reckoned with henceforth in the whole world's trade.

BRITAIN'S ATTITUDE TO THE CANADAS

The circumstances of the Canadas were more complex. Lower Canada, although ice-locked from December to April, had some of the mercantilistic merits of a maritime colony. These virtues grew during the shortages of the French wars, for not only did Lower Canada prove very productive, but the Richelieu River carried immense supplies of all kinds from the tributary section of Vermont and other parts of the

United States. Disgruntled Americans declared that Montreal ought to erect a statue of President Madison when the War of 1812 greatly swelled this traffic.

Upper Canada seemed a liability. "Examine the map of the globe throughout every Quarter, and there shall not be found a single district of an equal number of acres, which is more perfectly removed from all possibility of benefiting us, by settling it as a colony, than upper Canada," declared an orthodox pamphleteer. And, while Lower Canada might be defended from the ocean, "Upper Canada can no longer be expected to remain a British colony than the United States continue in Friendship with Great Britain."

THE INDIAN PROBLEM IN THE MIDDLE WEST

From 1782 to 1796, Britain had tried to avert a repetition of Pontiac's War and to mollify the fur traders of Montreal by retaining the fur-trading posts which were conceded to the United States in the Treaty of 1783—the head of Lake Champlain, Oswegatchie (Ogdensburg, N.Y.), Oswego, Niagara, Presque Isle, Sandusky, Detroit, and Michilimackinac. The excuse given was the failure of the United States to honor its promises affecting British and loyalist credits and property.

While this procedure undoubtedly helped the Montrealers to construct the fur empire which will be discussed in the next chapter, and while it greatly heartened the Indians, it was rendered futile by a vast flow of migrants across the middle passes of the Appalachians into the Ohio Valley. Beside that flow the stream north of lakes Ontario and Erie was a mere trickle. Swinging south of the Pennsylvania massif, about 1790 it was ready to break into the lands between the Ohio River and Lake Erie. The Indians, well aware of what the moving tide portended, tried to drive it back by raids on frontier settlements.

The ruling American oligarchy, which feared that "the Western people" might "ruin the Atlantic interests," nevertheless found that it could not contemplate their joining Spain or Great Britain. The admissions to statehood of Vermont (1791), Kentucky (1792), Tennessee (1796), and Ohio (1802) demonstrated this. The purchase of Louisiana in 1803 marked the submergence of tidewater timorousness.

THE UNITED STATES STRIKES

Late in 1793, the American government felt ready to act in the district north of the Ohio where the Canadian authorities were encouraging Indian resistance. The new American constitution had produced federal courts where British and loyalist claimants were securing consideration under the property-recovery clauses of the Treaty of 1783. In these circumstances John Jay was sent to England to obtain the western posts, and succeeded (as of June 1, 1796); Anthony Wayne was sent to cow the Indians, and did so in a brief battle near the western end of Lake Erie. Henceforth the American tides flowed into the Middle West irresistibly, and the Indians, towards whom the American government had little more policy than noninterference with extermination, felt that the Canadians were their only friends.

The Canadians, enjoying the easy international commercial relations which the indifferent negotiators of Jay's Treaty had conceded to the interior, traded with the Indians as of old, but tried to impress on them that they must come to terms with the Americans, since they could no longer expect military assistance. The distresses of the Indians mounted until they called for the talents of two gifted Shawnees —Tecumseh and his one-eyed brother, "The Prophet." When, in November, 1811, the governor of Indiana Territory, W. H. Harrison, marched against their headquarters in the Wabash Valley, they wiped out a quarter of his force before abandoning the area. In the eyes of western Americans, the issue of Indian resistance based upon Canadian supplies had to be dealt with.

THE STRANGE WAR OF 1812

In 1812 several long-accumulated, explosive American antipathies to Great Britain came to a head at once in hatred of her intolerably arrogant treatment of American ships, seamen, and commerce, her support of the Middle Western Indians, and her activities in chaotic Spanish Florida and Texas.

Conceivably the maritime issue was a sufficient cause, but it is nevertheless true that "the War Hawks," expansionists from the south and west, scored heavily in the elections of 1810 and put Henry Clay, one of their number, in the Speaker's chair in Congress. They were sure that Canada could be conquered by a few Kentucky riflemen, who could render the Indians helpless, and that a similarly easy conquest of Florida would preserve the delicate balance between free northern states and slaveholding southern states. Great Britain seemed to have engaged all her available energies against Napoleon. Whatever the equation of forces, Congress on June 18, 1812, bade President Madison declare war.

It proved to be a very strange war, largely because New England in particular would have none of it and traded defiantly with the enemy. Massachusetts negotiated for a separate peace and an alliance, as did one party in Vermont. New York troops refused to fight outside their state on several embarrassing occasions. Added to this, American strategy proved to be bad, partly because of obsession with the Indian problem of the Middle West, and partly because it was believed that most of the Upper Canadians would join forces with their invading brothers and leave Britain in possession only of the regions from Montreal eastward which she had already proved capable of conquering and defending, thanks to her navy.

Instead of striking hard at Montreal and cutting off Upper Canada, a series of expeditions toiled westward to Ohio so as to turn the Canadian flank from Detroit. After a few single-ship victories at sea, the American navy was smothered by the British, which dominated the entire Atlantic coast. On the other hand, Americans completely outclassed their enemies in fresh-water naval contests on Lake Erie and Lake Champlain and swept them back to the eastern end of Lake Ontario. The one great American military victory, that of Andrew Jackson at New Orleans, was won after peace had been signed.

Ridiculous or strange as were some aspects of this apparently unequal contest between eight million Americans and about half a million British colonists, yet it was a very serious war to the minority. They were saved in 1812 not by their own efforts so much as by the brilliance of Sir Isaac Brock, who used less than a thousand British regulars and his Indian auxiliaries to frighten William Hull and his force into surrender at Detroit and to drive out an invading force on the Niagara River. In 1813, Perry's American naval victory on Lake Erie enabled his baffled military associate, Harrison, to conquer and lay waste the settlements in southwestern Upper Canada, while raids, burnings, and pillagings made life hideous near the Niagara River and at York (Toronto). The Niagara campaign of 1814 was a bloody business which culminated in a drawn battle at Lundy's Lane.

While Upper Canada was suffering, Lower Canada got off relatively easily, thanks to sharp, resolute attacks delivered by regulars and by militia drawn from both English- and French-speaking colonists on invading detachments from the large, but lethargic and hopelessly led, American forces based on Sackets Harbor (Lake Ontario) and Lake Champlain.

By 1814, when Britain sent in thousands of experienced troops to the Richelieu Valley, they were entrusted to a commander, Sir George Prévost, who made such futile use of them that he was subsequently court-martialed. Down in the Maritimes, the war was an agreeable blend of cheering a triumphant British navy, indulging in some dashing privateering, and enjoying greater than customary profits from war needs and from the piquant determination of the dissident tidewater elements in the United States to maintain commercial relations.

The unsuccessful American attack of 1812–14 on what was expected to be the Achilles' heel of Great Britain deepened the weight of anti-Americanism among the British colonists. All of the colonies, even Upper Canada, had profited from war expenditures and from the contraband trade, and this prosperity was firmly, though illogically, credited to successful repulse of the American menace. Gratitude to Great Britain enhanced the prestige of British ideas and policies. The attitudes which the loyalists had brought with them were mightily reinforced, particularly in Upper Canada, where a reputation for lukewarmness or outright disloyalty during the war could easily be fastened on the American migrants who so substantially outnumbered the loyalist elect. The War of 1812, more than any other single circumstance, nourished anti-Americanism as a basic element in both regional British North Americanism and future Canadianism.

🍁 TRUCE BY TREATY

The peace treaty signed at Ghent in December, 1814, signified that Britain was tired of war and bent on the pacification of Europe. The treaty also indicated that the United States was determined to put an end to the internal schism that might destroy her and to the economic hobbles that were restraining her growth. The principal reason for Britain's surrender of her war-won advantages was the Duke of Wellington's demonstration that the United States was unconquered and unconquerable at any reasonable cost.

The treaty provided for restoration of the territorial *status quo ante bellum,* thus redeeming eastern Maine, and referred such matters as disputes over boundaries and fisheries to the arbitral adjudication of joint commissions. This procedure, initiated between the two parts of North America in Jay's Treaty of 1794, was to prove to be one of the great contributions of Great Britain and North America to the peaceful settlement of international disputes.

After two assaults by the United States, the eighteenth-century partition of North America had now been altered so that the Great Lakes furnished the dividing line. The "second war of American independence" had reasserted anti-British American nationality and the foundations of anti-American Canadian nationality. By a somewhat natural oversight, however, for over a century no one successfully insisted that the War of 1812 had abrogated the part of the third article of Jay's Treaty which provided that "it shall at all times be free to His Majesty's subjects, and to the citizens of the United States, and also to the Indians dwelling on either side of the said boundary line, freely to pass and repass by land or inland navigation, into the respective territories and countries of the two parties, on the continent of America."

The freedom extended to persons was not, however, extended to goods, in spite of British and Canadian efforts to that end. The United States had equipped itself with a tariff during the war, and, when Canadian traders rushed some goods into American territory after the peace and tried to bring out furs, the American authorities at Michilimackinac seized them for evasion of customs.

It is pleasant to record that the liquidation of remaining Anglo-American differences proceeded with unparalleled smoothness. Out of a host of border incidents involving desertion, Indians, smuggling, and so on, extending from the St. Croix to Lake Huron, there re-emerged John Adams' proposal to abolish the American and British navies on the Great Lakes. American initiative in the matter evoked favorable British response, for while the Americans could always outbuild and outnumber the Britons, both sides realized that the potentially competitive expenditures were foolish waste. The British navy, Americans admitted, could damage the United States more along the Atlantic than they could Great Britain along the Lakes. By the Rush-Bagot Agreement of April, 1817, mutual complete disarmament of a naval sort was achieved. It stood unimpaired until World War II, when it was suspended by Canada and the United States in order to allow the construction and movement of naval vessels upon which their joint cause depended.

The question of American fishing rights was obviously a difficult one, for Great Britain held that the war had terminated American "rights" and "liberties" in British waters and on British shores, whereas American fishermen had blithely rushed in to resume their old pursuits. Everyone concerned knew how complicated any set of regulations and its attempted enforcement must be. The main consideration was to reduce the risk of war, to obviate the dangerous situations created by arrogant American fishermen and British naval officers. Matters had actually reached the brink of war by the spring of 1818. Fortunately, however, certain boundary negotiations had ripened about the same time. Thereupon a sudden surge of determination on both sides to clean up everything in dispute produced the Convention of October 20, 1818. Its first three articles greatly reduced, if they did not completely eliminate, causes of friction between the United States and British North America.

By Article I the United States received certain fishing liberties "forever" and renounced others "forever." Americans might (1) fish, dry, and cure on the western half of the southern coast of Newfoundland and on the whole coast of Labrador, the drying and curing being limited to unsettled parts or elsewhere by consent of the inhabitants; (2) fish, but not dry or cure, on the entire western coast of Newfoundland and the shores of the Magdalen Islands; and (3) enter any bays or harbors of British North America "for the purpose of shelter and of repairing damages therein, of purchasing wood, and of obtaining water, and for no other purpose [notably securing bait] whatever." They renounced "forever, any liberty hitherto enjoyed or claimed . . . to take, dry, or cure fish on or within three marine miles of any of the coasts, bays, creeks, or harbors of His Britannic Majesty's dominions in America, not included within the above-mentioned limits."

By Article II the boundary between the United States and British North America was drawn due south from the northwest corner of the Lake of the Woods to the forty-ninth parallel and thence west to the Rocky Mountains. This arrangement, based on a false legend about the Treaty of Utrecht (1713), created a detached American peninsula on the lake, but it drew an oddly appropriate line between the valley of the American Missouri and the Hudson Bay Basin.

By Article III it was admitted that no agreement could be reached as to conflicting claims in the area between the Rockies and the Pacific. The *modus vivendi* adopted was that "any country that may be claimed by either party . . . shall . . . be free and open for the term of ten years . . . to the vessels, citizens, and subjects of the two powers." By treaties involving Great Britain, the United States, Spain, and Russia, made during the period 1819–25, the southern boundary of the disputed Anglo-American area became latitude 42° and the northern 54° 40'.

One of the joint commissions on boundaries under the Treaty of Ghent had managed in October, 1817, to complete the division of the islands in and near Passamaquoddy Bay in a manner distinctly favorable to Great Britain. Another bogged down trying to determine the Maine–New Brunswick boundary. Still another discovered that, because the old Valentine-Collins line along the forty-fifth parallel from the Connecticut to the St. Lawrence had been inaccurately surveyed, the United States had built its imposing "million-dollar" Fort Montgomery (Fort Blunder) on British soil at Rouses Point. It took until June, 1822, to allocate the islands along the Great Lakes waterway, and the line from Lake Huron to the Lake of the Woods, like the Maine–New Brunswick boundary and the wrongly surveyed forty-fifth parallel, had to await settlement until 1842.

A. L. Burt, the principal historian of these matters, concludes his account with one of those incidents of diplomacy that may mean little but in this case did mean much. In February, 1819, the leaders of Washington gave a ball in honor of Charles Bagot, the British minister who had worked so successfully towards Anglo-American understanding. Almost everyone of social or political importance attended. The ends of the ballroom were found to be decorated with the names of the minister and his wife and the supper tables were adorned in unprecedented fashion—"little flags of the two countries united." "Upon drinking our healths," reported Bagot, "the band, to my infinite surprise and somewhat to my apprehension for the effect, played 'God Save the King,' which the company heard standing. As this was a *pierre de touche,* I hinted to one of the managers to tell the band to play 'Yankee Doodle' the moment 'God Save the King' was finished, in order that it might be understood as a union of the two national airs, which I believe it was, for not a murmur was heard."

CHAPTER IX

Partition in the West (1690-1821)

One has only to recall how consistently the fur trade and monopoly had proceeded hand-in-hand in North America to be certain that the empty Far West would repeat the pattern. When the negotiators of 1818 drew their boundary along the forty-ninth parallel and agreed to disagree about "Oregon" on the Pacific coast, they were attempting to dispose of half the continent at a time when there were not more than three or four hundred white men in the entire area. Yet, during the preceding fifty years or so, it had been the focus, by land and sea, of rival energies in the fur trade emanating from Russia, New Spain, Hudson Bay, Montreal, New York, New Orleans, and St. Louis.

The directors of those energies knew very well what they were doing, but they had difficulty making their governments understand enough about it to come to their aid. And, since the vaulting imagination of John Jacob Astor contemplated western North America as the keystone of a world-girdling commercial structure which transcended national sovereignties, the history of these matters is interwoven with intrigue.

⚜ MONTREAL VS. HUDSON BAY

Groseilliers and Radisson had picked Hudson Bay as the ultimate winner in the quest for fur as early as 1660, but for a century and a half few persons would have agreed with them. The common impression then, and to some degree since, was that the Hudson's Bay Company sat idly ("asleep for eighty years beside the frozen sea") at its factories on the bay, waiting for whatever furs the Indians might choose to bring down the rivers after more energetic rivals in the interior had taken their pick of the lightest and best. In 1734, for instance, La Vérendrye asked a Cree chief "if the English [factor] knew that we were among the Crees and if he was not saying bad things." The Cree said that he had asked the factor if he was vexed and that he had replied "No, that we [British and French] were brothers and that he would never get angry first and that it was easy for us to get along together. . . . The French want oily beaver and I want dry beaver."

The truth was rather more complicated than that, a balancing of costs and returns in which the company enjoyed the advantage of bringing in its trade goods and taking out its furs by cheap ocean carriage to and from lightly manned fort-warehouses on tidewater. The company was not saddled with the costly business of shipment and handling involving ocean vessels to Quebec, river boats to Montreal, and lake boats, York boats, and canoes from Montreal to the deep interior.

The company did send men inland, in fact the first white man to reach the Canadian prairies was "the Boy Henry Kelsey" who, at fourteen, caught the spirit of the *coureurs* from those great exemplars, Groseilliers and Radisson, "Delighting much in Indians Company, being never better pleased then when he is Travelling amongst them." In 1689 he made a difficult circuit in the barrens north of the Churchill River, and from 1690 to 1692 he lived and traveled out from York Factory with the Indians of the Manitoba and Saskatchewan prairies, teaching them how to prepare furs ("work beaver") and encouraging peaceful commerce among the tribes so that as much as possible of the western drainage area should send its furs down to the company's post. He had the engaging habit of recording his travels in doggerel.

> Now Reader Read for I am well assur'd
> Thous dost not know the hardships I endur'd . . .
> Trusting still unto my masters Consideration
> Hoping they will Except of this my small Relation
> Which here I have pend & still will Justifie
> Concerning of those Indians & their Country
> If this wont do farewell to all as I may say
> And for my living I'll seek some other way.

Governor James Knight, who, with Kelsey as his Deputy, re-established the company on the bay after the Treaty of Utrecht, was another believer in seeking out the Indians. In 1715, the arrival at York Fort of an intelligent Slave Indian, a woman captive, enabled him to send William Stewart off on an unprecedented journey lasting almost a year which took him across the barrens to the wooded region south of Great Slave Lake and gave Knight news of the Coppermine River. By 1718 he had put together sketchy information about the interior from the Missouri to the Arctic and from the bay to the Rockies.

Unfortunately, in 1719 he and the company became obsessed with the idea that a passage could be found from the northwest corner of the bay around to rivers flowing out of the barrens where the Indians said gold and copper might be mined. Doubtless, they believed, the passage would also lead to the Pacific. The company raised new capital and dispatched Knight from Gravesend in June, 1719, with the "Albany" frigate and the "Discovery" sloop, to "find out the Streight of Anian in order to discover gold, and other valuable commodities to the northward." He and all his company perished on barren Marble Island, 350 miles north of York Factory, where they had chosen to winter after finding no passage.

The quest for gold, copper, and the Northwest Passage died away after Knight's fate was discovered in 1722. Now the company's problem became that of French competition from the Ottawa, the Great Lakes, and the Manitoba Basin. The company was relatively secure in its economic advantages, and A. S. Morton records that it enjoyed such excellent relations with the Indians (Eskimos were another matter), that during its first seventy years "not a single Englishman was struck down by the hand of an Indian, and not a single outrage is recorded as perpetrated by an English hand upon a native." Nonetheless, by 1730 Albany and York Forts were feeling threatened by the operations of French *coureurs* who were using brandy lavishly and inducing their Indian allies to attack and plunder bands of remoter Indians on their way to trade at the bay. Albany's yearly take fell by a half, York's by a third.

Yet it was not so much this decline that launched company men into the interior again as Arthur Dobbs's remarkable campaign (from 1731 to 1749) against the company's monopoly on grounds of its failure to seek and discover the Northwest Passage. It was partly to forestall English interlopers stimulated by Dobbs and partly to meet French competition that Governor James Isham sent Anthony Henday, an outlawed smuggler from the Isle of Wight, into the interior in February and again in June, 1754. He was to do as Kelsey had done sixty years earlier, but specifically to try to reach the Blackfeet in the shadow of the Rockies who had never come down to the bay to trade.

Henday had a good time once he reached the abundant game of the park belt, though it was disconcerting to be told by the Indians there: "We are conveniently supplied from the French House" (on the lower Saskatchewan). Since food was plentiful, there was much feasting. "I am not behind, thank God a good stomach, and as I am looked on as a Leader, I have Ladies of different ranks to attend me;

please to observe the men does nothing but hunt, and we Leaders hath a Lady to hold the thogin with water to our heads when we drink." He crossed the buffalo plains to the foothills of the Rockies, where he tried in vain to persuade the Blood group of the Blackfeet to come down to the bay. "The Chief further said they never wanted food, as they followed the Buffalo & killed them with the Bows and Arrows; and he was informed the Natives that frequented the Settlements were sometimes starved on their journey. Such remarks I thought exceeding true."

Next year, when Henday came out with a flotilla of sixty canoes, he saw the French in action at two points on the Saskatchewan. They neatly skimmed the cream of the furs: "They have the advantage of us in every shape, and if they had Brazil tobacco . . . they would entirely cut off our trade." Henday exaggerated; ultimately seventy canoes with what must have been considerable cargo went down with him to York Fort. That year the war began which expelled France from North America.

The company's next novel inland endeavor, therefore, was the astounding exploration of Samuel Hearne in the northern tundra from 1769 to 1772. Indians bearing chunks of native copper to Governor Moses Norton had revived the quest for the mines.

Hearne made two unsuccessful forays with the Indians out into the barrens from Churchill before his remarkable journey overland to the Arctic. Survival on the tundra was a great gamble. "It may justly be said to have been all feasting or all famine." Hearne's success may be attributed to the gifted Cree, Matonabbee, who ultimately managed things for him, "the most sociable, kind, and sensible Indian I had ever met with." "To the vivacity of a Frenchman, and the sincerity of an Englishman, he added the gravity and nobleness of a Turk." When Matonabbee heard that the French had taken the great stone fortress at Churchill in 1782, he hanged himself, "the only Northern Indian who, that I ever heard, put an end to his own existence."

Thanks to Matonabbee and his many squaws, "most of whom would for size have made good grenadiers," and thanks also to Hearne's own great qualities (not least as a writer), the area between Churchill and the Arctic mouth of the Coppermine, as well as Great Slave Lake and the Slave River, became known and recorded. The copper outcroppings did not amount to much, but, as Hearne said, he had learned from the Indians that "the Continent of America is much wider than many people imagine" and had "put a final end to all disputes concerning a North West passage through Hudson's Bay."

THE CONTEST FOR THE NORTHWEST

Meanwhile, however, British Montreal had come to life with a vigor and on a scale that made former French competition seem picayune. Americans, Englishmen, and Scotsmen, using French-Canadians as their rank and file, plunged into the Northwest, first as individual traders *en dérouine,* or "Pedlars," seeking out the Indians with their trade goods, and then in partnerships which after 1787 were fairly completely swallowed up in the North West Company.

About this time, moreover, news leaked out of St. Petersburg that Bering and Chirikov had discovered America from Asia. The Russians were soon deep in the world's richest fur trade—the fabulous sea otters, seals, and other rare furs of the northern Pacific which were not only eagerly desired in China, but could command there the Oriental products that were equally eagerly desired in the Western world. There has probably never been a more profitable quadrilateral trade.

At any rate, the unknown north Pacific coast of North America became a loadstone for the world. Spain acted first, launching expeditions by land and sea from New Spain to occupy Upper California. Juan Perez and Bruno Heceta in 1774 and 1775 coasted outside Vancouver and the Queen Charlotte Islands as far north as modern Sitka and saw the entrances to the Columbia River and Juan de Fuca Strait. Great Britain followed by dispatching her greatest navigator and geographer, Captain James Cook, on his third and last voyage in 1776. He achieved brilliant success in the North Pacific and sailed through the Bering Strait to the polar ice-pack during 1778, not only establishing the general outlines but probing the principal sounds and bays, including one, Cook's Inlet in southern Alaska, that apparently held some promise of a short cut to the Arctic.

One of his Marines was an ardent young man from Connecticut, named John Ledyard, who met the Russian fur traders on Unalaska Island and picked up some furs from the Indians at Nootka Sound on Vancouver Island. "We purchased while here about fifteen hundred beaver, besides other skins, but took none but the best, having no thoughts at that time of using them to any other advantage, than converting them to the purposes of clothing; but it afterwards happened that skins, which did not cost the purchaser sixpence sterling, sold in China for one hundred dollars."

Ledyard jumped ship at Long Island, New York, in December, 1782, published a journal of his experiences with Cook, and devoted the remaining five years of his astonishing life to spectacular, if unsuccessful, efforts in North America, Europe, and Asia to promote the North

Pacific fur trade. Naturally his ideas and the reports of Captain Cook's last voyage spread to interested persons in the United States and British North America.

The first non-Russian traders to break into the treasure house were British sea captains trading in India and China—Captain James Hanna from Macao in 1785, followed by captains Guise and Lowrie out of Bombay and trading to Macao in 1786. The Americans decided to reach what had become a free traders' paradise by sea around the Horn, starting with the "Columbia" and the "Lady Washington" in 1787. The master of the latter, Robert Gray, discovered the mouth of the Columbia on his second voyage in 1792, barely anticipating Britain's George Vancouver, whom he told of his experience.

Vancouver, a former midshipman under Cook, had two responsibilities. He was to meet at Nootka, for the purpose of defining boundary and property claims, the representatives sent by Spain under an Anglo-Spanish convention of 1790 that had abruptly terminated Spain's attempt of the previous year to assert her sovereignty that far north. He was also to complete in detail the mapping of the North Pacific coast, a task which he performed admirably in 1792, 1793, and 1794.

Meanwhile the Montrealers had become vastly interested in the new bounty of valuable furs. They had no merchant marine, but they did have knowledge of the interior of western North America that was shared only by their rivals on Hudson Bay. They were particularly excited by Cook's Inlet and the Alaskan river that entered its head, for their highways were rivers and it seemed reasonable to believe that they could either find the headwaters of Cook's River somewhere in the Northwest or at least find a portage to it from some of the rivers that they knew or that had been reported on by Hearne. Montreal's search for the Pacific was an inconspicuous but sturdy strand in the web of furious competition between Montreal and the Bay for the furs of the Northwest interior.

Confused and irregular trade, involving French Canadians and renegade company men, was going on in the Manitoba Basin at the time of Pontiac's Rising. After it, Prairie du Chien on the upper Mississippi became a great resort for free-lance traders aiming to profit from Spanish backwardness in the rich, almost unexploited, trans-Mississippi area which she had received by the treaty of 1763. Very quickly, however, Michilimackinac rose to transcendent importance, for it stood at the junction of the flows of furs to Montreal from the Mississippi (by the Chicago and the Green Bay route) and from Lake Superior, the Grand Portage, and the Far Northwest.

From about 1766 onwards, the Montreal fur trade swelled enormously at the hands of French-Canadian traders, backed and accompanied by American, English, and Scottish capitalists. They were past Lake Winnipeg by 1766, and the opening of the Indian trade by a British ordinance of April 15, 1768, sent them fanning out over the interior to the slogan *"La traite est libre."* From 1774 onward, the Bay Company had to fight for its furs, and in rapidly mounting, wasteful competition the rivals leapfrogged each other's posts, or built within hailing distance of each other as they raced up the waterways, singling out points of strategic advantage for interception of the eastward flow of furs.

THE WINNIPEG BASIN AND THE CHURCHILL AND MACKENZIE RIVERS

The map of Canada indicates the immense importance of Lake Winnipeg, "crossroads of the continent." Into it flowed the Red River of the North and the Assiniboine, which not only drained an immense area but provided access to the Missouri and its vast upper basin. The Saskatchewan poured into the lake's northwest corner, draining the middle prairies and the park land and furnishing a good water approach to the Churchill. From the upper Churchill, by the formidable, thirteen-mile Methye Portage, resolute men could reach the Clearwater and break into the third greatest drainage-basin of the continent—the Athabaska, Peace, Slave, and Mackenzie valleys.

Finally, it was on the plains south and west of Lake Winnipeg that the great buffalo hunts were conducted for the preparation of pemmican —the concentrated, almost imperishable mixture of dried and pounded meat with fat (and other odds and ends) that made possible the feverish, far-flung operations in the Northwest. Out of Lake Winnipeg, the Montrealers made their way by the Winnipeg and Rainy rivers to the Grand Portage and Lake Superior. The Bay "leaders" and their Indians usually avoided the mighty Nelson outlet from the lake because of its scarcity of game and the prevalence of great blocks of ice along its banks, but a convenient system of portages from Cross Lake put them into the more attractive Hayes River which reached the bay just east of the mouth of the Nelson.

William Pink, one of the Bay Company's vigorous servants in the interior, explored the upper Churchill from York Factory during 1767–68, coming close to the upper Mackenzie Basin. By 1774, Joseph Frobisher of Montreal was camped at Portage du Traite between Saskatchewan and Churchill, and in 1775–76 he, his brother Thomas, and Alexander Henry (late of New Jersey) broke into the Churchill country. By 1778, Peter Pond (late of Connecticut) had found the way to the Clearwater and the Athabaska which the Frobishers had been seeking and had built his post forty miles from Lake Athabaska, near where Crees and Chipewyans gathered before their very arduous journeys to and from the Saskatchewan or the bay. "They were, therefore, highly gratified . . . and were immediately reconciled to give an advanced price for the articles necessary to their comfort and convenience . . . [Pond] procured twice as many furs as his canoes could carry."

The above words were written by Alexander Mackenzie (actually, by his ghost writer, William Combe, author of *The Tours of Dr. Syntax*). Pond and Mackenzie had the intellectual, speculative qualities, coupled with the driving powers of far-ranging traders, which elevated them above their fellows and competitors. The former was an almost illiterate man, but philosophical and endlessly curious and imaginative about northwestern North America. Morose to a murderous degree, he got along badly with other traders and died poor in 1807 at Milford, Connecticut, but by his explorations, inquiries, and maps he made himself the bridge between the aspirations of Alexander Henry (who explored and traded until 1778 when he retired wealthy) and the achievements of Mackenzie.

All three communicated their ideas and findings to the learned men and the American, British, and Canadian authorities of the day. All three were principally concerned with the trade enjoyed by the Russians and with reaching Cook's Inlet on the Pacific. As Pond wrote to a friend in New York, "I make no doubt but Cook's River . . . has a communication with those parts of the North-west I was at, by which a road would be opened across the Continent."

Mackenzie was a Stornoway Scot who, like Pond, had been broken in to the trade at Detroit, and who had spent two years on the Churchill when he was sent in 1787 by the now full-fledged North West Company of Montreal and Grand Portage to replace Pond. Pond's withdrawal was dictated by deaths under suspicious circumstances of two of his rivals. Pond told Mackenzie of his deductions from his own direct knowledge and the reports of Indians, Hearne, and Cook. In short, Pond had decided that the combined Athabaska, Peace, and Slave rivers joined Cook's River to flow into the Pacific.

TO THE ARCTIC AND THE PACIFIC

From a new fort on the southern shore of Lake Athabaska, almost two thousand miles from the Grand Portage, Mackenzie started out, June 3, 1789, to explore that possibility. By July 10 he was in the delta of the river that bears his name, established his latitude, and concluded: "It was evident that these waters emptied themselves into the Hyperborean Sea." Having reached the Arctic and its ice pack two days later, he explored a little and, while a mob in Paris stormed the Bastille, set up a record post on Whale Island. He got back to his fort on September 12, 1789, two days after the first hard frost. It had all been a bitter disappointment, particularly since he knew that the Bay Company was now also questing for the Pacific.

In 1793, therefore, he set out on a far crueler journey from another new fort halfway up the mighty Peace River above Lake Athabaska. He had been studying in Montreal and in England in 1791–92 and had decided from what Pond and the Indians had told him that the Peace would lead him through the Rockies. He had learned of the Yukon River, and thought the Peace might lead him to its head. In an especially built canoe and carrying all his money except two guineas "to traffic with the Russians," he and his men struggled up the spring flood of the river, through and around the forbidding twenty-two miles of its canyon, into the mountains, and up the Parsnip from the forks. They found their way over a divide on the intermountain plateau to the headwaters of the Fraser and followed it south until its great volume, its canyon, and Indian reports convinced them that its road to the Pacific was too long by land and too dangerous by water.

Backtracking to the Blackwater, they took to their own feet and followed an Indian trail out of the high, dry plateau and through the Coast Range to the water-soaked Pacific slope. There, among the self-confident, irascible Indians in their imposing wooden villages, about seven weeks after George Vancouver's careful surveyors had felt their way along the same fiords twisting deep into the mountains, Mackenzie saw the ocean on the evening of July 19. Before hastening away from the threatening natives, he managed to make day and night observations for latitude and longitude and inscribed on a rock bluff in Dean Channel in vermilion: "Alexander Mackenzie, from Canada, by land, the twenty-second of July, one thousand seven hundred and ninety-three!" He had made the first truly transcontinental crossing, the Northwest Passage "by land."

Mackenzie is chiefly known to history for his great journeys to the Arctic and the Pacific, and he seldom gets credit for his early realization that the stern contest between Montreal and the Bay was a profound mistake. The marvelously intricate organization by which Montreal counterbalanced the advantages of the Bay was one of the most extraordinary achievements of North American man, but the credit costs, the duplication, the violence, the lavish competitive use of alcohol, and perhaps even some of the devastation of the Indians by disease and rapacity might have been obviated by a single monopoly based upon the Bay.

Upon this a world-girdling commercial structure might be based. On his way to Montreal in 1794, he called on Lieutenant Governor J. G. Simcoe at York and told him of his belief that the Peace and the Fraser (which he naturally believed to be the Columbia, "the River of the West") formed a route to the Pacific which could be exploited by North West Company methods, but most advantageously if they were conducted from Hudson Bay. He spent the rest of his life in unsuccessful efforts to create a great chartered company for the realization of his brilliant designs, but he was a generation ahead of his time.

Simcoe wrote to the British Privy Council:

It appears from the observations of Mr. Mackenzie who seems to be as intelligent as he is adventurous, That to carry on this Commerce to National Advantages, the privilege and rivalship, the claims and monopoly of great Commercial Companies must be reconciled and blended in one common Interest . . . the most practicable Rout to the Northwest was thro' the territories of the Hudsons Bay Company, that by this route from Great Britain all the Navigation from Montreal thro' the Chain of Lakes and their immense Communication to the more distant part of the interior Country and its consequent Carriage, would be saved, but that on the other hand the people of Canada being infinitely more capable of the hardships of the Indian life . . . than Europeans, from thence, must draw those supplies of men without which It would not be possible to pursue the Commerce. The Northwest Traders would find it their Interest to collect all the most valuable of the Furs, now brought from the Interior parts of America, and to pass them down the streams which fall into the Pacific Ocean . . . a post at Cooke's River and another at the Southerly limit of the British Claims would probably secure the whole Traffic . . . The East India Company, who possess the Privilege of the Chinese Market, It is to be presumed, would find the Utility of these Establishments and he seems to apprehend the diminution of the Quantity of Silver sent to China in Consequence of the increase of the Fur Trade would be a national advantage.

Five years after Mackenzie left the West the Nor'Westers, as represented by Duncan McGillivray, who shared his views, began the planning of their "Columbian Enterprise." This involved the discovery of what lay between the abrupt eastern face of the Rockies and the Pacific coast, by means of approaches from the Peace, the Athabaska, and both branches of the Saskatchewan. Following Simon Fraser's explorations from the Peace in the lake country of northern British Columbia and his almost incredible journey of 1807 to the mouth of the river which now bears his name, only northern British Columbia, or "New Cale-

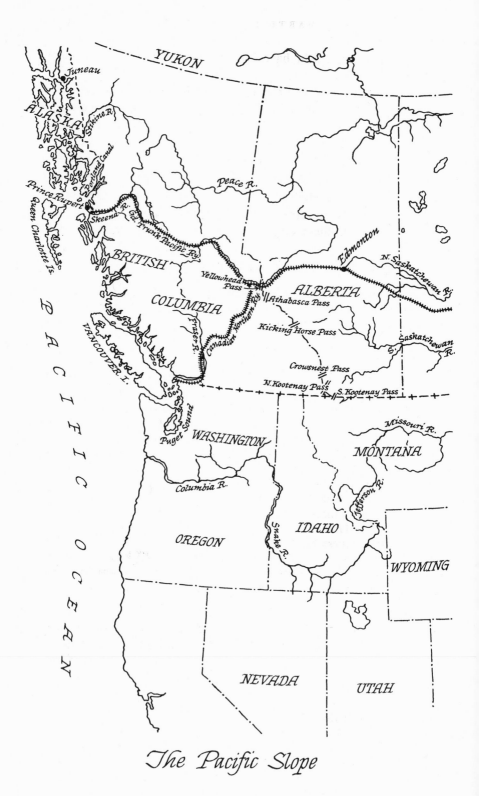

The Pacific Slope

donia," was found to be tributary to the rivers of the high plains. Fraser's exploit, in terms of endurance, will, management, and skill, transcended Mackenzie's, but it did not provide the desired route to the Pacific. It was to be a more southern set of enterprises which would bring success.

Those enterprises were mightily stimulated by the sudden and unexpected entry of the United States into the Far Western overland trading. Thomas Jefferson, who had never forgotten his exciting contacts with John Ledyard ("a man of genius, of some science, and of fearless courage and enterprise . . . unfortunately, he has too much imagination"), engineered the purchase of Louisiana from an embarrassed Napoleon during the first six months of 1803. During the same months he prepared an expedition "to trace the Missouri to its source, to cross the highlands and follow the best water communication which offered itself from thence to the Pacific Ocean."

This great publicly supported enterprise, under Meriwether Lewis and William Clark, left St. Louis on May 14, 1804, shortly after the formal transfer there of upper Louisiana. Admirably handled throughout difficult, dangerous, and unprecedented obstacles, this expedition reached the mouth of the Columbia on November 15, 1805, by way of the Jefferson, the Clearwater, and the Snake. Twelve years after Mackenzie reached the Pacific, a tree at Tongue Point was inscribed, "William Clark, December 3rd, 1805. By Land from the U. States in 1804 & 1805."

In order to understand fully what followed one ought to trace the wanderings imposed on the great snow-fed mountain rivers by the serried ranges between the high plains and the coast. The most important consideration to be borne in mind is that while the Columbia and the Kootenay rise in southeastern British Columbia within a few miles of each other, the former runs far to the north before coming back south to meet the Kootenay just north of the forty-ninth parallel after the latter has run far south and then north again. Near the northern bend of the Columbia, the headquarters of the Thompson River affords a tempting lure towards the West, but the Thompson flows into the Fraser. Near the southern bend of the Kootenay, the Missoula River system offers another temptation as a short cut, but it ultimately drains north to join the Columbia a very short distance south of the Kootenay junction itself.

The best passage for the fur traders from the high plains of the interior to the coast, therefore, was from the Saskatchewan to the Kootenay and thence down it and the Columbia. Amid great difficulties with the Indians, this route was painstakingly worked out between 1806 and 1811 on behalf of the North West Company by Duncan McGillivray and the ablest geographer and map maker of the day, David Thompson, once Philip Turnor's apprentice in the Hudson's Bay Company.

🍁 THE IMPACT OF ASTOR

Meanwhile an imagination as great as Mackenzie's and a much greater command of political influence and financial resources had been brought to bear by John Jacob Astor of New York. In 1787, within four years of his arrival as an almost penniless German immigrant, Astor was getting at the flow of furs to Montreal. Thereafter, using the Treaty of 1783 and Jay's Treaty on the one hand, and flouting American regulations by bribery and political influence on the other, he came close to dominating the Great Lakes trade. Quite swiftly he squeezed the Canadians out of their expected profits from operations south of the Lakes. Michilimackinac became the hinge of the closing door, and the Montrealers, thus diverted from Southwest to Northwest, shifted from the Grand Portage to Fort William and the Kaministikwia route in the season 1802–3.

By 1810 Astor was ready to operate a world-wide scheme which he calculated would put the St. Louis traders and both the Hudson's Bay Company and the North West Company at his mercy. He would assemble trade goods at New York and distribute them for the fur trade of the interior from Montreal, Detroit, Michilimackinac, St. Louis, and New Orleans. He sent both an overland and a sea expedition to set up Astoria at the mouth of the Columbia. In order to master the Pacific coast trade, he made an arrangement with the Russians of Alaska to exclude the two British companies and employ his Pacific Fur Company, at least in their supply trade with Spanish California and presumably in much else of an irregular sort. From the Pacific coast he would trade to China and from China to the rest of the world.

One of the results of the War of 1812 was the impairment of this scheme. The Canadians dominated the upper Great Lakes and cut off the Americans from the Far West by their control of Michilimackinac, Fort Dearborn (Chicago), and Prairie du Chien. Shortly after Astoria was founded in 1811, David Thompson turned up there at last, thus heralding the Montreal overlanders. News of the war reached Astoria in January, 1813, and, in default of American naval protection, the Astorians sold out to the Nor'Westers in October. In November a British naval vessel underlined the wisdom of that decision. The Pacific Fur Company wound up its affairs in 1814.

And, although Astoria was formally restored to the United States and "Oregon" was by the Convention left open to American and

Canadian enterprise in 1818, the over-all outcome was that Astor's American Fur Company monopolized (often through Canadian field managers) the trade on American territory only up to the Rockies. The more efficient overlanders from Montreal and the Bay rapidly cleaned the furs out of southern "Oregon" in anticipation of a day when they might be excluded by the kind of British political decision to which they had become accustomed.

❧ THE RED RIVER SETTLEMENT

Meanwhile the conflict between Montreal and the Bay had been mounting through violence to its natural conclusion. A new element introduced through the Hudson's Bay Company was to have lasting importance to Canada. This came about because of the entry into the Bay Company of Thomas Douglas, Earl of Selkirk, after quite intricate proposals made to him about 1807 or 1808 by that "Brother Scot," now Sir Alexander Mackenzie. Following modest purchases of stock and a reorganization of the company in accordance with a plan made by Selkirk's brother-in-law, Andrew Colville (known as Wedderburn), on February 26, 1811, it was "Resolved that Mr. Wedderburn be desired to request Lord Selkirk to lay before the Committee the Terms on which he will accept a Grant of Land, within the Territories of the Company."

Selkirk then bought a really large block of stock and embarked on the fateful business of attempting at the Red River a repetition of the Scottish colonizing in which he had already experimented in New York State, Prince Edward Island, and Upper Canada. Unfortunately for him and his settlers, his "Assiniboia" grant was blocked out to cover the basins of the Red and Assiniboine rivers and the lower half of the Manitoba lakes, that is, on top of the principal pemmican-producing area and across the routes from Montreal to the Far West. This flat assertion of enduring territorial sovereignty meant war with Montreal and it was promptly launched against "The Bible Peer."

For the grim details of the contest the interested reader is referred to the histories by A. S. Morton and J. P. Pritchett. From 1811 to 1817, Selkirk sent out successive batches of Scottish settlers and a group of Swiss mercenaries ("the Meurons") who had been stranded in Ceylon during the Napoleonic wars. The Nor'Westers responded by stimulating the half-breeds of the Red River against them, thus beginning the crystallization of a distinct and self-conscious future community there and elsewhere in the West—"La Nation Métisse." The first governor of the Selkirk Settlement, Miles Macdonell, sharpened the issue on January 8, 1814, by prohibiting "all export of provisions of what nature so ever for one year from this date," a direct blow at the pemmican trade which quickly produced strife.

On top of the perils of transportation from the bay and the harsh vicissitudes of pioneer farming on the Red River, the settlers were at first plagued in ingenious ways and then almost all frightened into leaving for Norway House and Upper Canada. When further reinforcements made it clear that Selkirk was determined to strike root, an open battle took place at the Seven Oaks on June 19, 1816, in which the new Governor, Robert Semple, and nineteen of his men were killed. Once more the settlers started to emigrate, but now Selkirk himself intervened with his Swiss and Canadian veterans.

He saved his settlement, but got himself into legal difficulties with the astute Montrealers under the Canada Jurisdiction Act of 1803 which in effect had given Lower Canada (i.e. Montreal) jurisdiction over "all offences committed within any of the Indian Territories or parts of America" not within the Canadas. Before he lavished his fortune and hastened his death (1820) in this prolonged and complicated litigation, Selkirk during the summer of 1817 personally made such excellent arrangements for the future working of the colony that it endured to become the natural place to which fur traders retired, particularly if they felt that their Indian wives and half-breed children would be happier there than in the outside world. Thus the only part of North America to be settled from Hudson Bay became a place where English and French (divided by the Red River), Indians and half-breeds lived in mutual tolerance.

❧ THE TRIUMPH OF THE BAY

The tolerance was enforced by the union of the two companies in 1821. The Montrealers were on the brink of bankruptcy and the lavish days of Far Western fur-looting were over. The Hudson's Bay Company had resumed its 4 per cent dividend in 1815 and maintained it. The Nor'Westers had won the last battle in the field for the trade of the Athabaska and Peace River areas and Ile-á-la-Crosse Lake, but their shareholders, unlike those of the Hudson's Bay Company, depended almost exclusively on the nonexistent profits of their trade. Negotiations inconspicuously begun in 1815 grew livelier when the Montreal combination faced renewal of its mutual contract in 1820. Long negotiations took place in London, Montreal, and among the "winterers" at the rendezvous at Fort William. It was Andrew Colville of the Hudson's Bay Company who detailed the terms of the merger which went into force March 26, 1821, about a year after the deaths of Mackenzie and Selkirk.

The Bay had won, one hundred and sixty years after its potentialities were first realized by Groseilliers and Radisson. Parliament by an act of July 2, 1821, tacitly recognized the old company's monopoly over Rupert's Land and the North West Territory. "The Fur Trade is for ever lost to Canada!" wrote William McGillivray, and indeed it seemed so as the old routes and forts between Montreal and the Red River fell silent, or almost so, and the whole trade was keyed to Hudson Bay. Ingenious shuffling and distribution of profit-sharing, rather large-scale retirements, and the emergence of an organizing genius in the person of George Simpson facilitated the absorption of the Nor'Westers and the ruthless elimination of wasteful duplication. In the summer of 1821, the field leaders of the two companies met at York Factory where John Tod, a Bay Company Scot who later became a Councilor of Vancouver Island, recorded the inevitable drama.

The Nor'Westers he saw as "a bold energetic race of breached Highlanders from the North; the heroes of the opposition who had fought and bled manfully," but who "had undoubtedly been defeated in the struggle, and their very name . . . now entirely defunct; yet they were by no means, apparently, humbled or in the least subdued in spirit." When the bell sounded for dinner, the whole mixed group entered "in perfect silence and with the most solemn gravity." "But that crafty fox . . . George Simpson, coming hastily to the rescue with his usual tact and dexterity on such occasions, succeeded . . . somewhat in dispelling that reserve in which both parties had hitherto continued to envelope themselves." Some of them began to smile and unbend. They then found that place cards had broken up the two groups, but that in some cases this meant that men who had actually tried to kill each other sat face to face. Of one couple Tod wrote:

I shall never forget the look of utter scorn and utter defiance with which they regarded each other the moment their eyes met. The highlander's nostrils actually seemed to expand; he snorted, squirted, and spat . . . between his legs, and was as restless in his chair as if he had been seated on a hillock of ants; the other looked equally defiant, but less uneasy—upon the whole, more cool. I thought it fortunate that they were without arms.

Out of the enforced union of these discordant survivors of "the rugging and the riving times when might was right and a man's life was valued at naught," George Simpson somehow built a fur monopoly of almost continental proportions which carried the Hudson's Bay Company, its lands, and their peoples into a period of profound peace and unparalleled prosperity. The use of rum in trade was almost eliminated and the Indians then responded quickly to the traditional tranquilizing measures of the old company. The Red River settlement, having received a great addition to its numbers, settled down so securely as to be able to survive such disasters as short and capricious growing seasons, the emigration of the Swiss to the United States, floods, and grasshoppers. Even the raids of unscrupulous "whiskey traders" from the United States were successfully countered.

As appropriate a concluding commentary as any on this achievement of the merged companies has been provided by Frederick Merk, the American editor of one of George Simpson's early journals, who has noted the contrast with the United States. "The territory of the Hudson's Bay Company . . . was an area of peace and order. . . . On the American side of the line, violence and murder were the order of the day." Consequently, when settlers came later to eclipse the fur trade, "on the American side [they] entered a region of already established strife and perpetuated there traditions two centuries old of Indian massacre and border retaliation. On the Canadian side civilization entered a region reduced by the Hudson's Bay Company to a tradition of law and order and the history of this frontier was one of almost unbroken peace."

BOOK 2

THE PARTS (1815–65)

CHAPTER X

Empire and Neighborhood (1815-71)

Before proceeding with the history of the several parts of British North America, consideration of some of the great forces that affected them all during the half century or so after 1815 will obviate a good deal of repetition. Most of those forces, of course, emanated from Great Britain and the United States.

For more than fifty years after the end of the Anglo-French wars in 1815, the colonies of British North America had to reconcile themselves to British indifference which mounted gradually to outright distaste. During the same years, the United States grew with unparalleled speed and also with the sense that its "Manifest Destiny" was to incorporate all North America, at least, and possibly all the Americas. Meanwhile, Great Britain and the United States never ceased to be occupied with the extraordinarily difficult adjustment of the embittered attitudes bred by the War of Independence and the War of 1812.

Caught up in this interplay of overpowering forces, the colonies had to puzzle out their individual courses as best they could in terms of their local interests and ambitions, and of the best accommodation to them that they could extract from each other, from Great Britain, and from the United States. Mere survival was an achievement in itself. Anything beyond that evidenced abilities of a high order in the colonial leaders.

BRITISH NORTH AMERICA OVERSHADOWED

Great Britain came out of the long contest with France the possessor of an economy unrivaled in the world. Her capital resources were immense, and she was practiced in lending from them; her industrial production of staple goods was unique; and her apparatus for carrying, warehousing, processing, and distributing her own and foreign goods made her the greatest trading nation on earth. The future seemed to promise extraordinary growth, but in every sector of the economy the

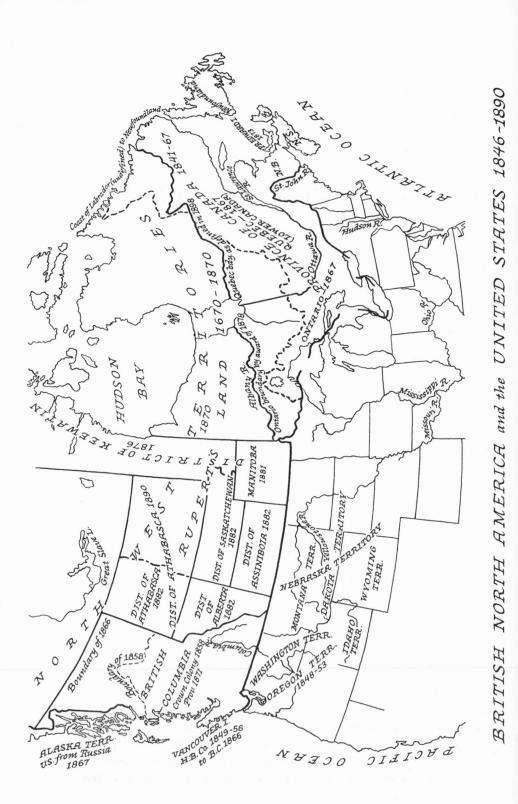

BRITISH NORTH AMERICA and the UNITED STATES 1846-1890

PACIFIC OCEAN

ATLANTIC OCEAN

HUDSON BAY

NORTHWEST TERRITORIES

DISTRICT OF KEEWATIN 1876

RUPERT'S LAND 1670

Coast of Labrador (undefined) to Newfoundland

CANADA 1841-67

PROVINCE OF CANADA 1867 (LOWER CANADA)

QUEBEC 1867

ONTARIO 1867

Quebec boundary as defined in 1898

Ontario boundary by award of 1878

Albany R.

St. Lawrence R.

Ottawa R.

P.E. Edward I. 1873

Newfoundland

St. John R.

N.S.

N.B.

Hudson R.

Ohio R.

Mississippi R.

Missouri R.

DIST. OF ATHABASCA 1882

DIST. OF ALBERTA 1882

DIST. OF SASKATCHEWAN 1882

DIST. OF ASSINIBOIA 1882

MANITOBA 1881

Great Slave L.

W. E. 1890

Boundary of 1866

Boundary of 1858

BRITISH COLUMBIA Crown Colony 1858 Prov. 1871

Columbia R.

Yellowstone R.

Missouri R.

MONTANA TERR.

DAKOTA TERRITORY

NEBRASKA TERRITORY

WYOMING TERR.

IDAHO TERR.

WASHINGTON TERR.

OREGON TERR. 1848-53

ALASKA TERR. U.S. from Russia 1867

VANCOUVER I. 1849-58 H.B.Co. to B.C. 1866

leading operators felt that they were working with as yet incalculable forces.

Great Britain, therefore, was the home of brilliant experimentation of all sorts—social, political, and economic—but the boldness was accompanied by constant fear lest something or other "rock the boat." The chief fear was of domestic revolution, since new ideas were in the air and the formulas adopted for postwar stability imposed almost intolerable burdens on the impoverished general population, already in the throes of a vast social dislocation brought on by industrialization. Second to it was the fear of new wars. Peace, domestic and international, on the other hand, seemed certain to pay on an unprecedented scale.

The slogan of the Liberal party which was gradually formed out of the business-minded members of the old Tory and Whig parties was "Peace, Retrenchment, and Reform." The new Political Economy meant literally what it said. The State must be run in accordance with the best bookkeeping practice, and its enterprises, for instance colonies, must justify themselves by balances on the credit side of the ledger. Reform meant essentially administrative reform, not any truckling to democracy or republicanism. And, finally, the best national economics, in the light of Britain's almost unchallenged supremacy in production and transportation, was free trade. Once the income tax could be seen as an acceptable substitute for customs revenue, the apparatus of mercantilism could be scrapped and the rest of the world, including British colonies, exposed to give-and-take, buying and selling, with the masterful British economy.

While the new British policies contained plenty of governmental regulation, the public emphasis was on freedom. Money poured out of the country for investment abroad. Raw materials flowed in with less and less tariff impediment. People moved out in such vast numbers that their individually small capitals combined to make huge increments at their destinations. The migrants carried skills with them and the knowledge, the blueprints, or the actual machines for industrialization abroad.

If in any case all the world must in its own interest trade with Britain, British territorial sovereignty overseas was of little account except insofar as it provided trading posts or the naval stations for the protection of world-girdling commerce, a conception which was neatly demonstrated when Britain took little more than a world-wide scattering of such places as her spoils at the end of the French wars. The name "Little Englandism" has been given to this antiterritorial creed of 1815–70, but Charles Dilke probed more deeply in 1866 when he wrote of a "Greater Britain" that commercially transcended national boundaries.

✿ AN EXPANSIVE UNITED STATES

As Albert Gallatin observed of the United States after the War of 1812, "The people . . . are more Americans; they feel and act more as a nation." Having at last really broken through the Appalachians, and receiving normally about 60 per cent of the large British emigration as well as other immigrants, they began to occupy the continent at an astounding rate. Since water transportation was a mighty consideration, at first the Ohio and Mississippi carried them west and south. "Hi-o, away we go, floating down the river on the O-hi-o."

The Indians east of the Mississippi were ruthlessly uprooted and pushed across the great river by 1840 to make room for white occupation of the near side of its valley. The Santa Fé Trail was opened early in the 1820's. American pressure produced an independent Texas by 1835 which was incorporated ten years later. Outright war against Mexico, coupled with some face-saving purchases, swallowed up the whole Southwest and California by 1848, just before the gold discoveries that catapulted California to statehood in 1850.

An odd combination of missionary enterprise beyond the Rockies, coupled with propaganda which made Oregon much more attractive than treeless, tough-sodded, fever-ridden Iowa and Missouri, launched so many settlers across the empty Far West to the valley of the Columbia in the early 1840's that by 1846 their presence dictated the end of Anglo-American mutual toleration south of the forty-ninth parallel. Small wonder that British North Americans feared that they would be swallowed up too.

The American economy was burgeoning. Eli Whitney's cotton gin (1793) followed hard on the discovery that the American South could easily outdo the West Indies in the production of a staple for which Great Britain had an inexhaustible appetite. Two years later, Étienne Boré demonstrated that Louisiana could profitably add sugar to the American list of "tropical" products. The eastern half of the Mississippi Valley proved to be immensely rich agricultural land, even if the grasslands beyond defeated the old methods of cultivation.

All in all the output of natural products was an ever-growing one, and an American merchant marine that almost surpassed Great Britain's during the golden days of the wooden ship (about 1850–60), carried, chiefly to Great Britain, surpluses of tobacco, lumber, naval stores, cotton, wheat, and coarse grains. British engineers and canal builders, spending British capital, helped to provide the cheap water transport that linked the interior with the coastal outlets to Europe. Imported British experts laid the foundations of an industrialized New England.

Whereas in Great Britain the oligarchy of property adjusted its changing balances of power internally, without yielding to democracy until 1867, in the United States "the people" almost triumphed in 1824 and did so behind Andrew Jackson in 1828. Fortress after fortress of long-established privilege was stormed by the people and their representatives. Public offices became party spoils in accordance with Jackson's dictum that wholesale removals following a change of administration "would . . . give healthful action to the system," although it should be noticed that the salaries were systematically kept very low, indeed too low.

The elective principle was extensively applied to judgeships. "The Money Power," that is, narrow control of credit, was resolutely attacked. Religious and educational monopolies were successfully sapped and mined. Prolonged battles were waged before victory was won for free, nonsectarian, publicly controlled primary schools where the curriculum would be popular and practical rather than traditional and abstract. In short, social and political democracy triumphed so thoroughly that Count Alexis de Tocqueville, traveling in the United States, was moved to write the most penetrating political treatise of the day, *Democracy in America* (1835).

Yet this expansive, energetic organism was in mortal danger from a cancer whose growth began in colonial days—Negro slavery, which had been rendered enormously more significant by the occupation of territory amenable to cotton, sugar, and other field crops cultivated under the extensive plantation system. Basically and persistently an ethnic problem involving ethics, color, and culture, it had ramifications of personal status, geographical region, economics, and politics which made it insoluble in any immediate sense.

The problem had been recognized during the framing of the Constitution, when it was expected to dwindle away. It had contributed mightily to the deep division of the republic during the War of 1812. Thereafter a series of delicate balancings of power between free and slave states served until the Southwest and California were acquired. The election of 1848 saw the emergence of "Free Soil, Free Speech, Free Labor, and Free Men" as a party slogan. Stephen Douglas, Henry Clay, and Daniel Webster pushed through still another compromise in 1850, but the Union was obviously breaking up. Douglas' Kansas-Nebraska Act of 1854 yielded more to the South than the North and the West could stomach, and in 1860 the election as president of Douglas' opponent, Abraham Lincoln of Illinois, prompted Southern secession from the Union. Civil war followed.

🍁 A YIELDING BRITAIN

British North Americans could do little to affect the impact upon them of the new might either of Great Britain or of the United States. What particularly embittered and frightened them was the recognition of Britain's almost continuous yielding to American pressure. The boundary settlements of 1783 and 1814 proved to be omens of the fact that British understanding with the United States was a more important consideration than all the interests of British North America put together.

After the Panic of 1837 was followed by American repudiations of public indebtedness, in large part to British investors, Britain allowed the settlement of some persistent North American disputes to be entrusted to Lord Ashburton, head of the banking house of Baring Brothers, and Daniel Webster, who had recently been paid by that firm while acting as go-between for British lenders and American borrowers. To these friendly negotiators the Maine–New Brunswick boundary, the acceptance of the crooked Valentine-Collins line instead of the forty-fifth parallel, and the determination of the frontier from Lake Superior to Lake of the Woods were troublesome but manageable preliminaries to the more important business of reconstructing Anglo-American financial and commercial confidence. Their treaty of 1842 aroused bitter criticism for some time in both the United States and the colonies by its blunt settlements, but most students of these matters today think that it was a remarkably fair compromise of nagging, inflammatory conflicts.

Again in 1846, when settlement of the Oregon question became imperative in American politics, it seemed to eastern British North Americans, who saw the issue in terms of territory long "occupied" by British fur traders instead of in terms of thousands of new American settlers, that Great Britain had meekly acquiesced in division by the forty-ninth parallel instead of by the Columbia River. Actually, about that time the British attitude towards the United States was hardening a little, as was evidenced by stands taken in the Caribbean region and Central America. But what neither Americans nor British colonists realized was that, diplomatically, the Americas were, and would continue to be, less important than Europe to Great Britain until the end of the nineteenth century. They barely figure, for instance, in British histories of British foreign policy.

Despite that comparative insignificance, it was nonetheless true that about 1850 some British statesmen who could rid themselves of conventional thinking in international relations were moving towards recognition of the United States as a potentially equal Great Power. These men formed a minority, and the party flux that followed the Repeal of the Corn Laws in 1846 permitted a great many obsolete considerations to govern British policy for another twenty-five years. This was most forcibly and regrettably demonstrated during the American Civil War, when a little hard thinking would have aligned Great Britain appropriately with the North instead of inappropriately with the South. Similarly a little less habitual arrogance and condescension towards the United States might have saved Great Britain from the stupidity (even in terms of her own future vulnerability) of allowing British territory to be used for the construction and maintenance of Southern land and sea power for use against the North.

Clearly, considering the difference in magnitudes between Great Britain and the United States on the one hand and any British North American colony on the other, the last was usually an almost negligible factor in the three-way operating relationship. Yet, in examining such triangles of forces, it is imperative to remember what few Britons or Americans bothered to remember, namely, that the colonists were confirmed North Americans, of varying views no doubt, but basically rooted in their continent, thoroughly alert to what might be made of their own localities, and utterly courageous in voicing and forwarding their views. By 1815, thanks to the long Anglo-French contest and the American embargoes, all of them were capable of self-support through the production, for sustenance and export, of fish, furs, wood products, grains, and other farm produce.

Their principal regret was that they, the "loyal" elements of the Old Empire, could attract so much less than the "rebel" United States by way of British emigration, investment, and general economic intercourse. Again and again they claimed as their due privileged treatment in assisted emigration, colonization companies, public works, defense expenditures, loans, guarantees of their public borrowings, entry to British and British colonial markets, and maintenance of their own or Britain's merchant marine. Moreover, they received much of this privileged treatment, sometimes so grudgingly and slowly that opportunities slipped away, and usually with more thoughtful consideration for the seaboard colonies than for those in the interior, but enough to show that Little Englandism could not prevail entirely over the tradition from the "Old Empire." And yet their potentialities could attract only fractions of the British increments to the United States— less than a third as many emigrants and still smaller proportions of capital, commerce, and carrying trade.

🍁 THE OBSTACLES TO COLONIAL AUTONOMY

Domestically the chief political preoccupation of the colonists was with an autonomy that would empower them to make their own experiments and, presumably, their own mistakes. In this matter they were confronted by a multiple force composed of three elements. One was the traditional mercantilistic idea that "it was better to have no colonies at all, than not to have them subservient to the maritime strength and commercial interest of Great Britain." Another was the antirepublican, antidemocratic temper of the oligarchy in Great Britain which, contemplating the forces let loose in the world by the French and American revolutions, was perhaps less capable of envisaging colonial self-government after 1800 than when it was demanded by other Americans about 1765. The last obstruction was the presence in the colonies of privileged oligarchies that attempted to maintain themselves by stressing proper colonial subordination and agreeing with the British oligarchy that authority should rest with the elect rather than with the majority of the people.

With minor exceptions and modifications, the institutional framework for this kind of empire was the "Royal Government" of the late seventeenth century. The governor, his Executive Council (or heads of departments), and the Legislative Council (or upper house of a bicameral legislature) were appointed by British authority and guided by the governor's commission and instructions and by the British laws of trade and navigation. The Assembly was elected by the people, often on a rather narrow franchise. Legislative action must not only have the agreement of governor, Legislative Council, and Assembly, but also the approval of the British government.

Executive action was not very amenable to Assembly regulation, even by the classical parliamentary device of control of the purse, for in most cases considerable funds were available from various sources for carrying on the administration without vote of the legislature. Moreover the patronage, direct and indirect, at the disposal of the executive was very large indeed by American standards. A colonial governor received ten times as much as a state governor, or about as much as the president of the United States. A colonial Chief Justice received half as much again as the Chief Justice of the United States. And the insiders skimmed the cream off most of the sources of colonial wealth—land grants, contracts, and an inappropriate apparatus of official fees.

Needless to say, the colonials saw, with Charles James Fox, that Great Britain had given them "something like the shadow of the British Constitution, but denied them the substance." The French

Canadians, for instance, who presumably had no previous understanding of such things, had exposed within a year or two the realities of the Constitutional Act of 1791. Most of the colonists, even the recent arrivals from the British Isles, had been infected in one way or another by what the Americans had been doing since 1775, and after 1824 had been much excited by news of the Jacksonian democrats. They were critical of some American procedures, but they could not resist using American achievements as criteria, not only for themselves, but for the colonial and British oligarchies. Party control of patronage, that inseparable accompaniment of parliamentary government, was particularly alluring.

Colonial democracy was relatively unhampered by the traditions which postponed in Great Britain until late in the nineteenth century recognition of what Durham called in 1839 "the necessary consequences of representative institutions." The Toronto reformers grouped around W. W. and Robert Baldwin perceived those consequences as early as 1828, not in American terms, but in terms of the Cabinet system which Britons had been working out for over a century but hesitating to accept in its fullest implications. After delimiting the logical area of colonial autonomy, the Baldwin formula conceded to the majority in the Assembly the nomination of the governor's Executive Council, and limited the governor's action to that taken on its advice. The Executive Council, not the governor, was to dispense the patronage. It would, of course, remain in office only so long as its measures commanded the support of a majority in the Assembly. This formula, a natural outcome of the heritage of Upper Canadian colonists, was taken up by the reform elements in the other colonies, usually under the name of "Responsible Government."

Irrespective of its objectionableness on democratic grounds, Responsible Government seemed logically ridiculous to the ruling class in Great Britain. How could a colonial governor, they asked, be at the same time the servant of British government and of the majority in a colonial assembly? Sovereignty could not operate when it flowed from both British and colonial electorates. As long as a colony remained a colony, its governor was answerable to the ministers of the British sovereign, who were in turn responsible by convention to the Crown, but in actuality to a majority in the British Parliament. Responsible Government in a colony, therefore, could only mean independence.

It took about twenty years to make the governors of Britain see the way out of that logical impasse. For the time being, the solution was simple enough. The thing to do, as the Baldwins suggested, was to divide the field of sovereignty into matters imperial and matters colonial and to make the colonial executive the servant of the British Parliament in the former and of the colonial Parliament in the latter. Moreover, as one shrewd governor, Lord Elgin, pointed out, it was likely that when the colonies were thrown on their own resources they would be more than ever anxious for continued association with the mother country.

🍁 FREE TRADE

The British mood of surrender to colonial insistence on Responsible Government was one part of the triumph of free trade. That triumph had been a slow one, for mercantilistic ideas were centuries old and the free trade alternative seemed very daring. Systematic propaganda for freer trade had begun about 1750 and was mightily strengthened by Adam Smith's *Wealth of Nations* in 1776 and by the American Revolution, but the French wars had arrested all possibilities of change; in fact, mercantilistic regulation of the surviving empire had played a large part in the life-and-death struggle with Napoleon. In many ways, as we have seen, it was the United States that set British free trade ideas rolling again, partly by its importance as a market and a source of needed commodities, but more specifically by its victory in the long, stubborn contest for entry into the West Indian trade.

At any rate, British tariffs were first systematized from profound confusion, and then in the 1820's began to decrease. While the postwar revenue problems remained serious and the harsh deflation onerous, the solution seemed to lie in reciprocal trade treaties, but very quickly the idea of general almost-free trade took hold, particularly when the Spanish Empire in the Americas broke up, thus opening immense new markets. The stumbling block was British agriculture, for the great landlords, long the keystone of the arch of government, were loath to expose the price structure on which the landed interest rested to the competition of the outside world. It was Sir Robert Peel, the only businessman to become prime minister during the nineteenth century, who in the early 1840's blasted that obstacle—and shattered his party —by practically eliminating the duties on grain.

Heartening as this freeing of trade and of prices was to the British manufacturer and to the general population that had borne the burden of debt and deflation for a generation, it seemed to spell disaster to the British North Americans. Their first prosperity had been founded on the preferential British market for all the fish, fur, timber, and farm products that they could extract or assemble for export during the French wars. Their acknowledged inferiority to the United States as producers, because of weaker capital, domestic markets, and communications, had been compensated for after 1815 by their privileged position in the British market.

As the duties (and their preferences) were whittled away, the protesting colonists cast about, as we shall see, for compensating advantages, and busied themselves with every possible enhancement of their productive capacities. The Maritimers succeeded remarkably well because of certain natural advantages, but the inland Canadians were so hard put to it by 1849 that those professional imperialists, the conservative businessmen of Montreal, burned the Parliament House, stoned and abused the governor, and went on record in favor of joining the United States as the only alternative to ruin.

Actually the inland Canadians, like the Maritimers, had by that time developed native strength sufficient to make the whole panicky episode ridiculous. Within five years all British North America was booming again and the American Civil War prolonged the boom until 1866. In 1854, out of a curious combination of American political needs and British North American economic ones, the British and American governments were able to negotiate the Reciprocity Treaty, which eased a dangerous situation in the North Atlantic fisheries. This agreement, establishing a ten-year period of reciprocal free trade in natural products between the United States and the colonies, was still in force when the American Civil War created an insatiable appetite for all kinds of goods.

AMERICAN ANNEXATIONISM AND BRITISH UNCONCERN

Yet that war unleashed in its most formidable form the threat that the triumphant American Union would take over a British North America to which Great Britain was ready to say "Good bye" if that could be done without too great offense to the colonists. As Edward Thornton, the British minister at Washington, told Hamilton Fish, the American Secretary of State, in June, 1869, Great Britain "did not wish to keep Canada, but could not part with it without the consent of the inhabitants."

As background for that situation of 1865–71, it is well to recall that every generation of the peoples who were to form a transcontinental Canada, from the founders in 1604 to the federators of 1864–67, faced outright attacks from what is now the United States. As Governor Cass of Michigan put it, "Americans had an awful swaller for territory." The phrase "Manifest Destiny" (what Tocqueville had called "a flood of men rising unabatedly and daily driven onward by the hand of God") seems to have been coined in 1845, but the idea was older than the republic. During the Revolution, Jonathan Mitchel Sewall had phrased a slogan for future American generations:

> No pent-up Utica contracts your powers,
> But the whole boundless continent is yours.

The crisis of 1837–42.—Although after the repulse of 1812–14 the inland waterways had the effect of drawing American pressure away from British North America to the south and west, it was inevitable that some American expansionists should covet British North America during their gloriously successful imperialism of the 1830's and 1840's. The precise occasion came after 1837, when severe economic depression created widespread unemployment in the northern states and when the presence of refugees from the Canadian rebellions of that time was taken to indicate that the Canadians would welcome American assistance in a war of independence. The simultaneous discovery by land-hungry "State of Mainers" that the Aroostook Valley contained really rich soils, coupled with a fairly characteristic lumberman's contest for timber and river rights in the same region, provided the combustibles for war along the New Brunswick boundary.

The response naturally followed the Texan model of the same times. From the Atlantic to Detroit, so-called "Hunters' Lodges" were set up and enlisted thousands of filibusters for the freeing of British North America. The movement spread even into the southern states. Its Cleveland convention of 1838 framed a constitution for Canada and arranged to issue invasion currency. The "Aroostook War" of 1839 came as near as might be to reality, but no lives were lost in spite of raids and counterraids and defense measures which involved Maine and the American Congress on one side, and New Brunswick, Nova Scotia, and Great Britain on the other.

The situation along the St. Lawrence was far more serious, for the forces in Vermont and New York not only kept the borders tense with small outrages and piracies but invaded Prescott in 1838 a thousand strong and withstood siege at a stone windmill there for five days. The Niagara River frontier was almost as spectacular in 1837–38 since it involved Canadian seizure and destruction of an American vessel, the "Caroline," on the United States side, and American reciprocation against the "Sir Robert Peel" on the Canadian. There was relatively little trouble farther west, but the state of affairs made it possible for rascals to indulge in murder, robbery, and arson at Canadian expense in the guise of "patriotism."

This dangerous situation took some time to liquidate and added its contribution to British North American fears of the United States. Returning prosperity diminished the numbers of the unemployed; the American federal government belatedly, but systematically, dragooned the states into rectitude; Lord Durham successfully cultivated Washington; and finally the whole business was consigned to the negotiations of Lord Ashburton and Daniel Webster. As we have seen, the treaty which they concluded in 1842 settled most of the surviving boundary problems and quiet reigned once more. It seemed about to be broken when the Americans in Oregon injected "Fifty-four forty or fight" as a slogan for James K. Polk in the presidential election of 1844, but Polk, when elected, had his hands full elsewhere and was glad in 1846 to settle peaceably for the forty-ninth parallel as the dividing line.

Civil War tensions.—Thereafter the American threat seemed to be eclipsed by the peaceful international commerce of the Reciprocity Treaty and by the fateful American plunge into the Civil War, but British and British North American behavior during that war made annexationism once again a powerful element in American national politics. The obvious preference of the British government for the South and the fatal errors of judgment and even of sheer inattentiveness to patient, proper American representations that allowed Great Britain to be used for the construction of fast (and very destructive) Southern commerce-raiders had built up one store of American hatred. The use of British North American soil and harbors to provide refuge and refreshment for Southern cruisers had built up another. The woes of Ireland, which had been transferred with hundreds of thousands of hungry emigrants to the United States, made "the Irish vote" of the great American cities an effective multiplier of native American resentments.

Filibustering Fenians.—Before the Civil War ended, the American government denounced both the Rush-Bagot Agreement for disarmament on the Great Lakes and the Reciprocity Treaty, and instituted harsh passport controls along the borders. Within a few months it thought better of the first and third of these reprisals, but the second was calculated to weaken the victim for the kill. Meanwhile the Irish Fenian Brotherhood had decided to imitate the Hunters' Lodges in filibustering against British North America. Its ambitions and activities were courted and encouraged by many prominent, indeed some leading, American politicians, who rang the changes on Manifest Destiny in Congress and at public meeting after public meeting from 1865 to 1871.

In such an atmosphere many persons decided that the simplest solution was to annex British North America as payment for American claims against Great Britain for the enormous damages done to shipping by the Southern sea-raiders. Out in the Red River Valley the northern column of westward American migration seemed ready to invade the Manitoba Basin. The American purchase of Alaska in 1867 left British Columbia as the only interruption of American sovereignty along the Pacific coast.

Fortunately for Canada, its peoples had strong "case-hardened" nerves. When the Fenians threatened, they patrolled the borders, sometimes armed only with farm tools and staves. When the Fenians invaded, captured Fort Erie, and laid waste part of the Niagara district, the Canadians abandoned their homes and the University of Toronto in order to resist—a cause which seemed hopeless before the regulars arrived and expelled the invaders. For seven years, with British help, they maintained their armed forces against invasion. American threats only drove the colonists closer together, finally into a federation which they proclaimed in biblical terms as "dominion from sea unto sea" and promptly, if hazardously, made good. When American negotiators made it plain to their colonial opposites that they expected termination of the Reciprocity Treaty to shake British North America like ripe fruit into "the magic circle of the American Union," the reply was that they would trade among themselves and substitute West Indian and Mediterranean markets for American.

The colonies despair of Great Britain.—Their deepest fear was of abandonment by Great Britain. Were they, as Disraeli asserted, a millstone around British necks? Was Viscount Bury right in his *Exodus of the Western Nations* (1865) to proclaim colonial independence as a natural law? How much British opinion did Richard Cobden represent when he wrote: "I cannot see what substantial interest the British people have in the connexion to compensate them for guaranteeing three or four million of North Americans living in Canada, &c, against another community of Americans living in their neighborhood." It was doubtless true that the War Office had decided that only a small part of British North America could be defended against a United States which had become a first-class Power.

In the face of these and many other evidences of British indifference, impatience, and distaste, the colonists still stood firm. When Great Britain hinted at their obvious destiny, they affected not to hear. When hints became warnings, they violently objected. And all the while they feverishly assembled their bargaining assets for what must be imminent readjustments in empire and neighborhood. The leaders among them who had summed up the situation most pessimistically had decided that, if Britain cast free of them, they would seek their future, not in the United States, but in independence.

In the remainder of Book 2, we shall try to discover in the histories of the individual colonies the wellsprings from which these men were able to draw their courage.

CHAPTER XI

Newfoundland (1783-1865)

Winston Churchill is said to have pictured Newfoundland as an orange in the mouth of a roasted sucking-pig. A less impish image would be the stopper in the long bottle of the Great Lakes and St. Lawrence system. Yet both of these views fail to conceive the island in its own terms. Except for Greenland, it is the easternmost part of North America, projecting to within 1900 miles of Europe and anchored like a great triangular raft at the center of the North Atlantic fishery. Its orientation and its history have been outward and maritime, not inward and continental. Others have exploited its position as "Atlantic bastion" and "Gibraltar of North America."

Half the size of Great Britain, the island is a good deal less attractive. Its surface is like a rough, rolling plateau rising on the west coast to mountains of over 2000 feet. Very little of it is fertile enough or climatically suitable for farming: forests fill the broad river valleys and clothe the west coast, and most of the rest is barrens, swamps, and a filigree of lakes and rivers. For almost three centuries, however, no one bothered much with the interior. Most people lived along the indented coast, about 6000 miles of fretwork on whose tumbling shores fishermen perched docks, fish flakes, and boxlike houses on timber stilts and platforms.

The climatic master was the cold Labrador current sweeping down both coasts and creating fog near the Banks where its chill air met the warm air rolling off the Gulf Stream. The winters were cold, the summers cool, and there was no dry season. The restless Atlantic kept the larger eastern and southern ports open all year, but by the end of the winter the frowning coast was clothed with ice. Inside the narrow Strait of Belle Isle on the north and the broader Cabot Strait on the south the Gulf of St. Lawrence was ice-packed for about four months.

THE COAST OF LABRADOR

Beyond Belle Isle, stretching over 1000 miles to Hudson Strait, was the Coast of Labrador, the hard northeastern rind of Canada. Its coast, too, was much indented, relatively low in the south, but rising to some of the earth's most forbidding, bare, and jagged mountains in the north. Viewed from the Atlantic, Labrador seemed a land scoured bare by wind and sea and cold. The northern third was just that, but inland in the middle third scanty vegetation appeared and increased in the southern third to sparse forests. Until the rifle practically exterminated the caribou about 1870, the interior was their range, but the soil was poor and there was little other animal or bird life—a land with no sound except the wind.

It was a cold land, for only summer winds and sun tempered the everlastingly refrigerated Labrador Current. The coast water froze along the upper third in October or November (even forming ground ice or "gru" sixty feet down), and along the lower third early in December. Boats ventured out into coastal strips of open water again about mid-May, but harbors might be closed and even the entry to Hamilton Inlet might be blocked by pack ice until mid-July. Labrador fog could snuff out in an instant the shores and reefs, boats and ships, or men sealing on the pack ice.

Originally this was a debatable land between coastal Eskimos and interior Indians, indeed the Eskimos could be found along the shores well inside the Gulf of St. Lawrence. As Europeans moved in, following the fisheries from inside the Gulf and from Newfoundland, Hamilton Inlet became an approximate southern boundary for the Eskimos and a northern one for the Indians and Europeans. From 1752 onwards the Moravian Missionary Society maintained stations among the Eskimos along the northernmost coast.

The widely scattered resident population was mixed: relatively pure Eskimos south from Cape Chidley to Hopedale, and mixed bloods or pure whites from there south. In 1824 at Hamilton Inlet, for instance, the count was 160 pure Eskimos, 60 half-breeds ("settlers" or "trappers") and 106 Europeans and Canadians ("liveyeres" or habitants). The visitors or transients were of two kinds: Indians of the interior, until they were gradually outdone in the fur trade by the resident half-breeds and whites; and the hundreds of schooners' crews from Newfoundland who came in annually, either to coastal stations from which they conducted a boat fishery, or to the Hamilton Inlet Bank and other offshore waters whence they took their fish "green" for curing in Newfoundland. By 1869 the population of Labrador totaled 2150, compared to 144,386 on the island.

ST. JOHN'S

Situated on the slopes around an excellent harbor reached by a narrow passage from the open Atlantic, St. John's on the Avalon Peninsula has been the capital of Newfoundland's society and economy since very early days. Scores of outports, hundreds of ships, and thousands of men have depended on the trading skills of the merchants of Water Street and of the piers and slips between it and the harbor. Since the merchants have "lived snug" while the hardy folk of the outports have seldom done so, Newfoundland society has been deeply split between privileged and unprivileged. Moreover, the unprivileged have been so scattered in such tiny groups along the coast of a roadless island that they have had little sense of solidarity. Generally speaking, therefore, down to quite recent times the will or action of "Newfoundland" has been largely that of the masters of St. John's.

THE WOEFUL TRANSITION

There can seldom have been a more mismanaged European dependency than Newfoundland during the half-century after the American Revolution, and yet the population multiplied from about 10,000 residents to about 60,000. That contradiction was only one among many; in fact, the history of the period is such a jungle of cross-purposes, of "boom and bust," of social savagery and humanitarianism, of economic and religious conflicts, and of obscure and violent politics, that no one has ever worked it out with precision. Basic to the situation was English west country refusal to countenance settlement in Newfoundland when every other circumstance was effecting it.

Two utterances within about a year of each other illustrate this neatly. In April, 1816, the governor, Vice Admiral Sir Richard Keats, reported to the British government: "Notwithstanding the clamour of a party for colonisation, averse to any restraints and hostile to the ancient system, I can discover no immediate necessity for any material alteration in the ancient system or laws as they relate to the fishery." An editorial in *The Times* (London) of July 4, 1817, on the other hand, asserted that maintaining the dependency merely as a nursery for seamen was like building a ruin to improve a landscape. The population at that time was at least 30,000. But the great critic of mercantilism, Adam Smith, had asserted that defense was more important than opulence, thereby excusing an alliance between the west country mercantile lobby and the even more effective lobby of the Royal Navy.

The ruling conception, therefore, remained that of William Knox in 1793: Newfoundland was "a great ship moored near the banks during the fishing season, for the convenience of English fishermen." It was the job of the naval governor to discourage settlers, as shrewd, cynical Lord North put it: "Whatever they loved to have roasted, he was to give them raw, and whatever they wished to have raw, he was to give it to them roasted." Where settlement was not supposed to exist, there need be no civil government. Naval officers could do the job.

☙ GROWTH

The wars of the eighteenth and early nineteenth centuries furnished the great stimulants to settlement and the great corrosion of the annual transatlantic fishery conducted by "servants" from the British Isles. The greater efficiency of a boat or small ship fishery, conducted by resident men on the sea and their women and children at the curing stages on shore, eventually brought about the islanders' victory. Social and economic distress in Great Britain and Ireland, demobilizations after wars, the lure of a new life in Newfoundland or farther west, and the legitimate and illegitimate profits that an English shipowner could add by substituting fish and oil for the annual "servants" as cargo on his return journey meant a persistent supply of emigrants. British naval superiority pretty well excluded foreigners from the fisheries for long periods and greedy markets beckoned from the Mediterranean, the West Indies, and Brazil.

The estimates of population, while abundant, were remarkably untrustworthy. A reasonable view is that population began to climb from 10,000 about 1782, had doubled in twenty years, doubled again by 1815, and was close to 60,000 by 1830. Later investigations indicate 96,295 in 1845, 122,638 in 1851, and 146,536 in 1869.

This peopling was still along the coasts, but it meant that few usable coastal areas were unoccupied and that, where a man could grow a few potatoes or some hay and oats without too much time taken from the fishery, a rough and capricious agriculture was established in spite of cultivation being forbidden. Roads were almost nonexistent. St. John's, which was a tangle of buildings pressing down on the coveted harbor front, and which was repeatedly devastated by fires (annually 1816–19, for instance), slowly and pugnaciously sorted itself out into an approximation of equity and efficiency in its streets, wharves, and warehouses after a semblance of landownership was tolerated in 1811 and a chartered corporation was provided for in 1824.

Meanwhile, in spite of terrible economic fluctuations, the fishery was growing vigorously. During the last decade of the eighteenth century it received a great adjunct from sealing. Every February the harp and hood seals of the Greenland-Labrador-Newfoundland area took to the ice floes for the birth of their young. Since each mature seal yielded ten or fifteen gallons of oil as well as its skin, from March to May the inhabitants slew seals in a perilous, if profitable, fury which soon induced them to build and outfit small schooners on shares, 150 of them with 2000 sailors in 1804, for instance, and over twice those numbers later. These ships were then ready for the Labrador cod fishery.

Sealing and cod fishing grew together. The number of seals taken annually passed 100,000 about 1807, 200,000 in 1819, hovered about 300,000 for six or seven years, and had reached a pinnacle of almost 700,000 in 1831. The winter season was thereby transformed from a period of idleness, drunkenness, vice, and near starvation into enterprise which could considerably enhance livelihood.

The cod fishery (normally an international enterprise) had reached a natural pinnacle of almost a million quintals (hundredweights) between the American and French revolutions, but owing to war and disorganization fell to little over 300,000 in 1802. From then on it rose steeply during the next twenty-five years to pass 900,000 quintals and thereafter fluctuate around the million mark. What mattered most to Newfoundland in this impressive achievement was that, whereas during the eighteenth century the resident population had taken a small proportion of the catch, about 1802 they began to take nearly all of it. The English transatlantic fishery was dead, more than twenty years before authority would admit it.

Yet it cannot be said that the people of Newfoundland had become masters of their economic fate. After 1796, war conditions pretty well compelled the English merchants and traders to stay in Newfoundland or leave agents there. As the transatlantic fishery was snuffed out, they simply took control of the resident fishery. Newfoundlanders had little or no capital beyond their own energies, and the activities they pursued kept them profitably employed for only part of the year in a region greatly dependent on the outside world for food and most of the commodities they consumed. St. John's, therefore, became the center of the nefarious "truck" and "supply" systems that reduced most of the inhabitants to peonage.

That situation was common all over the world (in British coal mining, for instance) wherever capital and mere physical energy worked in unequal partnership to exploit natural resources. The merchants certainly ran risks, as intermittent waves of bankruptcies attested. Yet the vulnerable residents of St. John's and the outports had to depend on the merchants for food, clothing, and marine equipment, going into debt for these things at prices generously calculated to take care of all possible costs and chances. They then turned over to the same merchants their fish, oil, and skins at prices settled upon by merchants' meetings in St. John's ("breaking the price") that were equally calculated to favor the masters of goods and credit. Finally, because of Britain's anachronistic refusal to give Newfoundland colonial status and appropriate civil government, the merchants were able to dominate what passed for justice in the courts, so that the poor had little or no redress.

Most Newfoundlanders lived in perpetual debt. Perhaps the most discouraging aspect of it all was that the profits of the successful merchants did not stay in Newfoundland. As A. H. McLintock, a close student of these matters, has said: "Though the fisheries had certainly become sedentary, the merchants and capitalists were almost entirely transitory, regarding the colony more as an exclusive investment, yielding rich dividends, rather than as a place in which to settle and form homes."

It need hardly be added that when in about 1840 steam navigation was applied to sealing as well as to the collection and carriage of fish and supplies, it was not the men of the outports who found broadened opportunities for profit in that new instrument of exploitation.

ADMINISTRATION

Subcolonial status.—A great deal of space could be filled in describing the absurd, corrupt, and ignorant administrative and judicial apparatus with which Newfoundland was saddled. After years of chaos, indeed of breakdown, Parliament established a regular judicature in 1791 and appointed an excellent Chief Justice in John Reeves. He did such a good job during his first year that the merchants lobbied against the court structure he suggested, but Pitt set it up. Unfortunately Reeves left in 1793, and all the merchants had to do in order to maintain what Reeves called their "dominion over the boatkeepers and poor inhabitants, whom they kept in perpetual thraldom" was to assert their dominance over the lesser magistrates. Reeves's successors as Chief Justice proved to be a sorry lot for the most part. Richard Tucker, 1822–33, for instance, had been a paymaster, and of his two assistants, Augustus Des Barres, although called to the bar of Nova Scotia, had never held a brief, and John Molloy had soon to be dismissed for swindling.

The executive branch of government was about as unsatisfactory, largely because of the basic contradiction between British policy and Newfoundland facts. The governors were admirals, for they were thought of as the controllers of the transient fishery, and until 1818 they came out in the spring and went home in the autumn. Naturally they defended the system that provided them with jobs and equally naturally they were unfitted for civil administration. Unhampered by council or assembly or official advisors, they looked, and usually acted, like autocrats, appointing and removing subordinate officials and the naval officers who served as surrogate justices in the outports. They issued proclamations which gradually amounted to a hotchpotch code of law—law which had no legality whatever. They even tried to levy rates and to dispute with the commander-in-chief in British North America the control of the island garrison. Civil liberties, of course, were beyond their ken.

Towards colonial status.—It was desperately hard for the New-foundlanders' grievances to find effective voice, to pierce the screen maintained between them and Westminster by the working alliance of merchants and navy. An occasional official like Chief Justice Reeves or Chief Justice Francis Forbes (1816–22) could make himself heard briefly, but what was needed was sustained and specific agitation, stemming unmistakably from the inhabitants.

Two men in particular stubbornly attempted to provide this. The first was William Carson, a Scottish medical man in St. John's. Like many another Scots "radical" of his generation, he was brave, loved a fight, and applied an icily dogmatic logic to manifest wrongs. Two pamphlets, *Letter to Members of Parliament* (1812) and *Reasons for Colonising the Island of Newfoundland* (1813), were the opening guns in his lonely campaign. Thereafter Dr. Carson was the core of a political committee which fostered a democratic spirit in spite of his own inability to evoke popular support. That lack began to be remedied in 1823 by his natural complement, a witty, controversial Irish merchant of St. John's named Patrick Morris. Morris poured forth a spate of pamphlets of which the warmth, sarcasm, and capacity to hit the target delighted the islanders and shook the authorities.

By the twenties, of course, Great Britain was emerging from the reaction that had gripped her since revolutionary France had gone to war thirty years before. Economic liberalism was breaking through mercantilism and moving towards free trade. The eighteenth-century anticolonialism of Tucker and Bentham was receiving systematic form at the hands of the Political Economists. The new wealth of finance, commerce, and industry was forcing the old landed oligarchy to adapt itself to change.

Recognition of Newfoundland as a colony instead of a ship and implementation of the new status with appropriate institutions was a slow and stumbling process. While it can be said that in a St. John's about evenly divided between Irish Roman Catholics and British Protestants (Anglican, Methodist, and Presbyterian), the Roman Catholics largely favored and the Protestants largely opposed self-government, that is too sweeping to be satisfactory. Then again, we know very little about the behavior of the outports and the bitter struggles there as the mercantile interest fought more ingeniously than fairly to hold off popular sovereignty. The numerous occasions when violence flared up among the unprivileged as they were thwarted by the privileged provides ample evidence of cunning in the overlords and passion in the people.

What broke down British inertia was a culmination in 1820 of tyrannical sentences (involving the lash) at the hands of naval officers who served as surrogate justices in the spirit of the old navy quarter-deck. The situation was so scandalous and inhuman that it evoked public castigation by Chief Justice Francis Forbes and also a public meeting and petition to Parliament directed by Carson and Morris.

The British government, resting on Governor Sir Charles Hamilton's stout Tory defense of the status quo, proposed no new policy, but Newfoundland's cause was taken up by British humanitarians and philosophic radicals who forced Parliament to discuss Newfoundland for the first time in a generation. Joseph Hume (then Francis Place's parliamentary Man Friday) added the neglected island to his quiver of anti-Tory ammunition. After the inevitable transatlantic correspondence, Parliament in June, 1824, at last recognized Newfoundland as a colony by three acts that reorganized and reformed the judicial system, empowered the 12,000 inhabitants of St. John's to set up municipal government, and enabled thousands of nominally unmarried Newfoundlanders to register their marital status.

Towards representative government.—Newfoundland was carried along the next stage of the road quite largely by the triumph of political reform in Great Britain. Indeed Lord Howick introduced a bill for a Newfoundland legislature on the very day that the British Reform Bill of 1832 received King William's assent. Again the achievement was thoroughly mixed, as it was bound to be for so peculiar and so primitive a society. A flamboyant, extravagant governor, Captain Sir Thomas Cochrane, had provided a good deal of the stimulus on both sides of the Atlantic for further reform by living up to his conviction "that a governor ought to go among them with all the attributes of consequence and authority belonging to the situation to ensure him that respect they are not over anxious to observe to those placed over them."

Carson and Morris had stirred up their political committee as soon as it was clear that the reforming spirit of 1824 did not extend to representative government. In two lively pamphlets of 1827 and 1828, addressed to William Huskisson, the Colonial Secretary, Morris let himself go in a mixture of sound sense, inaccuracies, calculated omissions, and numerous irrelevancies that nevertheless contained pungent, quotable observations on the central issue.

It is time to take us in Newfoundland out of leading strings. Three hundred years is in all conscience a sufficient minority. We are now of sufficient age to take care of our private affairs.

Do, sir, put an end to this quackery; like a good physician, infuse a little of the wholesome blood of the Constitution into the government of that neglected country; let it be no longer the theatre of experiment.

Meanwhile Carson worked on a sober, pointed petition for constitutional government which secured only five hundred signatures for its presentation to the Colonial Secretary in January, 1829; but its agitation evoked responses even from the outports. Parliament empowered the creation of a Newfoundland legislature by royal commission without argument, almost as a matter of course, during the uncritical reform mood of June and July, 1832.

Yet the issue was by no means clear, for not many persons would argue that Newfoundland could make the jump from despotism to representative government overnight. James Stephen, an able and informed legal adviser to the Colonial Office since 1813, had drawn up in December, 1831, a thoughtful survey of the situation that recommended a mixed unicameral legislature (modeled on the Dutch system in what became British Guiana) containing nominees of the Crown and elected representatives of the people. Lord Goderich wanted to try this and would have limited the number of nominated members to three and their role to that of explaining the proposals of the executive. When the first Newfoundland assembly met in January, 1833, however, its members were so exalted by their own importance that they decided that a united legislature "not being in accordance with the principles of the British constitution was in no wise applicable to the circumstances of the colony." Thereupon Newfoundland acquired the conventional apparatus of governor, nominated Executive Council, nominated Legislative Council, and elected Assembly.

Towards responsible government.—If that system, as we shall see, was working very badly in older and more experienced colonies, it was bound to be almost chaotic in raw Newfoundland. In fact, the political self-education of Newfoundlanders during the next nine years was thoroughly spectacular. Council and Assembly opposed each other automatically. The governor, the Chief Justice, and the Roman Catholic bishop were leading protagonists. Sectarian animosities poured oil on the flames. Two governors and a Chief Justice had to be withdrawn. The press was inflammatory, public meetings were battles, and elections sheer rioting.

Finally, after a wild election outbreak at Carbonear in 1840, the constitution was suspended from 1841 to 1843, and then the Legislature was resumed in a mixed unicameral form somewhat like Stephen's suggestion of 1831. With James Crowdy as Speaker and Sir John Harvey as governor, both bent on conciliation, and with a somewhat sobered population awakening to political responsibility, this system functioned awkwardly but successfully until Harvey's departure in 1847.

In that year, the British colonial world discovered that the Canadians and the Maritimers had won their twenty-year-old campaign for "responsible government." In her free-trade, anticolonial mood, the mother country had decided to grant domestic autonomy to the North American settlement colonies by making their executives responsible to the popular will as represented by majorities in the assemblies, that is, to concede cabinet government, in matters of other than imperial concern. Newfoundland, like the Cape of Good Hope and the Australian colonies, felt that it, too, must have responsible government.

While the agitation in this cause began in 1848 in the form of an alliance between the new Roman Catholic Bishop, John T. Mullock, and an able lawyer, P. F. Little, from Prince Edward Island, which aimed to improve the position of Roman Catholics, the achievement can hardly be credited to their "Catholic Liberal" party. British policy towards Newfoundland was already influenced by the concession of responsible government elsewhere.

Newfoundland, however, was not ready for domestic autonomy. The merchants were bitterly opposed to it and conniving in every possible way to keep counsels deeply divided. The superior organization of the Roman Catholics and their dominance in the legislature that would determine future electoral districts foreshadowed their mastery of a new and sovereign instrument. And above all, politics were still pervaded by a rash and irresponsible spirit, a kind of impatience towards necessary detail that promised ill.

Nonetheless, in 1854, the British government took the leap and sent out Mr. (later Sir) Charles Darling as governor to set up the new system. His position was prejudiced by a bad new structure of electoral districts and by incomplete authority and instructions from his superiors, but he did what he was told to do. His *ad interim* apparatus of August, 1855, consisted of an Executive or Ministerial Council of seven, a Legislative Council (from ministerial nominations) of fifteen, and an Assembly of thirty from ten constituencies. Little became prime minister and attorney general, and the Roman Catholics were in control.

Newfoundland had been almost unaffected by the imperial free-trade crisis of the forties because her dried fish had always been a constituent of international rather than of imperial trade. Her extreme vulnerability, like any other primary producer, was to the violent cyclical ups and downs that characterized the increasingly industrialized world. She had been hard hit by the depression at the end of the forties, but was booming with the prosperity of the fifties. Moreover, Great Britain had just put through the Reciprocity Treaty between the United States and the British North American colonies. Since this opened the vast American market to Newfoundland fish and fish products for over ten years, times were good when responsible government was initiated.

One wonders what politics would have been like had times been bad, for politics were anything but creditable during the next six years. To most British colonists everywhere, and indeed to the governing class of the day in Great Britain, the tangible prize in contest during the struggle for responsible government was control of the patronage. Britons themselves moved so slowly to political democracy at home that they were able to take their civil service from private patronage to a competitive basis before it could be made public spoils. Britain's offspring overseas, in the United States and in the empire, bound patronage and parliamentary government together from the beginning.

So it was in Newfoundland. The Roman Catholics won power again in the elections of 1859, but Bishop Mullock split with Premier John Kent and Speaker Ambrose Shea over a contract for steamer service. In 1860 and 1861 there was such trouble over poor relief and public salary payments (there had been a bad fishery in 1860) that premier and governor fell out and Hugh Hoyles, leader of the Opposition, was asked to form a new government which went to the country and won. The St. John's Catholics rioted so violently against the meeting of the new legislature in May, 1861, that when police failed to control them, the troops were ordered to fire on the mob, in the course of which Father Jeremiah O'Donnell was wounded.

How was this bitter brew of politics and religion neutralized? By an agreement to divide the patronage. After the riots of 1860 and 1861, the ruling principle and pacifier of politics in Newfoundland was an understanding that public offices, from the ministry at the top to minor jobs at the bottom, should be divided in thirds among Roman

Catholics, Anglicans, and Methodists. A similar denominational division was also applied to schools and school aid, with unhappy consequences in terms of efficiency.

✿ PROBLEMS OF EXTERNAL RELATIONS

Responsible government in mid-nineteenth-century British colonies was confined to their domestic affairs. Not until World War I did the Canadians consistently demand and largely exercise a positive extra-territorial sovereignty. Yet during the intervening two generations most of the self-governing colonies asserted fairly successfully an expanding claim to veto external relationships proposed to them by the mother country. Newfoundland, the center of an international fishery, was not least in this assertion, taking swift advantage of the anti-imperial mood in Great Britain. The rights and privileges of France and the United States in the North Atlantic fisheries had to be negotiated by Great Britain, but one of the great rewards of ordered government in Newfoundland was that the islanders now possessed an instrument for arguing their own case and for accepting or rejecting proposed settlements.

Great stacks of big books have been written recording and arguing the rival claims to the North Atlantic fisheries ever since their discovery at the end of the fifteenth century. No parts of Newfoundland history are nearly as thoroughly documented as the stories of "the French Shore" and of American fishing "rights" and "liberties." Probably Newfoundlanders poured more passionate energy into their own domestic differences than into these external controversies, but the records of international relations loom larger in bulk and in estimated importance.

The French Shore.—It may be recalled from Chapter VIII that during the peace negotiations of 1783 Great Britain and France made an exchange of declarations concerning French fishing rights, tracing them back to the treaties of 1713 and 1763 and altering the region to which they applied. In her pro-French mood after the Napoleonic wars, Great Britain maintained those rights in the treaties of 1814 and 1815. They amounted to "the liberty of fishing and drying" and erecting buildings "for the convenience of the fishery" from Cape St. John on the east coast round the northern tip of the island and down the west coast to Cape Ray. Great Britain sent out orders to remove British fishermen who might have established themselves in the region.

While the wording of these agreements furnished no justification for a French right to an exclusive fishery, France embarked on an effort to secure one. That effort clashed with the expansion of settlement in Newfoundland and with the determination of Newfoundlanders to control their own fisheries. The lamentable lack of British interest in New-foundland before 1833 worked against the islanders during the years when the French were reinforcing their claims by rather arbitrary actions.

Although British policy stiffened in 1836 with a blunt denial by Palmerston of the French claim, Newfoundlanders were convinced in 1842, 1846, 1852, and 1856 that for reasons of state in which they had no concern (e.g. the Crimean War alliance), the mother country was only too ready to sacrifice them. They petitioned and addressed the Queen and Parliament, but their worst fears were realized in the Pigeard-Merivale Convention of 1856 by which France secured an exclusive fishery in several vital areas.

When the legislature met in February, 1857, its unanimity in re-sistance was made clear by all manner of appeals, not only to Great Britain but also to the other British North American colonies. The pro-tests succeeded. The British government decided not to implement the convention. More important in the long run, Henry Labouchère, the Colonial Secretary, sent Governor Sir Alexander Bannerman a dis-patch of April 12, 1859, which Newfoundlanders thereafter regarded as the cornerstone of their sovereignty:

The proposals contained in the convention having been now unequivo-cally refused by the Colony, they will, of course, fall to the ground, and you are authorised to give such assurance as you may think proper that the con-sent of the community of Newfoundland is regarded by Her Majesty's Gov-ernment as the essential preliminary to any modification of their territorial or maritime rights.

Dealings with the Americans.—Contrary to her policy towards France, Great Britain held that by the War of 1812 the United States had forfeited her fishing rights of 1783. The Americans naturally in-sisted that they were perpetual. One of the valuable, precedent-making mixed commissions under the Treaty of Ghent hammered out a com-promise in the Convention of 1818. By it Americans might fish on the coasts of Newfoundland from the Ramea Islands on the south around Cape Ray and up the west coast to the Quirpon Islands at the northern tip, and also from Mount Joli, just north of the eastern end of Anti-costi in the Gulf of St. Lawrence, indefinitely east and north along the Coast of Labrador. They might also have "the liberty for ever, to dry and cure fish in any of the *unsettled* bays, harbours and creeks" of the south coast of Newfoundland between the Ramea Islands and Cape Ray. The American surrender was of the old right to fish within three miles of all the other coasts of British North America.

The Newfoundlanders' attitudes towards the Americans were rather mixed. They envied them their capital resources, cheaper supplies and commodities, more insistent and dependable market, and higher wages or shares. They knew that since 1763 they had been about as keen on trading for cured fish as on doing the job themselves, and quite ready to participate in smuggling.

In fact, the natural dependence of Newfoundland and Labrador on the United States for forest products, bread, flour, and livestock had qualified British controls until they dissolved into free trade. On the other hand, the Americans were often unbearably cocky, contemptuous of official controls, willing to fish on Sunday, and also to indulge in what Newfoundlanders considered harmful fishing practices. Thousands of islanders had settled the matter by signing on American ships and emigrating to the alluring United States, but other thousands had stayed at home.

It was Great Britain that secured the Reciprocity Treaty of 1854. An uninterested Newfoundland was expressly exempted unless its Legislature chose to enter in. Yet once it was realized that Great Britain had secured free entry to the American market for "fish of all kinds," "products of fish and of all other creatures living in the water," and "fish oil," in return for opening the shore fisheries of British North America to the Americans, the Legislature was prompt to approve (July, 1855).

Over the term of the treaty its benefits were so generally admitted that the Newfoundlanders pressed for its continuance and even hoped to modify it by persuading the United States to abolish its domestic fishing bounty and subsidy system. Never were hopes worse calculated. The victorious North denounced the treaty in March, 1865, and refused to change its mind next year. Newfoundland, like the other colonies in 1865 and 1866, was forced to consider its future in terms of the expansive energies of the United States.

CHAPTER XII

Nova Scotia (1815-65)

The over-all effect of the French wars and the War of 1812 on Nova Scotia was to enrich and consolidate that colony for what was probably the most satisfying half-century of its history. For over twenty years, by and large, there were about as many opportunities as takers while Britain's embarrassments increased her dependence on British North Americans for products and services.

During the same years the newly arrived loyalists hammered out a *modus vivendi* with their predecessors; sometimes they were uneasy and scornful of each other, but often enough an amalgam of North Americans alert to what could be done. The colony received its share of dispossessed Scots crofters, Irish malcontents, migrating Newfoundlanders, Englishmen out to better themselves, and, when the army and navy demobilized, members of those services.

THE GROWTH OF POPULATION

The population estimates of the late eighteenth century are dubious because of the separation of Cape Breton and New Brunswick, the ebb with peace and the flow with war, and the emigration of disillusioned loyalists and others. For instance, the estimate for 1784 was about 42,000 (English 28,000, French 14,000), and for 1790 about 30,000. Growth probably began with war in 1793, for the estimate in 1806 was 65,000, and a reasonably systematic census of the peninsula after the wars were over in 1817 showed 86,668.

This time peace did not interrupt growth. By 1827 the population was 123,630 with probably 20,000 more in Cape Breton, and the combined total reached 202,575 (38,000 of them in Cape Breton) in 1838. J. S. Martel has shown that between 1815 and 1838 immigration totaled at least 43,000 (Scots 22,000, Irish 13,000, English 2000) and emigration at least 3000, while Mrs. R. G. Flewelling has been able to add 16,000 immigrants and 1900 emigrants for the period 1839–51. These totals, particularly for emigration, are almost certainly too small. The emigration was chiefly to the United States, with a smaller movement to Quebec. The population of the colony increased to 276,854 in 1851, 330,857 in 1861, and 387,800 in 1871.

As late as 1835, T. C. Haliburton, who knew his colony thoroughly well, had his fictional hero, Sam Slick, say: "The old stock comes from New England, and the breed is tolerable pure yet, near about one half applesarce, and tother half molasses, all except to the Easterd where there is a cross of the Scotch." It is hard to see why he omitted some tens of thousands of Acadians, the original stock. By 1865 ethnic and regional origins had become secondary to the sense of being Nova Scotians and proud of it.

The South, or Atlantic shore, from Yarmouth to the Gut of Canso, settled down to lumbering and fishing towns, few of which had much substantial agricultural hinterland except Lunenburg (a German settlement of 1753), the Lahave River area, and Musquodoboit. West of Halifax the height of land was very close to the Bay of Fundy and long chains of rivers and lakes drained to the Atlantic through rough, practically uninhabited country, a folded and weatherworn apron of slate, quartzite, and granite.

In Cape Breton, broken up by its inland waters and its mountainous west coast, Acadians fished from the south and northwest, the evicted Highland crofters (often Gaelic-speaking) found new Highlands in the west, and anomalous coal-miners centered on Sydney in the northeast. Acadians combined fishing with lumbering, and farming of varying quality, from Cape Sable north to St. Mary Bay, and Acadians, Irish, and Scots worked the rather scattered good lands between the Gut of Canso and Pictou.

At widely scattered points there were meager, neglected little groups of Negroes, freedmen chiefly from the colonies to the south. There may have been as many as 2000 about 1790, but in 1792 nearly 1200 were induced to leave for Sierra Leone, where they were followed in 1800 by nearly all of five or six hundred "Maroons" recently brought in from Jamaica. Another inward surge of about 2000 accompanied and followed the War of 1812, 400 of whom were sent to New Brunswick in 1815 and 95 to Trinidad in 1821. In 1851 they totaled 4,908; twenty years later 6,212.

The good agricultural lands, diked and undiked, which supported the larger proportion of the population, were on the north or Fundy side: around the Annapolis Basin, up that narrow valley and across a short barrens to the much larger Minas Basin and its tributary tidal valleys.

A large proportion of the isthmus from which the peninsula hung was also good land, whether tidal marshes or the mild slopes leading down to the Minas and Chignecto basins on the south and the shores of the Northumberland Strait on the north. South of Minas Basin was a great apple-growing region, north of it mixed farming and animal husbandry. Gypsum deposits at Windsor and coal mining north of the Minas Basin added variety.

From its founding in 1749, many circumstances, most notably the magnificent harbor and the Bedford Basin, confirmed Halifax as the natural capital, but wealthy and influential Haligonians seem always to have had a powerful inclination to get away from its rather trying climate to the sunnier, drier, warmer Fundy side of the peninsula. The nearest desirable point was Windsor and there, as early as 1759, the privileged began to entrench themselves. It was there that the first annual fair was held, the first race track laid out, and there that the Church of England began to set up its University of King's College and tributary school in 1789. Windsor was quite largely a rural preserve and retreat for men of substance from Halifax and other parts of the province.

The capital itself was the lively, scheming center of politics, finance, commerce, and the Anglican Church, much colored by the troops of the garrison and by the navy. Its social "upper crust" was highly conscious of its station and "colonial-minded" in its deference to British birth and rank. Its lowest layers exhibited all the squalor and vice of a port town that was also an imperial garrison and naval base. In between was a group of climbers that refused to regard itself as middle class.

🍁 THE DAY OF THE WOODEN SHIP

Probably the most thrilling, satisfying activity for a Nova Scotian was boat or ship building. All over the colony skillful men drew upon their own forests to fabricate vessels, ranging from that crude yet cunning rowboat known as the dory up to sailing-ketch and swift and graceful clipper. Indeed it was Nova Scotia that produced Donald McKay, the acknowledged genius of the clipper, and Simon Newcomb, the industrious astronomer and mathematician of navigation, although both migrated to the United States to find scope for their abilities.

The Acadians of the southwest specialized in small boats and ships. The Germans of Lunenburg, converted from European peasants to North Atlantic mariners sometime about 1790, focused on a schooner for the banks fishery which became the finest thing of its kind. All this was done in spite of the fact that, except for some ironwork, Nova

Scotian builders had to depend on Great Britain and the United States for marine stores.

Most of these vessels were destined for the fisheries, but the larger ones entered into the world's trade in increasing numbers as long as wood and sail held their own against iron and steam. Nova Scotians, for instance, somewhat supplanted New Englanders as traders in and carriers of Newfoundland cured fish, not only the inferior brands for the West Indies, Caribbean, and Brazil, but the "merchantable" that went to Europe and the Mediterranean. Once out on the ocean, the "Bluenoses," like the New Englanders, were willing to go anywhere with or for cargo, so much so that in 1850 the combined tonnage of the Maritime colonies stood fourth in the register of the world's shipping.

By mid-century the British West Indies were declining in importance and influence in the British Empire, as was New England in the United States. Nova Scotian policy now aimed at inducing the mother country to urge the United States towards free trade and free (unsubsidized) competition in the fisheries. The colony's supposed trump card was exclusion of the Americans from her shore fisheries under the Convention of 1818.

STEAMSHIP, TELEGRAPH, AND RAILROAD

About the same time, Nova Scotia was greatly excited over its prospects as a pivotal point in the world of communications by telegraph, and transportation by steamer and railroad. It was heartening to have that human dynamo, Samuel Cunard of Halifax, establish the first regular transatlantic steamship service in 1840. Said the Halifax *Times,* "No one who knows the superior position of our port but must be convinced that the time is not far distant when it will become the center of steam navigation for the whole American continent."

Back in the days when Prince Edward, Duke of Kent, had been commander-in-chief in Nova Scotia (1794–1800), his visual telegraph system had linked Halifax with the Annapolis Valley and Fredericton (around the Bay of Fundy) and was even projected to Quebec, but it had been abandoned after his departure. Now Samuel Morse's successful electric telegraph (1837) had by 1848 threaded its way east from New York to Saint John. Thereupon several New York newspapers formed the Associated Press to marry the enterprises of Cunard and Morse. At once rivals entered the field, so that 1849 saw fast, small ships collecting news packets from Cunarders off Halifax, and galloping, pony-express riders racing along twelve-mile stages to Digby, where a little steamer waited to rush the news to the wire at Saint John. Later that year the wire reached Halifax and ended most of the glamour.

Railroads, too, were in men's minds. Boston was linked with Montreal in 1851, the Atlantic and St. Lawrence was pushing up from Portland, and the British (European) and North American was projected from Portland to Saint John, Moncton, and the Gulf of St. Lawrence. Why should not Halifax have its Halifax and Quebec (drawing in Canso by a line to Truro) which would supplant both Boston and Portland as the winter port for the ice-locked interior?

Actually these and certain other hopes of the time proved to be a feverish flush that accompanied the slowing-down of Nova Scotia's rapid economic growth. Advancing technology exposed the colony to severe trials. Rapid development of the marine engine and the iron ship was beyond Nova Scotia's competitive powers and narrowed opportunities for wood and sail. It also made Halifax secondary to New York, Boston, and Quebec or Montreal as a terminal in transatlantic services.

Railroads were so costly and depended so greatly on direct routes and settled, productive areas that even when nations, states and provinces, municipalities, and individuals gambled recklessly with railroad-building, Halifax was too far out on the bend of a hook to command attention and support as entry and outlet either for the United States or for interior British North America. Water transportation was much cheaper than by rail even in steamships. The ideal combination for interior North America was the shortest possible rail connections with year-round ports frequented by many ships, including steamships. No Nova Scotian port could meet those specifications.

🍁 SOCIETY

While there was always some tendency both for Nova Scotia to prosper for the greater benefit of her British and American associates and for the locally successful to take themselves and their gains away to more congenial parts of the world, there was also a sober, steady accumulation of domestic wealth. The heinous sin was to spend instead of increase one's capital, so much so that a century later it was disclosed that Nova Scotians held twice as much in bank stocks per capita as the inhabitants of any other Canadian province. Since nearly all of the easily negotiable wealth was present or controlled in Halifax, the bulk of the population thought of themselves as being the bond servants of an oligarchy of property and influence in the capital.

The great merit of this society was that, because of the varied elements it digested, because of its military and naval contacts, and because of its intense concern with the rest of the world, it could not be as provincial, as parochial, as some other colonies. D. C. Harvey has written eloquently of the "intellectual awakening of Nova Scotia" after the Napoleonic Wars and of its "age of faith" (in itself) between 1834 and 1867. The colony fairly hummed with social action, normally measured against British and American achievement—lively newspapers (at least eighty of them between 1840 and 1867), mechanics' institutes, libraries, literary, scientific, and agricultural societies, philanthropies, vigorous and combative churches, and unending debate about primary, secondary, and higher education among Anglicans, Presbyterians, Baptists, Roman Catholics, and Methodists. By 1834 Joseph Howe, the leading public figure of the time, felt that he could appeal to the Mechanics' Institute for a *native* distinction in Nova Scotia which should "win for her the admiration and esteem of other lands, and teach them to estimate Nova Scotia rather by her mental riches and resources than by her age, population or geographical extent."

AGRICULTURAL IMPROVEMENT

Probably the most notable example of organized self-help was the campaign of "Agricola" (a Scottish merchant of Halifax named John Young), 1818–26, to improve Nova Scotian agriculture, to set scientific field culture on a parity with haymaking and animal husbandry, and thereby at last to make Nova Scotia self-supporting in foodstuffs. "Agricola" wrote in all sixty-four letters of information and exhortation, fifty-seven of which appeared in one enterprising newspaper, the *Acadian Recorder*. Young failed in his final objective, but the Provincial Agricultural Society, of which he was secretary and treasurer, plus thirty local societies, aided by over £7000 of public and £1400 of private funds, did contribute to a better agriculture.

Cultivation and soil management improved, and new crops and rotations were established. Milling of oats and other grains expanded and new farm machinery was introduced. The attempts to improve livestock must be accounted a failure, but considerable reversion to grazing after 1840 led to remedying this deficiency. Perhaps equally important, after the central society collapsed in 1826, the agricultural interest remained and was reflected in the legislature, whose agricultural committees took over some of its functions until another Central Board of Agriculture was set up by statute in 1841. This Board had its troubles with the fishing, lumbering, and commercial interests, but persisted until well after federation in Canada in 1867.

Apple culture, later to be so important for export, got its recognition about 1858, when the local society in Cornwallis reported that "much attention is now paid to Orcharding and in almost any part of the County you will observe young orchards planted. In a few years we are in hopes not only to supply our own Market, but will be able to ship them to foreign parts."

🍁 EDUCATION AND CULTURE

This support of agricultural improvement can be thought of as one part of a long campaign for education in all its varieties and at all its levels. Sectarian schisms and rivalries bedeviled that effort and the conservative and radical wings of each religious group fell out among themselves.

In the higher education by which the churches hoped to recruit their ministers, the Church of England had a running start with King's College at Windsor, which the Scottish churches and the Baptists were able only gradually to approach with the Pictou Academy that contributed so largely to the functioning of nonsectarian Dalhousie University at Halifax (established in 1818) and the Horton Academy out of which Acadia University emerged at Wolfville (1838). The Roman Catholics managed to build St. Francis Xavier University out of some earlier colleges at Antigonish (1856), but the Methodists were dependent on Mt. Allison University (1839) just across the New Brunswick border at Sackville.

A struggle of greater popular concern was the long and tortuous campaign for publicly supported primary and secondary education. The story before 1825 might be summarized by saying that a bounty system had kept a few grammar schools and rural schools barely alive. In 1824 a grand investigation of the colony's voluntarily supported schools was made that revealed a lamentable state of affairs because of the inability of many areas to attract and hold teachers. Annapolis County West, for instance, with 5000 inhabitants, had no permanently established school. Cumberland County had nine schools and twelve places that needed them. Halifax itself had three common schools and a grammar school, and nine weak schools elsewhere in its county. The pathetic reports from the counties revealed backwardness and neglect that could be remedied only by the public treasury. Allegedly 217 schools served 5,514 children and it was believed that about 13,000 did not attend any school.

A committee of the legislature in 1825, having found this "altogether defective and totally unequal to the demand for tuition," recommended compulsory, assisted education "even in the remotest Settlement," on the model of what was done in Massachusetts (although allegedly in imitation of Scotland). Yet this recommendation and similarly enlightened and vigorous proposals of 1836 and 1838 foundered on the politician's fear of introducing the compulsory school-assessment upon which schools and teacher-training institutions must depend. J. W. Dawson of Pictou and Edinburgh University, brought in by Howe in 1850 as first Superintendent of Education, spent three years in hammering home the basic necessities, but it was not until 1865 that the premier, Charles Tupper, dared put a free school act into operation, and even then with adverse political effects.

It was during this period that Nova Scotia produced in Thomas Chandler Haliburton a literary giant of international popularity whose books went through over a hundred editions in the English-speaking world and were translated into various other languages—"a more general and more cordial recognition as a man of letters than has been secured by any other colonial author before or since." Haliburton was a Tory from Windsor and King's College who had a keen ear for the New England speech of his countryside and who in 1836 introduced to print "Sam Slick," the "gen-u-ine Yankee" clockmaker and notion-seller (peddler) from Slickville, Onion County, Connecticut. Through Sam he was able to satirize both American and Nova Scotian ways.

His relatively even balance let the colonists see themselves as others saw them, but it roused Professor (later President) C. C. Felton of Harvard to angry protest and James Russell Lowell to charge "a libel on the Yankee character and a complete falsification of Yankee modes of speech." Sam Slick came into the world along with Dickens' Sam Weller and for many years the two amused readers about equally. The early Sam Slick volumes possessed both humor and wit; indeed, they still attract a good many readers.

Haliburton had begun his literary career in 1823 with an anonymous pamphlet which he later expanded into a pioneering piece of careful scholarship and local patriotism, *An Historical and Statistical Account of Nova Scotia* (1829). As he became more and more willingly the literary "lion" and diner-out in Great Britain and elsewhere, and as the political conflict between oligarchy and people in Nova Scotia became bitter, Haliburton submerged his reforming spirit beneath what his principal biographer, V. L. O. Chittick, calls "an outworn and utterly discredited type of Toryism." This was "the backward-looking, contempt-provoking Haliburton" who, among many other faults, "never urged the adoption of a single measure or the undertaking of a single enterprise for his country's improvement in which it is certain that he had not a purely personal or selfish interest." He ended his life as an unhappy failure in the British House of Commons, 1859–65. As Andrew Shiel, the blacksmith poet of Dartmouth, put it, "none more famous living, less regretted gone!"

✤ THE VULNERABILITY OF SOME LEADING COLONIALS

Since a somewhat analogous degeneration of character affected Haliburton's contemporary and principal opponent, the radical reformer, Joseph Howe, as well as some leading statesmen in other colonies, the phenomenon calls for explanation. Part of that lies in Lord Acton's dictum that "power corrupts." These men had great popularity and fame, acknowledged prestige and influence, and could, and did, become careless, even cynical, about the relationship between the public origins of their power and the private uses that they made of it. It is worth remembering that the conflict over responsible government was also a ruthless contest for control of the spoils of office.

In the cases of Haliburton and Howe, moreover, another corrosive was distilled from their inability to transcend in British estimation the second-class status of "colonials." Haliburton, once his novelty in Great Britain had worn off, had to console himself with a shallow or narrow social approval, while the governing class, whom he had criticized, rather contemptuously refused him the kind of political recognition he wanted. At the pinnacle of Joseph Howe's career and reputation, he thought to commend himself irrevocably by building up a huge recruiting machine in the United States for British armies in the Crimean War. Partly by his own rashness, he involved Great Britain in the embarrassment of having the United States expel the British minister at Washington and several consuls.

Thereafter, whenever he could manage it, Howe vainly haunted ministers' anterooms and the country houses of the aristocracy, distributing printed copies of his single or his collected speeches wherever he thought they might help him towards imperial preferment, specifically a colonial governorship such as Francis Hincks of Canada had obtained. Both Haliburton and Howe revealed so often their sense of being thwarted in legitimate ambition that their regrettable last years must be credited in part to the British patronizing attitude, lack of imagination, and anti-imperialism that characterized the mid-nineteenth century.

Howe's early career had been glorious. In 1827 he emerged from self-education and apprenticeship as printer and journalist by purchasing part of a small weekly newspaper in Halifax. Next year he took over the *Nova Scotian* from a son of "Agricola" and was launched on his career. As editor, reporter (particularly of the legislature and the courts), and traveler all over Nova Scotia, he rapidly made himself the acknowledged voice of liberal reform, as well as of "the age of faith" in Nova Scotia.

He became the leader in assaults on every aspect of the oligarchical privilege that characterized the colony—in religion, education, politics, commerce, and finance. In an age of reform, he had a wonderful target in the outmoded apparatus of colonial government, the more vulnerable in Nova Scotia because the nominated executive and legislative councils were identical, that is, the same men helped make law as executed it. Among them there were the masters of capital, profitable public office, and political influence.

In 1835, Howe accused the Halifax magistrates of negligence and corruption at the rate of £1000 a year. Instantly sued for criminal libel, he studied its law and conducted his own defense in a six-hour speech, discovering his great powers of oratory in the process and reducing at least one juryman to tears. Nova Scotia had produced a Daniel Webster. "Yes, gentlemen, come what will, while I live, Nova Scotia shall have the blessing of an open and unshackled press." After ten minutes' deliberation, the jury acquitted him and Halifax went wild in a celebration that lasted through the night. Howe ran successfully as a Liberal candidate for Halifax County next year, dedicated to the cause of making the executive responsible to the people: "All we ask is for what exists at home [Great Britain]."

❧ THE FIGHT FOR RESPONSIBLE GOVERNMENT

He proved to be a superb popular leader—attractive, jaunty, and reassuring in appearance; master of the florid North American elocution of the day; apt at pointed quotation or evidence; emotionally magnetic and infectious; and a systematic collector and practiced teller of funny stories. Moreover he was the first leading figure of the colony who positively enjoyed mingling with the populace, for his upbringing and vigor made him as rollicking among the crowd as he was assured among their "betters." As John Allison Bell attested at this time, "Society seemed permanently divided into two classes, upper and lower. . . . There was no middle class of any amount or force." There are endless accounts of Howe's exuberant progresses and electioneering, but Bell's "upper-class" account of him during the election of 1836 is as good as any.

For the roughs in town and the fishermen along the shore it was simply a carnival—and a pretty coarse one too. Howe gloried in such scenes and was quite at home among them, carousing and gambling with the men or dancing with the girls night after night and frequently all night. His animal spirits and robust constitution enabled him to do such things with impunity.

Howe was also a statesman, caught up in the reform currents of his time, but judiciously and persuasively steering through them to the equitable and appropriate goal of self-government. He had able and equally devoted associates in the Liberal party, but there was seldom any question as to its leadership. The Liberals began in 1837 by pushing through Howe's Twelve Resolutions addressed to the Crown. These had the effect of inducing the British government to order separation of the councils, the opening of Legislative Council meetings to the public, the exclusion of the Chief Justice from both, and reform of their membership calculated to make both representative of the colony at large. The Halifax oligarchy succeeded in defeating the last demand. Responsible government was refused and Assembly control of the purse was made conditional on the certain provision of the principal official salaries.

After Lord Durham's mission to Lower and Upper Canada and his outright recommendation of responsible government there in his report of 1839, both the Nova Scotian oligarchy and the British government were thrown on the defensive, and for the next seven or eight years, that is, until Peel's free trade made empire seem pointless, Whig and Tory governments in Great Britain tried by every device to evade the concession. Howe's great contribution to this period of the campaign was in four remarkable letters to Lord John Russell, by which he exposed that overrated statesman in terms of logic, practicality, political realism, and racy humor. Their distribution in printed form to appropriate hands in Great Britain and elsewhere in the empire did much to enhance the effectiveness of Durham's report in securing the domestic autonomy of settlement colonies.

The material prize in the contest was control of the patronage. As the English colonial reformer, Charles Buller, said, "The patronage of the Colonial Office is the prey of every hungry department of our government." Britons who belonged to, or had worked their way into, the governing class, when irretrievably exposed in incapacity or fraud, were often sent to the colonies, if possible with a colonial office as a sheet anchor to windward. The Halifax oligarchy, having fought shrewdly to pre-empt their share of the local spoils, saw the advantage of alliance with British authority against the surrender of the whole to the popular majority. Howe and the reformers, like Andrew Jackson in the United States ten years earlier, made no secret of what they were determined that their victory would mean.

The battle was fought most vigorously and openly in Nova Scotia and the Canadas. Howe displayed exceptional powers of combining the novel and radical with studied moderation on crucial occasions. He managed to get one lieutenant governor, Sir Colin Campbell, recalled ("promoted" to Ceylon) for not going even as far as Russell had authorized. He then baited the rather unintelligent successor, Lord Falkland, who had revealed himself as a supporter of Howe's Conservative opponents, into some sad indiscretions which led to his "promotion" to Bombay.

Having resigned from the Executive Council and as collector of customs, Howe resumed editorship of the *Nova Scotian* and the *Morning Chronicle* in 1844. During the next three years his zestful, vituperative, sometimes coarse, pen and tongue kept politics in an uproar which ended only after his party won the election of 1847 and in January, 1848, entered upon responsible government at last.

THE RAILROAD PITFALL

Howe held office as Provincial Secretary in the Liberal administration from 1848 to 1854, but his gradually consuming interest became that pitfall for politicians, railroad promotion. His aim was an intercolonial railroad, and his belief, as stated in Halifax in May, 1851, was that "many in this room will live to hear the whistle of the steam engine in the passes of the Rocky Mountains and to make the journey from Halifax to the Pacific in five or six days."

For this he lobbied and negotiated with public authorities and private promoters in Great Britain, the United States, and British North America—on one occasion by an eloquent speech at Southampton virtually forcing a hostile British government to yield to his demand for support in the form of a guaranteed loan. When these activities ended in a tangle of cross-purposes in 1854, the colony set up a board of railroad commissioners whose chairmanship, at £700 a year, Howe took for himself when he might more properly have become premier.

That seven years of hobnobbing with the mighty in politics and finance had weakened Howe's rapport with the people was promptly and dramatically demonstrated. Charles Tupper, whom he had sneered at as "the little doctor" three years before, defeated him roundly in the general election of 1855, apparently the turning point in his career. Eight years later he received his only imperial patronage, a fishery commissionership under the Reciprocity Treaty that had been vacated by death. He needed it, for that year Tupper had defeated him again in one of the most relentless campaigns of Nova Scotian history.

UNCERTAIN DIAGNOSIS

It would appear that about 1854 Nova Scotians entered upon an interval during which they quite frequently misunderstood their situation. They had grasped the nettle of British free trade and as early as 1849 joined the other colonies in advocating it in their relations with the United

States, but a mixture of neglect and accident left them unrepresented when the Reciprocity Treaty was negotiated in 1854. They greeted it with truculent opposition because they thought that the Convention of 1818 and responsible government empowered them to use control of their shore fisheries to extract an even better bargain. They gave in when they realized that Great Britain had already fulfilled her obligation by opening those fisheries to the Americans, and they were greatly mollified when the United States remitted the duties that had been paid on imports of colonial natural products during the interval between negotiation and ratification of the treaty.

Then again, Nova Scotians were not sure about the effects of the treaty, although the prevailing impression was that it had been greatly beneficial. In a great speech Howe was largely instrumental in swinging an international convention at Detroit to supporting its renewal. Their exports and imports expanded during its term, but the long Civil War in the United States was an incalculable factor. Railroad building in the Maritimes during the same period brought in capital and goods and created both employment and a broadened market for local products.

Moreover, although the United States was becoming dependent on British North America for such products as lumber, it apparently contradicted that dependence by embarking on a high tariff policy at the end of the Civil War. Canada, too, had since 1847 been moving towards protectionism. It was all very confusing, and Nova Scotians became noticeably uncertain of what they should do. Their discovery of Canada's latent expansive strength in the railroad age, for instance, left them divided as to whether to unite the Maritimes in defense or climb on board the Canadian bandwagon.

Systematic protectionism, the iron steamship, and the railroad were components of a revolution in the world's economics and politics with which Nova Scotia could not grapple confidently. No clear indication of the future could be had from Great Britain. In fact it looked as if Britain had decided that her colonies would enter the United States. The public phase of British anti-imperialism was to last until Disraeli's Crystal Palace speech of 1872, and the subterranean schemes of the promoters of the "new imperialism" were but slightly known to Nova Scotians, who figured less weightily than the Canadians in their plans. The "golden age," when Nova Scotians felt masters, or at least potential masters, of their fate, was passing like the wooden ship, and henceforth they must exercise their wills and powers within a larger North American body politic. In the practical sense, they had only an expansive Canada and the United States to choose from.

CHAPTER XIII

Prince Edward Island (1767-1865)

Prince Edward Island, "the Garden of the Gulf," was the first truly salubrious part of North America to be discovered by Cartier in 1534. "It is the best-tempered region one can possibly see," he reported. Indeed one has to travel as far west as Montreal Island to find its rival in fertility. It is quite small—a crescent 145 miles long and at most 34 miles wide, cradled close to the mainland (this is the meaning of its Micmac name, Abegweit)—but nearly all of its gently rolling surface is cultivable.

Along the south, its fretwork shores reveal the underlying gently tilted red of Pennsylvanian sandstones; along the north is a series of white beaches with sand bars, frequently of great length, creating sheltered lagoons too shifting and treacherous, however, to compete with the south and east as harbors. The climate is more moderate than that of the mainland; spring begins with May, summer and autumn are warm, and winter is more notable for its heavy snows than for very low temperatures. There is remarkably little fog and the surrounding waters have a blueness and range of shades in the shallows that recall the Mediterranean.

THE TRIUMPH OF AGRICULTURE

In the gulf to the north were the fine fisheries of the Magdalen Islands, Bradelle, and Orphan Banks. Agriculture, therefore, for many years hung in an uneasy balance with the fisheries. As a shrewd north-shore Acadian put it to Lord Selkirk in 1803, "We be all farmer—all fisher—dat be de veri ting dat mak us all begars."

In spite of forest fires, it took a long time to clear away the trees. As late as 1820, a Scottish visitor reported: "The whole island, when viewed at a distance at sea, looks as if there were not a tree on it. The trees grow so close together, and are so equal in height, that in spring their dark colours resemble heath."

Gradually agriculture expanded, chiefly to supply lumbermen, fishermen, and traders in fish from and in such other regions as New Brunswick, Nova Scotia, and Newfoundland. The island's own fisheries diminished relatively and became specialized in shore activities, notably the lobster fishery and gathering the famous oysters of Malpeque and elsewhere.

🍁 LAND OWNERSHIP AND SETTLEMENT

Perhaps thirty Acadian families out of 4500 inhabitants were believed to have survived the expulsions and roundups of the Seven Years' War, so that the empty island called forth a flood of applications for shares of it. The British Board of Trade and Privy Council disposed of these in a wholesale manner during the early summer of 1767. By special favor and by lottery most of the island was handed over to nobles, British and colonial officials, lobbyists, ex-officers (quite the largest group, under the Proclamation of 1763), and some venturers in the gulf fisheries. Actually the Acadians seem to have been adroit in using the island as a refuge, for a report of 1771 recorded the somewhat improbable total of 1270.

No one knows precisely the population of Prince Edward Island before 1825. Some of the earlier estimates are fantastically contradictory, and there are manifest discrepancies between how many arrived and how many stayed. Many an immigrant from the British Isles or North America, expecting to be able to acquire lands for himself, decided to leave for Nova Scotia or New Brunswick when he discovered that the proprietors of 1767 owned the land already. Many arrived because honest or dishonest ship captains wanted to get rid of them or had business of some sort at the island. Still others were penniless and, failing to find employment, sought it in farms, fisheries, or lumber woods elsewhere.

If we assume that there may have been as many as 1000 settlers, chiefly French, on the island in 1770 when Governor Walter Patterson arrived to set up civil government, it seems safe to conclude that there were about ten times that many, chiefly Scottish, in 1815. The great Scottish enclosures and evictions ("the clearances") and some Scottish religious strife were reflected in the arrival of 300 Highland Catholics at Tracadie, on the north shore above Charlottetown during 1770–73, and 800 Scots, chiefly Protestants from the western isles, planted in the Belfast (*Belle Face*) area east of Charlottetown in 1803 by the Earl of Selkirk. Still other Scots, destined as they thought to join compatriots in North Carolina, had the misfortune to lose their ship and goods near the entrance to Malpeque Bay in 1770, but managed to strike roots near there with Acadian help.

There was some English and American immigration before the American Revolution. After it, of about 600 New York and New Jersey loyalists who were lured in by the proprietors and their agents to lands on the south shore for which they could not secure title, enough stuck it out to make the "loyalist vote" a small but compact power of discontent in island politics for ninety years. These Americans were notable among the settlers for their many frontiersman's skills: "The men make their own shoes, their ploughs, harrows and carts, as well as their sledges; the women spin, knit, and weave linens and coarse woollen clothes for domestic use."

There were also some Channel Islanders from Guernsey, and after the wars few years passed without little groups of immigrants, chiefly Scottish, being dropped off at one harbor or another. The Irish migrations did not affect the island much until the potato blight of 1834 started the great outward movement that reached its peak about the middle of the century.

Reasonably dependable figures indicate a population of about 23,-000 in 1827, about 32,000 in 1838, 62,678 in 1848, 71,496 in 1855, 80,857 in 1861, and 94,021 in 1871 (about 1000 less than in 1941). In religious persuasion the population seems to have been approximately 45 per cent Roman Catholic and 55 per cent Protestant.

🍁 RELIGION AND CHURCHES

The Roman Catholics were fortunate in having Father Angus McEachern arrive in 1790. He was a great missionary priest, ranging out in all directions from his large red sandstone house at Savage Harbor. He became bishop in 1821, and about 1826 founded the nearby college at St. Andrews, precursor of St. Dunstan's University. Except for the Gaelic- and English-speaking Roman Catholics, the early days were sadly deficient in religious services. The Acadians, save for brief attentions from Quebec, had to go in with the Scots and the Irish. The Anglicans, who had in Theophilus Des Brisay a rector from 1775 to 1828, did not have a church even at Charlottetown until 1800, and even then it was unconsecrated because the Church of Scotland had a right in it. Not until 1836 was a new St. Paul's ready for consecration by the Bishop of Nova Scotia.

Except for missions from Pictou, N.S., the Presbyterians, present in substantial number as early as 1770, had to depend on their own system of family religious observances until 1810, when two resident

clergy laid the foundations of a rapidly expanding Presbytery. Methodism, under part-time lay preachers, reached the island in 1775 through
Benjamin Chappell, a friend and convert of John Wesley, but it was
not until 1807 that the movement secured its first ordained minister.
It spread rapidly thereafter to become second only to Presbyterianism
among the Protestant denominations. The strength of these two churches
perhaps explains the relative failure of the Baptists, as compared to
Nova Scotia, to win a large proportion of the population. The first
organized Baptist church (at Bedeque) dates from 1826, although lay
preachers and missionaries had been active for about fifteen years before.
They did not form a distinct Baptist Association until 1868.

🍁 CHARLOTTETOWN AND SELF-SUFFICIENCY

Since everything was on a small scale in Prince Edward Island, except
absentee land proprietorship, beautifully located Charlottetown on
the south shore was also small, an unassuming little capital of government, commerce, religion, and finance that seldom felt any need to cut
a figure in the world. Once the system of land ownership was recognized
as an incurable ailment, the island as a whole could be seen as a comfortable, bucolic community largely wrapped up in its many domestic
controversies. Some folk might be poor, but they need not starve. Some
might be rich by island standards, but not rich enough to cut a swathe
elsewhere. Most lived well, but throughout the island's history those
who found its life dull or lacking in scope for their ambitions moved out
in impressive numbers.

The stay-at-homes, like similar isolated societies elsewhere, found
comfort and compensation for material inferiority in a noticeable sense
of moral superiority to the rest of the world. Perhaps naturally, the rest
of the world was not much interested in Prince Edward Island except as
an occasional pawn in interregional or international negotiations. One
consequence of this cumulative insularity has been that little of the
island's history has been critically investigated.

Yet it would be misleading to accept the axiom that happiness is
synonymous with a lack of history, for what is known provides the
usual pattern of human disappointments, frailties, and dissensions. The
valuable walrus fishery at North Cape ended with the practical extinction
of those oil-yielding mammals, and Prince Edward Islanders thereafter
burned cod-liver oil in their lamps. Plagues of mice (whence the city
name Souris) and locusts ruined harvests. The forests dwindled, skilled
shipbuilders emigrated, and the fisheries were reduced by competition.
Yet in the long run the island sustained its peoples. It was a market-
garden, the one great natural center of the "provision" supply for

fishermen, lumbermen, and other venturers in the Gulf and North Atlantic areas.

The harbors on the southern shore saw many ships, native and foreign, and if Prince Edward Islanders found it inconvenient to pay attention to British or local customs regulations when foreigners lured them into trade or barter, no one bothered about it very much. Why should one pay excise on a puncheon of Jamaica rum when it happened to be worth twenty bushels of island potatoes? Even ex-Governor Walter Patterson carried on an extensive illicit trade from his farm about three miles from Charlottetown with his brother John's father-in-law in New York. An added encouragement to the chronic barter and smuggling was the characteristic drain of specie. Various devices were adopted to cope with it, including leather currency, copper tokens, and double coins made by punching out the centers of Spanish dollars, but the main reliance was on the ancient colonial device of local treasury notes.

﹒ REPRESENTATIVE GOVERNMENT

Patterson's first government clearly had to be merely by officials and a council, and the proprietors contracted to support it by payment of the quitrents owed to the Crown. Since they failed to do so, the island was in financial difficulties and disrepute from the beginning. By 1773, Patterson decided that there were enough inhabitants to create an Assembly, "by taking the voices of the whole people collectively, as belonging to one county, and waiving all kinds of qualifications, except their being Protestants and residents." Its eighteen members met in July and the characteristic colonial combat between Council and Assembly got its start.

Patterson was on leave for over five years during the American Revolution, when the islanders suffered somewhat severely from privateering raids (in 1775 Charlottetown was plundered and the acting governor and two officials were carried off to Massachusetts). Dismissed in 1786, his successor, Edward Fanning, was merely a lieutenant governor theoretically under the governor general of British North America at Quebec. Fanning, an easygoing but greedy New Yorker, was fairly popular with the inhabitants until his retirement in 1805, partly because he went along with the enemies of Patterson (egged on by the disgruntled loyalists). Their representations about Patterson's efforts to escheat and sell lands in default for quitrents wrecked his fortunes.

In 1798 the legislature decided to honor the Duke of Kent by adopting Prince Edward Island as its name, a change authorized by the Crown in 1799.

A clash with autocracy.—After Fanning, J. F. W. Desbarres put in a lively governorship, 1805–13, much thwarted by the refusal or inability of the legislature to find revenue for public building and public works. This was during his eighty-first to ninety-fourth years of age (he died at Halifax, aged 102). His insolent, autocratic successor, Charles Douglas Smith, a wartime appointee (1813–24), distinguished himself by never traveling as much as twenty miles from Charlottetown and by summoning the legislature only four times in ten years, each time for exchange of hard words and prompt termination.

The winter of 1818–19 formed a kind of peak in this unseemly conduct when the Assembly laid charges against the Chief Justice and the lieutenant governor himself, and published their grievances in the *Gazette*. The lieutenant governor's son broke the Assembly windows, and his son-in-law commanded the Speaker to adjourn it or face its dissolution. Addresses were sent by the Assembly to the Prince Regent asking for their constitutional rights and for control of the purse. But Smith was a protégé of Lord Bathurst and managed to keep himself and members of his family on the island's payroll for another five years.

The principal leaders of the Assembly in this contest were the Speaker, Dr. Angus McAulay, and Mr. John Stewart of Mount Stewart, who after retiring from active public life emerged again in 1823. The High Sheriff, John McGregor, who co-operated by calling public meetings, was summarily dismissed. Nonetheless meetings were held and resolutions passed in all three counties. John Stewart, alone among the committeemen, managed to escape arrest and carry the islanders' petitions to England—by being smuggled aboard a schooner in a cask, it is believed.

Out of the violent agitation of 1823 came the removal of Smith and his tribe and the appointment in 1824 of John Ready, who came out from England accompanied by Stewart. A new Chief Justice, S. G. W. Archibald of Nova Scotia, was also appointed, but he resigned in 1828 because he was refused permission to go on living at home and visiting the island only during the summer. Ready's term of office, 1824–31, marked a definite turn for the better. He toured the island, making himself known and respected and learning its needs. He did everything possible to develop roads and bridges (largely by statutorily imposed labor). Realizing that agriculture must be the mainstay of the economy, he strove for its improvement, largely at his own expense, importing breeding animals to improve the degenerated livestock and encouraging good land and forest use. The Agricultural Society of 1827 was largely his creation.

Council versus Assembly.—Prince Edward Island politics have perhaps had a reputation down to the present day for greater novelties and eccentricities than other parts of Canada. In 1825, for instance, after an obnoxious petition had been ordered "to lie on the table," the Attorney General moved an amendment that it be thrown under the table, and this was carried. Other novelties have been more serious responses to the special characteristics of the society. The great issue in Ready's day was control of the purse, and over this Council and Assembly fought bitterly, exchanging arguments that ranged from correct constitutional principles to specious or merely ingenious devices.

The Assembly's case was that all supplies "are the sole gift and grant of the House of Assembly." The Council claimed "their right of deliberating separately upon every measure for which provision is to be made in the Appropriation Bill" from funds raised, or to be raised, by local action. Following a flat reproof to the Council late in 1827 from the Colonial Secretary, William Huskisson, a rather indefinite peace was patched up in the spring of 1829. It was not until 1830—a year after Catholic Emancipation in Great Britain, but long after its concession in many other colonies—that the civil disabilities of the Roman Catholics were removed.

EDUCATION

The problem of education was urgent about this time. An academy in Charlottetown was authorized in 1829, opened in 1836, and named Prince of Wales College when Edward, Queen Victoria's heir, visited it in 1860. There were grammar schools at Charlottetown, Georgetown, and Prince Town, plus a short-lived Lancasterian (i.e. monitorial) school of the English Society for the Propagation of the Gospel and scattered district schools where masters and local support were available. The masters were supposed to be examined by a central Board of Education and to receive £12 a year from the Treasury. The Board spent about £300 in this manner in 1830. In general, however, the struggle for a system of public primary and secondary education was destined to be long and progress slow, perhaps not so much bedeviled by sectarian controversy as elsewhere, but handicapped by a rural population's reluctance to find the money.

RESPONSIBLE GOVERNMENT

The islanders cannot be credited with an appreciable share in the winning of responsible government. Durham's phrase for it, "the necessary consequences of representative institutions," was as applicable to Prince Edward Island as elsewhere, and one can detect its implications in island politics from the beginning in 1773. But this colony was small and its politics were frequently marked by extravagance and irresponsibility. The eternal land problem, involving as it did an influential group of absentee landlords in Great Britain on the one hand, and a desperate body of colonists who found it intolerable to clear and cultivate lands they could not possess and erect buildings they could not call their own on the other, gave the colony the character of a small but active nuisance.

The island's progress to self-government, therefore, should be thought of as an especially reluctant part of the general British surrender to colonial aspirations. In 1839 Lieutenant Governor Young was ordered to create a separate Executive Council. A request of 1847 for a responsible executive was refused by Gladstone and Grey. The Assembly countered in 1849 by refusing to grant supplies.

But the dam was breaking, and bargaining and concession began over Crown revenues and the civil list, extension of the franchise almost to adult male suffrage, equitable division of office and patronage in terms of the size of the religious groups, and so on. Probably 1862, when the Legislative Council was made elective, is as good a year as any for dating the achievement of responsible government on the island. The land problem remained unsolved.

🍁 EXTERNAL RELATIONS

One hesitates to place much reliance on the commercial statistics of Prince Edward Island. It is more fruitful to think of it in general terms, selling its livestock, meat, grain, flour and meal, ships, fish, and lumber in Lower Canada, New Brunswick, Nova Scotia, Newfoundland, Bermuda, and occasionally still farther afield. In return it took rum, and sugar, and all manner of other goods, meanwhile regarding outward and inward manifests and declarations of cargo as rather silly and meaningless. About 1850 the island's exports were approximately 70 per cent agricultural products, 20 per cent forest products, and 10 per cent fishery products.

One can be fairly certain that the island was not much affected in a direct sense by British free trade, but it was the first part of British North America to pass an act (March 19, 1849) providing for reciprocal free trade with the United States in certain natural products, and to address the Crown (May 1, 1849) asking for admission of Americans to the shore fisheries. They had been operating there for generations anyway to mutual benefit. The island legislature persevered in this bargaining policy during the session of 1852 and ratified the ensuing Reciprocity Treaty promptly in November, 1854.

The prosperity of the fifties and early sixties on the island was reflected in a certain cockiness towards the rest of the world. Inevitably there had been several occasions when British or colonial statesmen had thought that so small a colony should be annexed either to Nova Scotia or to New Brunswick. The islanders themselves had occasionally argued that the only way to shake off the incubus of the land proprietors was to join one of their neighbors or even the United States. Yet, at a time when free trade was manifestly working to the colony's advantage, the feeling grew up that Prince Edward Island could make a go of it alone.

That independent spirit, natural enough in the circumstances, failed to take account of the economic changes that were taking place in the outside world. The railroad that reached Northumberland Strait from Saint John, New Brunswick, in 1860 and the iron ship were omens of repercussions undreamt of by Prince Edward Islanders. Just as the island seemed to have entered its reward in confident prosperity, it was to be confronted by world forces with which it could not cope alone.

CHAPTER XIV

New Brunswick (1784-1865)

The New Brunswick that was created in 1784 was an immense, rough, square pinery—in the density and size of its trees it was a worthy rival to the north shore of the St. Lawrence, the Ottawa Valley, and the Great Lakes Basin. The sea washed three of its four sides, with the District of Maine and Lower Canada along the other, and a few great river systems penetrated the pathless woods and proffered carriage for the light softwoods to the mills and ships at tidewater. The St. John River entered the colony from Maine at the northwest corner, flowed down the western boundary about halfway, and then swung east and south to enter the Bay of Fundy.

From the head of that bay a remarkable tidal river, the Petitcodiac, had its rise just east of a low height of land between it and the Kennebecasis tributary of the St. John, so that there was a passable inland route from the mouth of the Bay of Fundy to its head. Since the height of land between Fundy and the Gulf of St. Lawrence wandered very irregularly from the southeast corner of New Brunswick to the northwest, the rivers that flowed into the Gulf were sometimes short streams with tidal estuaries, like the Richibucto, and sometimes great river systems like the Miramichi and the Restigouche, whose headwaters were not far from the St. John itself.

✿ LUMBERING

The colony's geographical position and its combination of dense forests, generous precipitation, and omnipresent waterways made it, and similarly endowed Maine, great nurseries of the North American lumbermen who followed the white and red pine from Atlantic to Pacific ("letting daylight into the swamp") in less than a century. Those men, their works, and their techniques have disappeared with the forests that they ravished. The passing of the great trees has changed the very topography of the lands on which they stood, drying up lakes into ponds, and rivers into feverish little creeks. The traveler of today, who sees not only small pulp logs but also large saw logs being carried to the mills in motor trucks, may quite properly wonder how men got the original huge trees out of the trackless wilderness.

The answer, of course, was that they made snow and water do most of the carriage. The woodsmen entered a forest with the first good snow, and, operating from central log-shanties and stables, felled trees, sawed them into log lengths, and dragged them on horse-drawn sleds downhill over iced paths out onto the frozen surface of lakes or into piles along the banks of streams.

The crux of the matter was how to retain enough of the melted snows and ice so that the logs could be shepherded in stages down to waters that would run deep and strong towards the sea. This spring "drive" represented the highest art of the lumberman and tested him to the limits of his endurance.

The art, a kind of gigantic carpentry with axe, crosscut saw, and sledge hammer as tools, went into the construction of stone and timber dams at relatively brief intervals along the smaller streams and of squared timber troughs or "chutes" wherever falls or rapids would arrest the logs. The dams sometimes had apron gates, but were commonly blasted open by explosives or otherwise torn apart to provide successive "heads" of water as the drive worked downstream.

The main channels through irregular waters and towards chutes were bound into passageways by booms, that is, tree-length logs attached end to end by chains and kept in place by piers of cribwork. The same booms were drawn around enormous "rafts" of floating logs when they were moved by capstans, oars, or tugs across broad waters or when they reached the mills. Towards the mouth of a river worked by several companies there might be a "boom association" for sorting out the logs in accordance with the marks stamped into their butts.

The great risk was that logs might form a "jam" at some point and pile up like jackstraws above it. When that happened, the most skilled and responsible rivermen were called upon to search out and dislodge the "key log," with a huge mound overhanging them and usually "fast water" under foot, for a "hung-up drive" with thousands of logs stranded on the shores above shrunken waters was a financial disaster. Perhaps as many men were maimed and killed on the drive as in the primitive sawmills. Those who came through five or six months in "the bush" and six or eight weeks of unending toil, irregular food, and snatched sleep on the drive usually received their season's pay in a lump sum at the mill town. Many of them spent most of it in a spree during which respectable folk either left town or stayed indoors as much as possible.

Since the disreputable lumbermen passed on westwards, leaving little enduring record of their devastating activities except wilderness, impolite legends, and a very bad song or two, the written history of New Brunswick is chiefly the account of the respectable settled population. Historically that is regrettable, for almost the only basic wealth came from the forest. Most of the agriculture was poor and primitive, unable to compete with lumbering as a rewarding pursuit. The fisheries were relatively small. Most of the industry was the fabricating into ships, and most of the commerce the selling, of forest products which the lumbermen made available. Most of the "practical" politics centered in schemes of one sort or another whereby the politicians and the lumber operators negotiated to mutual advantage.

And finally, most of the wealth extracted by "timber barons," sawmills, shipbuilders, politicians, and merchants was taken out of New Brunswick to Great Britain, the United States, and central British North America. As Peter Fisher said in his *First History of New Brunswick* in 1825, "Such persons, then, who are to be found in all the ports of the Province add nothing to the wealth of the country, but rather act as drains to it." A huge piece of North America was looted of its natural riches in about a century, leaving a society that had acquired relatively little of them to devise new and better ways of living in New Brunswick.

🍁 THE COURSE OF SETTLEMENT

Europeans had begun settled life in New Brunswick quite early in the seventeenth century, for its longer rivers were good funnels for the fur trade and good sites for salmon fisheries. Saint John, and the mouths of the St. Croix, Petitcodiac, Miramichi, Nipisiguit, and Restigouche were such centers. There were small fishing groups on the islands of Passamaquoddy Bay. In addition, the fertile valley lands of the St. John, the tidal marshes and level lands at the head of Fundy, and an occasional pocket of good soil among the sandy shore areas along the gulf invited agriculture.

Acadian farmers set themselves up at such places and New Englanders and Yorkshiremen replaced them in some measure after the expulsion. There seem to have been 4500 settlers about 1775 (3000 English and German, 1500 Acadian), but the disturbances of the Revolution make it impossible to say what the population totaled just before perhaps fourteen thousand loyalists came in 1784.

The widely scattered settlements, the subsequent emigration of many loyalists, the high proportion of transients to the United States among immigrants, and the fashion in which American and colonial lumbermen took trees, transportation, and markets on the side of the ill-defined international border where they seemed most advantageous, make population estimates highly speculative before 1851. It is best to think of a fairly stable agricultural occupation in the St. John Valley from the apprehensive Acadians of Madawaska County on the north to the outskirts of commercial Saint John on Fundy; of similar, if rather more mixed, settlements along the Petitcodiac and on the Isthmus of Chignecto; and of fluctuating fishing and lumbering settlements on the fringes of an uninhabited wilderness where Acadians turned up mysteriously from refuges in the woods. The Napoleonic wars, the American embargoes, and the persistence of preferential British markets revived and expanded the dwindling colony after 1807, but it was progressively thrown back on its native strength as British free trade developed after 1820.

Immigration was large and continuous, from the British Isles, Newfoundland, Nova Scotia, and intermittently from the United States. The Scots predominated until the potato blight dislodged the Irish from their native country. For almost a hundred years, the lumber ships brought human cargo to every port, but since few of these immigrants were even faintly competent for work in the woods, most of them found passage farther on overland or in provision or gypsum ships and thus contributed heavily to "the second colonization of New England." Population estimates of varying credibility indicate that the colony held about 35,000 persons in 1806, just before the American embargoes; about twice as many in 1820, just before British free trade; 93,700 in 1831; 119,457 in 1834; and 156,162 in 1840. The census of 1851 reported 193,800, followed by 252,047 in 1861, and 285,594 in 1871.

Most of these people lived in the St. John Valley, for it drained the mightiest forests, contained the most arable land, and had the colony's natural economic capital around the fine harbor at its outlet. Its early sawmills had been perched at the mouths of creeks flowing into the great river, but, as lumbering grew into the exploitation of whole tributary basins and the mills grew with it, they tended to occupy strategic locations, like the entry of the Nashwaak at Fredericton, or of the Aroostook and Tobique farther upstream, or in the vicinity of Saint John itself.

Shipbuilding naturally bordered salt water, and New Brunswickers produced some of the best as well as some of the worst of the world's wooden ships. The best were the beautifully designed and constructed three-masted barks, square-rigged on fore and main, fore-and-aft on mizzen, and the slim, racing clippers whose forward-raking bows and aft-raking masts caught and held the maritime world's excited admiration for a generation at the mid-century. The worst were little more than rough floating boxes designed to carry lumber for as many trips as possible before they were wrecked or fell apart. New Brunswick, like Nova Scotia and Prince Edward Island, exported boats and ships, indeed it was common practice to sell a ship along with its cargo.

The same combination of lumbering, milling, and shipbuilding existed elsewhere in only slightly less degree. The St. Croix and Passamaquoddy Bay were the center of a remarkable international community that profited by paying little or no attention to trade controls or citizenship when it came to social and economic enterprise. Indeed the mild degree of competition and emulation between the British and the American shores probably benefited both. Another focal point was at the head of Fundy where the Shepody, Petitcodiac, and Memramcook rivers entered. Gypsum deposits there were an added encouragement to shipbuilding.

Probably Saint John's nearest rival, however, was the mouth of the Miramichi. This area had a powerful attraction for Scotsmen, perhaps because of the salmon which in early days were so numerous as to create an uproar when they fought their way up the shallows. The earliest comer was William Davidson of Inverness-shire, whose checkered career in fisheries, lumbering, and shipbuilding extended from 1765 to 1790. Many Scots followed, notably the firms of Fraser and Thom (1788–1837) and Gilmour, Rankin & Company, one of several soberly managed, long-lived, New Brunswick subsidiaries of Pollok, Gilmour & Company of Glasgow.

Meanwhile native Maritimers also saw the opportunity. Francis Peabody, from Maugerville on the St. John, set himself up in 1800 and founded Chatham four years later. Joseph Cunard, Samuel's huge, flamboyant brother, branched out from the family business in Halifax and staged a spectacular career until the equally spectacular collapse of his enterprises in the depression of 1848. In fact, during the boom days along the east shore, Cunard and Alexander Rankin fought for supremacy from the Richibucto to the Restigouche in almost feudal fashion. The "classic," generally tumultuous election of 1843, in which they backed rival candidates, assumed during the several days of the polling the proportions of a small civil war between Rankin men north of the river and Cunard men south of it with barricades, loaded (but unfired) cannon, prolonged fights with stones and coal as missiles, and mounted marshals of forces totaling several hundreds of men. Its chronicler, William Wyse, reported that after the Rankin victory "enmity between the parties was very bitter for a year or more, so that very few ventured to cross the river into the enemy's camp."

🍁 PRIMITIVE AGRICULTURE

For young and vigorous New Brunswickers agriculture seemed a tame life compared to the flaming excitement of the end of the river drives, or to the swagger of the skilled mill hands, shipwrights, and auxiliary artisans. There was excellent soil in the St. John Valley, behind the dikes at the head of Fundy, and in such scattered bands of reddish clays as along the Northwest and Little Southwest branches of the Miramichi, but relatively few persons could be induced to farm seriously. Many a possessor of extensive, well-chosen lands dreamed of an estate in the North American wilderness whose acres would be handed down from generation to generation in the European manner. To create it, however, he needed devoted labor of a kind that was practically unobtainable. Almost anyone could get land, but the temptation was to resort to the winter woods for some cash income which was only too likely to evaporate during the celebration that ended that ordeal.

To quote Peter Fisher again, "Instead of making a comfortable provision for their families [they] will wear out the prime of their days without making any permanent establishment; and keep their families shifting about like vagrants," thereby creating "a race of inhabitants who have no interest in the soil or welfare of the Province." D. G. Creighton has aptly compared the lumbermen to the *coureurs de bois*. There was a fairly well-sustained drive during the forties to put provincial agriculture on an improved technical basis, but even the optimistic predictions of Professor J. F. W. Johnston's report to the legislature in 1850 failed to reverse the prevailing neglect and backwardness. Until the lumber staple approached exhaustion, New Brunswickers would not devote themselves to agriculture.

Since they failed to supply themselves with food, a large proportion of the colony's imports consisted of flour, beans, salt pork, molasses for sustenance, and rum for exhilaration. Following New England's example, cotton manufacture, sugar refining, and leather-working industries sprang up on a small scale at the St. Croix and in Saint John, but the ships that came from Europe, the West Indies, and the United States, seeking lumber, fish, and gypsum, brought processed or manufactured goods with them that were either unobtainable in New Brunswick or more efficiently produced elsewhere.

🍁 DIVISIVE FORCES

British and American influences.—Economically this gigantic lumber-yard and shipyard was drawn in two directions, pulled at, as it were, by the more powerful British and American economies. No one could forget how the enhanced British preferences had put the colony on its feet, but no one was very certain how British free trade would affect it. The attempt to supplant the United States in the West Indies had failed, and anyway the sugar islands were in decline. Above all, in spite of British, American, and New Brunswick attempts at trade regulation, the colony persistently found itself involved in something very like a working partnership with New England.

During the War of 1812, New England had bordered on secession in her determination to trade with the Maritimes. In spite of the labors of diplomats and governments to define a boundary among the islands of Passamaquoddy Bay and from the mouth of the St. Croix to the height of land near the St. Lawrence, the bay area developed smuggling into a sustained, specialized, and large-scale enterprise. The disputes about the inland boundary that lasted until 1842 were pretty largely lumbermen's private contests for forests to loot and water carriage to the sea.

The bloodless "Aroostook War" that brought out troops on both sides of the border in 1839 may have been colored by Maine's delighted discovery that beyond miles of her unpromising forest uplands the Aroostook Valley contained broad fertile lands as well as fine trees, but the urgent problem was that its waters and the logs they carried reached the ocean through the St. John in New Brunswick. The Webster-Ashburton boundary settlement and river-navigation agreement of 1842 settled these problems peaceably.

The valley versus the rest.—Another divisive force in New Brunswick life was the lack of unity between the St. John Valley and the rest of the colony. The people of "the Valley" thought they were New Brunswick and regarded the Fundy and Gulf centers as mere dependencies. Not quite so obvious, but stubbornly disruptive of the colony, was the fact that the "gentry" of Fredericton, the political capital, and of a good many of the valley parishes looked down their noses at the crass mercantile elements of Saint John.

This phenomenon was a highly complex one, partly an ancient European attitude of landed property towards "trade" but more largely a social and political mechanism earlier perfected in the American colonies by the upper classes as a defense against the populace. The outcome was that a small group of shrewd politicians, judges, lawyers, and officeholders managed to persuade the larger group of loyalists, who really wrestled with the wilderness and made it yield their sustenance, that being a loyalist meant devotion to their cult and acceptance of their leadership. This maintenance of an English tradition that had become a façade in its birthplace, and was an absurdity in New Brunswick, lasted for about fifty years after the arrival of the loyalists and was responsible for such things as the exclusion of the commercial classes and Dissenters from the Legislative Council.

The loyalist tradition.—In other words, "the loyalist tradition" succeeded for half a century in imposing a threefold division in society —landed and political aristocracy, active entrepreneurs of all sorts, and the populace. It took a long time to break down New Brunswick society into the two-class structure characteristic of other colonies. The maintenance of an oligarchy was a subtle achievement. Miss K. F. C. Mac-Naughton has succeeded best in analyzing it because she has done so in terms of the British, American, and Nova Scotian traditional backgrounds at the time when self-confident, self-righteous American loyalists were lucky enough to have the management of a new colony put completely into their hands.

One can concede that New Brunswick received some benefits, particularly in learning and cultivation, from the aristocratic system and still deplore the strength of the position in which aristocrats entrenched themselves. While they were still negotiating for the creation of their new colony, Edward Winslow had announced that "it shall be the most gentlemanlike one on earth." Their ideal was a paternalistic Toryism that would have alarmed Edmund Burke, who was at least as agitated as they were over the forces let loose by the American and French revolutions. Their symbol of all that was most hateful was a crude and venomous caricature of life in the United States. In the words of R. P. Baker, "a proper hatred of the United States and an equally proper love of England became social decencies."

These men held the whip hand in government and in its spoils system of absurdly large official salaries and endless fees and perquisites. This minority imposed on the majority the assumption that the Church of England was "by law established" in the colony, whereas it was not. They even managed to substitute the alien parish for the native township as the unit of local government. In the matter of education, they took immediate pains to provide secondary and higher education for the sons of Anglican "gentlemen," and almost equal pains to hand over the primary and secondary education of others exclusively to teachers of the Anglican faith. In their eyes the Dissenters and the masses needed instruction only in submissive behavior and good morals.

One particularly unsavory episode in their triumph was their diversion of funds provided by the ancient New England Company for the education and Christianizing of the Indians into schooling for "children of the first condition in the neighborhood" (of Sussex Vale) and sinecure salaries for members of the governing class. Roman Catholics were denied the vote until 1810 and remained subject to certain civil disabilities until 1830. Dissenters were excluded from King's College, Fredericton, until 1829. The Provincial Act of 1832 that belatedly authorized marriages performed by Dissenting clergy was so illiberal that the British government sent it back for revision.

🍁 EDUCATION

It would be unfair to blame the oligarchy exclusively for the local deficiencies in primary and secondary education, since the problem of local assessment for common schools was as acute in New Brunswick as in other colonies. The provincially endowed and supported Fredericton Academy, which was to put forth the blossom of the College of New Brunswick in 1800 (King's College in 1829), was contemporary with King's at Windsor, N.S., and like that school and college owed a good deal to King's College, New York (1754). W. T. Baird, who attended it in the thirties, reported: "Many of the boys were sons of the so-called aristocracy of that day. . . . The school was divided by the scions of aristocracy . . . into two classes; and the Plebei thus proscribed were made to suffer many indignities."

The first sops thrown to others, aside from a few little missionary schools of the English Society for the Propagation of the Gospel, were the forty-two parish schools authorized under an act of 1802 and entitled to £10 annual subsidy. Since the parishioners had to build the schoolhouses themselves, none seem to have materialized. Three years later, a grammar school in Saint John and thirteen county schools were authorized with a £25 annual grant each for six years. New England's strong influence was seen in the provision that the school should move from parish to parish in rotation. In 1816, when only Saint John and St. Andrews had schools, the annual grant-in-aid was raised to £100. The amount was increased to £175 (if the county raised £100) in 1823, just after Westmorland and Northumberland managed to start one grammar school each. A new attempt in 1816 to secure parish schools failed completely.

At this point New Brunswick succumbed to the British craze for cheap education through the monitorial teaching systems of Bell and Lancaster. The Church of England's National Society was entrusted with the work, and a special New Brunswick committee was chartered in 1820 ("the Madras Board"). The original intention was to educate poor children along with the well-to-do, but little came of this. Moreover the monitorial system proved inadequate, so that about all that can be said for "the Madras Schools" is that they furnished the foundations for a few schools in the more populous centers where the pupils' parents could pay.

By 1830, however, some of the rural parishes had managed to set up and maintain schools. It was in that year that all clergymen were excluded from teaching in the grammar schools, a reflection of the utilitarian character of the education demanded by the well-to-do urban elements. In 1833 the parishes were authorized to receive £20 each up to eight satisfactory schools, and for the first time a maximum of two female teachers to a parish might receive £10 salary a year—half the rate paid to men.

REFORMS AND CONSERVATISM

These innovations were among the evidences that the reform spirit of the thirties was capable of breaking through even the fossilized oligarchy of New Brunswick, or, to put it in native terms, that new energies were cracking the fifty-year-old mold of loyalist tradition. This was partly a matter of mere numbers, the increase of the unprivileged; partly a response to change in Great Britain, the United States, and British North America; and partly a shift in the elements of political power.

It has been customary to lump these and other factors together, calling them "democracy" or "responsible government." In the case of New Brunswick, it would seem wiser to regard the upheavals as elements of a change similar to that taking place in Great Britain. Powerful new economic elements in both societies broke into an older oligarchy. In both cases the invaders made use of utilitarian, radical, and democratic allies, only to turn against them once the seats of power had been reached. Aristocracy and middle class achieved partnership, but had no intention of admitting the populace as well.

If events are regarded in that light, New Brunswick's persistent conservatism after 1830 is quite understandable, for the broadened oligarchy was almost as anxious as the old one to encourage submissiveness and to discourage the critical spirit, novelty, and, above all, invidious comparisons of quiescent New Brunswick with lively New England. In fact the loyalist *tradition* proved to be convertible into a loyalist *myth* as a bulwark against radicalism.

Furthermore, since the working understanding between the old oligarchs and their new associates meant a combination of philosophical opposites, it goes far to explain the puzzling temper of nineteenth-century New Brunswick—what has been called "an absence of clear philosophy, an inconsistency in attitudes and alignments, a failure to understand the true meaning of abstract principles, and a tendency to interpret such principles in terms of some practical effect on individuals, institutions, and practices." William Smith, comparing New Brunswick with the other colonies in the campaign for responsible government, observed that "while they were struggling to widen the sphere of self-government, New Brunswick confined itself to strictly practical objectives."

Once the old loyalist grip on the province began to weaken, there were very few aspects of life that did not feel some impact of new ideas and new forces. On the one hand, the banking monopoly was broken; on the other, Roman Catholics got free of their civil disabilities just as Irish immigration swelled, to the accompaniment of pitched fights with the professional Protestants of the Loyal Orange Lodges. Protestant Dissenters began to cut away Anglican privileges in piecemeal fashion. Some men hammered away, without much effect, at the necessity of improved agriculture; indeed, perhaps as neat a symbol of the times as any was the irreverent (and unsuccessful) proposal to convert King's College into an agricultural college and experimental farm.

The political radicalism that had made New Brunswick too hot to hold the reformer, James Glenie, a Scottish member of Assembly for the New Englanders of Sunbury County from 1792 to 1809, found new utterance. The Fredericton *Royal Gazette* of January 20, 1830, for instance, contained a letter signed "Without one touch of My Hat, Neither Your's nor any man's servant, A Manchester Turn-out," which lashed out eloquently with the author's disgust over "more *religion* and *loyalty* . . . more absurd credulity and fanaticism; more base servility and crouching submission to power . . . than I ever saw in Old England." He blasted the systematic indoctrination of school children with submissiveness, and the maintenance of the College "to perpetuate these abuses among generations yet unborn." Since no newspaper gave "the least idea that one is living in a land of liberty and an age of reason," the writer was off to Upper Canada where the spirit of Cobbett was abroad. The editor lauded that decision with the usual conservative New Brunswick censoriousness towards Upper Canada, "where we apprehend there are already too many who neither 'FEAR GOD' nor 'HONOR THE KING.' "

INTELLECTUAL AND AESTHETIC FERMENTS

The destruction of the insulation that the loyalists had maintained around New Brunswick meant that the isolationism inside it could not persist. One of the most striking episodes in Canadian cultural history is the sudden appearance of the distinguished Fredericton school of poets in the 1880's. Unquestionably they were an end product of the intellectual and aesthetic ferments that seem to have begun at King's College (which became the University of New Brunswick in 1859) some time about 1840. The notable feature of those ferments is that so many of them stemmed from what was going on in the outside world. New Brunswick was at last willing to admit that alien ideas and achievements were suitable measuring rods for her own, and nowhere was this temper more pervasive than in the stronghold of the loyalist tradition, Fredericton.

That little town in its rural retreat heard and discussed Abraham Gesner's geological survey and other scientific ideas (from 1838), Professor James Robb's Scottish learning in chemistry and natural history (1837–61), the agricultural program (1850) of Professor J. F. W. Johnston, a Fellow of the Royal Society, and, perhaps most novel and stimulating of all, the cosmopolitan romanticism and wit of that extraordinary son of an extraordinary father, Joseph Marshall de Brett, second Baron d'Avray, known as Marshall d'Avray in New Brunswick. His father, Dr. Joseph Head Marshall, a distinguished physician and diplomat, had been ennobled by Louis XVIII. The son was appointed Director of the new Normal School at Fredericton in 1847.

The principal influences on the colony's primary and secondary education were now unquestionably American, Canadian, and Nova Scotian, as personified by Horace Mann, Egerton Ryerson, and J. W. Dawson, although it was somewhat impolitic to admit that anything good could come out of the United States. Very gradually, and with many disappointing delays, patronage and sectarian squabbles, and blind alleys, the colony built up an apparatus of grammar schools, academies, parish schools, normal schools, an inspectorate, and text books (borrowed from the "National" Board of Education in Ireland) that was crowned in 1871 by the provincial establishment of free tax-supported, nonsectarian common schools.

RESPONSIBLE GOVERNMENT

While it could be argued that in a literal sense New Brunswick was the first British colony to receive the concession of responsible government, it would be misleading to award her a major share in winning or wanting it. The councils were separated and opened to non-Anglicans in 1833 and the Legislative Council made public in 1834 as part of general British imperial policy. Something very closely approaching responsible government was secured by Lemuel A. Wilmot and William Crane in 1837 when Britain surrendered control of Crown lands and territorial revenues (in return for the legislature's guarantee of a very generous fixed civil list) and assented to making the Executive Council one that commanded the "entire confidence" of the Assembly. This action, it was hoped, might induce other colonies to follow suit.

Yet that very Assembly refused to regard this as the establishment of the principle for which Canadians and Nova Scotians were contending so vigorously. In 1845, for instance, the Assembly explicitly rejected four resolutions of the Canadian Assembly that had precisely stated the colonial case in 1841. New Brunswick was still very much on good behavior, and in Sir John Harvey she had a skillful and conciliatory lieutenant governor from 1837 to 1842. Moreover, the revenues conceded in 1837 had amounted to £150,000, and the five years spent in "logrolling" their expenditure had been exciting, if not generally beneficial. Consequently the issue of responsible government slumbered under a mantle of somewhat bloated good feeling.

Not until Earl Grey disposed of alternatives and conceded responsible government in his dispatches of November 3, 1846, and March 31, 1847, to Harvey, now lieutenant governor of Nova Scotia, did New Brunswick wake up to what was at stake. Then, in common with the rest of British North America, New Brunswick greeted the Nova Scotian election of August 5, 1847, in which Howe and his Reformers beat J. W. Johnston and his Conservatives, as the passing of a milestone. Charles Fisher of New Brunswick, an able and trusted collaborator with Howe, wrote him: "It is a glorious thing this election, for Nova Scotia and all the other colonies. . . . Canada will strike the next blow." After the Nova Scotian Reformers had moved into their party inheritance on January 25, 1848, their emulators in New Brunswick followed suit and government began to be reorganized.

It was notable, however, that in New Brunswick the transition to pure party government was spread out over several years. Apparently Wilmot and his Reformers did not mind being a minority in a mixed ministry. The legislature and public office, in fact, quite neatly illustrated how an "aristocracy" in retreat gradually took its enemies into partnership. Political office and its patronage were not easily to be revolutionized in the colony where they had had all the sanctity of personal property for sixty-four years. The only pressing task was reduction of the extravagant salaries and perquisites.

While that was being done, Wilmot himself succumbed to the old tradition and ended his political career by accepting a puisne judgeship in 1850 under circumstances that his associate Charles Fisher thought so contrary to "my ideas of responsible government" that he resigned from the Executive Council. Wilmot's successor as leader of New Brunswick, Leonard Tilley, came from mercantile stock in Saint

John and personified the transition of power from landed or official loyalism to a blend with more appropriate characteristics. The Assembly, two years earlier, had voted down the proposal to move the seat of government to Saint John. Now Saint John came to Fredericton, but to occupy "the driver's seat."

✥ NEW TECHNOLOGIES AND A NEW ORIENTATION

In the twenty years prior to confederation New Brunswick was being confronted with the challenge of new technologies. In 1860, a correspondent who signed himself "Metallurgist" wrote to the editor of the Chatham *Gleaner* about the visible decline of the Miramichi area: "Our New Brunswick supplies of timber are annually diminishing, iron ships are competing strongly with our wooden ones. Can not we build iron ships with our own iron? I am prepared to show that iron far better than English or Scotch metal can be made here as cheaply as in England." Twenty-four years earlier the New Brunswick legislature had authorized the incorporation of two railroad companies. Yet an economy that lacked liquid capital, industrial population, and compact, contiguous domestic markets could only dream of rivaling Great Britain and the United States in the new forms of production and transportation. A good deal of the minor profits painfully accumulated by New Brunswick millowners and shipbuilders, for instance, was lost in ignorantly calculated surrenders to the railroad mania in such areas as the lower Petitcodiac Valley.

The end of the old British colonial system during the forties was the colony's initiation into this changed world. The world depression that began in 1847 and lasted until 1850, the flood of disease-ridden Irish emigrants, the abolition of preferential duties, and the repeal of the Navigation Acts in 1849 seemed to add up to unavoidable disaster. The mother country had apparently decided to secede from the empire, and New Brunswickers began to talk about annexation to the United States as the only alternative to starvation. When world conditions improved after 1850, they discovered that their forebodings had been extravagant, but it was clear that they must cast about for a new orientation.

The Reciprocity Treaty of 1854 seemed to provide this. Since New Brunswick had always had to import foodstuffs, the productive efficiency of American agriculture in the Middle West was no menace, and at a time when the American market for forest products was expanding, a colony, 70 to 80 per cent of whose exports fell in that category, was bound to profit. Imports from the United States increased by about a third over the term of the treaty; exports almost quadrupled. While the dislocations of the Civil War undoubtedly played a part, and while railroad-building in the Maritimes contributed temporarily to a general sense of prosperity, New Brunswick began to contemplate a future in which it would be keyed to a North American rather than the British economy. Even before the treaty, between 1831 and 1851, American goods had risen from 13 to 34 per cent of New Brunswick's imports and the American share of New Brunswick's exports had risen from 4 to 11 per cent. The corresponding figures for 1865 were 43 and 31 per cent.

The early interest in railroads in New Brunswick was an indication that the continental pull was making itself felt. Certainly the proposed projection of the British (European) and North American from Portland to Saint John, and then to Moncton and Shediac (opposite Prince Edward Island on the Gulf), looked as if the United States was drawing the colony into its orbit. When Wilmot attended the great international railroad convention at Portland, in 1850, he asserted in the course of one of the most enlivening speeches made there that "we of the provinces have made up our minds no longer to remain quiet in our present condition . . . we intend to open this line of railway entirely across the breadth of our province and bring ourselves into connection with the world."

Even before 1850, however, it was apparent that "the continental pull" might originate in Quebec and farther west as well as in Portland, Boston, and New York. One of the companies authorized in 1836, the St. Andrews and Quebec, had had Lord Ashburton of Baring Brothers on its board of directors. Various other intercolonial projects culminated in the British government's Robinson survey and its recommendation in 1848 of a route from Halifax to Quebec by way of Moncton and the thinly populated eastern shore of New Brunswick. For the next twenty years, therefore, New Brunswick was sadly divided about railroad policy. At great cost of effort and money a line was completed from Saint John to Shediac by 1860, but not until nine years later could that line be carried to the border of Maine ("the Western Extension") and a spur be built from near Moncton to the Nova Scotian border ("the Eastern Extension").

Meanwhile, politicians and promoters wrangled, not only over the comparative merits of lines from St. Andrews, Saint John, and Moncton to Quebec, but inferentially about the consequences of economic affiliation either with the United States or with a federated British North America. Great Britain had seemed to show signs of a willingness to facilitate the federation of the colonies by helping to construct an intercolonial railroad.

From the time of the Robinson survey onward, there was practically no likelihood that a railroad of such strategic importance would be authorized to run so near the international boundary as the St. Croix or St. John Valley. To the majority of New Brunswickers, who lived in the western third of the colony, a railroad on the outward margin of the eastward third seemed of dubious benefit. At the denunciation of the Reciprocity Treaty in 1865, therefore, New Brunswick was delicately balanced between the direct pull of the United States and the potentialities of a federated British North America in which she would serve, somewhat obliquely, as link between Canada and Nova Scotia.

CHAPTER XV

Lower Canada (1791-1841)

While the boundaries of Lower Canada embraced the region from the coast of Labrador, the Magdalens, and Gaspé on the east to the valley of the Ottawa on the west, and from the height of land south of the St. Lawrence to James Bay and the height of land north of the St. Lawrence, for human purposes it amounted largely to a great trough and a mighty river between the Appalachian and the Laurentian mountains. From just below Quebec to just above the entry of the Ottawa a basin of fertile lands broadened out on shelves and slopes above the river, was closed at its southwest end by a rocky bridge between the Laurentian and Adirondack formations and a long rapid-strewn stretch of the St. Lawrence, and was interrupted less seriously by rapids in the lower Ottawa. Its climate was favorable enough for tobacco to mature and for less sensitive crops to flourish.

The Ottawa Valley itself was another fertile basin broadening downriver from narrow beginnings about 150 miles from its mouth. Many large rivers came out of the Laurentian Shield into the Ottawa and the St. Lawrence from the north. From the south, the Richelieu drained the Champlain Basin, and the St. Francis and the Chaudière the northern slopes of the Appalachians. The whole area was originally densely wooded, with mixed forest on the better lands and closely ranked conifers on the uplands.

🍁 FOREST PRODUCTS AND COMMERCE

The region dictated man's activities in it. Since the excellent fisheries were chiefly conducted from the Gaspé, the Magdalens, and the approaches to Labrador, the fishing population hardly formed part of the main body of *Canadiens*. When the fur trade became based on Hudson Bay, its personnel became westerners, except in the relatively meager trade at the mouths of the rivers along the North Shore and

Labrador. Yet, well before the Bay triumphed over Montreal, Britain's needs during the French wars had virtually created the lumbering industry, the timber trade, and shipbuilding. Indeed the wealth drawn from the forest staple made past takings from fish and furs seem almost insignificant. The forests, the rivers, and tidewater to Montreal were bound together in a great apparatus of production, chiefly for the British market.

Moreover, Montreal, on its island in the throat of the St. Lawrence, received an expanding adjunct to its strength when North American settlers broke through the Appalachian barrier and poured into both sides of the Great Lakes Basin. These people soon had forest products, grains, flour, and potash to sell and needed to buy more processed and manufactured goods than had ever been consumed in the fur trade. Long before the War of 1812, the Montreal middlemen were in the saddle, picking up their consignments of European and other imports at Quebec, transporting them by fast sailing craft or, after 1809, by steamboat to Montreal, and shipping them into the interior by boat and wagon routes up the St. Lawrence.

The up-country folk sent down their bulky products, sometimes in rough, sturdy river boats, but more commonly along with large, choice "sticks" of nonbuoyant oak or other hardwood, staked or lashed on top of semiflexible rafts of square softwood timber. The similar commerce with northwestern Vermont and the Richelieu Valley pretty well escaped Montreal's control because its outlet was downriver towards Quebec, but that seemed unimportant while the island merchants dreamed of exploiting the northern half of the continent.

Although this new commercial empire was bound to grow mightily, it was clearly vulnerable not only to the distressing economic cycles that hit raw material producers so hard but also to other powerful external forces. The alluring preferences for colonial products in the British and imperial markets came under attack from the long-established Baltic timber and grain interests, the alert and aggressive Americans, and the rising school of free trade almost as soon as the Napoleonic wars were over. If the Great Lakes Basin were to be made tributary to Montreal, canals must be built around the St. Lawrence rapids, but the Upper Canadians were for long too poor to build them and the *Canadiens* were rural folk who resisted being taxed for transportation services that seemed calculated to benefit only Montreal businessmen.

Finally, New York was a winter port, whereas the St. Lawrence was open for only seven months of the year. If New York used the Hudson and built canals from it over the low heights of land to Lake

Champlain, Lake Ontario, and Lake Erie, as she did in 1822, 1828, and 1825, respectively, she could depress the Upper Canadian Welland Canal between Erie and Ontario (1829), the Rideau Canal between Ontario and the Ottawa (1831), and the early St. Lawrence canals (Lachine, 1825), into second-best routes from the interior to the Atlantic. Also it was so much cheaper, in terms of frequent fast ships, wharfage, pilotage, freight rates, and insurance, to ship from New York than from Montreal to Europe, that the northern port, as it added up the sum of its disadvantages, felt it absolutely necessary to be assisted by imperial concessions in trade and navigation.

Loyalty to Great Britain ought to be rewarded by these preferences over Montreal's competitors, the recently successful rebels in the United States. Otherwise New York would be likely almost to monopolize the incoming and outgoing trade of interior British North America as well as of the northern interior of the United States. The Montrealers, as D. G. Creighton has said, "were mercantilists on the Atlantic Ocean and free-traders on the Great Lakes."

As early as 1795, just after Jay's Treaty, commercial London in the person of John Brickwood had foreseen the situation clearly. "Mercantile Competition," he wrote, "will now most probably place these two Communications with the Sea, more strongly in opposition to each other." In these circumstances, Montreal wished the state in Britain and North America to become, again in Creighton's words, "the super-corporation of the new economy, dominated like any other corporation by commercial interests and used to its full capacity as a credit instrument in a grand programme of public works." Nonetheless, by 1835, New York was visibly attracting Canadian products that Montreal had deemed her due.

POPULATION AND SETTLEMENT

Settlement coincided neatly with the nature of the land and of men's activities in it. Most of the *Canadiens* lived on the fertile farm lands of the St. Lawrence Valley, practicing an easygoing, backward agriculture, and responding to the unaccustomed peace and prosperity that prevailed after 1760 by an astonishing display of fecundity. The 60,-000 or so of 1760 had become 146,000 by 1792, and the quarter million estimate of 1806 included only 20,000 non-*Canadiens*. Later totals, of which the English-speaking fraction probably never rose above one-sixth, were: 427,465 in 1822; 553,134 in 1831; about 600,000 in 1837 and about 700,000 in 1844; 890,261 in 1851; 1,111,586 in 1861; and 1,191,516 in 1871.

This growth was almost entirely by natural increase, for immigration was negligible except for about 15,000 Vermonters and New Yorkers who moved in to occupy some two million acres in the southernmost part of the colony (townships called "Eastern" because of their direction from Montreal) at the end of the eighteenth century. Most other English-speaking immigrants passed on to Upper Canada.

Actually there was a substantial amount of emigration from Lower Canada as the pressure of population began to be felt, and as the *Canadiens* discovered the rates of wages paid in the United States. From 1806 onward reports multiply of their presence as settled residents in New York, Vermont, and New England from Maine to Rhode Island. The *Canadiens* also began to spill over into New Brunswick and Upper Canada. The old hive was sending out new swarms of humble folk who did not possess capital or expect to inherit it—transient laborers on farms, canals, brickworks, and railroads, and, as the textile mills and shoe factories of New England prospered and extended, large families aiming at the wages available to women and children as well as to men.

Lower Canada's own urban centers were few and small. Quebec, as well as being the political and administrative capital, was the exporting nexus for square timber, sawn deals (thick planks), and more special wood products. Wolfe's Cove, just upriver from the town, was one of the greatest shipbuilding centers in North America. Three Rivers (the mouths of the St. Maurice) was busy milling grains and an endless flow of logs. Montreal hummed with commerce of all sorts and its attendant industries. Yet these places put together did not amount to 10 per cent of the colony's population. The "wolves" of Montreal felt bitter towards the "lambs" of Quebec, partly because of the older city's advantages as an ocean port, and in 1824 began their prolonged efforts to make their own harbor the ocean terminus. They also resented in Quebec what the Montreal *Gazette* called "an example of centralization of Military, Civil, Financial, Clerical, Commercial, and Marine power, worthy of the policy of the late Napoleon Bonaparte."

THE ETHNIC DIVISION

In the course of his famous report of 1839 on the disturbed Canadas, Lord Durham commented on the insoluble problem of relations between the *Canadiens* and their British overlords:

> The entire mistrust which the two races have thus learned to conceive of each other's intentions, induces them to put the worst construction on the most innocent conduct; to attribute the most odious designs, and reject every overture of kindness or fairness, as covering secret designs of treachery and malignity.

That statement might be made with equal truth about conquerors and conquered anywhere, particularly when, as in the case of Lower Canada, they differed in language and in their traditions of politics, law, economics, philosophy, and religion. By using the words "learned to conceive," Durham looked back towards some periods of good feeling, as for instance during the wars against the hated French Revolution, Napoleon, and the Americans. It seems true, also, that the officials, timber merchants, shipbuilders, armed forces, and service contractors in Quebec cultivated happier relations with the *Canadiens* than did the impatient, thrusting merchants of Montreal. Nonetheless there had persisted since 1759 a chasm between the two ethnic groups across which only temporary bridges could be thrown. Numerous hands were ready on both sides to dislodge them whenever circumstances multiplied the easy occasions for misunderstanding.

Durham and many others after him attributed the political impasse that developed in Lower Canada to the ethnic division, but that is a superficial view. Any attempt to lump all the English-speaking inhabitants on one side of a comprehensive conflict and all the French-speaking on the other is contradicted by social, economic, and political differences within as well as between the ethnic groups. The *Canadiens* have been able to achieve substantial unanimity only when major crises have seemed to threaten their survival as an entity, and only on such rare occasions of their united defense of *survivance* have English-speaking Canadians also responded to crisis by almost unanimous opposition to them. In other words, only in times of intense crisis between them have the two parties clapped on their ethnic blinkers and refused to recognize that there were normally just as many varieties of *Canadiens* as of Canadians. Politics, unfortunately, could fairly often be made to seem crucial.

The ethnic differences were obvious, but it is interesting to note that a number of leading *Canadiens* erroneously believed at first that the English language must prevail over the French. What happened instead was that more *Canadiens* than Canadians became bilingual. In politics, although the English tradition of the cabinet system of parliamentary government contrasted sharply with the French tradition of autocratic paternalism, the *Canadiens* almost instantly mastered the representative structure established for them in 1791 and exposed its logical absurdity. Unhampered by a reverence for tradition, the political neophytes demonstrated that parliamentary government in colonies was like the tale of the emperor's clothes.

In economic matters, both peoples were normally acquisitive, if not equally skilled, but the French and Roman Catholic tradition imposed fairly severe restraints, while the British and Protestant tradition amounted often to the abolition of them. Consequently the *Canadiens* for the most part contemplated a gradual *inheritance* of their land as their numbers grew, whereas the Canadians favored all sorts of devices, such as credit instruments and the use of public funds, for making it easy to *exploit* potential opportunity immediately and to the limit.

Philosophically, the French tradition was logical, authoritative, and systematic, whereas the British was commonsensical, individualistic, and pragmatic. Contrary to common notions, and in spite of the pretensions of Jacob Mountain, the Anglican bishop, differences of religion caused relatively little difficulty. As Durham said, there was "a degree of practical toleration, known in very few communities" and "the Catholic priesthood of this Province have, to a very remarkable degree, conciliated the good-will of persons of all creeds."

What then was the basis of the political impasse that blossomed in rebellion and bore fruit in unforgettable wrongs and some years of sullen intransigence on the part of the *Canadien* majority towards the invincible authority of the minority? Single causes are unsatisfactory explanations, but if there was an outstanding cause, it was the revolutionizing of the *Canadien* society and economy by exposing its rather lethargic rural population to the driving energies of a commercial element that saw boundless opportunity in exploitation of the continental interior. Commercialism corroded even Lower Canada's seigneurial land tenure and the customary civil law that went with it. Even granting that the conventional relationships of feudal society had seldom existed in New France, the conception of land as something to be bought and sold, mortgaged, speculated in, and made especially available to possessors of political influence divided the majority of the unprivileged, who were overwhelmingly *Canadiens,* from the privileged of both ethnic groups.

Even more disturbing was the fast alliance between the commercial element and the colony's administration, because this meant that political power was in economic opposition, not only to the majority of the people, but to the political leaders whom they threw up. There was little either in the tradition of the *Canadiens* or in their educational machinery that could train ambitious young men to excel in commerce, but a great deal that tempted them to become priests, doctors, lawyers, and functionaries in local business, land transfers, and inheritance.

To these men, with their training in the classics and in rhetoric, the new politics offered intoxicating scope, but almost exclusively scope in leadership of the unprivileged against an entrenched minority who monopolized economic as well as political power. A *Canadien* popular leader might easily find himself damning one and the same man for his activities as a councilor, official, or judge on the one hand, and as a land speculator, banker, or canal promoter on the other.

Three quotations will illustrate the radically opposed views that crystallized when commerce in alliance with political power assailed feudalism. A commercial pamphleteer of 1809 wrote:

> The population of this Province forms a small compact body inert in its nature, without one principle of percussion; and exhibiting its infant face, surcharged with all the indications of old age and decay. During a lapse of two centuries, little more than the borders of the St. Lawrence have been put under cultivation; in a few places only, have settlements slumbered forth, on the minor streams, with manifest reluctance and regret.

On the other hand, the editors of the newspaper *Le Canadien* wrote in 1806 and 1807:

> Some people wish to create a mercantile aristocracy, the most abominable, the most pernicious, of governments, equally detrimental to the authority of the Crown, to the interests of the landowners, and to the liberties of the people.

The "Yenkés" of the Eastern townships were taken to illustrate commercialism on the land:

> . . . a half-savage people, whose invasions are as much to be feared, in Canada, as those once made, in Italy, by the Goths and the Vandals.

Divisions within the ethnic groups.—Neither the *Canadien* nor the Canadian camp was a solid group, for each contained its conservatives and its radicals, its property-minded and its revolutionaries. Thus the great French Revolution, the innovations of Napoleon, and even the middle-class Revolution of 1830 in France had the effect of reinforcing the submission of the Roman Catholic hierarchy to "the powers that be" in Lower Canada and in London. Only an occasional parish priest, close to the uneasy people, foreshadowed the division between upper and lower clergy, probably because the fifty-odd clerics who fled from revolutionary France to Canada had great prestige, both as eyewitnesses of the overturn and as possessors of learning and culture that few *Canadiens* could rival.

Outside the church, however, there were many men who were deeply affected by the exciting courses of events and thought in France and in the United States, and who chose to align themselves with democracy against oligarchy in politics and with liberalism against authoritarianism in religion. As early as 1793, the Montreal merchant John Richardson detected one party among the *Canadiens* "infested with the detestable principles now prevalent in France." Citizen Genêt, France's representative in the United States in 1793–94, bombarded Lower Canada with revolutionary appeals that were at least in part reflected by popular outbreaks in 1793, 1794, and 1796.

The *Canadien* clergy and gentry did everything possible to counterbalance this by sermons, pastoral letters, subscriptions to patriotic funds, and public thanksgivings for British victories, but the revolutionary infections were not stamped out. *Le Canadien* might call Napoleon "the lawless leader of France" and Quebec might be illuminated to celebrate Trafalgar, but there were new ideas loose in the world that threatened any oligarchy.

In particular, the strange career and the brilliant, infectious writings of H. F. R. de Lamennais in France made themselves felt in Canada, and questing *Canadiens* followed his course from rationalism to ultramontanism and then from the narrowest Roman Catholic authoritarianism to unqualified religious freedom and democracy. Those who were frightened to abhorrence by Lamennais's revolutionary ideas, or obedient to papal denunciation of them, could hardly ignore radical, upsurging, Jacksonian democracy in the American republic and the general prosperity that seemed to go with it.

It was Durham who observed that, while the English of Lower Canada excelled in political and practical intelligence, "the greater amount of refinement, of speculative thought, and of the knowledge that books can give, is, with some brilliant exceptions, to be found among the French." Frederick Elliott of the Colonial Office had been surprised, when he visited Lower Canada in 1835, to find that the *Canadiens*'s "understanding of political science is superior to that of the men by whom they have been so arrogantly despised."

These commentators might have gone on to point out that "the English" were not a solid bloc, for they had their radicals and democrats as well as their conservatives and oligarchs. Just as the conservative *Canadiens* threw in their lot with their Canadian oligarchy, so did the Canadian radicals with the *Canadien* majority. The former Nova Scotian, James Stuart; the able Scottish journalist, John Neilson; the Briton, Dr. Wolfred Nelson; the Irishman, J. B. O'Callaghan; the Americans, Dr. Robert Nelson and Thomas Storrow Brown; and the Swiss Amury Girod—all had been potential members of the Canadian oligarchy who fought it instead.

SOCIETY, RELIGION, EDUCATION

Fifty years of conflict between a commercial oligarchy and its rural opponents piled up a mountain of well-remembered clashes which finally toppled over in rebellion. The components interacted in endless permutations and combinations, but it is possible to indicate and illustrate separately some of the social, cultural, and economic disagreements that found their way ultimately into the political arena. The legislature—of governor, Council, and Assembly—was the seat of power in Lower Canada. Conflicts were either settled there or came to the point where the exercise of legal power called forth first outright refusal to act, and then rebellion.

In the social sense, a minority of merchants, officeholders, higher clergy, and seigneurs held itself above a majority of farmers, lumbermen, and workers in and about the sawmills, shipyards, gristmills, and wharves. In between was another minority of professional men, politicians, and small merchants and entrepreneurs, many of whom gave allegiance as well as leadership to the majority, although many others succumbed to inducements that looked like a start up the ladder to the upper class. Stewart Derbishire, a detached, industrious, and acute investigator of Lower Canada in 1838, wrote an astringent description of the huge rural matrix of the *Canadiens* that is persuasive because it catches the psychology of a conquered and isolated people.

> The *habitans* are a sluggish race, fond of indolent pleasures, light-hearted and gay. . . . They consider themselves superior to all other peoples, and too good to mix with any other race. . . . They are, I believe, an innocent and virtuous race, have retained a character of primitive simplicity, & even in the lowest orders have that naturally good manner, mid-way between servility and familiarity, which distinguishes the same class among the natives of the old country. The ambition of bettering their condition seems never to have visited their minds: Locomotive faculties they seem to have none.

His remarks probably echo Papineau's statement to an English gentleman:

> Our people don't want English capital nor English people here—they have no ambition beyond their present possessions, & never want to go beyond the sound of their own Church Bells.

Religious differences of Catholic and Protestant caused very little trouble except between the two persuasions of Irishmen, who fought bitterly on numerous occasions and were used by others for such non-religious ends as electoral intimidation. There was also some trouble within Catholicism because Irishmen and Scotsmen felt that the *Canadien* churchmen denied them recognition of the linguistic difference.

The nearest approach to a great religious issue was connected with education. The general dissolution of the Society of Jesus had left its Canadian estates at the disposal of the Crown in 1801, and the Anglican Bishop and others proposed to devote the revenues chiefly to an elaborate engine of Anglicizing education known as the Royal Institution for the Advancement of Learning. Somehow or other the Roman Catholic hierarchy failed to block this scheme. As Bishop Plessis remarked to Governor Craig, "You say our Church never sleeps, but nevertheless you will grant that we were asleep, and very soundly asleep, when we let this bill be adopted."

The Bishop need not have worried, for the Royal Institution never faintly threatened *Canadien* religion or culture. The Jesuit Estates Fund became a Jack Horner's pie for political insiders. Of £49,000 net revenue for 1801-31 remaining after 35 per cent had been charged to "administrative expenses," £37,000 was spent on general purposes, that is, salaries, expense accounts, and pensions of noneducational officials, and £12,000 was devoted to Protestant education, that is, to the Royal Institution itself and the three Royal Grammar Schools of Quebec, Montreal, and Kingston (Upper Canada).

Meanwhile a slowly increasing number of parish schools, conducted by the priests, underlay an uneven apparatus of *Canadien* secondary and higher education that was designed *ad majorem Dei gloriam*. The *émigré* clergy of the French Revolution had done much to establish the curriculum for a few classical colleges that combined secondary and higher education along seventeenth- and eighteenth-century lines. Durham strongly commended this secondary education, while deploring the paucity of primary, and said it "greatly resembles the kind given in the English public schools, though it is rather more varied." The classical colleges served only a tiny minority, but they were the stepping stones to the priesthood and to the professions, then studied by apprenticeship. Some of the religious orders also conducted schools of varying quality at their monasteries and convents. The Petit Séminaire and Grand Séminaire at Quebec were the keystones of the educational arch, and the latter was appropriately chartered as Laval University in 1852.

ECONOMIC ISSUES

The economic conflicts could be lumped together to form the classic model of colonial strife between farmers and manual workers on the one hand, and the possessors of capital, credit, and political office and power on the other. A triple alliance of the merchants with officialdom in Lower Canada and of both with authority in Britain emerged soon after 1791 and grew to be commonplace by 1820. Indeed, the Montrealers became professional imperialists, as they had good reason to be, mouthing the clichés of "the British connection," "the prerogative of the Crown," and "the glorious Constitution," and damning democracy as subversive, revolutionary, and despotic. They maintained lobbyists in London, where their organization blossomed out into the North American Colonial Association in 1831.

The extravagant salaries, fees, and perquisites of the official oligarchy were used from early days to attach a few conservative *Canadiens* to the administration. The *Canadien* share of office and profit was so utterly out of line with its proportion of the total population, however, that about the commonest weapon of the democratic leaders was recitation of the contrasted ratios of population and patronage. Another favorite weapon was the indefensible case of John Caldwell, the Receiver General of the colony, whose speculations with the public funds crashed in the depression of 1821, leaving him and the revenues short by the immense amount of almost £100,000.

The situation was similar in land-granting and land speculation. From the days (1795) when John Jacob Astor and others began to connive with officialdom for grants in the Eastern townships and along the Ottawa, down to and beyond the grant of more than half a million acres to the British American Land Company in 1832, land provided a great avenue to wealth for the influential. Empty lands awaiting speculative profits provided powerful provocation at a time when poor *Canadiens* were emigrating for want of them. Naturally the Canadians were as strongly in favor of immigration as the *Canadiens* were opposed to it. Indeed, when the famine migrations from Ireland brought cholera and typhus with them, some *Canadien* leaders allowed their accumulated feelings to betray them into accusations that the immigration was a plot to decimate them.

The great aggravation of this series of economic conflicts grew from Montreal's awareness of the money to be made from the expanding productivity of the Great Lakes Basin. The merchants wanted to build canals; the *Canadiens* saw enough benefits to their own people from the Lachine Canal to support its construction (1815–25) from the public treasury, but called a halt on wrestlings with the unruly St. Lawrence above that point. The merchants wanted to reunite Lower and Upper Canada (for political as well as economic ends); the *Canadiens* fought such proposals with intense and successful energy. The merchants wanted to raise revenues for public works by a land tax; the *Canadiens* not only successfully insisted on confining taxation to customs and excise duties but were dilatory and obstructive in reaching agreements with the Upper Canadians as to equitable division of a customs revenue that reflected the growth of the inland colony. When the imminence of British free trade made it seem to the merchants that only some kind of annexation of the interior could save them, the *Canadiens* were unmoved.

🍁 TRANSLATION INTO POLITICS

All of these inner contradictions and imperial conflicts affecting Lower Canada were thrown into the political hopper. The *Canadiens,* who took to representative government like ducks to water, were untroubled by traditional British beliefs and conventions as they explored and revealed the innate contradiction between appearance and reality in colonial parliamentary government. By sheer weight of numbers and on grounds of common sense they had fought and won in the legislature of 1792 the recognition of bilingualism, thus rounding off the rights of religion, civil law, and property conceded to them by the Quebec Act of 1774.

While the governmental apparatus set up under the Act of 1791 was the conventional one of nominated governor, Executive Council, and Legislative Council on the one hand, and elected Assembly on the other, the nonelective group enjoyed unusual advantages. The governor, since he was also governor general of British North America, had large military funds at his disposal; the Jesuit Estates Fund was another reserve; and the Crown revenues (chiefly territorial, plus the customs duties of 1774) were unusually large. Even after Caldwell's defalcations of 1821 had rendered the Executive distinctly more dependent on the Assembly for revenue, it was practicable in an emergency to carry on government in defiance of the Assembly's supposed power of the purse. The sense of frustration that arose from this situation had a great deal to do with the ultimate resort to revolution.

Union with Upper Canada defeated.—Most of the issues had emerged in recognizable form before the War of 1812, including the clear, if general, suggestion by Pierre Bédard in 1809 that the executive should be responsible to the legislature, and the question of reunion with Upper Canada. The war, in which both the "Yenkés" of the Eastern Townships and the *Voltigeurs Canadiens* under Lieutenant Colonel Charles Michel de Salaberry played distinguished parts, was an interlude. Thereafter tensions grew, over such matters as the Assembly's claim to control the annual estimates, until the ambitions of the oligarchy prompted a bill, quietly introduced in the British Parliament in June, 1822, to unite the Canadas. The depression of 1821 and the construction of the Erie Canal had heightened Montreal's sense of urgency.

This attempt to short-circuit *Canadien* resistance to the merchants' designs evoked instant resistance and served to arouse the population generally, for under it a high property-franchise would have excluded most of the people, the French language was to be discontinued in the legislature in fifteen years, and the Roman Catholic Church was to be brought under civil authority. *Canadien* opposition was so explicit, so widespread, and so well argued and presented in Parliament (chiefly by the Philosophical Radicals), that the political union was dropped and only legislation as to trade with the United States and division of the Quebec customs duties between Lower and Upper Canada was passed.

Papineau.—One of the two *Canadien* emissaries to London at this time had been Louis Joseph Papineau, the gifted orator and romantic leader of his compatriots in their agitated responses to injury and frustration. He, as a member of this wronged people, shared their subordination, and voiced it to them and to their oppressors with memorable, infectious eloquence. Then carried away by his own emotional impetus, he drove on to the point where force responded to force. Much had been expected of Papineau even as a schoolboy; in the Assembly he became Speaker, not in the constitutional but in the popular sense; and behind him for twenty years radical leaders of both tongues instinctively arrayed themselves.

Indeed, it was to John Neilson, in 1828, that Papineau revealed the weakness that ultimately robbed him of full effectiveness. "You," he wrote, "are worth much more than I am, for you have the same sensitiveness as I have, and the strength that I have not. . . . The injustice done to my country overthrows me and agitates me to such a degree that I am not always capable of taking counsel only of an enlightened patriotism, but rather of anger and hatred against its oppressors."

After ten years of preliminary skirmishing, from 1822 to 1837 Papineau fought uncompromisingly against the oligarchy, drawing some of his arguments from French and British radicalism, but gradually coming to depend chiefly on the democratic republicanism of the United States. In fact, it might almost be said that, despairing of the extension of true British constitutional practice to Lower Canada, he seized upon the sweeping application of the electoral principle in the United States in order to provide at one and the same time a contemptuous slap at the British tradition and political equity for the *Canadiens*.

His great error was that he was incapable of recognizing and profiting by either the Tory liberalism (economic) of the twenties or the Whig liberalism (political) of the thirties in Great Britain. Many of his actual or potential associates and followers, however, realized that the dam was breaking. In spite of being gibed at as sellouts (*vendus*), placemen (*gens en place*), and deserters (*Chouayens*), they preferred legality to revolution and accepted office within a regime that they hoped to modify and reform.

British concessions rejected.—The British Tories may have committed themselves to union of the Canadas in 1822 on the basis of one-sided advice, but they went far to redeem themselves by the thorough examination of the Lower Canadian problem that was made by parliamentary committee in 1828. While it would have been too much to expect recommendation of the responsible government that was merely in the process of its first systematic formulation by the Baldwin group in York, Upper Canada, the committee report was remarkably reflective of *Canadien* representations. It agreed to various particular reforms and, on the central issue, declared "that the real interests of the province would be best promoted by placing the receipt and expenditure of the whole public revenue under the superintendence and control of the house of assembly."

Papineau insisted on interpreting this literally, that is, on excluding the Legislative Council from any share, and on refusing to countenance any bargain as to the simultaneous provision of a civil list, or the assurance of a few basic official salaries. During 1830–34, the exciting years of Tory defeat, Whig victory, and parliamentary reform in Great Britain, Papineau's intransigence in the face of almost complete Tory and Whig surrender to Lower Canada's demands is explainable only in terms of his and others' belief that the colony was immediately destined to parallel Jackson's triumph in the United States.

This prophetic mood culminated in the Ninety-two Resolutions introduced to the Assembly as the *Patriote* creed on February 17, 1834, by Elzéar Bédard. Although full of overtones from the American Declaration of Independence and suggesting strongly that Lower Canada was entering on the same course, the resolutions were more like the English Grand Remonstrance against the government of Charles I in 1641. John Neilson, who had regretfully broken with Papineau only the year before, wrote that of the resolutions, "eleven stood true; six contained both truth and falsehood; sixteen stood wholly false; seventeen stood doubtful; twelve were ridiculous; seven were repetitious; fourteen consisted only of abuse; four were false and seditious; and five were good or indifferent."

The extravagance of the document accelerated the falling away from Papineau of the church (Papineau had become obviously anticlerical as early as 1829), the conservatives, and the moderates. Even Bédard cut himself free and accepted a judgeship. Papineau and those whom his emotion kindled went on. The merchant element organized a powerful counteroffensive that combined unremitting pressure on the administration with systematically provocative strong-arm gangs in the streets of Montreal.

Efforts made then and earlier to induce Papineau to accept office, to become a member of councils that now contained more *Canadiens* than Canadians, were indignantly repulsed, and Papineau has been harshly criticized for this. Doubtful as it is that he had really worked out the principles of responsible government, that criticism seems unjust, in the light, say, of Wilmot's opposite course in New Brunswick. What was blameworthy was Papineau's prolonged use of his majority in the Assembly to prevent the legislature from functioning at all. Moreover, his passionate surrender to his own revolutionary emotions gave extremists their chance and carried many of his followers to hopeless rebellion and its consequences in death and destruction.

The rebellions.—Three external events contributed to the uprisings. The first, and probably the most potent, was the combination of crop failures in 1836 and 1837 with the world-wide financial panic and depression of 1837 which rendered thousands in the Richelieu Valley and western Lower Canada literally desperate by the spring of 1837. The second was the apparently calculated revelation during the winter of 1836–37 by Sir Francis Bond Head, lieutenant governor of Upper Canada, of instructions issued to Governor Lord Gosford and a British Royal Commission of inquiry and conciliation in Lower Canada that precluded them from recommending either an elected Legislative Council or Assembly control of Crown lands. The third was the blunt and arrogant series of Ten Resolutions, carried through the British Parliament during March by Lord John Russell, which flatly denied the elective Legislative Council demanded by Papineau and authorized the governor to appropriate revenue without the authority of the legislature.

The Twelve Resolutions, or Declaration, adopted in response at a *patriote* meeting at St. Ours on May 7 and circulated throughout the colony at many inflammatory gatherings, became the manifesto of the rural rebellions that began in the face of stern repressive measures in mid-November. The Declaration had openly threatened Lower Canada's entry into the United States. This had evoked a British patriotism and the enrollment of ill-disciplined volunteers who were spoiling for a fight.

The half-dozen skirmishes and pitched battles of November and December were pitiable, tragic affairs in which half-armed farmers faced regulars backed by artillery, and, after their defeats, saw their villages and farmsteads looted and burned by uncontrollable, vengeful volunteers. When Robert Nelson tried to retrieve the cause by bringing in American filibusterers and declaring a republic, he failed completely in an invasion in February, 1838, and by a second effort in November exposed his followers and sympathizers to still more ruthless treatment.

Courts martial condemned ninety-nine of the prisoners to death, of whom ten were executed and fifty-eight were exiled to the penal colonies in Australia. The remainder were later set free. One of the odd features of the rebellions, later to be paralleled in South Africa, was that many of the leaders (e.g., Papineau, Wolfred Nelson, Lafontaine, Morin, Taché, Cartier, Brown, and Bouchette) subsequently became prominent in Canadian public life, four of them prime ministers. No one can say that the blood of the *patriote* martyrs, nearly all of them humble men, won self-government for the *Canadiens;* it is even doubtful that they greatly hastened its coming; yet no one can deny that they were men rendered desperate enough to venture their lives by grossly inequitable and inadequate colonial administration.

Durham and his recommendations.—Discredited by the Lower Canadian outbreaks of 1837 and by almost simultaneous rebellions in Upper Canada, the Whigs in Great Britain had to make another attempt to settle the colonial problem. As their principal agent they chose "Radical Jack" Lambton, Lord Durham, socially an aristocrat, but politically so much a democrat that he had embarrassed as well as stimulated his cautious colleagues during their reform activities of the thirties. Durham had picked up from the Political Economists and the Philosophical Radicals their new technique of investigation and report by a *corps d'élite* drawn from the rising administrative class. He rapidly surrounded himself with such agents, ignoring or evading the Cabinet's social objections to some of them, and was hard at work in Lower Canada before the end of May, 1838.

His white horse, his theatricality, his large *entourage* at the Château St. Louis and the legislative buildings, and his whirlwind self-confidence and arrogance were a very real part of his impact on history. So also was his peevish resignation and sudden return to England in November after his Whig colleagues in Parliament failed to defend his highhanded banishment to Bermuda of certain rebel prisoners under pain of death. These things served to make his brilliantly written, completely assured report of 1839 exciting news in Great Britain and to elevate the colonial question in national politics for the first time since the American Revolution. His death from tuberculosis in July, 1840, furnished a kind of copestone of publicity for the colonial problem and for Durham's assertion that it might be solved easily and completely by the concession of responsible government.

Durham's report may have been a *tour de force,* and he may have got the idea of responsible government from the Baldwins and the idea of Union from the Montreal merchants, yet it is unrivaled as a landmark in the world's, as well as in Great Britain's, imperial history. While it is substantial enough to stand and to convince alone, its appendices and the Durham Papers at the Public Archives of Canada reveal how broad and deep and intelligent were the investigations upon which it was based. Its general offensiveness to the *Canadiens* has unfortunately meant that it is not well known to their descendants today, yet there is nothing to equal it in revealing the painful circumstances and the difficult issues that had to be mastered at the mid-nineteenth-century turning point in Canada's development.

While Durham made clear his underlying assumption—that the colonies "are the rightful patrimony of the English people, the ample appanage which God and Nature have set aside in the New World for those whose lot has assigned them but insufficient portions in the Old," his report was designed to effect two principal ends. One of these dictated a third that may have been secondary in Durham's thinking, but was actually so fundamental as, at least temporarily, to eclipse all else in the minds and hearts of the *Canadiens*. The assumption and the aims illustrate well his blithe capacity for ignoring or overriding contradictions.

Durham would concede responsible government; he would unite the Canadas in order to end the ethnic and other conflicts; and he would anglicize the *Canadiens*.

Every purpose of popular control might be combined with every advantage of vesting the immediate choice of advisers in the crown, were the colonial governor to be instructed to secure the cooperation of the assembly in his policy by entrusting its administration to such men as could command a majority, and if he were given to understand that he need count on no aid from home in any difference with the assembly that should not directly involve the relations between the mother country and the colony.

The pretensions of the French Canadians to the exclusive possession of Lower Canada would debar the yet larger population of Upper Canada and the [Eastern] Townships from access to the great natural channel of that trade which they alone have created, and now carry on. The possession of the mouth of the St. Lawrence concerns not only those who have made their settlements along the narrow line which borders it, but all who now dwell, or will hereafter dwell, in the great basin of that river.

I entertain no doubts as to the national character which must be given to Lower Canada; it must be that of the British Empire, that of the majority of the population of British America, that of the great race which must, in the lapse of no long period of time, be predominant over the whole North American continent. Without effecting the change so rapidly or so roughly as to shock the feelings and trample on the welfare of the existing generation, it must henceforth be the first and steady purpose of the British government to establish an English population, with English laws and language in this province, and to trust its government to none but a decidedly English legislature.

He wished to elevate the *Canadiens* by anglicizing them.

There can hardly be conceived a nationality more destitute of all that can invigorate and elevate a people, than that which is exhibited by the descendants of the French in Lower Canada, owing to their retaining their peculiar language and manners. They are a people with no history and no literature.

Thus Durham, who seems to have been in lengthy close communion with the conservatives, advocated the union of the provinces which had been foremost in their minds for a generation or more. On the other hand, he advocated the responsible government that in one form or another had been dreamed of and worked for by the radicals of the same generation. He expected these two devices to better the *Canadiens* by giving them the cultural, economic, and political character that he expected to prevail in North America. "He performed the remarkable feat," wrote D. G. Creighton, "of joining the Lower Canada merchants and the Upper Canadian radicals in approval of his measures and of uniting the French Canadians and the Toronto tories in outraged disapprobation."

Once Union seemed certain, the mercantile Montrealers turned against responsible government, this "insane principle of Colonial Government," this "Chartism of the Colonies," as the *Gazette* called it. On the other hand, François Xavier Garneau, who had been moved by Durham's personal graciousness to write an ode to him that concluded by declaring that "Canada would be the last defender of old England on this great continent," was now moved by Durham's blunt condemnation of his people's qualities to start work on the romantic, epic history that remains the best-loved, central strand in the tradition behind their nationalism.

The *Canadiens* generally, beaten down, sullen, and seeing no hope, abandoned themselves to an inert despair. Lord John Russell sent out as governor Mr. Poulett Thomson, late of the Baltic timber merchants and the Board of Trade, soon to be first Baron Sydenham of Sydenham in Kent and Toronto in Canada, with orders to unite the Canadas and "to refuse any explanation which may be construed to imply an acquiescence in the petitions and addresses" upon the subject of responsible government.

CHAPTER XVI

Upper Canada (1791-1841)

The most important factor in the formation of the Upper Canadian community was that the colony penetrated southward so deeply into the United States that it lay across some of the principal continental migration routes from the coastal slope to the interior. In a formal sense, Upper Canada was bounded by the Ottawa River, the Great Lakes, and the height of land to the north of them, but practically it amounted to the fertile lands south of a line drawn westward up the Ottawa Valley from Montreal to Georgian Bay. The main lines of travel and transportation, of course, were along the water margins.

🍁 A FOCUS OF CONTINENTAL MIGRATIONS

The triangle of southern Upper Canada (about 24,000 square miles) had its long base open to the United States. Migrants from New England and New York and, to some extent, from New Jersey and Pennsylvania, found themselves considering the relative attractions of British and American lands because so many natural travel routes led to that choice—the Hudson-Champlain-Richelieu gap; the Hudson-Mohawk avenue either to Lake Ontario or across New York State to the Niagara River; and the curling courses of the Delaware and Susquehanna rivers to points not far from the basin of the Great Lakes. Upper Canada's land system, or lack of it, was nothing to cheer about, but New England's good lands were exhausted, upper New York was largely in the hands of great land speculators, upper Pennsylvania was rough uplands, and upper Ohio was swampy and malarial. Finally, relations with the Indians were much better on the British than on the American side of the boundary.

The lands were relatively cheap and attractive, for the most part plains and gently rolling hills with soils of clay or sandy loam. Not only did they yield some of the largest white pine in eastern North America, but most of them were "strong" enough to nourish magnificent hard-woods. Numerous streams came down out of the rough Laurentian Shield across the deeper soils to the Ottawa or the Lakes, so that timber could be floated down and mills kept busy. The booming textile industry in Great Britain provided such a market for potash and pearl-ash that a pioneer could girdle the trees, cut and burn them after drying, leach out the coveted chemicals from the ashes, and have a "cash crop" before he had done much more than plant some potatoes and grain among the stumps. These he would later grub out to serve as spiky fencing or to be burned for more potash.

Montreal reached out directly and through agents (Kingston was Montreal's outpost on the Lakes) to bind this combination of rough exploitation and cheap water transportation to the outside world. The colonists exported wheat, flour, peas, provisions, lumber, and potash in order to pay for tools, firearms, tea, woolen cloth, and printed cottons. The ease with which they could make their own whisky (it sold for ten or fifteen cents a quart) soon reduced their dependence on West Indian rum.

Patterns of settlement.—The earliest nodes of settlement had been around the "western posts," that is, Detroit, Niagara, the Toronto harbor and portage to Georgian Bay, and Kingston at the eastern end of Lake Ontario. During and after the American Revolution these points continued to attract settlers and served as refuges, particularly for military loyalists of the ranger type and persons connected with the fur and Indian trades. In 1785 there were some 6800 loyalists in the old province of Quebec and perhaps 4000 of these, chiefly New York and New England frontiersmen, were ushered into new townships be-tween Lake St. Francis on the St. Lawrence and the Bay of Quinte on Lake Ontario.

From these centers, and fed by a constant influx from the United States and after 1815 from Great Britain, settlement expanded with great rapidity. The movement of Quakers and German Mennonites and Dunkers from Pennsylvania, for instance, antedated considerably the similar but larger exodus to Indiana. From the beginning there was a certain amount of migration across Upper Canada from the eastern United States to the American Middle West; the War of 1812 naturally produced some emigration; and about the time of the Upper Canadian Rebellion and critical relations with the United States, 1837–42, move-ment to the Middle West began which was to be characteristic for at least two generations, largely because the impassable Laurentian Shield lay between Upper Canada and the plains that began in the Manitoba Basin.

John Graves Simcoe, the first lieutenant governor, who was indefatigable in advertising for settlers and facilitating their establishment, built two useful roads—Yonge Street from York to Lake Simcoe and Dundas Street from the western end of Lake Ontario to Lake St. Clair. Lord Selkirk achieved a little at Baldoon, near Lake St. Clair, between his Prince Edward Island and his Manitoba enterprises. An eccentric, unbending, Anglo-Irish Tory, Colonel Thomas Talbot, created a vigorous duchy for himself north of Lake Erie after 1803 by his careful planning, great influence with authority, and boundless energy.

The anti-Americanism that expanded with the War of 1812 made it difficult for Americans to secure land, but they continued to move in for another twenty years or so because they were greatly in demand as the best possible pioneers. After 1815, assisted emigration from Great Britain, while generally regarded as a failure, did bring in a good many distressed English, Scottish, and Irish migrants. Since few of them had the skills requisite for frontier existence, they tended to cling to the urban centers or hire themselves out on public works or under practiced pioneers until they had acquired competence. The United States, with more and larger urban centers and public works, attracted a great many of them soon after their arrival.

There was an extraordinary fluidity of population and disregard of political boundaries in eastern North America, partly because, as one group of Scots reported, "It was a' America tae us," and partly because it took some time for a European to find his niche or for a North American to settle down. Indeed some of the latter never did, but moved this way and that all their lives in search of greener pastures farther on.

Nationalism, of the sort that has become so deep-rooted and insistent since about 1870, did not affect much of the population in spite of the American Revolution and the War of 1812. Family connections were frequently international. As a New Yorker observed in 1831, when war talk was in the air: "Well, sir, I guess if we don't fight for a year or two we won't fight at all, for we are marrying so fast, sir, that a man won't be sure but he may shoot his father or brother-in-law."

Thanks to the original loyalist townships and some early quasi-military townships east of the Bay of Quinte, the eastern half of Upper Canada tended to be regarded as "British" and "Tory," in spite of much American immigration. Since the southwest lay between New York and Michigan, with the Erie Canal leading up to it after 1825, it tended to be regarded as "American" and "Radical," in spite of the truculent Colonel Talbot and provocative gangs of Orangemen.

Yet certainly, once the War of 1812 was over, the Canadians from about midway on Lake Ontario westward belonged to a distinct segment of North American society, as their speech attests to this day. As early as 1824, E. A. Talbot observed after five years' residence: "It is very remarkable, that . . . there should be so little difference in their manners, customs, and habits of life. Germans, Hollanders, French, English, Scotch, and Irish, after a few years' residence in Canada, forget their national customs and peculiarities, and become, in almost every particular, entirely assimilated to the people of America."

The founding of the Canada Company in 1826 can be taken as a kind of milestone. Supported by British capital and well managed, it enjoyed a modest financial success in settling "the Huron Tract" and some smaller holdings, chiefly between Lake Ontario and Lake Huron. Many accomplished pioneers moved into these good lands, development of which was accelerated by roads, supply depots, and so on. Successful pioneers served as magnets for relatives and friends in Europe and the United States. Since a considerable number of the incoming Europeans could afford steerage passage on the swift and dependable New York packets instead of on the ill-found lumber ships, and settlers' effects could pass through the United States in bond, the company maintained agents in New York and Detroit who managed water-passage from the Atlantic to Lake Huron.

Needless to say, American land-agents were busy too, indeed it was held during the thirties that two-thirds of even the St. Lawrence entrants ended up in the United States.

One unique element in the population resulted from the attraction of freedom on British soil for American Negroes. Quite soon after emancipation was provided for in Upper Canada (1793), they and their white supporters began to make small settlements along Lake Erie and the Thames River which served as asylums for fugitives. After 1833 no Negro could be extradited to the United States except for violent crime. This was reflected in the refrain of a Negro song:

> Farewell, old master,
> Don't come after me.
> I'm on my way to Canada
> Where colored men are free.

The total rose to perhaps forty or fifty thousand by 1861, but fell to less than twenty thousand after the Civil War.

The growth of population.—The early population estimates were rather wild guesses or the propaganda of settlement, but there seem to have been about 20,000 inhabitants in 1792, 26,000 two years later, and 60,000 in 1800. A calculation from assessment rolls in 1811 yielded 77,000. In spite of the emigration and dislocation inseparable from the War of 1812, the colony continued to grow and the total seems to have risen above 90,000 by 1815. When regular censuses began in 1824, the first total was 150,066. Growth was respectable rather than spectacular during a grand agitation over citizenship and land tenure in the twenties, but a great spurt took place from 213,156 in 1830 to 397,489 in 1837. Political and economic disturbances, involving "truly alarming & astonishing" emigration through Buffalo and Detroit, then slowed growth for two years, but the 1840 total was 432,159. It was this irresistible expansion during a single generation that brought Upper Canada to within hailing distance of Lower Canada's 650,000 people and assured Durham and others that, if the colonies were combined in one, Canadians would soon outnumber *Canadiens* and rapidly increase the advantage.

🍁 THE AGRICULTURAL FRONTIER

In lumbering and farming, Upper Canada presented an almost classic example of frontier society in the interior of North America. Lumbering soon pulled away from the farmlands except for the crude marginal production of hay, oats, potatoes, and a few hogs that was to cling to the fringe of forest operations until the internal combustion engine supplanted the horse. The lumbermen, therefore, were outside ordinary society, as were the unskilled workers who sought the shelter of the towns.

There was little manufacture before 1841 in spite of the constant immigration of "millers and mechanics" from the United States and "artisans" from Great Britain. Sawmilling, of course, was important, but industrial operations were small in iron smelting and foundry, gypsum extraction and processing, tanning and leatherworking, wagon and carriage manufacture, glassmaking, distilling, and brewing. Field & Cahoon's Colbourne Furnaces near the Detroit River were notable for employing sixty to seventy men. Two Americans, Simeon Morrell and E. W. Hyman, gave London an industrial complexion by their progressive methods in tanning and bootmaking, as did the Gurneys of New York in Hamilton by their stove works.

For the most part, the Upper Canadians were farmers struggling with the resources and forces of nature on the one hand, and with the merchants, bankers, and politicians on the other. Capable of a high degree of self-sufficiency themselves, they regarded those possessors of power as parasites and Montreal's powers as a still higher parasitism. Once agriculture stopped merely hugging the shores of the Lakes, the farmers wanted roads and bridges. They could see the desirability of canals, but less immediately. The Welland was no more useful than the

Erie for the western half of the colony; the Rideau was easily outdone by the Oswego branch of the Erie. Canalization of the St. Lawrence made a good deal of sense, but of the hundred miles of river southwest from Montreal about sixty demanded circumvention, a task so expensive that Upper Canada could not finance it. Private capital had been thoroughly frightened off during the metamorphosis of the Welland Canal from private failure to public enterprise.

Yet agriculture was rewarding and rural life was bountiful. The temperate, changeable climate meant good precipitation and long growing seasons. The Lakes moderated the climate of their region all year round so that even during the dull and humid winters temperatures below zero were rare and brief except up the Ottawa Valley where continental forces were felt. January in Ottawa (originally Bytown) was closely comparable with January in Moscow. The summers were hot and sunny.

Mixed farming flourished for generations before specialization developed in some areas. All the cereals were successful and fine forage and root crops encouraged dairying and stock raising. Along the Lakes and in the Niagara Peninsula fruits, tobacco, and vegetables gradually increased from being parts of farm production to become exclusive ends in themselves for the growing urban markets. Particularly fine hard, or winter, apples and pears were grown as successfully as soft and small fruits and vegetables. Ontario, Upper Canada's successor of today, with little larger arable area than in 1840, remains Canada's richest agricultural province.

A HOTBED OF CONFLICTS

S. D. Clark, after studying this society, detected a change in its character after the War of 1812. Before it, a self-sufficient "pioneer economy . . . inherited the simple, primary social institutions of the American frontier." Loyalist and other Americans and clannish Highland Scots cohered in natural groups of family and neighborhood, often around Methodist, Quaker, Moravian, Roman Catholic, and Presbyterian spiritual leaders.

Change came between 1812 and 1820 with the growth of towns, administration, the timber trade, and assisted immigration. The price system separated those who had capital from those who had not. More elaborate government created hierarchies in politics, the military forces, and religion, particularly in relation to efforts to make the Church of England a privileged, established church. Town and country drew apart. The large labor force of the lumber industry formed a self-conscious separate group that troubled the townsmen during its off-seasons. Problems of social welfare which rural societies were spared or solved relatively easily were so conspicuous and urgent in the towns that they required the organization of poor relief and work houses, the erection of jails, churches and parsonages, and the establishment of education along both upper-class and commercial lines. Disease and mental disturbances demanded hospitals.

The new immigrants from Europe were a mixed lot and created endless problems. They lacked the frontier skills that were necessary for survival there. They cherished for years the social distinction between those who paid their own steerage fare ("Passengers") and those who had it paid for them ("Emmy Grants"). Their very family structure and their habits of looking outside it for satisfactions often failed them in frontier conditions, producing nervous breakdowns among the women on isolated farms and drunkenness among the men.

Much has been made of the horrors of the Atlantic passage in the lumberships and even in the packets, but the highest social costs had usually to be paid at the immigrants' destinations, and Upper Canada had special burdens to bear in disbanded soldiers and sailors, exported ne'er-do-wells and paupers, and, heaviest of all, the flood of distressed fugitives from the Irish famine. "The pioneer began unable to afford the decencies of life; he often ended by losing an appreciation of their worth." One of the commonest manifestations of this indifference was in education. "The influence of the frontier upon a population unequipped to deal with its demands tended to a general lowering rather than a raising of standards, and this tendency became more pronounced when standards became increasingly diversified."

In short, Upper Canada was a hotbed of social, economic, and political conflicts from 1812 to 1841 with a host of lines drawn across local communities, rural and urban, a basic clash between town and country, and a sense of frustration by such remote powers as the merchants of Montreal, the shrewd managers of the United States, the British government, and the *Canadiens*. All of these conflicts were poured into the hopper of political life, for politics and evangelical religion gave existence most of its warmth and color beyond the "bees" or neighborhood gatherings for clearing, mowing, sugar making, barn-raising, apple-paring, wool-picking, or quilting. Every appeal to passion was made during the political contests, and violence, which ranged from intimidation by superior numbers to kidnaping, assault, and even murder, was systematically organized, often in such group forms as Irish Roman Catholic navvies on the one side and their avowed opponents, militant Protestant Orangemen, on the other.

Social and cultural clashes.—The acknowledged social pinnacle was membership in the colonial oligarchy, civil or military, coupled with membership in the Church of England or, less desirably, in the Church of Scotland. Within the privileged group, of course, there were varieties of status. The remainder of the population either damned the whole structure, root and branch, or tried to find places in it.

The Constitutional Act of 1791 had endowed the Church of England by adding in its behalf to all grants of land an amount equal to one-seventh of similar quality and situation. Not until forty years later were the proceeds from that endowment shared, moderately equitably, first with the Roman Catholics, and then with the Presbyterians and Methodists. All over the colony lay blocks of unimproved lands, the Clergy Reserves, waiting for disposal until the improvement of other lands had built up their value. By an order in council, the Crown set aside for itself (i.e. the colonial executive) Crown Reserves in the same proportion. Church and State formed a powerful, privileged alliance.

The oligarchs liked to justify their power by simplifying the colony's issues of disagreement into "loyalists" versus "Americans," and "gentlemen" versus "boors." It was true that the egalitarianism that sat naturally and well on native or acclimated North Americans often went to the heads of emancipated European immigrants and made them act foolishly. At the same time, as Susanna Moodie observed about 1850: "The native-born Canadian regarded with a jealous feeling men of talent and respectability who emigrated from the mother country, as most offices of consequence and emolument were given to such persons."

Basically, however, the hopes entertained in 1791 of creating an Upper Canadian aristocracy could not be fulfilled, but degenerated into land speculation. Where there was no stable servant class, and most men, to Simcoe's disgust, "kept but one table," the rural "gentry" were not so much the largest landowners as the most capable land managers, irrespective of birth and origin. The outcome was that the oligarchy of Church and State drew its Canadian recruits from wealthy and acquiescent townsmen, and thus intensified scorn and neglect of the rural population, along with the mass of the town dwellers. Since "the aristocracy" provided little or no moral or cultural leadership for "the people," and the latter were too busy to do much for themselves, time had to pass in confusion and frustration before a purposeful democracy could unseat its overlords, assume responsibility, and try out its own ideas.

Churches and sects.—"It seems to me," wrote J. J. Bigsby, an English observer, in 1850, "that the Episcopal clergy are taken from too high a class for colonial service. . . . Their early nurture has been too nice, and their education too academic." Whatever the causes, the

Anglican Church, lacking enough adaptable clergy, failed to hold even its own adherents among the rural newcomers. The Presbyterians did somewhat better because of their clannishness and congregational discipline, but their theology demanded highly trained clergy, and the power of congregations to call and dismiss their pastors discouraged some Scots or Ulstermen who might otherwise have come out to risk missionary work in Canada.

The strictness of both the established churches in theology and in dispensing the sacraments was ill-calculated to fulfill the needs of frontiersmen, but, instead of grappling with the problem, those churches gave themselves up to condemnation of the antinomian evangelists who did. The Roman Catholics—French in the west, Scottish in the east, and Irish everywhere—were nurtured by the remarkable Father Alexander Macdonell, who became Bishop of Kingston in 1826. By 1840, after a half-century of effort, the leading denominations claimed 77 per cent of the population in the following totals: Anglicans, 96,014; Presbyterians, 88,643; Methodists, 73,933; Roman Catholics, 49,601; Baptists, 19,021.

The religious need and hunger of the colony called for evangelism, and not only Methodists and Baptists, but small sects such as the Davidites and the Millerites, responded. The Methodist apparatus of lay leaders, itinerant preachers, and conferences that assigned clergy was especially successful. Methodism had serious internal problems, most notably intense zeal accompanied by routine rousing of emotions in some of its evangelism, and struggles for dominance between the British Wesleyans and the American Episcopal Methodists. Yet it proved to be the most appropriate church for frontier conditions and about 1840 may be said to have become Canadian rather than American or British.

Gradually, however, just as in Britain and the United States, it produced an organizational machine that was based upon the democratic aspirations of the colony. Yet the very ability of Egerton Ryerson, the leader of the Methodists, to "deliver the Methodist vote" had its effects upon him and upon substantial elements in his church which were stressing respectability and conservatism. The Baptists, through their distrust of overriding organization, continued to be a free church whose congregations manifested a diversity of views. And where the organized churches were inert, evangelical sects rushed into the vacuum.

Education.—Gross inadequacies and inequalities in education before the mid-century can be attributed partly to adverse elements in frontier society but quite largely to the contradiction between the conservative ideals of the oligarchy and the needs of the society at large. The testimony of observers is uniformly damning. Robert Gourlay in 1822 explained why "education was neglected . . . until the neglect became habitual," but felt that the wealthier class was now determined to provide it. E. A. Talbot in 1824 declared: "The inestimable advantages resulting from a well-educated and enlightened population, cannot be experienced in Canada for many years to come." Anna Jameson in 1838 told of passing a few wayside schools in her travels, but "of these, several were shut up for want of schoolmasters; and who that could earn a subsistence in any other way, would be a schoolmaster in the wilds of Upper Canada?" In 1844, "a Four Years' Resident" reported: "Education, notwithstanding legislative efforts which have existed from an early period in the settlement of Western Canada to the present time, continues still in a very unsatisfactory state."

Patrick Shirreff in 1835 said: "I find much less refinement than in the lower province or in the United States," and R. H. Bonnycastle in 1841 found that what he called "the family compact" or "the aristocracy of Little York [Toronto]" resisted rather than forwarded efforts to raise the cultural level of the capital. "The public amusements in Toronto are not of a nature to attract much attention."

In 1838, "Out of a population of 450,000 [in Upper Canada] . . . there were only about 300 children in the 13 district grammar schools [begun in 1807], and only 24,000 in the 800 common schools [begun in 1816]; and in 1844 only 55 per cent of the children of school age attended school." Durham was distressed: "Nor can even wealthy landowners prevent their children from growing up ignorant and boorish."

Higher education was originally designed to be exclusively for Anglicans. John Strachan, a former Presbyterian whose dynamic energies raised him to be Bishop of Toronto, secured a Royal Charter in 1827 for an Anglican King's College, but, since its exclusive character proved too much to be swallowed, it became a political football. Teaching in it did not begin until 1843, it was secularized in 1849, and in 1853 became University College in the University of Toronto (1850). Strachan had been so incensed in 1849 that he put his amazing energies into founding a new Anglican University of Trinity College in Toronto in 1851. By 1841 the Methodists had a charter for Victoria College at Cobourg and the Presbyterians another for Queen's University at Kingston.

Probably the best educational institution in the colony before 1841 was the generously endowed preparatory school known as Upper Canada College, opened in 1830 at Toronto with an Anglican staff drawn largely from Oxford and Cambridge. It was small, self-consciously aristocratic, and a recognized avenue to preferment. Egerton Ryerson, as second Superintendent of Education, 1844–76, was to be the architect and creator of a general system of education. It took thirty years to complete universal schools, a normal and model school for teachers and to effect the general use of the Irish public school textbooks, which supplanted the earlier hodgepodge of American and British books.

Economic clashes.—For the most part the economic issues between the oligarchy and the people were of the classical sort—abuse of privilege on one side, and rather unconstructive resentment on the other. Land granting and speculation symbolized it neatly. Durham's assistants reported that although practically all the available lands had been granted by 1838, "a very small proportion, perhaps less than a tenth, of the land thus granted has been even occupied by settlers, much less reclaimed and cultivated." The Clergy and Crown Reserves worsened the situation. British parliamentary investigators in 1828 declared that they "retard more than any other circumstance, the improvement of the colony, lying as they do in detached portions of each township, and intervening between the occupations of actual settlers, who have no means of cutting roads through the woods and morasses which thus separate them from their neighbors."

As elsewhere, the alliance between political and financial power seemed aimed against the producers. Profits for capital seemed unwarrantably high, and the merchants owned the ships and boats, the mills, the distilleries, and the tanyards. Banking was a monopoly of the Bank of Upper Canada; twelve of its original fifteen directors were in public office. The churchman, Strachan, was a director of the Bank and pamphleteered for the Welland Canal.

The canal was not only indebted to the Bank, but depended on the government for at least a quarter of its support—in the form of taxation that most of the farmers would have preferred to use to improve their roads and bridges. "Is all to be subservient to this great Moloch, and everything bow to it?" In 1835, William Lyon Mackenzie, a radical leader, moved to request the king to negotiate for free passage of Upper Canadian exports and imports through the United States (via the Erie Canal at Buffalo and Oswego)—"We had a right to go to Oswego with our produce; and buy our Tea wherever we could buy it best." Upper Canada, he argued, had always been a free trade area, raising its revenue from a land tax. As for the Bank, no elected representative of the people had ever been chosen for its board—"In the hands of our irresponsible governing faction, it becomes a political curse of the first magnitude —a prostituted instrument of corruption, of all others the most powerful and insidious."

One economic problem peculiar to Upper Canada was its dependence on Lower Canada for an ocean port of entry and departure. Although the Montreal merchants advocated union of the Canadas as the solution, not all the Upper Canadians saw matters in the same light. J. B. Robinson commented: "I gather that some of those in U. Canada resident near Montreal, or rather nearer to it than the seat of Government in Upper Canada are in favour of the Union, while those in York and above are with very few exceptions against it." It was all very well to propose to meet the situation by canals on the St. Lawrence, but Upper Canada's credit was strained as early as 1833. About that time there was a formidable, but unsuccessful, attempt to secure the annexation of Montreal to Upper Canada. Only a broader base for credit and a more productive system of taxation could enable Upper Canada to realize its potentialities.

🍁 THE POLITICAL FORUM

Much has been made, then and since, of the political iniquities of Upper Canada, but it seems more sensible to think in terms of immaturity. The region had to be governed somehow, even if Great Britain had little interest in an inland colony. Upper Canada was given the conventional structure of government, and a mercantile and financial group shared the seats of power with a moderately capable group of officeholders.

Aileen Dunham's summary is apt: "Now the infant settlement of Upper Canada lying adjacent to the United States, and yet a British province, peopled half from Great Britain, half from the United States, formed a battle-ground on which were fought out the conflicting ideals of religion, education and government of the two states." In short, it required about fifty years for the Upper Canadians to expose the inadequacy of the old colonial system and a far more difficult task, produce their own blend from new British and American ideas. Canadianism, not Americanism or Britonism, had to emerge, mature, and make itself felt.

A roll call of the political agitators in Upper Canada shows that they were more British than American, even if the loyalist strain is regarded as American. The most radical Assembly, that of 1829, contained four Irishmen, six Scots, seven Englishmen, thirteen Canadians, three men born in other British colonies, and fifteen Americans. The British influence in Upper Canadian reform was due partly to the many strains of radicalism brought in by English, Scottish, and Irish emigrants, partly to the resentment felt by able British immigrants who were cold-shouldered by the entrenched oligarchy, and partly to the inexpediency of "Americanism." As everyone recognized, however, the great criterion was the United States, and the great motive force was the passionate desire to bring Upper Canada to within hailing distance of the lively communities just across the border. T. R. Preston, for instance, in 1840 summarized his three years' residence in Canada, an American traverse, and return, as "supposing that you have plunged unconsciously from a stagnant pool into a vivifying stream and tumbled from the latter back into a miry slough."

Upper Canadian reform ideas were democratic and North American during a time (until 1867) when the governing class in Great Britain was antidemocratic. The fortunate outcome of this conflict was that the Canadians found British constitutional *forms* for contradictory North American *functions*.

The tedious annals of unending contest between oligarchy in the legislative and executive councils and democracy in the Assembly were galvanized by a few strong personalities on both sides. John Strachan, as priest, archdeacon, and bishop, was indefatigable, imperious, and obdurate throughout the contest. John Beverly Robinson, the orphaned son of a Virginian loyalist who became Attorney General during the War of 1812 before he had been called to the Bar, and Chief Justice in 1829 at the age of 38, was an able, benevolent, but arrogant man who held the masses in contempt politically and exercised every ounce of available power and influence without compunction. Of the lieutenant governors after Simcoe, Sir Peregrine Maitland (1818–28) was a prejudiced Tory guardsman of limited intellect and no flexibility or tolerance whose tyrannical behavior almost provoked rebellion in 1828; Sir John Colborne (1828–36) was much abler and a good administrator who obeyed British orders the more easily because his imagination did not greatly transcend them; and Sir Francis Bond Head (1836–37) was a dangerous megalomaniac whose demonstrated energy and abilities were accompanied by very bad judgment.

On the radical side, sheer frustration destroyed most of the agitators or induced their surrender. Of three very active Irish critics before 1815, Judge Robert Thorpe was dismissed after two years of shrewd and comprehensive attacks; William Weekes was killed in a duel; and Joseph Willcocks, sheriff of York County, came a cropper when he tried to woo the heiress sister of Peter Russell, a wealthy member of the inner circle. A little later he was shot while a member of the American forces in the War of 1812. C. B. Wyatt, the Surveyor General, and J. M. Jackson, Thorpe's associate, were efficiently cold-shouldered by the oligarchy as soon as their exploitation of agrarian discontents became troublesome. When Robert Gourlay, a brilliant, well-educated, but utterly indiscreet and frequently unstable Scot, conducted a remarkable two-year campaign (1817–19) against the conditions of land settlement, employing questionnaires and the fashionable "statistical" methods of inquiry and report, the terrified official clique railroaded him out of the colony with a callous and scandalous disregard for legality.

Barnabas Bidwell, a Massachusetts politician and officeholder who had fled to Canada about 1810 under charges of speculation and forgery and who was elected as a reformer in 1821, was vindictively expelled from the Assembly in 1822. When his American-born son, Marshall Spring Bidwell, was elected in his place, he too was at first expelled as an alien, only to be returned in 1824 when the position and rights of American-born settlers were regularized. He then became the moderate, capable leader of the reformers. In a brief but spectacular nine months during 1827–28, a noted English equity lawyer, J. W. Willis, who had been sent out by the British government as puisne judge, fell foul of J. B. Robinson and the oligarchy in a contest to succeed the Chief Justice (his titled wife challenged the social primacy of Lieutenant Governor Maitland's wife), and was dismissed by Maitland for an attack on the Court of King's Bench as then constituted.

Meanwhile, William Lyon Mackenzie, a redheaded, melodramatic Scottish radical who had shifted from shopkeeping to journalism in 1824, had pushed himself forward as an irrepressible agitator, attacking every evil he could find with an amazing armory of provocativeness and little or no attention to the relative magnitude of the issues. While Bidwell quietly marshaled his reformers in and out of the Assembly, while Egerton Ryerson (the son of a loyalist American) focused his attacks on ecclesiastical abuses and the Clergy Reserves, Mackenzie let himself go in all directions. It was fitting that he and Sir Francis Bond Head should be the final adversaries in 1837, and a great pity that Bidwell, to whom the Colonial Secretary urged Head to offer a judgeship, was instead perversely driven by Head into voluntary exile for the rest of his life. Ryerson changed sides in 1832–33 when an understanding with the British Wesleyans opened the way for state support of the Canadian Methodists.

The idea of responsible government.—Meanwhile the sober, informed discussion that produced the ultimate solution of the political problem had been centering in the York home of Dr. W. W. Baldwin, a wealthy Irishman from Cork who had come to Canada at the end of the eighteenth century. The discussion had all been very Whiggish, deliberate, and even obscure, but at least as early as 1828 it had arrived at the principle of introducing the Cabinet type of executive in the colony, that is, responsible government. This was still rather cumbrously phrased, but it should be remembered that the Cabinet system in Britain was as yet vague because untested by the strains of the reform agitation there, and that in the United States Andrew Jackson's triumph had been accompanied by frightening excesses. The Baldwin group had also been sufficiently thorough to arrive at the corollary dogma that colonial autonomy through Cabinet government could operate only if matters of imperial concern were reserved to the British Parliament.

The group included, at one time or another, the Bidwells; John Galt (Scottish author and founder of the Canada Company); three influential, if changeable, radical editors (H. C. Thomson, Thomas Dalton, Francis Collins); John Rolph, an English doctor who became an able, though enigmatic, politician; and, during his brief Canadian career, Judge Willis. By 1830, Dr. Baldwin's son Robert had become the chosen vessel to bear the sacred principle of responsible government, an unrevolutionary task which he began in the Assembly of that year and sustained with singular uncompromising devotion.

The Upper Canadian explosion.—The thirties were distinctly wild in Upper Canada. Control of £33,840 in annual customs duties was surrendered to the Assembly in 1831 in return for a guaranteed civil list of £6500, but the Executive retained £28,230 in casual and territorial revenues. Chief Justice Robinson obeyed British orders by resigning from the Legislative Council, but remained in the Executive Council. In a society well inflamed over freedom of the press, Mackenzie, like John Wilkes, was five (or more) times expelled from the Assembly after legitimate elections. The newly incorporated city of Toronto (York) followed the Wilkes precedent by choosing Mackenzie as its first mayor.

When the reformers won the election of 1834, Mackenzie prepared his Seventh Report on Grievances, a worthy companion to Papineau's Ninety-two Resolutions. Like Papineau, he had visited England (in 1833), but, also like him, what positive reform proposals he made amounted to little more than general adoption of the American "elective principle." It has proved futile to seek a systematic political philosophy in Mackenzie.

On the eve of retirement in 1836, Sir John Colborne provided a final bombshell by yielding to his own religious inclinations, Lord Goderich's private persuasions, and the pressure of Strachan and the Executive

Council by endowing no less than fifty-seven Anglican parishes and rectories with over 27,000 acres of Clergy Reserves in lieu of the support hitherto received from the Society for the Propagation of the Gospel. All the classical colonial issues, plus those peculiar to Upper Canada, were now boiling in the political pot. In 1837, crop failure, a world-wide financial panic, and depression were added to the brew.

So it went, but the actual goads to rebellion came from Colborne's successor, Sir Francis Bond Head. This hitherto obscure person had the self-confidence of a demigod, towards the British and Upper Canadian governments as well as towards everyone else, and little or no ballast to steady him. After he went to the country in his own behalf and won the election of 1836 (largely because Ryerson and the Methodists abandoned the reform cause), there was no holding him. The moderate reformers and the voters had fallen away from Mackenzie, just as they had from Papineau.

Head believed that he must govern personally and lead the monarchists against the republicans. He had thoroughly confused the issues by taking Robert Baldwin, Dr. Rolph, and J. H. Dunn into the Executive Council. There Baldwin converted three Tory colleagues to his view of responsible government, only to have Head take up their resignations as the alternative to accepting it. Head met the Panic of 1837 by ordering the banks to pay in specie, that is, call in their loans, and he countered the unprecedented refusal of the Assembly to vote supplies by stopping all government payments. Nothing could have been better calculated to deepen prevailing distress. His fantastic egocentricity and imperviousness to any man's advice, even to orders from the British government, filled 1836 and 1837 with actions that made his recall inevitable.

But Mackenzie's defeat in the 1836 election, coupled with his conviction that government had reached an impasse of disaster in both Canadas, drove him also into political insanity. Head's gleeful revelation of the restrictive instructions issued by the British government seemed explicitly corroborated by Lord John Russell's Ten Resolutions of March, 1837, denying responsible government. Greatly excited by the activities of the *Canadien* radicals, Mackenzie persuaded himself that Upper Canadians too had entered on what he called "this bold, dangerous but delightful course" to revolution and independence.

In July and August, 1837, he organized and issued declarations on the American model of sixty years earlier, and on December 7, a pitiful little band of his followers was attacked and dispersed by a large volunteer force just north of Toronto. Mackenzie had no greater gifts than Papineau as a leader of rebellion and had many fewer followers. Dr. Charles Duncombe's loyal attempt to rouse the western part of the colony to aid him failed because of Mackenzie's poor planning. These two and most of the other leaders of impotent distress in Upper Canada fled to the United States.

The protest they personified so feebly and pathetically was widespread and deep, but too immature to find assured voice either in a solid party program or in truly substantial revolt. Indeed there is great reason to agree with Lord Durham's view that the flamboyant antics of Head and Mackenzie concealed a systematic counterrevolution somewhat like the cumulative provocations that were organized by the Lower Canadian oligarchy.

It certainly appeared too much as if the rebellion had been purposely invited by the government, and the unfortunate men who took part in it deliberately drawn into a trap by those who subsequently inflicted so severe a punishment on them for their error. It seemed, too, as if the dominant party made use of the occasion afforded it by the real guilt of a few desperate and imprudent men, in order to persecute or disable the whole body of their political opponents.

In Upper Canada, as in Lower Canada, the aftermath of the rebellion was a disgraceful exhibition of the kind of revenge that follows victory in primitive politics. In the western part of the colony, for instance, where there had been no actual conflict, Colonel Allan MacNab distinguished himself by employing bands of armed Indians in war paint to round up reputed rebels and add terror to a swashbuckling campaign of arrests, looting, and so on, that singled out, rather than spared, the peaceful Quakers. Fortunately, Sir George Arthur, Head's successor, managed to exercise mercy in various quiet ways. Only two men, the American-born Samuel Lount and the Canadian-born Peter Matthews, were hanged. Others had their death sentences reprieved, but the victory of reaction drove scores of "rebels" into exile in the United States (twelve were transported to Australia) and persuaded thousands of other persons to emigrate in despair.

The American menace.—Unquestionably the triumph of reaction in Upper Canada was greatly facilitated in 1838, 1839, and 1840 by the menace of American filibustering, which sprang up from economic depression and unemployment and found justification in the Canadian rebellions. As A. B. Corey has shown, Canadian-American relations were considerably disturbed from 1830 to 1842, and for three years they bordered on war, with thousands of men from Maine to Wisconsin organized in American secret societies and bent upon repeating the expansionist techniques that were working so well in Texas. Their organization extended even into the South and their conventions produced plans that were complete with proposed constitutions and invasion currency.

The list of half-forgotten border "incidents" is long and the scale of the activities astonishingly great. The Canadians started a series of raids and counterraids by seizing on the American side of the Niagara River the steamer "Caroline," which supplied a force that Mackenzie and others had gathered on Navy Island, and destroying it. One American force of about 1000 men attacked Prescott in November, 1838, and was defeated only after five days' fighting at Windmill Point. The situation involved not only quite large casualties, destruction of property, and defense expenditures, but years of anxious efforts of British, Canadian, and American authorities to curb the movement and prevent overt war. In many ways, the most valuable achievement of Ashburton and Webster in their treaty-making of 1842 was their stifling of this menace to British North America.

Durham, Thomson, and union.—Lord Durham and his report went down very badly with the conservative masters of Upper Canada and delighted the recently discomfited reformers. J. B. Robinson, making much of the fact that Durham had spent only five days in the colony, chiefly junketing at Toronto and Niagara Falls, marshaled his great powers in a skillful refutation of the report. The Baldwins happily contemplated their surprising conversion of an English peer to the backwoods' invention of responsible government. For the moment, however, constitutional principles were less relevant than political practice. An expiring Whig Government, through the action of the inflexible Lord John Russell, sent out Charles Poulett Thomson in October, 1839, as governor general, with instructions to secure reunion of the Canadas and to deny responsible government. In Lower Canada this could be done by *fiat,* since the constitution was suspended, but Upper Canada, reflecting agrarian fears of subjection to Montreal's commerce and finance, was reluctant to reunite.

Thomson proved to be a superb politician. Playing adroitly on the economic dislocations since 1837 and on prevailing uncertainties, he ignored party and painted a glowing future based upon British willingness to find the money for completion of the St. Lawrence canals and other public works. He even somehow led Baldwin to believe that responsible government would be conceded. It took him less than three weeks to carry both houses of the legislature for union on terms of equal representation for the two former colonies, a sufficient civil list, and a charge against the new united colony for the proportion of Upper Canadian debt that had been incurred on works of a general kind. Since the former Lower Canada would elect some English-speaking members, it was assumed that union meant subordination of the French.

Thomson revealed his zestful sense of accomplishment in a letter to a friend. "My ministers vote against me. So I govern through the opposition who are truly 'her majesty's.' " The British Parliament promptly passed the necessary legislation, Thomson was rewarded with the peerage of Sydenham and Toronto, and the Province of Canada came into existence on February 10, 1841.

CHAPTER XVII

The West (1821-66)

The union of the Hudson's Bay and North West companies in 1821 meant that, after two generations during which Montrealers, at least, had spoken of "the North West," Canadians and Americans alike reverted to the old term "The Hudson's Bay Company's Territory" or "Rupert's Land." The advantages of the Bay route had given it victory over the St. Lawrence, the Hudson, and the Mississippi, and the combined field force of Bay men and Montrealers was now master, if not quite monopolist, of the fur trade from the coast of Labrador to Russian Alaska and thence south to Spanish California.

Americans exploited the upper Mississippi and the Missouri valleys and the lands south of them to the Spanish border, but, except for isolated ventures, their competitive strength failed them beyond the Continental Divide, so that the immense basin of the Columbia and its tributaries (notably "the Snake River Country") and the similar basin of the Fraser yielded their furs to "the company." Even the maritime trade of the Pacific coast, which had drawn ships of all nations in search of the now-dwindling sea otter, began to be yielded more and more to the company's accumulated skills and unremitting enterprise. The first steamship on the Pacific was the "Beaver," a stout little craft, barely over a hundred feet long, which the company put into service in 1836. Although in other hands after 1874, she was still going strong when wrecked on the way out of Vancouver harbor in 1888.

🍁 MANAGEMENT OF THE INDIAN TRADE

Naturally no single, simple code of operating rules was applicable to so vast and so varied a territory. It took seven years, for instance, to get British goods to Fort Yukon and the Yukon furs they bought to the British market. In George Simpson, who became governor of the Northern Department (governor-in-chief in 1826) and managed the amalgamation of 1821, the company possessed an administrator of the first order. Until his death in 1860, he practically commanded the company, marshaling its energies and directing them, not only at the strategic level, but often at the tactical. He was an artist in managing men.

He and the twenty-four Chief Factors cultivated prestige. In those days, for instance, out in the wilderness a Chief Factor "dressed every day in a suit of black or dark blue, white shirt, collars to his ears, frock coat, velvet stock and straps to the bottom of his trousers. When he went out of doors he wore a black beaver hat worth forty shillings. When travelling in a canoe or boat, he was lifted in or out by the crew; he still wore his beaver hat, but it was protected by an oiled silk cover, and over his black frock he wore a long cloak made of Royal Stuart tartan lined with scarlet or dark blue bath coating. . . . Salutes were fired on his departure from the fort and on his return." Simpson himself made his remarkable travels in special express canoes or boats, accompanied by his personal servant and bagpiper, whose strange music pulsed and vibrated in the North American wilds while his master dined in special state. Simpson was a great note-taker and correspondent, with quite different methods for public and private records, so that we may learn today what he thought and what he said about the servants of the company and how some public reproofs were neutralized by private explanations.

Relations with the Indians, having become conventionalized under monopoly, were seldom troublesome. For one thing, since the inrush into their territories after 1760 the tribes had been very hard hit by the white man's epidemics, particularly by smallpox and venereal diseases, but also by milder diseases like measles against which they had no immunity. No one has demonstrated the proportions of these casualties, but they were very large, often wiping out whole bands or almost destroying certain tribes. The survivors became shrewd traders, particularly during the conflict between the company and the Nor'Westers. In 1821, like their predecessors in 1760, they had suddenly to accommodate themselves to having only one string to the bow of their trading position. Not least remarkable among Simpson's achievements was the fact that there was no equivalent to the Conspiracy of Pontiac after 1821.

His task was not made easier by the necessity for gradually restricting the supply of beaver because of the swiftly expanding vogue after 1810 of the silk hat, a Florentine invention of half a century earlier. The trade in every kind of fur had always been calculated in terms of tallies representing "one beaver." The tallies were retained, but beaver lost the pre-eminence it had enjoyed for over two centuries. The company's long record of relations with the Indians was practically unblemished by death or violence because of the mutual interests that were involved. The use of liquor, which had been abundant during the Montreal-Bay conflict, was immediately halved and progressively reduced until small amounts became a mere special inducement twice a year in competition with the American "whisky traders" of the Missouri, or to rouse lethargic salmon-fed Indians west of the Continental Divide to the business of fur gathering.

The Red River settlement.—Many of the white or partly white employees of the company had to accommodate themselves to the reduction of waste in its field operations. A few went over to the American side; a few retired to the Canadas or even to Great Britain; but most of them, with their Indian or half-breed wives and families, settled down in the lower valley of the Red River. "Valley" is a somewhat misleading term, for the Red and its tributaries were the writhing, slowly descending channels which drained a vast, treeless, fertile plain that had been the bottom of shallow Lake Agassiz in postglacial times. The extraordinary richness of the soils, combined with good precipitation, hot summers, and a growing season of from 160 to 170 days, destined it to become one of the world's great granaries, but its past and immediate role was to nourish huge herds of buffalo with its grasses.

Because of Lord Selkirk's activities, the Red River Settlement was distinct from the company until 1836, a landed nobleman's estate at the crossroads of the continent. To people and defend it, he had brought in Scots, *Canadiens,* and an ethnically mixed lot of Swiss mercenaries of the De Meuron regiment. An additional 165 Swiss (chiefly French-speaking) were introduced in 1821, an unpromising lot which did, however, provide wives for some of the De Meurons. It is believed that reduction and redistribution of the field force of the Indian trade after 1821 in effect doubled the population, chiefly with half-breeds, the *Bois brulés.* At any rate, there were over 2000 settlers in 1824, the only society of European stock that had been brought into the continent mainly by its northern entry.

Simpson characterized them neatly. "The Meurons and Swiss . . . are wretched settlers." The Scots "are steady and well-disposed, and consider Red River as much their home as the land of their nativity formerly was," but they grumbled, talked "nothing but Gaelic," did not mix with the other settlers, and were "honest in their dealings with all, except the Company and executors." "The Company's old Canadian servants are the least troublesome and most attached to us; either in starvation or in plenty we can do anything with them." "The freemen and half-breed population is now growing very formidable in point of numbers and lives entirely by the chase [of buffalo] . . . unless early means are taken to bring them round to industrious habits . . . I do most seriously apprehend that they will in due time be the destruction of the colony. They never inter-marry with the whites, but on the contrary all the best looking women among them are picked up by the whites, and this produces everlasting jealousies."

This strangely assorted community was subjected to great strains between 1818 and 1826 which winnowed out the misfits. Grasshoppers darkened the skies and completely devoured the crops in 1818 and 1819. In 1820 they destroyed part of the crops before disappearing again for decades. In 1826, as at long intervals since (for instance, 1950), the Red River could not rid itself of the spring freshets fast enough, and a twenty-two-day rise (and slower fall) inundated the colony, washing away everything that would float. This, following a winter of dreadful snowstorms, scarce buffalo, starvation, and other disasters, was the last straw. "Hardly a house or building of any kind was left standing in the colony."

The De Meurons and Swiss moved out, 243 of them to "squat" near the American Fort Snelling (Minneapolis) on the upper Mississippi or to seek new homes farther east, and about 60 of them to Canada. It was a tough and self-reliant society that persisted and slowly increased. The population reported for 1831 was 2390; for 1835, 3649; for 1840, 4704; for 1849, 5391; and for 1856, 6691. By that time eastern North Americans had begun to enter, and the statistician's estimates for the area now Manitoba are 15,000 in 1867 and over 25,000 in 1871.

La Nation Métisse.—During the fight between the companies, the Montrealers had found it advantageous to cultivate strong group sentiments among the métis (half-breeds), sentiments which not only persisted but deepened. Indeed *La Nation Métisse* became so vigorous and problematical an entity in the history of Canada then and since that it has evoked much study, notably an immense investigation by Professor Marcel Giraud of the Collège de France. The mixblood community was more French than English because the Montreal traders, roaming the interior, had sorely needed Indian wives as interpreters, canoe-menders, snowshoe makers, seamstresses, food and fur handlers, and helpers in travel by canoe and portage; whereas "to the normal English trader or hand in the post by the Bay an Indian woman was rather a surreptitious luxury than a necessity." Both English and French tended to be solicitous of their children, sometimes sending them to be educated in Great Britain or Canada, but by the early nineteenth century their preference was for schoolmasters and clergy to be drawn to the Red River Settlement.

The company and its retired servants made great efforts to persuade the *Bois brulés* to accept a sedentary life, but most of them, particularly those active in the buffalo hunt and the preparation of pemmican, were nomads who claimed basic ownership of the lands but were almost completely uninterested in their cultivation. Thus the true settlers near the forks, English-speaking on the west bank (now Winnipeg) and French-speaking on the east (now St. Boniface), and the nearby farmers along the Red and the Assiniboine rivers formed a small core of stability in a society of hunters on horseback who ranged in bands up to a thousand strong.

Theirs was a triple society, composed of a large central core with much smaller fractions breaking off to join either the white or the Indian community. Only a few of them, emulating the former bourgeois of the fur trade, emerged as merchants and traders. A perceptible proportion of those with British blood became farmers. Gradually the influence of religion and the churches, more than schools, public policy, or marriage, sorted out the sedentary from the nomads. A continuous Roman Catholic mission dated from 1818; an Anglican one from 1820; James Evans, the Methodist who invented a syllabic system for the commonly used Cree language, arrived as one of four western missionaries in 1840; and John Black, the Presbyterian pioneer, in 1851.

In economic terms, agriculture was victorious over nomadism, but the nomads were not to be subdued until 1885. By that time the buffalo had been almost exterminated. During the interval, *La Nation Métisse* was involved in several conflicts. Generally speaking, the métis disliked the company as much as it disliked them, chiefly because it employed, particularly after it resumed control of the Selkirk Grant in 1836, every possible device, even a proviso in land deeds, to prevent them from trading on their own. These attempted bonds on their freedom of buying and selling where they pleased (that is, in the United States) were far too weak to hold the nomads. The two-way smuggling went on and matters reached a climax in 1849 when Jean-Louis Riel, father of the more famous Louis, marshaled 500 or 600 métis to intimidate with musketry a court which was trying Guillaume Sayer for illegal trade. When he was convicted, but unpunished because the frightened judge fled on horseback, the cry was raised *"Le commerce est libre —vive la liberté."*

🍁 THE UNITED STATES FRONTIER

Before 1860 the initiative in relations between the Red River and the United States had come chiefly from the British side. Following the boundary settlement of 1818 and Astor's successes in confining the American fur trade to Americans, the company dismantled Fort Daer and its post at Pembina, but as early as the grasshopper plague of 1819 seed grain and supplies had been secured at Prairie du Chien. During succeeding years cattle and sheep were driven in to meet eager demand. When Fort Snelling was begun in 1819 and American fur companies became active on the upper Mississippi, the upper Red, and the Missouri, it became a resort for illegal traders as well as for the discouraged Swiss from the Red River Settlement.

The American fur trade of the area declined after the Panic of 1837, but about the same time St. Louis emerged as a quasi-independent supply center for the upper Mississippi and the Missouri. The Mississippi entry and the steamboat triumphed over New York just as the Bay entry had triumphed over Montreal. It was moderately easy to reach the Red River Valley from the headwaters of the Mississippi or of its tributary, the Minnesota.

The natural consequence was that legal and illegal trade between the Red River Settlement and the Mississippi grew steadily and was conducted chiefly by the métis in long trains of Red River carts. These awkward but efficient vehicles were constructed almost entirely of wood and leather, and the noise they made even on level plains was loud and unmistakable. Yet the company could not stop the smuggling. By 1843 there was a regular cart line from Pembina to St. Paul or Mendota which used 200 carts by 1850. By then both the American Fur Company and the Hudson's Bay Company were losing money in the Red River Settlement and Great Britain had committed herself to free trade. Small wonder that after steamboats began to operate on the Red River at the end of the fifties, the company itself found it advantageous to import by way of the Mississippi.

About 1860, the frontier of American settlement appeared to be no great menace. Wisconsin, east of the Mississippi, became a territory in 1836 and, in 1848, having passed the 200,000 mark, the area east of the Mississippi and St. Croix became a state. Five thousand persons in the river triangle to the west of them obtained the creation of Minnesota Territory in 1849, but geography and railways diverted the American frontier of agricultural settlement into Iowa, Kansas and Nebraska. Also, problems of high plains agriculture discouraged settlement, and the Civil War and its preliminaries absorbed attention and energies until 1865. By the time lumbering began to be substantially supplemented by agriculture in Minnesota (a state in 1858) and farmers out of Iowa and Nebraska dared to tackle the American portion of the Red River Valley (the Dakotas), there were about as many inquisitive and enterprising adventurers from Canada in the old Red River Settlement as their counterparts from the United States.

Yet the United States was a convenience for the métis in political as well as economic ways, and they used it as a lever in their contest with the company. The *Bois brulés,* English as well as French, began to play off against each other the interests in them of Great Britain, Canada, and the United States. By 1849, after two years' efforts, Alexander K. Isbister, a quarter-breed born at Cumberland House on the Saskatchewan and now an English barrister, had persuaded the British Cabinet and Parliament to investigate the company's charter and the settlers' rights under it. Métis from British territory were elected to the legislature of Minnesota in 1857.

The movement of the day towards colonial autonomy was being extended to embrace the remote and peculiar society on the Red River. Progress was to be slow, tortuous, and finally violent, but it was unquestionably accelerated because the liberty-loving *Nation Métisse* consciously and unconsciously drew upon the expansive energies of Canada and the United States against the company. Neither country was congenial to, or sympathetic with, this anomalous North American community, but the company was the enemy. Ironically enough, the nomads were ultimately to be pushed aside by the North American agricultural frontier, while the company was able to adapt itself, survive, and even prosper.

WEST TO THE PACIFIC

A semicircle with the forks of the Red River as its center and the transcontinental forty-ninth parallel as its diameter would have fairly neatly embraced the company's field of operations except for a southward projection in Oregon. Over this enormous, forbidding area a course network of routes was laid down with trading posts at strategic positions, like knots in the net. Chief Factors, whose incomes averaged about £720 a year, commanded the twenty-five districts; Chief Traders, at about half that income, commanded important single posts. Both shared in the company's profits during their terms and to a lesser degree for seven years after retirement.

Simpson's restless habit of touring the territory nearly eliminated the old practice of having the Chief Factors and Chief Traders assemble annually for a council with the governor. Attenuated meetings were

held, first at York Fort on Hudson Bay where the incoming and outgoing cargoes met, and, from the thirties onwards, at Norway House
at the northern end of Lake Winnipeg astride the principal route to
the bay. Toiling little groups of Indians and *voyageurs* all over that
almost empty land were organized to transport furs and goods by the
best routes to and from the "factory" on the bay. Naturally the trade
of the area east of Hudson Bay, insofar as it drained to the St. Lawrence, converged on Montreal.

The great problem of the western half of the territory was the area
between the abrupt eastern face of the Rockies and the Pacific coast.
In a practical sense it amounted to two distinct districts: New Caledonia,
or the high, dry, interior plateau west and north of the upper Columbia,
which was at first tied in to the continental apparatus by Edmonton
and the Yellowhead Pass; and the huge basin of the Columbia and
its tributaries which could also be reached from the North Saskatchewan
by the Athabaska Pass and the Columbia itself or, preferably, by Howse
Pass or White Man's Pass to the Kootenay tributary.

Since the lower Fraser, which drained the northern interior, was
not navigable for long stretches of deep canyon and insuperable rapids,
New Caledonia was not directly tied to the Pacific coast. The mouth
of the Columbia, on the other hand, was the most used Pacific port.
The outcome was that after 1826 New Caledonia was joined to the
Columbia system by a pack-horse route from the Fraser and Thompson
rivers to the Okanagan tributary of the Columbia, thus channeling the
imports and exports of the whole mountain region for the long voyage
round Cape Horn. Only dispatches and special commodities such as
snowshoe webbing traveled by fast express through the mountains.

The Oregon Question.—By 1821 the formerly intense international
competition in the Pacific maritime trade was quieting down because
of the increasing scarcity of sea otter, but the company was in fairly
continuous competition with American interests for a *modus vivendi*
with the Russian fur traders of Alaska. Not until February, 1839, at
Hamburg did the company seal its gradually achieved triumph by an
agreement (for 1840–50) to lease what is now known as the Alaskan
Panhandle, thereby securing direct access to the northern interior, and
to enjoy exclusive commercial relations with the Russians. This ended
the American maritime interest, but did so at the very moment that
an irresistible overland interest was being created by the immigration
of settlers from the eastern United States. Thus the company had succeeded in Simpson's policy of keeping the American overland fur traders
out by hunting "as bare as possible all the Country South of the
Columbia and West of the Mountains," only to face the astounding

anomaly of farming frontiersmen who traversed the dry and empty western half of North America to reach the well-watered Pacific slope at the mouth of the Columbia.

There were a host of elements involved in "the Oregon Question" of 1840–46, but the determinant was that thousands of Americans poured in voluntarily to settle the area, whereas the best the company could do was to bring in 116 settlers from the Red River to work for the Puget's Sound Agricultural Company north of the Columbia and produce farm products for the Russians. Life and the problems of high plains agriculture in the trans-Mississippi region had been thoroughly discouraging to eastern American farm migrants, and glowing propaganda made the Pacific slope sound like a paradisal version of what they had been accustomed to in the East. There is no other way to account for their willingness to undergo the horrors and perils of the Oregon Trail, although such elements as nationalism and Manifest Destiny undoubtedly played their parts. Westward-bound Canadians were at the same time being diverted into the United States by 1500 miles of impassable Laurentian Shield. The farmers of the Red River Valley felt no call to leave the area they had learned to master.

Simpson was no fool. For twenty years he had been hammering on the necessity for agriculture as an adjunct to the fur trade. He argued that this would cut down imports and, on the Pacific, be built into the profitable maritime trade. He did his best in the area north of the Columbia, and during the early forties the company hoped that the river might be the international boundary, but their best was not enough compared to the American achievement south of the river. Moreover, the bar at the mouth of the Columbia greatly reduced its usefulness as a port. North of San Francisco the Puget Sound area afforded the first fine natural harbors.

In 1846, therefore, after a great deal of misleading bluff and bluster, both Great Britain and the United States were glad to avoid war by extending the international boundary westward along the forty-ninth parallel through the Rockies and round the southern end of Vancouver Island to the Pacific. In the circumstances, Britain (and the later transcontinental Canada) may probably be considered to have been lucky to secure 5° 40′ of the Pacific coast between Russian Alaska and the United States.

Vancouver's Island.—The determinant on the British side, of course, was pre-eminence in the fur trade, and it is significant that three years before the surrender of the Columbia, the company had moved its Pacific headquarters from the mouth of that river to the original focus —from Fort Vancouver to "Vancouver's Island." Not at bleak, buffeted

Nootka Sound but at sheltered Camosack Harbor inside Juan de Fuca Strait was Fort Victoria founded in 1843 to exploit the Russian contract and focus the trade. New routes had to be worked out through the southern mountain ranges between the Coast Range and the Rockies and, in particular, the avenues across the panhandle of Alaska into the northern interior afforded by the Nass, the Stikine, and the Taku rivers had to be explored and developed.

In 1849 Great Britain granted Vancouver's Island to the company as a colony on the impractical condition of bringing in settlers within five years. A year later a governor and Council were appointed, and in 1856 an Assembly of seven members from four districts was added. Great Britain had learned from Oregon that only British settlement could stand up against American settlement. Victoria slowly developed into a solid little enterprise with about 500 inhabitants, and the discovery of easily accessible coal at coastal Nanaimo gave the colony an important role in the boom that accompanied the gold discoveries in California, American since the Mexican War of 1846. San Francisco was a portent of "a new world a-coming" on the Pacific coast.

GOLD ON THE FRASER

The greatest early difficulty was the almost irresistible pull of the California gold fields. And then, in 1856, gold was discovered in the river bars of the Fraser. Within two years the whole coast was convulsed by the news. Victoria was transformed during a single summer into a miniature San Francisco, and settlements sprang up below Fort Langley at the mouth of the Fraser. The spectacularly altered circumstances demanded new and thoughtful policies. The first governor, R. C. Blanshard, had been replaced in 1851 by James Douglas, Chief Factor at Victoria. His intelligent energies on the spot prevented what might easily have been chaos with over 10,000 miners on the Fraser by the autumn of 1858—a territory which had no legal governor. Douglas, following his practice during an ephemeral gold rush to the Queen Charlotte Islands, 1851–52, had assumed the powers on his own in December, 1857.

The American inundation.—The legal and constitutional outcome was that the company became a simple business corporation west of the Rockies, for in 1858 the British Parliament repurchased Vancouver Island and set up the additional colony of British Columbia on the mainland. Douglas, on resigning office under the company, was named governor of both colonies and the learned Matthew B. Begbie was sent out from England to act as judge. The practical situation, of course, was infinitely less simple, for thousands of not very law-abiding persons, carried along by the extraordinary excitement of the gold rush, were at first little inclined to be regulated by Douglas and Begbie. Yet the two officials succeeded in imposing law and order with almost none of the defiance and violence that accompanied gold rushes elsewhere. The reason for their success was that, even during the most turbulent early days, they knew what it was practicable to do and demonstrated that it was not merely practicable but serviceable as well.

F. W. Howay and other students of this period have recounted some of its fantastic elements, such as the notorious Ned McGowan's arrival at Victoria in early July, 1858, with 460 adventurers from San Francisco. "He felt an uncontrollable itch to twist the Lion's tail, and accordingly marked his advent . . . by touching off a salute of one hundred guns from the *Pacific*'s two small cannon, which Ned had manned with a crew of gold hunters, most of whom had just returned from Walker's disastrous filibustering jaunt to Nicaragua."

Next Christmas, on the Fraser, McGowan, acting as a special constable, took part in a comic conflict of jurisdictions between two makeshift magistrates that became known as "Ned McGowan's War" because the alarmed authorities sent a mixed force of Engineers, Navy, and Marines seventy miles up the ice-encumbered river to investigate it. The magistrates were dismissed and the San Franciscan was commended. During the celebration of Washington's Birthday two months later, Ned was challenged to a duel by J. W. Bagley, another former San Francisco ruffian, but replied "that he would not fight in British territory, but was willing to meet him in United States territory." It is believed that the duel was not fought, but the respectful McGowan left the country shortly afterwards with $4700 worth of dust in his poke.

These and other incidents involving American miners' sentiments, national holidays, flag, customs, law, and currency in British territory were the froth that floated over really substantial issues. Most of the Americans were serious, practiced men and they speedily found that the authorities were of the same sort. The United States had inundated a large, undeveloped piece of British territory. Could the incomers be induced to regard themselves as immigrants on an equal footing with the residents? That is, could the truculence of the men who had "taken over" California a few years before be met and modified by authorities willing to accept the mining and administrative practices that had been worked out in California?

The answer depended on the promptness, assurance, consistency, and evenhandedness with which authority acted. Douglas filled the bill. Although he exceeded his legal powers, and was reprimanded for it by London, he made it clear that neither lawlessness nor local autonomy would be tolerated, but that he was open to suggestion as to practical arrangements. His task was made much easier by the presence of a small detachment of the Royal Engineers that had been sent out from Great Britain in 1858 and by the presence of Begbie as personification of British law.

British Columbia had no Vigilantes. The only lynching was done (in 1884) by eighty men from the State of Washington who took a fugitive murderer from a British Columbia jail and hanged him near the border. H. H. Bancroft's summary was based on abundant knowledge: "Considering the circumstances surrounding the beginning, the unruly, wild men and the unruly gold-gatherers, society during these incipient stages was, I say, a marvel of order and obedience to law."

Gold on the mainland had brought about the situation that the colony of Vancouver's Island had been designed to prevent and, if the Americans had called on their country to extend its laws and protection to them, the American government, as Lord Grey admitted, would have been unable to refuse. "Fifty-four Forty or Fight" might well have been a more potent slogan about 1860 than in Polk's presidential campaign of 1844. As it was, American institutions were accepted, but British sovereignty maintained and all men treated equally.

Mining licenses were a little more expensive than in California, but both foreigner and Briton paid. Mining supplies came from California, but import duties were low. The administration kept its accounts in sterling, but all transactions were in dollars or dust. When, in 1861, £6900 in silver currency was brought in, the florins were called half-dollars, the shillings quarters, and the six-penny pieces one bit. That year Douglas imported a minting plant from San Francisco to coin $10 and $20 gold pieces, but that anomalous currency did not pass into circulation.

In the courts, the juries were mixed and arrangements were made, but not needed, for American lawyers to practice. The first newspaper, the *Gazette,* founded in 1858, was American-owned, but fought for British ideas of order. The transportation services licensed by Douglas were American, as were the two express services, those of W. T. Ballou and Wells, Fargo & Co. The first bank was that of the Californian Scot, A. D. Macdonald. The early improvised administration by a few gold commissioners, justices of the peace, and constables was a compromise between slight legal or administrative knowledge and common sense. Nobody bothered about the frequent displays of the American flag or the Californian custom of wearing a revolver on one hip and a bowie knife on the other, for both practices died a natural death.

There were four really large issues. In December, 1857, Douglas, still a company officer as well as colonial governor, tried to assert his company's monopoly of trade by a system of licenses, but was to be checked, as he learned in October, 1858, by the British government. The new colonial structure for British Columbia which went into force November 19, 1858, endowed Douglas for five years with autocratic powers, including taxation, but trade was to be free.

In the second place, the Indian problem was aggravated by recent and contemporary wars, not unmarked by Indian successes, in Washington and Oregon. Indian and American tempers were alike high, and in August, 1858, the miners themselves conducted a campaign to cow the Indians who had been harassing parties at Big Canyon, twenty miles above Yale. On this and a couple of other occasions, Douglas emphatically forbade both parties to take the law into their own hands. Having prohibited the sale of liquor to the Indians, he successfully insisted on recourse to the courts where "the laws would protect the rights of the Indians, no less than those of the white man."

The third large issue was between the local mining regulations that were imported from California after a decade of experimentation and the general regulations that Douglas improvised. In this the hard-won knowledge and conclusions of the miners as to size of claim, water rights, and so forth triumphed, and by a proclamation of early 1859 Douglas authorized the creation of local mining boards composed of six to twelve elected members, regardless of nationality, and possessing wide regulatory, but not judicial, powers. "The mining boards," declared Douglas, "will be fostered and encouraged as long as they confine their influence to its legitimate object, that of improving the conditions of the gold fields."

Finally, there was the issue of connection with the outside world. Should it be overland from American Puget Sound or the interior of Washington Territory, or by sea through exclusive control points at Victoria, Fort Langley, or New Westminster to the controllable channel of the Fraser and beyond? Douglas found that he had to depend on American supplies, but he did succeed for the most part in imposing the Fraser as the sole route of entry. By employing the surveying skill and experience of Col. R. C. Moody and his Royal Engineers in the construction of roads along the old company brigade trails, he convinced the miners that British administration could serve as well as regulate.

During the idleness enforced by the high water in the summer of 1858, Douglas secured the co-operation of the miners in cutting out a pack trail by Harrison River and Lake to Lillooet in the upper Fraser. The narrow wagon roads hacked out of, or shelving out on props from, the canyon walls of the Fraser and Thompson, and the meandering tracks that paralleled the Fraser from Lytton to Quesnel and Barkerville ("the Cariboo Road"), or threaded eastward across a series of ranges between Hope and the Kootenay ("the Dewdney Trail"), were evidences of a useful kind of sovereignty. They were financed largely by levies and tolls; they greatly reduced prices; but they had a way of being finished just as a gold field petered out, leaving heavy burdens on the colonial treasury.

🍁 INTERCOLONIAL CONFLICT

The old colony of Vancouver's Island did not take kindly to being overshadowed by the new colony of British Columbia. The land-boom and the mercantile and financial prosperity that had visited Victoria in 1858 could be maintained only as long as it remained the official port of entry for both colonies and housed the upper ranks of the administration. The New Westminster community at the mouth of the Fraser bitterly resented its subordination and a feud began which persists in slightly altered forms to this day. Yet the mainland was notoriously unstable because placer-mining quickly exhausted its "diggings" and prospectors ranged the mountains, touching off "rushes" to regions as far away to the north as the *T*-like east and west division of the Fraser near Fort George ("the Cariboo"), or to the west near the twin headwaters of the Columbia and the Kootenay. Adventures like these in the otherwise empty wilderness put an insupportable burden on administration and revenue.

Matters came to a head in 1860 with the building of the Cariboo Road, and Douglas found himself caught between entrenched Victoria and the communities of the lower Fraser Valley. The issue became that of representative government for British Columbia and control of its taxation. Douglas fought a stout fight against this on reasonably good grounds and instituted such conciliatory services as direct steamship entry to New Westminster (1862), but mainland agitators and press could not resist the invitation to indulge in the customary extravagances —"the insulting despotism of a Governor whose continued absence from the colony amounted to a betrayal of the trust confided to him," and so on. They did not want union with the Island lest Victoria remain privileged, but they insisted on self-government.

In Victoria, meanwhile, a former Nova Scotian and pupil of Joseph Howe named Smith had renamed himself Amor de Cosmos and had become the stormy petrel of politics, aiming, perhaps, to be the Howe of the Pacific coast. He found plenty of ammunition in the rather primitive procedures of the legislature of Vancouver's Island. Both colonies bombarded the British government with petitions and memorials.

The details of the turmoil, descending as they did to the cost of bedding straw for Colonel Moody's horse and the authorship of election squibs, do not justify repetition here. British Columbia received a Legislative Council of its own in January, 1864, composed one-third of Victoria officials, one-third of local magistrates, and one-third of elected representatives from the five principal inhabited areas. Douglas, made Knight Commander of the Bath in 1863, was succeeded in 1864 by A. E. Kennedy as governor of Vancouver's Island and by Frederick Seymour as governor of British Columbia.

But by 1865 the Cariboo placers were almost exhausted and a great emigration was about to begin. The new Kootenay field was far more easily reached from the American Columbia than by the Dewdney Trail from the Fraser. Moreover, new methods of mining, requiring advanced techniques and large capital but employing few men, were replacing the hordes of the semiskilled. Both colonies were deeply in debt and no one could see where future revenues would come from because the exodus of miners depressed everything (except absurdly high official salaries) from land values to mercantile incomes. Each colony demanded the best of two worlds by insisting that, if union took place, it should have the capital. Vancouver's Island wanted free trade. British Columbia needed the revenues from customs duties.

The union under the name of British Columbia that was imposed (without resistance) by a puzzled British government in 1866 made Victoria the capital (in 1868), but equipped the colony with the conciliar apparatus of British Columbia, instead of the representative system of Vancouver's Island. The hope was that a new public spirit, visible, for instance, in Amor de Cosmos in spite of his insistence on responsible government, might thus find acceptable local solutions for the really profound problems of this divided and rapidly dwindling society. Vancouver's Island lost its Assembly and Victoria ceased to be a "free port."

But would the united colonies now be gobbled up by a United States that was in process of buying Alaska from the Russians? Only a British-American transcontinental railroad could keep the coast between 49° and 54° 40′ from the Americans. The American agricultural frontier seemed close to threatening the Red River settlement, but it, too, might perhaps be saved by such a railroad. We must turn, therefore, to the combination of energies which grew up, chiefly in Canada and in Great Britain, and dared to propose such an astonishing enterprise.

CHAPTER XVIII

The Canadian Keystone (1841-65)

The united Canada created in February, 1841, introduced a new quality into British North America, largely because of its size and its keystone position in the continent. Hitherto the colonial units had been small in terms of population and bristling in terms of independence. Now an immense area, which enclosed one of the principal entries to the continent and reached far down into the United States, had had union imposed on it for economic and political ends. Even if it had stood still after 1841, it could not have been ignored in North America.

Instead of that, it grew mightily. The population, which was about 1,100,000 to start with, rose to 1,842,264 in 1851 and to 2,507,677 ten years later. Production for export, chiefly of wood products and grains, grew also. Continental transportation routes, waterway or railroad, drained and traversed the southern margins of this huge tract, not only to carry Canada's own exports and imports directly to and from Europe or the United States, but also to convert wheat into Canadian flour for the British market.

SELF-REALIZATION IN A DIVIDED SOCIETY

Political and economic union could not unite the society. Thomas Chapais, a most temperate modern commentator, has drawn an unforgettable picture of the apathy and sullenness that lay over most of Canada East during the early forties. To nearly all *Canadiens* the union of 1841 meant conquest, conquest in a hopeless sense that had been absent even in 1760 and the succeeding years, for Canada West was growing far more rapidly than the older Canada, hemmed in as its farmers and woodsmen were by uncultivable uplands, as yet not industrialized, and losing more and more of its people to the United States.

Alarmed by the emigration, the church began to throw its weight behind assisted colonization in the Eastern townships, the Saguenay, and the regions that the lumbermen had cleared in the St. Maurice and Ottawa valleys. Popular as this movement was, it had little relative effect. There had been more Canadians than *Canadiens* as early as 1837, but they had been politically divided. During 1850, apparently, Canada West surged past Canada East in total population, and thereafter increased its advantage in spite of the high *Canadien* birth rate.

This was a period of maturing and enterprise for both societies. It was as if each had to shake off or ignore some of its earlier obsessions and some of its European traditions in order to set its house in order. There might be no single overriding Canadianism as yet, but its two principal components were taking self-confident forms. These societies were facing the implications of the democracy to which they aspired. If they were to govern themselves it must be in terms higher than mere diatribes. They must discover what it was in them to be.

And so, in apparently detached enterprises, life began to be raised above mere survival, subsistence, conflict, and acquisitiveness. The churches were recruiting and educating Canadian clergy, and the infant universities at Toronto, Cobourg, Kingston, Montreal, and Quebec, whose function had usually been thought to be religious education, found themselves responding also to the demands of an eager lay world.

At the bottom of the educational ladder, primary education was now considered a common necessity, and in order to bring it about the *Canadien* classical colleges and monastic schools, and the high schools, collegiate institutes, and normal schools of the Canadians, had painfully to be organized, expanded, and equipped, thereby providing both primary teachers and an intermediate secondary education. Here, too, strong utilitarian demands were in contest with traditional conceptions of classical education. No one, as it were, as yet stepped back to take an over-all view of what was happening, but from the Detroit River to the Gaspé Peninsula devoted educators were at work in response to the birth pangs of Canada.

There had, of course, been imported culture of various sorts in the Maritimes and in both the Canadas, indeed there was something approaching sophistication in a number of individuals or small circles throughout British North America. The new note, however, was the native one, colonial in the sense that it emulated and borrowed heavily from the French and British traditions, while at the same time venturing to express the Canadian experience.

F. X. Garneau in 1828 responded to a fellow law-clerk's sneers at the conquered *Canadiens* by announcing that he would write their glorious history. Subsequent years of study, travel, and contacts with enlightened men in Canada, the United States, Great Britain, and France hardened his determination. With Durham's scathing comments ringing in his mind, he wrote a history that was both French and *Canadien,* and imbued with the romanticism and nationalism that were sweeping Europe.

The *Canadien* refrain, often narrow and strident in political pamphleteering, was broadened and deepened by the youthful George (for George III) Étienne Cartier's song, *Canada! mon pays! mes amours,* of 1835. In 1846 Pierre Chauveau sounded a new and lasting note in his novel *Charles Guerin* by exalting the life of the frontiersman above that of the intellectual, and in 1860 the "Patriotic School" of writers took form at the able and inspiring Octave Crémazie's bookshop in Quebec. They published chiefly works of a historical character such as those of Abbé J. B. A. Ferland and P. A. de Gaspé (the younger), but A. Gérin-Lajoie's *Jean Rivard* of 1862 was a sociological justification, inspiration, and guide for the frontiersman. The 1855 visit, in the interest of Napoleon III's expansive ambitions, of the French naval vessel, *La Capricieuse,* evoked from Crémazie poetry which movingly blended the French tradition with *Canadien* history. It has been well said that he and Louis Fréchette put Garneau's history into verse.

It seems significant, too, that of the twelve English-speaking poets who published work before 1867 that was judged worthy of inclusion in A. J. M. Smith's *The Book of Canadian Poetry* (1943), three were born in England, three in Ireland, two in Scotland, two (Oliver Goldsmith and Joseph Howe) in Nova Scotia, one in New York State, and one (Charles Sangster) in Canada. All of them were highly imitative of English poetry, but all of them succeeded in communicating some sense of the North America in which they lived.

The same mixed expression can be seen in architecture, wood carving, and painting. The more ambitious public buildings and churches were usually copies, often on a reduced scale, of famous French or British edifices, but Canadian themes crept into their carvings and decoration. Domestic architecture of an ambitious sort proceeded from European models, but responded to North American environment. Stone and brick were somewhat more frequently used in Canada than in New England and New York, but in general wood was far more abundantly employed than in Europe, and a variety of devices, from more steeply pitched roofs to abundant flues and chimneys and covered passages between farm buildings, were responses to severe winters and heavy snows.

Many amateurs sketched or made water colors and itinerant painters picked up a precarious living from portraiture, but Paul Kane (Irish),

Daniel Fowler (English), O. R. Jacobi (Prussian), Cornelius Krieghoff (Dutch), and G. T. Berthon (French) were foreign artists of enduring achievement who found stimulation in Canada and won support because they translated some of its essences to canvas. As early as 1834 Toronto had an art exhibition and by 1847 a Society of Arts. The *Instituts Canadiens* in Quebec, Montreal, and Ottawa, and the Canadian Institute in Toronto were literary and scientific societies which persisted because they expressed the intellectual aspirations of the times.

NEW CAPITAL AND NEW TRIALS

Sydenham, in addition to being a great politician, had also the advantage of being able to refund the public economy of Canada by a British guaranteed loan of £1,500,000 to be spent on employment-creating public works. Semi-bankrupt Upper Canada, unable to carry its debt of £1,200,000, joined solvent Lower Canada, whose debt was only £95,000, to form a new credit structure under the pleased eyes of a British Chancellor of the Exchequer who just happened to be a Baring. This moved Pierre Chauveau to write a very bitter, very bad, poem on the theme, "It's the day of the bankers," but Cartier, who came of old merchant stock, could see further. Canals, roads, and other public works were creating a new and stronger St. Lawrence economy from which both *Canadiens* and Canadians must benefit, and, thanks to British aid, they were being built faster than the Canadian economy could have provided them. A deepened Welland Canal and deep canals along the St. Lawrence should offset the Erie and pour wealth into Montreal that might otherwise have gone to New York.

Sydenham had barely constructed the new edifice, however, before it began to be shaken by blasts from Great Britain, Ireland, and the United States. When Peel became prime minister in 1841, he promptly initiated a program that destroyed the old idea of empire. With the income tax as an offset to loss of customs revenue, he used a series of five budgets to convert Great Britain to "virtual" free trade, finally repealing even the protection of agriculture. The colonial corollary of all this was that it ended the protected markets for staples that had been the economic cement of the old system of empire. Once preferential markets were gone (by 1846), navigation laws lost their justification, and in 1849 they too disappeared. Free trade, however, meant free (and exposed) empire.

The Irish blast was the export of poverty, misery, and disease during the elimination, by an incurable blight, of the people's principal foodstuff, the potato. Canada's sufferings in consequence could not, of course, compare with Ireland's tragedy, but the colony was ill-prepared to receive and sustain the helpless, cholera-ridden Irish who were carried up the St. Lawrence. About 100,000 of them arrived during 1847 alone. Devoted doctors, nurses, and public officials risked and often lost their lives in relief measures; camps were built and serviced; and schemes of distribution were devised; but the burden on the central treasury, on local authorities, and on private charity was almost insupportable.

Finally, the United States had no intention of letting the managers of the St. Lawrence drain off the products of the Great Lakes Basin. The Canadians had been astute, for in 1843 they had managed to bully Peel's government into virtual (and still preferential) acceptance of American produce as Canadian if it were processed in, and exported through, Canada, but two could play at that game. The New Yorkers not only set about improving their Erie Canal, but they also persuaded the federal government to pass drawback laws in 1845 and 1846 that facilitated the passage of Canadian exports through their state. In 1847 world commodity prices crashed and credit was tightened everywhere, to the profound distress of a Canadian milling industry built up in speculative anticipation of turning American grains into Canadian flour.

The really crushing blow, however, was the discovery in 1848 and 1849 that the now completed St. Lawrence canals were not enough. While they made it much cheaper to ship grain, let us say, from Illinois to tidewater, the disadvantages of Montreal and the dangerous lower St. Lawrence compared with New York and the open Atlantic, in abundance of ships and rates for pilotage and insurance, meant that it cost about $13.75 to ship a ton of grain from Chicago to Liverpool by Montreal and about $10.50 a ton by New York. The present seemed disastrous and the future, without some special consideration from Great Britain, seemed hopeless indeed.

At this time, too, the conviction in the colonies deepened, to last for about a generation, that the victory of the bookkeeping British burghers over the landed aristocracy meant the end of empire. The Free Traders argued that colonies did not pay their way, particularly in costs of defense, and that anyway as free trade expanded it would eliminate the causes of war. This Little Englandism, in the air since before Adam Smith, had clearly conquered the governing class even though it had not become conspicuous public policy.

Lord Grey, the liberal Whig Colonial Secretary, for instance, was writing privately to Lord Elgin, the liberal Tory governor of Canada: "To us except the loss of prestige (no slight one I admit), the loss of Canada would be the loss of little but a source of heavy expense and great anxiety." In reply, Elgin compared himself to a ship's captain who had through great perils saved a rickety lumber vessel and its cargo only to have its owners mutter: "It would have been better for us if the whole concern had gone to the bottom, as we should then have realized the Insurance."

In 1848, when revolution swept the Continent, invaded Ireland, and seemed about to blaze up as Chartism in Great Britain, Grey expressed the hope (again privately) that Canadian intercourse with the sharply divided United States might be subtly encouraged and possibly effect two new states, "British America with some of the Northern States forming one Nation and the Southern States another. This would be no such bad result and in the meantime our trade would prosper and emigration would flourish." It took Elgin years to bring Grey around to another way of thinking and to reassure the Canadian leaders who smelled what was in the air.

THE CAULDRON OF POLITICS

Such was the social, economic, and political background between 1840 and 1850 for what Canadians have been accustomed to think of, chiefly, as the struggle for responsible government. Thanks to their scholars' researches into what was locally, in the British Empire, and in world history a remarkable innovation, a "play-by-play" account of this contest has been recorded. Fascinating as it was, it must be generalized here.

Sydenham tried to obey Russell and stave off surrender to a democratic colonial executive by a number of brilliant personal conquests and other improvisations, but was gradually thrown back on the single device of himself heading an executive drawn from several groups, *Canadien* and Canadian, and drawing its voting support from a coalition, a "governor's party," in the Assembly. Thanks to the clearheadedness of the reform leaders, Louis Hippolyte Lafontaine and Robert Baldwin, that device had begun to fail Sydenham even before his accidental death in September, 1841. The day before Sydenham was buried at Kingston, the electors of York took Baldwin's advice and chose Lafontaine as their representative, a gesture that was reciprocated by Rimouski next year when Baldwin lost his Upper Canadian seat to the Tories.

In other words, the naïve expectations of Durham and of Russell that union would be followed by the opposition of two parties, minority *Canadien* and majority Canadian, were disappointed. Papineau and others were to revive its essence fairly often in succeeding years, but it was never to establish itself. Instead, men divided, irrespective of tongue, into conservatives and radicals. In addition, once some of the naturally conservative *Canadiens* had detected a way out of their subjection by uniting with the Canadian radicals to secure control of the executive and its alluring patronage, the result was a foregone conclusion.

Sir Charles Bagot, Sydenham's successor and the appointee of Peel and of Lord Stanley at the Colonial Office, saw clearly why Sydenham had courted failure. Stanley continued Russell's policy of no surrender to responsible government, but Bagot told him plainly that "it was only by dint of the greatest energy, and I must add . . . unscrupulous personal interference . . . combined with practices which I would not use . . . in addition to the promise of the Loan and the bribe of the public Works, that Lord Sydenham managed to get through the Session."

In spite of Tory fury in Canada and Tory bewilderment in Britain, Bagot yielded to the combined majority of Lafontaine and Baldwin after a dramatic series of plays and counterplays during the legislative meeting of September, 1842. Stanley acquiesced, but urged Bagot to revert to *divide et impera* and, when Bagot died suddenly in the following May, sent out the dutiful Sir Charles Metcalfe to turn back the clock.

Metcalfe was a prodigy, for although he saw clearly the hopelessness of British policy and was himself stricken by a painful and incurable disease, he obeyed orders, put together a "governor's party" in the manner of Head and Sydenham, and won an Assembly majority in 1844. He was rewarded with a peerage, but his system was breaking up when, in 1845, he went home to die. His successor was Lord Elgin, serving under Grey and the uncertain Whigs after Peel's defeat in 1846. Before Elgin left England in January, 1847, he and the British government had accepted the logic of events, and as the occasions for surrendering to it arose, in Nova Scotia in 1847 and in Canada in 1848, responsible government came into force.

Robert Baldwin supplied the principle behind this peaceful colonial revolution; a mounting Little Englandism concurred in it; but the actual political achievement was largely Louis Hippolyte Lafontaine's. He had resisted Sydenham's attempts to "buy" him with the office of Solicitor General for Canada East and had withdrawn his Assembly candidacy at Terrebonne in 1841 when the governor's "bludgeon men" were sent in to beat him, but his election manifesto had been precise and clear—responsible government and alliance with the Canadian reformers. "Our cause is common." Of course it was, for he and Baldwin, Francis Hincks and Augustin Morin, had reached agreement on the principle before Sydenham reached Canada. All three of the others wavered, if only slightly, from their singleness of purpose, but not Lafontaine. He built up a group of disciplined *Canadien* followers until it could exercise a balance of power. As early as 1842 he successfully defied the exclusive use of English that Sydenham had written into the Act of Union. (It was Elgin who signalized that victory by giving the Speech from the throne in French and English in January, 1849.) The combination of Lafontaine's following and Baldwin's forced Bagot to accept their terms almost completely in 1842.

Lafontaine also stood firm through the confusions created when Papineau came back from exile in 1845, was elected to the Assembly and, full of the revolutionary and nationalistic ideas he had discussed in France, created a new group, the Rouges. Lafontaine exalted collaboration with the Canadians on equal terms over retrospective, introspective *Canadien* nationalism and demonstrated that the Rouges were "outs" trying to get in. Baldwin and Lafontaine also exposed the futility of René-Edouard Caron's variation on John C. Calhoun's recipe for similar division in the United States, that is, government by "concurrent" or "double" majorities in the Assembly.

Baldwin, so wholehearted in his devotion to Lafontaine's kind of union that he sent his daughters to be educated by the Ursulines in Quebec, stood by his redoubtable ally through the storms and confusions of Metcalfe's regime until the Lafontaine-Baldwin ministry was candidly accepted by Elgin in March, 1848. Throughout the fluctuating contest both men had clung to the criterion of success that everyone concerned in Britain and British North America had long known to be not only the victors' immediate prize but also the great lubricant of parliamentary government everywhere—control of the patronage. Elgin knew well what he was doing when he paid that price for a colonial executive that had the backing to get things done. He believed from the beginning that much would be solved "if the French would split into a Liberal and a Conservative party, and join with the Upper Canadian parties which bear corresponding names." In the meantime he would act towards any working majority as his queen must towards one in the British Parliament.

A great many things were achieved during the forties by the emerging democracy, ranging from local government and common school systems to the undermining of seigneurial tenure and of the Crown and Clergy Reserves, but the copestone was laid in 1849 amidst arson, riot, and treason by the despairing Montreal merchants. An act had provided compensation for rebellion losses in Canada West. Lafontaine and Baldwin carried another for Canada East early in 1849 that would reimburse even actual rebels. Elgin tried to cool the atmosphere by delaying his assent a few weeks, but when he gave it, April 25, 1849, all the shattered hopes and ancient hates of Montreal's businessmen broke forth, for they were in the depths of economic depression and hope-lessness.

This led to disgraceful scenes in Montreal, the capital of the province. The governor was booed in the House and assailed with rotten eggs and any convenient missiles when he went to his carriage. A mob was raised at the Place d'Armes that night, burst in on the busy Assembly, sacked the Parliament Building, and destroyed it by fire. For days they ruled the city, sacking reformers' houses, attacking the Assembly at the Château de Ramézay, and stoning the governor again on his way to and from the meeting there. The mob's backers, the mercantile and financial lords of Montreal, indulged in extremities of hysterical abuse, made themselves ridiculous by "expunging" the governor's name from the records of the principal Scottish societies and exclusive clubs of Montreal and Quebec, and ended up in October by circulating and subscribing to a manifesto advocating entry into the American union.

Even granting that 1849 represented a climax of economic hopes in apparent ruin, of a subject people set free and triumphant, and of oligarchy beaten by democracy, it was a petulant, disgraceful episode. Canada was still far from mature. Elgin remained unmoved, and the British government, in spite of fierce and most venomous pressures, sustained him. Within a few months, business began to pick up and the shamefaced masters of Montreal looked around anxiously for a way of retreat from the extravagances that had earned them appropriate reproach in Britain and British North America. The recently beloved United States conveniently provided a way out by the law of 1850 which put federal agencies at the service of the pursuers of fugitive slaves, and the Montreal *Witness* grasped at the straw:

> We have hitherto advocated annexation, but rather than consent to the annexation of Canada to the United States, while the slave-catching law remains in force . . . we would be willing not only to forego all the advantages of annexation, but to see Canada ten times poorer and worse governed than she is.

It was a poor excuse, but anything was better than none.

🍁 A NEW ECONOMIC ORIENTATION

Back in the thirties, when Huskisson was making reciprocal trade treaties for Great Britain, the worried Upper Canadians had complained several times of their inability to manage their own commercial system. The economic earthquakes of the forties, culminating as they did in an economy as free and as exposed as a raft, intensified their anxieties and, in particular, focused attention on the way in which the New Yorkers blended their geographical advantages into their nation's economic policy. Free trade was the talk of the day, with reciprocal trade treaties as the avenues that were supposed to lead gradually to it. Down in the Maritimes, self-government was being celebrated by efforts to keep Americans out of the inshore fisheries. In the United States the conflict between North and South was increasing rather than diminishing, and men were talking of resort to war. Perhaps everything could be shaken up and settled on a new and peaceful basis by arranging North American production, transportation, and trade in more rational ways.

In this whole matter, Elgin was the devoted and able agent of Canadian ambitions from beginning to end. He believed in helping Canada to be strong because he believed that it would voluntarily associate itself with Great Britain. Indeed some of his letters to Grey are like prophecies of the future free association in the British Commonwealth of Nations. After his courageous tour of Canada West in the autumn of 1849, he wrote to Grey: "Canada cannot be saved unless you force the selfish scheming Yankees to concede reciprocity."

This was the economic cornerstone of his theory of empire as it affected British North America. But Elgin's stimulus came from vigorous, farsighted North Americans, most notably William Hamilton Merritt, the builder of the Welland Canal and a restless North American entrepreneur; Thomas Coltrin Keefer, Merritt's protégé and a leader in North American engineering well into the twentieth century; and Israel De Wolf Andrews, an American free trader and brilliant lobbyist who had been Consul at Saint John.

Merritt and Keefer were experts in transportation during the transition from canals and waterways to railroads, men who could envisage (and map) northeastern North America in terms of the shortest and most efficient movement of its products to the European market. They even pointed out the advantages of the Hudson Bay route. Andrews was in his element as a confidential agent of as many American, British, and Canadian public authorities as he could impress, renting suites at the big hotels, buying up legislators and newspapers, organizing delegations and conventions for his project, and radiating rumors about the governments and other powers for whom he was acting and by whom he was paid. Andrews claimed to have spent over $200,000 to secure a reciprocity agreement. In spite of extensive governmental compensation, he died in debt.

Elgin negotiated the Reciprocity Treaty providing for free trade in natural products between the United States and the British North American colonies in 1854. In effect the colonies traded the use of the Lakes and St. Lawrence waterways, which the Lakes States and Middle West wanted as a supplement to and lever against the Erie, and access to the inshore fisheries (and smuggling), which New Englanders claimed as of right, for the free access of their produce to a market that was already showing signs of being receptive.

The treaty was slipped through an otherwise-obsessed American Senate on the ingenious argument to the North that it was the first step to annexation and to the South that by strengthening the colonies' independence it would preclude that addition to the voting strength of the North. The American administration was behind it because it eliminated dangerous friction over the fisheries at a time when civil war seemed imminent. The British government saw it as part of a world movement, as compensation to the colonists for their loss of British preferences, and as enabling them to stand on their own feet, be better credit risks, and even relieve the British Treasury of the costs of their defense. It was the splendid consummation of Elgin's Canadian career.

THE RAILROAD

During the forties, everywhere in North America the railroad became the passport to a new and glorious future. Marvelous and profitable as the waterways and canals had been, their limitations were summarily exposed by the machine that could conquer mountains, go where it was wanted, and do it all year round. The conversion of canal men like Merritt and Keefer, for instance, was reluctant at first and then marvelously quick.

Moreover, the railroad, as Britain's speculative booms and crashes of the thirties and forties testified, produced an almost new quality in finance by the quantities of investment and gambling that it introduced, and that new quality infected politics. Finally, the railroad was an apt instrument for political designs, for knitting together the pieces of a polity, and for expanding it in desired directions. A British North America linked by rail into a transcontinental state, for instance, would also be a road to the fabled Orient.

We have already seen the ferments at work in the Maritimes, and their effects on the Canadian keystone may easily be imagined. What was perhaps most remarkable there was that they dominated the imagination of a great *Canadien* for twenty years and made him a leading figure in Canadian politics. This leader was G. E. Cartier. Lafontaine and Baldwin retired in 1850 and the future national leader, young John A. Macdonald, had to be content to work in Cartier's shadow for another ten or twelve years.

Cartier was a lively, industrious, efficient, little man whose briskness was nicely tempered by gay cordiality and charming urbanity. Coming from the fourth generation of a prosperous merchant family, he was

Canadian Railways with Extensions in the United States

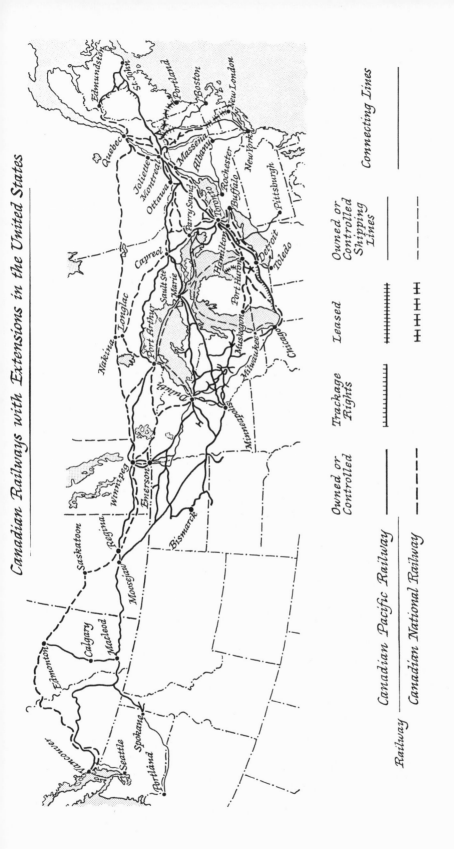

Railway

Canadian Pacific Railway

Canadian National Railway

| Owned or Controlled | Trackage Rights | Leased | Owned or Controlled Shipping Lines | Connecting Lines |

one of the few *Canadiens* in whom business was instinctive. A fighting rebel in 1837 and refugee in 1838, he returned to become a leading lawyer and supporter of Lafontaine. His first speech after being elected a member of Assembly in 1848 was in support of public aid for a railroad to unite Montreal with Portland, Maine. Then and thereafter, he also worked for the improvement and the extension of the Canadian canal system, but the railroad was his love. After five years of determined education of the apathetic and even hostile *Canadiens* in this matter, he was made legal advisor of the Grand Trunk Railway when it was incorporated in 1853. His political slogan was: "I build for the future."

In Canada's first period of railroad building, the decade of the fifties, about 2000 miles were added to the previously existing sixty-six miles of "portage railroads." In addition, two unprecedented structures, the Suspension Bridge at Niagara and the Victoria Bridge at Montreal, were added to the engineering marvels of the time. Most of the capital came from Great Britain where certain great construction firms were already seeking new employment in India and North America as well as in Europe. They were devising ingenious arrangements of loans and guarantees, made through the government in combination with such private bankers as Baring Brothers and Glyn, Mills and Company, their investing customers, and colonial governments, for what has been called "public risk and private profit."

In Canada the central government incurred a debt of about $30,-000,000 in support of the railroads, not to speak of private investment and the subscriptions of towns and cities that hoped to gain by railroad connection. The colony's roads were atrocious and not everyone lived beside a waterway. Whatever the political advantages of railroads in Canada, water transportation was decidedly cheaper for the movement of most of its exports. The dream, however, eclipsed the actuality.

The railroads that were built demonstrated the Canadian dilemma. The politico-economic objective was represented by the Grand Trunk and the Great Western (its first sod was turned by ancient Colonel Talbot at London in 1844!) which aimed to bring the products of the American Middle West to Hamilton and Toronto, and thence to Montreal, Lévis, and Rivière du Loup on the St. Lawrence in the summer, and to Portland in the winter; and by the Northern Railway, connecting Toronto with Collingwood on Georgian Bay (modernizing the old portage route towards Chicago and the Upper Lakes).

Mere economics, on the other hand, was evidenced in the many privately built north-south lines that were designed to carry Canadian and Upper Lake products as directly and cheaply as possible to the

United States, sometimes by direct or close rail connections, but often by connections with water carriage. New York proved more potent than Montreal and Portland. Canada fed the United States in spite of generations of hopes and designs to the contrary. Yet even second-best was proving profitable. Would things be still better if an intercolonial railroad reached out from Rivière du Loup to the Maritimes?

Public works and public credit.—It is a reasonable generalization about railroads in North America to say that until recently the only ways to make money out of most of them were in original underwriting, in building them and supplying their builders, and in reorganizing them when they went bankrupt. The investing public and the taxpayers paid the bills, and in the case of the Grand Trunk, in particular, they were unmercifully and unjustifiably high for many not very reputable reasons, not least of which was the adoption of English standards (expensive construction for low upkeep) in conditions about as unlike their original habitat as possible. Canada had borrowed to build canals before 1850; she now borrowed for railroads, almost trebling her debt, from $18,782,565 in 1850 to $54,142,044 in 1859. Much of the money was spent in Canada, creating the boom conditions of the time, but the money had to be paid for somehow.

Canada did not have, could not have, an income tax, and excises could not be high because it would be so easy to evade them. The fiscal burden, therefore, fell heavily on customs duties. If Canadians were determined to have costly transportation services, they must pay for them in higher prices for imported goods, prices which Canadian producers of similar goods would see no reason to undercut by very much. A much larger and more compact market enabled American manufacturers to undersell their northern neighbors. So the Canadians began about 1845, and more purposefully in 1858, to organize in favor of protective (and revenue-producing) tariffs; and the consumer paid the bill.

Canadians discovered then what they have accepted ever since: a slightly lower standard of living was the price of the transportation services that enabled them to maintain political independence of the United States. For the moment, however, and in spite of the fact that manufactured goods had been expressly excluded from the Reciprocity Treaty, the disturbing consequence of higher Canadian tariffs was that disgruntled Americans began to oppose renewal of the treaty at the end of its term in 1865. Their indignation was mild compared to that of startled British manufacturers at the same time, but of the two the American mood was the more ominous.

Public works and public men.—For the most part, political morality is highly relative. When one finds, for instance, first private bankers and then industrialists and railroad builders at the very heart of British government between 1775 and 1875, one should recall their mercantile predecessors in influence. Similarly, when one finds that the leading politicians of the Maritimes and Canada were publicly up to their ears in unsavory railroad building and privately not above taking advantage of their inside knowledge, one is apt to forget that their predecessors were British spoilsmen saddled at outrageous cost upon struggling little colonies.

Who were some of the "new" leaders? Cartier has been suggested as one of the greatest and most influential among them, and Francis Hincks might be taken as his "opposite number" among the Canadians, although his career was uniquely interrupted in 1855 by a lively twelve-year term as governor, first of Barbados and the Windward Islands, and then of British Guiana. A "radical" who played a key part in both Canadas during the struggle for responsible government, his great financial abilities made him equally important in public finance and in its relations with the British government, British bankers, and the railroads.

A. T. Galt, son of John Galt of the Canada Company, got his start in the British American Land Company in the Eastern townships, but he, too, rose rapidly to the top in the combination of politics, finance, and big business. As that unregenerate old Tory, Sir Allan MacNab, said, railroads were his politics. He might have added that they were world politics too, for Galt became an imperial figure when he lectured British manufacturers on the relation between his new tariffs and responsible government.

One might add such others as the nimble-witted Rouge, A. A. Dorion in Canada East, the brusque Toronto journalist, George Brown, and the inconspicuous, influential, discreet, and acquisitive John Rose of Montreal. About 1860, however, all of these men were beginning to be overshadowed by the future nation-builder, John A. Macdonald. No one excelled him in the tricks of the political trade. As yet he seemed to play second fiddle to Cartier in the conservative equivalent of the Lafontaine-Baldwin radical alliance, but when the time should come for transcending the concerns of half-a-dozen little colonial capitals, his ten years of rather futile Liberal-Conservatism would stand him in good stead. In fact, in spite of its apparently irreconcilable *Canadien* and Canadian conservative elements, his party was to provide Canada with most of its political management from its founding in 1854 until 1896.

✤ DIMINISHING POLITICAL RETURNS

After the retirements of Lafontaine and Baldwin, Canadian politics entered on a downward spiral the subtle course of which cannot be charted here. A considerable amount of constructive business was done for two maturing societies and for the single economy, and both public and politicians became accustomed to power and responsibility on a new scale. New Radical movements, notably the Rouges in Canada East and the Clear Grits in Canada West, voiced new aspirations against old powers, only to lose either their fighting qualities or their marginal members when their new causes grew stale.

It was a prosperous, scandalous, but curiously frustrating time, rather like the period when a young man has more strength than wisdom to direct it. Now that Canada West was more populous than Canada East, Brown and the Grits wanted "Rep [resentation] by Pop [ulation]." The system of basing cabinets on double majorities, *Canadien* and Canadian, became so precarious that finally almost the same heads could pop up in different offices, as in the notorious "Double Shuffle" of 1858. Politically union was failing, for much the same reasons as Calhoun's proposal for government by "concurrent majorities" in the United States.

✤ THE AMERICAN CIVIL WAR

The American failure issued in the Civil War, an event that immensely complicated the course of British North America. The colonies, as we have seen, profited from its demands for goods and services. Some 53,532 persons born in the colonies, perhaps two-thirds of them *Canadiens* dislodged by the waning of opportunity in Canada East, served in the Northern armies. In general, as their early prohibition of slavery and conspicuous asylum for fugitives demonstrated, the colonists favored the North, but their position was impaired by the clear preference of the British government for the South and by the activities of Southern maritime and military agents who used colonial ports as refuges or bases and threatened to (and very rarely did) conduct raids against the United States from the colonies.

The only raid that amounted to much was against St. Albans, Vermont, in 1864. It involved the killing of one man, the wounding of another, and the looting of $200,000 from three banks. Unfortunately the law and courts of Canada were unprepared for such an eventuality, and that failure was built up imposingly in the United States. Actually the Canadian authorities managed to do so much by way of discovering and exposing to Washington the plans of the Southerners that the latter declared they could do nothing. In any case, the United States had been far more injurious to Canada between 1837 and 1842. But the land menace and the usefulness of colonial ports to Southern vessels were amalgamated into a substantial Northern grievance.

Even this might not have been serious but for the bad blood between the North and the British government. It is hard to explain the folly of British diplomacy, particularly in allowing the destructive Southern commerce raiders to be built, armed, provisioned, and facilitated in their escapes from British and British colonial ports. No country would be more vulnerable than Britain to such tactics on the part of others. The British people overwhelmingly favored the North, but few of them had the vote before 1867. The "Ancient Grudge" between Mother Country and Independent Daughter was given plenty to feed on for four years.

The North American colonies were obviously Britain's Achilles' heel. The victorious Northern army and the technically advanced American navy could easily gobble up a region that British military leaders had long ago decided it would be impossible to defend. The United States harbored hundreds of thousands of Irishmen who saw an easy revenge for their own and their country's woes, and from Secretary of State downwards American politicians saw advantages in appealing to Manifest Destiny, the Ancient Grudge, and Irish ambitions. On November 23, 1864, notice was given of intention to terminate the Rush-Bagot Agreement for naval disarmament on the Lakes. On December 17, rigid passport regulations were instituted on the borders. On January 16, 1865, Congress instructed the president to give notice of termination of the Reciprocity Treaty. The two earlier reprisals were dropped in March, but the third was carried out.

When one recalls that at the same time the Red River Valley and British Columbia seemed threatened by expansive American energies, it can be seen that Britain and her North American colonies had grave causes for concern in the spring of 1865. In the colonies themselves, particularly in Canada, politics seemed to have come to the end of a road and, with reciprocity ending in 1866, perhaps economics had come to a dead end too. Fear, then, and frustration served as urgent goads to ambition and daring in the great design of a British North American federation.

CHAPTER XIX

A Mari usque ad Mare (1857-73)

"Some peoples are born nations, some achieve nationhood and others have nationhood thrust upon them. Canadians seem to be among these latter." This wry, astringent dictum by a Canadian historian, A. R. M. Lower, invites its own sequel. Who did the thrusting? What reinforcement, and what resistance, did it find in British North America? One might, indeed, put together a kind of algebraic formula or polygon of forces from the many external and internal elements that converged in pressure upon British North America to unite, but it would be an inexact thing at best. Some of the strongest elements seem to have been like icebergs with most of their mass out of sight. Moreover, there were no constants in the situation, for forces waxed and waned, attracted and repelled each other.

The nearest thing to a certainty was that in the railroad these scattered communities saw an agency that was capable of binding them together. The greatest area of uncertainty was the push and pull between the general nationalistic sentiment and several deep-rooted particularisms. Every aspiring politician had to ask himself whether to come out for a larger stage on which he and his colony might play their parts or to appeal to the narrow but reassuring ways of their own localism. Young Alexander Morris, McGill University's first graduate in arts, might lecture glowingly about a "Nova Britannia" extending from ocean to ocean; D'Arcy McGee might even more effectively transmute his Fenian eloquence into stirring appeals for "a new nationality"; but Joseph Howe might secure revenge by persuading the Nova Scotians that Tupper had sold them out to the Canadians at "eighty cents a head."

FACTORS AND INFLUENCES

The British factor.—Canadian federation was the business of governments, not of the peoples themselves, and British governments played a decisive part. Yet here the contrast between appearance and reality was bewildering. Superficially the years between 1850 and 1872 were the great period of anti-imperialism. Disraeli, Gladstone, Cobden, Bright, practically all political leaders, declared that colonies of European stock were an unjustifiable expense and were bound to grow into independence anyway. Indeed, in 1865, Viscount Bury in his *Exodus of the Western Nations* drew upon the experience of six European nations in the Americas to frame a kind of natural law of colonial independence. "One by one, the last rags of the commercial system have been torn away. We receive no tribute; we expect no advantage . . . yet we undertake the burden of defending them against attack."

Perhaps some of the Little Englanders hoped to have an empire for nothing, but the reasonable conclusion from the evidence relating to Canada is that public opinion was anti-imperial, apathetic, or persuaded that federation was merely a decent way of helping some troublesome little colonies to band together, either for future independence or, more likely, for absorption into the United States. Parliament showed so little interest in the enabling legislation that Macdonald believed the members compared it to "a private bill uniting two or three English parishes."

Some of the sources of the British policy that drove federation along, indeed overrode the opposition of Nova Scotia and, to a lesser degree, of New Brunswick, lay in the shadowy realm of high finance. About 1850, just after the old mercantile colonial system was destroyed, many quiet indications appeared that the big British banking houses, shipping interests, and railroad builders could make governments help them in protecting or extending colonial investments, in sustaining such ventures as steamship services to Asia, Africa, and America, and in taking some of the risk out of contracts to build or operate railroads abroad.

This tacit alliance was seldom admitted publicly or debated in Parliament. It was the product of lobbying at a very high level, sometimes directly between Cabinet ministers and representatives of the interests concerned, sometimes through civil servants to the Cabinet, particularly in a Board of Trade that had been transformed into a board of industry, finance, and communications now that free trade had triumphed. This lobbying could seldom be recognized as the single determinant of policy, but obviously it could often be grafted onto other policies and contribute a substantial adjunct.

The American factor.—American influence on Canadian federation was equally contradictory. Ever since the Revolution, men had been echoing in one way or another Jonathan Mitchel Sewall's exhortation of 1778:

No pent-up Utica contracts your powers
But the whole boundless continent is yours.

The speed of American expansion had been astounding before the railroad, and now that engine of still swifter land conquest had crossed the Mississippi and Missouri and was on its way to "golden California." Another line, the Northern Pacific, chartered in 1864 to run from Duluth to Puget Sound, seemed bound to embrace the Red River Settlement and British Columbia. The electric telegraph had brought Alaska into the picture as the route to Asia, and Secretary of State Seward, who arranged its purchase from Russia in 1867, had been active for years in telling the British North Americans where their manifest destiny lay. "I know," he said in 1867, "that Nature designs that this whole continent, not merely these thirty-six states, shall be, sooner or later, within the magic circle of the American Union."

The United States wanted revenge on Great Britain and demanded $25,000,000 damages for some 284 ships lost to the Southern commerce raiders. British colonies might make a suitable *quid pro quo*. There was a general willingness, too, not to obstruct the Fenian Brotherhood too greatly in their attempts by force of arms against the British North American colonies to get back at Great Britain. The manufacturing interest exercised high tariffs against the colonies after the termination of the Reciprocity Treaty, expecting that they would be unable to stand alone and, as in 1849, would seek admission to the United States. The Taylor Bill of July 2, 1866, even laid down the procedure for their entry.

Widespread and intense as American annexationism was for about six years after the end of the Civil War, particularly in angling for the Irish vote, it never became the avowed national policy. It was argued in the American Cabinet; it was used adroitly within and between the parties during the hectic and unsavory politics that followed Lincoln's death; and it figured frequently in formal and informal diplomatic exchanges and occasionally in such unauthorized adventures as General B. F. Butler's meddling in Prince Edward Island politics. Yet probably the nearest it came to overt policy was in President Grant's hectoring reference in his annual message of December 5, 1870, to the "unfriendly way" in which Canada, the "semi-independent but irresponsible agent" of British jurisdiction in the North Atlantic, had been treating American fishermen, and in his threats to end the bonding privilege and the entry of Canadian vessels to American ports.

Thus the annexation of Canada by force, much as the colonists feared it, never moved up to the forefront of American ambitions. The postwar United States bubbled with what were thought more important opportunities and problems. Canada would probably fall in anyway sometime soon. If the Canadians persisted in their curious obduracy, perhaps Great Britain could be persuaded to give them a shove.

The fate of British North America continued to be secondary to the necessity for understanding between the two Great Powers. The United States and Great Britain needed each other so much and regarded the rest of the world so similarly that war between them must be avoided. Nonetheless, Britain must be made to demonstrate her acceptance of the United States as an equal. There must be an end to what James Russell Lowell in 1868 called "a Certain Condescension in Foreigners." In the meantime, Hamilton Fish, who had explored the Anglo-Canadian situation with shrewd thoroughness, summed it up for Grant's Cabinet: "Great Britain is quite willing to part with Canada when the latter requests it, but will not cede it, in any negotiations, as a satisfaction for any claim."

The Canadian factor.—The leaders of Canada, although profoundly depressed by Little Englandism, did not want to join the United States, which was their manifest and persistent enemy (since the seventeenth century for the *Canadiens,* since 1776 for the Canadians). A. T. Galt, an annexationist in 1849 but a frequent visitor to England on public and private financial business during the fifties, lamented: "It is very grievous to see half a continent slipping away from the grasp of England with scarcely an effort to hold it." His response, clearly, stubbornly, and realistically maintained, was federation of British North America—an independent federation, if necessary. It was he who told the Committee of Ways and Means of the American House of Representatives, after fruitless negotiations for resumption of the Reciprocity Treaty, that the colonies would turn to advantageous intercolonial trade and to trade with the West Indies and Mediterranean.

During the decade following the depression of 1857, there was a curious, half-defiant margin of confidence over doubt in Canada. Prosperity had a great deal to do with it, but denunciation of the Reciprocity Treaty threatened that. Land hunger, the need for a Canadian Middle West, figured significantly. A railroad was needed to reach the Red River Valley, but the Grand Trunk was already in such a mess as to shake public credit.

Defense against serious American attack was impracticable. The seven years of intermittent Fenian menace along the borders from New Brunswick to the Red River, involving one small war with considerable loss of life and property in the Niagara Peninsula and weak raids from Vermont and Dakota, proved dubious and costly even with British help, and that help was very clearly being given for the last time. In

1871, after twenty-five years of effort to make the colonials take over their own defense, the British garrisons were withdrawn, thus fulfilling the expectations expressed by the *Times* (London), March 1, 1867: "We look to Confederation as the means of relieving this country from much expense and much embarrassment." One is forced to conclude that the colonists did not believe that the United States would attempt to conquer them outright.

Some of the Canadian decisiveness was simple determination to find an alternative to political stalemate. There must be some possibility other than the confusions of the fifties, and in one sense those confusions bred federalism as the way out. The "double majority" system became so precarious that it produced two elections and four governments in three years, but it also emphatically demonstrated the insistence of *Canadiens* and Canadians on controlling certain of their own affairs. A federation of Canada East and Canada West could achieve the same ends, leaving joint concerns to the federal authority. And if the federation could be extended to the Atlantic colonies, the joint structure might be a large enough base for the public credit that would permit railroad construction to bind them all together and perhaps to reach out to the Red River and on to the Pacific.

The Maritime factor.—Down in the Maritimes, as we have seen, the economic changes in the world after the mid-century had involved the colonists in forces not very amenable to their wills and therefore productive of indecision, confusion, or, as in Prince Edward Island, misplaced confidence. The great era of lumbering and of the wooden sailing ship, during which they had risen to prominence and prosperity, was drawing to its close. The steamship and the steam railroad, which had raised high hopes during the forties, began to disappoint those hopes, the ships bypassing Halifax and Saint John, and the uneconomic railroads suspended in space, as it were, pending their integration with New England and the United States or with Canada East and the interior.

The natural center of this Atlantic region was Boston rather than Montreal or London, indeed strict utility would have dictated the colonies' entry into the United States. Old loyalties were to Great Britain, and Britain had been more interested in maritime colonies and their naval bases than in inland ones, but she was now plainly impatient over their cost.

The new note in the Maritimes was a growing suspicion that, in Britain's anti-imperial mood, the alternative to joining the United States was coming to terms with the Canadians, a strange, violent, expansive, and not very congenial lot of people who seemed to have caught the hang of the new technologies and their political and financial accompaniments rather better than the Maritimers. Maritime moral superiority towards *Canadien* and Canadian alike grew in proportion to Maritime material inferiority, a cover for uneasiness.

W. M. Whitelaw, the best-informed student of these matters, has provided two reasoned summaries. Of the obscure, halting explorations of the possibility of a Maritime Union, he says:

> Sometimes regarded as an important or essential preliminary to the larger union, frequently as a necessary antidote to it, maritime union was seldom urged, or even thought of, except in some relation to Canadian expansion eastward.

His remarks on the new balance of power in British North America created by the railroad are enlightening:

> Canada, and more particularly Upper Canada, was beginning to turn its eyes toward the West. This left the maritime provinces behind them. It might be said . . . even Great Britain was behind them. . . . With this new outlook there was to come to an end the older designation of Great Britain as "home." English-speaking Canadians were now to join their French-speaking brethren in speaking and thinking of Canada as home, and the old land merely as the mother country. . . . It is significant that when . . . the call to British North American federation came to be heard, French-speaking Canada was swinging to the advantage of admitting the maritime provinces as a counterpoise to the overweening strength of English-speaking Canada, while Upper Canadians were inclined to look hopefully to the West as the ultimate answer to the French challenge to supremacy.

Other regional factors.—Newfoundland, of course, was as far removed as possible from the seat of westward energies; indeed, except for a rather distrustful commercial relationship with Halifax, her outlook was east and south, not west. Her external relations were locked into the diplomacy of Great Britain with France, and the United States and the record of the past made Newfoundlanders continuously uneasy lest their assets be given away. The only time the island colony thought of turning to the mainland for help was in 1857 when the Crimean War alliance of Britain and France threatened to eventuate in some such way.

There was little or no sense of identity with Canada in the Red River Settlement and British Columbia. *La Nation Métisse* wanted to be left alone, by the company, the Americans, and the Canadians. Its leader, Louis Riel, dreamed of a high-minded, free, almost independent republican existence. The trouble was that the time had arrived when the métis had become pawns in contests which they could complicate, but not control. Out on the Pacific coast, the colonists were chiefly Americans, and their only neighbors were either Americans or Russians about to give way to Americans. Their prosperity depended on gold rushes, feverish adventures which brought in more Americans. The Canadian settlements were almost three thousand empty miles away. What substantial reason was there to believe that British Columbia had any other future than incorporation in the American Pacific coast?

FEDERATION

If one disregards the quite natural, if impractical, proposals for federation of British North America that were made at intervals from the American Revolution to Durham's day, the actual achievement took place, with starts and stops, within nine years, 1857–66. The depression of 1857 led the credit-minded Galt to propose a general federation, a cause which he made the condition of his entry into the Cartier-Macdonald conservative ministry after the "Double Shuffle" of 1858.

Galt failed utterly to evoke British interest in a careful formulation of the project during two successive visits to London on railroad and financial business, and it looked as if Cartier and Macdonald had used it as a red herring in their contest with the reformers, for they dropped it from their program for six years. There was talk about it in all the colonies, but as little more than a gambit towards some other end. It figured fairly largely, for instance, in the fervid oratory that greeted Edward, Prince of Wales, during his tour of the colonies in 1860, and there are indications that the idea took root in the mind of the Duke of Newcastle, the Colonial Secretary, who accompanied him.

Next year an English businessman temporarily galvanized the project. Edward W. Watkin of the International Financial Society represented a new phase in capitalism: the reorganization, recapitalization, and repair of distressed enterprises so large and intermeshed with politics that their salvation required both financial skill and persuasive lobbying. Watkin's Society acquired a major interest in two embattled North American corporations—the chaotic Grand Trunk and the "outdated" Hudson's Bay Company. As he saw it, both could be saved by a British North American federation. He set himself the task of persuading the British government to forward this while he roused the colonials to a glorious future.

"Expansion" was the word. He described how he would at the same time nourish the debilitated Grand Trunk between Rivière du Loup and Michigan and swell real estate values in Rupert's Land:

. . . the best route for a Railway to the Pacific was, to commence at Halifax, to strike . . . to Sarnia; to extend that system to Chicago; to use, under a treaty of neutralization, the United States lines from Chicago to

St. Paul; to build a line from St. Paul to Fort Garry by English and American capital, and then to extend this line to the Tete Jaune Pass, there to meet a Railway through British Columbia starting from the Pacific. . . .

In September, 1861, he arranged that governmental delegations from Nova Scotia and New Brunswick should be taken at Grand Trunk expense to Portland, Montreal, Detroit, and Chicago before a conference with a similar Canadian delegation at Quebec. Taking back with him to London the colonists' renewed offer to aid in building the intercolonial railroad link from Rivière du Loup to Moncton, he plunged into conversations with Newcastle. Those conversations and the subsequent representations of a mixed colonial delegation abruptly lost their impetus, however, because of the Anglo-American crisis that was caused when a Northern naval vessel stopped the British mail steamer "Trent" and insisted on removing two Southern diplomatic representatives.

Britain immediately sent military reinforcements to Canada. Although their inability to get up the frozen St. Lawrence except in sleighs added weight to the argument for an intercolonial railroad, Watkin now had to proceed more slowly and substantially. For one thing, the Canadian legislature soon bore out the worst expectations of the anti-imperialists by defeating their government's Militia Bill in May, 1862.

It was with Newcastle's blessing that delegations from Nova Scotia, New Brunswick, and Canada met at Quebec in September, 1862, to discuss the railroad, commercial union, and political union. They learned a good deal about each other, enough at any rate to sheer off from the union proposals and to bid their delegates to London to confine themselves to the railroad. In London they even differed among themselves and with the British government about that, but the Canadians decided to proceed on their own with a new survey of the route by Sandford Fleming.

The year 1863 proved to be a turning point, largely because of bitternesses arising out of the Civil War. The military might and productive strength of the North grew more ominous daily, and threats were freely uttered that not only would the Reciprocity Treaty be terminated, but the privilege of moving colonial goods across the United States would be withdrawn, thus presumably reducing Canada to impotence. It was during the summer of 1863 that the eloquence of D'Arcy McGee, a former Fenian and rebel of 1848, found outlet in magnificent pleas "for British American Nationality," delivered in the course of a lecture tour of Canada and the Maritimes. That winter, policy began to harden in Great Britain.

In December, a troublesome Confederate raider named the "Chesapeake" (a captured Northern vessel) was abandoned at Sambro, just outside Halifax. The Northern navy took her into Halifax, but the courts refused to authorize her return to her original owners, thereby intensifying Northern anger against Great Britain and Nova Scotia. A firm and comprehensive policy in British North American affairs became urgent. Watkin later published an obviously selective account of his activities in Great Britain and North America at the time, but much of the relationship between high policy and high finance must still be surmised. At the Cabinet level, however, it was decided to put Britain's weight behind coalition of the colonies.

The opportunity at Charlottetown.—The focal occasion proved to be a meeting of Maritime delegations at Charlottetown in September, 1864, the outcome of an apathetic, doomed exploration of union among themselves that had been engineered largely by Lieutenant Governor Gordon of New Brunswick rather than by the colonial governments. The vital spark came from Canada where, in June, 1864, legislative futility had culminated in the surprising combination of archenemies, the reformer George Brown and the conservative J. A. Macdonald, with Galt and Cartier in the background, and the enthusiast Alexander Morris as the go-between. The governor, Lord Monck, had been tactfully active. The price paid for getting the Canadian legislature off dead-center was that Brown and the Clear Grits retreated from "Rep. by Pop.," or federation merely of Canada West and East, to join Cartier and Macdonald in promoting a more general federation at Charlottetown.

All the guns of the federation battery were brought to bear on the target with great rapidity. The new Colonial Secretary, Edward Cardwell, sanctioned the enlarged meeting at Charlottetown. Having secured their invitation, the Canadian Cabinet settled down to hard work on their big federal scheme. Meanwhile General Manager C. J. Brydges of the Grand Trunk, along with McGee and Sandford Fleming, organized a magnificent preparatory junket of Canadian legislators and journalists by train to Portland and by boat to the Maritimes, which roused New Brunswick and Nova Scotia considerably during August.

When the Maritimers met in a curiously uncertain way at Charlottetown on Thursday, September 1, they put off their own agenda to await the arrival of the Canadian ministerial party. When the latter arrived at noon on their government steamer "Queen Victoria," W. H. Pope, the only notable island advocate of the broad federation, rowed out to explain that, because a circus was straining the little capital's accommodations, most of them would have to live on the boat.

The well-prepared newcomers began to present their case in highly systematic fashion next day. Cartier led off on provincial rights; Brown introduced the balancing of numerical representation in the lower house of the legislature by sectional representation in the upper; and Macdonald took all day Saturday for advocacy of a strong central government for matters of common concern. On Monday Galt dazzled the conference with a brilliant exposition of federal finance.

After some discussion of details on Tuesday, the Maritimers, unprepared for such seasoned discussion, met alone on Wednesday, postponed Maritime Union, and consigned everything to informal and formal discussions that took place during a loosely organized grand tour that included the island's north shore, Pictou, the coal mines, Truro, Halifax, Windsor, Saint John, Fredericton, and Shediac. At Halifax on the twelfth it was agreed to meet on October 10 at Quebec in a formal conference on the larger federal proposal. Newfoundland was invited. From Charlottetown on, a Mr. Levesey, representing the Intercolonial Contract Company of London, had been trailing the Maritimers and negotiating to build the railroad between Truro and the Bend (Moncton), but although he followed them to Quebec, Brydges and Watkin were "in on the ground floor."

It was at Halifax that Macdonald marked the turning point in his life. Hitherto he had been politically adroit and the power behind Cartier, but the essential futility of politics in Canada had been reflected in his notoriously flippant and dissolute life. Now he summed up the past and welcomed the future:

I have been dragging myself through the dreary waste of colonial politics. I thought there was no end, nothing worthy of ambition, but now I see something which is well worthy of all I have suffered in the cause of my little country. . . . There may be obstructions, local prejudices may arise, disputes may occur, local jealousies may intervene, but it matters not—the wheel is now revolving and we are only the fly on the wheel; we cannot delay it—the union of the colonies of British America under the Sovereign is a fixed fact.

It was tragic that Howe, who had felt similarly thwarted even earlier, could not reach out towards the same vision.

The Quebec Conference.—Public opinion had been sounded and found on the whole favorable, and all parties were better prepared for their task at Quebec, although because of certain domestic vicissitudes the Newfoundland representatives carried little authority. All the colonial capitals were linked by telegraph and cable, but, since the Atlantic cable had broken down, the Colonial Secretary, Cardwell, was out of touch with the conference. In it the Atlantic colonies had four votes to Canada's two, but Canada was outvoted by all of them only once, whereas Prince Edward Island opposed all the rest at least half the time. Having feared absorption by Nova Scotia or New Brunswick for almost a century, the minute colony was still more apprehensive of a proposed federation in which it would be almost lost to sight.

Since the delegates completed their work between October 10 and October 29 (at Montreal) in the form of the seventy-two Quebec Resolutions which, with little alteration, formed the subsequent federal constitution, they have sometimes been credited with prodigious abilities. One needs to remember the work put in by the Canadian Cabinet before and after Charlottetown, and the six weeks during which the Maritimers had the bones of the matter to chew on.

At Quebec, once agreement in principle on an over-all federation had been voted, there were stormy and prolonged debates on its details. In general, the Canadians knew what they wanted and were united on it and the Maritimers were just the opposite, but the Canadians were willing to give the Maritimes greater weight than their wealth and numbers called for.

Throughout the discussions, the general belief that the American Civil War demonstrated the need for a strong central government possessing the residuary power worked mightily against over-great "states' rights." Indeed, by a nice analogy to Watkin's promotional methods, the central government was to be like a holding company and the local governments like subordinate companies. The conference broke up with Resolution Seventy-two declaring that the delegates' signatures to the resolutions merely authenticated them for submission to their respective governments.

The final flourish was a tour of Upper Canada and an irregular revelation in the press of what had been agreed upon. This committed the Colonial Office to unequivocal support, although it was ignorant of public opinion. It was the more willing to be favorable, however, because along with the conference report it had another from its defense expert, Lieutenant Colonel W. F. D. Jervois, to the effect that the Canadians were willing to accept Jervois's proposals for defensive works provided that the costs should be levied upon the future federation.

Recall that Northern victory was in sight and that reprisals against British North America began in November. The St. Alban's raid took place during the meetings at Quebec. Recall also that the Canadians had expressed their anxiety to extinguish the Hudson's Bay Company's territorial title and to take the Red River and British Columbia under the federal wing.

These seem to have been the reasons why Cardwell sent out his unanticipated approval of the general federation to Governor Monck at Quebec without waiting to hear from lieutenant governors MacDonell of Nova Scotia and Gordon of New Brunswick. They had both written condemning it, partly because they thought they were expected to promote only Maritime Union, but largely because the people of their colonies were drawing back in alarm from what their representatives had involved them in.

Britain overrides resistance.—It took two years and the full weight of Britain's resources to get a federation established and extended. The Canadians did not consult their electorate, but they did fight the matter out thoroughly in their legislature during February and March, 1865. This patient, searching debate found most of the upper Canadians favorable, but a substantial number from Canada East, *Canadiens* and Canadians, liberals and conservatives, opposed. Cartier and Galt were able finally to reassure most of them and the resolutions passed both Houses of the legislature by large majorities.

But in a March election the people of New Brunswick rejected the government of S. L. Tilley for favoring the measure. At the same time, Howe thought he saw his chance to overturn Tupper in Nova Scotia, but the latter was smart enough to avoid an election in which he, like Tilley, would certainly have been defeated. The lieutenant governors, Gordon and MacDonell, courted popular favor by their opposition to federation. Prince Edward Island would have none of the scheme. In Newfoundland the matter was submitted to the electorate in November, 1865, and sustained, but the new legislature quickly began to reflect popular doubts, and the government in March, 1866, decided to wait and see. Newfoundland was to wait for eighty-three years.

The one omen of the year favorable for general action was the meeting at Quebec in September of a "Confederate Council" representing all the colonies and bent upon intercolonial and other substitutes for trade with the United States.

The Canadians would have federated merely the two Canadas, but the British government could not give up so easily a scheme that seemed able to settle so many problems at once. The financiers and railroad-builders could not bear to have the cup dashed from their lips, and a benign, if uninformed and uninterested, British public thought it a splendid idea to throw the colonies together and trust to the agglomeration to look after itself.

Two successive British governments, therefore, one Liberal and one Conservative, felt that they had to act. Gordon was called home and sent back with explicit, urgent orders. MacDonell was shifted to Hong Kong and a Nova Scotian officer in the British Army, Sir W. Fenwick Williams, the heroic defender of Kars during the Crimean War, went out to replace him bearing instructions similar to Gordon's. Monck in Canada was left in no doubt as to what to do.

The American goad finishes the work.—Yet the Fenians in a sense did it, for they raided and ravaged the Niagara Peninsula and threatened New Brunswick in 1866. As the American Congress refused to renew reciprocity except on ridiculous terms, it ended on March 17, 1866. The alarmed New Brunswickers brought back Tilley in a May–June election. This nerved Tupper to accept London's invitation to send delegates to an intercolonial conference in December.

At Westminster the British guarantee for an intercolonial railroad was made explicit at last, and, except for some modest modifications of the Quebec Resolutions, the job was done. "Federation" was misleadingly altered to "Confederation"; the really appropriate name, "Kingdom of Canada," was dropped at British insistence to avoid offending the United States; and Tilley found the substitute in Psalm 72—"He shall have dominion also from sea to sea, and from the river unto the ends of the earth."

Parliament passed the British North America Bill in an apathetic way, although Howe and a delegation from Nova Scotia went to England to oppose it. The bill became law on March 28, 1867, and a federal Canada composed of Nova Scotia, New Brunswick, Quebec, and Ontario came into being on July 1, the date chosen long before as terminal date for one of the putative intercolonial railroad schemes.

Macdonald pierced the vaporous clouds of self-congratulation: "We are all mere petty provincial politicians at present; perhaps by and by some of us will rise to the level of national statesmen." When the baronetcies and knighthoods were distributed to the leading "Fathers of Confederation," it was notable that Watkin was knighted, as was the purposefully inconspicuous Canadian financier, John Rose. Men like these unfortunately see to it that the details of their work must be left largely to the imagination.

A CONSERVATIVE CONSTITUTION

"Whereas the Provinces . . . have expressed their desire to be federally united into one Dominion . . . with a Constitution similar in principle to that of the United Kingdom: etc." These apparently contradictory opening words of the B.N.A. Act meant what they said. The federal principle was adopted, but the form of the institutions and their working were to be British, although already considerably Canadianized by local practice. Canada thus received a written constitution, but also a good deal of the important unwritten constitution.

Government was vested in a governor general; a Senate of seventy-two persons nominated for life, equally divided among Ontario, Quebec, and the Maritime Provinces; and an elected House of Commons in which Quebec had sixty-five members and the others totals in the ratio of their populations to Quebec's, to be revised after decennial censuses beginning in 1871. The executive was to be in "the Queen's Privy Council for Canada," part of which formed a Cabinet responsible to Parliament. That is, sovereignty was in Parliament and its electors, and reliance was rested on the sensitive functioning of a dependent executive rather than on the fixed American structure with its checks and balances and supposed division of the executive, legislative, and judicial powers. Neither prime minister nor Cabinet was mentioned in the act, but the "privileges, immunities, and powers" of the British Parliament were expressly assumed.

The Canadian model was naturally the old semifederal relationship of the imperial Parliament and the colonial legislatures. The British North American colonies had not been sovereign states creating a federal authority by delegation; the British Parliament had heard their wishes and created both it and their rights under it. Macdonald had previously summed it up: "The General Government assumes towards the local governments precisely the same position as the Imperial Government holds with respect to each of the colonies now."

This was evidenced in unlimited federal powers of taxation, the federal appointment of provincial lieutenant governors as "officers of the Dominion," and arrangements for possible federal disallowance of provincial legislation. The provinces pretty well retained their former governmental structures, but were restricted to "direct taxation," that is, of real estate.

To counter "the weakness of the American system" or "the point where the American Constitution breaks down," in the distribution of legislative powers "all the great subjects" were assigned to the federal Parliament, plus residuary powers, while what were thought to be carefully specified local matters were assigned to the provinces. Time and ingenious lawyers were soon to expose this naïve confidence in having precisely distributed the powers. In particular, the apparently innocent, but unlucky, thirteenth category of local authority was "Property and civil rights in the Province," a marvelous invitation to expansion that was not neglected.

The intercolonial railroad was to be undertaken by Canada within six months. The grave differences in "Revenues; Debts; Assets; Taxation" were accommodated by the single trading and fiscal area and by highly ingenious federal subsidies to the provinces written into Section

VIII of the act. What were regarded as adequate safe-guarding clauses protected religion and education, language, and the *Canadien* civil code from being overridden, but there was then no general "bill of rights" protecting the citizens against the state.

Ontario, New Brunswick, and Nova Scotia were to adopt uniform civil law, English criminal law with statutory additions was to be general, and the judges, with minor exceptions, were to be appointed "during good behavior" by the federal government on the advice of the several provincial Bars, subject to removal by address of both Houses of Parliament. Provision was made for the admission of "Newfoundland, Prince Edward Island, British Columbia, Rupert's Land and Northwestern Territory into the Union by Order in Council," with careful specification of the Senate representation of the first two that was distinctly more considerate towards the larger island.

ADDITIONS AND AN ATTEMPTED SUBTRACTION

Grabbing for the West.—Ontario wanted Canada to get possession of the West at once; indeed two Toronto journalists, George Brown and William McDougall, had been beating that drum for almost twenty years. Brown's representations in this matter to Jervois and the British government in the autumn of 1864 followed the challenging of the company's rights, by charter to Rupert's Land and by license to the Northwestern Territory, which had emanated from the Red River Settlement and engaged the British Parliament after 1857. Between 1857 and 1861 Canada expended a good deal of money and energy on exploring for an all-British route to the West.

In 1861, as we have seen, Watkin and his banking associates began to eclipse such petty ventures. To make a long story short, in 1865 the British government agreed when Brown, Cartier, Galt, and Macdonald "proposed to the Imperial Ministers that the whole British Territory east of the Rocky Mountains and north of the American and Canadian lines should be made over to Canada, subject to such rights as the Hudson's Bay Company might be able to establish; and that the compensation to the company (if any were found to be due) should be met by a loan guaranteed by Great Britain." Federal Canada got to work as soon as it came into existence, and the British Parliament passed the enabling legislation in July, 1868.

Macdonald and the federal government behaved with shocking ignorance and carelessness of *La Nation Métisse*. They ignored the settlers by arranging to incorporate the huge area under an appointed lieutenant governor and council. Louis Riel, who reflected his people's feelings, made himself dictator of the settlement and proclaimed a provisional government in December, 1869, after Canadian surveyors and other agents had moved in in a truculent and exploiting manner. W. B. O'Donoghue, a Fenian conspirator, tried to use his membership in Riel's government to wrest the territory from Great Britain. Riel, in the meantime, effectively frightened the bumbling McDougall, intended lieutenant governor, off the ground, but his somewhat unstable personality ran away with him and he ordered the execution of a provocative and uncontrollable Ontario Orangeman named Thomas Scott who opposed him. The passions excited in Ontario and Quebec by that regrettable act have tainted Canadian politics ever since.

There was a prodigious to-do among the British, Canadian, and Red River elements during the winter of 1869–70, with Bishop Taché, Grand Vicar Thibault, and Colonel de Salaberry negotiating from the *Canadien* side, Donald Smith of the company from the Canadian, and an expedition of British regular troops and Canadian militia making its way through the wilderness from Lake Superior to take over the region and thereafter transfer it tranquilly from Britain to Canada. Riel withdrew to the United States, but his resistance to Canada, while he professed loyalty to Great Britain, had been highly salutary.

The negotiators worked out an acceptable compromise of views: Canada accepted the transfer of the West, the area roughly corresponding to Selkirk's Assiniboia became the self-governing province of Manitoba (July 15, 1870), and the remainder was administered by an appointed governor and council as the North West Territories. Watkin did well for the company which his society had taken over. It began to prosper on the basis of a cash payment of £300,000, ownership of 45,000 acres around its posts, and the right to claim blocks of land up to one-twentieth of the fertile areas. Canada had rather crassly secured room to grow and it hardly deserved Riel's effective assistance in 1871 when John O'Neill and his Fenians tried to upset the exclusion of the United States by an invasion from Minnesota.

Nova Scotia's attempt to withdraw.—One reason for insufficient attention to the situation in the West was Howe's attempt to take Nova Scotia out of federal Canada. That province sent poor Tupper alone with eighteen of his opponents to the first federal Parliament, and the provincial elections returned thirty-six antifederationists out of thirty-eight seats. Once more it was Great Britain that met the shock. Howe and a delegation representing Nova Scotia's determination to withdraw were met by London's refusal to permit secession, whereupon frustration found expression in threats to join the United States. Macdonald, sensing that that was the turning point, personally negotiated the way out. Howe was taken into the federal Cabinet and later made lieutenant governor of Nova Scotia, while the province's subsidy, written into the British North America Act only two years before, was increased by $140,000.

British Columbia's turn.—The Canadian acquisition of the West to the Rockies interested the colony beyond them, sinking under its debt of $1,000,000 and with emigration still unchecked. The controlling group in the colony held out for its British complexion, but hardly thought of doing so through remote Canada. Opposing them, a substantial group believed in the inevitability of entry into the United States.

Here again the British government put its effective strength into play, replacing a diffident, even obstructive governor with a dutiful, aggressive one. After four years of confused and confusing activities on the part of various groups in various places, including De Cosmos' lively British Columbia federationists, Macdonald made the breathtaking decision to secure British Columbia by the promise to begin a railroad to the coast within two years and complete it in ten—this on the part of less than four million people separated from the Pacific by about 700 miles of towering, precipitous mountains, 1000 miles of plains, and 1200 miles of Laurentian Shield. This was Macdonald at his adventurous best. British Columbia was admitted July 20, 1871.

Prince Edward Island falls in.—Prince Edward Island "made it seven" on the sixth anniversary of the dominion because there was nothing else to do. Having been seduced into building a railroad, the island quickly found itself helpless. The contract set the construction rate per mile. The contractors chose the easiest routes, thereby increasing the mileage, and 2½ per cent added to the customs duties could not meet interest charges on a colonial debt that climbed from $250,000 to $4,000,000 in a decade. The contractors pledged their payment in 6 per cent debentures to the bank (one of them held $120,000 worth with a capital of $97,000), and the banks could not sell the debentures in Halifax or anywhere else.

After some face-saving amendments were accepted by the opposition, a hasty deal with Canada was made by the government, January–March, 1873. The island did remarkably well for itself. Canada took on the railroad guaranty and communications with the mainland, provided $800,000 to buy out the island's absentee proprietors, and granted an abnormally generous subsidy.

🍁 ACCEPTANCE BY THE UNITED STATES

It should be remembered that this daring, almost foolhardy, nation-building was carried on during continuous threats of annexation by the United States and in the face of overwhelming American power to make those threats good. Congress expressed its dislike of the original federation at the time, and, once the impeachment and trial of President Johnson were over in 1868, Senator Charles Sumner, chairman of the Foreign Affairs Committee, let himself go in an unbalanced fashion until he reached the point of inflating the "Alabama" claims with "indirect claims" for the prolongation of the Civil War to at least two, possibly eight, billion dollars. He and others then demanded that Britain pay the bill with British North America, indeed in January, 1871, Sumner demanded her withdrawal from the entire Western Hemisphere. This mad extravagance assured his retirement as chairman of the powerful Senate committee, but the annexationist threat remained.

The point to be observed in all this is that Canada's fate was secondary to a crucial Anglo-American conflict. If it could be settled, perhaps Canada would be spared. Through Sir John Rose, the Canadian go-between and partner of the American banker-politician Levi P. Morton, the Gladstone government had unsuccessfully sounded out the new Grant administration in July, 1869, in an effort to find a way of retreat from the position taken by Lord John Russell concerning the Southern commerce-raiders.

The Canadians, aware that action by the big Powers would certainly affect them, began assembling their assets—the inshore Atlantic fisheries resumed with the termination of the Reciprocity Treaty, the St. Lawrence waterway, and their claims for losses and expenses incurred from the Fenian menace. There is evidence that the Canadian government valued the Fenian claims chiefly as leverage towards other ends. Efforts to enforce sovereignty over the fisheries by licenses having been ignored by the Americans, Canada set up an enforcing squadron and began to seize offending vessels in 1870.

It looked like 1854 all over again, a situation that might be made to yield renewal of commercial reciprocity. The startling course of the Franco-Prussian War meanwhile increased Britain's anxiety to settle relations with the United States. The fall elections of 1870 did something to quiet the stridencies of American politics.

Rose went back to Washington in January, 1871, prepared, in response to a proposal from Hamilton Fish, Secretary of State, to admit that Britain had been wrong and to promise that she would now cooperate in an International Joint Commission in Washington to settle all outstanding disagreements. Sir John Macdonald was appointed one of the British commissioners, that is, to act for the British government instead of his own. He thereupon made himself the monkey wrench in the smoothly prepared machinery while Britain acted nervously anxious to please and the United States vigorously exploited the situation. It was fortunate that Macdonald's stubborn rearguard action did not upset an Anglo-American accord, for that was Canada's prime requirement, little as most Canadians realized it.

At the end of a superbly calculated performance, Canada came out of the melee, having surrendered access to the inshore fisheries for ten years (plus two years for notice of termination), having failed to secure commercial reciprocity, and with no consideration of her Fenian claims. For the same term of years, however, she secured free access for her sea fish and fish oil to the American market, joined the United States in reciprocal arrangements for the use of inland and Alaskan waterways and of the bonding privilege, and had her claims to compensation for the fisheries and to a boundary through the San Juan Islands between Washington and British Columbia submitted to arbitration. Great Britain agreed to submit the "Alabama" claims to arbitration under a previously extracted definition of neutrality that undermined Russell's untenable position.

Very few Canadians could understand what had happened, but Macdonald, who did not expect to be understood, had secured a clause in the Treaty of Washington requiring ratification by the Canadian Parliament. His ace in the hole was a promise from the Gladstone government that it would compensate Canada for its Fenian claims against the United States! Canada, in Gladstone's view, had suffered for Britain's sins in Ireland. Macdonald stiffly refused any money payment, but indicated that a British guarantee for a large railroad loan would be acceptable. Actually, after some rather ignoble British maneuvers, in 1872 the guarantee for a loan to build the now unnecessary Jervois fortifications of 1864 was converted into one for an intercolonial railroad.

It required over seven years to implement the Treaty of Washington, and the often sordid details need not be repeated here. In the arbitration of claims one commission awarded the United States $15,500,000 for damage done by the commerce-raiders; another levied $5,500,000 against her to balance matters in the fisheries; and a third awarded Great Britain almost $2,000,000 in settlement of other claims. Macdonald got the treaty through the Canadian Parliament in May, 1872, by holding his hand until his opponents had committed themselves to positions which he could destroy by pointing out that he had signed as commanded by the British, not the Canadian, government. In 1872 the German Emperor repudiated the Canadian line through the San Juan Islands and accepted the American. After the large award against the United States in the fisheries (in 1877), it was announced that the

United States would denounce the fisheries clauses of the treaty as of July 1, 1885, the earliest possible date.

Yet all these things added together were less important to Canada than two general considerations: the achievement of Anglo-American understanding and the formal acceptance of transcontinental Canada by the United States. Superficially neither seemed secure; actually both were to endure.

CANADA'S APPEAL TO IMPERIAL SENTIMENT

Macdonald was a notoriously unsentimental man and an outright, even passionate, Canadian nationalist. Unlike Galt, he thought it "simply nonsense" to think that Canada was ready for independence, but, unlike the colonial-minded, he thought it equally ridiculous that Canada should take orders from Great Britain. In other words, his objective was the free association, what he called "a healthy and cordial alliance," that had been refused to the Americans a century earlier.

Macdonald had been quite properly alarmed by the sustained campaign of Edward Cardwell and the Liberals in Great Britain that had culminated in notice given February 12, 1870, that aside from a small imperial garrison in Halifax and another to be left for one year at Quebec, all else would be withdrawn and the defense facilities handed over to Canada. It was even suggested that Canada should assume her naval defense. In very emphatic public dispatches and private letters Sir John had tried to overthrow that Liberal orthodoxy. A considerable backfire developed in Britain's press and Parliament during the alarm engendered by Prussia's swift triumph over France, but "the legions" were resolutely withdrawn in 1871 to the tune of "Good-bye, Sweetheart, Good-bye" and "Auld Lang Syne." The same procedure was followed elsewhere throughout the world in Britain's self-governing colonies, at an annual saving of about £4,000,000.

In his appeal of May 3, 1872, to the Canadian Parliament to ratify the Treaty of Washington, Macdonald embodied his aims very subtly and successfully:

Let Canada be severed from England—let England not be responsible to us, and for us, and what could the United States do to England? . . . England has got the supremacy on the sea—she is impregnable in every point but one, and that point is Canada; and if England does call upon us to make a financial sacrifice; does find it for the good of the Empire that we, England's first colony, should sacrifice something. I say that we would be unworthy of our proud position if we were not prepared to do so. [Cheers.] I hope to live to see the day, and if I do not that my son may be spared to see Canada the right arm of England, [cheers] to see Canada a powerful auxiliary to the Empire, and not a cause of anxiety and a source of danger.

About seven weeks later, on June 24, 1872, the astute Disraeli, seeking for a new and persuasive Conservative policy with which to counter Gladstone's triumphant Liberals, pulled out all the stops of the organ in praise of imperialism at the Crystal Palace. The *Times,* as usual defending the *status quo* as long as it was deemed not seriously threatened, took up arms against him and, as usual, used Canada as the ungrateful, bad example. An especially savage attack of October 30, 1872, on Canada, along these lines, roused Tennyson from his romantic Arthurian epics to address a poem of curiously mixed, but strongly royalist and imperialist, sentiments "To the Queen." Among the millions who had recently offered up prayers of thanks for the recovery of the Prince of Wales from serious illness, he chose to note the people of London:

> And that true North, whereof we lately heard
> A strain to shame us, 'Keep you to yourselves;
> So loyal is too costly! friends—your love
> Is but a burthen; loose the bond, and go.'
> Is this the tone of empire? here the faith
> That made us rulers?

Events were to reveal that Macdonald, Disraeli, and the Laureate had caught the turn of the imperial tide.

CHAPTER XX

Integration vs. Disintegration (1873-85)

In the circumstances prevailing in Canada and elsewhere in the world at the end of the sixties it was almost inevitable that idealistic nationalism would emerge and be blended with more material considerations. This was not to be expected in the upset and overridden Maritimes, for they were not even connected directly with central Canada by rail and in their various moods of unease were resentful and suspicious. Indeed, for another two generations they were apt to greet a visiting compatriot from Ontario with the remark "So you're down from Canada, eh?" But in Ontario there was too much of a new sense of mission not to be given some formal expression. Much as in the new German Empire or in Italy, the missionaries of the new order took the name "Canada First," not first among the nations, but above local particularisms.

Significantly, they were entirely an English-speaking group, stemming from Toronto, with some affiliations at Ottawa, the national capital. More enthusiastic than systematic or disciplined, they gave all sorts of national ideas an airing from 1868 to 1875. When their group broke up, the members entered other groups which had borrowed their ideas and grafted them onto sometimes flatly contradictory policies. Their leaders, William Allen Foster, a lawyer, Charles Mair, a poet and novelist whose imagination was fired by the West, and G. T. Denison, who became a fire-eating militarist and imperialist, deserve mention as symbols rather than for any great intellectual, aesthetic, or political merits.

They left behind them a club in Toronto, a good but short-lived weekly, *The Nation,* and a Canadian National Association that was soon swallowed up by others. The ideas in Foster's declaratory speech of 1871, "Canada First," were in the air at the time—protectionism, a voice in treaty-making, internal reforms, advances towards national character and status, imperial federation, and so forth, and they were formulated principally by two earlier political groups, the one looking towards something like independence and the other banking on the British connection. The ideas persisted, though the movement died, and they were, of course, much muddied when interested persons interjected annexation to the United States.

🍁 THE BLIGHT OF ULTRAMONTANISM

In Quebec, the Rouges were nationalists, but, unfortunately for them, they were tarred by the brush that the Vatican had recently been wielding vigorously against nationalism and liberalism in Europe. The *Syllabus of Errors* of 1864, the end of the papacy's temporal power, and the dogma of papal infallibility in 1870 were links in a chain of conservative reaction to the events of 1848. In Quebec it took the form of a revival of the ultramontanism that *Canadiens* had had to cope with since the days of Laval, now greatly strengthened by the prevailing rejection of France, Gallican to the point of godlessness, and by an inclination to substitute the Vatican as the principal outside enhancement of Quebec's particularism.

Hence the curious and often tragic conflict within *Canadien* nationalism—on the one hand, the Rouges and their liberal successors urging the independence of the state and of the national church in terms of democracy, and, on the other, the ultramontanists, who, while advocating the same things, favored in addition the subordination of the state to the church and the extension of papal infallibility on faith and morals to bishop and curé on all matters. Non-Catholics might find it useful to recall that ultramontanism could be a serious nuisance to the Vatican, indeed it sometimes gave more trouble than all the rest of Christendom. Some ultramontanists (including *Canadiens*) carried their extremism to the point of asserting that the pope could err, and of course had erred, in matters of fact. The Red River "rebellion" greatly complicated this already confused mixture of racism, nationalism, liberalism, and ultramontanism because Quebec held that Riel had been unfairly treated. Indeed the nickname for the ultramontanists was *Castors* (beavers), a reference to the Jesuit dream of the seventeenth century. In politics, of course, they were the *Bleus*.

French Canada's *Kulturkampf,* or conflict of philosophies, coincided with Germany's, and was every bit as intricate. Its character was pretty well epitomized in *l'affaire Guibord*. Joseph Guibord was a printer who belonged to the *Institut Canadien,* refused to renounce it, and died, deprived of last rites, in 1869, just after the ultramontanist Bishop Ignace Bourget of Montreal, with papal authorization, had announced that the sacraments would be denied to its members. His body was refused burial in consecrated ground. His friends sought redress on civil grounds and carried the case through the courts to a favorable decision in the British Privy Council. When they attempted the burial, an ultramontanist mob prevented them. When they secured military assistance and completed their mission in Côte des Neiges cemetery in November, 1875, protecting the coffin with a cover of reinforced concrete, Bishop Bourget deconsecrated the ground. The *Institut* and the Rouges were smashed and many priests instructed their parishioners that to vote for a Liberal was a serious fault, some even that it was a mortal sin, an assurance of hell.

It was not until 1877 that a young barrister and journalist named Wilfrid Laurier hit upon a way out of this dangerous impasse. In an address to the *Club Canadien* of Quebec he made the distinction between the Continental liberalism condemned by the Pope and the British liberalism to which he adhered because only it could prevent the fatal division of Canadian politics on purely ethnic lines. Gradually, too, the church in Canada and Rome moved to hold ultramontanism in check. It required papal missions in 1878 and 1897, not to speak of less imposing efforts, to curb the use of ecclesiastical sanctions in politics. Meanwhile the *Canadien* voter was swinging in behind Laurier, in spite of the ultramontanists.

This savage campaign by the ultramontanists had sad effects on a literary and aesthetic life that had recently been promising. The destruction of the *Institut Canadien* at Montreal and the dispersal of its fine library were grievous enough, but the stifling of new voices and thoughts was worse. The only notable new literary artist between 1867 and 1900 was the poet, Louis Fréchette, who took refuge in Chicago for a number of years, and then courageously sat as a Liberal in the federal Parliament. When the French Academy crowned his *Fleurs boréales et oiseaux de neige* in 1880, even ultramontanism could not submerge *Canadien* pride, but gradually even he was overwhelmed in abuse. Historical writing, also, was subjected to such tendentious criticism that only a gifted writer like Abbé H. R. Casgrain, also crowned by the French Academy in 1885, or an entertaining antiquarian like Benjamin Sulte, could be at all faithful to the proper standards. Fréchette also wrote many popular tales, little stories of French Canada which worked a new and innocent vein and found many imitators.

🍁 LITERATURE, ARTS, AND SCIENCES

There was, about this time, a marked inclination towards nationalistic historical writing among English-speaking Canadians. As a Methodist reviewer said in 1881: "It is an evidence that the pulse of national life beats more and more strongly among us, that so many books by Canadian authors on Canadian subjects, and especially upon Canadian history, are finding publishers and readers." J. C. Dent wrote on the period from 1835 to 1880; William Kingsford embarked on a ten-volume history of Canada which he carried to 1841; Egerton Ryerson wrote his *Reminiscences* and two volumes on the loyalists; Francis Hincks, Canniff Haight, George Bryce, G. M. Grant, Andrew Begg, and others combined their recollections with the public record; and there was a great outburst of church histories to accompany the organization of national churches.

Little of this writing was systematically critical, but the foundations for that form were being laid. Daniel Wilson's chair of history at the University of Toronto (1853) was paralleled at Queen's in 1870, Dalhousie in 1880, and McGill in 1895. Archival collection in North America and by transcripts from the United States and Europe, begun by Andrew Brown in eighteenth-century Halifax and Georges Faribault in mid-nineteenth-century Quebec, was accompanied by the publication of documents after the establishment of the Public Archives of Canada under Douglas Brymner in 1871–72.

The new method of rather arid reliance on the sources emerged most clearly in the work of Beamish Murdoch, Duncan Campbell, and T. B. Akins in the Maritimes during the sixties and seventies, but it soon began to be blended with literary and synthetic art. The foundations for critical scholarship were completed after G. M. Wrong succeeded Sir Daniel Wilson at Toronto in 1894. Alert to contemporary developments in the United States, Great Britain, and Continental Europe, he and H. H. Langton succeeded in launching (February, 1897) the annual *Review of Historical Publications Relating to Canada* (since 1920, the quarterly *Canadian Historical Review*). This forthright, usually expert periodical, to a greater degree than its predecessor, the *Bulletin des Recherches Historiques* (1895), covered the ground and exposed the new works to explicit criticism.

The same nationalistic tendencies were apparent in the creation of the Royal Canadian Academy of Arts in 1880 and the Royal Society of Canada in 1881. Both were brought to life largely through the efforts of the governor general, the Marquess of Lorne, and his wife, Princess Louise, and both followed British models. The former provided a general focus for an interest in painting that had been greatly increased by the collections, particularly of French painting, at the Centennial Exhibition in Philadelphia in 1876, and effectively carried along by Thomas Eakins and others at the Pennsylvania Academy of Fine Arts, where so many Canadians studied. In fact, there was a notable loss of Canadian character in some of the best painting during the next generation because so many artists rushed off to the United States, Great Britain, and France to study and work. The Royal Society of Canada, however, in its specialized sections for literary, social, and scientific studies, succeeded remarkably well during the same generation in winning the loyalty of the most zealous and mature scholars, and its early *Transactions* contained a respectable share of the best work that was being done in Canada.

In Ontario most of the available literary talent went into journalism and politics. Some of the political speech and writing was of a distinctly high order, but the malodorous, violent politics of the day made that seem such feeble stuff that it was savored (and supported) by very few, and such periodicals as *The Week,* an excellent Toronto production, were usually short-lived. Some good poetry was written by Miss I. V. Crawford of Toronto, who was probably Canada's first professional woman writer, and by G. F. Cameron, an exile from Nova Scotia in Boston during his productive period (1872–82) and later an editor in Kingston (1883–85). There was also some rollicking humorous and satirical verse of better than ordinary quality.

The aesthetic surprise of the time was that in 1861 and 1862 four poets were born whose voices were to be warmly applauded in the United States and Great Britain. Two of them, Charles G. D. Roberts and Bliss Carman, were trained by a Fredericton educator, George R. Parkin, who transplanted Thomas Arnold's ideas from Rugby to the Collegiate School and the University of New Brunswick. Roberts was a versatile writer of marked lyric and narrative gifts who gave his country and its makers two unrivaled poetic statements of the nationalism of the federation movement, and reached much of the English-speaking world with poems, romances, and a series of animal stories. Carman also had true lyric gifts, but became a rather shallow poseur because he could turn out rapidly quite salable poems and essays of either faintly "pagan" or vaguely "inspirational" tone. Both Roberts and Carman wrote their really fine poetry on Canadian themes, but earned their highest incomes by more broadly popular literary work in the United States.

The other two poets, Archibald Lampman and W. W. Campbell, came from strong Anglican backgrounds, taught school or ministered in the Church of England, and ended up in the safe haven of the federal civil service. Lampman was notably successful in combining the classical and the English literary traditions with his quiet joy in the Ottawa country he knew so well. His poems were like impressionistic paintings, literary forerunners of a movement in Canadian painting a generation after his death. Campbell wrote a few excellent lyric poems about Lake Huron and Georgian Bay and some powerful, unsuccessful "poetical tragedies" before his conversion to British imperialism turned him into an inferior political bard.

ECONOMIC ADVERSITY

All of these aspiring Canadian voices were raised from the depths of profoundly discouraging, long sustained, economic depression. For twenty-three years, 1873–96, a downward secular trend in prices produced a world-wide series of long depressions and brief, feverish recoveries. If as mature and varied an economy as Britain's regarded this period as "the Great Depression," its effects on the shaky new Canadian economy may be imagined.

Here was an energetic population in a country of obviously enormous natural resources and yet the total of its export and import trade in 1895 was almost exactly the same as in 1874. Producers, exporters, and importers who saw prices fall and profits vanish did not have the comfort of knowing, as we now do, that the economy as a whole was gaining; their distresses, innumerable commercial and industrial failures, and recurrent unemployment were far more immediate.

In general, Canadians were accumulating operative capital of many sorts which did not yield obvious dividends in the form of a more abundant life. Actually the terms of trade, or price ratio of their exports to their imports, favored them, but this was small comfort to traders. Their exports to Britain and their imports from the United States increased, while their British imports and American exports decreased, thus underlining their traditional and not entirely reasonable belief that resolute American protectionism might bring them to their knees. The "unfavorable" trade balance that characterized the whole period except 1880 and 1895 indicated a sustained inward flow of capital which would yield dividends as soon as the secular trend of prices was reversed.

Moreover the economy was fundamentally altering towards useful diversification. Relatively, lumbering was declining; agriculture was expanding and specializing in such things as cheese-making, fruit-farming, and livestock-finishing; and industry, although on a small scale, was reaching out in many directions, notably cotton textiles, milling, wheeled vehicles, agricultural machinery, furniture, and iron.

How little Canadians felt these basic benefits, and how greatly they suffered from their incidental hardships, are revealed in the following discouraging picture of population.

Decade	Population at Beginning	Actual Increase	Natural Increase	Immigration	Emigration
1871–81	3,689,000	636,000	799,000	342,000	505,000
1881–91	4,325,000	508,000	686,000	886,000	1,064,000
1891–1901	4,833,000	538,000	612,000	321,000	395,000

The United States was sufficiently more mature and diversified economically to take in 2,000,000 immigrants from Canada in thirty years. Except perhaps Scandinavia, no modern nation has had such a drain upon a meager population as Canada had at this time.

🍁 RAILROAD POLITICS

The fall of Macdonald.—In a sense, Sir John Macdonald was the first great Canadian casualty of the Panic of 1873. He had managed to get construction of the intercolonial railroad by the gulf route started as a national project in 1869, financing it by a loan of £4,000,000 (1867), three-quarters of which was guaranteed as to interest by Great Britain. The road, as completed in 1876 from Halifax and Saint John to Quebec, incorporating earlier short lines, cost $34,000,000 instead of $20,000,000, largely because Sandford Fleming secured approval for steel rails, iron bridges, etc., suitable for a through freight route with little local traffic. The line was never economically profitable.

It was, of course, an essential part of federation, and the precedent for the Pacific railroad promised to British Columbia in 1871. The economic underpinning of that railroad had been forecast in the Manitoba Act of 1870, by which federal Canada retained control of the natural resources (notably land of the West), with the clear intention of using them in opening up the country. But hard cash had to be found to build the railroad, and Macdonald found himself in a whirlwind of rival routes and rival contractors, with Montreal and Toronto as deeply interested, if not as financially powerful, as New York and London.

The struggle for the contract in 1871, 1872, and 1873 was a wild one, for as part of the statutory arrangement with British Columbia it was decided that the Pacific railroad should be built and operated by a private company on the basis of not more than 50,000,000 acres of land and $30,000,000 in subsidy. After the Grand Trunk had dropped out because it opposed the construction of a line across the Shield to the north of the Lakes, the fight narrowed down to two groups, both of which aimed to appear Canadian but were largely American in terms of resources and had a way of containing a strong representation of Northern Pacific interests.

When the risk of Americans dominating Canada's transcontinental railroad became too embarrassing, Sir John, as the Toronto *Globe* said, "made an Act of Parliament" incorporating a new company, February 5, 1873, with only Canadian subscribers named, of whom Sir Hugh Allan of Montreal, a successful operator of transatlantic steamships, was the most prominent. Allan, having satisfied himself, as he said, "that the whole decision of the question must ultimately be in the hands of one man . . . Sir George E. Cartier," went out into the Quebec constituencies, subsidized the press, and by great effort and expenditure claimed to have captured twenty-seven out of forty-five members of the legislature, whose pressure, coupled with that of Cartier's own constituents, persuaded him that the charter must go to Allan "in the interests of Lower Canada."

By the time the new Parliament assembled, too many people were "in the know," and it was inevitable that the Liberals, who had made considerable gains in the election of 1872, should bring forward allegations of deception as to exclusion of the Americans and of corruption in the form of huge payments (of American money) by Allan to Macdonald for the winning of the general election. Resistance to these charges was broken down in July by the publication in the Montreal *Herald* of irrefutable evidence in the form of correspondence stolen from the office of J. C. Abbott, Allan's counsel. A royal commission found that, in response to urgent letters and telegrams from Macdonald and his ministry that were barely distinguishable from commands, Allan had furnished $350,000 for the election. The clincher was Sir John's telegram: "I must have another ten thousand; will be the last time of calling; do not fail me; answer today." Macdonald resigned. Meanwhile Allan had of course utterly failed to get financial backing in London in the face of the Panic of 1873 and opposition by the Grand Trunk and traditional banking circles.

The inadequacy of the Liberals.—Macdonald's mantle fell on Alexander Mackenzie, the utterly upright and utterly unglamorous leader of the Liberals. He was sustained in a general election early in 1874. The ever-confident George Brown, regarding himself as the power behind the throne, went off to Washington to persuade the Grant administration to concede commercial reciprocity in return for Canada's abandonment of a cash consideration for the inshore fisheries, which would thus give Canada and the Liberals a fresh start. Fish played him along into an understanding that would have been humiliating and unsatisfactory to Canada and then demonstrated that even it would be impossible. Mackenzie and his ministry had to grapple alone with depression and the promise to British Columbia.

They were a curious team, with the able young Edward Blake, self-confident to the point of unpredictability, as Mackenzie's strongest associate. Behind them the Liberal party was divided and uncertain (for it could count on slight support from the beleaguered Rouges), had made little attempt to win the Maritimes or the West, and in Ontario had lost its rural crusading fervor as its elder statesman grew wealthier and more property-minded. Brown, for instance, had recently made himself conspicuous by trying to smash a Toronto printers' union. Macdonald had promptly countered by a statute, ironically based on Gladstone's, legalizing trade unions and affording them scope. In brief, the Liberals lacked the resilience, the enterprise, and the imagination necessary to chart a new course.

During their four years of office, they had to try to build the Pacific railroad as a public enterprise because private undertakers other than the undesirable Americans could not be found. All that they could manage was surveying the Pacific route, and trying to patch together very cautiously a makeshift route by rail from Ottawa to Lake Nipissing and Georgian Bay, by water to Fort William, and by rail thence to Selkirk, north of Winnipeg. Since American railways would have to serve in winter, a connection from Pembina to Selkirk was built, and a line begun westward. British Columbia was so thoroughly thwarted and estranged by the Liberals' inability to fulfill the promises of 1871 that it was on the brink of secession, in spite of manifest British displeasure. Only 127 extremely difficult miles of railroad along the Fraser were tackled in that province before 1878.

The only notable achievement of the Liberals resulted from Edward Blake's attempt, 1875–77, to abolish appeals from Canadian courts to the British Privy Council and to limit the governor general to actions on the advice of his Canadian ministers. Blake got a Canadian Supreme Court, but failed to find a way to get around British desires to retain the appeals, with most unfortunate consequences which he had foreseen. He did, however, make it constitutionally impossible for the titular executive to act as the instrument of British instead of Canadian policy.

Macdonald comes back.—By 1878, Macdonald, the political artist and opportunist, was the only leading person who knew precisely what he wanted to do with Canada, had the nerve to try it, and could communicate that confidence to the voters. The Liberal-Conservative team he drove bordered on the unbelievable in its combination of contradictions—Ontario Orangemen and Quebec *Bleus;* protectionist manufacturers, businessmen, railroad interests, and their trade unionist employees; Maritimers mollified by larger federal subsidies, and Westerners won by disproportionately large parliamentary representation and assurances that a Canadian transcontinental railroad would be built and built at once.

He certainly held it under control in part by quite flagrant appeals to the baseness, prejudice, and even violence in the politics of his day, but he did so in a jaunty, funny, man-to-man spirit of complicity in human strengths and frailties. If he did not say that the electors would sooner listen to him drunk than to Alexander Mackenzie or Edward Blake sober, he repeatedly implied it. A Macdonald political meeting was a disreputable, but exciting, affair.

Yet the touchstone of his success in putting Canada together and keeping it so during appalling adversity was a consideration that men felt was larger and deeper than Macdonald's antics. He succeeded in conveying the conviction that a Canada could be built and maintained if the people would back him up in the effort. In 1891, aged seventy-six, having incredibly survived labors and excesses that would have killed an ordinary man, he died of a paralysis brought on by his efforts during his most desperate and least creditable general election. His Canada was still a kind of mixed grill, skewered on the transcontinental railroad that he gambled the national credit to build.

For electoral purposes, and drawing upon the interest aroused by the Canada Firsters, Macdonald spoke of "The National Policy." That was a fair description of what he and his Liberal-Conservatives aimed at, but it was a single thing made up of many parts. For Macdonald himself, as for the Canada Firsters, its core was the ascendancy of Canada over its constituent parts. Its protectionism dated back to the Canadian response to British free trade in the forties, and was necessitated by the carrying charges on the public debt.

The tariff, which had been reduced a little after the abrogation of the Reciprocity Treaty in 1866 in order to reassure the Maritimes, was increased again in 1870, and protectionism became a party plank two years later. After 1873, when both Great Britain and the United States unloaded their ever-cheapening manufactures in the Canadian market, Canadian industrialists, themselves hard hit by depression, organized to agitate for higher protectionism. The Liberals were apparently willing to concede a higher tariff on grounds of the need for higher revenue, but they missed their chance through timidity in 1874 and 1876, thus presenting Macdonald with his chief instrument of victory in the elections of 1878.

In party politics Macdonald's ascendancy was a subtler thing than mere protectionism, for in effect he made the Liberals seem seekers of independence, "Americans," or "continentalists," while he won for the Conservatives a reputation for submissive loyalty to Britain that would have astonished British manufacturers or the army and navy circles that mistakenly expected Canada to provide troops for British wars. Somehow Macdonald's "The Suez Canal is nothing to us," his rejection of any return to centralized empire, and his basic nationalist's idea of an associational, nonsubordinate relationship with Great Britain could always be smothered in such bombastic appeals to uncritical feeling as appeared in his last manifesto: "A British subject I was born —a British subject I will die."

In terms of political affiliation, self-governing Canadians, still believing themselves threatened by their mighty neighbor, had become, as Elgin predicted, rather more British than Britons themselves. There was, of course, no risk to Canadian autonomy and nationality from Britain unless Canadians chose to reverse the whole course of their history. For the Liberals, however, the only alternative to Macdonaldism was admittedly risky negotiation with Canada's only historical enemy, the United States. It is a striking circumstance that when the Conservatives were driven by adversity to undertake this, they shed the implied consequences like water rolling off a duck's back. Macdonald had made it unthinkable that the Conservatives would consider a continental alignment.

The Canadian Pacific Railway.—Fascinating as Macdonald's opportunism in party politics was, and helpful in creating at least an illusion of national unity, his most enduring achievement was the transcontinental railroad. He had the great luck to come into office during a brief cyclical recovery and to happen on a group of Canadians who had just pulled off an extremely profitable coup in American railroading, or, more correctly, in American railroad finance. His Man Friday, J. H. Pope, bade him "catch them while their pockets are full."

No financial help could be obtained from the British government, but D. J. McIntyre, manager of the Canada Central (Ottawa Valley), emerged from negotiations in London during the summer of 1880 with a contract to build the Canadian Pacific Railway in ten years, on the basis of a subsidy of $25,000,000 and 25,000,000 acres of land "fit for settlement" in alternate sections within 24 miles of the line across the plains. The company might issue $25,000,000 in bonds, to be held and sold for it by the government, but its plan from the beginning, in George Stephen's words, was "to limit the borrowing of money from the public to the smallest possible point . . . to have looked for a return of our own capital and a legitimate profit entirely to the growth of the country and the development of the property." Among the secondary privileges of the company was protection against competition between its main line and the international boundary.

Where was the rest of the money to come from? Largely from a characteristically intricate bit of bankruptcy proceedings, reorganization, and so forth, by which the ownership of the St. Paul, Minneapolis, and Manitoba Railway escaped from the hands of its European bondholders into the more practiced and immediate hands of a mixed Canadian and American group, who thereby made sudden, large fortunes for themselves. This line was the only railroad entry to Manitoba and its new masters knew that the recent grasshopper plagues that had weakened it were comparatively rare occurrences.

Montreal emerged once more (having beaten down a feeble challenge from Toronto) with a design for mastery of the West, for George Stephen and R. B. Angus were the former president and general manager of the Bank of Montreal, McIntyre's Canada Central had its terminus there, and Donald Smith was a Hudson's Bay Company man of great shrewdness who understood the expansion of Canada and was determined to profit by it. The only Ontario man was James J. Hill, the true architect of the St. Paul, Minneapolis and Manitoba coup, but he had become much more an American and was so deeply committed to the schemes which ultimately gave him the railroad mastery of the American Northwest that he broke with his C.P.R. associates when they agreed to build the costly and unprofitable line across the Shield north of the Lakes.

Ironically, the brilliant American construction engineer and railroad operative, William Van Horne, whom Hill had successfully recommended for the C.P.R., built the line that deprived Hill of the chance of drawing western Canada into his railroad empire. Sir John Rose, through Morton, Rose and Company, represented London's modest interest and facilitated the inconspicuous but large American one in the daring gamble, and continental European investors used Kohn, Reinach and Company or the French Société Générale.

The swiftness of the actual construction was breathtaking. W. J. Wilgus, an eminent modern railroad engineer, regarded it as the greatest achievement in North American railroading up to that time—"one of man's most marvelous accomplishments." This achievement, however, was largely the result of what had gone before. It is well to recall both the 700 miles of already completed line and Sandford Fleming's ten years of exploratory surveys. It is well also to condemn the Conservatives' political savagery that drove Fleming into retirement in 1880. He had penetrated the *terra incognita* of the Shield between Ottawa and Winnipeg and found ways through it. He had chosen to follow the better-watered northern portion of the plains to Edmonton because he was aiming at the Yellowhead Pass (3733 feet), which by general agreement and his own extensive explorations seemed the best way through the Rockies. His greatest problem was the route across the British Columbia ranges; this was much complicated by Victoria's insistence on Bute Inlet and bridges to Nanaimo while every other consideration argued for following the Thompson and Fraser rivers to Burrard Inlet (Port Moody, near Vancouver).

Work began at the eastern end of Lake Nipissing in 1882 and by May, 1885, the Shield had been conquered. Some old and some new devices were employed, but the significance of the achievement lay in the unprecedented distance across rock, muskey, and a filigree of lakes and rivers. The plains section was, of course, much simpler and more orthodox. Here for a number of reasons, chief of which was the competitive position with American railroading, a southern route across dry lands to Medicine Hat and Calgary was chosen, leading to the Kicking Horse Pass (5300 feet) through the Rockies and the conveniently revealed Rogers Pass (4316 feet) through the Selkirks. By using night gangs in supply and bridge-building, the top of the Kicking Horse was reached from the east in June, 1883.

British Columbia, where the line had to tunnel great mountains and their innumerable projections, climb long steep grades, and perch on shelves cut out from canyon walls, was probably the hardest assignment, but with Van Horne on the spot and another American, T. G. Shaughnessy, marshaling the supplies at both ends of the line, the job was done by November, 1885. On November 7, the telegraph reported:

> The first train from Montreal is approaching Yale, within a few hours of the Pacific Coast. The last spike was driven this morning by Honourable Donald Smith at Craigellachie, in Eagle Pass, some 340 miles from Port Moody. On reaching the coast, our running time from Montreal, exclusive of stoppages, will be five days, averaging twenty-four miles per hour.

There are good reasons for believing that the builders of the C.P.R. and Sir John knew each other thoroughly well. He knew that they had money, experience, and great expertness in finance and management as well as in construction. They sized him up equally accurately and, expecting him to pledge the nation's credit if necessary, planned to make their fortunes less from the usual siphoning techniques during the construction or from the usual manipulation of credit and securities than from the values that their road created and from the profits of its operations and land sales.

Almost from the beginning, however, the money they expected to take in from sale of lands, land-grant bonds, and common stock failed them disastrously, for the six-year depression after 1873 was followed by another of about the same length after 1882, and the C.P.R. was being built faster than money could be found to pay for it. The Northern Pacific went bankrupt in 1883 and C.P.R. stock fell from 100 to 40. The bank of Montreal advanced funds on securities pledged by Stephen,

Smith, Angus, Van Horne, and Shaughnessy, who thus risked their fortunes, but these were not enough. At this point J. H. Pope claimed he woke Macdonald one night after hearing that he had told the C.P.R. that a large loan was as unobtainable as the planet Jupiter, and brought him down to earth by saying: "The day the Canadian Pacific busts, the Conservative party busts the day after."

From 1883 onwards, therefore, Macdonald and Tupper had to extract public loans from a Cabinet that had cold feet, and said so, and from an increasingly dubious Parliament, alarmed by the nation's ordinary bookkeeping in such times and by the hostile commentary from Grand Trunk interests in Canada and Britain, from the embittered Hill in the United States, and from Canadian newspapers that implied the whole business was a patronage apparatus designed to keep the Conservatives in office forever. Tupper put through a first mortgage loan of $22,500,000 at the end of 1883, but money ran out again in 1884 and during the spring of 1885 it looked as if, to use Galt's illustration of twenty years earlier regarding the Grand Trunk, the Canadian government was "in the position of the man who had the good luck to win the elephant." C.P.R. stock fell to 34.

At this point, Louis Riel saved the railroad by rousing the métis to rebellion in Saskatchewan. Van Horne declared the C.P.R. should erect a monument to Riel. The speed with which the C.P.R. delivered the armed forces there gave Sir John the leverage he needed in Cabinet, party caucus, and Parliament. In July the Government's $35,000,000 worth of stock was canceled; from an equal amount of new stock the company received $15,000,000, and $20,000,000 was held to cover that amount of its debt. Another $9,800,000 of debt was converted into a mortgage on lands, and the government lent the company another $5,000,000 against $8,000,000 of it. Finally, the Barings bought $4,000,000 worth of bonds at 90, half of which they were unable to persuade the public to take and had to carry themselves. Next year the company retired its debt to the government, but the most casual review of the first six years of its financial history refutes any claim that it was a private enterprise.

The construction of the C.P.R. did a good deal to moderate the effects of depression by creating employment and a market for Canadian farm and forest products. It was estimated that about 40,000 persons entered the West to work on the railroad. Rails, locomotives, cars, and equipment came in from Britain and the United States, but many other kinds of supplies were Canadian. Moreover railroad building had its usual effects, outside the Shield, at least, in creating land speculation.

Banks and loan companies sent capital to the West; land-hungry

Eastern farmers, or those who insisted on wheat-raising when Ontario was diversifying its agriculture, or those who preferred the fertile, treeless plains to the margins of the forest, went with it. The free homestead of 160 acres was available from 1872 to the extent of perhaps one-quarter of the fertile belt, but the Hudson's Bay Company and C.P.R. lands were astutely chosen and, as usual, land companies sprang up, accumulated desirable blocks, and offered special inducements. The big real estate gambling, however, was at town sites, and "booms" developed in Winnipeg, Regina, Calgary, and in the New Westminster–Port Moody–Vancouver area between the mouth of the Fraser and Burrard Inlet.

When construction stopped, the bubbles burst. The truth was that even Westerners did not as yet know how to farm the West. The Red River Settlement, for instance, had never been able to depend on its agriculture, but had had to supplement it by "plains provisions," i.e. buffalo meat. Farther west, aridity and short growing-seasons, not to speak of plant disease and gophers, defeated many a farmer who was bemused by the deep rich soil. Governor Simpson has been much blamed for his stubborn insistence to the Parliamentary investigation of the late fifties that the West was not suitable for agriculture, but he was right until new techniques, new seeds, and new prices changed the situation forty years later. At any rate, depression and discouragement fell on the plains in 1886 and rapidly weeded out all but the most determined.

Out on the coast, things were a little better, for lumbering, the mining of coal and gold, and the new (1870) and booming industry of canning salmon at last took up some of the slack after the collapse of placer mining. The following census statistics reveal the disappointing results of the immense effort put into the West.

Area	Population		
	1871	1881	1891
Manitoba and N.W. Territory	73,228	118,706	251,473
British Columbia	36,247	49,459	98,967

The single great tragedy of this westward movement, however, was the dying outburst of *La Nation Métisse*. After the establishment of Manitoba, most of the nomadic element withdrew from that advance of the uncongenial Canadian frontier to regions where they could carry on as before, notably the Saskatchewan Valley. Their brothers, the Indians, were quietly shepherded by treaty into reservations, and after 1874 about three hundred well-chosen, well-directed men in the North

West Mounted Police maintained the rude, but on the whole equitable, order among men that the Hudson's Bay Company had established on the plains.

And then, with startling rapidity, the buffalo, the underlying basis of the hunters' lives, were exterminated. Almost innumerable west of the ninety-fifth meridian in 1850, they had been slaughtered in the United States by the "robe-hunters" who came with the railroad and by the United States Army in its efforts to cope with the mounted Western Indians. The "southern herd" had disappeared by 1876, the "northern herd" did not return from its migration, and now the railroad invaded western Canada. For a few years, the nomads fastened on the dwindling herds like desperate wolves until by 1880 they had destroyed them. A way of life had ended for the Indians and the métis. The surveyors, land-grabbers, and other attendants of the C.P.R.'s invasion repeated 1869 on the Red River in even more threatening forms.

In their extremity the métis called upon the now unbalanced Riel in Montana and he, though an American citizen, responded in a sense of divine mission. His proposal to dethrone the pope, shake off the Catholic clergy, and make himself prophet and chief of a new nation failed to disqualify him among his own people then or diminish his martyrdom for *Canadiens* later. Once more, in 1884, a fairly reasonable petition went to Ottawa; once more Macdonald inexcusably delayed. Once more, in March, 1885, a provisional government was set up and this time, unlike 1869, the English-speaking element fell away from Riel. The horrified clergy had given him up in despair. When the police intervened, they were routed at Duck Lake on March 26, and then some bands of Indians rose and sacked three posts and settlements with small massacres.

But now Van Horne showed what he could do by transporting almost 8000 troops, *Canadiens* and Canadians, to the scene over the route of the new C.P.R. All was over by the beginning of July. Riel had surrendered early in May, but Gabriel Dumont fought on until hope was gone. This time, after a furious controversy between Quebec and Ontario, an appeal to the Privy Council, and great pressure on Sir John to extend pardon, Riel was hanged at Regina, November 16, 1885. *La Nation Métisse* was to live on in the form of a rending issue between *Canadien* and Canadian. Its symbols were the "political murders" of Thomas Scott and Louis Riel.

CHAPTER XXI

Emergence of a New Symbol (1885-96)

In 1880, Edward Blake, who was inclined to pessimism, said in the Commons:

> We have been running ahead of our resources. We have increased our expenses more than three times as fast as our tax-paying power. . . . I believe hard work, rigid economy, prudent management and gradual progress and accumulation is the fate of this country as a whole and of its population individually. I regard it as no unhappy fate.

Five years later much of the weight of the C.P.R. had been added to the load of debt, and emigration from the country suggested that it was standing still. Commercial depression lay heavy over the land and no one saw any likely way out. It looked as if the great gamble was to fail, not suddenly, but in a slow decline to a marginal kind of existence as a "poor relation" of the United States. Canadians have always had to wrestle with the many problems created by their perceptible material inferiority to their neighbor, but never so grimly and hopelessly as between 1885 and 1896.

🍁 SIGNS OF DISINTEGRATION

The underlying factor in the situation was, as we have seen, the downward secular trend of prices that made the troughs of the business cycles both broad and deep. Knowledge of such fluctuations had been increasing as they became more and more obvious accompaniments of the world economy under industrialism, but it was as yet merely summarized in a few rule-of-thumb terms by bankers, tentatively handled by economists, or squeezed and pressed as readers of the Old Testament tried to make it fit the pattern of "lean years" and "fat years" in the ancient Levant.

Most Canadians knew only that they were having a bad time economically and tried to find economic remedies in local terms. And in

Canada, as elsewhere, the margins of the economy and the producers of its raw materials carried more of the burden of depression than the owners of capital and the processors. The cities of central Canada, harassed though they were by commercial failures, were obviously better off than the rest of the country.

The Maritimes.—The Atlantic provinces were particularly hard hit, even though the American market was open until 1885 to their fish products and to some degree dependent on their wood products. Other markets were diffident and paying lower and lower prices. The Canadian tariff and the railroad exposed many Maritime manufactures to competition from the larger and better placed establishments of Quebec and Ontario that they could not meet. Perhaps the saddest symbol of the times was that the railroad and the steamship did not combine to make Saint John and Halifax great ports of commerce, for the summer traffic moved by the St. Lawrence and even in winter American ports were more advantageous. Since the old days of free or almost free trade seemed blissful by comparison, it was not long before the Maritime case came to be that even the enlarged federal subsidies were not enough and that the tariff must come down. The threat of secession bubbled continuously just below the surface of politics and became explicit in 1886.

Central Canada.—The economic troubles of central Canada were surface manifestations of great and fairly rapid changes that dislocated many men's lives and sent many *Canadiens* and Canadians into the United States. In both Quebec and Ontario the good farm lands were occupied, the marginal ones suffered as the lumber industry advanced to the upper lakes or deeper into the Shield, and land agriculture generally had to alter or improve in competition with the Middle and even the Far West of the United States. Primitive extensive soil-mining would no longer do, and Quebec, in particular, discovered its backwardness. Many men migrated to cheap distant lands for want of the knowledge, adaptability, or capital needed to keep up in the swift transition from unprofitable grain farming to dairying, fruit-growing, stock-finishing, and other specialization for urban and overseas markets.

Many others, like their European predecessors, left the land for the factory and the city in Canada or, more often, in the United States. The proportion of urban and rural population in Canada was changing rapidly: from about 85 per cent rural in 1867 to about 65 per cent rural in 1896. Life could be miserable enough in the cities during such times, but for many there was no place else to go, and already urban society was organizing itself to look after the casualties of fluctuating industrial and commercial life.

Other factors also contributed to central Canada's economic discontents. Many persons felt that the Atlantic and Western provinces had proved to be dangerous liabilities instead of assets, and that their support, either by federal subsidies or by underwriting railroads, was an unfair burden on the central Canadians.

In addition, the alliance between political power at Ottawa and financial power at Montreal was resented and suspected. Quebec City, accommodating itself to the decline of the timber and lumber trades and of shipbuilding, contemplating river and harbor improvements for the benefit of Montreal, and wracked by its own transformation into an industrial center, found being the provincial capital slight compensation for Montreal's overlordship. Toronto, after having fostered the acquisition of the West, felt that whatever profit could be made of it would find its way, like the C.P.R., to the "bloated" financial capital at the head of tidewater on the St. Lawrence. The country folk of Quebec and Ontario distrusted urban merchants, bankers, and their like on principle and thought of Montreal as the ultimate residence of such insuperable powers.

Although the central Canadian economy was being basically and comprehensively strengthened and was better off than the rest of Canada, yet the society was shaken and torn by change, uncertainty, resentment, and hopelessness.

New economic sinews.—While most of the industrialization of central Canada was of conventional North American kinds, indeed largely part of a continental pattern of development, some of it faintly presaged a time when the region would have a special economic character and when the Canadian Shield would be an asset instead of a liability. On the American side of the boundary, such an amazing nexus of iron, steel, and heavy industry had been growing up near the Great Lakes (particularly south of Lake Erie) that it was changing the whole shape of two national economies. This nexus was built around the happy combination of iron ore from northern Michigan and Minnesota and coal from Pennsylvania, Ohio, and Indiana brought together by cheap water transportation, hundreds of miles of "coastal navigation" in the interior once a canal had been built round the "Sault" and the rapids of the St. Mary's River between Lake Superior and Lake Huron.

Central Canada, lacking both iron and coal in her part of the Lakes Basin, became dependent on the United States for most of her coal and much of her iron and steel. Some British coal, as ballast, and soft coal from Nova Scotia moved in during the summer. Boston and Montreal capital began in 1893 to put together a great iron and steel combination in Nova Scotia, using Newfoundland ore and local coal. Central Canada's iron and steel industry was small and scattered. This dependence rankled, particularly in the matter of coal for steam power, and had much to do with the persistent efforts to use water power wherever possible. During the seventies and eighties, however, an international group of inventors worked out the practical principles of the electric dynamo, the power for which could be provided by the hydraulic turbines on which French inventors had been successfully at work since about 1827. By the nineties, small beginnings in the hydroelectric power which central Canada could produce in abundance opened broad vistas to the future.

The most exciting of these were in enterprises that might be conducted within the wilderness of the Shield at places where dependence on coal would be prohibitive, even at places some distance from the railroad. Such enterprises were the manufacture of paper pulp and mining. As the supplies of trees suitable for saw logs dwindled (first grade pine had almost disappeared by 1894), a shift was made during the seventies to the production, chiefly for export, of groundwood pulp from spruce logs. Three Rivers was the first great center of this enterprise, which expanded very rapidly with the introduction of the sulphate process about 1887. As yet the industry consisted almost exclusively of cutting and exporting large spruce as pulpwood and small spruce as wood pulp, but by the mid-nineties it was obvious that the production of paper, particularly newsprint, was on the brink of great expansion. Here accessible raw materials, abundant water, cheap water power, and cheap water transport would be topped off by hydroelectric power.

The mining possibilities of the eastern Canadian wilderness had been tantalizing since Cartier's day, but most mining had depended on scattered, small, rich bodies of iron, copper, silver, gold, and so on. Railroad construction exposed new deposits, most notably the asbestos near Thetford, Quebec, discovered in 1876, and the nickel at Sudbury, Ontario, discovered in 1883, that were to make Canada the world's leading producer of both. But what of the hundreds of thousands of square miles away from the railroad? The Shield was obviously an extraordinary conglomeration of minerals, but its rocks must be broken and ground up and separated. For these processes great quantities of power and water were needed. The water was there and if it could produce transmissible power in the form of electricity, the possibilities seemed endless.

At this point a digression seems justified to signalize a group of devoted men who contributed enormously to Canada's well-being, but whose names and work are known to very few—Sir William Logan and the leaders of the Geological Survey of Canada. The survey began its work in 1842, following urgent representations made by that busybody, W. L. Mackenzie, as early as 1836, and by the literary and philosophical societies of Toronto, Montreal, and Quebec. Logan carried the survey through its first phase, Lower and Upper Canada, in 1842–69, and Alfred R. C. Selwyn expanded its work for the larger Canada in 1869–95, but there were other great investigators serving under them who rose to succeed to the directorship: George M. Dawson, whose activities west of the Lakes, 1872–1901, ranked with Logan's in eastern Canada; Robert Bell, who began spending his summers with the survey in 1856 at the age of fifteen and made his greatest contribution between Lake Superior and Hudson Bay; and A. P. Low, who started in 1881 while still a student at McGill and made his name in Labrador, the unpopulated area between the St. Lawrence and Hudson Strait, and in Canada's eastern arctic.

Some of the most thrilling Canadian history is contained in the sober words and pioneering maps of the Geological Survey, and one wishes that some gifted scholar and writer would systematically bring it to the attention of the public. Yet it is fair to say that even a Canada whose annual mineral production has soared from about $10,000,000 in 1881 to over $1,000,000,000 in 1950 has failed to produce such an account, and that the interested person has to put the great story together for himself.

The members of the survey, in canoe, York boat, Red River cart, pack train, covered wagon, and on foot found out what Canada was like and what lay below its surface. They did most of the mapping of the country and more often preceded the mining prospector than followed him, more often suggested where he might go, and for what, than moved in to systematize what he was uncovering. Who can say how much wasted effort Logan forestalled by pointing out that the subsurface of Lower and Upper Canada could contain no coal because all of it was older than the earliest coal-bearing formations?

Logan was a Montrealer who went to Great Britain in 1814 at the age of sixteen and seemed settled in business there when he became first interested in coal and then obsessed by geology. His paper on coal for the Geological Society in 1840 established his reputation internationally, and a visit to Canada, Nova Scotia, and the United States that year whetted his appetite appropriately for the invitation of 1842. He was at work in Gaspé next year. Fortunately he was a wealthy man, for the government kept him on meager supply. He lived as simply and devotedly as a man can and worked harder than most could. His "city overcoat," for instance, lasted him from 1862 until he left Canada in 1874, and both his living and his working quarters were Spartan. He made the survey and established its character by choosing the ablest men he could find and inspiring them with a devotion that emulated his own. The rest of the world honored him even if his fellow Canadians either never heard of him or thought him a freak.

Selwyn was an Englishman who, having come to Canada after seventeen years spent in inaugurating the geological survey of Victoria, Australia, naturally interested himself chiefly in the gold fields of Nova Scotia and British Columbia when he could shake free of the immense responsibilities occasioned by the federation and expansion of Canada. J. B. Tyrrell, whom he recruited, led in 1893–94 the first white party to cross the great Barrens west of Hudson Bay since Samuel Hearne in 1769–72. Engaging in perilous expeditions, inland and on Hudson Bay, the group managed to map the area meticulously. Tyrrell's narratives should be as classic as Hearne's.

The slight, apparently delicate G. M. Dawson was the son of Sir John William Dawson of Pictou, N.S., himself a great geologist, a colleague of Sir Charles Lyell in studying the substructure of the Maritimes, and the founder of popular education in Nova Scotia and New Brunswick before he converted McGill University from blueprint to actuality. His son, one of the greatest scientists that Canada has produced, made his reputation on the plains and in interior British Columbia between 1875 and his death in 1901. He was the principal discoverer and explorer of the Yukon region, and a notable contributor to anthropology.

Bell was a Torontonian of similarly broad curiosities who took degrees in engineering and medicine at McGill before plunging into his chosen work. He worked all over Canada, including the arctic, with a basic interest in fossils that yielded to such other considerations as petroleum and the copper nickel of Sudbury. Low was a Montrealer and McGill graduate who was a prodigious wilderness traveler in winter as in summer. He once snowshoed with a toboggan from Lake Mistassini in the heart of the Quebec uplands to Ottawa. His greatest work, which included the discovery of the remote Quebec-Labrador iron fields, was in the unmapped and forbidding interior between Hudson Bay and the Atlantic.

The obdurate plains.—

The story of the settlement of the Northwest begins with an ignorant optimism, passes on to disillusionment and even to despair, then shows the adjustment of the settlers' methods of farming to the necessities of the climate; it ends with what might be called a modest victory over nature and a prosperity moderated by the vagaries of the climate and of the price of wheat in the world market.

This reasoned judgment by A. S. Morton, the most thorough historian of the Canadian West, was made as recently as 1938. Historians before and since tend to gloss over the first two phases in Morton's progression. The first might be dated from about 1812 and was overlapped fifty or sixty years later by the second, which reached its nadir about 1895. Why did the incalculably rich soils of the plains disappoint optimistic Easterners and shatter wave after wave of them in despair?

Although they had the tremendous advantages of previous American experience and of an eager industrialism in the forms of the railroad, barbwire, the steel plow, and the steel self-regulating windmill, western Canadians had still to conquer aridity and short growing seasons, not to speak of spottier evils such as animal and insect pests, plant diseases, and storms of rain, hail, or erosive winds.

The plains were dry grasslands. Even in winter they were dry, not mantled in deep snows. They received from 60 to 70 per cent of their moisture between April 1 and August 31 and this was too little to permit the successful cultivation of the land every year. The average annual precipitation on what came to be regarded as arable land might be as little as eight or nine inches a year where evaporation was least, or, in such a relatively favorable region as the Red River Valley, reach twenty-one inches, but averages of precipitation are treacherous because of the extremes and the irregular intervals between falls. The rainfall of western Canada can be shown in perspective by a consideration of the annual average precipitation in the various Canadian centers. The averages are St. John's, 54 inches; Halifax, 56; Charlottetown, 39; Moncton, 37; Montreal, 41; Ottawa, 34; London, 38; Regina, 15; Lethbridge, 15; Edmonton, 17; Penticton, 11; Vancouver, 57; and Prince Rupert, 95.

Grass could look after itself because its leafage caught the rains and snows and protected the loose mat of stubble and roots from transpiration. Plowing broke up and gradually destroyed the thick prairie sod, exposing the soil to the blazing sun and heat of summer. The basic problem of dry farming, therefore, was how to retain as much as possible of the precipitation. Men are still wrestling with that problem, complicated as it is by wind erosion and the infection of stem and stubble by destructive insects. The early procedure was deep plowing and frequent shallow cultivation to make a spongy layer and protect it with a loose, fine, soil cover, but, if the land was used every year, it dried out.

About 1863 some Scandinavian settlers in Utah are said to have accidentally discovered the principle of summer fallowing, which gradually spread over the West. Crop land of one year was thoroughly

plowed during the wet June and July of the following one and thereafter cultivated to keep a moist subsoil as the base for the light winter
precipitation during the dry spring. Wheat deeply planted in such fallow
would flourish when drought killed off ordinary planting. Wind erosion
and infected stubble could be countered by alternate strips of sown
land and fallow, with the fallow lightly undercut to leave a trash cover,
and by trap rows of wheat or grass with a bare space between them
and the crop.

What could be done about the short growing season? A. S. Morton
decided from his extensive researches into its history before 1871 that
on the Red River spring wheat required, on average, 137 days between
sowing and harvest. W. L. Morton's more recent researches led him to
conclude that from 1850 on the period was from 110 to 120 days. The
explanation lies, of course, in the gradual development of more suitable
seed. The British fall and spring wheat of 1812 failed completely and
died out. Soft spring wheat brought in from Prairie du Chien in 1820
did better and its surviving strains became one standard. In 1847 South
Russian wheat was introduced to combat drought, and strains of it,
too, survived, while Scottish and Irish varieties were experimented
with and natural selection got in its work. Contrary to the common
impression, natural selection also produced a ripening variety of corn
in the West.

Yet by 1871, wheat farming was very precarious, even on the lands
near the river that were kept moist and meadowy by the natural reser-
voirs formed during periodic overflows. Sixty years of a slovenly, small-
scale, squatter agriculture that was always less esteemed than the buffalo
hunt had provided no basis for predicting a brilliant future for the
plains, and the neighboring United States was little better. Indeed Iowa
was desperately trying out Red River wheat in 1860.

Commercial agriculture had to do better, even though this meant
using hard wheats that necessitated a revolution in milling. Red Fife,
a Ukrainian wheat which reached the West by way of Scotland, Ontario,
and the American Middle West, proved to be the principal basis for
experimentation and crossbreeding in the United States and at the
experimental farms of the C.P.R. and the Canadian government. It
required thirty years more of careful and laborious work by devoted
men (in Canada most notably William Saunders and his two sons) before the great succession of northern wheats began, wheats that would
mature sturdily and bountifully in 98 to 105 days and yield abundantly
the best milling wheat in the world.

When, therefore, the men and women who somehow managed to
stick it out in the Canadian West between 1870 and 1900 damned the

money lords of the East, the C.P.R. monopoly, and the Canadian tariff, they were at bottom testifying to their failure to solve the problems of high plains agriculture.

One interesting consequence of their relative failure was that much of the West remained available for its most natural crop—the cattle which took the place of the buffalo. The North American Cattle King-dom was born after the Civil War when cheap Texas longhorns were driven north with free grass along the way. During the winter of 1864–65 some cattle turned loose to fend for themselves on the Laramie Plains of Wyoming pawed through the light snow and fattened on the northern grasses. Ranching became big business, with better stock and careful arrangements for transportation and marketing that reached north to the C.P.R. country. A twenty-year spiral boom collapsed in 1885, sifting out the speculators and the merely frivolous, but in western Canada cattle ranching had come to stay.

Contrasts in British Columbia.—The Vancouver boom collapsed as heavily as the Winnipeg boom when the C.P.R. was finished, and the falling prices for British Columbia's products were thoroughly dis-couraging. Yet here the foundations were being laid for a rich and diversified economy that might have a feverish, speculative cast and be every bit as vulnerable to technical and cyclical changes as any large producer of raw and semifinished goods, but nevertheless would grow and prosper in the long run. Salmon, lumber, coal, and nonferrous metals promised a much more enduring society than placer-mining. The supply of salmon and of giant trees seemed inexhaustible and both were procured at the edge of tidewater. Almost the same thing seemed true of Vancouver Island coal. Perhaps the most exciting new economic element, however, was the advance of the "hard-rock miners" from Montana, Idaho, and Washington into the several long, narrow, north-south valleys that lay between the ranges in southern British Columbia.

At first these areas were tributary to the United States, as six or seven spur-lines from Hill's Great Northern testified. Rich deposits of silver, lead, zinc, copper, and gold were looted extremely wastefully, largely because transportation was so costly and because the smelters were in the protectionist United States. And then rich coal deposits were developed in the folded Rockies just west of the Crowsnest Pass. This combination of rich ores and good coal to smelt them was suffi-cient in the mid-nineties to induce the C.P.R., in an agreement with the Canadian government, to drive one of the world's most remarkable rail and water routes from Lethbridge over the Crowsnest (4500 feet) and then by narrow, tortuous valleys, ribbon-like lakes, and high passes (seven of them over 3000 feet) to the lower Fraser at Hope. In the 1930's this became an all-rail route.

British Columbia's complaints, then, were basically against the persistent circumstances that robbed the present of a prosperity that everything else seemed to promise. Macdonald was blamed and bullied for help and for pressure against the American tariff; "the East" was pictured as uninterested in the West except insofar as it could milk it; and the prevailing belief was that the masters of the Atlantic money market would see to it that British Columbia never accumulated enough capital to become independent of them.

An almost unexplored element in the economic situation was that British Columbia was passing beyond importance merely to the coast and the cordilleran region to importance in the world economy. Transportation costs by rail to eastern North American and thence to European markets were high and even cheap water transportation was comparatively costly, if only to the Panama Railroad, let alone around the Horn. The British Columbian producer felt that the odds were stacked against him by American protectionism and geographical remoteness.

Harassed Newfoundland.—Although formally outside Canada, Newfoundland was so deeply embroiled with Canada during this period, and ended up so embittered against her, that the histories of the two countries must be considered together. As may be imagined, Newfoundland had an exceedingly rough time of it economically from 1873 onwards. In its frustration and despair, the island saw enemies everywhere and, lashing out against them, became involved in angry, stubborn, and almost unavailing disputes with Great Britain and France, Canada and the United States, singly and in combination. The complexities of these multiparty struggles were great, and a lucid account would require art and space not available here. Yet it should be pointed out that, from the Labouchère dispatch of 1859 to the Hague Convention of 1910, Newfoundland's course constituted the principal pioneering effort within the British Empire to extend the principles of responsible government from internal affairs to external. Canadian and other students of British imperial development should know, for instance, that in 1885 Newfoundland initiated, and in 1890 carried out, independent diplomatic negotiations with the United States.

In addition to the problem of falling prices, Newfoundland was struggling with the need for such improved services as a new drydock at St. John's, new harbor facilities, and the $10,000,000 railroad that was begun in 1881 to link St. John's by a semicircular route across the upper part of the main body of the island with Port aux Basques at its southwestern tip. In the world market, and particularly in the Mediterranean countries that had taken half Newfoundland's cure of fish, foreign competition was severe, notably from France, which subsidized cured fish by as much as 72 per cent of its value, and from the expanding Norwegian fishery.

All these things were reflected in a burden of poor relief that from time to time taxed both private charity and the public treasury to the limit. Inevitably there was steady emigration, as the population figures attest: 1874, 161,374; 1884, 197,335; 1891, 202,040; 1901, 220,984. There was also an irresistible pressure of population on the French Shore, where, in spite of serious deterrents, there were about 9000 settlers in 1881 and almost twice as many twenty years later.

In her distress, Newfoundland aimed at two things—the end of the French bounty system (or of French rights in Newfoundland), and free entry for her fisheries' products to the American market. As bargaining assets she had treaty rights which, thanks to technical changes in the fisheries, pretty well boiled down to control of bait supplies upon which others depended. She began to use the leverage of bait immediately after the Labouchère dispatch and never let go of it.

The struggle with French pretensions on the French Shore over settlement, local government, lobster canning, etc., and bait purchase elsewhere produced a long series of vain efforts by Great Britain to shake off the problem by an Anglo-French agreement which Newfoundland might accept. But, as a Newfoundland minute in council of 1873 said, "No minister in this country would dare to compromise the right of Newfoundlanders. . . . Not an inch of their soil, not an atom of their concurrent rights in the fisheries on the so-called French Shore, would any permanent resident of sound mind in the Colony, consent to part with." That intransigence persisted until Great Britain imposed an Anglo-French *modus vivendi* in 1889 which evoked an address to the queen and delegations to Great Britain and Canada. When this resistance had no effect, Newfoundland capitulated by enacting and renewing temporary legislation until 1904, when Great Britain liquidated the French claims as part of the great bargain for the Anglo-French *Entente Cordiale*.

Relations with the United States were immensely complicated because Canada could not be kept out of them. The term of the Treaty of Washington (for Newfoundland, May, 1874, to July, 1885) was fairly tranquil, and Newfoundland's $1,000,000 share of the arbitral award of 1877 for the fisheries was very welcome, but an attempt at Fortune Bay, January 6, 1878, to enforce on American fishermen Newfoundland regulations as to Sunday fishing, etc., raised an issue that was not settled until the Hague Arbitration of 1910.

After July 1, 1885, fisheries' relations with the United States fell once more under the Convention of 1818, but what Newfoundland wanted and was willing to pay for by bait privileges and preferential tariffs on many American goods was free entry for her own products to the United States. In 1890, Robert Bond successfully negotiated such an agreement with J. G. Blaine, the American Secretary of State who was pursuing a calculated policy of weakening British North America for its probable entry into the United States.

Doubtful as it was that Congress would have accepted the Bond-Blaine Convention (it rejected the similar Bond-Hay Convention in 1902), the result was a first-class conflict between Newfoundland and Canada over the special concessions to the United States, involving bait legislation, tariff war, and very bitter feeling. Canada's aid after the great St. John's fire of July, 1892, helped a little, but a week's conference at Halifax that November failed to reach any agreement about the issues. Two years and a month later, Newfoundland's woes culminated in the collapse of her banks, including the government's financial agent, the Union Bank. An irritated Britain would not aid without the acceptance of an investigating royal commission with power to make political as well as financial recommendations. The Canadian Bank of Montreal and the Bank of Nova Scotia, having stepped into the vacuum created by the island's bank failures, stood idly by while lost confidence threatened the existence of the government's Savings Bank. The only thing to do was to treat for entry into the Canadian federation.

Overtures were made in February, 1895, and detailed terms were discussed at Ottawa, April 4–16, embracing the whole range of debt, railroad obligations, steamship and postal services, fisheries, and so forth. But Canada, too, was shaken by twenty years of adversity and hopes deferred, and Macdonald had died in 1891. There was no daring left in his party, so that ultimately about $5,000,000, or better, the interest on $3,500,000, was allowed to separate the parties.

Britain, appealed to, but also deep in depression, would not bridge the gap without exposing Newfoundland to possible political regression as well as financial overhauling and direction. Bond pulled the Savings Bank through by a small temporary loan secured in Montreal on his personal resources and rushed off to London where, a few days before the July 1 deadline for interest on his colony's securities, he secured in the money market a long-term and a short-term loan which carried Newfoundland and the Savings Bank through to the better times that began in 1896.

The fundamental economic (and political) status of Newfoundland had revealed itself during the depression between 1873 and 1895. A little more knowledge, imagination, and magnanimity on the part of Britain or Canada in 1895 might have given the much maltreated island colony a better existence than it was to have during the next half-century. But Britain was out of patience and Canada was timid and distrustful. A. M. Fraser, a Newfoundland historian, recently summed up the results of 1895 very aptly.

For a generation Newfoundland could neither forgive nor forget the apparent indifference of the Canadian banks and of the government of Canada to the fate of the Colony. The very mention of union became a reproach and would in itself have been sufficient to damn any political party in the eyes of the people of Newfoundland. The events of 1895 killed confederation.

❦ DISINTEGRATION IN NATIONAL POLITICS

Newfoundland was not the only region to translate its economic woes into political terms. Indeed most of our histories of these times are a labyrinth of party politics because, except for the railroad builders, the politicians were about the only figures in the public eye. Fred Landon's reminder is to the point:

Industrial development had not yet proceeded sufficiently far to bring the business man as such into first-rate prominence, nor had public attention yet been turned to mining magnates, promoters of power development, owners of metropolitan newspapers, or university professors. Canadians as individuals still loved and hated, with about equal measure of intensity, the leaders of their own and the opposite party.

The very impotence of the politicians reduced politics largely to adulation of party leaders, notably Macdonald, depreciation of opponents, and such unreasoning party loyalty that Lady Macdonald, for instance, never entertained Liberals or members of their families. Blake's powerful destructive criticism and reasoned constructive proposals could make little progress in so blind and delusive an atmosphere. Faced by insuperable adversity, the voter preferred fireworks, torchlight processions, and retrospective or pugnacious oratorical taradiddle.

Friedrich Engels' impression of Canada in 1888 was that "at first he thought he was back in Europe, but later that he had entered a decaying and retrogressive country . . . ripe for annexation by the United States." This was also a time when evangelicalism, as typified by gifted, quiet Dwight L. Moody and many theatrical revivalists, warmed the chilled lives of Canadians, east, central, and west, and the Salvation Army sprang into vigorous life. Macdonald attended Methodist revival meetings, singing heartily and manifesting his personal concern for salvation.

Each section of Canada voiced its particular claims on the national government. The Maritimes threatened secession if they could not get "better terms" by way of federal subsidies. Quebec put all its woes into Honoré Mercier's short-lived single *Canadien* party, Rouges and *Bleus,* fanning the coals of ethnic singularity and "nationalism" with the emotions aroused by Riel's execution, by the transformation of Manitoba from a predominantly *Canadien* community to a Canadian one, and so on.

Ontario, in the person of Oliver Mowat, hit upon the device of challenging the overriding federal power in a series of appeals to the Privy Council, whose Judicial Committee showed its ignorance of federalism by reversing the intentions of "the Fathers," establishing provincial sovereignty as co-ordinate with federal, and, by concentrating on Section 92 of the B.N.A. Act instead of on Section 91, greatly broadening provincial powers.

Manitoba was determined to assert its British and American character over its French, and to break the C.P.R. monopoly clause by chartering other railroads, even south of the C.P.R. main line. The territories writhed under nondemocratic administration. British Columbia suspected that Robert Dunsmuir, its coal magnate, by associating the "Big Four" of the Union Pacific–Central Pacific in his Esquimalt and Nanaimo Railway, was easing the way into annexation, and at the same time lamented that Canadian indifference to the great mineral field just north of the forty-ninth parallel was "enough to make a citizen of West Kootenay weary and tired."

The pinnacle of the swelling antifederalism was reached in 1887, when Mercier succeeded in holding an unprecedented and unconstitutional conference at Quebec of the prime ministers of Nova Scotia, New Brunswick, Quebec, Ontario, and Manitoba. They passed resolutions providing for larger federal subsidies and for certain constitutional reforms, notably abolition of the federal power to disallow provincial legislation. That same year a substantial movement for close economic relations with the United States came out into the open vigorously, braving the inevitable charges of annexationism. Neither the Quebec conferees nor the advocates of commercial union knew how they could realize their ambitions, but it looked as if Canada would break up or enter the United States.

Macdonald's grip.—Yet Canada did neither, for Sir John won not only the general election of 1887 but also that of 1891. There is little use bewailing his political methods during those five years, even though they ran the whole gamut of fraudulence, bribery, gerrymandering, and mere expediency. Macdonald was fighting for his nation's continued existence at a time when its political morals and his were as low as its economic fortunes and its spirits. His office enabled him to appease Nova Scotia by tariffs and subsidies calculated to assist her coal, iron, and steel industry, and Quebec or Manitoba by ceasing to disallow their provincial legislation.

As a larger instance of his technique, the C.P.R. was forced to give up its monopoly clause in 1888, but it was helped to acquire and complete a line from Montreal across Maine to Saint John by 1890 in very advantageous competition with the Intercolonial and the Grand Trunk. It also acquired the North Shore line from Quebec to Ottawa that Macdonald had formerly assisted as a sop to Quebec. By a series of complicated maneuvers (including ownership of a strong interest in Hill's Great Northern), the C.P.R. crossed southern Ontario towards Chicago and bought two American lines that connected Winnipeg and Moose Jaw with St. Paul, Duluth, and the Sault by lines south of Lake Superior. "My own position as a public man is as intimately connected with the prosperity of the C.P.R. as yours is, as a railway man," Macdonald wrote to Stephen in 1889, and he was rewarded by very efficient C.P.R. support in the constituencies and in Parliament.

The revival of British imperial interest furnished another striking example of Macdonald's flexibility. This movement, resting as it did on protectionism, was a dubious venture in free-trade Britain, but it grew nonetheless, feeding on doubts bred by the Great Depression and on considerations of prestige and advantage at a time when international competition for weakly defended territories everywhere had become obvious. It enjoyed the eloquent support of such able, if different, publicists as Ruskin, J. R. Seeley, W. T. Stead and his assistant, Alfred Milner, R. L. Stevenson, Rider Haggard, the American Admiral Mahan, and Sir Charles W. Dilke. It was to culminate in Rhodes, Chamberlain, Kipling, and the lamentable South African War. From the beginning, Canada loomed large in the imperialists' calculations and leading Canadians took prominent parts in the significant chain of organizations which included the Royal Colonial Institute (Royal Empire Society), 1868; the Revivers of Trade Association, 1870; the National Fair Trade League, 1881; and the Imperial Federation League, 1884. The Canadian, Jehu Mathews, drew up in 1872 the first detailed plan for an imperial federation. The Queen's Jubilee and the Colonial Conference of 1887 were studiously used towards it. The imperialists produced the Imperial Federation League (1884–93), with its amalgamated creed of union and strength through a revived mercantilism and a centralized empire.

Macdonald had worked for this revival of British interest since 1864 and now the emergence of the movement for commercial union with the United States had provoked the establishment of branches of the Imperial Federation League in Canada, beginning at Montreal in 1885. Yet he sent Sir Alexander Campbell, lieutenant governor of Ontario, and Sandford Fleming, president of the Ottawa branch of the League, to represent Canada very noncommittally at the Colonial Conference of 1887 which was intended to be a meeting of governments. In other words, Macdonald saw as clearly as the British government that a free-trade Britain could not build a customs union and he was determined not to have Canada drawn into schemes of imperial defense or of central direction in Great Britain.

But, as the Liberals became identified more and more in the public mind with commercial union, and as that connection became translated popularly into Liberalism and Annexation, he had no compunction whatever about exploiting latent Canadian anti-Americanism to the limit and thumping the drum of his own and his party's pro-Britonism, their "loyalty" *vs.* Liberal "disloyalty." To *Canadiens* the cry was "Remember Louisiana," to Canadians it was "Remember the South," and to the colonial-minded it was "A British subject I was born—a British subject I will die."

The underlying fact was that if Canada preserved her existing autonomy, that is, maintained Macdonald's idea of "alliance" or free association of equals in sovereignty, the relationship with Britain was likely to be less burdensome than almost any with her overpowering American neighbor. (The McKinley tariff of October, 1890, by its disastrous effects, for instance on Canadian barley growing, was a reminder of how the United States could unconsciously, or half-consciously, damage Canada.) Imperial federation and commercial union were equally impracticable. The Toronto *News* hit the nail on the head in 1888:

The colonies do not ask "Will federation further military schemes, will it assist territorial aggrandizement, will it help emigration?" but they ask "Will it assist trade?" and until it can be shown that it will assist trade— assist it so largely that nothing further in that direction can be desired— the imperial federation idea is a meaningless one to colonists, and especially to Canadians.

✤ THE NEW SYMBOL

Macdonaldism barely sufficed in 1891. The next five years of depression and frustration completed its breakdown under no less than four quite able, if elderly, Conservative prime ministers: Sir John J. C. Abbott, Sir John S. D. Thompson, Sir Mackenzie Bowell, and Sir Charles Tupper. There was a widespread conviction that Canadian politics had sunk to the lowest tolerable point, for on the one hand an enigmatic *Canadien* politician, J. Israel Tarte, exposed even more thoroughly than in 1873 the relationship between public contracts and Conservative party funds, and, on the other, the methods of the triumphant Mercier in Quebec, when similarly exposed, were so sordid that, for the only time in Canadian history, the lieutenant governor dismissed a provincial premier and his ministry.

Superficially, the final crash of Conservative rule came over the vexed and complicated situation created by Manitoba's insistence on nonsectarian public schools, but actually the voters were rejecting the old hands in state and church, the old cynicism in politics, and the hardened disdain for principles other than frankly materialistic ones. To its surprise, the country came out of the election of 1896 with a *Canadien* as its prime minister.

Henri Charles Wilfrid Laurier had climbed to that eminence by a rough path. Touched by tuberculosis as a young man, his health had always been delicate. He went to a conservative classical college carrying his father's liberalism, his own two years of experience among Scottish Presbyterians, and much of the faith of Papineau and Garneau. He studied law at McGill and in the offices of Rodolphe Laflamme, a Rouge. When, after some false starts, he began in 1867 at the age of twenty-six to practice law and journalism at Arthabaskaville in the Eastern townships, the ultramontanist Bishop L. F. Laflèche of Three Rivers effectively squelched his liberal weekly, *Le Défricheur*. In those days, even a whiggish Rouge like Laurier was fair and easy game for the Ultramontanes, and Laurier, moreover, had been active in *L'Institut Canadien* of Montreal.

The young man had plenty of time for study and meditation in the country, from which he emerged with a mastery of modern British political and constitutional history and with some basic convictions. He was a liberal democrat in the parliamentary tradition. He believed that federation, by giving the *Canadiens* security in their own traditions, also created an opportunity that must be seized for an all-embracing Canadianism. A Catholic party in Canadian politics, he believed, would be as fatal as a *Canadien* party, and therefore, while the priest had the dubious right to discuss politics, he must not reinforce his views by ecclesiastical sanctions. As Laurier said in 1877, "It is perfectly legitimate to alter the elector's opinion by argument and all other means of persuasion, but never by intimidation."

Even while still struggling with ominous hemorrhages, he had been elected to the provincial legislature in 1871 in the small Liberal opposition to the easygoing Conservative administration of Pierre Chauveau, poet, novelist, and educator. He instantly made his mark, justifying the natural prestige he had enjoyed all his life. In the years of their triumph at Rome, the Ultramontanes had once more marked him down, but he had beaten them at the polls. Bishop Bourget's astonishing "Catholic Program" of April 20, 1871, was a declaration of war. The Ultramontanes had made over a Conservative party in their own image by 1875, yet Laurier beat them again for a federal seat in 1874.

In June, 1877, he made his brilliant statement of political principles to the *Club Canadien,* and in October Bishop Conroy of Armagh, as Papal delegate, called a halt to Ultramontane extravagances. Laurier had then become a national figure and was a member of Mackenzie's Cabinet at Ottawa. When he stood for the necessary re-election, scandalous methods secured his defeat in his own constituency by twenty-nine votes, but Quebec East soon returned him by 315. Time was to prove that he had cut the Gordian knot of Ultramontanism for the *Canadien* voter. French Canada need not follow France and Gambetta in a war against clericalism unless the Ultramontanes provoked such a war.

Laurier had a profound admiration for Blake, whose intellect and scholarship seemed to him commanding, and he persisted far longer than most Liberals in urging him to retain or resume the leadership of the party that he had taken over from Mackenzie after the great defeat in the election of 1878. But Blake's independent, original, complex character made him an impossibly undependable politician. He was a leader who for seven years did not lead his party.

When Blake finally gave up the leadership after electoral defeat in 1887, he chose Laurier to succeed him in what seemed a hopeless task. Somehow this gay and friendly, yet reserved, studious and philosophical man had built up the solidest reputation in a sorely harassed party. He had also risen to become the most brilliant and skilled member of Parliament. His courage in seeking out his enemies and speaking with great eloquence and conviction on vexed subjects in Ontario and Quebec, and his unfailing elegance, courtesy, and fastidiousness stood him in good stead.

A number of political issues raged between 1885 and 1896—Riel, the Manitoba schools question, disposition of the Jesuit Estates, and the unreal choice between imperial federation and commercial union. Laurier trod cautiously except when he was caught up in the wild year of excitement over Riel's execution, the year that produced Mercier's solid *Canadien* party. He tried and failed to find a way for easier trade relations with the United States. What he really achieved during that grim period was to win the voters of Quebec in spite of the bitter opposition of a great part of the church to which he and they belonged.

It was in this contest that he revealed the strong will and courage that made him the acceptable symbol of a new Canada—a *Canadien* and a Catholic with unrivaled, almost unblemished, claims to transcend those particularities and bespeak national generalities. "I am a Liberal of the English school," he asserted. "I am here the acknowledged leader of a great party, composed of Roman Catholics and Protestants as well, as Protestants must be in the majority in every party in Canada. . . . Am I to be told . . . that I am to be dictated the course I am to take . . . by reasons that can appeal to the consciences of my fellow-Catholic members, but which do not appeal as well to the consciences of my Protestant colleagues? No."

In Quebec during the election of 1896 he fought a large part of the church hierarchy, Conservatives in control of the federal and provincial political machinery, and all the varieties of provincial particularism. With the former *Bleu,* Tarte, managing the campaign on his side, he won 49 of the 65 Quebec seats. In Ontario it was 44 to 41, in the Maritimes about even, in Manitoba 4 to 2, and in British Columbia and the territories 6 to 3. And then, in the inexplicable way in which such things seem to happen, the long decline of prices ended and Canada entered on the rewards of her long endurance.

BOOK 4

CONSOLIDATION (1896–1920)

CHAPTER XXII

A Profitable National Economy
(1896-1913)

The statisticians record that, according to their indexes, Canadian
wholesale prices rose 48 per cent from 1897 to 1914, sharing, of course,
a similar rise in world prices. When translated from mere arithmetic
into Canadian history, that increase meant the difference between an
economy whose stagnation threatened decline and the fastest growing
one on earth.

The exhilaration of the swift swing from frustration to fruition gave
Canadian life a new quality. It raised Canada to a new status in the
world, especially in relations with Great Britain and the United States.
Population, particularly in industrial Europe, was pressing on the
world's food supply; the free or almost free arable land of the United
States was exhausted; the African gold that had so much to do with
rising prices had hardly begun to be mined in quantity; and great
technical changes were cheapening and speeding transportation. It
seemed as if Canada had been expressly (if painfully) groomed to win
in the twentieth-century sweepstakes.

The outside world thought so too, and bet on Canada in the form
of immense investment, not only in federal, provincial, and municipal
securities, but in railroads, forests, mines, and factories. In 1900, the
year's inflow of investment (chiefly British) and of settlers' capital
(chiefly American) amounted on net balance to $30,000,000, but by
1905 it was $110,000,000, by 1910, $308,000,000, and in 1913, at
its climax, $541,000,000. There were speculation and folly aplenty in
this foreign gambling on Canada, but once the capital was placed in
the country most of it and of its increment stayed there. Every phase
of Canadian economic life, from iron and steel in Cape Breton or

harbor improvement at Saint John to the grocery business in Ontario, railroads on the plains, and real estate in Vancouver, received new vigor.

The peopling of the country underwent a tremendous change. The year 1896 is believed to have been the lowest point in the rate of Canadian population increase since the end of the seventeenth century, probably less than 1 per cent during the year. During the decade 1901–11 population increased by 35 per cent, and during the next decade the Canadian-born population of the United States decreased instead of increasing as heretofore. That is, instead of losing to the United States practically the sum total of natural increase (about 12 per cent per decade at this time) and immigration, Canada began to hold almost that total. The annual inflow of Americans (including many of Canadian stock) and Europeans went up like a rocket: 16,835 in 1896, 41,681 in 1900, 131,252 in 1904, 143,326 in 1908 (world depression), 331,288 in 1911, and 400,870 in 1913.

This general change, as M. C. MacLean has most ingeniously demonstrated, involved a great deal of internal migration in Canada and a considerable amount of temporary clustering in the cities, which served as distribution points. Why emigrate to farm in the United States when Americans were rushing in to western Canada by the hundreds of thousands? Yet at the same time the eastern pull of the cities and of industrial employment was operating in and between the two countries, so that something like a continental redistribution of population was taking place as well as an unparalleled immigration from Europe. From 1897 to 1914, inclusive, Canada received 1,154,709 immigrants from Great Britain, 1,026,678 from the United States, and 842,689 from other countries.

The following figures indicate the effects on the pattern of Canadian settlement. The decade 1911 to 1921 is included because the decisions as to destination made at the distributing points took some time to reveal themselves.

	Population			
Area	*1891*	*1901*	*1911*	*1921*
Maritime Provinces	880,737	893,953	937,955	1,000,328
Quebec	1,488,535	1,648,898	2,005,776	2,360,510
Ontario	2,114,321	2,182,947	2,527,292	2,933,662
Western Plains	251,473	439,641	1,334,628	1,964,225
British Columbia	98,173	178,657	392,480	524,582

For the first time since federation, Canada had something like well-distributed, if still thin, flesh on her immense bones.

🍁 PRODUCTION SOARS

Agriculture.—The excellent northern wheat that Western Canadians had painfully learned to grow, and could now market at prices and transportation costs that made life worth living, naturally occupied the center of the agricultural stage. In the plains area few men considered mixed farming. All the land a man could till or get tilled went into wheat; indeed it was already apparent that, in a region where the long-term average yield was about fourteen bushels to the acre, the quarter-section of 160 acres was too small a farm. A good year in yield and price on a full section might put a man on Easy Street, whereas if both were bad he might as well be killed for a sheep as for a lamb. "Wheat-mining" was a gamble in which you risked nearly all you had on each year's play.

Yet one must see the West in its proper place in the national economy, that is, as the producer of a world commodity in amounts far beyond Canada's capacity to consume. Twentieth-century Canada produced many farm goods besides wheat; indeed in a national economic sense it was the variety as well as the abundance of her farm production that made her predominantly an agricultural country down to about 1920. Hay, oats, and other grains were immensely important before the internal combustion engine vanquished the horse. Potatoes, vegetables, fruits, sugar beets, and tobacco; hides, wool, honey, maple products, and furs; all sorts of valuable crops came off the farm lands. Some were sold in their natural state; many others were processed for consumption, notably in the rapidly expanding milling, canning, and meat-packing industries.

A resort to statistics demonstrates this abundance and variety. Recall that wheat and livestock were produced in every province of Canada.

Item	Dollar value in		
	1891	1901	1911
Wheat	31,667,529	36,122,039	104,816,825
Total field crops	194,766,934	237,682,285	384,513,795
Total livestock & poultry	Unknown	274,375,000	630,113,000
Total dairy products	30,315,214	66,470,953	103,381,854
Wheat & flour exports	2,971,662	10,887,165	59,375,924
Total exports of vegetable products	13,742,557	25,541,567	84,368,425
Total exports of animals & their products	36,399,140	68,465,332	69,693,263
Total exports	88,671,738	177,431,386	274,316,553

The forests.—By 1896 the original thick-set pine forests of eastern and central Canada were nearly gone and lumbering had become a matter of balancing cost and yield for surviving remote stands, or picking over thin old and new areas, or turning to spruce, fir, and hemlock. Mills and mill towns shut down, dams and chutes crumbled, and a strange cautiousness appeared in what had been a rampant industry for a century. Some mill sites became valuable for the water power and hydroelectric power that they could develop, but in lumbering itself the bookkeeper and the accountant worked with skilled estimators of standing timber and its transportation ("timber-cruisers") before deciding that such-and-such a river might still support a mill or two, or that it would pay to put so many hundreds of thousands into a new mill (with a regional monopoly) in northern Quebec or Ontario, or along the north shores of Huron and Superior.

When the railroad broke out of the Lakes Basin and the St. Lawrence and Ottawa valleys, deep into the Shield and across it north of the height of land, the lumberman was alert to the possibilities of monopolizing the basins of rivers flowing into James Bay. The good pine faded out just north of the new National Transcontinental, but that railroad and the Temiskaming and Northern Ontario ran through stands of smaller, less desirable softwoods and crossed many useful rivers.

The Canadian timber "crop" was three-quarters softwoods, but hardwoods were so much in demand for construction, furniture, and vehicles that expensive methods of collection were employed. Black walnut fence rails, for instance, were traded for wire; skilled agents toured the countryside "boosting" coal over cordwood for stoves and furnaces; and unspoiled stands could justify the building of a woods railroad. In other words, eastern lumbering became big business.

This was, of course, most notable in the pulp and paper industry which required large quantities of capital as well as of water and trees. Statistics of pulp and paper production rather unaccountably were not collected until 1921, but it is significant that the turbine horsepower installed in Canada rose from 71,219 in 1891 to 1,363,134 in 1911, the number of electric powerhouses grew from 80 to 266, and the value of wood, wood products, and paper exported rose from $25,351,085 to $56,334,695. Since 1913 Canada has been the world's leading exporter of newsprint paper.

Yet if the eastern forest industries were in decline or transition, the western were gaining. The well-watered area between Lake Nipigon and the Manitoba Basin contained some good stands of pine, particularly near the international boundary; indeed reasonably good timber (not including white pine) could be taken from the margins of a crescent-shaped area the horns of which touched the international boundary in southeast Manitoba and southwest Alberta. Here the milling was chiefly in small units and for local consumption, as it was among the ponderosa and lodgepole pines, the Engelmann spruce, and Douglas fir of interior British Columbia.

The booming, expanding, western lumber business was along the Pacific coast, where high precipitation and temperate climate produced gigantic Douglas fir, cedar, hemlock, and Sitka spruce. This highly mechanized industry, with its donkey engines, airy cableways, and steep skids on rough mountainsides, and its specialized topping, felling, and log-making techniques, moved its huge logs on land by rail and by sea in odd, cable-bound, cigar-shaped rafts to tidewater mills; their machinery dwarfed what the East had known. It is estimated that the "infant" growth of this industry was as follows: 1881–90, 550 million feet of board; 1891–1900, 1327 million; and 1901–10, 4754 million.

The fisheries.—During the preliminaries to the Treaty of Washington in 1871, Hincks wrote confidentially to Macdonald that "the fisheries are a mere expense." This central Canadian parochialism has persisted in large degree, in spite of the fact that the fisheries have remained sustenance and profit to large numbers of Canadians on the Atlantic and Pacific coasts, not to speak of Newfoundlanders whose entire well-being depended on the fishery. Moreover, the marketed value of Canadian fishery products grew steadily from $17,714,900 in 1890 to $35,860,708 in 1915.

Within that period a number of significant changes took place. It was in 1895, for instance, that salmon established itself above cod as the leading commercial fish, a place that it held until Newfoundland's entry to Canada in 1949, with lobster and herring competing with cod for the second place. Also within that period, the immense fresh-water fishery of the Great Lakes Basin was subjected to inroads by new methods and by pollution from which it has never recovered.

The shore fisheries on the oceans were still carried on from small boats and fish traps and the banks fisheries from dories carried in sailing schooners of 70 to 125 tons, but the internal combustion engine was about to effect great changes. Refrigeration, usually the lavish use of ice, was allowing fresh fish to supplement cured on the Atlantic coast and was stimulating the catch of salmon and halibut, by purse seine, drift nets, trolls, and setlines, along the narrow shelf and banks of the Pacific coast. Mechanical freezing of fish was just beginning to be established about 1910–14. On the Pacific, in contrast to the Atlantic, the greater part of the commercial catch was canned, notably the varieties of salmon taken in and near the rivers during their successive annual runs. In succession from June 1 to late November, Spring, Sockeye, Cohoe, Pink, and Chum were caught.

Mining and hydroelectric power.—Canadians of the early twentieth century knew of their country's great mineral resources and its expanding production, but lamented the location of its iron and coal and the exhaustion of its petroleum and natural gas. The coal deposits were almost as far apart and as distant from the great consuming centers as possible—in the Maritime Provinces and in western Alberta and British Columbia. Canadian iron was unable to compete with Minnesotan or Newfoundland ores because it was of poorer quality, harder to extract or purify, or situated at remote points like the Belcher Islands in Hudson Bay or the interior of Ungava.

As we have seen, Canada was instantly receptive to hydroelectric power, and only the United States has exceeded her installations. Niagara, of course, and the Ottawa, St. Lawrence, St. Maurice, and Montmorency rivers were most conveniently situated for the industrial heart of Canada once high-frequency transmission conquered distance. In spite of immense capital costs, the 173,000 installed horsepower of 1900 became 977,000 in 1910 and 2,515,000 by 1920, with the end far from being in sight. Characteristically, about 90 per cent of the developed water power has been for sale, with the remainder part of mining, pulp and paper, and other industries. In addition, steam plants either produced power or served as stand-bys.

The people of Ontario were so impressed by their chance to reduce dependence on American coal that between 1900 and 1906 they created a public hydroelectric power commission that moved, with public approval, into almost monopolistic production (or purchase) and sale of power. It is impossible to calculate the influence of this energy on the rapid transformation of Canada into a predominantly industrial nation. One horsepower is commonly held to equal the working capacity of ten men, and the delivery of electricity to the motor on each job is infinitely preferable to the complex and costly apparatus of shafts, belts, and pulleys by which steam power was delivered to the machine. Moreover electric power could be cheaply delivered to mountaintops, isolated places, and the depths of the earth.

The general public heard of mining chiefly in terms of exciting new developments. The most celebrated of these was the Klondike gold rush of 1896–1903. (Placer-mining had been going on along the Yukon since about 1880, particularly on Forty-mile Creek, but the big strike on the Klondike tributary was made in 1896.) The difficult accessibility of this region in the Yukon Territory and the consequent fantastic accompaniments of travel, transportation, international relations, and life in and around Dawson City brought back to life the Californian, Australian, and British Columbian rushes of fifty years earlier. They also evoked a popular rhymester in Robert W. Service and a popular novelist in Jack London. The madness seems to have infected between 200,000 and 300,000 persons, of whom perhaps 50,000 reached the interior at a cost ranging from $500 to $10,000. It was a godsend to Seattle and Vancouver, but a wild business for the Klondikers.

Gradually the region came under the control of large American capital as the opportunities for individual effort disappeared and it was succeeded by costly hydraulic and soil-thawing enterprises, and finally by dredges. Production reached its peak of $13,000,000 in 1903, about half the total Canadian production of gold that year, and fell away to $5,000,000 in 1914; population was 27,129 in 1901 and 8,512 ten years later. Oddly enough, no great lodes have been found either in the Yukon or in the Cassiar country south of it, whereas along the coast the Treadwell on Baranoff Island, Juneau near the mouth of the Taku River, and Premier on the Portland Canal have been very rich hard-rock mines. The rich hard-rock mines of the area far to the south near Lillooet at the beginning of the Cariboo Trail were staked in 1897, but proved very slow in coming into their own.

The second exciting new development came when the province of Ontario embarked on the doubtful business of building a railroad north from North Bay across the Shield in order to colonize the Clay Belt, a roughly triangular area stretching 300 miles east to west about halfway between James Bay and Lake Huron, where a rather limited kind of mixed farming had been shown to be practicable. The adventure paid off in an unexpected fashion, for in 1903 the railroad builders uncovered slabs of almost solid silver about 70 miles north of Lake Nipissing—the "silver pavements of Cobalt." Next year the railroad was ready to bring in the miners and their equipment and the camp developed in a progressive way from rich surface operations ("open cut") to deep mining, stamping, concentrating, and milling. Here the new hydroelectric power came into its own at considerable distances from the railroad.

Cobalt became a great focus for advanced mining and milling technology at about the same time that the copper nickel ores of Sudbury about 100 miles to the southwest were efficiently mastered by new methods of ore treatment, smelting, and refining. Moreover, at Cobalt were assembled the capital, the skills, and above all the urge towards further prospecting in the Shield. In rapid succession strikes were made along the railroad line and to east and west of it, not only of silver, but of gold, copper, zinc and other nonferrous metals in concentrations that advanced metallurgy made profitable.

By 1913 it was apparent that the Shield, not only in Quebec and

Ontario but probably also in its great swing up to the arctic, might be converted from a mighty obstacle to Canadian growth into a mighty asset. Already its crumpled gray and green surface was gridironed here and there by railroad, road, and electric transmission lines; dams impounded some of its rivers and lakes; and tall chimneys launched thin plumes of smoke across the empty land from smelting ores. It was these mining, plus pulp and paper enterprises that were to sustain (precariously) Clay Belt agriculture, for it would otherwise have been too marginal to persist.

Ontario became the principal mineral-producing province of Canada in 1907 and as her silver declined, nickel, gold, and copper took its place, keeping her ahead of British Columbia. This coalless province became a great testing ground for costly, but advanced, technique and its abundance of water not only provided power, but the washing and flotation processes that made it profitable, for instance, to mine and mill a ton of rock that contained a good deal less than an ounce of gold. Canada as a whole was on the march in mining, as the value of the production showed: 1895, $20,505,917; 1900, $64,420,877; 1905, $69,078,999; 1910, $106,823,623; and 1915, $137,109,171.

Manufactures.—About 1920 the net value of Canadian manufactures, that is, their total value less the cost of the power and the materials used in their production, passed the net value of agricultural production; Canada became a predominantly industrial country. This was not, as many thought then, primarily the result of the demands made on the Canadian economy by World War I, but rather the natural outcome of a long-established trend which was confirmed twenty years later when the net value of industrial production exceeded that of all other production. The immense growth of wheat and mineral production since 1896, however, overshadowed this development; since the world regarded Canada chiefly as a bread basket, Canadians did too.

This manufacturing was of two kinds: the varied production for domestic consumption of most of the commodities that entered into the high North American standard of living, and a few large-scale industries which processed Canadian raw materials for the world market. Textiles or shoes would fall into the first category, flour and newsprint into the second. The main deficiencies in the over-all structure were the large dependence on the United States for many kinds of iron and steel and a considerable technological lag in nearly all manufacturing which, combined with the relatively small market, meant that the more intricate, advanced, and refined products were imported.

Thus Canada could export agricultural machinery in successful competition almost anywhere in the world, but the automobiles she produced were assembled very largely from parts imported from the United States. Or, for another example, Canada smelted her own ores, but exported most of them to the United States and Great Britain for refining.

It was natural that most industry, and practically all its financing that was not done by London and New York, was located in Quebec and Ontario. They contained the oldest and largest compact populations and geographically they belonged to the great North American industrial complex that had grown up inside the Appalachian Barrier. Hamilton and Cleveland, Toronto and Buffalo, even Montreal and New York had more in common with each other than with Halifax, Gloucester, St. Louis, Kansas City, Winnipeg, Denver, San Francisco, and Vancouver.

The statistics of the distribution of Canadian manufacturing about 1913 are complex and subject to qualification, but the percentage of the value of manufacturing production contributed by each province was roughly as follows: Ontario 52, Quebec 30, British Columbia 6, Nova Scotia 5, Manitoba 3, New Brunswick 2, Alberta 1.6 and Saskatchewan and Prince Edward Island under 1 per cent. Of the total value, iron production accounted for 29 per cent, wood and paper for 20, vegetable for 14, chemical for 10, animal for 10, textile for 9, nonmetallic minerals for 5, and nonferrous metals for 3.

☙ TRANSPORTATION

As might have been expected, Canadians really let themselves go when it came to providing transportation for this production. They improved the St. Lawrence Ship Channel, deepened the canals to fourteen feet, and completed a 900-foot lock at the Sault. They even embarked on a scandalous and harebrained 240-mile Trent Canal from the Bay of Quinte to Georgian Bay which finally collapsed in absurdity and disgrace. They built endless roads and entered upon the costly business of providing hard-surfaced roads for the motor traffic that was swelling so swiftly.

They thickened the previous railroad networks, built the Timiskaming and Northern Ontario (now Ontario Northland) halfway from North Bay to James Bay, and added two transcontinental railroads. They began a line from The Pas in Manitoba towards Port Nelson on Hudson Bay; pushed three lines northward in Alberta to the Athabaska River and the Peace River country, and launched one of the world's most extraordinary (and scenic) railways from Squamish, north of Vancouver, through the mountains to the upper Fraser. Meanwhile Newfoundland completed her trans-island railway from St. John's to the Cabot Strait.

The Great Lakes waterways of modern times should not be passed over without comment, especially since even most Americans and Canadians are blissfully ignorant of their greatest common possession. How many of them know that twice as much freight passes through the Sault canals during the open season (eight months or less) as through Panama and Suez together in a year, or that more freight moves each year on the Lakes waterways than the total ocean-borne foreign trade of both countries? Most of the traffic is coastal to one country or the other, and cargoes down, chiefly wheat and iron ore, are twice as heavy as cargoes up, chiefly coal and the bulkier manufactured goods.

The desirability of speed in bulk carriage across the Lakes and through narrow, shallow passages and locks produced special shipping and loading devices. For the grain traffic from Lake Superior to Georgian Bay or Buffalo and the ore traffic from the same lake down as far as Lake Erie, the "upper laker" was developed, a great self-propelled, subdivided steel barge, perhaps over six hundred feet long, but not over seventy feet in beam or thirty-three feet in draught when fully loaded. The "lower laker" or "canaller" operated in waters limited by the fourteen-foot canals, but might be 260 feet long and 44 feet in beam and carry 2500 tons. The loading and unloading apparatus for wheat, ore, and coal was elaborate and amazingly efficient, employing elevators, railroad car tippers, bins, chutes, suction, conveyors, etc., on a scale justified, in particular, by the short period between harvest and freeze-up. The best way to take in the scale of this water transportation was to watch the endless procession of huge vessels through the Sault locks or on the St. Clair and Detroit rivers.

Stated summarily, Canadian railway mileage grew as follows: 1891, 13,838 miles; 1901, 18,140; 1911, 25,400; 1915, 37,400. In those days before the ubiquitous motor truck, the railroad not only reached out for customers but opened up areas where it hoped to create custom. In addition, a nation intoxicated by long-deferred prosperity encouraged its legislators (municipal, provincial, and federal) to put public funds into transportation projects that could not possibly pay. The largest components in this situation before 1914 were the two new transcontinentals, the Canadian Northern and the National Transcontinental.

The former was the creation of two former C.P.R. contractors, William Mackenzie and Donald Mann, who got their start by making capital out of western dislike of the C.P.R. monopoly. They knew all the tricks of the trade and, in particular, were expert in using federal and bank loans, bond guarantees, and subsidies in land and money to form a financial pyramid of subsidiary companies designed to keep the use of all possible credit and profits.

Their construction was so cheap that the tracks were said to jump up and hit the trains from behind. Their operating methods were ingenious and highly adaptable. Somehow their trains seemed to have a high percentage of cars belonging to other lines (under the pool system); their train crews would pick up or unload freight here and there with slight regard for regular stopping places or timetables; and the second-hand equipment which they acquired from the small, local roads they absorbed made Canadian Northern "mixed trains" (freight and passenger) fairly fantastic.

Once they had broken through the C.P.R.'s mid-continental toll gate in Manitoba, they built and acquired lines in the better-paying parts of the West to serve as the base for the costly, unproductive stretches across British Columbia (by the Yellowhead and moderate grades) and the Shield. The complete story of this last great North American railroad adventure has never been told, but it contained all the traditional elements as well as some new. When one disregards the piquancies and the gossip, the swashbuckling and the lobbying, the achievement stands out clearly as one facet of Canadian exuberance at the time. Completed in 1915, it comprised 9,362 miles of line. Mackenzie and Mann still held nearly all the common stock.

The National Transcontinental, on the other hand, was obviously a "political" railroad. The Conservatives had built the C.P.R. Now it was the Liberals' turn. Unfortunately they planned to build upon the base of the slightly revived Grand Trunk and, instead of forcing it to combine with the Canadian Northern and its large network on the plains, they gave up that idea too easily (1902–3) and allowed the two private lines to pursue their separate (and wasteful) ambitions —another surrender to infectious optimism.

The intricacies of the Liberals' lavish railroad policy cannot be pursued here. The outcome was a white elephant. The national government built a new and more direct line from Moncton across New Brunswick to Quebec, thus increasing the deficits of the Intercolonial, for this part of the line involved the unprecedented problems of bridging the St. Lawrence at Quebec, a task completed, after two costly failures, in 1917. From Quebec the line ran north and west to the Clay Belt and Winnipeg through the empty and even unsurveyed Shield for about 1500 miles. Costs exceeded estimates by 200 per cent and amounted to $88,600 a mile. This line, built to expensive specifications, was to be leased to and operated by the Grand Trunk.

That company, supported by the government's guarantee of bonds amounting to about 75 per cent of the cost and by subsequent large direct loans, built its new Grand Trunk Pacific from Winnipeg by Edmonton and the Yellowhead Pass to Prince Rupert on the Pacific coast near the Alaskan boundary. By the most charitable interpretation, through the National Transcontinental New Brunswick got an advantageous new line; the plains got more competition for the C.P.R. and better access to northern areas that they were learning how to cultivate; and Quebec, Ontario, and British Columbia got an inappropriately well-constructed line for colonization purposes in northern areas that could not support even moderately dense population. The taxpayer was soon to have to cope with railroad bankruptcies.

🍁 AN INTERNATIONAL TRADER

In 1913 almost any Canadian would have said that the past few years had equipped his country to supply the world with an enormous surplus production, chiefly of foodstuffs. The west-east lines of the international boundary and the transcontinental railroads pointed to an export chiefly to Europe, and most Canadians thought of their foreign trade as a two-way affair with wheat, flour, cattle, meat, and nonferrous metals going to Great Britain for consumption or distribution, and with British textiles, tropical products, and manufactured goods coming back. The reality was considerably different—a triangular to-and-fro movement of peoples, capital, and goods among Canada, Great Britain, and the United States.

The determinants of this triangular interplay were many, and their interaction was complex. To begin with, the great influx of foreign capital, chiefly British, allowed Canadians to buy abroad more than they sold from 1902 onwards, but the United States produced manufactured goods more desirable to North Americans more cheaply and more speedily deliverable than did Great Britain. In the second place, the terms of trade, or the price ratio between the products Canada had to sell and what she bought, were favorable every year from 1896 to 1913 (except 1900 when they were even) and were so from 1909 to 1913 by over 10 per cent. Thirdly, larger Canadian production permitted both the large-scale economies and the specialized production that had hitherto been lacking.

This was a period of industrial combinations or trusts, what a Canadian poet has called "the joint stock frontier." The number of manufacturing establishments between 1900 and 1915 increased only from 14,650 to 15,593, but the capital represented increased from $447,-000,000 to $1,959,000,000. Finally, it became apparent that the swelling population and industrial production of the United States had become dependent on Canada to a considerable and growing degree. About 10 per cent of American newsprint came from Canada in 1913, for instance, and Canadian fish, lumber, grain, meat, dairy products, and minerals, metallic and nonmetallic, went to the United States in significantly increasing quantities.

In the most general terms, Canada sold much more to Great Britain than she bought from her and bought much more from the United States than she sold to her. Though part of a much larger pattern of multilateral trade, this was a clear-cut triangle nonetheless. Canadians bought their needed American dollars with their surplus of British sterling, and Americans used the sterling to meet their obligations either to Great Britain or to Latin America and Oriental countries whose products had come to the United States. The ability of Canada to sell her surplus production practically every year from 1896 to 1913 at a profit was associated with a rising standard of consumption for the rising population within Canada.

The expansion and directions of Canadian external trade can be summarized statistically.

Item	1891	1901	1911
Total foreign trade	$200,205,692	355,362,305	727,041,156
Exports to U.K.	43,243,784	92,857,525	132,156,924
Imports from U.K.	42,018,943	42,820,334	109,934,753
Exports to U.S.	37,743,420	69,983,673	104,115,823
Imports from U.S.	52,033,477	107,377,906	275,824,265

Canada's double economic affiliation stands out clearly, indeed it almost monopolizes Canada's external trade. Yet not many Canadians made this part of their thinking, for reasons arising out of their history. They liked to forget their economic relationships with the United States and to stress those with Great Britain because they feared the former and not the latter. They had so much invested in competitive transcontinental transportation systems that they thought in terms of business for them rather than for lines running north and south. In brief, since they had made a nation in defiance of transverse obstacles across the continent they tended to think of trade as functioning almost exclusively that way.

Seen in perspective, there were two striking characteristics of the general Canadian economy of 1913 that were ominous of the future. One was the involvement of the municipal, provincial, and federal authorities. In addition to governmental financing (such as in the transportation industry), there was government ownership (for example,

the Ontario Hydroelectric Power Commission), and government operation of great public services (Manitoba's public telephone system).
The state was less obvious, but at least as pervasive, in nearly every
aspect of production and marketing, by subsidies and bounties, by
tariffs and special freight rates, not to speak of the contracts it was
awarded or the lands, forests, mines, and water powers that it gave away.
The politician held the keys to many doors of opportunity. Moreover,
the state had begun to assume responsibility for several kinds of economic regulation, for instance, in trade unionism, public relief, railroad
rates, and industrial combination. The state had always been interventionist in Canada and now it had to adapt its interventionism to
Canada's swift industrialization and what went with it.

The second characteristic was also one that called for state action
—the need for conservation of the natural resources that Canadians
had been exploiting for three centuries. Conservation had become a
public cause in the United States shortly after the Census of 1890 had
alarmed some observers by revealing the imminent exhaustion of certain
national resources. Efforts to save forests, grazing lands, and so on
provoked conflicts near the center of the political stage.

When the movement was echoed in Canada, its supporters met
ridicule and indifference in spite of the fact that the eastern forests
had gone the way of those in the United States and that the Pacific
salmon were being fished out. In the face of interested or ignorant
claims that Canada's resources had been "barely scratched," all that
the conservationist could achieve was the reservation of a small number
of provincial and national parks as game sanctuaries and scenic or
vacation resorts. The successful preservation of the valuable Pribiloff
Islands' seals was the outcome, by four-power treaty in 1911, of a
generation of international controversy. The Canada of 1913 saw too
much immediate opportunity to worry about less in the future.

CHAPTER XXIII

The Canadian Peoples (1896-1913)

There was, of course, no single Canadian people in 1914. The political unity of 1867 and after, and the economic unity that grew so rapidly after 1896, had few parallels in society. The peoples of Canada were various, and their loyalties to their regions were more urgent than their responses to Canada as a whole. One out of four had been born outside Canada; hundreds of thousands spoke neither French nor English; and many were tentatively poised here and there across the country without any strong sense of having struck roots, liable to move within Canada or into the United States or back to their place of origin. The feverishness of 1896–1913 had culminated in a deep depression and second thoughts were rife in 1914.

Of the population of 7,200,000 in 1911, the Canadian-born formed 78 per cent, the British-born 12 per cent, the American-born 4 per cent, and others 6 per cent. In terms of racial origin, the British stock formed 54 per cent and the French stock 29 per cent, the only other large elements being German, 5 per cent, and Scandinavian and Indian, each about 1½ per cent.

Yet these percentages applied to the country as a whole, not to its parts. The Maritimes were by racial origin overwhelmingly British (74 per cent) and French (19 per cent). Quebec, in spite of cosmopolitan Montreal, was 80 per cent French. Ontario, in spite of *Canadien* and other immigration, was 79 per cent British. The plains provinces (where American-born formed at least 15 per cent of the whole and in some areas 35 per cent) were ethnically mixed, with 56 per cent British, .6 per cent French, and most of the remaining 43 per cent a highly variegated mixture of Continental European stock. British Columbia, which was 74 per cent British, contained many more of Chinese and Japanese stock than of French, not to speak of a small group of East Indians.

On the plains there had been a natural tendency for the "New Canadians," the immigrants who spoke neither English nor French, to settle in groups, some of which, the Mennonites and Dukhobors from Russia most notably, strongly resisted efforts to Canadianize them. Yet it could be confidently predicted that the plains population would in general become English-speaking and would respond to the North American plains environment.

In a cultural sense, it was important to Canada that the New Canadians should inject into the drab life on the plains some of the color and glow that centuries of rural life in Europe had produced. The Germans, Austrians, Scandinavians, Ukrainians, and Russians tried to do so, with some lasting effects, particularly in music and literature.

⚜ TWO WAYS OF LIFE

The great dichotomy of *Canadien* and Canadian remained—two ways of life, each deep-rooted in tradition, each having acquired a set of harsh attitudes towards the other that made instinctive understanding impossible for all save an infinitesimal few. No intelligent person believed that the two cultures would merge or that one would submerge the other in the foreseeable future.

A few *Canadiens* believed in the possibility of a separate people and state astride the St. Lawrence and gradually spreading by sheer fecundity over the Maritimes, New England, and Ontario in much the same way that they had inundated the smaller American stock of the Eastern townships. This view neglected both the probable response of the rest of Canada to having its principal eastern avenue at someone else's mercy and the probable loss of *Canadiens* by assimilation into the larger societies they were expected to submerge.

A few Canadians still thought of anglicizing the *Canadiens* by persuasion or by force. Yet talk of dragooning the *Canadiens* was so silly that it could not properly be called dangerous except in its effects on the more lightheaded in both groups.

The prevalent differences and antagonisms may be quickly recalled. Basic to them all were contradictory views as to the nature and function of man, and it did not lessen the intensity that one stemmed from the French Reformation in John Calvin and the other from the French Counter-Reformation in the missionary Order of Jesus, both being markedly evangelical and puritan. Almost as fundamental was the fact that the Canadian believed in the separation of church and state, while the *Canadien* emphatically did not.

This made education a principal battleground when *Canadiens* spread beyond Quebec into neighboring provinces and states. It also gave the priest or pastor a natural leadership (not necessarily domination) among *Canadiens* that he once had but rapidly lost among Canadians. The *Canadien* emphasis was on communal, homogeneous things—the family, the church, adaptation to tradition and natural environment, life after death. The Canadian emphasis was on individual, variegated things—"planned parenthood," churches, mastery over tradition and natural environment, and the highest attainable material standards of life. Marriage outside one's group, for instance, was a commonplace to Canadians, but shocking to *Canadiens*. *Canadiens* were excessively resistant to innovations, Canadians excessively receptive to them.

The clash was not one between rural and urban dwellers, for the Quebec that had been two-thirds rural in 1891 was only 44 per cent rural by 1921. It was more truly a heritage from the superior power, privilege, and material possessions of the Canadians in French Canada, accentuated by their greater aptitude and training for modern business and by their creed or ethic of success measured in terms of money. From 1760 onwards, the *Canadiens* had been severely handicapped in these regards; they showed all the traits likely to develop in a group regarded as inferior. In fact they behaved like minorities everywhere by insistently setting their survival as a distinct ethnic entity above all else. Whether conquered and subjected or not, they felt themselves to be so and often carried their defensiveness to the point of inability to change with the times.

Distress was unavoidable, for the majority seemed and often were callous and the minority seemed and often were hypersensitive. Common criteria were seldom applicable, for they had a way of being material when Canadian and immaterial when *Canadien*. French Canada, driven in on itself by British Canada just as British Canada was often driven in on itself by the United States, tended to be ingrown and to seek enhancement from Rome rather more than from its French tradition, while British Canada made matters worse in the relationship by exaggerating its Britonism as its principal assurance against Americanization. Neither dared seek reinforcement from the United States lest it weaken itself for annexation or absorption.

Clearly the only remedy could be some larger loyalty, to be attained very slowly. Neither Canadianism nor North Americanism was as yet attainable and Britonism was both repugnant to *Canadiens* and unreal to Canadians. Industrialism was effecting a revolution which might some day produce a dominant culture, but even that powerful process carried no promise of a common society. Canada, like Belgium or South

Africa, could not shed her dual ethnic nature. In the meantime the church of the *Canadiens* remained the leader in their struggle for *survivance*. *"Canadiens français soyons nous-mêmes!"*

THE DISTRIBUTION OF CITIES

It should be observed that cities were distributed along the transcontinental ribbon of settlement with remarkable evenness. Every province except Prince Edward Island had at least one large city and most of them more than one, even the plains provinces and British Columbia.

Every province was a rural-urban mixture with a pronounced trend from country to town as mechanization reduced the needs for manpower in the extractive pursuits and "city lights" beckoned. Everywhere in Canada the cities felt the burden of the seasonal unemployment that affected industry as well as other activities. Many Canadians sought shelter in their cities during adversity and many who felt thwarted in Canada made for the larger cities of the United States, even while self-confident Americans were pouring into Canada by hundreds of thousands.

SOCIAL STRATIFICATION

As late as 1914 the traditional leaders of society still persisted in some strength. In nearly every province some long-established families had developed habits of public service and social responsibility, more often than not accompanied by enduring wealth. They formed, as it were, the backbone or core of the group invited to call on the governor general or at the provincial Government Houses on New Year's Day and similar symbolic occasions. Academic society was usually included in this group.

Religious leadership was very secure among the *Canadiens* at all levels, in spite of the differences provoked by the intransigent ultramontanists, but among the Canadians it suffered from the variety of churches; indeed, although Anglicans, Methodists, and Presbyterians were about equal in number, the first enjoyed quite the highest status, partly by reason of tradition and partly by default. Mere wealth, unaccompanied by public spirit or support of the other kinds of distinction, was still contemptible.

Yet gentility was only moderately secure because the appearance of it had been so grossly exploited for three or four generations and because it was still exploited by ne'er-do-wells unloaded on Canada from the British Isles—the "remittance men." H. A. Kennedy, for instance, a shrewd observer of the West, wrote in 1907:

Here and there you meet a gentleman of leisure, but he is called a tramp. . . . Unhappily there are certain members of the English leisured class who find themselves in Canada without either the necessity or the inclination to work for their living . . . the average "remittance man" . . . is by universal testimony a failure.

At all levels of society, of course, new leadership was breaking through old crusts. Most conspicuous were the successful adventurers along "the joint-stock frontier," the men whose aptness in business and politics enabled them to drain off huge shares of the wealth Canada was borrowing and producing. E. B. Mitchell reported in 1915 that "the British mind is startled to discover that here business is socially at the top of the tree, and land-owning does not count at all."

While numbers of the business magnates, with their fortunes, left Canada, perhaps "for their country's good," many more remained and a significant number of these, perhaps because they had read or been influenced by Andrew Carnegie's *The Gospel of Wealth,* embarked on great philanthropies of many sorts. These were the days before the income tax, but the wave of philanthropy between about 1900 and about 1921 was (relatively) unrivaled before or since.

New intellectual or aesthetic leadership was not nearly so noticeable, indeed Canadian culture was generally derivative, parochial, and timid in the face of vested interests. In the churches the usual pattern existed of respectability and complacence at the top, particularly in the wealthier and more solidly established communities, and radicals or sectarians at the bottom. Urbanization and immigration, particularly where non-English-speaking persons were concerned, posed religious and social problems beyond Canada's capacity to solve, but the men and women, singly and in new associations, who made the effort got less attention and aid from the unseeing conservatives than might have been given. Foreign missionary enterprises somehow had more appeal than domestic ones.

The prevailing social tone in Canada was that of a middle-class, businessman's civilization (with all the great merits and defects that that implied). If old wealth and family found it crass and distasteful, they could put their money in land, mortgages, or impersonal bonds and stocks, and insulate themselves in exclusive associations and clubs. The materially successful and undiscriminating could afford to laugh at the old leaders and often did, in their confidence of present well-being and future improvement.

More important was the permeation of English-speaking society by the creed of "getting on" in a world of apparently endless opportunities.

Very few *Canadiens* entered the business world, for in the first place English-speaking Canadians of the business type had entrenched themselves too thoroughly to be dislodged and, in the second, the defensive *Canadien* culture stubbornly scorned mere acquisitive success and exalted other values. The church and the professions of law and medicine formed the cream of *Canadien* society and, with or without the politicians, provided its leadership. The merely wealthy were made to feel second-class, somewhat as in medieval European society.

The *Canadien* on the land called himself "habitant," not *paysan,* and the similar Canadian or New Canadian called himself "farmer," not "peasant." That is, the combination of landed proprietorship, freedom from military service, and open opportunity created an enviable rural status in which almost no one ordered another man around, expected him to touch his cap, or condemned him to subordination. Even if the lands in eastern and central Canada could not employ the natural increase of population, a man could go west or to the cities and industries nearby. There was little sense of being locked into the situation in which one was born, as the records of internal migration and of emigration testified.

In the West things were different, but the differences were rather blindly held to be transitory. What chiefly impressed visitors was the emptiness and loneliness of the plains. To begin with, land speculators encircled even the smaller cities with belts of vacant "city lots" that might be three to five miles wide. Then, out on the countryside, the Hudson's Bay Company and the C.P.R., not to speak of lesser land and railroad companies, mottled the whole landscape with unused lands, some in the original grass (and gophers), and some, because once broken, a wilderness of weeds.

The characteristic western township, based on a single accurate and uniform survey under the system adopted April 25, 1871, was a checkerboard six miles square containing 36 sections, each of 640 acres, subdivided into four, and bounded by a 66-foot road allowance. The 16 (or 16¼) free homestead sections were separated by 16 railroad lands sections, 2 school lands sections, and 1¾ or 2 Hudson's Bay Company lands sections. The smallest farm, therefore, was 160 acres, and most were twice or four times that size once the compulsions of plains agriculture took hold, so that there was no telling how far away your nearest neighbor might live even if you happened to have a neighbor or two in your township.

Whereas mixed farming could take farmers out of themselves in its variety and in the care of animals, wheat farming held little of this or of human companionship except in large families. About 1914, Mitchell found that the individualistic Anglo-Saxon had often planted himself in empty country or among New Canadians with the nearest English-speaking neighbor miles away.

I had an old-timer friend, a sort of mother to all her district, and at dish-washing time in the kitchen she told me stories of the prairie. It seemed as if her acquaintance might be divided into three sets—the "lovely" people, the "nice young fellows that don't know the first thing about farming," and the men and women who went mad. The prairie madness is perfectly recognized and very common still; the "bachelors" suffer most, and the women.

It was against the individual and social results of this gridiron pattern of settlement that the New Canadian and *Canadien* plains farmers struggled by means of group settlements, the alien ethnic islands that Canadians so often and so ignorantly deplored. Almost anything that could mitigate the awful loneliness of pioneering life on the plains was justified in the beginning, and time and technology have since then provided some reassuring answers to the problem. A Norwegian-American novelist of genius, O. E. Rölvaag, in a trilogy published from 1927 to 1931, has interpreted the grim plains ordeal, Canadian as well as American, in enduring human terms.

City life had its dolors, too, for the industrial and commercial workers, for the misfits and casualties of Canadian life who sought shelter, and for the abundant, pitifully paid, and often abused domestic servants. According to the *Report of the Social Survey Commission of Toronto* (1915), "The commonest occupation of girls who go wrong is that of domestic service." Goldwin Smith had seen the problems in 1888, years before the great influx, when he said to a charities conference in Toronto:

These cities of the New World have traversed in half a century the distance in the race of progress which it has taken the cities of the Old World ten centuries to traverse; young in years they are old in magnitude, and the liabilities and cares of maturity have already fully come upon them.

Seasonal unemployment, which affected many pursuits besides the extractive industries, was a tremendous problem. Men outnumbered women by over 6 per cent in 1911, and each winter thousands of them poured into the cities, where employment also decreased. Trade unionism was a feeble protection, indeed the whole position of the laboring classes was bound to be vulnerable, even during a boom, when so great an increase in population had to be digested.

Serious, too, were the various consequences of shipping to Canada British boys and girls from reform schools and other socially maladjusted persons. The record of those who responded happily to the new environment was eclipsed by the common belief of social workers that such immigrants created most of their problems. Dr. Bruce Smith, Inspector of Hospitals and Charities, said to a charities' and correction conference at Toronto in 1905:

Too often of late years by the pernicious system of bonusing emigration agencies abroad, mental and physical degenerates have been landed on our shores and have finally drifted, either through mental, physical or moral deficiencies into one or other of our great public Charities. The majority of the feeble-minded girls, who having fallen an easy prey to some designing villain, are sent to our Rescue Homes, have only been a short while in this country.

That complaint had been made at intervals for almost three centuries in Canada, but its intensity was great during the mass immigration of the early twentieth century.

Yet the evidence of success was plain to see in the same cities. One of the manifestations was the very rapid rise and decline of exclusive neighborhoods in the heyday of the streetcar and the beginnings of the automobile. Any city housewife or grocer or churchman could make a diagram of any city in terms of the gradation in wealth of its inhabitants. Only a real estate man or banker or mortgage expert could keep up with the often speculative rise in favor of one district and the irresistible blight that descended on another.

With so much at stake, the pressures on city administrations for favors by way of urban services were very great and very corrupting. The ordinary citizen was in no position to know much about all this, but he did know that some persons were prospering mightily in the Canadian cities; indeed had perhaps made the magical progression "from rags to riches" that was declared to be within the grasp of every alert, industrious, and "right-living" Canadian. The very social isolation that was built up around the successful in dozens of ways became the badge of the ordinary man's desire.

☙ LIVING CONDITIONS

There is little use in attempting to record the best and the worst in Canadian living conditions. Unquestionably most resident Canadians and newcomers bettered themselves in housing, diet, clothing, and amenities during these twenty years of economic growth. At the same time, however, it was reported of the Canadian cities that not only were all existing houses occupied, the older and cheaper ones in shocking congestion, but "respectable people have had to live in stables, tents, old cars, sheds (others in damp cellars) where we would not place a valued animal, let alone a human being." Because the Canadian climate was on the whole somewhat colder than the American and population was spread out thinly along a long ribbon of settlement, the Canadian standard of living was perceptibly lower than the American; but for the majority of the people both North American levels were so far above the European or Asiatic that the discrepancies between them were almost irrelevant.

It is worth remembering that these were the years when the horse and his companion, the domestic fly, were in retreat, and sanitation, at last firmly based on the new science of bacteriology, was moving on from triumph to triumph in the prevention and cure of disease. "Swat that fly," pure water, pasteurized milk, "crusades" against tuberculosis, compulsory vaccination, and the antiseptic smell of bigger and better hospitals would be not inappropriate symbols of a generation that felt increasingly competent to reduce, perhaps dispel, some of man's old plagues.

In many ways, it was defeat on the frontiers of rural and urban poverty that goaded on private persons and public authority in these matters, for a slum epidemic or a rural maniac could strike at any level of society. When, as so often happened, a defeated or unemployed husband and father simply vanished without trace to "the woods," "the States," or "the West," he shifted the intolerable burden of his family to the community at large.

In the face of rapid economic and social change, and armed with new wealth, many organizations, public and private, grew up every-where to combat child labor, illiteracy, alien ways, desertion, bad factory conditions, alcoholism, insanity, disease, juvenile delinquency, and crime. On religious and philosophical grounds there was less concern with mere health and physical well-being among Roman Catholics than among Protestants. Characteristically the Roman Catholic Church owned and operated charitable institutions with private, and some public, support. Wage rates and, for the most part, hours of work were still held to be matters of individual, possibly trade union, but certainly not social, contract.

The idea that social work required specialized training as well as charitable inclination was very dimly perceived, as witness the puzzle-ment and angry despair of a Humane Society official because Toronto newsboys preferred sleeping on the floor of a dive to "nice clean beds . . . with texts on the wall . . . and appropriate mottoes" at the Newsboys' Home. One of the most tragic accompaniments of these times was the extensive use of jails as workhouses, poorhouses, and even asylums for the insane, because some parts of the country were unable rapidly enough to organize and maintain more specialized in-stitutions. Halifax and Quebec formed interesting exceptions, having had the problem of army and navy society for at least a century and a half, but in New Brunswick "the poor were also farmed out by auction to the lowest bidder" (1900).

The effects of rural depopulation were being felt in some areas in the loss of responsible leadership, deterioration of the human stock, and greater neglect and abuse of children than in neighboring urban centers. There seems to have been more of a sense of inadequacy in dealing with children's problems, urban and rural, at this time than in anything else.

⚜ SOCIAL INSTITUTIONS

Up to 1914 the family was unquestionably the most important Canadian social institution. In spite of the forces that might scatter its members, or some of them, here and there in North America, there was a strong tendency to maintain or replace family centers. This was partly owing to the persistence of the intoxicating sense of status that lay in actual ownership of land, as well as to more general human considerations. With the family went a great cluster of loyalties, associations, and responsibilities that contributed heavily to social stability and moral rectitude. Divorce was extremely rare, even if desertion was only too common. The very rich and the very poor might be led or driven to offenses against the family, but the great body of society cherished and defended it, often with unthinking blindness or cruelty. The normal ambition of Canadians was to marry and own a home and, even during an exciting era full of beckoning opportunities, to settle down.

The churches.—Second only to the family was the church. In French Canada it had become the great agency in *survivance,* the arm on which the *Canadien* most often leaned, consciously and subconsciously, in his single-minded determination to preserve his sense of distinctness in a world in which he and his kind seemed fated to be a misunderstood and abused minority. When these attributes were added to the custodian and dispenser of spiritual life and of the sacraments that marked every important stage in human existence, the church possessed great breadth and depth in *Canadien* society.

Yet the common description of French Canada as "a priest-ridden society" was badly off the target, in fact a good case could be made for "a society-ridden priesthood." *Canadiens* and their clergy were as variegated as human beings and their spiritual pastors anywhere, and interacted in just as varied ways. They could ally instantly to meet threats to *survivance,* but they could vehemently differ over whether or not to vote for Laurier. They could agree absolutely on dogma and differ profoundly on practice.

The only times that French Canada has possessed anything like the monolithic character commonly ascribed to it have been when some external force has seemed to menace its distinct existence. At other times this society, with its delight in differences of taste and philosophy, has displayed the full spectrum of human differences. It might be added that the church of the *Canadiens* succeeded only partially in identifying itself with the *Franco-Américain* communities and with the colonies it fostered in Canada and the United States, for in such circumstances there was a large shredding-off into the surrounding alien societies.

The Protestant churches of the time were changing rapidly in a number of ways. Their doctrines had been hard hit by the historical and textual criticism of the nineteenth century and by the positivism and materialism that accompanied and followed the recent discoveries and hypotheses of natural science. Their individualism deprived them of any such armory of dogma as the Vatican provided. They had responded to the idea of a Canadian nation by organizing national churches; indeed the Anglican Church of Canada at the Lambeth conferences of 1867, 1878, 1888, 1897, and 1908 found itself paralleling in an interesting way, within the Church of England, the pros and cons of the political development of Canada within the British Empire.

The national churches could and did marshal strong resources to meet the challenges of a rapidly growing Canada, rural and urban, but their number made for some unfortunate duplication of effort. Moreover, while each national church was big enough to embrace various ecclesiastical enterprises, it was inevitable that these should reflect sectional patterns and the differences between them rather more than rapid adaptation to such general problems as the New Canadians presented in town and country, or the novel and intense difficulties of urban and industrial society.

The middle classes naturally dominated; the working classes failed to find understanding sympathy; and the evangelical sects on the margins of or outside the national churches rushed in to fill the vacuum at least partially. The Salvation Army, for instance, although its proportion of the total population did not vary much, had 14,000 members in 1891, 10,000 in 1901, 19,000 in 1911, and 25,000 in 1921. Eight or ten other fairly well-known sects and many small ones, after marked declines between 1891 and 1901, grew sturdily during the next twenty years. The Mormons, for example, approximately tripled in number, chiefly in an arid, but irrigated, section of southern Alberta. In the West, settlement very largely outran the churches. "Routine church-going almost disappears in the Western country, and a man may drive a very long way to find only five or six assembled," Mitchell reported.

A Joint Committee of the Methodist, Congregational, and Presbyterian churches set to work just before 1914 to investigate and report on their work across Canada. They concluded that central and downtown churches had been tardy in adaptation to the changing cities; that the working classes were on the whole friendly and responsive to suitable overtures; that the well-to-do increasingly tended "to grow careless in their religious life and loose in their Sabbath observance"; that home mission work for the English-speaking population was reasonably adequate across Canada; that the countryside of the old provinces and the small towns of the new "are over-churched rather than under-churched"; and "that the Protestant Churches have as yet scarcely touched the fringe of the non-English-speaking immigrants who have flocked in upon us during recent years." At about the same time there were many, if scattered, premonitions of a "social service" Protestant church that had not yet crystallized.

Groups.—It was a great age of "joiners," a heyday for associations of all sorts. One's church and one's political party were usually acquired at birth and neither was easily shed. Loyalties of this sort were intense even when extended to butcher, baker, grocer, or department store. The rich had their clubs; the poor were going through the transition from the livery stable to the garage. The saloon was definitely disreputable and on the defensive before the abolitionists. The billiard parlor or pool room was not much better. Ethnic societies were strong and sentimental, not only among those of French, English, Irish, and Scottish stock, but especially among the New Canadians who needed so badly the reassurance from the group.

Loyalties were also focused on athletic teams—not only the local amateur or semiprofessional clubs for hockey, lacrosse, football, rowing, bowling, curling, and so forth, but on American professional baseball teams as well. Indeed professional sports gave the ordinary man a sense of proprietorship that he indulged fantastically when he felt he somehow "owned" part of a ballplayer, a prize fighter, or a Marathon runner. Compared to these loyalties, those of professional associations, even of college fraternities or trade unions, were weak indeed. Secret societies and similar fraternal organizations were numerous and strong, stressing their exclusiveness, their hierarchies of office, and their brotherly activities. Urban society nourished most of these groups, for in the countryside organizations of a public and general sort had much stronger appeal.

Amusements.—In the matter of diversion, Canadians were in the course of transition from what modern jargon calls "participation activities" to "spectator activities." While it is reasonably doubtful whether the members of any society have received as much release and satisfaction from watching things happen as from sharing in making them happen, for city dwellers particularly the entertainment industry now offered a great deal for relatively little. Many moving-picture theaters were literally "nickelodeons" as late as 1910, and the cheapest seats in the theaters and at baseball, hockey, and lacrosse matches could be had for twenty-five cents.

Yet in those cities the churches, the Y.M.C.A., Y.W.C.A., and various athletic and social clubs provided men and women with opportunities for exercise and contests and with conviviality, dancing, and so on at a good many levels of expenditure. The tremendous vogue of the bicycle during the 1890's was a great outlet for energy and gregariousness. About 1910 women's sports had won places for themselves not only in the schools and colleges and not only among the leisured members of society. Golf was expensive and exclusive, but tennis, which had been both, was becoming more available. In winter skating and bobsledding, in summer swimming and boating, were available to everyone at relatively small cost.

Rural diversions consisted overwhelmingly of informal pastimes, whether the endless series of fetes, family parties, saints' days, and holidays among the *Canadiens* or the hayrides, sleighrides, basket parties, "bees," and picnics among the Canadians. Here the automobile was the thin edge of a wedge opening up a new scale of mobility and expenditure. Instead of a short drive in a polished light carriage or sleigh (cutter) with his lady, behind groomed and spirited horses, the rural lad who could secure a car could whisk her in to the nearest town or city with a dash (and a privacy) that could not be equaled by train or by interurban electric railway.

Even before the inflation that accompanied World War I the scale of money expenditure on amusements, rural or urban, had risen a great deal since 1896. Fairs and circuses, moving pictures and theaters, automobiles and travel, athletic contests and famous musicians—all these diversions were obviously attracting more cents every year out of the dollar of income. Even the summer cottage or hunting cabin in the woods, where men, women, and children played at the frontier lives of their predecessors, was ceasing to be a rough shack or tent platform and becoming city comfort transplanted.

EDUCATIONAL INSTITUTIONS

Naturally the various parts of Canadian society were hard put to it to provide adequate educational apparatus. The universities and the classical colleges (of French Canada) managed very well on the whole, for it conferred prestige on an individual to give to them and they knew how to spend the gifts. Here the great problem was to keep up sufficiently in the swift advances of science and technology by developing expensive equipment and leadership in such professions as medicine and such engineering pursuits as mining. The habit in ambitious young Canadians of pursuing advanced studies in the United States and Great Britain provided constant stimulus to development at home, even though many of these students did not return.

The *Canadien* classical college, which corresponded to the Canadian senior high school or collegiate institute plus the nonspecialized first years of a college education, seemed in its emphasis on philosophy, classical literature and such arts as rhetoric to be something of an anomaly in North American life, but it was a useful anomaly because it cultivated serious thought and the arts and graces of existence in a rather unsympathetic environment. The classical colleges, however, served a very small proportion of *Canadien* youth, and a still smaller group went on from them to advanced or professional studies at the universities in Quebec and Montreal.

The undergraduate honors courses of Toronto and the older Canadian universities could be used towards purely intellectual and aesthetic ends, but more often than not were ladders for advancement in higher professional studies and in high school teaching. It was apparent by 1914 that the provincial or the semipublic university, receiving most, or at least part, of its support from public authority, would predominate in the future. Indeed the new universities in the West granted permission to practice to the members of the principal professions—a privilege which in the East was jealously guarded by the professional societies. On the whole, by generous support of institutions that blended French, British, and American ideas in varying proportions with local experience and demand, Canada did distinctly better than might have been expected in higher education.

Outside French Canada the common ambition was to provide all children with at least the opportunity to proceed beyond primary to secondary education. The public high school or collegiate institute had something of the quality that had been represented in New England and the Middle States by the academy, an institution as much social as educational, a kind of college or technical school for those who could not or did not want to proceed further, and an intensive training ground for those who did.

Canada did not go so far or so fast as the United States in making the high school an end in itself, complete with "collegiate" trappings, elaborate graduations, and so on; indeed, for reasons too complex for discussion here, far less intelligent use was made at that time of high schools and primary schools for general social purposes. Somehow Canadian schools and their grounds were usually opened grudgingly in the morning, closed as soon as possible, and sternly guarded against intrusion by zealous caretakers at other times.

The privileged few went to private schools that were practically all rather slavish imitations of the English "public school" as developed by emulators of Thomas Arnold. The usually high quality of their intimate methods of instruction and group life was more fruitful socially than the snobbery and borrowed plumes that went with it. Good secondary education was available rather generally in Canada except among the *Canadiens,* whose tradition it was to confine it to the most promising few.

The great battle, of course, was being fought with varying results on the democratic front of primary education. In the growing cities it was relatively easy to recruit good teachers and the schools erected in new municipal areas were as up-to-date as possible. The problems existed in slum areas, areas in transition from gentility to squalor or to business, and the areas on the lightly taxed margins of municipalities where land-proud immigrants built their "shack towns" in the confidence that a few years would see them on Easy Street, relatively unaware that their land and houses must carry the tax-burden for education as well as for minimal urban services.

In all of these areas poverty, the root of most evils, was frequently accompanied by linguistic and other ethnic difficulties and by definite hostility on the part of parents to their children being at school instead of being at work. Yet, on the whole, in the cities and in the townships on their margins compulsory attendance was quite well enforced.

In general, Ontario led the provinces in education by reason of its wealth and long exposure to American and British standards, but, education being a provincial concern in the federal system, variation in the other provinces was extreme. Even where school attendance was compulsory, the law was frequently not well enforced in the large, let alone in details of age, regularity of attendance, and length of school year. An informed observer reported in 1909 that even in Ontario there were "at least 150 to 200 districts where the law is not put into force."

Matters were much worse in parts of the Maritimes, and on the plains, even with wheat, the great "cash crop," as fiscal underpinning, the rapidly expanding school problem was too big to be handled even moderately well in many areas. Yet the intention was unmistakable, the prevailing "climate of opinion" demanded it, and devoted individuals gave their lives to the work. In the circumstances of the time Canadians of the old as well as the new parts of the country achieved an immense amount and there was little inclination to sit back in contentment with things as they were. Education as the duty as well as the right of every child was one of the main articles of the Canadian creed.

In considering Canadian education, the newspaper and other periodicals should not be overlooked and the ubiquitous mail-order catalog should be included. One of the main reasons for the stress on education was that there was so much cheap reading matter. In the days before the inexpensive automobile, when roads were bad, moving pictures available only in large communities, and the radio not invented, rural dwellers read a great deal and discussed what they read. Most farmers took a city weekly, perhaps an additional agricultural weekly or monthly, and probably a local weekly as well.

There was a large market for cheaply printed fiction, not in book form, but in "dime novels" and fiction magazines that made up in bulk for their other deficiencies. In urban centers, the public library movement was strong, stimulated by Carnegie's philanthropy, but in the countryside only Sunday school libraries and rare private libraries were available. Canadians were much less addicted to book-buying than, say, New Zealanders, but cheap paper and American mass production of magazines and paperbound stories kept them supplied with reading matter of a sort. As yet the Canadian public thought it got so much more for its money from many American, and a few British, magazines and periodicals that Canadian ventures of the sort were starved and anemic.

🍁 CANADIANISM

By 1914 many Canadians had been asking themselves for at least fifty years what, if anything, Canadianism amounted to. Had these peoples an over-all recognizable culture of their own? Notwithstanding a number of common traits, the answers had always had to be in the negative because of the fierce local loyalties of the five or six regions of Canada and most notably because of the chasm between *Canadien* and Canadian. Moreover, as we have seen, each people in Canada tried to strengthen its feeling of distinctness by borrowing heavily and often unrealistically, not only from the traditions of the several parent peoples, but from the Vatican or from a sense of being part of a British Empire or from something else. Such borrowing might make for survival, but not for native development, which must come from within.

Moreover, any foreign observer could tell them what they themselves felt compelled to deny—that the greatest force exerted on their development was the stimulating example of the people of the United States in adapting themselves to and mastering the North American environment. Canadians had proved eminently capable of doing this too, but the similarities between their performance and that of the Americans were so much greater than the differences that it was futile to try to separate them. Perhaps, therefore, the best evidence of Canada's frustration was the endless, almost desperate, quest for solace in forced and often fallacious claims of Canadian primacy and general superiority in the common continental adventure.

Historically, the importance of all this was that the aspiration for nationhood was there: all sorts of Canadians wanted a common Canadianism, wanted to be a nation in the fullest sense of the word. Their progress towards it had been considerable, but the obstacles within and without were appalling. The only thing to do was to hold on and see what the future might bring.

CHAPTER XXIV

Potential Independence (1896-1913)

It is perhaps natural to exaggerate the importance of political party differences in Canadian, as in British and American, history, but when any long period in any of their modern histories is examined carefully, it becomes obvious that usually the two parties, ordinarily supposed to be in bitter opposition, had more in common than in dispute.

In other words, political aims and actions have been the responses made by these peoples through their elected representatives to circumstances and forces that have been much deeper and more compelling than the reputed party shibboleths of the politicians. While it must be granted that some men tend to be conservative and others to be radical, yet both are compelled to react to change inside and outside their country, and frequently the changes are so powerful that they leave little choice. The politician and the political party do not create and seldom master such forces; they adapt themselves to them.

Two general matters were historically more important than the battles between the political parties. One was the growing political independence of Canada, dramatically revealed in her capacity to say "No" to Great Britain and the United States. The other was the painful, reluctant, but inescapable adaptation of the *Canadiens* to the industrialization of Quebec and to the international relations of the dominion as a whole.

Laurier's victory of 1896 or the South African War might appropriately be taken to mark the end of mere separatism, withdrawal, or negation as *Canadien* political solutions, powerful as these urges remained. They could and did try all of these things in passionate defense of *survivance,* but the forces arising from their own industrialization, the rest of Canada, or from potent external circumstances were frequently so powerful that they could be neither ignored nor completely defied.

🍁 LAURIER IN POWER

The omens for Laurier's success after 1896 were auspicious. In Quebec the ultramontanism that had assumed itself to be more Catholic than the pope had been unmistakably repudiated at the polls. In Israel Tarte, Laurier had the most efficient party politician in French Canada to manage elections and party organization. Moreover, it seemed as if the imposing threat of a purely *Canadien* party, the "National" party that Mercier had created out of Quebec's almost unanimous espousal of Riel in 1885, had been utterly dispelled by Mercier's meteor-like fall in 1891, so disgraced that Quebec returned only seventeen of his party in the provincial elections of 1892.

Arthur Buies, the brilliant, caustic, and precise journalist who, in his lonely way, had since 1868 exposed so much pretense in *Canadien* life, summed up Mercier's destruction by saying: "He had in his hands the most brilliant role which has ever been given to a Canadian states-man; his vanity, his egotism, and his absolute absence of moral sense lost everything." Even so, Mercier had, in an attack of 1888 on the Imperial Federation League, phrased almost unforgettably a festering *Canadien* suspicion that was to break out again and again during Quebec's subsequent painful education in world affairs. "It is pro-posed," he said, "to impose upon us a political regime which through conscription could scatter our sons from the ice-fields of the North Pole to the burning sands of the Sahara."

The rest of Canada was feeling the stirrings of economic vigor that were to transform the country, and it was natural to connect them with the end of the long Conservative sway. The Maritimes expected to bene-fit from lower tariffs and from the system of imperial preference invented by W. S. Fielding, Laurier's Nova Scotian minister of finance. The in-dustrial, business, and railroad interests of central Canada discovered from Fielding's budget of 1897 that they were not threatened by any serious reductions in the protectionism from which they had benefited for twenty years.

Manitoba realized, a little slowly, that a *Canadien* prime minister could oppose his bishops and defend its provincial right to alter its school system, even when that alteration robbed its French-speaking children of privileges established twenty-five years before. "The smallest measure of conciliation," he said, "was far preferable to any measure of coercion," and his negotiation of a subsequent compromise some-what fairer to Roman Catholics was directly related to the dispatch of Monsignor Merry del Val by the pope in 1897 as an envoy to repress *Canadien* ultramontane extremism.

Domestically Laurier aimed, as he had for over twenty years, at an embracing Canadianism—a structure of compromises bridging the ethnic chasm—rendering it undesirable for the *Canadiens* to form an ethnic party and thereby disarming all save the extremist Canadians, best typified by the Orangemen's toast to "the glorious, pious and immortal memory of the great and good King William who saved us from popery, slavery, knavery, brass money, and wooden shoes."

Internationally he was confronted by both American and British ambitions to subordinate Canada. The American threat was represented by the Continental Union League in New York, an association representative of aspirations in the Republican party and among certain especially interested businessmen to reduce Canada to such economic straits as would induce her to seek annexation. The British threat was "Chamberlainism" in the form of the Imperial Federation League with its hope, essentially futile as long as the majority of Britons believed in free trade, of combining the autonomous colonies and the empire in an imperial customs and defense union. Laurier would have none of either, for he thought Canada ready and able to act independently in her relations with her great associates.

The basic decisions.—External events forced Laurier to make a series of such basic decisions almost at once. He and Canada were fortunate that his decisions maintained continuity with the policies of Macdonald at their best, just as Borden, Laurier's successor, also followed him in conforming to Canada's interests and capacities rather than to party cries. In the United States, the uneasy balance that was symbolized by the Democrat Cleveland's election as president in 1884, defeat in 1888, and re-election in 1892, only to yield again to the Republicans in 1896 had affected Canada principally by the increasing (and damaging) protectionism of the McKinley tariff of 1890 and the Dingley Tariff of 1897.

Meanwhile Joseph Chamberlain, the former "Red Republican" and Radical Liberal, was becoming an imperialist and a protectionist in Great Britain and had surprised beholders by claiming the despised office of Colonial Secretary in the Conservative government of 1895. The tide of the "new imperialism" of Ruskin, Seeley, Dilke, and Rhodes was rising to its disgraceful peak in "Anglo-Saxon" racism, the South African War, and Kipling's appeal to the United States to "take up the white man's burden" in the Philippines. Chamberlain and others chose to make Queen Victoria's Diamond Jubilee of 1897 not only an unparalleled display of imperial pageantry but the occasion of a colonial conference which should be aimed at greater imperial centralization for British economic and military strength.

Laurier went off to this brilliant tournament armed with a good lance and a good shield, the former being Fielding's offer of tariff preference to Great Britain without apparently asking anything in return, and the latter Canada's long and unimpaired record of autonomy. Actually Britain's acceptance of imperial preference from Canada revolutionized her commercial relations with other countries, notably France, Belgium, and Germany, for Canada demanded and got freedom from British commercial treaties. The resulting disturbance lasted from 1898 to 1910 and Britain gave up distinctly more in foreign commercial privilege than she gained, except in the imponderables of imperial association. The *Canadiens,* thanks to the activities of the imperial federationists in Canada, were wide awake to what they considered the threats of Chamberlainism. The Canadians, more aware of recent American menaces, thought it might be used in some ways to offset the United States.

Laurier himself, a conspicuous, picturesque figure who was feted, swooned over by duchesses and their like, and knighted somewhat against his will, managed to keep his head and resist pressures surprisingly well. "I am not sure whether the British Empire needs a new constitution," he wrote home, "but I am certain that every Jubilee guest will need one."

Imperial preference could not nullify Canada's continued protectionism. Laurier's occasional rhetorical excesses could not nullify his flat resistance to any form of central imperial authority and to Canadian contributions to the British navy. He once fell into the suggestion that "it would be the proudest moment of my life if I could see a Canadian of French descent affirming the principles of freedom in the parliament of Great Britain," but he quickly reverted to the prophecy that "in a few years the earth will be circled by a series of independent nations, recognizing, however, the suzerainty of England."

Meanwhile he and Fielding had been sounding out the McKinley administration, chiefly on the prospects for easier commercial relations, and in conferences at Washington in November, the United States, Great Britain, and Canada made the preliminary arrangements for a Joint High Commission on the Atlantic and Pacific fisheries, the Bering Sea seal fishery, the Alaska boundary, commercial reciprocity, and other minor matters. Newfoundland was also to be represented, and the Commission subsequently met in Quebec from August 23 to October 10, 1898, and in Washington from November 10, 1898, to February 20, 1899.

The negotiations for the Commission were the occasion for shrewd, if bitter, American and British characterizations of how the newly confident Canada was trying to balance her powerful associates against each other. Ambassador John Hay wrote home confidentially from London about the British diplomats:

> They frankly avow their slavery to Canada and chafe under it, and yet they rather resent our talking to Canada directly, and make this a pretext for declining adhesion to the Convention [on pelagic sealing] . . . It is far more to Canada's advantage than ours to be on good terms with us. Lord Salisbury, in a private conversation the other day, compared her to a co-quettish girl with two suitors, playing off one against the other. I should think a closer analogy would be to call her a married flirt, ready to betray John Bull on any occasion, but holding him responsible for all her follies.

Yet the startling and highly significant feature of the Joint High Commission, which failed in all its objects, was that the United States proved anxious, and Canada, not "a married flirt," but truly resistant to the offer of the commercial reciprocity that it had profited by forty years earlier and had been trying to resume ever since. From the very beginning the Americans described themselves as "heartily committed to the policy of commercial reciprocity," but the Canadians were fascinated by the growing, profitable productivity of their long-dormant country under the stimulus of a rapidly expanding British market and the industrialists were worried lest their protected enterprises be jeopardized.

The Laurier administration kept its ear to the ground at home while negotiating actively with the Americans over the full range of natural and manufactured products. And then to the surprise and even anger of the Americans, just when by Laurier's own admission "we can at any moment make a very fair treaty," the commission was allowed to disband without one. Laurier's explanation to the Canadian Commons was at once general and specific.

> I think I am not making too wide a statement when I say that the general feeling in Canada today is not in favour of reciprocity. There was a time when Canadians . . . would have given many things to obtain the American market; there was a time not long ago when the market of the great cities of the union was the only market we had for any of our own products. But, thank heaven! These days are past and over now.

The touchstone of South Africa.—The climax of British imperialism in the South African War was the severest imaginable test of Laurier's position. Here was the event that Mercier and alarmed, defensive *Canadiens* had predicted ten or more years earlier, the potential involvement of Canada in Britain's wars that Macdonald had so bluntly resisted, but to which Laurier might be induced to yield. Although the *Canadiens* still formed 31 per cent of the population as they had in 1871, they had been misled by the recent swell of British and other immigration into believing themselves an increasingly helpless minority. A generation's influx of conservative, even royalist, *émigré* clergy from republican France had nourished a sense of dedicated separatism among the *Canadiens* by planting the conviction that Providence had chosen French Canada to maintain and extend the faith that France had betrayed for a second time after 1871.

The approach and outbreak of the war in South Africa had stirred some Ontario emotions to the point of damning the *Canadiens* in the press as "disloyal," "an inferior people," "a section of the Canadian people speaking a foreign language and maintaining," through Laurier's dependence on their "massive vote," "an ideal foreign to the dominant race in this country." The governor general, Lord Minto, who conceived it to be his job, with all due caution and constitutional correctness, to encourage Canada to help, nonetheless was moved to comment:

> The writing of the leading Opposition [Conservative] papers in Ontario has been positively wicked, simply aiming at stirring up hatred of French Canada. It is perfectly monstrous . . . I believe myself that the French Canadians are very much maligned as to their disloyalty. French Canada does not wish to be mixed up in imperial wars, and is lukewarm, but at home you do not call a man disloyal, if he disapproves of the war. Here, if he is only lukewarm, and is a French Canadian, he must be a rebel.

The Laurier government met the issue appropriately by authorizing the enlistment of volunteers whom it would equip and transport for service with the British armies. It also both allowed the Militia Department to be used for other forms of recruiting and provided a battalion to relieve British troops at the Halifax and Esquimalt naval bases. It spent about $2,800,000 and provided about a third of the 7300 Canadians and *Canadiens* who went to South Africa.

There they truly distinguished themselves, but their importance was so exaggerated in the British and Canadian press that a Buffalo journalist pictured Lord Roberts as saying before every battle: "Are the Canadians present? Then let the advance begin." One untoward accompaniment of the war was the enforced withdrawal in February, 1900, of Major General Edward Hutton, who had come out with Minto to command the Canadian militia, but whose assumption that he served the British rather than the Canadian government disqualified him.

Laurier's position concerning British wars was summarized in two statements of the time:

> I claim for Canada this, that, in future, Canada shall be at liberty to act or not to act, to interfere or not to interfere, to do just as she pleases, and that she shall reserve to herself the right to judge whether or not there is cause for her to act.

While every Canadian admits that he would be ready to contribute our treasure and our blood, and the resources of Canada at the disposal of this country, for the rescue of England, were she engaged in a life and death struggle, there are many Canadians who are not ready to take part in the secondary wars of England.

This was the ground upon which he chose to fight, or better, to disarm his brilliant young protégé, Henri Bourassa, who otherwise seemed bent on creating an ethnic party of the *Canadiens*. Bourassa, the grandson of Papineau, was one of the best-informed *Canadiens* of his time, a brilliant orator, but a difficult politician to work with. He began, like the Canada Firsters of a generation earlier, by preaching a transcendent Canadianism, and Laurier indulged and encouraged him as a disciple of unimpeachable character and unusual cultivation. The war, however, so heightened his fears of the British imperialists, and his deep religious convictions so endeared him to the conservative clergy, that the threat of separatism became obvious, and Laurier, who had been through it all before, set to work to redeem Bourassa, if not his impetuous associates, Armand Lavergne and Olivar Asselin, lest Mercierism revive.

Bourassa had become the idol of the students at the branch of Laval University in Montreal. During and after the siege of Ladysmith, there were fairly serious clashes with the English-speaking students of McGill. As *La Presse* said: "We French Canadians belong to one country, Canada; Canada is for us the whole world; but the English Canadians have two countries, one here and one across the sea." Bourassa chose this moment for a particularly provocative and long speech in the Commons against Canada's participation in the war.

Laurier's reply was a masterly exposition to *Canadiens* and Canadians of his chosen position. On logical grounds it drove Bourassa back to his earlier all-embracing Canadianism, but it could not change the minds and emotions of many of his followers. It was in this speech that Laurier agreed with Bourassa that the constitutional relationship with Britain would have to be altered if it were assumed that Canada should take part in all British wars. Canada would have to say: "If you want us to help you, call us to your councils."

Chamberlain was quick to try to exploit this opening and Laurier had to extricate himself by insisting to Lord Minto that it be read in its hypothetical context. Minto was loyal to him, and wrote to Chamberlain:

He recognizes the fact that his Canadian fellow-countrymen must follow the Anglo-Saxon lead, and will do his best to educate them up to it; but I believe it to be much more with the idea of the welding together of a Canadian nation than of forming part of a great Empire . . . I suspect that he dreams of Canadian independence in some future age.

Laurier's ascendancy was demonstrated in the overwhelming rejection of Bourassa's proposals in Parliament and by the Liberals' easy victory across Canada in the general election of 1900, held during the war. The immediate problem then became the forthcoming trial of strength between Chamberlain and Laurier at the colonial conference of 1902. Bourassa judged that he must keep Laurier in line by speaking, and publishing, in English and French, largely on the theme: "In short, military contributions from the colonies to Great Britain, in men and treasure, but mainly in men, constitute British Imperialism." It was this, he declared, that set *Canadien* against Canadian, endangered the British connection, and thereby heightened the likelihood of annexation by the United States. Laurier, for his part, declined a proffered peerage before the conference.

At the conference, Chamberlain, with Australian and New Zealand support, argued for a "real council of the Empire, to which all questions of imperial interest might be referred," but Laurier successfully opposed this, responding to Chamberlain's "Gentlemen, we do want your aid" by offering to assume responsibility for the naval defense of Canada. This was a logical enough consequence of his view of Canada's position, but its practical seriousness may be doubted when it is recalled that that same year Laurier told Lord Dundonald, the British commander of the Canadian militia, not to take the force seriously, "for though it is useful for suppressing internal disturbances, it will not be required for the defense of the country, as the Monroe Doctrine protects us against enemy aggression."

Laurier's performance at the conference won back Bourassa who asserted, "I become once more your firm and sincere supporter," but the "Nationalist" movement that he had started was having obvious appeal. Tarte, who had broken with Laurier and endeared himself to the industrialists of central Canada by a new protectionist doctrine ("Outbuild the Americans in canals, harbors, ships; build a tariff wall as high as Dingley's"), set out to organize the *Canadien* Conservatives in such a way as to embrace the Nationalists. Bourassa saw through him and, to anticipate events a little, publicly exposed and utterly crushed Laurier's then most dangerous enemy in Quebec during a single debate at La Prairie on September 19, 1903. By that time Asselin and others had founded La Ligue Nationaliste (March 1, 1903), and its existence was made public late in August.

The lesson of Alaska.—That year Laurier, his associates, and many among the Canadian peoples received a bitter lesson at the hands of Great Britain and the United States over the boundary between British Columbia and Alaska. Since 1895 the two great powers had been in-

The Alaskan Boundary
and the Klondike

• • • • • Provisional Line near Mouth of Stikine River,
agreed to by U.S. and Britain in 1878

• • • • • • Line claimed by British High Commissioners, 1898

═══ Provisional Lines (3) near head of Lynn Canal,
agreed to by U.S. and Britain in 1899

—•••— Line claimed by U.S. before Alaskan Boundary Tribunal
in 1903

—×— " " " Britain " " " " "

++++++ Alternative Lines at Lynn Canal and Glacier Bay
Claimed by Britain in 1903

═══ Line according to award of Alaskan Boundary
Tribunal in 1903, and Notes of 1905

volved in differences and mutual embarrassments before the world concerning Venezuela and British Guiana, the South African War, the Spanish-American War, the suppression of the Filipinos, and American monopolistic seizure of a canal route at Panama. The situation might not unfairly be summarized by saying that Great Britain, recognizing the power of the United States, surrendered treaty rights and withdrew from the Caribbean in order to make an ally of the United States in an unfriendly world.

The Canadian government, which had been trying since 1896 to get from the United States a port on the Lynn Canal through which direct access to the Klondike might be had, made the mistake of overestimating Britain's strength and determination vis-à-vis the United States and assumed that such a concession could be a *quid pro quo* in the course of Britain's almost continuous surrenders to American dictation. Their misfortune was that the rampaging Theodore Roosevelt, who became president in September, 1901, was thoroughly enjoying American ascendancy and, fired by the ideas of Admiral A. T. Mahan, was bent on exploiting it to the limit.

When, in 1903, the issue was finally, by mere Anglo-American agreement, submitted to a supposedly impartial and judicial tribunal, Roosevelt flouted and prejudiced its formal and its implied character outrageously, and even took pains to inform the British government repeatedly that if the American case were not sustained he would ask Congress for funds "to run the line on our theory," that is, he would challenge war. In the circumstances, the unfortunate British Chief Justice, Lord Alverstone, whose vote was the deciding one, not only granted the reasonable principal American contention, but yielded so obviously to additional American claims that there could be no doubt of his motives.

To President Roosevelt this was "the greatest diplomatic victory during the present generation"; to Canadians it was one more instance of their serving as a burnt offering on the altar of Anglo-American understanding. Laurier said to the Commons: "It is important that we should ask the British Parliament for more extensive powers, so that if we ever have to deal with matters of a similar nature again, we shall deal with them in our own way, in our own fashion, according to the best light that we have."

Rebuff to colonialism.—Before the Liberals went to the country again in the general election of 1904, Laurier had another brush with British assumptions of Canada's colonial subservience. The point to be remembered about such assumptions is that they were almost incurably natural in Britons and have remained so in many instances. Winston Churchill, who came sharply up against Canada's insistence on autonomy at intervals from 1911 onwards, repeatedly ignored it, with unhappy consequences. W. A. MacIntosh, who worked with the brilliant Lord Keynes during the intimate triangular economic relationships of London, Washington, and Ottawa during World War II, reported that Keynes comprehended intellectually Ottawa's direct relationship with Washington, respected it, and was even patient with it, but "never really understood it."

In such lights, the behavior of the Earl of Dundonald, who succeeded Hutton as commander of the Canadian militia in 1902, is easily intelligible. Ultimately he clashed directly and publicly with the Canadian minister under whom he served over a militia commission cancelled by the minister on political grounds and, to his indignant amazement, was dismissed by order in council. This helped Laurier among the *Canadiens,* but angered those in Ontario who were still bathed in the emotions of belated victory over the Boers.

In dealing with the matter in Parliament, Laurier momentarily made one of his very rare mistakes in English by referring first to Dundonald as "a foreigner" before immediately correcting it to "a stranger" (*étranger*). His enemies most unfairly exploited this slip during Dundonald's subsequent campaign of imperialistic public meetings, but the Liberals saw to it that their new Militia Act provided that the commander should henceforth be Canadian.

In the election of November, 1904, the Liberals won a sweeping victory in every province except Prince Edward Island, thus demonstrating that prosperity and national self-assertion were more popular than Chamberlainism and its accompaniments. The Liberal majority (149 to 75) was now about twice as great as in 1896, and even the Conservative leader, Robert Laird Borden, who had succeeded Tupper in 1901, lost his seat in his own province of Nova Scotia.

✦ INTERNAL AND EXTERNAL STRAINS

Almost at once, however, the great Canadian schism began to reassert itself. The occasion was the creation in 1905, from the North West Territories, of the new provinces of Saskatchewan and Alberta. This raised the old Western issue of education, and now Laurier had in Clifford Sifton, the energetic, self-confident Minister of the Interior, an associate who was determined to mold the Westerners in the English-speaking image. In the Cabinet and in inner policy-making with Laurier, his personal rival was the Roman Catholic Minister of Justice, Charles Fitzpatrick of Quebec, who had been counsel for Riel in 1885 and for the past ten years a mediator in Canada and at Rome during the war of the ultramontanists against Laurier.

In the act creating the new provinces Laurier, claiming to follow Blake's prescription for Manitoba in 1875, reversed his stand of 1896 by providing separate schools for Roman Catholics, of whom now more were New Canadians than *Canadiens*. Moreover, it became known that Fitzpatrick had consulted Bourassa and the apostolic delegate to Canada, Monsignor Sbaretti, about the bill.

Sifton came rushing back from a Florida holiday and the fat was in the fire, with both extremist camps behaving their worst. When Sifton resigned and the Liberal party divided, Laurier called the Quebec members together and persuaded them (and the apostolic delegate) to accept a compromise negotiated by Sifton and Fitzpatrick. By-election results in Ontario and responses from the West seemed to approve this statesmanlike move. Subsequently, however, Laurier judged Sifton's price for re-entry to the Cabinet both too high and too presumptive of succession to him.

The compromise lost Bourassa to Laurier, for he and Lavergne had refused to be won over; indeed 1905 might be taken to mark what largely amounted to Bourassa's substitution of *Canadien* nationalism for the all-embracing variety to which he had hitherto been reasonably faithful. This shift quickly came to involve first an understanding and then an alliance with Laurier's enemies in Quebec conservatism and the church. La Ligue Nationaliste, which put nationalism before religion, and L'Association Catholique de la Jeunesse Canadienne (A.C.J.C.), which did the opposite, began to work in combination. In 1906 Bourassa enjoyed a personal triumph when his candidate defeated the Liberal nominee at a by-election in Quebec County itself. Next year the A.C.J.C. established a journal, *Action Sociale,* and the alliance against Laurier became so serious that he openly employed the patronage weapon to keep the province in line. Political separatism was now a visible threat. The emerging question was whether or not the federal Conservative party would try to work with Quebec nationalism to dislodge Laurier.

Laurier's behavior towards Chamberlainism was a kind of touchstone for Bourassa and his Nationalists. In a minute of council, November 13, 1905, the Canadian government typified its resistance to a renewed proposal for an "imperial council" by describing what henceforth came to be called an imperial conference as "a more or less unconventional gathering for informal discussion of public questions . . . possessing no faculty or power of binding action."

By the time of the Conference of 1907, the British Liberals were in

power with an unprecedented majority won by opposing Chamberlainism. Laurier was the only member who had attended in 1897 and
1902 and his view, "We are all His Majesty's governments," officially
prevailed, thus characterizing what came later to be called dominion
status. As he told the Commons, his conception "that the proper basis
of the British Empire was that it was to be composed of a galaxy of
nations under the British Crown" prevailed over "the principle that
the young daughter communities should be simply satellites revolving
around the parent State."

Already, however, the challenge of Germany to Great Britain was
modifying Canada's international position to a point that would test
severely Laurier's reliance on the mere power to say, "No." He had
repulsed Chamberlain's effort to build on his remark, "Call us to your
councils." Now the time was coming when Canadians as a whole would
have to decide whether or not to accept his differentiation between
"the secondary wars of England," in which they might not care to take
part, and "a life and death struggle," to which he had declared every
Canadian "would be ready to contribute our treasure and our blood."

An ominous preliminary was the naval scare in the British Parliament during the spring of 1909, just before a special London conference
of the empire on defense. Laurier and his associates had to settle upon
a clear-cut policy. In Ontario there were loud cries for immediate
contributions to the British navy; in Quebec there were equally loud
cries against involvement in "imperialist wars."

At the defense conference in July, 1909, Canada agreed to a plan
whereby it would create and command its own navy, based on Halifax
and Esquimalt, train it in uniformity with Britain and the other dominions, and, if it chose to put it at the disposal of Britain during a war,
accept Admiralty control for the duration.

Brilliantly consistent as this was with Laurier's principles, the
urgency of the times made it utterly inacceptable to *Canadien* and
Canadian extremists, for the former regarded it as surrender to Great
Britain and the latter as no guarantee of help at all. Each attitude aggravated the other. During the debates on the Navy Bill of 1910,
although Borden, Leader of the Opposition, declared that he agreed
with its policy rather than with one of contribution to the British navy,
it became apparent that Laurier's position was being undermined by
the mounting numbers in the "imperialist" and "anti-imperialist" camps.
Only the most cynical could conceive that they might be brought together to engineer his downfall, but while the Liberals were patiently
putting their bill through Parliament, Bourassa was becoming the idol

of Quebec, armed with his own newspaper, *Le Devoir,* and with hosts of young men at the bidding of Lavergne, Asselin, and the A.C.J.C.

With conscious symbolism, Bourassa chose finally to focus his forces on an election in Laurier's own countryside and first constituency, Drummond-Arthabaska in the changing Eastern townships. The general issue, of course, was the Canadian navy, but with great shrewdness and acumen Bourassa had pierced to the heart of the argument by claiming Canada's right to neutrality.

In response to a question during his introduction of the Navy Bill in the Commons in mid-January, 1910, Laurier had said: "When Britain is at war, Canada is at war; there is no distinction. If Great Britain, to which we are subject, is at war with any nation, Canada is exposed to invasion; hence Canada is at war." That was certainly good international law of the day, but Bourassa, seizing upon the first two phrases, was ingenious and determined enough to propose changing international law. In a long and closely reasoned lecture to an immense public meeting a week later, his thesis was: "As British subjects, we owe to England only the preservation of that part of the empire which has fallen to our share." He painstakingly rejected all imperial considerations and demanded a plebiscite in order to discover the will of the people.

Six months later, he broke finally with Laurier, and early in September he completed his conquest of the *Canadiens* by brilliantly taking advantage of an opportunity presented to him by the British Cardinal-Archbishop Bourne at a public meeting held in Notre Dame Church, Montreal, during a Eucharistic Congress of the Church of Rome.

Bourne curiously and unexpectedly made a most maladroit speech urging the church to give up its almost exclusive link with the French language and to use the growing influence of English as the vehicle of the Faith, particularly among the New Canadians. Taking advantage of two intervening speeches, Bourassa pocketed his own proposed address and improvised another. When he spoke, the great assembly hung on his words; when he finished in a breathless hush the papal legate rose and shook his hand. Then a tumult of emotional release broke out; bishops stamped their feet; strangers embraced each other; and people danced and rejoiced outside in the Place d'Armes.

Laurier's reasoned and "political" efforts in and out of Parliament could not stamp out this new and swelling Mercierism. At the November election, the Nationalist candidate Arthur Gilbert, a relatively unknown young farmer, took Laurier's home constituency from the official candidate by two hundred votes after an election marked by many almost incredible excesses.

🍁 LAURIER AND RECIPROCITY

By this time the political wolves had scented blood and were gathering to bring down the leader of the Liberal herd. Almost fifteen years of power during an ebullient, extravagant age had saddled the Liberal party with some rascally hangers-on and careless or corrupted heads of departments. Laurier had escaped taint because he had initiated the practice of the prime minister not taking a departmental portfolio, but unquestionably substantial demoralization of his party had set in and scandal was in the air. At the end of 1910, therefore, the leader must reassert himself, purge his party, and confront the country with some truly national proposal that would transcend sectional differences if his power was not to crumble and his vision of understanding and compromise between *Canadien* and Canadian come to an end.

One day late in January, 1911, Laurier's enemies would have admitted to his friends that he seemed to have saved himself and his aims, for W. S. Fielding, Minister of Finance, had acquainted Parliament with an agreement on commercial reciprocity with the United States that was better than anything generally imagined possible. The Republican president, W. H. Taft, whose party had instituted the aggressive Payne-Aldrich tariff in 1909, found himself deeply embarrassed, not only by its bludgeoning provisions against any country judged to discriminate against the United States, but by a revolt of the progressives in his own party. He worked out a face-saving compromise with Canada during the spring of 1910, but by then it had become apparent that the Democrats were riding a wave rising against the tariff, egged on by the newspapers of the country which wanted free entry of Canadian newsprint.

Taft got to work at once exploring the possibilities of a broad reciprocity agreement, the details of which were worked out in Ottawa and Washington during the autumn and announced in January. Meanwhile, the "off-year" elections of November swept the Democrats into control of Congress. Inevitably every special American interest that imagined itself threatened by the agreement plunged into the Washington lobbies, but in July, at the cost of a special session, the enabling measure became law in the United States, to remain on the statute books for ten years.

Laurier could have made it law in Canada too, but, sincere parliamentarian that he was, disdained to do so without reference to the people after this long-hoped-for boon surprisingly evoked opposition. In the most unexpected and dramatic reversal of their modern history, the people of Canada savored to the full the unprecedented joy of rebuffing their overpowering American neighbors.

Economically the rejection was confirmation of the almost forgotten precedent of 1899. Practically every large financial, industrial, and transportation interest in Canada rushed to the defense of the protected transcontinental economy that had been functioning so profitably in terms, presumably, of the British rather than the American market. The percentage of Canadian exports going to Great Britain had been declining slowly since 1898, but was about 50 per cent in 1911; that of exports going to the United States had been rising slowly during the same period, and was about 37 per cent; but no one paused to discuss anything as "academic" as trends during the heady uproar of 1911. When old Sir William Van Horne was asked what had brought him out of retirement in his art gallery in Montreal, he exclaimed that he was "out to do all I can to bust the damned thing." Clifford Sifton managed the campaign that he judged could give him a most ample revenge.

Politically, the rejection embraced many things that were seldom allowed to rise from the emotional to the rational level. Two of these deserve especial mention. In terms of votes, the lesser one was fear of annexation by the United States. Taft himself, during his efforts to force the agreement through Congress, several times spoke in ways that could be interpreted to mean that it was a first step in an association that was bound to become more intimate. Others were much less discreet. Champ Clark, Speaker of the House of Representatives, jested that "We are preparing to annex Canada," and, when prodded, announced that he supported the agreement "because I hope to see the day when the American flag will float over every square foot of the British North American possessions clear to the North Pole."

Useful as such remarks were to the Conservatives, their alliance with Bourassa was politically more important. Almost as in the days of Macdonald, an election saw English-speaking Conservatives fighting an imaginary and imaginative war against Laurier as the personification of Catholicism outside Quebec and allying themselves with Catholics inside Quebec who judged Laurier no true Catholic. It was useless for the Liberals to castigate this "Unholy Alliance," for the infectious separatism that Bourassa had built up over the Navy Act went hand-in-hand with the ecclesiastical enemies of Laurier, and the Conservatives could not resist the obvious invitation to unseat the man who had triumphed over that ethnic threat to an over-all Canadianism in 1896, 1900, 1904, and 1908.

The election results were striking in their demonstration of what brought Laurier down. The Liberal majority of popular votes, 25,000 in 1908, became a minority of 47,000, and the majority in seats (45) was almost precisely reversed. The decision was made chiefly in the economic headquarters of Canada, for Ontario returned 72 Conservatives to 14 Liberals, and in Quebec the Nationalists and Conservatives succeeded in wresting 30 of the 65 seats from "French Canada's prime minister." Even if the Nationalists should subsequently desert him, Borden, the new prime minister, ought still to be able to count on a bare majority.

🍁 DOMESTIC AND FOREIGN AFFAIRS

Of course, no such election could alter the course of Canadian development in any fundamental sense, but before turning to Borden's stern wrestlings with the abiding forces, brief mention, at least, should be made of some secondary political developments during the lively period, 1896–1913. There is no great object to be gained by crediting them to particular persons or parties. Both Laurier and Borden, for instance, recognized that the new Canada could not risk getting along with a civil service that was loaded to the gunwales with political appointees under the patronage system, and their pressures on rather unregenerate members of parliament brought about reforms in the service that were to yield useful dividends in the future.

Domestically the principal achievements were by way of piecemeal, inadequate, and uneven social adaptations to industrialization and urbanization in areas where municipal and provincial action had failed. The Board of Railway Commissioners of 1904, corresponding roughly to the American Interstate Commerce Commission, possessed powers to fix rates, set up operating regulations, and settle disputes, subject to appeal on points of law. It collaborated easily and well with the United States over the many lines of each country that entered the other. The Lord's Day Act, made law in 1906 in spite of Conservative exploitation of Quebec's resistance to it, was social as well as sabbatarian in its aims.

Next year, Mr. William Lyon Mackenzie King, grandson of the rebel of 1837 and now, after social studies in the United States, deputy minister in the Department of Labor (1900), saw his Industrial Disputes Investigation Act (the "Lemieux Act") become law as a protection against suspension of public services. His department then became a separate ministry. The act worked quite well until shortly after the War of 1914 when ingenious lawyers managed to persuade Lord Haldane and the Judicial Committee of the Privy Council that it was *ultra vires* of the federal government. In 1908, a niggardly attack was made on the problem of old age by instituting a system of contributory annuities. In 1910, previous American and British efforts to check business and industrial monopolies were reflected in a practically negligible Combines Investigation Act.

In general, however, the social conscience even in the provinces, let alone in the great federal arena, was weak in its resort to the state, and there were plenty of appeals to "rugged individualism" and judicious private charity as the tested, acceptable procedures. Trade unionism suffered from this mood as well as from being torn by conflicting American, British, and Roman Catholic aspirations. Its numbers were small, the courts and the public were hostile, and the Trades and Labor Congress of 1886 was expert chiefly in keeping its head down and in exploiting its "international" relations with the American Federation of Labor. The Ministry of Labor, with the social reformer King as its deputy minister, was timorous and conciliatory towards both "big business" and a public that resented such interruptions as the railroad strike of 1910.

In external affairs there had to be a number of milestones along the road to recognition of Canada's power to exercise external as well as internal sovereignty. In effect, Canada got her way by a variety of devices that spared the diplomatic sensibilities of Great Britain. The problem of commercial treaties, for instance, that arose with Canada's imperial preference of 1897 was resolved, after a great deal of trouble, usually by having Canadians negotiate the treaties or conventions with foreign consuls general while acting as British plenipotentiaries, and by having the appropriate British diplomat associated only in their signature. In 1908 Laurier secured the British promise that no imperial treaty should be binding on Canada without Canada's explicit consent. Next year he set up a Department of External Affairs which he combined with the office of prime minister, but provided with a separate deputy minister.

In one quite urgent problem, that of Oriental immigration, Canada characteristically resorted to personal missions and negotiations of a secret and informal sort in order to avoid embarrassing Great Britain. British Columbia, which, like California, proposed to deal with this matter on her own, was held firmly in check by the overriding federal power. The head tax on Chinese immigrants rose from fifty dollars in 1885 to a hundred in 1901 and to a practically prohibitive four hundred in 1904, without protest from China. When Japan took advantage after 1905 of Canada's acceptance of an Anglo-Japanese commercial treaty by sending 10,000 emigrants in 1906 and 1907, thereby provoking serious riots in Vancouver, Rodolphe Lemieux went off to Japan and negotiated an understanding which cut the ingress to a few hundred a year. A similar arrangement for China was in process when Laurier went out of power in 1911.

India represented a special problem, for her peoples were British subjects and their entry too began to be very noticeable in 1907. Mr. King conducted the ensuing difficult negotiations in London and Calcutta (stopping off for direct negotiations at Washington on the way). The ingenious exclusion device adopted in 1909 was challenged in 1914 by a somewhat conspiratorial adventure which transformed H.M.C.S. "Rainbow" into the excluding authority and ended in serious Sikh riots in India when the emigrants were returned. An important by-product of these problems was Britain's recognition in 1910 of Canada's right to control and regulate British immigration.

Canada's relations with the United States improved quite rapidly after Roosevelt's insulting antics of 1903 over Alaska. After his re-election in 1904, Elihu Root, his Secretary of State, achieved an understanding with James Bryce, the British ambassador, that was soon broadened to include Laurier. Root set out to "mend fences" in the Americas after getting firsthand information in Newfoundland (1905), Latin America (1906), and Canada (1907).

In 1905, Canada and the United States set up an International Waterways Commission to survey their greatest common possessions, and in 1909 by the Boundary Waters Treaty a code of international law regarding them was agreed upon and a permanent International Joint Commission was established (1) to pass upon applications for use, diversion, or obstruction; (2) to investigate any question involving rights along the common frontier referred to it by the two governments jointly; and (3) to act as a court of arbitration on any disputes submitted jointly for decision. This remarkable body has since performed highly varied and difficult duties with practically unbroken success in the first two fields, but this very prowess in purely engineering problems has rendered it so unsuitable for the third more general power that it has not been put into exercise.

Finally, by action in the Permanent Court of Arbitration at The Hague in 1910, the long-vexed disputes over the North Atlantic fisheries among Britain, the United States, Newfoundland, and Canada were for most practical purposes brought to an end. This settlement also liquidated a long period of Newfoundland bitterness against Great Britain.

After the failure in the United States and Great Britain of the Bond-Hay Convention of 1902, Prime Minister Robert Bond of Newfoundland discovered that, while the Convention of 1818 specified the entry of American vessels into the bays, harbors, and creeks of Labrador, it spoke only of the coast of Newfoundland. With this new arrow in his quiver, he went on to pass the Foreign Fishing Vessels Act of 1905 which ended the licensing system and prohibited the sale of bait to foreign vessels. The colonial patrol vessel "Fiona" proceeded to enforce these policies, provoking American protests, but also leading to the ingenious device of hiring Newfoundlanders who did the fishing legally for the American ships.

When Bond carried a new act in 1906 forbidding this, the British government withheld assent and once more overrode Newfoundland by arranging a *modus vivendi* with the United States. The Labouchère Dispatch of 1857 was once more invoked in vain by Newfoundland, but now Bond's hold began to weaken, for the west coast preferred the working arrangements to fighting.

Bond appealed to Canada, where the matter was discussed in Parliament, and, thus reinforced, he succeeded in getting his idea of submitting the whole matter to the Hague Court before the Colonial Conference of 1907. Great Britain agreed, the United States concurred, and Canada was included because of her situation in the Magdalen Islands. Bond's bitterness during the interim was intense, but in one of Newfoundland's perhaps characteristic parliamentary upsets he found his party in a tie with its opponents after the elections of November, 1908. The governor refused him a dissolution, accepted his opponent, E. P. Morris, as prime minister, and granted the latter a dissolution for a second general election in which he won a solid majority.

Bond had gone down fighting, and it must have been some satisfaction to him two years later when the Hague Court in general confirmed his views of British rights and American presumptions. The arbitration was so complex and difficult even after the terms of reference were agreed to in February, 1909, that the specially interested must consult the legal treatises that deal with it. Here it must be sufficient to say that the British view of the Convention of 1818 was accepted and the American view rejected, that is, Great Britain through Newfoundland and Canada had the sovereign right to regulate in a reasonable manner their inshore fisheries. This basic decision was implemented by various arrangements as to reasonableness, American employment of Newfoundlanders, the boundaries of bays, separation of trading and fishing rights, and so on, made by the Court, its commissioners, and conferences in Washington in 1911 and 1912.

🍁 BORDEN'S INITIATION

Robert Laird Borden, Laurier's successor as prime minister, was a Nova Scotian lawyer (of constitutional bent) who had been chosen leader of his party after Tupper in 1901 and who had had an unusually rough time of it, even for a leader of the Opposition, during the following ten years, largely because he preferred principles to expediencies at a time when Laurier seemed to monopolize the useful principles.

Like Macdonald and Laurier, he was a nationalist, but he never equaled them either in political grace and magnetism or in ability to drive *Canadien* and Canadian in the same team. He was much more affable than he looked and also tactically more astute than his apparent devotion to strategic principles indicated. Basically he was a patiently determined man of upright character and great dependability, not well known across the country, and seriously handicapped by insufficient reputation and prestige in dealing with his own Cabinet, some of whom were sure that they had won the election that put him into power. (F. D. Monk, as leader of the Quebec Conservatives, offered Bourassa and Lavergne portfolios which they declined.) It took Borden almost five years to win unquestioned loyalty from his colleagues.

The naval question.—The immediate problem that almost eclipsed everything else was, of course, the naval one. Laurier had gone off to the Imperial Conference of 1911 in the midst of the reciprocity conflict, and there, for the first time, the dominion prime ministers had been taken somewhat into the confidence of the British Committee on Imperial Defence and had been warned of the existing emergency. Laurier was in no position to go beyond his Canadian navy, and during the election campaign Borden had carefully avoided the issue.

The truth was that external events had raced ahead of Canada's readiness to cope with them, and Borden, caught between the Quebec Nationalists and the Ontario and Maritime imperialists, was trying to decide what step a Canadian nationalist could take beyond Laurier's policy, and having to do so at a crucial time in British affairs. He proceeded with great deliberation.

His central and persistent idea was a sound one. If Canada were to contribute to imperial defense, Canada must have a voice in imperial foreign policy. In 1910, he said: "If we are to take part in the permanent defense of this great empire, we must have some control and some voice in such matters." Laurier had seen this connection in 1900, the moment Chamberlain had tried to exploit his "Call us to your councils," but he knew he could not carry French Canada with him, in fact, even his clever alternative of a Canadian navy had failed him there. Borden judged that the emergency was so great that Britain would yield a voice in foreign policy in return for help. He went to England in the summer of 1912, received moderately satisfactory assurances of this, and in December, 1912, put his policy before Parliament. In Winston Churchill, First Lord of the Admiralty, he had an urgent, impetuous imperialist who was impatient to scrap the Laurier policy and get things done in terms of a single imperial navy.

Borden asked Parliament to vote $35,000,000 to build three battleships of the latest and most powerful sort to be incorporated in the imperial navy for the time being, with the possibility that they might subsequently be recalled to form the core of "a Canadian unit of the British Navy" somewhat along Australian lines. In return, the Committee on Imperial Defence was to be open to a Canadian Minister in London and "no important step in foreign policy would be undertaken without consultation of such a representative of Canada."

Not only did Laurier and the Liberals oppose this move on the grounds that current utterances by the most highly placed Britons had declared that there was no emergency; that Canadians, not Britons, should man Canadian ships; and that the proposed voice in policy must be illusory; but the Quebec Nationalists asserted as well that Canada should do nothing since she did not have any voice in British foreign policy. Mr. Churchill injected himself and his views into the controversy by two published communications that were utterly oblivious of Canadian national feelings.

Finally Borden, adopting the closure that Laurier had refused to use in 1911, carried his bill in the Commons, indeed on its third reading it won one Liberal and all but four of the Quebec Nationalists, a result that qualified very seriously the sincerity of their recent campaigns against Laurier.

And then, to general surprise, the Senate rejected the bill. Owing to its system of appointment, it was over 60 per cent Liberal, and it had been giving Borden a good deal of trouble by its treatment of his legislation, but its leader was Sir George Ross, generally regarded as an imperialist. Yet when he moved rejection, using the very words that Borden had used in opposing Laurier's Navy Bill in 1910, "that this House is not justified in giving its assent to this bill until it is submitted to the judgment of the country," the Senate agreed, 51 to 27. Ross offered to vote the $35,000,000 to be spent in terms of the existing Navy Act, but Borden did not take him up. Neither did he go to the country for a mandate.

A good deal is now known about Borden's own feelings in this matter and about the rather frenzied and prolonged correspondence between him and Churchill. In effect, Borden and the Conservatives did as little as possible about Canadian naval defense under the Navy Act from their victory until World War I. One reason was that the sense of emergency in Great Britain really did diminish considerably after the panic of 1909. Another was that Churchill did aggravate the national feelings in Canada that he was never to be able to understand. A third was that Borden discovered how unreal British promises of a voice in foreign policy must be, since Britons like Asquith and Grey simply did not (probably could not) ascribe the same meaning to words about foreign policy as Borden did. In fact, they "put his back up" and drove him back to ideas that were to startle conventional British statesmen when war came.

Yet all these reasons added together were less than one other—the depression that struck the gaudy speculative economy of Canada like a thunderbolt during the debates on the Navy Bill. Bubbles burst, speculative profits vanished, values wilted, foreign lending dried up, and the "seasonally unemployed" of the winter of 1912–13 remained unemployed. The slowly formulated, excellent new Bank Act of July, 1913, came just in time.

The great symbol of all manner of economic distresses from Atlantic to Pacific was the plight of Mackenzie and Mann's "miracle," the Canadian Northern Railway, attended as it was by the very serious financial embarrassments of Montreal's too aspiring rival, Toronto. So much of the national credit seemed threatened that the nation's political leaders pretty much disregarded party considerations in coming to the rescue (as it proved, temporary), to the tune of $15,640,000 to the National Transcontinental in 1913 and of $45,000,000 to the Canadian Northern in 1914. The favor in which Borden himself, other Conservatives, and now Laurier beheld public ownership in transportation had a long tradition behind it. Meanwhile Canada had urgent problems nearer its consciousness than either the British or the Canadian navy.

🍁 CANADA AND THE ARCTIC

One of the least noticed and, in a sense, prophetic Canadian activities of this time was a curious interest in the arctic. Until more is known of its motivation beyond the facts that the arctic islands (except Axel Heiberg and the Ringnes Islands) were discovered and named by British explorers, and that, after acquisition of the Hudson's Bay Company's rights and later British surrenders, Canada could reasonably claim them by exercise of jurisdiction, little can be done except record the fact of systematic Canadian attempts to make such claims.

The cumulative process began with a British order in council of 1880, confirmed by statute in 1895, which transferred to Canada all British territories in North America except Newfoundland. In 1895 and again in 1897 Canadian orders in council defined the boundaries of the Northwest territories so as to include practically all the Arctic Archipelago. This declared intention to exercise jurisdiction was followed by five separate expeditions to the Arctic "with instructions to explore the region, to maintain peace and order, and to establish police, customs, and post offices at strategic points where such governmental services were required."

In 1903–4, A. P. Low and a detachment of Northwest Mounted Police made a great circuit from the west coast of Hudson Bay up Davis Strait, Baffin Bay, and Smith Sound to embrace Ellesmere and north Devon Island and Baffin Island. A second expedition to set up police posts also operated in 1904–5 from the west coast of Hudson Bay. A third, of 1906, patrolled the western Arctic, hoisting the flag on various islands and depositing records of annexation.

The fourth, of 1908–9, entered by Lancaster Sound, formally claimed some five large islands, and erected a tablet of record (July 1, 1909) at Winter Harbour on Melville Island, claiming the Canadian territory to the North Pole. On its return journey, the great Canadian arctic navigator, Captain J. E. Bernier, had the unique pleasure of collecting a symbolical $50 fee from the American sportsman, Harry Whitney, for the license issued to him for a motor whale-boat. Five whaling licenses (for 1906–9) were issued to whalers operating from stations on the Canadian side of Baffin Bay and Davis Strait. The fifth expedition of 1910–11 had trouble with ice, but operated overland and by water in such ways as to patrol whaling operations and to attempt to enforce licensing jurisdiction.

World War I interrupted such activities, but meanwhile Norwegian, American, and Danish claims had made the matter sufficiently serious for it to be brought before the Imperial War Cabinet in 1917, and after 1918 the Canadian governments resumed the patrols, police operations, and so forth, upon which her claims were based. Captain Bernier's formal taking of possession in 1909 was thereby validated, Norway recognized it, and the unimplemented claims of Denmark and the United States were nullified in the great sector extending to the North Pole. Aviation after 1918, especially after World War II, was to add point to this achievement and to stimulate international concern and legal disagreement over sovereignties north of the Arctic Circle.

✷ CANADA IN 1914

All in all, the Canada of 1914 had attained economic and political, if not cultural, nationhood. She was locked into an economic and political triangle with Great Britain and the United States, but she had recently said "No" in spectacular fashion to each of them. When the United States threatened, the ties to Britain were stressed, and, when Britain presumed too far, Canada, if not Newfoundland, could and did successfully insist on autonomy, not only internally but externally as well.

Moreover Macdonald's realization in 1871 that Anglo-American understanding was so valuable to Canada as to justify Canada paying something for it had slowly but effectively become an underlying assumption in Canada's external relations, sore as Canadians still were over the manner of the Alaska boundary decision. Not many Canadians seriously considered independence, though John S. Ewart was exploring the legalities and the actualities of such status, with an interested eye on the less parochial aspects of Bourassa's nationalism. Americans and Britons, knowing little or nothing for the most part about Canadian development, acted and spoke in ways that angered Canadians and made them resolve somehow to impose their conception of themselves on the outside world.

Yet the truth was that Canadian developments, and still more Canadian thinking about them, were uneven, and exploitation of Canada was so exciting that only a few persons were absorbed by matters of legal and constitutional status. Moreover, most Canadians knew that their deep ethnic schism was normally operative in politics, perhaps even to the point of making full nationhood impossible. If *Canadien* separatism had been one of the mightiest forces in bringing about Canada's dominion status in its negative aspect, it could also very seriously modify its positive exercise if the majority chose to move in directions that a 30 per cent minority were not prepared to follow.

CHAPTER XXV

The Tests of War (1914-18)

Between 1914 and 1918 an astonished and unprepared Canada discovered that it could carry the burdens of over four years of all-out participation in a world war and grow in the process. Moreover, the English-speaking majority found that it could impose its will on the French-speaking and other minorities without destroying the national political structure. Few, if any, Canadians would have prophesied as much on August 4, 1914, when, Britain being at war, Canada accepted that state too.

Yet it was gradually revealed that about seven and a half million divided people could put 628,000 men in the armed services and send 425,000 of them overseas, forming an army corps of their own and serving in Canadian or British forces on every front—sea, land, and air—of a widespread war. At the same time Canadian productivity was transformed and grew, in volume by about 20 per cent, and in value from about $1600 millions to about $3700 millions, carrying the national income from $2200 millions to $3700 millions. Instead of being a net borrower, Canada became a net lender. By the time the war was over, Canada's performance was recognized as having been so substantial that the outside world was ready to accord her, internationally, the autonomous status that she had been exercising within the British Empire for over twenty years.

Few countries have undergone such profound, swift transformations. Moreover World War I, far more than any preceding event, was a tragically painful step in the reluctant discovery by French Canada of its inescapable implication in world affairs.

🍁 THE COMING OF THE WAR

The Canadian Cabinet was scattered on holiday in Europe and North America when war became imminent, but Borden hurried back from the Muskoka lakes in Ontario, arriving in Ottawa on August 1. In the absence of the governor general, he cabled to the British government, expressing his own government's hope for peace, but saying: "If unhappily war should ensue, the Canadian people will be united in a common resolve to put forth every effort and to make every sacrifice necessary to ensure the integrity and maintain the honour of our Empire."

An incomplete Cabinet then put into force a number of orders in council planned earlier in the year on the British war-model of 1909; the decrepit, half-manned, and feebly armed "Rainbow" was ordered south from British Columbia to protect two small British naval vessels against the German Pacific fleet. (She escaped certain destruction by the "Leipzig" off San Francisco by about three hours.) Two submarines built at Seattle for Chile were purchased and rushed to Esquimalt before the U.S. navy could prevent it. Parliament was summoned to meet on August 18.

Meanwhile the dynamic, eccentric Minister of Militia, Colonel Sam Hughes, was reaping the benefits of the patient efforts of Sir Frederick Borden (1896–1911), Sir Percy Lake (1907–11), and General Colin Mackenzie (1912–14) to organize Canada's small permanent force (3000) and her large, but ill-trained militia (58,000). Their design was somewhat along the lines of co-operation between regulars and territorials worked out by Lord Haldane in England and carried to Canada by Sir John French in the course of consultations about a Canadian expeditionary force in 1910. In 1907 Lake had planned a central mobilization camp at Valcartier near Quebec, so that Borden, Lake, and Mackenzie had at least the blueprints for mobilization. Hughes affected to scorn the professional soldiers and to scrap their painstaking plans, but most of what he achieved of a substantial sort before his resignation was demanded two years later was in accordance with their work.

Parliament, like the Cabinet, accepted the state of war and proceeded to pass a War Measures Act, modeled on Britain's Defence of the Realm Act, which not only validated the arbitrary ordinances of the Cabinet since August 2, but surrendered Parliament's powers to the Cabinet almost insofar as it should choose to exercise them. Members of Parliament vied with one another in expressing unanimous solidarity with Great Britain in her support of France and Belgium. Laurier excelled himself; Borden expressed his gratitude; indeed after the conflicts of the preceding fifteen years there was an enormous wave of emotional relief that *Canadiens* and Canadians stood shoulder to shoulder.

The higher Quebec clergy rallied quickly to the allied cause, asserting the duty to support the war and the expectation that young *Canadiens* would not hesitate to serve in it. French and Belgian reservists were cheered to their ships in Montreal and Quebec. British reservists and thousands of British-born immigrants either made for England or swamped the Canadian recruiting offices. In spite of British suggestions that German and Austrian reservists should be interned, the government offered to protect them unless they tried to leave the country. Actually it subsequently proved necessary to confine only about 6000 of perhaps 200,000 recent immigrants from Austria-Hungary and Germany.

During the autumn of 1914 nearly all Canada was enthusiastically dedicated to an enterprise of which its peoples had very little understanding. Of the tiny group of dedicated *Canadien* Nationalists, Bourassa was busy escaping from Germany on foot; Lavergne ominously asserted that Canada was bound to defend only herself; but Paul-Emile Lamarche committed himself to saying that it was every Canadian's duty to defend the empire. On August 6, however, Omer Héroux stated the Nationalists' then very unpopular case in *Le Devoir:*

We persist in believing, along with the great statesmen of the past, that the proper duty of Canadian troops is to ensure, along with the defense of our territory, for which we are ready to consent to any sacrifice, freedom of communications and free export of the wheat necessary to the life of the English nation.

French Canada falls away.—As the first shock wore off, and reality broke through imagination, the enduring essentials in Canadian life began to assert themselves. On the whole, the 12 per cent of the population who were British-born and the 55 per cent who were ethnically British were almost unqualified in their support of the war, and only gradually were doubts and confusions displayed, chiefly by farmers and trade unionists.

Yet it was apparent that outright enthusiasm dwindled in rough proportion to length of establishment in Canada, and the *Canadiens,* in particular, had little sense of, or liking for, active participation, since they had very little general sense of identity with France or Britain. *"France notre coeur, Albion notre foi"* was an evasion of obligation, for the uneasy affiliation with republican, anticlerical France was chiefly useful as a defense against British and Anglo-Canadian forces, and the reliance on Britain was a shield against both anglicizing Canadians and the potentially overpowering United States. A host of historical circumstances combined to make the *Canadiens* natural isolationists, and the small group among them, chiefly in military or other public service, who saw and accepted Canada's international role came to seem to the others almost like the *vendus* (sellouts) of earlier political struggles.

In terms of ordinary human nature, however, it was necessary for the *Canadiens* to have, or to invent as an excuse for their dissent from the general mood, some great wrong done to them which must be righted before they might be expected to co-operate. Since 1912 they had had one at hand in Regulation Seventeen of the Ontario Department of Education which prescribed English as the dominant language of instruction in the schools, even where, as in eastern and northern Ontario or in some sections along the Detroit River, the population was French-speaking.

The city of Ottawa, where, as in the United States, the Irish Catholics opposed the *Canadiens* on the language question, was a natural and conspicuous battleground. The war against "the Prussians of Ontario" quite quickly became the focus of *Canadien* passion and devotion, eliciting very large sums of money from private and public sources for support of French instruction, and gradually becoming the most satisfying substitute for orderly consideration of French Canada's position in a larger world.

Second only to the Ontario school question as grounds for dissent was the persistently bad management of recruiting in Quebec and the ill-calculated treatment of the *Canadiens* who volunteered. Hughes was an Orangeman, and it seemed as if he and his intimates hoped that the war would accelerate the amalgamation of *Canadien* and Canadian instead of recognizing that the best to be hoped for at the time was collaboration. The language of command and instruction in the armed forces was English; senior rank and important responsibilities seemed unattainable for *Canadiens;* and their natural ambition to build up by solid battalions, batteries, and so forth, to their own brigade and possibly division was diverted and thwarted in time-consuming and discouraging ways.

In this time of crisis, English-speaking Canadians simply did not possess the imagination and magnanimity needed to foster and enhance the devotion to the cause of those *Canadiens* who were willing and anxious to face unpopularity in its behalf. During the autumn of 1914, the *Canadien* would-be collaborators undoubtedly outnumbered the Nationalists, but English-speaking Canada seemed fated by tradition to act in ways calculated to evoke the equally traditional distrust of the *Canadiens* instead of to encourage their co-operation.

Early in September, back from his studies of ethnical division in Alsace and Belgium, Bourassa elaborated his position in such a deliberate, tentative, and logically elaborate way as to confuse rather than clarify the immediate situation. In brief, he held that, not as a British colony, but as an Anglo-French nation, it was Canada's duty "to contribute, in the measure of her strength and by the means of action proper to her, to the triumph and above all to the *endurance* of the combined efforts of France and England. But to render this contribution effective, Canada should begin by resolutely surveying its real situation, making an exact account of what it can and cannot do and assuring its internal security, before launching on or pursuing efforts which it perhaps will not be able to maintain until the end."

Such counsels suited almost no one in any camp, prowar, antiwar, or open to conviction, but in the long run they furnished ample support for *Canadien* inertia and resistance. Indeed, by the end of October, Bourassa's own criticisms of the government's war policies had become so sweeping as to amount, substantially, to opposition to active participation in the war. By May, 1915, nearly all his energies were being poured into the war for the defense of the French language in Ontario and into an appeal to Rome against the Irish clergy there.

BRITISH NORTH AMERICAN CONTRIBUTIONS

Newfoundland.—It is a striking evidence of the prestige and might of the British navy in 1914 that during the war 7000 Newfoundlanders enrolled themselves as soldiers, as compared with 1500 as sailors. Since the German navy was bottled up, the immediate way to help was to fight the German army, as Newfoundlanders did, with appalling casualties—1300 killed and 2314 wounded, chiefly in the battles of the Somme. Only after submarine warfare became severe in 1917 and 1918 was the strategic importance of Newfoundland prominent, and by that time the Canadian and American navies had adopted the convoy system in the North Atlantic and the endless, painstaking procedures devised to cope with submarines and mines.

Newfoundland's main task, economically, was to produce dried cod for the Iberian and Mediterranean markets and make up for the deficiencies of her usual European competitors. A boom in prices and the carrying trade resulted, which distorted the realities of Newfoundland's enduring position and saddled the island with contradictory aspirations and burdens. In her enthusiasm, Newfoundland spent $13,000,000 on the war, $10,000,000 of which was added to the colony's debt, and the burden of war pensions and allowances became disturbingly large.

Yet the people carried over from their four years of prosperity new habits of expenditure on a scale that optimism thought might well continue. The future reckoning was to be severe.

The Canadian forces.—Canada, thanks to her rich and variegated economy, fared better. It is impracticable to convey any precise sense of what her fighting men achieved. All warriors are valiant, just as all brides are beautiful.

The navy redeemed itself from its absurd beginnings in practical ways. Its two old cruisers, "Rainbow" and "Niobe," were converted into depot ships at Esquimalt and Halifax, while Japan took on the serious naval responsibilities of the North Pacific and Great Britain and the United States those of the North Atlantic. The two ex-Chilean submarines may possibly have made Esquimalt seem to the Germans more dangerous than it was until Admiral von Spee went round the Horn to meet destruction at the Falkland Islands in December, 1914.

Thereafter the Canadian navy turned to sloops, patrol vessels, a destroyer, trawlers, drifters, mine sweepers, tugs, and motor launches, because the best service it could render was to protect the immense flow of North American goods to Europe. The Atlantic Coast Patrol of 123 vessels (including six American submarine chasers and one torpedo boat), assisted by a Naval Air Service largely American in its inspiration and equipment, succeeded almost completely in protecting the convoys in Canadian eastern waters. Meanwhile the naval dockyards at both Halifax and Esquimalt were kept continuously busy repairing, refueling, and reprovisioning allied warships.

No one has accurately calculated Canadian enterprise in air warfare because Canada had no air force of her own. She built training aircraft and, during 1917 and 1918, was the home of a large-scale training branch of the Royal Flying Corps. From the beginning of the war, Canadian soldiers, once overseas, transferred by the thousands into the Royal Flying Corps and Royal Naval Air Service. Altogether they seem to have provided about a quarter of the fighters in those forces, and they were early recognized to have unusual aptitude in air combat. Many of them made extremely large numbers of "kills," and W. A. Bishop, who survived, seems to have been the most successful airfighter in the world with his astonishing total of seventy-two. This passion for flying was to have important consequences after the war, for down to 1939 the aircraft of Canada carried the largest recorded total annual tonnages in the world.

To most Canadians, however, "the war" meant membership in the Canadian Expeditionary Force in France, an army almost exclusively of volunteers that distinguished itself from beginning to end. The first division was at sea by October 1 and in France, after a dreadful winter of training on Salisbury Plain, by early February, 1915. Late in April it was its lot to meet the first gas-attack in history, and its fame that its steadfastness prevented a breakthrough. The arrival at the front of the second division during the late summer created a Canadian Corps that grew to four divisions, with a fifth as reserve in Great Britain. During 1915 the grim Ypres salient became familiar ground; indeed until the autumn of 1916 the corps earned its principal laurels by weeks of dogged defense there and a series of repulses of crucial, "set" attempts by the Germans to break through.

In September, 1916, they took the offensive so successfully during the bloodbaths at the Somme that they were henceforth to be depended upon as trench-raiders and assault troops. In April, 1917, they captured Vimy Ridge, a powerful key position and fortress which the Germans had held against a great French assault eighteen months before. This was a costly operation, but it had an unprecedented completeness and "perfection" hitherto lacking in British and French efforts.

It is fitting, therefore, that Canada's beautiful principal memorial of the war, the work of Walter S. Allward, stands broodingly, defiantly, and triumphantly, facing Germany from that height. Early that winter it fell to the Canadians to complete the work of the British and Australian forces in the capture of Passchendaele after a very long grueling struggle in seas of mud, a "holding" operation designed to counter the defection of Russia and the mutiny in the French army. Canadian casualties during November were almost 31,000.

Like everyone else, the Canadians were thrown on the defensive by the immense German assaults of March, April, and May, 1918, but following them they were groomed in great secrecy for the attack again. On August 8, Ludendorff's "black day of the German army," they embarked on their "Hundred Days" of victory, a series of assaults on prepared German positions which began at Amiens, broke a "switch" line at Drocourt-Quéant, pierced the Hindenburg Line, crossed the Canal du Nord, captured Cambrai at frightful cost, and carried them, symbolically, into Mons on the morning of the armistice that ended the war. It had been a war unparalleled before or since for casualties in battle. About 61,000 Canadians were killed or missing, and over 175,000 wounded.

Throughout the war Canadian nationalism continued to assert itself. On the sea and in the air, British direction was accepted, as it necessarily was for ground forces when individuals or small detachments were engulfed in large British or Allied enterprises. The Canadian Expeditionary Force in France was another matter, in spite of the original British assumptions that it was merely an obedient part of the British armies. Canada did not presume to claim that her statesmen were more inspired or her generals more gifted than Great Britain's, but Borden was quite certain that both at least measured up to the responsibilities undertaken and that Canada was entitled to "fuller information" and "consultation respecting general policy in war operations."

During the summer of 1915 he discovered a good deal that was disquieting to him in England and France, and before he returned to Canada he served notice on Asquith and Bonar Law that he could not urge Canadians to continue at their present intensity unless he could find better evidence that Britain herself "takes the war seriously, realizes the immensity of the task, is making preparation accordingly, and there is no more cry of 'Business as Usual.' "

Canada insisted that her large army must be a distinct formation. When they tried to put him off with soft words and talk of impracticality, he blazed out angrily about the Canadian-born Bonar Law:

It can hardly be expected that we shall put 400,000 or 500,000 men in the field and willingly accept the position of having no more voice and receiving no more consideration than if we were toy automata. Any person cherishing such an expectation harbours an unfortunate and even dangerous delusion. Is this war being waged by the United Kingdom alone, or is it a war waged by the whole Empire? If I am correct in supposing that the second hypothesis must be accepted, then why do the statesmen of the British Isles arrogate to themselves solely the methods by which it shall be carried on in the various spheres of warlike activity and the steps which shall be taken to assure victory and a lasting peace?

Once Sam Hughes was out of the way in Canada, some profiteers and their Cabinet patrons exposed and disgraced, and the Lloyd George management established in England, most of the difficulties were straightened out. In the field, the popular and successful British commander of the Corps, Sir Julian Byng (later Lord Byng of Vimy), was succeeded by the Canadian, Arthur W. Currie, who had left the real-estate business in Vancouver to earn recognition as the ablest and most dependable of the now professionally competent Canadian commanders.

In London, the Canadian Cabinet tightened up its control of the forces which had hitherto been rather uncertainly exercised by the High Commissioner for Canada and by some curious devices of Hughes, such as the Ministry of the Overseas Military Forces of Canada, established in October, 1916. Two months later the Canadian General Staff was set up in London. And finally, in February, 1917, the dominion prime ministers, or their deputies, became members of the Imperial

War Cabinet, the tight little directorate of political authority in the manifold, but now unified, management of the war.

꧁ CONSCRIPTION SPLITS CANADA

Borden's announced aim had been to put half a million men in the field. Voluntary enlistments had been falling at an accelerating rate during 1916; 250,000 men had been sought, but 160,000 obtained, 120,000 of whom had enlisted during the first six months. In the period from January to May, 1917, inclusive, enlistments were 34,580 and casualties 56,860. The losses in the Somme Valley and at Vimy, the defection of Russia, and the French mutiny, even in the light of American entry to the war in April, 1917, convinced him that his aim must be sustained. This could only be done by strengthening his domestic political control, which had been weakened by scandals, frauds, inefficiencies, and the falling away of the *Canadiens,* and by using that enhanced authority to distribute the burden of war as evenly as possible across the nation.

In other words, about May, 1917, he aimed at parliamentary coalition and military conscription, if possible without a general election. Parliament had already extended its own life and in agreement could do so again. Laurier, whose dream of a Canada united in compromise was already dimmed, rejected the idea of a coalition, declared that conscription was indefensible without a referendum or a general election, and suspected that the real urgency lay in the bankruptcy of the railroads and its ramifications in public credit. Paul-Emile Lamarche, the Nationalist, was quite blunt. "Consult the annals of Canada for the past fifty years at random, and whatever party may be in power, what do you find?" he asked. "The government is building a railway, buying a railway, selling a railway, or blocking a railway."

Since sometime in 1915, most of French Canada had been conducting a rearguard action or retreat in the face of English-speaking Canada. There was pride in the demonstrated prowess of the *Canadien* Twenty-Second Battalion and other units composed of *Canadiens* who felt moved to serve in the war. The hierarchy of the church and other traditional leaders constantly reaffirmed the rightness of the war and the duty of serving in it. But the lower clergy and the mass of the people were simply not committed to it and their distaste found excuse in the Ontario school question, and intensification in the mounting torrent of condemnation and abuse from English-speaking Canada. The result was that for over two years the higher clergy, leading patriotic *Canadiens,* and *Canadien* soldiers at home and abroad preached to increasingly deaf ears. For example, Captain Talbot Papineau, a grandson of the *Patriote* leader, and Captain Gustave Lanctot, who had been an officer in Asselin's battalion, wrote eloquently and urgently from the front asking Quebec to do its share, but without avail.

It is evidence of the sincerity of the more thoughtful Nationalist leaders that they were profoundly troubled when their "chickens came home to roost" in this way. Some of them, like Olivar Asselin, threw themselves into military service and efforts to stimulate voluntary enlistment. Others vacillated from one extremity to the other. Bourassa himself largely withdrew to the consolations of religion. For the most part, however, they and their people pulled back deeper and deeper into sullen or angry retreat from a world that would not let them alone. In his reply to Papineau, for instance, Bourassa said:

> The simple truth is that the abstention of the French Canadians is no more the result of the present attitude of the Nationalists than the consequence of the Liberal campaign of 1896 or the Conservative appeals of 1911. It relates to deeper causes: hereditary instincts, social and economic conditions, a national tradition of three centuries . . . strengthened by the constant teaching of all our political and social leaders from Lafontaine, Cartier, Macdonald, Mackenzie to Laurier inclusively.

Borden's procedure during and after the late summer of 1916 emerged from clouds of negotiations. His principal lieutenant was Arthur Meighen, an intense, sharply focused, and rather ruthless agent who was prepared to hew to the line and let the chips fall where they might.

The foundation of the design, as the *Canadiens* had suspected, was the structure for national registration set up in October, 1916, but securing parliamentary sanction for using this in conscription was a serious problem. The year 1916 had demonstrated that only a small proportion of *Canadien* manpower was available for the armed forces and that opposition to the war was growing. Patient negotiations with Laurier made it clear that his long-held views of Canadianism by compromise forbade him to accept either coalition or conscription because they would result in Quebec's withdrawal. The church hierarchy in Quebec was showing clear signs of surrender to the sentiments of the lower clergy and the masses of the people.

Meighen had, in August and September, 1916, put through his Military Voters Act and War Times Election Act, which were ingenious, but flagrant and, it would seem, unnecessary devices to disenfranchise possible opponents of conscription—particularly aliens naturalized since 1902, and to multiply and manipulate the votes of those committed to the war—servicemen and their wives, widows, and female relatives. The Conscription Act, which came in June, 1917, following British and American adoption of this practice, served to split the Liberal party.

After some nasty struggles within the party, those dissenting from Laurier secured very generous representation in a coalition government.

The act may also be said, with substantial justice, to have driven the church hierarchy tacitly into the opposition camp with its people. A motion by J. N. Francoeur in the Quebec provincial legislature for secession, if the other provinces wanted it, was debated and discussed, but withdrawn on January 23, 1918. An election held in December, 1917, was, of course, a hysterical affair, but it was also a tragic denial of what the best *Canadiens* and Canadians had been building up since the days of Lafontaine and Baldwin. Laurier at seventy-seven, ardently committed to the war and to acceptance of the electoral decision, campaigned across the country. Although hissed and heckled in Quebec, he attracted large and on the whole respectful audiences elsewhere. In effect, 62 out of 65 Quebec constituencies and twenty others scattered across Canada opposed the aims of an overwhelming majority—115 Conservatives and 38 Liberal Unionists.

And then 1918 revealed that the conscriptionists of 1917 had wounded their country sorely in quest of the unattainable. The Canadian government had committed Canada to more than its peoples could be brought to achieve, even when, faced by the Conscription Act's failure to secure the expected results, it was intensified by resort to order in council. Popular resistance to the intolerable took the forms of very extensive requests for exemption, unsuccessful tests of constitutionality, flight, and desertion, although the German offensives of March–May, 1918, combined with more conciliatory procedures in Quebec and elsewhere, undermined resistance a little and somewhat stimulated recruiting.

The statistics of the operation of the act, the order in council, and other determined administrative procedures are both contradictory and dubious, but it is believed that, instead of 100,000 recruits, it secured perhaps 61,000, of whom over 47,000 were sent overseas, most of them too late and too unsuitable to see much action. Obstruction was, of course, most determined in Quebec, but it affected every other province. In parts of Ontario, farmers attended coalition government or recruiting meetings for the satisfaction of honking their automobile horns in derision from outside. Rioting, some dynamiting, and other forms of protest and destruction had been sporadic in Quebec before 1917, but during that summer anticonscription demonstrations in Montreal had reached the brink of systematic assassinations when the terrorist agitators were arrested. The most serious outbreak occurred in the city of Quebec, where violent disturbances and destruction, which involved four deaths and many woundings, lasted from the night of March 29 to the afternoon of April 2, 1918.

Industrial workers, torn between demands to produce goods and soldiers, proved vulnerable because they were city dwellers and easy to locate unless they cleared out for the United States. Farmers, at their wits' end for labor, sent stormy delegations to Ottawa, inundated the boards with appeals for exemption, and connived with men who took to the woods. Desertion was almost uncontrollable at times, indeed some Quebec detachments were encouraged and even financed by their officers in effecting it.

It was noteworthy that the pope, in a pastoral letter of June, 1918, took a strong and explicit line about the separate school question, declaring that the *Canadiens* might quite justly appeal to government for modification of Regulation Seventeen or other concessions "but all these advantages and others which may be useful must be invoked and sought for by Catholics without the least appearance of revolt and without recourse to violent or illegitimate methods." No one was to appeal to the courts in the matter without the knowledge and consent of his bishop, who was himself to consult other interested bishops. Every discouragement to division by language and race was to be used. "Let all priests endeavor to acquire the knowledge and use of both languages, English and French, and, setting aside all prejudices, let them adopt one or the other according to the needs of the faithful."

🍁 THE WAR ECONOMY

The immense Canadian war effort had to be paid for, or, in the fashion of states, "financed," and in the prevailing circumstances Canada had to learn how to do it herself since adequate borrowing abroad was out of the question. Fortunately the world made demands on the Canadian economy which it was equipped to fulfill, indeed, in an economic sense, 1914–20 was a continuation of 1896–1913. The outcome of this situation might briefly and reasonably accurately be described by saying that Canada sustained the war out of production, inflation, and borrowing—from her own citizens.

The discovery that Canadians could and would provide huge sums (of inflated dollars) that had hitherto been believed to be available only in Lombard and Wall streets was so surprising as to be shocking to the borrowers. Indeed for some years there was a modest fund of stories about how various loan committees timidly approached rich men in the hope that their patriotism would induce them to take up a respectable fraction of the local "quota," only to discover that such men's appreciation of 5 per cent on 10-year bonds selling at 97½ per cent and backed by the highest available security made them anxious to lay their hands on all they could get.

The annals of borrowing were revealing. To begin with, London set up a credit of about $60,000,000 for Canada until a balance could be struck between Canadian expenditures in Europe and British purchases in Canada. Very soon the latter exceeded the former, indeed before the end of 1917 the president of the Canadian Bankers' Association rather smugly told its members in annual meeting: "For the present I consider that we have loaned as much as we should to the British Government."

He was disregarded. During 1917, 1918, and 1919, his country was putting successively $100,000,000, $112,000,000, and $221,000,000 at the disposal of Great Britain in Canada. When accounts were made up at the end of March, 1920, Canada's net lending abroad since 1914 amounted to $150,000,000. The first response to London's difficulties in 1915 had been that Canada borrowed for the first time in New York, on a very modest scale ($45,000,000). The second was an attempt to borrow $50,000,000 at home that autumn, to which the startling response was subscription of over double the amount. The state had "struck oil." During 1915-19, inclusive, it drew off about $2,000,000,000!

The technicalities of Canada's inflation were complex and need not be repeated here. Gold payment was suspended at the beginning of August, 1914, and the banks were given great freedom in credit expansion. National revenue from customs and excise, even at rapidly increased rates, was hopelessly insufficient; a retroactive business profits tax brought in inadequate amounts; and the new income tax of 1917, added to the other sources, barely met the domestic current account and interest obligations, let alone the costs of the war and the so-called ordinary capital expenditures, in other words, railroad deficits.

The only thing to do was to print money and borrow it back from those who accumulated it. The inflation may be approximately measured by the fact that the index of wholesale prices rose from 100 in 1913 to 209 in 1919 and the cost of living index from 100 to 164. Recipients of fixed incomes suffered, but real income increased for a great many.

New and increased production.—Matters would have been disastrously worse, of course, had not Canada increased her production and increased her exports even more. It was as if the great productive capacity that had been rendered partly superfluous by the depression of 1913 was stimulated to its limits by the war and by its assured markets. The land could produce foodstuffs and a rapidly altered and expanded industry could produce munitions. The rising prices ensured profits and export prices rose higher than import prices.

The acreage in field crops grew from 35 million in 1913 to 53 million in 1919, largely because of an 80 per cent increase in the wheat acreage on the plains. Meat exports rose from $6 million to $85 million; live-stock exports from $10 million to $35 million; and a half instead of a quarter of farm production was exported. The demands of war ac-celerated mining and some highly important technical advances in ore-handling and metallurgy. Production of copper, lead, zinc, and nickel rose from $29 million to $74 million. War news and war advertising expanded newspapers and periodicals, particularly in the United States, where pulp and paper resources had dwindled since Scandinavia was no longer a supplier. Exports of newsprint rose from $20 million in 1913 to $105 million in 1920.

The catalog might be continued, but historically the great basic eco-nomic phenomenon, generally unobserved then and for years after-wards, was the rise of manufacturing. One of the principal stimulating agents in this matter was the Imperial Munitions Board, an agency of the British government, manned by Canadians, which managed specific war production. The usual index of its importance is that by 1917 and 1918 between a quarter and a third of the shells used by British forces on the Western Front came from Canada.

Yet this emphasis on shells is misleading, even though the plants for their manufacture could be and were converted to other industrial ends after 1918. Actually every branch of manufacturing was sharply stimulated: to supply the Canadian forces with food and clothing; to satisfy a public at home with money burning holes in its pockets; and to fill gaps in civilian production abroad. In particular, American branch factories, which had been increasing since 1905, both expanded their operations and spurted in number in 1916 and 1917. While foreign demand for Canadian manufactured goods was obviously abnormal, it was capable of persisting in some categories, so that the rise in the percentage of the total net value of manufactured goods exported from about 6 to over 40 was significant.

At this stage of Canada's industrialization the emphasis lay on the large-scale processing of raw materials—the milling of grains, meat-packing, pulp and paper making, the milling, smelting, and refining of metals, and so on—manufacturing which could continue to be exported in times of peace. Intricate industrial products such as internal com-bustion engines or electric motors and dynamos were usually imported from the United States for "assembly" into vehicles or for other uses. The manufacture of such consumers' goods as textiles or shoes had advanced to a stage where it hardly needed the protectionist wall behind which it had grown.

International accounts.—Even if the distortion by inflation is taken into account, the amounts and directions of Canada's triangular trade with Great Britain and the United States are revealing:

	In Millions of Dollars	
	1914	*1918*
Total imports	619	963
Total exports	455	1586
Balance	−164	623
Imports from the U.S.	396	792
Exports to the U.S.	177	441
Balance	−219	−351
Imports from G.B.	132	81
Exports to G.B.	232	861
Balance	100	780

The complicated triangular movements of bullion, securities, and currency were affected by "pegging" after the United States entered the war, but in general Canada's productivity and savings in the form of lending to the state not only kept the Canadian dollar near parity but probably assisted in sustaining the pound sterling. The vast importance of the income tax by way of freeing Canada from her great dependence on tariff revenues was little appreciated at the time.

The railroads.—No one, however, could fail to know that the nation's credit had been irretrievably pledged to save the railroads. Borrowing was their lifeblood, and private lending had vanished. We need not follow their collapses in detail. The C.P.R. was fortunate enough to have ended its dependency on the public treasury before 1900 and to have developed an excellent, matured, and profitable system, reinforced by transatlantic and transpacific steamship lines. Extensive double-tracking and building or acquisition of branch lines took place after 1907. Its reserves and credit enabled it to profit from the increased traffic of war, even though immigration had dried up and land sales with it.

The Canadian Northern and the Grand Trunk Pacific, on the other hand, were not even completely built when war came, in fact they were like the C.P.R. about 1883–90, and their collapse in the face of the dead money market and rising costs and wages was prompt. The outcome, after elaborate investigations and much argument over such things as public ownership, public operation, fairness to the C.P.R., and so on, was that a public corporation, the Canadian National Railway Company, modeled after the Suez Canal Corporation, gradually took over the bankrupt lines as well as the Canadian Government Railways during the period 1917 to 1923.

Meanwhile grim parliamentary and court battles went on in the interests of the private security holders. The Canadian Bank of Commerce, for instance, held $51,000,000 of the $58,614,000 common stock of the Canadian Northern standing in the name of Mackenzie, Mann and Co., as pledge against advances. What would happen to the bank if the stock were held worthless? In Great Britain thousands of investors had been holding on to Grand Trunk securities of various kinds, although that railroad had been in trouble since its beginning in the mid-nineteenth century and had invited more by its recent line to Prince Rupert.

In the case of the Canadian Northern, the outstanding stock was ultimately valued at $10,800,000 by arbitrators, but the Grand Trunk stockholders learned through another arbitration that their preferred and common stocks were worthless. Undoubtedly their railroad had suffered from its foreign control, and unjustified dividends had been paid, but the general disaster arose from yielding negligently to the optimism that gripped London as well as Canada in 1903. It was the Canadian people, moreover, who really reaped the whirlwind. The consolidated balance sheet of 1923 for the Canadian National showed a long-term interest-bearing debt of about $2 billions on assets worth little more, and a current deficit of $283 millions.

SOCIAL CHANGES

Increased money income accelerated the economic betterment of Canadians that had been going on since 1896. Even when prices were rising and scarcities resulted from greatly increased exports, the majority of the Canadian people were better off and their savings increased.

The interruption of immigration, except from the United States, made for a period of social digestion, of Canadianization, that went on in spite of a good many outbreaks of xenophobia and spy mania. The discovery of, and pride in, Canada's capacities in war made for self-confidence and a sense of nationality that imbued most English-speaking Canadians and, appearances to the contrary notwithstanding, a considerable number of *Canadiens* as well. The movement and stationing of troops across Canada gave many servicemen their first concrete ideas of the country as a whole, and their journeys to Europe and other parts of the globe broke down the parochialism of all except the stubbornly unimpressionable. A popular song of the day, with the refrain "How ya goin' to keep them down on the farm after they've seen Paree?" was a pointed commentary on what happened to hundreds of thousands of Canadians.

Money to spend and new ideas of how to spend it made deep inroads on what had been a notably puritanical code of manners. The Roman Catholic Sunday (holiday after religious observance) and the pagan Sunday eroded a sabbatarianism which was already yielding to golf, the automobile, and weekending, but, except in Quebec, the Lord's Day Alliance kept a firm, prohibitive hand on commercial amusements.

The desirability of saving grain for foodstuffs, signalized by an order in council of November 5, 1917, forbidding its use in making alcoholic drinks, tipped the balance heavily in favor of those who aimed to prohibit the drinking of alcohol. This movement, borrowed from the United States, swept rapidly over the Canadian provinces under the enabling powers of the Canada Temperance Act of 1878. Had the war not ended in 1918, the last holdout, Quebec, would have yielded. Probably public opinion, as a whole, favored this bold, indeed rash, social experiment, but it angered the servicemen and made some of them the readier to circumvent it. Its accompaniments in corruption, crime, and violence were not greatly apparent during the war.

There was a good deal of public indignation over profiteering, particularly during the period of confused, graft-ridden, and inefficient beginnings in the supply of the forces. Hughes was incurable in his reliance on friends and acquaintances, some of whom deeply betrayed his confidence. Borden resolutely cleared up these messes during 1916, not sparing his own Cabinet in the process. Profiteering there undoubtedly was, but the public failed to see that with the volume of business growing and prices rising, even the most carefully calculated margins of narrow profit accumulated into large totals.

Public indignation in this matter easily attached itself to the knighthoods and hereditary titles of honor which the British government used, rather lavishly, to express its gratitude for Canadian aid, and which had a way of going to the big businessmen to whom the Canadian government felt most indebted. After the great shower of titles that accompanied the end of the war, the House of Commons voted an address to the Crown asking that no more be granted except on the advice of Canada and for professional distinction only.

This climate of opinion, coinciding with the decent civilian's almost desperate feeling that nothing he could do faintly approached the sacrifices of the serviceman, produced a remarkable outburst of philanthropical giving and of unpaid war service. William Wood discovered, for instance, that in the city of Quebec alone there were over a hundred separate Canadian war activities, of which about a third were civilian. The symbolical central national philanthropy was the Canadian Patriotic Fund designed to supplement the allowances of servicemen's dependents. In addition a few very wealthy individuals raised and equipped special military units; voluntary funds bought machine guns beyond the ordinary military establishment; hospitals were equipped and maintained; servicemen's lives were insured; canteens were operated; the Red Cross expanded; relief funds for allied peoples were raised; and so forth. No systematic investigation of all this conscience-easing charity has been made, but it has usually been estimated as amounting to $100,000,000.

One other development, of an almost accidental sort, was the concession of votes to women. The woman suffrage movement in Canada, as recorded by Catherine L. Cleverdon, had a curiously apathetic history considering the proximity of the United States and the aggressiveness of Australasia in this matter. Except for lively and ingenious minorities in the various provinces, notably Ontario and the West, most Canadian women were passive about the whole thing, in fact feminism has never been as active a cause in Canada as in other English-speaking countries.

Women's enterprise was another matter, an old story, and it was largely their contribution to national objectives during war that made it ridiculous to deny them the vote. In 1916 the plains provinces conceded it, in 1917 British Columbia and Ontario followed suit. The partial federal concession of the War Times Election Act was completed in the Dominion Franchise Act of 1920. The Maritimes fell into line, Nova Scotia in 1918, New Brunswick in 1919, and Prince Edward Island in 1922, but Quebec held out until 1940. Newfoundland had made the concession in 1925. It was notable, however, that very few women were elected to public office.

🍁 NEW ECONOMIC INTERVENTIONS BY THE STATE

As we have seen, the almost all-absorbing political issue of the war years was the handling of the ethnic schism. What was less apparent and partly temporary, though portentous, was that the state, in its determination to mobilize the national economy for what became an economic war, very boldly intervened in economic life. Of course, throughout Canada's history "laissez faire" was quite unreal. Whenever Canadian business needed state help, it demanded and got it, and whenever it found the state's attentions hampering to "rugged individualism," for instance in legalizing trade unionism, its appeals for "Hands off Business" were neither entirely sincere nor entirely successful.

Historically the state in Canada had always been involved in the economy—the nature of its intervention merely changed with the character of the economy. The striking thing about the new interventions of 1914–18 was that they were so frequently made for the benefit of society as a whole. It was as if the industrialization and urbanization that were expanding in Canada, under the stress of war, brought with them the emphasis on general social legislation that had been gaining momentum in industrial Britain since 1832.

Here it must be sufficient to do little more than list the new economic activities of the state, with the idea that such precedents seeped into public opinion and, combined with similar experiments abroad, prepared the way for similar action later. Among other things, the movement revolutionized the nature of the statistics needed by government. The now indispensable Dominion Bureau of Statistics was organized in 1918. New activities of the state created a new kind of civil servant and new kinds of enterprise for him. The Shell Committee of 1914 blundered its way into becoming the Imperial Munitions Board of 1916 which went into production in an immense way. The Military Hospitals Commission of 1915 emerged as the governmental Department of Soldiers' Civil Re-establishment, engaged, among other things, in the business of life insurance and in land settlement. Commissions were set up for natural resources and wool supply.

Manpower began to be allotted in 1916, prices began to be fixed in 1917, and a flood of orders in council tried to prevent the economy from getting out of hand. A startled, inadequate, uninformed Department of Labour was saddled with responsibilities which it could not perform for lack of staff and sheer unavailability of knowledge; particularly unamenable to control was the rise in the cost of living. The Food and Fuel Controllers of 1917 did their best, but no one knew how to enforce their demands.

The Food Board of 1918 had somewhat greater success by controlling the prices and movements of the bulk purchases of cereal, meat, and dairy products for export and thereby affecting domestic consumption. A licensing system made distributors feel that they were under some sort of supervision. The supply of coal and the wages of miners caused great concern and evoked stern controls in 1917 and 1918. The War Trade Board of 1918 was a kind of copestone which controlled exports and imports and directed the transportation and destinations of many commodities from wheat to platinum. Some of the apparatus was needed during the economic gyrations and the reconstruction immediately after 1918. As a whole it left a distinct collectivistic residue in the Canadian state and in the minds of Canadians.

BORDEN'S NATIONALISM

Throughout the war, Borden's bulldog determination had repelled every assumption of Canadian subordination to Great Britain. He had been astonishingly alert to check and correct even official phraseology lest it weaken his country's position. When the war came to an end, he was strengthened in this cause by three great auxiliaries—the imagination of Lloyd George, the understanding of Jan Christiaan Smuts, and the self-confidence of the Canadian people. The British prime minister had seen what Borden and Smuts meant and was sincerely prepared to operate in terms of self-governing dominions that wanted to co-operate but insisted on doing so without subservience. Smuts, coming like Borden from an ethnically divided country, thought in Borden's terms and, with his philosophic turn of mind, was subtler and more successful in informing and persuading the uninformed and uninterested.

The Canadian people were not very sure what it was all about and were conspicuously careless of its subtle constitutional details, but they were quite certain that they had exercised greater weight in the world than many recognized independent nations and they saw no reason why the world should not admit it formally. Canada had become a distinct entity in world affairs, but saw no incompatibility between that and mutually respectful association with Great Britain, or, for that matter, with any other country.

BOOK 5
INTERNATIONAL ENTITY (1919–59)

CHAPTER XXVI

First Steps (1918-21)

In October, 1921, Sir Robert Borden, delivering the Marfleet lectures at the University of Toronto, distilled his experiences and his views concerning Canada's status into terse, dry, and occasionally ironic or indignant form. He had turned over leadership of his party and of Parliament to Meighen, and, as an elder statesman, now tried to explain to his people what had been done to protect and secure recognition for their nation's autonomy. In effect, he attempted to outline and explain how Canada had developed up to and after the milestone of a resolution of the Imperial War Conference in 1917 which had asserted "full recognition of the Dominions as autonomous nations of an Imperial Commonwealth." His one gnawing dissatisfaction, which had been troubling him since 1911 or 1912, was his skepticism about Canada's share in imperial foreign policy:

"If the self-governing Dominions may not have *adequate* voice and influence in the direction of the Empire's foreign policy, it is not improbable that some of them will eventually have distinctive foreign policies of their own; and that may mean separation."

🍁 BADGES OF NATIONHOOD

Borden saw the issue in six principal aspects: formal pronouncement of equal partnership among Great Britain and the dominions, direct communication between their governments, equal exercise of Crown prerogative, extraterritorial exercise of sovereignty, separate diplomatic representation, and individual acceptance at the peace conference and in international organizations. He felt that the pronouncements of 1917 and afterwards, supported as they had been by Lord Milner's declaration of July 10, 1919, that "the only possibility of a continuance of the British Empire is on a basis of absolute out-and-out equal partnership between the United Kingdom and the Dominions," were clear enough, but he thought the issue had been somewhat blurred at the 1921 conference of prime ministers, largely because the British Foreign Office could not or would not alter its thinking to embrace the dominions' right "to an adequate voice in foreign policy and in foreign relations."

Direct communication between prime ministers, without using governors general or the Colonial Office as intermediaries, which had become customary during the war, seemed assured. His own action, embodied in a Canadian order in council of January 30, 1917, rejecting British authority to requisition Canadian ships, was on record as declaring that the exercise of the prerogative of the Crown so far as Canada was concerned must be upon the advice of the King's Canadian, not his British, ministers. This matter of shipping implied the extraterritorial exercise of Canadian sovereignty more widely, perhaps, than the ministerial control of the Canadian forces in Great Britain and France. It was finally accepted on Canada's terms in 1929.

Canadian representation abroad was, of course, a tender point between Borden and his real or imaginary enemies in the British Foreign Office. Here his array of precedents was a strong one. Canadians, Liberal and Conservative, had been advocating and arguing about the matter at fairly frequent intervals since 1882, but Laurier had dropped the agitation late in 1909 because James Bryce, the British ambassador at Washington, had been serving Canada so remarkably well. Early in 1918, however, the Borden government had established, by order in council, a War Mission at Washington and had built upon its usefulness to conclude in May, 1920, an agreement with Great Britain that Canada might henceforth have a minister plenipotentiary of her own at Washington who would, moreover, act for the British ambassador during his absence. For a number of reasons, this representation did not become actual until 1927, and the substitution for the British ambassador was withdrawn, but the principle had been conceded.

International recognition of separate Canadian entity had come swiftly at the end of the war. The process was summed up in Borden's statement that "the British Empire Delegation [at the Peace Conference] was really the Imperial War Cabinet under another name." Yet the achievement had been no mere acceptance of an accomplished fact. Borden had raised the question in behalf of his Cabinet in a dispatch to Lloyd George of October 29, 1918: "The press and people of this country take it for granted that Canada will be represented at the Peace Conference."

The solution of this unprecedented problem was dual and came only after continuous watchfulness and difficult negotiation. In the first place, Borden, for Canada, was a member of the panel acting in behalf of the whole British Empire, whose members were allotted various responsibilities from day to day. The other dominions (except Newfoundland) were conceded similar status. In the second place, Canada and the other dominions enjoyed separate representation "similar to that accorded to the smaller Allied powers." This novel diplomatic procedure was first fought for and won in the Imperial War Cabinet, then accepted at a London conference with France and Italy, and, after presentation to a surprised and resistant Peace Conference on January 12, 1919, pushed through to adoption there. Lloyd George's support, with Milner also committed and with Smuts and Borden, in particular, enjoying considerable international prestige, finally overrode objections, particularly American fears that the British countries would have a disproportionate number of votes.

The victory was rammed home with Borden-like thoroughness. Not only did Canada sign the peace treaties under plenipotentiary powers issued from the Crown through a Canadian order in council, but the treaties went to the Canadian Parliament for debate and ratification before their imperial ratification and approval by the Crown. Following a parallel course outside the empire, Canada secured separate membership in the Assembly of the League of Nations and, after Borden threatened to withdraw from the League if Canada were excluded, in the International Labour Organization. Membership in the League Council was regarded, by the United States in particular, as out of the question, but Borden was not to be downed. Finally, on May 6, 1919, he secured a signed declaration from Clemenceau, Wilson, and Lloyd George that "representatives of the self-governing Dominions of the British Empire may be selected or named as members of the Council," a privilege that Canada secured in 1927.

RENASCENT ISOLATIONISM

Canada as a whole had little clear appreciation of what all this amounted to, but was, of course, inundated by the violent and confused politics of the United States following President Wilson's loss of control of Congress at the beginning of November, 1918. Consequently the debates on the treaties in the Canadian Parliament revealed less appreciation of the niceties of status than fears of foreign conspiracy and entanglement. In other words, after having acted positively on an unprecedented scale for five years, Canada was strongly inclined to fall back on her capacity to say "No."

Isolationism achieved an ambiguous electoral victory in November, 1920, in the United States. A somewhat different isolationism in Canada excused itself by membership in the League of Nations and in the association of the British Empire. In both countries, problems of reconstruction during the economic hurricanes of 1919 and 1920 tended to make international organization and collective security rather remote and unreal. It is worth recalling that most North Americans living during the first third of the twentieth century thought that international peace was the normal state of affairs.

While there was never any serious doubt that the Canadian Parliament would ratify the treaties and the League Covenant, as it finally did without reservations or amendment, the debates revealed some of the future characteristics of Canadian international behavior. A few imperialists preferred exclusive association with the British Empire to membership in the League. A few idealists disliked some parts of the settlements so much that they were ready to "throw out the baby with the bath water." A few nationalists believed that Canada had exchanged subordination to Great Britain for subordination to Geneva.

The main burden of criticism, however, which came chiefly from the Liberal Opposition since the Union Government was sponsoring the measures, took the form of attacks, particularly from Quebec but also from the Maritimes and the West, aimed at Article X of the League Covenant, by which "The Members of the League undertake to respect and preserve as against external aggression the territorial integrity and existing political independence of all Members of the League."

Now the striking thing was that, unknown to Parliament, the Canadian peace delegation had also attacked Article X, even before it became the target of Wilson's enemies in the United States. As early as February, Borden's Minister of Justice, C. J. Doherty, had drawn up and circulated in the Canadian delegation a memorandum condemning this commitment to maintaining what time might make indefensible. Borden fought the issue at Paris, but failed to alter Wilson's conviction that it was "the heart of the Covenant."

He later faithfully secured approval of it in the Canadian Parliament, but for the next four years Canada tried continuously, if unsuccessfully, to have it deleted or substantially amended in the League itself. The Article meanwhile had proved to be the chief effective obstacle to American adherence to the League. Canada's almost united stand in this matter owed something to factions, something to fears of impairment in her national status, something to reflection of a common North American mood, a good deal to Quebec bitterness against the Union Government, but most of all to an inclination to withdraw from the confusions and tensions of international affairs.

Canadian isolationism during the twenty years after World War I was an exceedingly complex thing. It was palliated by membership in the League, but in 1938, J. W. Dafoe of Winnipeg, the Canadian journalist who had done most to bring their international position to the attention of his people, took a skeptical view of that saving grace.

The comfortable idea took possession of the Canadian mind that the war era was over and that permanent peace was guaranteed by the League of Nations, an institution for which they had a vague detached regard resting upon a mysterious belief that it had occult means for keeping the peace without any obligation resting upon its member nations to see that it had either the power or the will to enforce any such programme on a turbulent world.

Canadian isolationism was consciously and unconsciously reinforced by the isolationism of the United States and by the very conditional commitment of Great Britain to collective security.

At bottom, however, it was rooted in individual Canadians' sense of identity with a unique place that was Canada and with ways of life there that seemed not only different from, but preferable to, ways of life elsewhere. That kind of particularism was neither restricted to Canada nor unusual in its assumptions of moral superiority, fears of foreign contamination, and reluctance to attempt to understand other peoples. Yet insulation by Atlantic, Arctic, and Pacific, and the habits of depending on the British navy and the Monroe Doctrine for protection made Canada much more negative and passive than positive and active in international affairs, much given to urging less happily placed nations to follow her peaceable example, and much obsessed with her domestic affairs. The *Canadiens,* who had been in Canada longest and whom circumstances had separated from France, Great Britain, the United States, and English-speaking Canada, behaved almost instinctively in isolationist ways. And after 1918 their sixty-five seats in the federal Parliament normally constituted an almost solid block which no prime minister or government could safely ignore.

If one thinks of Canada then as being involved in three associations —with Britain and the other dominions, with the League of Nations, and with the United States—her attitude towards all three was almost the same. Americans inveighed against "entangling alliances." Canadians cried "no advance commitments." This was particularly noticeable during Canada's resolute resistance to efforts made by France and her friends to create some substitute for the Anglo-American protective guaranty to France that had disappeared with the American withdrawal from international responsibilities.

As in the case of Doherty's objection to Article X, Canadians, "keenly alive to the horror that was involved in the World War," looked "with a critical eye indeed" on proposed arrangements "so easily susceptible of being read as making everybody's wars their wars." Moreover they began to reinforce their own withdrawal by the belief that the withdrawal of the United States made it difficult, perhaps almost impossible in some cases, for Canada to pursue courses diametrically contrary to those of her mighty neighbor.

THE SHELVING OF THE ANGLO-JAPANESE ALLIANCE

The foregoing circumstances, and a few others, made understandable Canada's success in suspending the renewal of the Anglo-Japanese Alliance in 1921. They also explained why at that time there were British and Australasian charges that Canada had become a mouthpiece for the United States. The whole incident was so unusual in its general character, its particular circumstances, and the behavior of the actors in it that it demands special attention.

In effect, Canada, at first single-handed, checked and altered the previously determined direction of British and imperial foreign policy. The principal agent in the matter was the Canadian prime minister, Arthur Meighen, whose sentiments and bearing had hitherto seemed to be distinctly more pro-British than pro-American. The United States disliked the alliance because, although an Anglo-American treaty of September, 1914, precluded its operation in overt conflict between Japan and the United States, it seemed to tolerate Japanese aggression against China. Canadian sentiment, with minor exceptions, followed the same line. Yet Meighen's remarkable feat in 1921 was neither pro-British nor pro-American. Like his master Borden's work, it was pro-Canadian.

The independent Canadian line of action may well have emerged from exasperation at the diplomatic gossip in Geneva and other centers during the winter of 1920–21 to the effect that the renewal of the Anglo-Japanese Alliance would certainly dispel any likelihood that the rest of the world might have to dance to the piping of an Anglo-American partnership. The gifted legal advisor of the Department of External Affairs, Mr. Loring F. Christie, explored the situation in London on his way home to Canada and, probably after consultations with Borden, enlisted the prime minister.

As early as February, Mr. Meighen set to work to fulfill his and indeed most Canadians' conception of Canada's most useful role— fostering Anglo-American understanding—by advocating a general conference about Pacific affairs. Borden had been most emphatic at the councils of the empire in expressing the basic need for understanding with the United States, thereby earning the distrust of Prime Minister W. M. Hughes of Australia. By his own account he told them that "if the future policy of the British Empire meant working in co-operation with some European nation as against the United States, that policy could not reckon on the approval or the support of Canada," and "that the best asset we could bring home from the war would be future good relations between the British Empire and the United States."

Correspondence with London about a number of Canadian suggestions got Meighen nowhere, but in June a conference of dominion prime ministers was to meet the British government, professedly to consider the formalities needed to recognize the changed imperial constitutional relationships. When the conference met, the tangled constitutional problem was quickly and to general relief pushed into the background and foreign policy moved into its place.

Lord Curzon put on, during two sessions, one of his most monumental performances, a full-dress rehearsal of world affairs, building up to the necessity of renewing the Anglo-Japanese Alliance, long ago redrafted to preclude Anglo-American war and now revised in acceptable League of Nations form. Japan had observed it even beyond the bond and with great benefit to the empire during the war; the Japanese were a peculiarly sensitive people and failure to renew might excite their vengefulness; and they had been meticulously correct and helpful in the new apparatus of collective security under the League. The United States had withdrawn from world affairs and could not be depended upon. Japan was the only substitute available to exercise her strength beneficially in the Pacific area. The Committee on Imperial Defence, the British Cabinet and the armed services, Australia, New Zealand, South Africa, India—the whole conference and its auxiliaries favored renewal, except that Meighen took the opposite view.

Meighen had first earned a reputation as a successful criminal lawyer in Manitoba fifteen years earlier; he was a redoubtable fighter, quick to detect and exploit his opponents' weaknesses; and he was at his best in cutting to pieces a generally or uncritically accepted view. The case he had been presenting since February was simple, direct, and forcible, and, if he was right in thinking that it would draw the United States back into active participation in world affairs, Curzon's case was by comparison ponderous, retrospective, roundabout, and fatally oblivious of the fact that the United States had become the world's greatest power.

Meighen wanted to put the bilateral alliance on the shelf and work for a multilateral Pacific agreement in which the United States would have to be involved and through which, the alliance gone, Anglo-American understanding might be increased, not diminished. Moreover the occasion could serve to terminate the tacit toleration which Britain had extended to Japanese economic and territorial aggression at the expense of prostrate China. Multilateralism in the Pacific would be much more in harmony with League principles than bilateralism. And, of course, every degree of improved Anglo-American understanding meant many degrees of improvement in Canada's international position.

The violence and venom with which Hughes greeted Meighen's cool performance seem to have shocked Lloyd George into a rapid reversal. He had hitherto been having to divide his energies and attention between the conference and a coal strike, the Irish problem, and Egyptian unrest. Now, while a docile Curzon began to recompose the British case in Meighen's terms, the British prime minister deftly and forcefully wheeled the conference (except a baffled Hughes) in the new direction. The co-operative Lord Chancellor (Birkenhead) excelled himself in demonstrating how legally possible and meritorious the turnabout was.

A week later, the British imperial proposal was blended with the hitherto secret plans of the American Secretary of State, C. E. Hughes, towards similar ends, chiefly in the interest of naval disarmament, and the Powers were invited to meet in Washington. Canada came near to being overlooked during the Washington Conference, but that did not matter greatly, for the emergent Four Power Treaty initiated naval disarmament by the famous ratio of $5:5:3:1.75:1.675$ for Great Britain, the United States, Japan, France, and Italy; and the Nine-Power Treaty bound its signatories to respect the sovereign integrity of China and to uphold the principle of the Open Door there. Moreover, Senator Henry Cabot Lodge, once President Wilson's implacable opponent, dragooned the American Senate into ratifying the treaties with only a few grumbling reservations. Canada did not have to pay for Anglo-American understanding at the Washington Conference of 1921–22 as she had at the Washington Conference of 1871. The ghost of Macdonald must have envied Meighen.

❧ THE EMERGENCE OF KING

Meighen's achievement was not only the unique example in Canada's history of ability to bring her two great associates together by making one of them change its mind, but it was also the high-water mark of the positive Canadian action that had begun in August, 1914. In December Meighen and the Conservatives were overwhelmed in a general election, and the premiership passed to Mr. William Lyon Mackenzie King, who, after Laurier's death, had been chosen leader of the Liberals in 1919 by the unprecedented method of a national party convention.

For reasons to be discussed in the next chapter, Mr. King and his

Liberals did not enjoy a plurality in a House now divided among three parties, but they were the largest group and the Conservatives were the smallest. During the succeeding thirty years, King was to achieve a success in parliamentary leadership unequaled in the history of parliaments, largely because he best personified in domestic and international affairs a blend of the cautious, conservative, retiring inclinations of his compatriots. The adventurousness of 1921 was put into storage.

Since King lived and moved behind a dense screen of tedious verbiage, the real and imagined contradictions in his personality and his career have not yet been resolved into an accepted characterization or estimate of his statesmanship. Although passionately concerned with family and with his own descent from one grandfather who led the radicals and the other who served with the British regulars during the Rebellion of 1837, he himself remained a bachelor. A devoted patriot who bequeathed practically the whole of his large fortune to the nation, he escaped and avoided the tense issues of 1911-19 by electoral defeats in 1911 and 1917 and by serving as Director of Industrial Research for the American Rockefeller Foundation.

An expert in industrial relations in the United States, Great Britain, and Canada from 1896 onwards, he was always well in the rear of the advanced views in these matters, indeed in social legislation generally. The most astute and ruthless parliamentarian of his day, he developed almost a contempt for Parliament, committing the nation without consulting it, and in various ways subordinating it to the Executive.

An inordinate public speaker and private recorder in his field of politics, he could not bring himself to express precisely what he had distilled from the mash, but imbedded it so obscurely in masses of words as often to baffle even shrewd parliamentary journalists and often to serve years later as the triumphantly resurrected "principle" upon which to base some disconcerting new move. A man who yearned after friendship, his inability to lay himself open or to take for granted unliked but quite ordinary idiosyncrasies in others made him seem too cold, aloof, and intolerant for comradeship and conviviality.

One could go on with a catalog of such contradictions and doubtless historians and others will do so for a long time to come. The principal tactical clues to King's retention of power were, on the one hand, his rare ability, even under expert goading, to be inert, not to "cross bridges," not to commit himself, his party, or his country in advance; and, on the other, a shrewd readiness to adopt planks taken from his opponents' platforms at moments when he judged that he could both weaken them and strengthen himself politically by doing so.

His chief claim to statesmanship was his unremitting loyalty to the

dream of the radicals of the 1840's, of Macdonald, and of Laurier—
a Canada united by tolerance and compromise of the great ethnic
differences. He retreated instantly from any internal or external situation that threatened it. For this cause King was willing to risk anything
short of violence—parliamentary upheaval, local civil dissension, national or personal humiliation and abuse. By it he was able to bring
Canada through World War II perceptibly less rent and divided than
by World War I and to hand over the reins to a *Canadien* successor who
ventured to commit Canada to more positive courses.

CHAPTER XXVII

Vulnerable Strength (1919-29)

World War I required long and often painful digesting by Canada, indeed the process took about seven years. Almost everything had been changed, not so much in nature as in magnitude. Thus the schism between Quebec and much of the rest of the country had been broadened and yet the rapid industrialization and urbanization of Quebec were giving her many of the same problems and much of the same economic outlook as her ethnic enemy, Ontario.

The economic "maturity" of central Canada in finance and industry was based to a large degree on the development of the West and the acquiescence of the Maritimes. For at least a decade after 1911 the grievances of those "marginal" regions were met by what they considered neglect.

The Canadian farmer, forest worker, or fisherman, bewildered by price changes and self-righteous about his objections to conscription, felt that he had been made a fool of by the protectionists in 1911 and by both the old parties since. Trade unionists, casting about for explanations of their comparative weakness in an industrialized society, blamed it on the law, the courts, and the Industrial Disputes Act, and, instead of settling down to the hard work of recruitment and organization within the structure they possessed, became inquisitive about syndicalist and communist panaceas emanating from Europe, Australia, and the United States. The ease with which the Union Government had been formed heightened many men's suspicions that there was no great difference between Liberals and Conservatives.

⚜ ECONOMIC CHANGES

Probably the single greatest factor in Canada's long unease was her now immense dependence on the ability to export goods profitably. This was the chief price she had paid for her steep increase in productivity since 1896. For a little less than two years after the war, the world's appetite for Canadian products and its real or imagined capacity to pay for them remained very high, indeed inflation increased more steeply than during the war. When the inevitable crash came, Canadian producers, in competition with other harassed producers, had to adapt themselves to what the consumer could or would pay for what Canada had to sell, in amounts far and away beyond her own people's capacity to consume. Such adjustments were notoriously hard upon major exporting countries, much harder on Canada, for instance, than on the United States.

Canada's postwar ups and downs might be summarized as follows: boom to the autumn of 1920, deep depression until two years later, modest recovery during 1923, considerable depression during 1924, recovery during 1925, and another boom, 1926–29. Primary producers (in fishing, farming, and forestry, rather than in mining) suffered most, employment in services crept up on employment in manufacturing, and female employment steadily increased. The most disconcerting circumstances were the rapidity and violence of the economic fluctuations.

The briefest way to demonstrate what happened to the economy during the decade, 1919–29, is by means of some statistics.

When one looks beyond these statistics, a number of significant economic changes appear. For one thing, whereas the debt of the federal government rose sharply from 1914 to 1920, to flatten out and even decline by 1930, we know that the debts of the provinces and municipalities grew at a smooth, inexorable rate that nothing seemed to interrupt. That is, local governments were constantly assuming responsibilities of many sorts that they could not pay for outright from local revenues.

For another, although the economic triangle of Canada, the United States, and Great Britain was still maintained, the United States figured more powerfully and Great Britain less powerfully in the Canadian economy. The growing Canadian investment abroad, for instance, was chiefly in the United States, and, as Canada's positive trade balance with Great Britain grew, her negative trade balance with the United States grew also.

One hopeful sign for greater Canadian freedom in commercial action was the slightly increasing proportion of her trade with countries other than her two traditional associates. Not many observers noticed that the Canadian economy as a whole had become "a mature debtor," that is, was reducing its relative indebtedness abroad and in fact lending there.

The continued loss of population by emigration was disconcerting.

Item	1920	1925	1929
	(All figures, except percentages, are stated in hundred thousands)		
National wealth	22,195(1921)	25,673	31,276
National debt	2,249	2,417	2,226
National revenue	350	352	460
National expenditure	786	351	389
British capital invested in Canada	2,577	2,346	2,774
American capital invested in Canada	2,128	3,219	3,794
Canadian capital invested abroad	942	954	1,958
Canadian balance of international payments (excluding movements of capital)	−216	+250	−114
Movements of capital	+309	−34	+80
Population	8.631	9.269	9.797
Immigration	.117	.111	.168
Emigration (Decade, 1911–21)	1.298	(Decade, 1921–31)	.926
Net value of production	3,682	3,325	3,947
			(1928–4,123)
Chief categories of production (by percentages of net value)	Agric. 41	Mfg. 41	Mfg. 51
	Mfg. 33	Agric. 40	Agric. 26
	Forestry 11	Forestry 9	Constr. 10
			Forestry 9
			Mining 8
Leading provinces in production (by percentages of net value)	Ontario 38	Ontario 38	Ontario 42
	Quebec 26	Quebec 24	Quebec 27
	Saskatchewan 8	Saskatchewan 11	British Columbia 8
Canadian exports to Great Britain	489(39.5%)	396(37%)	430(31.5%)
Canadian imports from Great Britain	126(11.9%)	151(19%)	194(15.3%)
Canadian exports to the United States	464(37.4%)	417(39%)	500(36.7%)
Canadian imports from the United States	801(75.3%)	510(64%)	868(68.6%)
Canadian exports, all countries	1,239	1,069	1,364
Canadian imports, all countries	1,065	797	1,266

Most of it was to the United States, but the movement back to Great Britain and to other parts of Europe was also substantial. The American restrictions on immigration after 1920 contained quotas for Europeans, but not for native North Americans. This had the effect of accelerating in Canada the displacement of the Canadian-born by less demanding immigrants. The much swifter and more assured rebound of the United States from the postwar depression made opportunity there seem boundless while it was distinctly limited in Canada.

Probably at least a quarter of the million and a quarter persons who were "missing" from the Census of 1931 were Canadian-born emigrants to the United States. The immigrants to Canada who managed in one way or another to get across the American border were, of course, usually less valuable to Canada than her lost natives, a high proportion of whom belonged to the professions. Within Canada the relative movement of population inward to Quebec and Ontario corresponded to central Canada's continued possession of about two-thirds of the nation's wealth and strength and voting power.

The kinds of products which Canada principally exported were revealing of both the strengths and the vulnerabilities of a country that characteristically exported over a third of its production. In 1920, the percentages of total exports ran: vegetable products 34, animal products 25, wood products 17, with iron and its products next at 7. In 1925, the corresponding figures revealed the impact of pulp and paper production: vegetable products 41, wood products 24, and animal products 15, but nonferrous metals and their products, with 8, had moved past iron and its products, with 5. In 1929 the order ran: vegetable products 47, wood products 21, animal products 12, nonferrous metals and their products 8, and iron and its products 6.

Closely related to the increase in pulp and paper plants, the growth in the production of hydroelectric power (over 96 per cent of the total electric power capacity) was truly startling, for installed horsepower grew from 2,516,000 in 1920 to 4,338,000 in 1925 and 5,717,000 in 1929, and the corresponding generation of kilowatt hours was 5,497,-000, 10,110,000, and 17,963,000. The capital investment in these central electric stations was very large and rose from $448,000,000 in 1920 to $1,056,000,000 in 1929 with no end in sight. The production of this "white coal" began to cut down Canada's relative dependence on imported coal and coke about 1918, for the consumption of them fell from 21,611,000 tons then to 16,332,000 in 1925, and was only 17,-724,000 in the boom year, 1929. Normally well over half the Canadian consumption of coal and coke was imported, chiefly from the United States.

Grain growers' co-operation.—This was a period when the grain growers attempted to unite and break free from the discrimination exercised by the grain companies, the elevator owners, and the railways. The long slow work of education and experiment, which owed much to the United States and to immigrant Americans, had begun seriously about 1901 in a number of regional grain growers' associations. By 1909 they had a manual of information and action in their journal, the *Grain Growers' Guide*. The Grain Growers' Grain Company of 1905, which had fought its co-operative way into politics and some ill-judged purchase of elevators before 1914, learned during the war that the state could control prices for the benefit of the consumer and saw no reason why, after the war, it could not do so for the benefit of the producer.

Out of the price collapse of 1920 and an opinionated and complicated mixture of producers' co-operation and farmers' party politics there emerged in 1923 and 1924 the so-called Wheat Pools of the plains provinces. They organized co-operatively the collection, storage in their own or leased elevators, and orderly sale of a large proportion of western wheat. During the crop year 1923–24, with only the Alberta organization at work, membership was 25,601, acreage 2,416,413, and bushels handled 34,218,980, but by 1928–29, with three provincial pools in operation, the figures were 131,728, 16,152,904, and 244,-248,200.

The pools then operated 1634 country elevators and eleven terminal elevators on the Great Lakes and the Pacific. Their selling agency sent grain to ninety ports in nineteen countries, and the total turnover was over $288,000,000. They had their own cereal research station, had entered the insurance business, and were riding "high, wide, and handsome," when the inflated world economy collapsed in 1929.

The railroads.—It was inevitable that another deep economic concern of the time should be with the railroads, for no magic could alter the fact that the Canadian producer had to ship his goods long distances by land or water or both. Someone had to get to work on making a rational, unified system out of the hodgepodge brought together in the Canadian National Railways, and it had to be done in the face of demands for special consideration by local voters and local politicians. The C.P.R., too, had to consider the competition it faced and prime its representatives to defend it against real or potential unfairness.

The man chosen for the C.N.R. task was Sir Henry Thornton. He had made such a notable reputation with the Pennsylvania Railroad that he had been called in by the London and Northeastern in England and had been knighted for his success there. To Canada, in October, 1922, he brought great abilities, dynamic drive, and a determination to keep up with the C.P.R. He was given a remarkably free hand (and access to the national treasury), and he proceeded to establish higher standards in everything, from running schedules and new branch lines to dining-car service and new hotels.

Only by his systematic reduction of duplication did his regime differ from that of the boom decade before 1913. His creed was: "The success of the National System . . . is not entirely to be obtained by methods generally applied to railways which are not producing returns, *viz.,* improving the physical condition and operating methods—it is a matter of building up the country to support the railways." His good fortune was the economic upturn towards the end of 1924 which was accompanied by a marked increase in immigration. Between 1922 and his resignation in 1930, he greatly improved the C.N.R. (and the C.P.R., by response), and at the same time reduced the ratio of operating costs to operating receipts from about 90 per cent to about 80 per cent.

During 1925–30, inclusive, Canada added over 480 miles of new railroad line a year, meanwhile scrapping some old mileage, so that the total rose from 40,352 to 42,049. The upper and lower Peace River country in Alberta and British Columbia were reached and served, although neither the upper Peace River line nor the Pacific Great Eastern was pushed on to connect with the other or with the C.N.R. route from Edmonton to Prince Rupert.

Manitoba's long agitation for a line to Hudson Bay which would give Montreal competition by its shorter land and sea routes to Liverpool was met in 1926 by the government's decision to repair the "Muskeg Special" line from The Pas to a point about seventy-five miles from Port Nelson, but to divert it to the more desirable harbor at Churchill and to build a grain elevator there. The first two cargoes of wheat by that route moved out in 1931, but, in view of the high insurance rates for ships operating on the bay, the whole enterprise was economically unsound.

The province of Ontario also reached out to Hudson Bay by extending its Timiskaming and Northern Ontario (now Ontario Northland) across the National Transcontinental at Cochrane and on to Moosonee, near the old Hudson's Bay Company Moose Factory, a port unimproved for large ships. Both these northern lines became of more importance to forest operations and mining than to the movement of goods to Europe. Toronto, in particular, gained largely from its advantageous connections with the gold, silver, and nonferrous mining activities and the pulp and paper production of northern Ontario and of northwestern Quebec.

A C.N.R. steamship line operated five combined passenger and freight vessels between Halifax and the West Indies, and, under the Maritime Freight Rates Act of 1927, in effect all rail freight from the Maritimes was subsidized by about 20 per cent. The Crowsnest Pass rates on western grains and grain products were suspended from 1918 to 1922, revived, and in 1925 extended to Vancouver in reflection both of the effects of the Panama Canal on that port and of a broadening market for Canadian cereals in the Orient.

Canadian freight rates were, for obvious reasons, the lowest in the world, but the contributions of the taxpayer to make them so did not evoke effective opposition either from the shareholders of the C.P.R. or from competitive railroads in the United States.

Foreign trade.—As always, for most Canadians the economic barometer was the record of foreign trade, and most of them believed that Canada must export more than she imported in order to achieve economic health. Indeed, not until 1926 did the Dominion Bureau of Statistics begin the much more subtle business of attempting to measure all the principal elements in Canada's balance of international payments.

From 1919 to 1929 the picture of external trade was a confused one because of the violent fluctuations in prices, in foreign demand, and in Canada's own production of wheat, that great component in her exports. In bad crop years like 1918–20, 1924, and 1929, the yield fell below 300,000,000 bushels, whereas the average yield was close to 400,000,000 bushels and in 1928 it was 567,000,000. Meanwhile prices did strange tricks, falling steadily from $2.36 a bushel in 1919 to 67 cents in 1923, bouncing back to $1.22 next year and staying above a dollar except in 1928. Other basic commodities had their ups and downs in production and prices, but none of them had quite the spectacular range of wheat.

Great Britain was the great market for Canadian goods, the United States the great market for Canadian purchases. Moreover, since the United States had surplus capital to export and foreign tariff walls to climb, there was a marked increase of American branch factories and enterprises in Canada.

This was an old movement, strong enough to persist through wars and depressions, but it now became very conspicuous, for American firms were doing over a fifth of the manufacturing in Canada. Everyone knew that they almost monopolized the automotive industry; but they also had over 60 per cent of the electrical industry, the rubber industry, and the production of nonferrous metals, and over 40 per cent of nonmetallic minerals, machinery, and chemicals. The Canadian market could take up only part of this production; some of it climbed back over the American tariff wall; but much more went abroad under imperial preferences not extended to the United States.

From the Canadian point of view the advantages lay in the employment of Canadian labor and in the great diversification and deepening of the economy as the American plants progressed from the assembly of imported American parts to more and more outright manufacture in Canada from Canadian materials. The strangest aspect was the obliviousness in the United States to the fact that Canada was rapidly becoming her most important single economic associate, about as important as the combined Latin American countries which figured so largely in American economic discussions.

Canada sold to Great Britain chiefly grains and their products, meats, furs, and dairy products, and bought about 45 per cent as much in return, chiefly textiles, alcoholic beverages, and metal goods. To the United States she sold chiefly newsprint, wood products, animals and animal products, and nonferrous metals and bought three quarters as much again, in a great variety of products, chiefly machinery of all sorts and its parts, coal and petroleum, cotton, fruits, rubber, silk, and so on.

The dependence on the United States for coal, oil, iron, and steel was particularly unwelcome, for it increased in almost direct proportion to increases in Canadian economic activity. The far eastern and far western distribution of Canadian coal seemed a bad geological joke. As E. S. Moore summed it up, "The total production of coal in Canada to the end of 1938 has been less than 600 million short tons, a quantity less than that produced in the United States in one year of maximum production, in spite of the fact that she has the second largest coal resources in the world." The deficiencies in iron ore and oil were galling, and the American lead in the capital and technology of iron- and steel-making seemed irreducible.

Thanks to the degree of multilateral trading in the world, Canada could use her surpluses of sterling to balance her deficits of American dollars. Indeed the movement of goods, money, and services to-and-fro in the economic triangle of Great Britain, the United States, and Canada was the mightiest thing of its kind on earth.

By 1929, inconspicuous but persistent trends were establishing themselves by way of altering the balance of the triangular forces. The industrial growth of the United States and Canada, as compared with Great Britain's relative standstill, created one trend. Britain's weakening position in international trade, partly because of her own defective productivity and partly because of foreign tariffs and quotas, constituted another.

The least apparent, but in the long run to be most important trend, however, was the basic and growing dependence of the United States upon Canadian products as her own natural resources diminished and her consumption increased. The whole picture of the Canadian-American economic relationship was complicated in the extreme, involving as it did unbalanced trading and investment, the rapid increase in Canadian production of gold and its sale in the United States, and the even more rapid expansion of American tourists' expenditures in Canada as the automobile and good roads made travel easier. Tariff wars obscured the underlying circumstances, but what was slowly and irresistibly taking form was an economic interplay analogous to the physical interdependence of inseparable Siamese twins.

🍁 SOCIETY

The cities.—The chief outward sign of the changing Canadian economy was the growth of cities and urban centers. Halifax and Saint John were not great industrial cities, but they gained somewhat from the immense federal expenditures on their harbor installations and from the devices designed to encourage their use as winter ports instead of American Atlantic outlets. The coal, iron, and steel industries near Sydney, Cape Breton, built up that region into an urban cluster even though the greedy market for steel rails had tapered off.

Well up the Saguenay River near Lake St. John, lumber and farming had yielded to hydroelectric power of which the development on an immense scale made the region the most efficient producer of aluminum in the world. Here there sprang up a group of modern towns in the wilderness like the anomalous urban communities that were being created by mining and papermaking at widely scattered points in the otherwise empty Canadian Shield.

Even Quebec City was caught up by urban growth, and industrial slums began to spread across the flatlands along the St. Charles River below the ancient citadel hill. Three Rivers grew as the center of the expanding pulp and paper, power, and chemical industries of the St. Maurice River. Montreal, of course, in itself overshadowed the other cities of Canada, but it was also the core of a huge industrial "conurbation" that spilled off the great island towards the south and west.

Up the Ottawa River, the city of Hull across from the federal capital became the industrial inheritor of the cheap power generated on the neighboring rivers. In Ottawa itself Mackenzie King belatedly brought to life the commission that since 1899 had been supposed to beautify and improve the federal district, but had been unable to make much headway. The Federal District Commission faced serious problems, but as it was given increasing powers and resources it set about ordering the region, developing parks and driveways, and even restraining the eccentricities of federal and other architecture in harmony with the handsome new parliament buildings on the great cliff above the river.

In Ontario, a string of small industrial communities bordered the St. Lawrence and Lake Ontario, but a large metropolitan district, four-fifths the size of Montreal's, centered in Toronto. Hamilton, at the head of the lake, was closely related to another industrial cluster around the Welland Canal and the power development of the Niagara River. Here, distinctly more than elsewhere to the eastward, was an international industrial area, often with American and Canadian branches of the same enterprise within a few miles of each other.

That pattern was emphatically repeated near Windsor, where the Michigan-dominated automotive industry operated on both sides of the river. In both these international areas the "border commuter" became notable, that is, the Canadian or American who traveled daily to work outside his own country. Indeed, better amenities, and the possibility of securing alcoholic beverages, meant that a substantial number of Americans lived in Canada and worked in the United States.

The western urban areas were commercial, financial, and transportation centers for the most part, although some of them contained special industries like milling, meat-packing, smelting, and small industrial assembly plants. The great surprise of the postwar decade was Vancouver's surge in population past Winnipeg to become third among the seven Canadian cities of over 100,000 persons. The Panama Canal had made the tremendous natural resources of British Columbia more available to the world.

In Saskatchewan, Regina had grown to pass almost static Saint John, N.B., and in Alberta, Calgary, with oil and natural gas to bolster its cattle and grain economy, managed to retain a slight lead over Edmonton, the provincial capital, whose connections with the barely exploited North seemed likely to add to its strength. In the West, Thornton's C.N.R. built hotels in Saskatoon and Edmonton that were naturally more modern and appealing than the older C.P.R. ones, and these seemed to presage a greater wealth in the northern section of the Canadian plains than in the arid southern section across which the C.P.R. had been laid out. The C.P.R. launched many branch lines northward in order to feed the old "Main Line."

Social tremors.—The times were feverish, both during the "boom and bust" of 1919–24 and the surging prosperity of 1925–29. So much needed to be done during the first five years after the war and the resources for doing them were felt to be so precarious that the successful civil and military demobilization seemed almost miraculous. Veterans' hospitals were built and manned, pensions services set up, and a notable scheme for soldiers' civil re-establishment operated far better than might have been expected.

The most intractable problems were those connected with the cities. Housing had fallen far in arrears, schools seemed never to catch up with demand, and charitable or semicharitable institutions were hard hit by the inflation. The social difficulties that had been growing before 1914 mushroomed up ominously everywhere after 1918, and municipalities and provinces, distinctly more than the federal government, discovered that they must extend and professionalize all manner of social services, must go into housing, transportation, and other businesses if their citizens demanded it, and must revolutionize their fiscal and financial procedures in order to do such things.

Particularly in thickly settled, industrialized central Canada, the insatiable demand was for expensive hard-surfaced roads for the use of automobiles and motor trucks. Expenditures of all sorts, public and private, acquired an oddly unreal quality for those whose habitual standards had been set before 1914. And then the soaring prosperity of 1925–29 seemed to justify any optimism and to make the older generation's caution ridiculous.

The increasing worldliness of society and its standards accelerated after 1918 in many forms. Social utility or efficiency, for instance, was a generally accepted criterion for action even in the religious sphere and had much to do with the union of most of the Methodist, Presbyterian, and Congregational churches in 1926. "The social gospel," in degrees of intensity that usually varied inversely with the wealth of the congregations, affected both Protestantism and Catholicism, making it difficult for religious leaders to maintain emphasis on other-worldly values and strengthening tendencies towards broadening the churches into elaborate centers for decorous social, educational, entertainment, and even athletic diversions.

French Canada.—The situation in Quebec was especially complex as industrialization and commercialization corroded older values, and, whereas the provincial Liberal government and the church hierarchy could and did accommodate themselves to the alien capital that was transforming the province, the rural clergy and a new school of economic nationalists fought back against "American," "materialist" ways. An ominous anti-Semitism in the Montreal region was evoked by the Jews' success in small business.

The Abbé Lionel Groulx, much influenced by Comte de Gobineau's racism and the antidemocracy of Maurice Barrès and Charles Maurras, emerged as an extreme nationalist leader about 1920, when he became editor of *L'Action Française*. First professor of Canadian history at the University of Montreal, he made the history of *Canadien* "racial" survival the central strand of a cult of antifederal separatism that fired the young students and for some years drew to it a large number of defensive causes—*refrançisation;* the development of *Canadien* labor unions, co-operatives, and credit unions; ultramontanism; corporativism of the Italian or Portuguese type; political authoritarianism; redevelopment of mixed rural economy; and so on.

Gradually, however, as depression died away and King re-created a national Liberal party, the alliance broke up. The gifted and cultivated Edouard Montpetit gave his voice and pen to pleas for better education, particularly economic, so that French Canada could take its proper place in the nation. The economist Esdras Minville devoted himself to creating in his native Gaspé the mixed economy he advocated.

Unhyphenated Canadianism (*Canadiens tout courts*) rose again, and a notable group of men began to contribute purposefully to a Quebec that should acknowledge itself a part of Canada—the anthropologist Marius Barbeau; Ivanhoe Caron, Thomas Chapais, and other historians; the Belgian Henri Laureys at the *Ecole des hautes études commerciales,* Augustin Frigon at the *École polytechnique,* and Frère Marie-Victorin at the Botanical Garden which he created as a teaching center and a breathing space in the midst of a Montreal working-class district; Robert Choquette and other poets; novelists like Adjutor Rivard and Félix-Antoine Savard whose devotion to their land was not exclusive; or that stormy petrel in journalism and letters, the Byronesque Jean-Charles Harvey.

English-speaking Canada.—In English-speaking Canada there was somewhat franker surrender to materialistic standards, more buying of automobiles (which for the young, at least, supplanted the traditional home veranda), more transfer from the responsibilities of houses to the irresponsibilities (and anonymities) of apartments, and more expenditures on amusements or on rapidly obsolescent radio receivers, music machines, and so on. Men's ideas of the desirable amenities were changing and social institutions such as the family, the home, and the neighborhood were changing in the process.

Many newspapers, or "chains" of them, became mere businesses. Those which prospered mightily gobbled up others, went into the broadcasting business, and set out to titillate and entertain. Either they substituted neutral tones for their former editorial partisanship or they indulged in such extravagances and contradictions of editorial policy that their readers counted on them more for distraction, some underlining of their prejudices, and a modicum of world news than for sober discussion of Canadian affairs. There were, of course, marked exceptions in all the provinces, but they found it hard to maintain their standards, circulations, and advertising revenues against the commercialized journals. In general Canadian communities got about what they deserved in journalism.

Aesthetic and intellectual developments were curiously uneven. The universities and colleges grew mightily. Canadians did not often contribute conspicuously to scientific research, but one discovery, that of the insulin treatment of diabetes by the team of F. G. Banting, C. H. Best, and J. J. Macleod, brought Canada its first Nobel Prize.

There was a curious fallow period in literature, a kind of pause to search for new and native soundings which was to be rewarded during the next decade by a notable outburst of poetry. The one great exception at this time was the rapid revelation of the gifts in narrative, fantasy, and imagination of E. J. Pratt, whose five volumes of poetry between 1923 and 1930, devoted to non-Canadian subjects for the most part, won him an international audience. His sense of the sea, of human energy and heroism, of man's technology, and of extravagant fun made him a unique figure.

In scholarly writing, as perhaps might have been expected, the most notable feature of the new Canada was the extensive reinterpretation of Canadian history. The students of constitutional development, headed by W. P. M. Kennedy, had much to work on along old lines of interest, but the principal new note was the immensely influential work of H. A. Innis in economic history and political economy from 1923 onwards. Adam Shortt and O. D. Skelton had been the notable pioneers in this field, but their world of scholarship had been unresponsive. Now the moment seemed ripe, and a large band of researchers and writers embarked on the re-explanation of Canadian developments of all kinds, using the overlooked economic tool with increasing knowledge and assurance and starting a flow of historical works of unprecedentedly high quality.

There were signs, too, of an awareness of the North American continental factors that a jaundiced attitude towards the United States had hitherto excluded. It was perhaps a tribute to the discipline of the long road which Canada had followed to nationhood that, on arrival, her historians did not succumb merely to nativism, but instead set their country's story in its French, British, and North American traditions.

The great aesthetic excitement of the time was caused by the painting and other graphic arts of the Group of Seven, which represented a clean break with the academic tradition and an exultant emphasis on the Canadian scene—the Shield, the mountains, the cities, and the countryside, seen usually in clear light, rich primary colors, and patterned strong outlines. There had been premonitions of their work in the notable Canadian war pictures assembled by Lord Beaverbrook, but the public was plainly shocked in 1919 when the Group first exhibited together. Associated with the Group were F. Carmichael, L. S. Harris, A. Y. Jackson, F. Johnston, A. Lismer, J. E. H. MacDonald, Tom Thomson, and F. H. Varley. Johnston left the Group early and there were some subsequent shifts. Their acknowledged leader, Tom Thomson, had recently been drowned on one of the solitary canoe trips during which he had for long struggled to find original, successful expression for the unique Canadian scene. Although he and the group found what was at first too much for the public to swallow, by the end of the decade their strong and often studiously simple modes had entered Canadian consciousness; people were buying Canadian pictures with pride and appreciation, and new artists found encouragement and instruction. Canada began to be uniquely represented in foreign exhibitions and galleries and, the note of independence once struck, her artists of all kinds began to feel less need for particularism.

❦ NATIONAL POLITICS

The national politics of this decade, the beginning of "the King era," were tortuous and infinitely ramified, but they might be roughly summarized as the rise, decline, and containment of a farmers' third party movement in the face of King's unobtrusive, cautious, astute, and finally successful re-creation of a national Liberal party. The Conservatives, less patient, pliable, and adroit, and saddled with the unpopularity of conscription, failed in the same effort and, except for one term during the depression of the thirties, did not in this era succeed in finding a unifying and persuasive political gospel.

In fact, it might be argued that with the enormous rise in the responsibilities and activities of the provincial governments and their often sharply differentiated interests, national parties could succeed only by blurring the outlines of policy, compromising local differences in vague generalities, and, once in power, managing the federal patronage shrewdly. F. H. Underhill's comment that "Mr. King for twenty-five years was the leader who divided us least," hit the bull's-eye, and it was significantly followed by his discussion of the close analogies to Canada in American federal politics, particularly the modern expression of Calhoun's "concurrent majorities" in the form of national parties composed of loosely allied, significant, yet possibly inconsistent interest groups.

The challenge of progressivism.—The great challenge to the Conservatives and the Liberals after 1918 was the abrupt emergence of a redoubtable farmers' movement. It, too, was made up of local parties, but they were alike in representing agrarian revolts, roughly analogous to, and indeed borrowing considerably from, American rural Progressivism. This appearance of a class party roughly coincided with the organization in 1921 of the Canadian Labor Party and with the Winnipeg General Strike of 1919.

The latter grew out of an attempt by metal workers to secure the right of collective bargaining at a time when hysterical fears of Bolshevism were easily enlarged and when government was easily convinced that revolution was being fomented. Labor in Winnipeg had abundant just causes for dissatisfaction and, in spite of some radical efforts to marshal it behind the Australian and American syndicalist banners of One Big Union and Industrial Workers of the World, it was proceeding in a Canadian or British fashion to secure a right denied it. Sympathetic strikes in industry and the public services forced the strike committee to take over several municipal functions. Labor's clearly peaceful intent was then challenged forcibly by the Royal Canadian Mounted Police, which had developed a political branch during the war. When other public agencies took the offensive instead of attempting conciliation and understanding, the strike collapsed in confusions and uneasy second thoughts which showed how thoroughly the situation had been mishandled.

For the interesting and varied details of Canadian Progressivism the reader must be referred to W. L. Morton's careful study of the movement and to W. K. Rolph's biography of Henry Wise Wood. There were at least as many kinds of farmers' movements as there were provinces in Canada, but a central theme persisted. As E. A. Partridge, "the fiery old prophet" of the Western movement and moving spirit in founding the Grain Growers' Grain Company and the *Grain Growers' Guide,* phrased it:

The history of Canada since Confederation—the outcome of a politico-commercial, or a commercio-political conspiracy, if consequences are any indication of motive—has been a history of heartless robbery of both the people of the Maritimes and of the Prairie Sections of Canada by the Big "Vested" Interests—so called from the size of their owners' vests—of the politically and financially stronger Central Provinces.

This theme served as a magnet that drew to it all sorts of discontents—antiprotectionism, anticonscriptionism, hostility to big business and big finance and their reputed dominance and corruption of the two old parties, worry over rural depopulation, and even such apparently remote causes as evangelical religious movements, feminism, prohibition, and various forms of puritanism. In several senses, Progressivism was a subconscious revolt against many of the accompaniments of the increasing predominance of modern industrialized society over the individual.

Deeply imbedded in the movement was a set of political notions that were part of an ancient pattern, but which reached Canada largely from American Progressivism. These notions represented a passionate democratic revolt against political bigness and against the discipline of the party caucus that so often compelled a member of a national party to vote in direct contradiction of the wishes of his constituents.

The radical Progressives, particularly H. W. Wood's followers in Alberta, rejected party government, even their own, in favor of group government, or thought they did. They insisted that the constituencies choose their candidates; many of them wanted to institute the direct political action of initiative, referendum, and recall; in brief, they aimed to implicate the ordinary man nearly continuously in the conduct of political affairs locally, provincially, nationally, and, presumably, internationally. In effect, delegation was to supplant representation.

On grounds of size and contiguity, the farmers could succeed in single constituencies and in single provinces. The coincidence of farmers' movements all across Canada between 1917 and 1926 even made them look like a third party at Ottawa, but their intense individualism there, their refusal to be bound by their own caucus, seemed anarchical to the rest of Canada and made them a fairly easy prey to the disciplined behavior and sustained focus on power of King's Liberals.

"The Progressive Movement," wrote T. A. Crerar, in 1922, who had grown up with it, "particularly in Western Canada, was built largely on the individual Member of Parliament, that is, he was to be free from the old party machinery and to follow his own judgment." Three years later, Grant Dexter, the able parliamentary reporter of the *Winnipeg Free Press,* said flatly, "No one pretended that a vote in caucus bound the group as a whole." Such tactics were better calculated to prevent government than to facilitate it, unless Canada was prepared to abandon the two-party conventions of her traditional parliamentary system—the leader and caucus system that had reconciled local differences for almost a century—in favor of the Continental European mode of group government.

After the Union Government and the general election of 1917 had dissolved old party loyalties and roused new discontents, farmers' revolts began popping up all across Canada, and in November, 1918, the Canadian Council of Agriculture formulated and adopted "The

New National Policy" in avowed opposition to Macdonald's National
Policy of 1878 which had become the Liberals' policy after 1896.

Yet it was notable that the farmers sought representation rather than
the responsibilities of power. After ominous and substantial upsurges
in the Maritimes and Quebec, their movements there died away for
lack of organization and of consolidation in a national movement. In
the Ontario election of October, 1919, however, the United Farmers
were embarrassed to discover that they had 43 seats, the Liberals 28,
the Conservatives 6, Labor 12, and Independents 2, and, as the largest
group, the U.F.O. must form a government. They did so in an understanding with Labor and governed somewhat eccentrically until 1923,
when their internal schism over solidarity as contrasted to occupational
representation, their diffidence in national affairs, and some gross mal-
administration brought about their defeat.

In Manitoba and Saskatchewan, reform governments which were
loyally local, substantially agrarian, and moderately reformist managed
to stem the farmers' revolt fairly successfully by astute concessions to
their aims. In fact, a powerful Manitoba group entertained strong
hopes of creating a new and liberal Liberal party until King defeated
them by various means.

Alberta, "the farmers' last frontier," and the most American part
of Canada, proved to be the stronghold of Progressivism in its economic
and its peculiar political aspects. Henry Wise Wood, a native of Missouri, educated as a Campbellite preacher and a participant in the
American Farmers' Alliance and the Populist Party in the 80's and
90's, was the Moses of the movement. His early preference for economic over political activities by farmers' organizations had developed
into the idea of occupational representation and representatives' direct
responsibility to constituents. It worked in Alberta, where the United
Farmers of Alberta governed from 1921 to 1935, when they were overwhelmed by a new political sect, William Aberhart's Social Credit.

Nationally, however, Thomas Alexander Crerar of Manitoba, the
first leader of the Progressive party of Canada, parted from Wood's
uncompromising localism when he declared, on accepting the office
in December, 1920: "A man's duty lies largely to the people who elect
him, but in a larger, and I venture to say a more complete sense, his
duty lies to the whole people of Canada." Mackenzie King at once
slammed a wedge into that crack in the farmers' edifice and hammered
it until he had separated the Crerar and Wood groups and won enough
of the former to create a national Liberal party. In Morton's words,
"the Crerarites were reformers only; the Woodites, though constitu-

tionalists in profession and practice, were in concept revolutionaries."

Mackenzie King's response.—King's course was slow, often subterranean, and shrewd, marked by natural and by calculated confusions, many proffered bargains by way of Cabinet or other office, and exploitation of weaknesses and differences. The national election of 1921, in which Meighen had committed the Conservatives to protectionism and King had studiously avoided commitments on the subject (indeed he had been plainly contradictory), was a kind of contest among Meighen, King, and Crerar for a formula that would win the nation. Meighen's protectionism and his conspicuous appeals for national unity could not counterbalance Quebec's will to revenge for conscription. (In fact, Bourassa supported the forlorn cause of the United Farmers of Quebec!) The West and most of Ontario seemed dedicated to Progressivism. What hope could there be of a national party majority?

The results of the election showed "a Liberal East, a Progressive West, and a divided Ontario." The Liberals had 117 seats, 90 of them east of the Ottawa and the few others in Ontario and British Columbia, with only three on the plains. The Progressives had 65 seats, all but one west of the Ottawa (24 from Ontario). The Conservatives had 50 seats from industrial and eastern Ontario, Vancouver Island, and the lower St. John Valley of New Brunswick. Yet the Progressives declined the role of official opposition, handing it over to the Conservatives by default.

There was thus no national party, not even a national farmers' party, in spite of the omens of the past four years. For a while, at least, Canada was destined to wrestle with the grave problems of postwar depression depending upon a Parliament in which most of the Progressives felt perfectly free to vote for or against the government and to put the wishes of their immediate constituents above national considerations. King knew, however, that they would be reluctant to throw him out and make Meighen prime minister.

In general, the Manitoba and Saskatchewan Progressives drifted back towards the Liberals, the Ontario movement crumpled through dissension and disgrace, and only Alberta held out stubbornly. Yet Progressivism was not the only political problem that King had to face: national finance, problems of industrialization and urbanization, variations in Quebec's separatism, the social legislation that increasing collectivism required, wheat-marketing, national railroad policy—a long catalog might easily be compiled. The Senate, moreover, contained a substantial Conservative majority.

In these circumstances, King took as little positive legislative action as possible, meanwhile "building political fences" in a determined, if not very promising, effort to strengthen his party. By the summer of 1925, after the tide had on the whole set against him in provincial elections and federal by-elections, he decided to ask for a new mandate at elections in October. There appeared to be no general issue except King's really eloquent appeal for national unity, and meanwhile the Conservatives had carried Ontario, Nova Scotia, and New Brunswick. The West was groaning under the effects of the bad crop of 1924, low prices for wheat, and a burden of debt incurred during the period of inflated prices.

The second and third rounds.—The outcome of the confused campaign of 1925 was a "moral" victory for the Conservatives, whose 117 members came from every province, although only four were from unforgiving Quebec. King's Liberals had won only 101 seats, 59 of them in Quebec. Progressivism, with two exceptions, had become purely the revolt of the plains and even there had contracted to 22 members. Now, however, these dissidents possessed the definite balance of power.

In these circumstances, King announced that he would exercise his constitutional right to meet Parliament in January, 1926, and seek its verdict. Meanwhile he set to work bargaining for Progressive support. Meighen used the interval to woo Quebec by a speech at Hamilton whose substance he later reiterated in Quebec itself. Concerning Canada's possible future declaration of war and action in it, he said:

The decision of the Government, which, of course, would have to be given promptly, should be submitted to the judgment of the people at a general election before troops should leave our shores. . . . The Government would have to decide and decide quickly what was best in the interest of Canada. The Government would have to act on its own judgment, but before there was anything in the way of participation involving the despatch of troops the will of the people of Canada should first be obtained.

After sizing up the offers of King and Meighen, the Progressives gave their support to King on condition of a known program of legislation, thus affording him a narrow and rather unpredictable majority to maintain his retention of power. Meanwhile, however, the Conservatives had unearthed such a scandal in the Customs Department, where bootleggers' bribes got liquor out of Canada into the United States and cheap, highly excised articles such as cigarettes out of the United States into Canada, that a vote of censure in late June appeared certain to win enough Progressive votes to defeat the King government.

The ensuing political and constitutional mess has produced dissension and debate ever since, for, instead of waiting for the vote or resigning in Meighen's favor, King asked the governor general for a dissolution and was properly refused. He thereupon broke all precedent by resigning without the conventional delay to permit discussion with a successor, thereby leaving Canada without an administration. Lord Byng then could only call on Meighen to form a government.

Meighen felt that he must do so in order that public business might be carried on, although he could not be certain of a majority. The outcome was that his administration was defeated within three days in spite of some quite novel devices of dubious constitutionality to preserve it. Meighen then asked for a dissolution and got it from Lord Byng.

Now the advantage was King's, for he could appeal, even though on specious grounds, to strong, if varied, Canadian nationalism against the alleged unconstitutional actions of the British peer whom Canadians had asked to be their governor general. King's campaign was an ignoble, but masterly, political performance during which he endeavored to subordinate the customs scandal and every other issue to the alleged danger of Canada's being reduced to colonial status again. His additional good fortune was that prosperity had visibly returned during the winter of 1925–26, permitting long-desired budget reductions in income and sales taxes, postal rates, and tariffs.

Moreover, while King was a neutral rather than a winning personality, his opponent was much more effective in opposition than in leadership. Meighen was so intense and unsparing in his attacks that some listeners were alarmed at the prospect of his heading the country and unexpectedly found themselves defending the man and the party he denounced. In spite of the fact that 529 candidates, representing six parties and various brands of independents, ran for 245 seats, Canadian politics in essence now got back to the two-party system.

After an election in which about 100,000 minority-party votes switched to the Liberals, the Liberals numbered 119, the Conservatives 92, the Liberal Progressives 11, the United Farmers of Alberta 11, the Progressives 8, Labor 3, and Independents 2. Progressivism had in the course of eight or nine years rejected its chance to create a liberal national party, largely because the truly determined Progressives were incapable of transcending local particularisms. The residuum of the movement was Western, the persisting sense of grievance against the outside world that had burst out in Selkirk's day and under Riel in 1870 and 1885, that had disturbed Canadian politics from 1910 to 1926, and was to emerge later as "Social Credit" in Alberta and "Socialism" in Saskatchewan. Meanwhile King had created a strangely mixed team from all parts of Canada that he was to drive artfully, with a single interruption, until he surrendered the reins over twenty years later.

⚜ FOREIGN AFFAIRS

Great Britain becomes a "dominion."—That autumn an imperial conference in London finally found words for the relationship among Great Britain and the dominions. It might, said the Declaration, rather impishly, "be readily defined." "They are autonomous communities within the British Empire, equal in status, in no way subordinate one to another in any aspect of their domestic or external affairs, though united by a common allegiance to the Crown, and freely associated as members of the British Commonwealth of Nations."

Punch, after consideration of that deft definition of tangible and intangible, expressed its relief that Great Britain had decided not to secede from the empire. Or, as A. R. M. Lower put it, "the Commonwealth had evolved a metaphysical position exceeding in complexity as seven exceeds three the metaphysics of the Trinity. Surpassed was mystic One in Three and Three in One: God in three persons was outnumbered by the British King in seven persons, the Septennity." For Canadians the Declaration of 1926 meant formal recognition of the status their leaders had claimed and, except in the matter of Alaska, had exercised for thirty years. Neither Great Britain nor any other dominion might act so as to bind another member of the Commonwealth without its consent. Canada's capacity to say "No" was recognized. The question now became that of deciding how and when Canada would say "Yes" in Commonwealth and international affairs.

Isolationism vs. involvement.—The record for thirty years had been overwhelmingly negative and, since the circumstances of Canada and of the outside world since 1918 had discouraged positive action, it would have been startling had Canada set herself against the general tide of isolationism that began to flow everywhere promptly after World War I. We have noticed Canada's opposition to Article X of the League Covenant, to renewal of the Anglo-Japanese Alliance, and to a protective guaranty of French security. In each of these stands, an admitted component of the Canadian attitude was harmony with the attitude of the United States. This policy became still more pronounced and explicit during 1924 and 1925 in Canada's rejections of the draft Treaty of Mutual Guaranty and the Geneva Protocol.

Even where the United States was not concerned, Canada reiterated her withdrawal. In 1922 an ineptly handled British appeal for aid in defending the internationalized zone at Chanaq on the Dardanelles was met by King's declaration that Parliament would have to be summoned to authorize such action. When a new treaty with Turkey was negotiated at Lausanne in 1923, King declared that "not having been invited, not having been represented directly or indirectly, and not having signed, Canada had no obligations." Canada was not represented during the negotiation of the Locarno Treaty of 1925, and an express reservation in the treaty excused the Dominions and India from obligations under it unless they chose to assume them.

Even when accepting the Pact of Paris of 1928, King was careful to distinguish between collective action in general and the obligation to exercise sanctions in undefined cases, and to reassert that the Covenant of the League must not be interpreted as imposing such burdens as the latter "automatically or by the decision of other states." Canada's sense of positive responsibility in maintaining collective security could hardly have been thinner and still have existed at all.

Yet Canada could not be entirely inert in external affairs. Her first conspicuously positive assertion was her independent negotiation of a treaty for the conservation of the Pacific halibut fishery with the United States in 1923, a treaty which the British ambassador at Washington proposed to sign in the old fashion in behalf of Canada, only to be refused. This symbolical action created a good deal of confusion at the British Foreign Office and in the American State Department and Senate, but ultimately the Canadian stand was accepted.

Canadian diplomatic representation abroad was hastened by the precipitate opening in 1924 of a legation in Washington by the Irish Free State. Yet the Canadian High Commissioner in London, the ministers in Washington (1927), Paris (1928), and Tokyo (1929), and their "opposite numbers" posted in Ottawa were less important than the quiet building up of the Department of External Affairs and the recruitment through careful competitive examinations of a small but remarkably able staff by O. D. Skelton, the Undersecretary. The secretaryship, perhaps inevitably, but somewhat unfortunately, continued to be combined with the office of prime minister (until 1946), but Mr. Skelton deserved well of his country for his almost anonymous services after 1925 in finding and training the civil servants who made their corner of the old East Block of the Parliament Buildings an acknowledged storehouse of knowledge and expertness. Naturally there continued to be great reliance on the British Foreign Office for information and other services, but Canadian policy and the most vital Canadian representation abroad were in Canadian hands.

The Labrador boundary award.—In 1927, Canada, and particularly Quebec, received an unexpected shock in the decision of the Privy Council concerning the undefined boundaries of Labrador. The territorial dispute between Canada and Newfoundland was an ancient one, going back to the eighteenth century, but problems of coastal jurisdiction had been compromised in Newfoundland's favor in 1825 and the issue remained fairly academic, although raised and ineffectually discussed in 1888 and 1892. It was, of course, the pulp and paper industry which made the problem of the interior of considerable importance, and trouble began inside Hamilton Inlet about 1902.

After negotiations involving Great Britain, Newfoundland, Quebec, and Canada, it was agreed in 1907 to submit the matter for decision to the Judicial Committee of the Privy Council. Not until 1920 did Newfoundland and Canada agree on the terms of reference, which were amended in 1922, and not until 1926 did the Committee face its task. After voluminous written and oral argument (the record fills twelve large volumes), the Committee advised an inland boundary around the headwaters of the rivers and river basins emptying on the coast that made the former "Coast of Labrador" an addition of about 112,000 square miles to the territory of Newfoundland. Since this was the result of an agreed-upon submission to judicial arbitration, there was nothing for Quebec or Canada to do except express injured surprise.

Alcohol and the international boundary.—Prohibition greatly complicated relations with the United States, for, on the one hand, the complexities of Canadian federalism permitted the manufacture of alcoholic liquors even where their sale was illegal, and, on the other, the provinces during the twenties abandoned prohibition and its attendant evils for various devices of government monopoly of sale. Since the United States remained allegedly "dry" until 1933, the international situation became impossible to control and a disgrace to both countries that they could not wipe out except at unwarrantable expense. In 1930, for instance, when Canada finally prohibited clearance of liquors to the United States, the business and the Americans and Canadians engaged in it merely moved its base (in part) to the French islands of St. Pierre and Miquelon.

United States vs. Karnuth.—Few Canadians were aware of a decision in 1928 of the United States Supreme Court that was to have profound effects on Canada. The case of *United States* vs. *Karnuth* ended the freedom of Canadians to enter the United States. Ever since Jay's Treaty of 1794, it had been commonly assumed that Canadians and Americans had the right, in its words, "freely to pass and repass by land or inland navigation." After 1920, the right had been hedged about somewhat by restrictive regulations connected with the new American restrictions on non-North American immigration, but it had been possible, for instance, to regularize the "border commuting" in the international industrial areas. Now the highest American authority held that the War of 1812 had nullified the provisions of Jay's Treaty.

It took some time for the effects of the decision to be felt and realized, but potentially it deprived Canada of a safety valve that had operated, probably beneficially in the sense that it kept American and Canadian standards of living pretty close to each other, for about a century and a half.

🍁 A TRANSITIONAL DECADE

In retrospect, some of the developments in the period 1919–29 seem more significant than they did then. Canada had become a powerful economy, capable of great expansion, but vulnerable to the fluctuations of world prices and world trade. Canadian society was still divided into three parts—*Canadiens,* Canadians, and New Canadians—but obvious as these divisions were, they were probably no more important than the general social maladjustment caused by the lag between the industrialization and urbanization of Canada, on the one hand, and the institutional arrangements designed to cope with them, on the other. An increasingly collectivized society was jerking along on a long individualistic leg and a short collective one.

Sectionalism, too, in the form of resentment against central Canada on the part of the Maritimes, the plains, and the Pacific coast, demanded more than the palliative measures of unsystematic federal subsidies or the draining off of the enterprising from the margins to the center. In domestic politics, King's achievement of national unity was a very great one, but it was at the cost of postponing or submerging positive leadership in petty compromises and rather negative sectional bargains. This threw burdens on provincial governments and municipalities which they were not ready, or sometimes simply unable, to shoulder. And, internationally, a generation of saying "No" was poor preparation for imminent times when affirmations would be called for. All in all, impressive as Canada was at the peak of the boom, she was vulnerable and unready when the economic roof of the world began falling in on October 21, 1929.

CHAPTER XXVIII

Depression and Sectionalism (1929-39)

It is as dangerous to be assured about recent history as about an iceberg, for no matter how clear and precise the view of what is above the surface, it is certain that much more is submerged. We know a great deal about what happened in Canada and to Canada during the second quarter of the twentieth century. We can even put our fingers on certain apparent general trends. We know a good many of the things that leading, influential Canadians did and the reasons they gave for doing them. Yet we can be sure that things were not quite what they seemed.

It seems probable that we do not know the decisive considerations that governed prime ministers King and Bennett, and their opponents, on many important occasions. We know a little of President Roosevelt's conceptions of Canada, but almost nothing about how King conducted himself during his numerous personal negotiations with the American president. We know that, although French Canada fought conscription and although the cautious King government studiously concealed the comparative statistics, yet *Canadiens* took a far larger share in World War II than in World War I. The historian ought to be frank in admitting that his account of recent events is subject to substantial revision.

☙ THE IMPACTS OF DEPRESSION

The depression that struck Canada during the autumn of 1929 and lasted in several of its chief aspects for ten years was an unprecedented phenomenon. The world economy disintegrated into a host of separate regions each trying desperately to protect its own for its own, and the devil take the hindmost, until Japan, Italy, and Germany exploded in violent insistence on conquest. Buyers no longer sought primary products in the cheapest market, but either did their best to get along with home produce or did without. World prices, that is, chiefly the prices for primary products, fell to the lowest recorded levels. Wheat in Winnipeg, for instance, sold for thirty-eight cents a bushel. Cash and credit became so scarce that a world dependent on them was submerged by wave after wave of bankruptcies. Gold increased spectacularly its power to buy goods and services. Currencies were set free to find their own levels.

Manufacturing was throttled down towards decreased purchasing power, far more in terms of output than in terms of lowered prices, because industrial capital in the form of buildings and equipment was more capable of lasting out the dreadful process of deflation than under-employed or unemployed industrial workers, farmers, forest-workers, miners, and fishermen. Meanwhile the possessors of salaried income or liquid capital were able to buy most goods and services and even capital assets, or the securities representing them, at bargain prices. The differences between the fortunate few and the unfortunate many were extreme, flamboyant, indeed invitations to violence.

As if to underline Canadian misery, wheat, the traditional economic symbol, put on a spectacular show of its own. Every country tried to grow wheat; a handicapped Russia, bent upon industrialization, put its people on short rations in order to export grain and acquire purchasing power abroad. Wheat prices fell far below remunerative levels, and wheat accumulations rose. Meanwhile the Canadian high plains were stricken by drought, the worst years being 1929, 1931, and 1933–37. For every year from 1929 to 1938, inclusive, the yield in bushels per acre was below the long-time average, and the 1937 yield was the lowest ever recorded. The hard, uninterrupted plains winds picked up the dusty soil and banked it over abandoned buildings and machinery, or carried it so high into the air that on occasion it visibly darkened the skies thousands of miles away in central Canada. In an over-all sense, the Canadian West went bankrupt.

Seen as an impersonal whole, the economy could be said to have been plunged in depression from 1929 to 1933, to have begun a halting, spotty recovery when the American economy broke the rigidities of its gold-dollar standard by devaluation in 1933; to have fallen back again in 1937–38; and to have resumed its growth with the world's rearmament in 1938–39. The net national income has been estimated (in millions of dollars) as follows: 1929, 4,689; 1932, 2,582; 1935, 3,117; and 1939, 4,289. Since federal, provincial, and municipal revenues were deeply affected by the state of the economy, and since their expenditures had to expand to meet human distress, taxation and deficits operated in a somewhat inflationary manner, that is, gradually tended to counter the deflation of 1929–33 and to assist the rise in prices thereafter.

The Canadian dollar had gone off gold as early as 1928 and, symbolically, stayed approximately half-way between the British pound and the American dollar after their devaluations. The Bank of Canada, set up as a semiprivate central bank in 1934, and nationalized in 1938, was given powers "to regulate credit and currency in the best interests of the economic life of the nation, to control and protect the external value of the national monetary unit and to mitigate by its influence fluctuations in the general level of production, trade, prices and employment, so far as may be possible within the scope of monetary action, and generally to promote the economic and financial welfare of the Dominion." Keynesian interventionist economics had invaded national finance.

New factors in population.—Precision about population changes at such a time is impossible. There was, of course, a series of inrushes towards the towns and cities from drought-stricken farms and from the forests and mines, and yet there was also an increased dependence on subsistence agriculture in better-watered regions and, indeed, on subsistence fisheries, although at a grimly lowered level of well-being because the prices of manufactured goods were distinctly better maintained than those of natural products. Adventurous young people took to the roads or stole rides on freight trains in spite of belated and sometimes harsh efforts to hive them in work camps and to use them in building a transcontinental highway or landing fields for a national transcontinental air service.

Perhaps as great as the inward movements to urban centers and to central Canada was the emigration to the United States, in spite of the stern steps taken by both countries to restrict migration and to repatriate each other's dependent nationals. After 1930, there was a marked emigration to Europe, particularly to the shelter of the British social services. The statistics of these movements are admittedly unsatisfactory because of the impossibility of controlling the international boundary, but it is clear that many American-born returned to the United States, that many Canadian-born and others followed them legally and illegally, particularly after the United States began to recover in 1933, and that the actual population of Canada grew more slowly than natural increase and immigration gave grounds for expecting.

The deficiency of perhaps 150,000 for the decade 1929–38, however, was undoubtedly very much less than it would have been had the United States not instituted both border and internal controls of increased effectiveness. In fact, for the first time in her history, Canada had been pretty well deprived of her social and economic safety valve to the south, a circumstance that was to have interesting consequences in succeeding years. There might be adverse results in the relative standard of living, but after 1930 Canada seemed destined to grow approximately at her natural rate plus the immigration she attracted.

Some casualties and an exception.—One inevitable casualty of the depression was the Central Selling Agency of the provincial wheat pools. In effect, the federal government gradually took over the basic credit aspects of wheat marketing from 1930 on, while the provincial cooperatives, in spite of aid from their governments, "went through the wringer" before undergoing a long, slow process of reorganization and recovery. The emergent federal Canadian Wheat Board of 1935 served as a rather leaky umbrella for the Western farmers until war and its demands after 1942 brought fair weather again.

Another set of victims was in pulp and paper, where slashed prices and narrowed operations could not pay interest on the borrowings that had been needed for these costly enterprises, and bankruptcy came close to being the rule. The Canadian National Railways leaned on the public treasury; the Canadian Pacific stopped paying dividends.

The one industry that indubitably boomed during this dismal period was gold mining. Important as it was in the balance of payments before 1933, it was given a mighty fillip by the devaluation of the American dollar and other currencies. One of the most spectacular episodes in Canadian economic history was the increase in gold production from 1,928,000 fine ounces in 1929 to 5,095,000 in 1939, still more spectacular when represented by $39,862,000 and $184,145,000 respectively. Nonferrous metals and the chemical industry also did fairly well during these difficult times.

The nation's account.—Among the curiosities of economic development to the ordinary man is the fact that a total economy may be improving its "bookkeeping" position during a period of depression, deflation, deficit financing, widespread misery, and unemployment. Canada has been a convenient subject for such studies for a generation or so, and it can be said that after about 1930 she cut down her indebtedness abroad and at the same time increased her investments there. Foreign investment in Canada ranged from $6003 millions in 1926, to $7614 millions in 1930, and $6913 millions in 1939; whereas Canadian investments abroad ranged from $1296 millions in 1926, to $1443 millions in 1930, and to $1876 millions in 1939.

On current account from 1933–39, Canada acquired average annual credits of $140,000,000, partly by large credits in transactions with the

United Kingdom and other overseas countries, but also by immense reduction of her characteristic debits in transactions with the United States. The principal ingredients in this apparently paradoxical development appear to have been the abrupt decline in international investment after 1929, Canada's ability and determination to supply at home both capital and many commodities previously imported, and the successful use of sterling surpluses and increased gold production to reduce indebtedness the principal and interest of which were payable in American dollars, as well as to redeem Canadian securities held in Great Britain.

Increased provincial responsibilities.—When depression began in 1929, the common assumption was that charity and local government, municipal and provincial, would take care of the casualties. The rise in the scope of provincial government during the twenties, when the federal government was doing little, was thus taken for granted. Following a dominion-provincial conference in 1927, a number of steps had been taken to strengthen the provinces—the new western ones were given ownership and control of their lands and natural resources, with Manitoba receiving over $4,500,000 as special compensation for her earlier subordinate position; additional annual grants ("better terms" again) were made to each of the Maritime Provinces; and steps were taken to subsidize Canadian coal and coke, the harbor activities of Saint John and Halifax, and the Atlantic fisheries.

Innocent in intention as these gestures may have been, they seemed like "passing the buck" when depression bit into the income taxes, and the revenues from liquor monopolies, automobile licenses, gasoline taxes, and so on, upon which the provinces had been depending for their educational expansion, their road building, and their social services.

Ottawa's conscience was especially clear in this matter because of recent interpretations of the British North America Act's division between federal and provincial powers made by the Judicial Committee of the Privy Council. In effect, Lord Haldane handed down a series of "advices" to the Crown which carried his admired predecessor's (Lord Watson) development of "provincial rights" during the nineties to an obvious and dangerous contradiction of the intentions at Charlottetown and Quebec two generations earlier. He denied the federal government's right to "trench upon" a broadly interpreted provincial jurisdiction over "property and civil rights," except when war or peril enhanced Ottawa's specified power to legislate "for the peace, order, and good government of Canada."

Thus Canada's reliance upon a "neutral" British legal committee for interpretation of her constitution—a federal one unfamiliar to Britons—had carried her to a point where many obviously national objectives could be attained only by special, ingenious, *ad hoc* agreements between the federal and provincial governments. It was not until after Haldane's retirement that the Judicial Committee called a partial halt by finding control over radio broadcasting and civil aviation within the competence of the federal government, but by then the damage had been done in that a trend of precedents stretching over more than forty years was reducing the constitution of Canada to absurdity in a number of vital aspects.

Meanwhile, however, depression was imposing burdens on the local governments which they could not carry unaided. The situation was bad everywhere—in industry, farming, forestry, mining, and fisheries—but it was simply intolerable in the southern dry plains of Manitoba, Saskatchewan, and Alberta. The reluctant devices of the past were not enough. The nation could not survive provincial or municipal bankruptcy. Gradually, therefore, by loans and so-called loans and direct grants the federal government assumed about 40 per cent of the burden of relief, with its heaviest commitments to the primary producing areas, the plains, the Shield, and the Pacific coast. The whole Canadian structure, quite properly, rested for six or seven years on confidence in federal Canada's promises to pay.

Upheavals.—The social costs of this catastrophic setback were enormous—mature persons rendered penniless and dependent, perhaps uprooted; youths jobless, unexpectant, and "on the loose"; and a decade during which social services in education, health, and relief during dependency at best held their own and usually retrogressed. Next door, Roosevelt, the jaunty experimenter, opened a Pandora's box of bold new devices and his people took the enormous chances which their powerful and resilient economy seemed to justify.

Canadians, who probably listened to and read about Roosevelt's "New Deal" as avidly as Americans, could not compete in daring. Their economy was harder hit and in general much less self-reliant. Their industrialization had been later than the American and their contradictory combination of "rugged individualism" and reliance on governmental aid to enterprise had been very little eroded by systematic thought and discussion about collective society. They were hamstrung by their constitution, cautious because of past and present vulnerability to external forces, and for the most part resigned to tightened belts and minimal relief while they waited for the depression to pass.

There were, of course, exceptions. Indeed almost every variety of panacea and salvationism cropped up in one corner or another of Canada. Evangelical religious sects flourished. Fascism was advocated here and communism there. Industrial unionism fought its way into

Canada from the United States against craft unionism, the Catholic syndicates, and the opponents of any kind of powerful collective action. "Funny money" projects of many sorts found advocates, indeed William Aberhart, a high school principal and an infectious broadcaster from the Prophetic Bible Institute in Alberta, promised a new economic and political dispensation if Albertans would only believe in the dogma which the Briton, Major C. H. Douglas, called "Social Credit."

Less eccentric Western Progressivism took a different line, reminiscent of some hopes that had withered during 1919 and 1920, and closely connected with the "one-man Socialism" of J. S. Woodsworth, the Labor member from Winnipeg in the Canadian Parliament since 1921 and respected advocate of many fundamental social reforms. The Co-operative Commonwealth Federation, Fabian in name and nature, although much more fundamentally democratic than its parent, represented an attempt to ally Western Progressivism with Eastern trade unionism and to use the knowledge and advice of academic intellectuals in the affiliated League for Social Reconstruction. Yet when all these movements, and more, were added together, they merely contributed some interesting minor variations to the general resignation to "sticking it out."

Quebec.—Quebec represented a special case. The depression gave the real and the pretended economic nationalists a second chance. Closed paper mills, abandoned power developments and aluminum works, and smokeless factories provided marvelous ammunition for the *anti-trustards* or critics of "irresponsible" foreign capital. The vanishing dream of a paternalistic, contented, rural society returned with new emphasis. Separatism mounted confidently to assertions of independence. Corporative and authoritarian doctrines and admiration of the Italian Mussolini and the Portuguese Salazar were carried by some believers to the outright avowal of fascism.

Some men dreamed and talked of a "Laurentie," like Eire in the British Commonwealth, which should have privileges without responsibilities. Others even anticipated a combination of an Eastern Canada and a Northeastern United States where former *Canadiens, Acadiens,* and *Franco-Américains* would achieve working arrangements with English-speaking compatriots who could understand what that part of North America needed. Once again, however, it must be said that all these vagaries, and more, counted for less than resignation to endurance until better times.

Perhaps the one new feature of the Quebec scene was an anticlericalism different, more intense, and more widespread than anything like it before. Its most frequent manifestation grew out of shock and re-sentiment when the traditional charity of the church and its agencies was abdicated in favor of the state and its agencies. The bitterness of destitution and despair were for perhaps the first time directed against the religious institutions which had been created, enlarged, and supported by the people themselves. This mood, which lingered in both rural and urban societies, evoked a variety of responses, not only among the clergy and intellectuals who still hoped to set the clock back, but also among those who felt that the time had come to study what other industrialized societies and states had thought and done about such far-reaching change.

Aesthetic and intellectual responses.—Canada was, of course, flooded by French, British, and American literature of the depression—the poetry of "social conscience"; the painting and sculpture of distress, dogma, bewilderment, or retreat into private worlds; the "proletarian" novel or the fiction of "values" sometimes so dubious and relativistic as to approach nihilism. A good deal of the Canadian equivalent was derivative and bad. Pratt's gifts, for instance, under the goading of his conscience, were temporarily diverted to efforts less fruitful and satisfying, if evidencing experimentation and growth, than what he wrote before and after the shock of the depression.

On the other hand, a new generation of good poets found eloquent voice, partly native and partly cosmopolitan. Anne Marriott in "The Wind Our Enemy" and F. E. Laight in "Soliloquy" commemorated unforgettably the desperation, the local loneliness, and the stubborn determination of Canadians under drought and depression, as well as their distrust of the politicians and the ensconced leaders of society. A number of other poets, with British Columbia heavily represented among them, were equally evocative and feelingly expressive of new depths in Canadian self-discovery.

The cosmopolitans, perhaps naturally, were for the most part in the East, in Montreal and Toronto, many of them connected with secondary or higher education. If F. R. Scott be taken as an example, his poem "The Canadian Authors Meet" ("To paint the native maple, and to plan/ More ways to set the self-same welkin ringing") might serve as a symbol of their revolt against parochialism, or, if the sardonic epigrammatist L. A. Mackay, his "Battle Hymn of the Spanish Rebellion" which began:

> The Church's one foundation
> Is now the Moslem sword.

Yet these two, although characterizing their company, were perhaps less notable in breadth and depth than others such as A. M. Klein, who blended profound consciousness of the Hebrew tradition with full sense and knowledge of English and American literature, or sensitive, distinctive experimenters like A. G. Bailey, Ralph Gustafson, and A. J. M. Smith. Canadian fiction was less remarkable, in French or in English, except in the form of short stories or sketches or in at least one of the novels of Morley Callaghan. It was as if Canadian writers in this form were in process of discovering the city, its wage earners, and their relation to society at large, and were not yet assured enough to distill their essences. The scholarly world was immensely concerned and active in studies of Canadian economics, society, and politics and at last venturing into the difficult field of systematic social history.

The leader principle.—Both Canada and her provinces surrendered in some degree to the so-called "leader principle": in their desperation, large numbers of Canadians were prepared to hand over large amounts of power to individuals who had the gift of persuading them that they knew what needed to be done and were prepared to override conventional legal and constitutional safeguards if they stood in the way. This was the mood in which dictatorships were born elsewhere, but it also characterized the Great Britain of J. Ramsay MacDonald and his "Doctor's Mandate" and the United States during Franklin D. Roosevelt's fight against the "Nine Old Men" of the Supreme Court. In Canada, Richard B. Bennett in federal politics, and Maurice Duplessis in Quebec, Mitchell F. Hepburn in Ontario, and William Aberhart in Alberta, not to speak of some others, demonstrated a combination of supreme self-confidence and disregard of established legal and constitutional restraints.

The hypercautious Mackenzie King was an early victim of this temper in Canadians, for nothing in his make-up qualified him for the sweeping, dramatic, decisive action that the voters wanted. Indeed his own doubts and confusions must have been extreme, for he burst out in Parliament with one of his rare lapses in temper and discretion when the provinces began to turn against his party and the Conservatives were demanding that he do something about helping them to cope with unemployment.

He was reported to have said, although he disputed the accuracy of the report:

I might be prepared to go a certain length, possibly, in meeting one or two of the western provinces that have Progressive premiers at the head of their governments, but I would not give a single cent to any Tory government . . . With respect to giving moneys out of the federal treasury to any Tory government in this country for these alleged unemployment purposes, with these governments situated as they are today, with policies directly opposed to those of this Government, I would not give them a five-cent piece.

Such invidious distinction, at a time when distress affected all manner of men, was marvelous campaign material, and in the general election of July, 1930, the voters replaced King and the Liberals with Bennett and the Conservatives. Now the latter held 138 seats, the Liberals 87, and the minor parties 20.

🍁 BENNETT'S SWAY

Bennett was an able, vigorous New Brunswicker who had made a fortune as a lawyer and businessman, first in the West and later in central Canada. Material success, working upon his sincerity, humane concern, and self-certainty, had developed in him habits of dominance and assurance that commended him to bewildered Canadians in 1930 but that made him an unacceptably masterful and inconsiderate leader of a Cabinet. Perhaps he came to high office too late in life and with too little experience of the give and take that must characterize the federal executive in Canada. Whatever the case, he treated his Cabinet colleagues as subordinates and with little or no concern for their feelings. The classic story about him pictured him as talking to himself, that is, "holding a Cabinet meeting."

His attitude towards Parliament showed even less concern, and towards the people passed beyond paternalism to something approaching dictation. He announced that he would end unemployment by retaliatory protectionism and other devices aimed principally to cut down purchases from the provocative United States by placing "Canada first and then the Empire," and by "blasting" a way into the markets of the world. He often refused to let Parliament spend time discussing appropriations, but forced it to vote lump sums to be spent as he (or the Cabinet) saw best.

One of the most interesting and in the long run significant aspects of his single term as prime minister was his discovery and use of the knowledge and ability of the civil service. Canadians in general had hitherto held the permanent administrative staff in distinctly low esteem, regarding it, with some justice, as a safe refuge for successive generations of the politically faithful who did as little as possible as slowly as possible and could not be fired.

They overlooked the fact that a Civil Service Commission had been at work for some years instituting entrance by competitive examinations, classifying positions in terms of the accomplishments required, and arranging promotion by merit. Moreover, the needs and demands of the executive and legislature had since 1914 greatly increased in volume and difficulty, forcing the heads of many departments to recruit the ablest men they could find. Even Mr. King's hesitant administrations had come increasingly to rely on the service, but to a man of Bennett's legal and business experience it was completely natural to use its members like law-office juniors and junior executives.

Bennett had no compunctions about departmental specialization. When he found a good man, he used him for whatever he needed. Thus the Dominion Bureau of Statistics at times seemed like a bureau of legislative drafting; it was often impossible to disentangle the activities of key men in the departments of Finance, of National Revenue, and of Trade and Commerce; and some of Skelton's men in the Department of External Affairs found themselves negotiating trade agreements, serving as economic advisors, acting as secretaries and writing the reports of royal commissions on such technical matters as wheat marketing or price spreads, and traveling about with Bennett to serve him in manifold and sometimes unpredictable capacities.

One dubious feature of this procedure was that he tended to treat the Royal Canadian Mounted Police in somewhat the same way, building up its political and secret branch for the surveillance and discouragement of radical activities. These were practically negligible in Canada even before the depression lifted, but Bennett seems to have been genuinely afraid of "dangerous thoughts." He also insisted on making Canada's principal diplomatic representatives political, that is, party appointees. He flouted the established ban against titles of honor for Canadians by securing a number of them from the Crown before his fall from power.

"Canada First."—Within Canada, Bennett's high protectionism had the obvious and predictable effect of sheltering central Canada and still further exposing the desperate margins. In 1934, N. M. Rogers startled not only the Nova Scotian Royal Commission to which he submitted the statement, but the rest of Canada as well, by his calculation that the tariff in effect subsidized each person in Ontario by $15.15 a year, and in Quebec by $11.03, but cost each person in the other seven provinces as much as $11.67 in Nova Scotia or $28.16 in Saskatchewan. Bennett succeeded, however, in using protectionism forcefully in the international area. In fact, Canada's reprisals for the stupid Smoot-Hawley tariff of the United States in 1930 and the still more stupid fiscal tariffs of 1932 were probably the most effective wakening shocks that the Americans received.

When Bennett rushed over to England in 1930 and demanded that the Labour Government institute protection so as to permit the creation of a Commonwealth and Empire walled against the world but conceding mutual preferences, those orthodox free traders were sufficiently angered to dismiss his scheme as "humbug." Two years later, however, the British Conservatives were back in power and had instituted protection, thus giving Bennett his chance, which the Americans enlarged by their panicky rearing of still higher tariff walls.

In 1932, therefore, during the summer heat at Ottawa, the Commonwealth fought out a series of five-year bilateral trade agreements. The British delegation, representing multilateral trade, wanted low tariffs, but Bennett wanted both to eat his cake and have it. For the sake of imperial understanding in an unpredictable world, the Britons gave way. Tariffs stayed very high, with preferences extended under them. Britain paid for Canadian economic nationalism, for she granted a privileged market to Canada's principal exports without getting much for her own products in return. Canadian manufacturers still demanded and got protection, particularly against the textiles that Britain was so anxious to export. Canada was deeply concerned about Russian and Argentinian competition in the British market for primary products and received considerable aid against it.

Stated summarily, in each year from 1927 to 1932 current payments by Canada to the United Kingdom exceeded receipts, whereas in each year from 1933 to 1939 they were emphatically the reverse. Canadian exports to Britain improved steadily after 1932, although the values were a little lower because of the fall in prices, the increased volume being chiefly in bacon and other food products, lumber, wood products, and nonferrous metals. Canadian imports from Great Britain did not get above the 1932 level until 1935 and averaged less than a fifth of her imports during the thirties. Although the percentage of Canada's total trade with the mother country was a little higher during the thirties than during the twenties, and the percentage with the United States slightly lower, yet Great Britain was steadily losing on current payments account with Canada and the United States was gaining.

The Ottawa agreements, British rearmament, and World War II had the effect of twisting the Canadian economy so that the inescapable problem of a much better balance with the United States was not recognized. The American economy might be so colossal and variable that even minor fluctuations in it could rock Canada from end to end, but by the thirties it was unmistakably the trend that each country would be the other's most important economic associate. Americans could disregard that at some cost, but without disaster. Canadians could not.

The Statute of Westminster.—Bennett's practical nationalism conflicted again with his emotional imperialism when the attempt was made to put the 1926 declaration as to status in the Commonwealth into legal form. This time the balance was tipped apparently towards imperialism, but actually towards further disintegration of the Canadian federation.

G. H. Ferguson, the Conservative premier of Ontario, successfully advanced the theory that that federation had been a treaty or compact among the provinces and therefore could be altered only with their consent. The immediate result was that the Statute of Westminster, 1931, while it enunciated the individual full sovereign competence of Great Britain and the dominions except over one another, also contained safeguards for the provinces of Canada against constitutional amendment without their consent. That involved the rather undignified procedure of calling upon the British Parliament to legislate Canadian constitutional change when unmistakably requested to do so by Canada and her provinces.

Provincial revolts.—Ferguson's action was an early symptom of the provincial revolts that were to unseat Bennett. Needless to say, he did not end unemployment, indeed by 1935 it was calculated that a tenth of the population was on relief. One after another, the provinces rejected the Conservatives locally and threw up strongly particularistic leaders who promised to remedy Ottawa's deficiencies by looking after individual Canadians instead of after large industry and the national bookkeeping position.

The Liberals under A. L. Macdonald won office in Nova Scotia in 1933 and under A. A. Dysart in New Brunswick in 1935. These Liberal premiers chanted "Maritime Rights" and other voices hinted at secession. In Quebec, the shaken Liberals under L. A. Taschereau were undermined by the nationalists, the separatists, and all manner of demands for social legislation from within the party and without. After sundry maneuvers, the astute Maurice Duplessis capitalized the discontents with a new party, the *Union Nationale,* which was essentially separatist, conservative, autocratic, and extravagant, but earned popularity by fulminations and overt actions against Ottawa, against foreign financial domination, and against "Communism." After barely missing victory in November, 1935, Duplessis achieved it in August, 1936.

In Ontario, M. F. Hepburn carried the province for the Liberals in 1934 by a curious alliance between discontent, rural and urban, and the mining and financial interests of Toronto. He staged spectacular attacks against American and Quebec "power interests" and "foreign" industrial unionism, which he subsequently compromised, and kept in the limelight by vituperative campaigns against the Ottawa governments, Conservative or Liberal. In the West, the C.C.F. (Co-operative Commonwealth Federation) was strong enough outside Alberta to force open or tacit alliances of the older parties against it. Aberhart carried Alberta in 1935 by promises to pay all adults a "social dividend" of twenty-five dollars a month.

Canada was breaking up into rather demagogic principalities. Even within Bennett's Cabinet, H. H. Stevens, Minister of Trade and Commerce, became so disturbed by, and outspoken about, the social and economic abominations in commerce and industry, uncovered by the Royal Commission on Price Spreads of 1934 that, after being forced to resign, he founded a political party of his own.

Tory radicalism.—Bennett's response to this situation was superficially shocking, but in keeping with his character. In a series of radio broadcasts during January, 1935, he announced an immense program of federal state intervention, relying considerably upon Ottawa's emergency powers for "peace, order, and good government," and on its treaty-making power in the form of accepting conventions of the International Labor Organization, so as to get round the obstacles set up by the Judicial Committee of the Privy Council. Practically, however, his legislation defied the constitutional interpretations of the past forty years. His brother-in-law, W. D. Herridge, while Canadian minister at Washington, had been intimate with some of Roosevelt's "Brain Trusters" who had found it useful to try out their ideas on an intelligent North American who had no local political commitments.

Now Bennett and Herridge, with the rather feverish aid of some able civil servants, prepared for Parliament, which dutifully passed them except for some amendments in the Senate, bills involving the federal government in the export marketing and interprovincial trade of natural products; agricultural debts and loans; minimum wages; maximum hours; prevention of child labor; unemployment insurance; antimonopoly; prevention of unfair and misleading business, commercial, and financial practices; relief; housing; public works; and so forth. Bennett's "Tory Radicalism" harmonized both with his nationalism and with his authoritarianism. A striking feature of some of the Bennett legislation was that certain breaches of it were made criminal, not civil, offenses.

This was certainly, as he said, "more comprehensive, more far-reaching, than any scheme of reform which this country has ever known," and it not only blew his big-business supporters into the federal Liberal camp at once, but, perhaps more significantly, secured their support provincially for Duplessis, Hepburn, and other local defenders of the economic status quo. Actually Canada had reached the point where she must choose between apparently unregulated economic enterprise and the kind of state intervention and control that had grown up elsewhere in industrialized states. Great Britain, for instance, had begun it effectively as early as 1833. Few Canadians, however, were sophisticated in these matters and most of them did not know that outside North America such intervention or "planning" had historically been as congenial to the politico-economic Right as to the Left, with the liberals of the Middle holding it off as much as possible until political democracy destroyed their position.

It was in the midst of provincial revolts and of considerable confusion and muddled thinking, therefore, that King and the federal Liberals swept Bennett and the federal Conservatives out of power, indeed almost out of existence, in the autumn elections of 1935, in spite of promises of still further social and economic legislation from Bennett. The Liberals had 171 seats, the Conservatives 39, Social Credit 17, and the C.C.F., with twice the vote of Social Credit, 7. Mr. Stevens won only his own seat, although his Reconstruction party's vote almost equaled that of the C.C.F., and there was a scattering of variegated dissidents. The Liberal percentage of the vote was little larger than in 1930, but the voters saw to it that the Conservatives were defeated.

KING AGAIN

King promptly turned Bennett's legislation over to the Privy Council, which rejected nearly all of it. He also yielded sufficiently to push through a treaty of substantial reciprocal trade concessions with the United States which Bennett had been negotiating for about three years in a more obdurate manner. King's good fortune was that economic conditions improved during the first two years of his term, thereby seeming to justify his policies.

When the Social Credit Government in Alberta found itself in impossible difficulties about redeeming its extravagant promises and had to default on its bonded debt, it resorted to ordinances and legislation which were either found invalid by the Alberta courts or the Supreme Court of Canada, refused assent by the lieutenant governor, or disallowed by the federal government. Aberhart, beyond his depth, had to watch his party settle down, after violent dissensions, into a fairly typical, honest, Western rebellion against central Canada, with some unhealthy authoritarian and reactionary aspects in its attempts to muzzle the press, its anti-Semitism, and its suspicious isolationism. King sat on the lid at Ottawa, cautiously assisting bankers and financiers in their struggles with Alberta's bankruptcy, but Albertans remained suffused with self-righteousness and a unique sense of mission in an unregenerate world.

Reconstruction of the economic triangle.—As the Ottawa agreements approached termination in 1937, Canada, the United States, and Great Britain systematically re-examined and rearranged their triangular interplay. The American Reciprocal Trade Treaties Act of 1934 was Secretary of State Hull's favorite device, indeed freer trade seemed to him a panacea for the world's woes. The British Conservatives still smarted from Bennett's bludgeonings of 1932, were highly realistic about the benefits to Britain of enlarged world trade, and wanted Anglo-American understanding above all else in the world. King was therefore in clover, with everything favoring his real or imaginary antiprotectionist views.

Naturally the outcome was no abandonment of protection by the three nations, but they systematically re-created the most advantageous and practicable arrangements for their interplay. In effect, a penitent United States bought its way back into world trade by retreats from Hawley-Smootdom, indeed it started on its path towards becoming a proponent of freer international trade. By 1938 each of the three countries had made new agreements with the other two in a carefully interlocked commercial structure.

The Rowell-Sirois Commission.—Meanwhile, however, the ever more absurd state to which the federal constitution had been reduced by the Judicial Committee of the Privy Council obviously threatened Canada with disintegration into nine principalities. To meet this threat, King in 1937 resorted to the Canadian agency of a Royal Commission on Dominion-Provincial Relations, under the chairmanship first of N. W. Rowell and, after his illness, of Joseph Sirois. This able body, appropriately financed and calling on experts and conducting hearings all over the country, conducted a patient, thorough national inquest before reporting in 1940.

The Rowell-Sirois Report, with its appendices, was not only the most important state paper ever produced in Canada, but became at once a significant document in the general history of federalism. Its historical, descriptive, and analytical materials constituted a tribute to Canadian intelligence and maturity. Its recommendations proved to be more than the country could swallow, particularly in time of war, but they were the blueprint for political and economic, if not cultural, Canadian unity, and many subsequent developments have been in accordance with them, although sometimes effected in devious face-saving ways.

The report met separatism head-on by demonstrating the unevenness of wealth and prosperity across Canada and recommending that national revenues be raised and distributed in such a way as to ensure that no part be allowed to fall below a minimum level of well-being and security. This would involve federal responsibility for unemployment relief and insurance, and a new and flexible dispensation in the federal subsidies to the provincial governments so that they might maintain a uniform average level of social services.

Such national burdens would necessitate a new federal-provincial division of taxation. It was recommended, therefore, that Ottawa assume the provincial debts and receive the exclusive right to collect income, corporation, and inheritance taxes. Ontario, Alberta, and British Columbia rejected the proposals flatly; indeed, Hepburn behaved with such spectacular offensiveness at a dominion-provincial conference on these matters in January, 1941, that it broke up on the second day without Quebec having to shoot at its favorite target, "centralization."

It fell, therefore, to the able and forceful Minister of Finance, J. L. Ilsley, subsequently to initiate and carry through individually under the pressures of war a series of temporary "tax bargains" with the separate provinces by which, in the financial field at least, considerable advance towards national unity was attained. In 1940, after previous agreement by the provinces, the constitution was amended so as to bring unemployment insurance under federal jurisdiction; it was instituted on the basis of contributions by employers, employed, and the national treasury.

NEWFOUNDLAND'S COLLAPSE

While Canada stumbled through depression by using the national credit to sustain her distressed parts, Newfoundland had had to try to get along alone and had failed. The cod fishery, her principal source of outside revenue, had been under constant competitive pressure after 1918 from Scandinavia and from British and other operations off Iceland with whose costly new equipment and technology Newfoundland could not compete on even terms. A certain amount of diversification in terms of exports was derived from the large iron deposit at Bell Island, from two great paper-making enterprises at Grand Falls (1923) and Corner Brook (1925), and from a copper-lead-zinc mine at Buchans (1928). Yet even when (1935-40) fish and fish products constituted 24 per cent, forest products 48 per cent, and mineral products 26 per cent of exports, about half of the working population still depended on the fisheries, as did most of the commercial life in which others were engaged.

"If Newfoundland no longer has her export eggs all in one basket, all her baskets are fragile." To this comment by R. A. MacKay another might be added: "The contrast between the many and the few in Newfoundland society is more glaring than almost anywhere else north of the Rio Grande, except possibly in the deep South of the United States, or in derelict areas, such as former mining communities."

This economy and this society suffered greatly from 1920 to 1925; recovered, a little dizzily, from 1926 to 1929; and then, in effect, collapsed. Prices plummeted, foreign markets dried up, the railway deficits mounted to become half the national debt, the safety valves of emigration to Canada and the United States were shut, remittances from emigrants dwindled away to a quarter of what they had been, and every available asset was mortgaged to the hilt by the state, even to landing rights in transatlantic aviation.

The average annual budget deficit from 1920 to 1932 was $2,000,000 and the public debt more than doubled. The Ottawa Agreements of 1932 were inadequate to remedy the situation, although the hospitable British market was a great help. In 1931–32 two Canadian banks and an oil company advanced funds in return for prior liens on the customs revenue and certain monopolistic privileges; in 1933 the Canadian and British governments made loans; but the disease was too radical to be cured by transfusions.

A Royal Commission of February, 1933, therefore, recommended that Great Britain take over the country temporarily; that it meanwhile revert from its proud self-governing status; and, in order to shake free from accumulated, habitual, political and financial abuses, accept control from a nominated governor and commission of six members (three Britons and three Newfoundlanders) who should be responsible, not to Newfoundlanders, but to the British government. Newfoundland swallowed this pill in February, 1934.

Although the commission government had the advantage of an improving world economy, its task was an unenviable one, for it started with the conviction that its first objective was to clean up the mess and tangle of domestic inequities, the spoils system, the extravagantly wasteful effects of the old denominational bargain in political patronage and education, the corruption, and so on. Certainly there was much that had been scandalous, and the exploitative hold of the St. John's mercantile group on the rest of the country divided it sharply into Haves and Have-nots, but if the "outsiders" of the commission government had the advantage of neutrality, they also had the disadvantage of not knowing how many Newfoundland toes they trod on.

In the circumstances, they did a notably good job, and Britain's continuous financial generosity to the island meant that it was slowly regaining economic strength and was possessed of an improved financial structure and social and economic administration when World War II gave Newfoundland "the greatest period of prosperity it has ever known." It has been estimated that Saskatchewan suffered more from the world depression than did Newfoundland, but Newfoundland's standard of living was much lower to start with and, with no Ottawa to call on, British authority had to supersede local autonomy.

☘ THE INTERNATIONAL MAELSTROM

While Newfoundlanders and Canadians were wrestling with depression and were seeing the outside world chiefly in terms of how to re-establish the export trade upon which their well-being so greatly depended, the international situation was degenerating with accelerated rapidity. Canada, with troubles enough at home, became uncomfortably aware that, in similar circumstances, Japan, Italy, and Germany were resorting to force in order to shatter what seemed intolerable bonds on their development. Canadians, like Americans, in general responded to this situation by intensifying their isolationism. King described his government's policy in 1936 as "to do nothing itself and if possible to prevent anything occurring which will precipitate one additional factor into all the important discussions which are taking place in Europe."

The beckoning American orbit.—President Roosevelt and his administrations, as representing the greatest world power, began early in 1937 the long, slow task of educating their people in its responsibilities. Bennett and King and their Cabinets, knowing that, however independent Canada might be constitutionally, her cause in world crisis must in large part be determined by Britain's, found themselves trying to avoid or to diminish actions abroad that might affect the uneasy polygon of forces in which the Great Powers were involved.

There seems also to have been a realization, at least after Britain's economic crisis of 1931, that British power was waning and thus exposing Canada, perhaps more than ever before, to the enormous potential power of the United States. At any rate, Canadian governments were scrupulous in avoiding or liquidating any obligations to the United States. The two countries did negotiate in 1932 a treaty providing for the construction of a deep waterway and immense power developments on the rapids section of the St. Lawrence and improvements of the upper canals, channels, and lakes to permit vessels of deep draught to proceed from tidewater to the head of the lakes. An agreement negotiated in 1941 affected only the International Rapids Section of the St. Lawrence. Yet Canada submitted without much protest to the repeated refusals of the American Congress to implement the schemes, partly because Ottawa found Ontario and Quebec rather recalcitrant about having the matter pass entirely out of their hands.

Roosevelt's "Good Neighbor" or "Hemisphere" Policy, as it developed from 1933 onwards, might be described as a modified isolationism designed to be a gradual re-education of his people in world politics. It presented Canada with an opportunity for a new international alignment that was quietly, but firmly, rejected. There was something of an upsurge of interest in the Pan-American Union, particularly in French Canada where some leaders saw a chance of withdrawing from implication in British policies while at the same time offsetting the might of the United States by affiliation with other "Latin" nations, but tradition and forebodings about American domination robbed the movement of any strength.

When Roosevelt at Chautauqua in 1936 launched a trial balloon in Canada's direction, it was almost completely ignored except by some *Canadien* separatists. In the midst of the Czechoslovakian crisis of 1938, when Roosevelt opened the Thousand Islands Bridge and received an honorary degree from Queen's University at Kingston, he became more specific, saying: "The Dominion of Canada is part of the sisterhood of the British Empire. I give you assurance that the people of the United States will not stand idly by if domination of Canadian soil is threatened by any other Empire." Two days later, King spoke at Woodbridge, expressing his gratitude, but asserting clearly and specifically that the international situation imposed on Canada the duty of defending herself against invasion so that "should the occasion ever arise, enemy forces should not be able to pursue their way, either by land, sea, or air to the United States, across Canadian territory."

Studied withdrawal.—Until the beginning of 1939, perhaps even until March, when Hitler revealed himself completely by disregarding his bargain of 1938 and by occupying all of Czechoslovakia, Canada hoped to avoid war by keeping out of war-breeding situations. Yet at the same time she gradually succumbed to the agonizing feeling that war would come, that Britain and France would be involved in it, and that Canada would have to follow suit.

The progress from about 1930 to September, 1939, was marked by grave differences within Canada and many writhing efforts to avoid involvement. French Canada, in general, and both rural and urban groups in other parts of the country persistently sought and advocated various ways out of the predicament, gradually focusing on neutrality or the newly invented "passive belligerency." At a time when international behavior had shattered all conventions, nonaggressive Canada could be pardoned for her continuous attempts to reject the destiny towards which external, rather more than internal, forces seemed to be driving her.

When Japan invaded Manchuria in 1931, bombed and burned Shanghai in 1932, and set up both the puppet state of Manchukuo abroad and a terroristic military government at home, Canada was incensed, partly because China was an important field for both Catholic and Protestant Canadian missionary enterprise, and partly because it was confidently expected that the League of Nations would bring Japan to book. Similar sentiments in the United States carried the Hoover administration into open collaboration with the League, and Secretary of State Henry L. Stimson attempted to reach agreement with Great Britain on ways to enforce the Pact of Paris and the Nine-Power Treaty.

Yet Sir John Simon believed, probably correctly, that American administrative opinion could not be supported by American action, and the British government was fearful that Japan would leave the League if forcefully checked in China. Sir George Perley, Canada's delegate to the League, had begun by blunt expressions of Canada's views. C. H. Cahan, his successor, surprised and grieved Canada by following Simon's line of conspicuous considerateness toward Japan. The Bennett government completed this stage of Canada's painful education in her own impotence by supporting Cahan and awkwardly trying to justify itself to the country.

The same reaction, now complicated by internal dissension in Canada, followed Italy's attack on Ethiopia and Franco's rebellion against the Spanish Republic, for *Canadiens* and indeed a large part of the Roman Catholic community across Canada favored Mussolini for his corporativism and Franco for his representation of his cause as a crusade against Communism.

When W. A. Riddell, Canada's representative at Geneva, supported the League's attempts to restrain Italy by economic sanctions to the point of proposing that they be made really effective by embargoes on oil, coal, iron and steel, the King government swiftly disavowed his action, explaining that Canada did not intend to take the initiative and that Riddell's views were his own, not those of his government. Similarly, when some Canadians began to aid the Spanish Republic by enlistment in the Mackenzie-Papineau detachment and by sending other aid, the King government in 1937 passed a Foreign Enlistment Act under which by order in council such assistance was fairly effectively checked.

External forces take command.—By 1937, Canadian fears of what this degeneration in international relations might entail were beginning to find rather bewildered expression. In February, for instance, Ernest Lapointe, King's masterly lieutenant for Quebec, was saying: "If international leaders or gangsters ever come to assail us on a mad impulse—because the world is mad at the present time—we cannot meet them with a declaration of neutrality," but at the same time Maxime Raymond, a Quebec isolationist, was declaring: "Our army, our air force, and our navy must be called out only in defense of Canada and solely within her territory."

These utterances were made during the revealing debates on Canada's greatly increased defense estimates. The government's case, as put by Ian Mackenzie, Minister of National Defense, was that "the more you believe in, the more you subscribe to doctrines of Canadian nationalism, the more you must provide for the defense of the Dominion of Canada. You cannot any longer lean upon the alliances or the implied alliances of the past; you can no longer lean upon the implications of the Monroe Doctrine."

The contrast in the reception of these views could be found in a British Columbian member's remark: "As a Canadian I do not want to be riding on the coat-tails of Uncle Sam," and in a Quebec member's comment: "As regards imperialism, I think that American imperialism is not any better, nor any brighter, nor any more desirable than British imperialism." The C.C.F. opposed the increases, as did various Liberal, Liberal-Progressive, and Social Credit members from all over the country, but the prime minister and the caucus drove them through, with the cordial approval of most of the little band of Conservatives.

If 1937 be regarded as a period almost of chaos in Canadian (and American and British) foreign policy, 1938 represented a hardening into resentful acceptance of the imminence of war. The Hoare-Laval proposals for the partition of Ethiopia and Neville Chamberlain's description of continued sanctions after the fall of Addis Ababa as "midsummer madness" had offended the moral sense of many Canadians; the calculated agonies of the Hitler-Chamberlain negotiations which culminated at Munich in the dismemberment of Czechoslovakia in 1938 took place so near the brink of war that relief at first eclipsed shame.

Yet had Britain gone to war in September, 1938, the Canadian Cabinet would have followed suit, and during that winter disillusionment with Chamberlain's hoped-for "general scheme of appeasement" (February 21, 1938) grew tardily but steadily. More significantly, British opinion also hardened so unmistakably that when Hitler shamelessly took over Czechoslovakia in March, 1939, Chamberlain's policy was considered bankrupt. The British prime minister then figuratively drew a series of lines across Europe whose transgression by Germany would mean war with Great Britain. Canadians agreed, for the most part. As W. A. Mackintosh remarked of his country early that summer, "Yet in large measure she is still on the world's circumference. She can support world policy better than she can initiate."

The preliminary debate took place in late March and early April, 1939. It was a sober, grim affair, little relieved by the flashes of angry, frightened rejection of the apparently inevitable by representatives drawn from all three great divisions of the Canadian peoples. King, who had personally visited Hitler during the summer of 1937 to tell him that Canada would enter war "at Britain's side," seems to have been almost sure as early as January, 1939, that it would come. Yet, since to him the maintenance of precarious Canadian unity was the basic objective, he spoke very cautiously, if ominously, in the debates, reverting to his January declaration that war in alliance with Britain was a matter "upon which the Canadian Parliament will have to pronounce and will have to decide in its own best judgment."

The *Canadiens,* Liberal and Conservative, made the principal appeals for neutrality, for the C.C.F., while opposed to war, was divided and confused in opinion, as were the Western radicals. It fell upon *Canadien* members of the Cabinet to disillusion them. Lapointe, after eloquently supporting King's insistence on the paramount importance of national unity, warned his compatriots that whatever Canada's right to neutrality in a British war, its exercise would involve such things as interning British seamen seeking shelter in Canadian ports. "I ask any one of my countrymen whether they believe seriously that this could be done without a civil war in Canada . . . the right itself is meaningless. There is only the policy of neutrality, which would be rather a hazardous policy, hardly compatible with the national situation of Canada."

The only small comfort to be drawn from the debates was the prevailing belief in Britain and Canada that a war would not require the dispatch of forces to Europe and that therefore the problem of conscription could be ignored. The enlarged defense estimates in May were carried with an enhanced display of national unity.

Early that summer King George and Queen Elizabeth made their contribution to solidarity in the course of a month's visit to Canada, during which the king met his Canadian ministers and, acting on their advice, temporarily supplanted the governor general in receiving a new American minister and signing the new Canadian trade agreement with the United States. The admirable tact and easy friendliness of the sovereigns conquered the whole country in their personal behalf, and the queen's farewell—*"Que Dieu bénisse le Canada"*—reciprocated the emotional and gay welcome they had received from Quebec.

Yet the dread of war remained, and two defiantly despairing utterances of King's have become almost classical expressions of Canadian feelings in 1939. On March 30, he said:

The idea that every twenty years this country should automatically and as a matter of course take part in a war overseas for democracy or self-determination of other small nations, that a country which has all it can do to run itself should feel called upon to save, periodically, a continent that cannot run itself, and to these ends risk the lives of its people, risk bankruptcy and political disunion, seems to many a nightmare and sheer madness.

At a banquet in his honor at Toronto one month before war broke out, he replied to criticisms that he had not stated Canada's foreign policy precisely by saying:

One thing I will not do and can not be persuaded to do is to say what Canada will do in regard to a situation that may arise at some future time and under circumstances of which we know nothing.

Canada could only "wait and see," but by then not many Canadians had much doubt about what the outcome must be.

CHAPTER XXIX

The Forcing-Frame of War (1939-45)

World War II, like World War I, effected an extraordinary surge in Canadian development. In armed forces, in production, in aid to others, and in domestic enlargement of all sorts Canada grew into unpredictable strength. Not only was her used and unused capacity of the thirties in brains, manpower, production, and transportation drawn upon to the full, but immense quantities were added, and the fruits of the whole made Canada known and felt internationally as never before. Perhaps most significantly, in spite of the rapid decline of Great Britain and the rapid rise of the United States as world powers, Canada was able to maintain an exceedingly close relationship with her mighty neighbor in which her actual and her potential independence were preserved, indeed were perhaps enhanced in the sense that American awareness of Canada increased and was accompanied by respect for her individuality.

In a world that was becoming one of Great Powers and satellites, that relationship seemed incredible to an American isolationist like Charles Lindbergh or to the Russian government. It was a curious connection, functioning at various levels and in various depths, variegated by new approvals and old distastes, and pregnant with possibilities of both benefit and disaster, but it worked, as almost no one would have dared to prophesy a decade earlier. All this in spite of the fact that the United States could not in reason evoke the warmth of emotional attachment that perhaps half the Canadian peoples felt towards Great Britain. Indeed the roots of the relationship's strength lay in the sense that the United States and Canada were allied in support of Britain's defiance of tyranny and defense of traditionally cherished values.

🍁 CANADA ENTERS THE WAR

It was a saddened and reluctantly resigned Mackenzie King who accepted the imminence of war in late August, 1939. The Russo-German

Pact of August 21 eased his position a little by putting Nazism and Communism in the same camp, but he knew that, in spite of Quebec's sympathy for Catholic Poland and her special fears of Communism, a great war carried with it the threat that one part of Canada would demand a greater share in it than another part was prepared to undertake. Believing as he did in March that "a divided Canada can be of little help to any country, and least of all to itself," he knew that the maintenance of a united Canada to which he had wholeheartedly devoted himself was in great peril.

After announcing on August 23 that the government was prepared to use its powers under the War Measures Act of 1914, and on August 25 that Parliament would be summoned if war became inevitable, he proclaimed on September 1 that a state "of apprehended war exists and has existed as and from the twenty-fifth day of August," and summoned Parliament to meet on September 7. With Great Britain's declaration of war on September 3, he announced that his government would recommend co-operation and he took several precautionary steps in view of, but without formally recognizing, the state of war. This allowed Roosevelt to postpone bringing the American Neutrality Act into force against Canada, thus permitting some useful Canadian purchases from the United States. It meant that theoretically Parliament might decide on active belligerency, passive belligerency, or neutrality.

The Speech from the Throne that greeted Parliament was vague, and King himself spoke at great length without being specific about what Canada would do beyond the defense of Canada and Newfoundland and the provision of Britain's needs in supplies and air training facilities. Not until September 9 were Parliament and the country informed that approval of the Speech would be followed by a declaration of war.

The three-day debate was marked by an able appeal from Maxime Raymond for a friendly neutrality, which Lapointe rejected in the most eloquent and effective speech of his career. After J. S. Woodsworth, leader of the C.C.F., had announced that he spoke only for himself in commitment to unconditional pacifism, M. J. Coldwell explained the party's policy, which was to accept Canada's involvement, but limit contributions to home defense and economic aid. Liguori Lacombe's amendment against "participation in war outside of Canada," while seconded by Wilfrid Lacroix, was attacked by G. H. Héon, a Quebec Conservative, on grounds of its alienating the majority group, and was overwhelmingly rejected. When less than five members rose to oppose approval of the Speech, no division was necessary.

On Sunday morning, September 10, the Canadian High Commissioner in London received the King's written approval for the Canadian government's declaration "that a State of War with the German Reich exists and has existed in Our Dominion of Canada as and from the tenth day of September, 1939." No one was prepared to declare either what "State" had existed during the previous week or what Canada was going to do about positive belligerent action. All parties pledged themselves against conscription, and the vote of $100,000,000 in war appropriations was opposed by only ten *Canadien* and six C.C.F. votes.

The early lull.—During the lull of the succeeding seven months, the "phony war" during which neither side attacked in the West, Canada waited for a lead that was not forthcoming. King emphatically did not take the country into his confidence, striving as he was to maintain unity. There was no inrush of British orders for munitions and supplies, no indication of what thinking lay behind the dispatch of the First Canadian Division to Britain in December and the preparation of the Second to follow. In the United States, Roosevelt was still bound by the strength of popular resistance to implication and by the great web of precautionary legislation under which the United States was prepared to sacrifice her foreign trade and financial interest, her carrying trade, the free movement of her citizens, and her cherished concepts of neutral rights and freedom of the seas in order to keep out of war. Only the Pittman Act of November loosened the web by permitting "Cash and Carry" sales of munitions. The really provocative six months' notice in July, 1939, to Japan of the American abrogation of the commercial treaty of 1911 had passed almost unnoticed.

King used the lull very shrewdly in the face of mutually aggravating challenges—Duplessis's calling a Quebec election against participation in October and Ontario's mounting demands for a less "practical" and more dramatic participation.

The first challenge was met and crushed when Lapointe and his three *Canadien* colleagues in the federal Cabinet announced that they would resign, leaving Quebec without representation in the national Executive, if Duplessis were sustained, but would prevent conscription if he were not. A dramatic reversal took place in the Quebec house: instead of 75 Union Nationale members against 15 Liberals, 69 Liberals faced 17 others.

The second challenge was countered by raising and sending the military forces to England, by strenuous attention to the navy, particularly in its antisubmarine and escort capacities, and by the establishment of the British Commonwealth Air Training Plan, under which, with Canada providing over half the cost and four-fifths of the personnel,

20,000 pilots and observers a year were to be provided for Great Britain, Canada, Australia, and New Zealand, and the number was later expanded.

When, even so, Hepburn of Ontario continued his attacks to the point of a legislative vote of regret "that the Federal Government at Ottawa has made so little effort to prosecute Canada's duty in the war in the vigorous manner the people of Canada desire to see," King called the federal Parliament for a three-hour session which amounted to nothing, in spite of protests, beyond the announcement of a general election on March 26. With his enemies off balance, and having provided them with no clear targets to shoot at since the outbreak of the war, he appealed for national unity and a general mandate. He secured a tremendous majority, 183 out of 245 seats. He and his party again gave the specific pledge against conscription for overseas services.

The crisis of 1940.—Hitler's blitzkrieg (and Italy's "stab in the back") of April-June, 1940, produced something approaching panic in North America, for Britain, minus the equipment of her expeditionary force, though surprisingly spared most of its men by the daring feats at Dunkirk, now stood nearly alone against the Axis powers in Europe, the Mediterranean, and the Far East. But with Churchill's moral courage and infectiously defiant eloquence as a rallying point, and Anglo-American alliance as the all-embracing objective, Canada committed herself to all-out war just as beleaguered and almost weaponless Britain did after months of complacent inertia which had almost rivaled that of France. Churchill's reputed aside after his famous "We shall fight" speech of June 4—that it would have to be with beer bottles because they were the only weapons available—was a grim commentary on Chamberlain's War Office as well as on the losses at Dunkirk.

When the United States rearmed Britain during the last days of France's collapse, it could be said that North America as a whole had begun to fulfill Churchill's prophecy that "the New World, with all its power and might," would step "forth to the rescue and the liberation of the old." Canadians were less aware of American implication than of their own, for Canadian sailors and airmen were in actual combat for over two years before the Americans, but the great war against the Axis powers was underway during the summer of 1940 with Britain as the spearhead, the British dominions, Yugoslavia, and Greece as auxiliaries, and the United States and Canada as the "arsenal of democracy." Russia's involuntary involvement during the summer of 1941 and the crippling losses incurred by the United States and Great Britain when Japan struck at the end of that year placed still heavier burdens on North American productivity.

Triangular collaboration.—The basic understanding achieved among Great Britain, the United States, and Canada during the summer of 1940 made collaboration possible. Britain was rearmed in June; during the last week of July the Pan American Union organized its republics in mutual self-reliance and respect against the Axis. King and four members of his Cabinet had vacationed near Washington during April and had conducted purposeful conversations with the Roosevelt administration. On August 18 King and Roosevelt announced at Ogdensburg, N. Y., their agreement to create a "Permanent Joint Board on Defense" to "consider in the broad sense the defense of the north half of the Western Hemisphere." Two days later, Churchill forewarned the British Parliament of a bargain with the United States by which, on September 3, the United States received, gratis, leases for bases in Bermuda and Newfoundland, and leased for ninety-nine years six others from the Bahamas to British Guiana in exchange for fifty "overage" destroyers. Britain also promised never to surrender or scuttle her navy. The American Congress voted huge sums for rearmament, and peacetime conscription was inaugurated for the first time. In the November election Roosevelt and his unsuccessful opponent, Wendell Willkie, were agreed upon all-out aid to Britain "short of war."

Lend-lease in March, 1941, and the Hyde Park Agreement between Roosevelt and King in April eliminated the financial problem. A series of international committees progressively constructed a single economic, strategic, and policy apparatus to manage the joint effort. The United States, having lost her first merchant vessel to a submarine in May, began in July to take over from Canada and Britain the defense of Iceland, to which it was already convoying supplies. For a number of reasons it seemed advisable to Britain and Canada for the United States to assume protection of Danish Iceland and Greenland. In August Churchill and Roosevelt met at Newfoundland and issued a declaration of principles, the Atlantic Charter. By September and October, American destroyers and German submarines were at outright war in northern waters. In November, Congress repealed the Neutrality Act, and on December 7 a Japan that refused to be deterred from exploiting irresistible opportunities in the Far East destroyed half the American fleet at Pearl Harbor, fatally impaired American and British Far Eastern outposts, and made the war a world war.

Canadian frustration.—Canadian recorders of this time report that a feeling of frustration followed the fears felt during the great Battle of Britain in the air and on the island's surrounding waters during 1940, and that it lasted until almost the end of 1942, to be succeeded by an exhilarating sense of fulfillment. The ingredients of the frustration were many: distaste for British policies of the thirties, pessimism over American isolationism, disillusioned resignation to the necessity of fighting Hitler, puzzlement as to how he could be defeated in less than decades, and the almost complete lack of anything dramatic or victorious to show for the dispatch overseas of hundreds of thousands of Canadians and astronomical amounts of supplies. The two Canadian battalions sent to Hong Kong in November, 1941, were lost within a month. The daring Canadian raid on Dieppe in August, 1942, although conducted with the utmost gallantry, was in itself almost a complete failure since few of its objectives were attained. Of almost 5000 men embarked, only 2211 returned, including 1000 who could not land. It was apparently necessary to take prefabricated harbors along as substitutes for destroyed port facilities or as installations at beaches. But the lessons learned for later successful landings and particularly for D-Day, 1944, were small consolation.

It was hard for Canadians to hear of the exploits of Britons, Indians, Australians, New Zealanders, and South Africans while their own troops were held in Great Britain. The grim, swiftly expanding activities of the Canadian navy in the North Atlantic and along the American coast after Pearl Harbor were almost completely shrouded in secrecy, and Canadian airmen in Britain, Malta, Africa, Ceylon, and elsewhere were for the most part anonymously cloaked in reports of the enterprises of the Royal Air Force.

It was hardest of all to be overshadowed in British and American utterances by the United States, almost from the moment of disaster in which Churchill became prime minister and Minister of Defense. Canada had rallied to the cause at its beginning, her concrete donations to it were greater than the American until well after Pearl Harbor; indeed her total effort in the war relative to her population and national income was greater. (This remained true until the Marshall Plan came into operation in 1947–48.) Yet Canada was continually being overlooked and occasionally misused by both of her great associates. Logically American support and involvement were the assurance of victory and Anglo-American understanding was the keystone of Canadian foreign policy. Emotionally these considerations were often distinctly less than satisfying.

Two classical instances might be cited. Although King is reported to have played an important part in the destroyers-for-bases deal, Canada, which was already defending Newfoundland, found that her interests and rights there were ignored in the Anglo-American agreement, and only after prolonged diplomatic pressure on Great Britain were they partially accommodated in a special triangular protocol of March, 1941. The Goose Bay air base in interior Labrador which furnished the necessary alternative to Gander in Newfoundland on the crucial North Atlantic ferry and transport route provided an outrageous instance of American arrogance. The astonishingly favorable site, in terms of level, drainable terrain and accessibility to Hamilton Inlet and the Atlantic, had been discovered by Canada and the original base was built by Canada and in operation before Pearl Harbor. Yet when news of it was released, certain American periodicals not only "scooped" the agreed-upon date of publication, but claimed Goose Bay as an American achievement.

🍁 FIGHTING THE WAR

The army.—By the spring of 1942, the First Canadian Army of three infantry divisions, two armored divisions, and two armored brigades was being organized in England, but the invasion of North Africa in November found the forces raised and trained during the past three years still unengaged and, except for Dieppe, without battle experience. Their commander, Lieutenant General A. G. L. McNaughton, had been encouraged to think of them as a special highly integrated force for the assault on Europe and he found himself unable to agree to their being broken up and "lost" in British armies, or, as the British land and air forces were during the initial invasions of North Africa, disguised as Americans.

His government, faced by vigorous and vocal, if not very well-informed, public opinion, had to entertain other ideas, the outcome of which was that some hundreds of Canadian officers and noncommissioned officers were sent to Africa to learn the ropes early in 1943. At the beginning of July, the First Canadian Division and the First Canadian Army Tank Brigade, as part of Montgomery's Eighth Army and without McNaughton, took part in the invasion of Sicily, thus beginning over two years of outstanding achievement by the Canadian troops. McNaughton resigned in December, 1943, in a cloud of controversy, misunderstanding, and mistrust which had produced some loss of confidence in him by Churchill, the British War Office, the Allied High Command, and the Ottawa government—an unhappy ending to his truly distinguished services during the preceding years.

The Canadians, reinforced to form a full corps of the Eighth Army, fought their way through the successive stages of the bitter Italian campaign. Their victories were notable and their casualties were heavy. By Christmas, 1944, they had almost reached Bologna after playing conspicuous parts in breaking the Adolf Hitler line behind Cassino and the Gothic Line at its eastern end near the Adriatic. In February, 1945, they were transferred to join the First Canadian Army in Germany.

That Army had been brought into being on July 31, 1944, under Lieutenant General H. D. G. Crerar after various units had played various parts in the initial landings by air and sea in Normandy. At first it contained a British Corps, a Dutch and a Belgian Brigade, and a Polish Armored Division. The Canadians were destined chiefly to constitute the left flank of the great advance from Normandy to Denmark. They began at "the hinge" between Bayeux and Caen, where the Germans massed their armor and fought a series of fanatically intense battles between June 6 and August 22 before their awful slaughter at the Falaise Gap and their retreat across the Seine. Canadian losses here were so heavy as to upset previous calculations as to the need of reinforcements, but the reward was the successive captures of the Channel ports, especially Dieppe, and the buzz-bomb sites and long-range guns in the Calais area.

When Antwerp was taken intact early in September, the problem arose of making it the chief port of entry by clearing the Germans out of the strong defenses between it and the sea—a watery network of canals and dikes and islands that demanded many novelties in land, air, and sea warfare and exacted heavy losses before it was conquered early in November. Major General Guy Simonds had been in command during these operations because of Crerar's illness, and following them the Canadians had a lull and refitting until early February, when Crerar's Army took the offensive again.

From then on, the Canadian Army sometimes had more non-Canadians than Canadians in it, for its strength on occasion was built up to almost 400,000 men when British or American units were assigned to it, the chief interplay being with the British Second Army. Meanwhile some Canadian units served outside it and one of their inventions, an improvised armored personnel carrier, was in great demand by other forces. After almost a month's battle during February in the Reichswald and Hochswald quagmires at the northern end of the Siegfried Line, and the crossing of the Rhine, part of the Canadians gradually cleared northern Holland while the Second, Third, and Fourth divisions drove through northern Germany towards Denmark.

After the German surrender, those who volunteered for the continuing war in the Pacific were withdrawn first from Europe, but as early as January, 1945, Great Britain had been warned by King that it might not "be politically possible to provide Canadian occupation forces in view of the fact that the plans for control of Germany give the Canadian government no voice in the direction of policy." In spite of re-peated British appeals, the Canadian forces were withdrawn during the winter of 1945–46 as rapidly as shipping could be found. An occupation force of about 20,000, however, functioned in the British Zone from September 1, 1945, to April, 1946. The Great Powers then took over.

The forces in general.—Of over a million men and women in the Canadian armed forces (986,000 of them volunteers), over 730,000 had been in the army. In substantial units, they had served in the defense of Britain, Hong Kong, and the Pacific coast. The Canadians had served in garrisons at Newfoundland, Iceland, Gibraltar, British Guiana, Bermuda, and the West Indies; and they had fought through Italy from Sicily to the Po and along the northwestern flank of Europe from the Orne to the Weser.

Although, as compared with World War I, a larger proportion (40.6 per cent) of the men between 18 and 45 had been in the services, and the war had lasted almost two years longer, the changed character of war was reflected in a third fewer casualties, about 42,000 killed, 17,000 of them airmen. The forces had been composed much more of born Canadians, and although the *Canadiens* for the most part served in army regiments, batteries, and so forth, of their own, this was not always the case, with the result that in army, navy, and air force there was a constant mingling of English-speaking Canadians, *Canadiens,* and New Canadians. The size, mixed character, and authority of the commands entrusted to Generals McNaughton, Crerar, Simonds, and E. L. M. Burns (in Italy) evidenced the increase in Canada's weight and maturity.

The airmen.—It was natural that Canada excelled in the air considering her record during World War I and in civil aviation after it. Unfortunately for the historian who wishes to award Canada her due, the Canadian achievement cannot be separated from the British, the Commonwealth, and, to some degree, the American achievements. In spite of determined efforts by C. G. Power, the Air Minister, it proved impossible to secure either autonomy ("Canadianization") or appropriately high command for the Royal Canadian Air Force, and, as Terence Sheard has since observed, from a nationalistic point of view "it must be recognized that Canada's participation in the air war overseas was not a satisfactory pattern."

The R.C.A.F. attracted a quarter of a million men and women; the British Commonwealth Air Training Plan, which was largely its achievement, turned out 131,500 air crew; and it has been estimated that Canadians provided between a fifth and a quarter of the air crew under

British tactical command. Canadian airmen bombed, fought, reconnoitered, photographed, and ferried all over the globe except (with minor exceptions) Russia and the Japanese sector. They dropped parachute troops, dive-bombed, furnished air cover, intercepted buzz bombs, supplied partisan forces and underground resistance forces, and sank submarines. They were maintaining forty-eight operational squadrons of their own overseas and twenty-three at home when war ended in Europe. Their relative casualties were by far the highest among the three services.

The navy.—Although the smallest of the services (106,500 all ranks), the navy demonstrated the most astonishing growth and assumption of responsibility. Here again, the problem of "Canadianization" proved a somewhat insoluble one, and the numerical submergence of the "regular" by the "wavy" navy occasioned considerable difficulty. But from the moment that Halifax, "an Eastern Canadian Port" in the language of censorship, began to figure in the newspapers, the Canadian Navy (and Air Force) grew with the responsibilities of the North Atlantic life-line to Europe.

The navy began with 15 vessels, and ended with 374 fighting ships and over 550 auxiliaries, all small ships except for two cruisers and two "baby" aircraft carriers. Its tough core consisted of the early armed merchantmen and the destroyers, corvettes, and frigates which Canada learned to build for herself and which guarded the Atlantic convoys or sought out submarines. Its responsibility for close escort on the vital North Atlantic route, where the terrible battles with commerce raiders, submarines, mines, and aircraft went on until the last day of the war, rose rapidly from about 40 per cent during 1941 to 100 per cent in 1944.

In addition, four "Tribal" destroyers formed half of a very aggressive and successful flotilla in the Channel, where two lively torpedo-boat flotillas were also posted. Infantry landing ships and their escorts served in Greece, the Aegean, Italy, southern France, and Normandy. Minesweepers plied their dangerous tasks chiefly off Halifax and St. John's, but after the meetings of the Joint Board on Defense at Halifax in October, 1940, a band beginning in Massachusetts and extending, 500 miles broad, up to Iceland came under intensive sea and air supervision from many harbors and airfields.

In this war the St. Lawrence itself was successfully invaded by submarines, and during the awful destruction of shipping along the American Atlantic coast during 1942 and 1943, when the United States was concentrating on the Pacific, Canadian ships helped greatly to curb the menace from Iceland and Greenland to the Caribbean. Two naval colleges trained both veterans from the lower decks and newcomers to become officers in such great numbers that Canada was able not only to officer her own ships, but lend a surplus to the Royal Navy.

The northern transportation routes.—Mention should also be made of the Canadian-American co-operation in military transportation. Even before the war, discussions and investigations had taken place concerning air and land links across Canada between the United States and the Alaska Territory. The Joint Board on Defense speeded them up. After Pearl Harbor, they materialized in the rapid expansion of the C.N.R. terminus at Prince Rupert, within sight of the Alaskan Panhandle; the construction of the northwest staging route and Mackenzie River air route complete with landing fields, directional aids, and so forth, from Edmonton to Fairbanks and to Aklavik; the building of the Alaska Highway (1523 miles) through almost untouched wilderness from Dawson Creek to Fairbanks; and the completion of oil pipe-lines connecting Norman Wells on the Mackenzie with Whitehorse, Watson Lake, Skagway, and Fairbanks.

Less well known were the northeast staging routes for ferrying aircraft and for other transport services from the United States and Canada to Europe. Disregarding the various alternative routes and services, three main operating lines and one unneeded one were arranged for with landing fields, weather stations, and directional aids. One stretched from assembly at Regina, by The Pas, Churchill, Coral Harbor (on Southampton Island), Frobisher Bay (Baffin Island) and either Bluie West Eight or Bluie West One on Greenland to Iceland and beyond. Another extended from assembly at Montreal, either by Sydney and Newfoundland, or by Goose Bay (Labrador) and Greenland. A third reached from assembly at Presque Isle near the Maine–New Brunswick boundary, either by Newfoundland, or by Labrador and Greenland. The route from the American Middle West by Moosonee (James Bay) and Fort Chimo (Ungava Bay) to Frobisher Bay or Bluie West One was practically unused.

The expenditures on all these services were enormous, but Canada was scrupulously careful to avoid infringement of her sovereignty through sharing costs of installations on her territory. The postwar use by the United States of such facilities as at Churchill, Frobisher Bay, Mingan (near Anticosti), or Chimo has been by Canadian permission.

Applied science.—Great Britain, Canada, and the United States pooled their applications of science to warfare so thoroughly that most of the contributions of each were inseparable from those of the others. Before the war, General McNaughton, as president of the National Research Council, C. J. Mackenzie, who succeeded him at that post in

1938, and Sir Frederick Banting and Dr. C. H. Best, at their Medical Research Institute at Toronto, had set going research in radio, ballistics, chemical warfare, aviation medicine, and biological warfare. War immensely accelerated and expanded such work. The Council grew from 300 employees and an annual budget of $900,000 to 2000 and $7,000,-000, and its subsidiaries multiplied all across the country. In addition, both private industry and public corporations turned to highly technical and novel production.

Among the more outstanding achievements were the dried blood serum of the Banting-Best institute and the Connaught Laboratories at the University of Toronto; the perfection by a mixed industrial and academic team of an inexpensive method for producing the explosive known as RDX; the antigravity flier's suit developed by Banting's assistant, Dr. W. R. Frank; the early and immense production of radar equipment so valuable not only to Great Britain on land and sea and in the air, but especially to the United States for Panama and for her post-Pearl Harbor navy; the National Research Council's early (1941) automatic antiaircraft gun-laying device (GL); and both the production of uranium and radium from Great Bear Lake ores and the nuclear research that culminated in the atomic bomb.

🍁 THE WAR ECONOMY

The expansion and diversification of the Canadian economy under the pressures of war defy brief, comprehensive description. Canada may well have furnished the world's most successful example of resolute, intelligent, co-ordinated state economic direction and control, for her people, in individual and in joint activities, gave the co-operation and local supervision necessary for the efficient and reasonably equitable operation of a national system in production, consumption, and taxation.

The apparatus proliferated with astonishing speed and scope after rather modest, if fundamental, beginnings between September, 1939, and May, 1940. The Executive possessed enormous powers under the War Measures Act of 1914 and the National Resources Mobilization Act of June, 1940, and used them. Canada was governed for over six years largely by hundreds of orders in council, and Canadians, on the whole, accepted that kind of dictatorial control dutifully and with little by way of scandalous defections such as black markets.

The state set out to mobilize men and women, materials, and all kinds of productive capacity, meanwhile combating inflation by using very heavy taxation and both voluntary and compulsory savings to reinforce rationing, fortify price and wage controls, and pay for the war as much as possible out of income. The rate achieved, 56 per cent, was distinctly higher than in Britain or the United States. On March 31, 1940, the national debt was $4700 million and the annual interest charges of $115 million represented 2.4 per cent of the national income, or 20 per cent of the national revenue. The comparable figures for March 31, 1945, were: $14,600 million; $273 million; 3 per cent; and 10.1 per cent. The large degree of success testified unusual skill among the policy-makers and self-discipline among the citizens. The cost of living, for instance, rose by only 20 per cent, and the standard was at least maintained.

During the war, government expenditures rose from 15 per cent of the gross national income to 40 per cent, but that income itself more than doubled. The most striking expansion, as might have been expected, was in manufactures, which grew from 39 per cent of the net value of production to almost 60 per cent. Moreover this industrial development both deepened and broadened: steel production doubled; aluminum production became six times as great; complex ships, advanced types of aircraft, tanks, and military vehicles were built; and great quantities of explosives and chemicals, as well as such specialized products as serums, penicillin, optical glass and instruments, artificial rubber, and electronic equipment, were turned out. In 1945 the ten leading industries in terms of gross value of production were, in order: meat packing, pulp and paper, nonferrous metals, aircraft, sawmills, electrical, automotive, grain milling, dairy, shipbuilding. It has been calculated that war production reached the total value of $10 billion, only one-third of which was for the use of Canada.

Since Canada's allies could not pay for all the goods they needed for war and sustenance, she gave them over $4 billion worth. She did not avail herself of American lend-lease, but made arrangements through the Hyde Park Agreement to achieve a more even balance with the United States and to work up British lend-lease materials drawn from the United States without debits to her own account. In any case, American investors were pouring capital into Canada at a very high rate, partly by reinvestment of earnings there but also by purchase of Canadian securities. The American capital investment rose from $4,151 million in 1939 to $5,157 million in 1946, half directly in enterprises and half in securities. There was a good deal of talk about Canada being a better place than the United States for one's money.

Impressive as the industrial growth was, the transformation of agriculture was in some ways equally remarkable. Agriculture had declined from 22 to 20 per cent of the nation's net value of production, and over 120,000 persons had left the western plains during the war. Yet agricultural production increased in value by 60 per cent. In other words, "the wheat economy" was being "rationalized" in size of holding, mechanization, and manpower, and western agriculture was being diversified. A cattle center like Calgary was processing thousands of grain-fed hogs and liking it, or, perhaps more surprisingly, turning out tons of powdered eggs. In addition to grains, flours, and meals, Canada could sell all the pork products, beef, eggs, cheese, flax, oil seeds, etc., her farmers could produce.

Agricultural prices more than doubled from 1939 to 1945, and the average values of both farm capital and farm lands greatly increased. Yet there were few signs of the "runaway" agricultural speculation that had characterized 1914–18. After "the years of the locust" between 1929 and 1939, Canadian farmers were sobered, prone to suspend judgment about how long the return of good fortune would last, and meanwhile inclined to pay off their debts and save their gains. The food contracts which the state selling agency negotiated with Great Britain reflected this cautious mood by accepting lower than world prices in return for guaranteed postwar markets.

Forest production a little more than doubled in value during the war, and the fisheries almost tripled the value of their product particularly after 1943, when relief needs in devastated areas made a hungry market for dried and canned fish. Mining on the whole presented a picture of increased demands on production at a time when manpower was in short supply. Thus gold production, being somewhat irrelevant, was encouraged to decline from over five million ounces in 1939 to half of that in 1945. Yet total mineral production increased in value by about 5 per cent, largely because of the expanded demand for nickel, copper, lead, zinc, and asbestos.

The really tantalizing portion of the mining picture was the prospect of Canada's being able substantially to remedy her deficiencies in iron ore and petroleum. Two mines in the Lake Superior region, both amenable to opencut operations, emerged after 1940 as substitutes for the declining supplies of iron ore in northern Minnesota, and the huge surface deposits along the Labrador-Quebec boundary, noted by A. P. Low fifty years earlier, were considered rich enough to justify a 360-mile railroad from Seven Islands on the lower St. Lawrence. A large deposit of ilmenite, an ore which yields highly valuable titanium and iron to electric smelting, was discovered in 1946 at Allard Lake, near Havre St. Pierre, 125 miles farther down the St. Lawrence. It was to be carried upriver to Sorel by water and smelted by power from a new development on the St. Maurice River.

The new prospects for petroleum were in Alberta where, although the

Turner Valley field had begun to decline, the geology in the vicinity of Edmonton and extending to the Saskatchewan boundary seemed to promise compensation. This expectation was more than fulfilled in 1947 when a series of wells began to come in of such great richness as to justify a pipeline to the Great Lakes. These developments and the abundance of natural gas accompanying them seriously threatened the never very satisfactory coal industry of Alberta and British Columbia.

The astonishing expansion—42 per cent from 1938 to 1944—in the output of electrical power was chiefly in response to the demands of wartime industry in central Canada, most notably the sixfold growth of aluminum production based upon the Saguenay and its tributaries, where completion during the war of the Shipshaw development raised the capacity to almost 2,000,000 horsepower.

⚜ NEWFOUNDLAND

The war lifted Newfoundland out of bankruptcy and meager livelihood. At its outbreak over 50,000, one sixth of its people, were in receipt of public relief, but with the impact of Canadian and American defense expenditures (and wage rates), there were not enough hands for the jobs to be done. The national income was at least doubled, probably a good deal more. The cost of living almost doubled, but now Newfoundlanders could sell their goods and services, and the prices of exported pulp, paper, iron, nonferrous metals, and fish rose as well as wages.

There was some rationing, but the standard of living improved notably. The new social services did a good deal to ease the lot of the unfortunate. The merchant group made phenomenal profits, as always during a boom; recipients of fixed incomes had a hard time. The expansion of the fisheries after 1942 and its continuance after the war carried many Newfoundlanders smoothly from the abnormalities of 1939–42 back into their traditionally most important occupation. Newfoundlanders served in, and were paid by, the British and Canadian armed services, except for certain bonuses paid to those in the British forces.

The transformation was most dramatically reflected in the statistics of public finance. Modest beginnings were made in direct (income) taxation, but customs duties, the chief source of revenue, mushroomed in volume. Whereas the over-all national deficit for the seven years before 1940 had been $16,700,000, at the expense of the British taxpayer, budget surpluses for the next five years amounted to $23,000,000. With the addition of internal loans of about $8,000,000, these funds were used to pay off some Canadian and British loans, to meet sinking fund and interest requirements on others, to make outright gifts or extend interest-free credits to Great Britain, and still leave about $12,000,000 as a reserve for postwar eventualities.

Not many countries emerged from World War II with reduced public debts, but Newfoundland, which in 1933–34 had a debt of over $100,-000,000, the service of which swallowed up 65 per cent of the average revenue, ten years later had a debt of $88,000,000, with a service cost of 14 per cent of the revenue. Peace, of course, was expected to throw Newfoundland back on her own resources, which normally would be insufficient to maintain her people at, say, the standard of living in the Maritime Provinces of Canada. Great Britain had been too sorely damaged to be asked for help.

Before the war ended, therefore, there were obvious signs, perhaps most particularly a great enquiry into Newfoundland's past history and enduring circumstances conducted by the Canadian Institute of International Affairs, that Newfoundlanders must soon choose between standing alone and entering the Canadian federation. The war, on the sea and in the air, had demonstrated that their greatest bargaining asset was their island's strategic location as a strong sea-bastion, "a focus of United States, Canadian, and British power in the North Atlantic."

CANADIAN DOMESTIC POLITICS

In spite of the federal government's almost dictatorial powers during the war, Canadian politics were anything but dull. To begin with, there was the crucial problem of the now vested and emotional, rather than reasonable, *Canadien* resistance to conscription, supported as it was by smaller groups in other parts of Canada and badly aggravated by English-speaking Canadian and American extremists. Western and other Progressivism was substantially diluted by a prosperity that public economic controls had prevented from being dissipated in inflation, but sectionalism was not dead, as was demonstrated by the abrupt failure of the dominion-provincial conference of January, 1941, on the Rowell-Sirois recommendations.

The Maritimes and the Plains lamented the accelerated growth of central Canada and the suction there that drew off their young people, notably women, who were systematically recruited for industry. British Columbia, rising rapidly in realized wealth and comparative economic weight, tended to stand alone, and many a Canadian in the services who discovered the unique beauty and mild (if rainy) climate of "the coast" vowed that after the war he would go there and turn his back on the rest of Canada. Finally, there was the problem of the Japanese Canadians, whose presence in British Columbia created a panic there that managed to overwhelm Ottawa and produce discreditable national policy.

The conscription issue.—King's handling of the conscription problem was probably his greatest achievement as a Canadian politician, a kind of copestone for the edifice of national unity to which he had dedicated himself. Yet that end had to justify some very ignoble means. If politics is the art of the possible, its practices must offend purists. Some of King's purposeful obscurities and his tricky devices could hardly be described as candid or honorable, but he felt that if he could hold the country together, could avoid the wounds of 1917 and 1918, the achievement would eventually outweigh personal disrepute. Apparently he had seen the writing on the wall as early as 1938. From then until his baffling personal triumph in the Commons in December, 1944, he conducted a masterly, if devious, retreat from his repeated promises that he and his party would never countenance conscription for military service overseas.

Once again in Canada's history external forces upset the delicate balance of internal compromise, but King's surrender was so long drawn out and adroit that the final act in it was a quite unexpected political victory. Throughout it all, it should be remembered, *Canadien* volunteers were serving in large numbers overseas, brilliantly on many occasions. King's decision to make it impossible to compare the contributions in manpower of the *Canadiens* with other Canadians was characteristic of him. The contrast between what the *Canadiens* would do freely and their almost uniform resistance to compulsion was not the least confusing element in a situation where tradition and feeling triumphed over actual circumstances and logic. A *Canadien* who would do his utmost in patriotic duty at home, who was proud of the services of his children and relatives in battle, would nevertheless feel committed to resisting the advent of conscription in every possible way.

Out of the fears of 1940 came national registration of manpower in August, to be followed almost at once by peacetime conscription in the United States. King's policy was gradually to introduce, expand, and extend short-term compulsory military training at home for young single men, using the powers secured from Parliament in the National Resources Mobilization Act of June, 1940. This policy had been quite calmly accepted by Quebec. When Mayor Houde of Montreal in early August advised his people not to register, he was promptly arrested and interned by Lapointe's Department of Justice without provoking any strong outburst of sympathy. In April, 1941, what had been first thirty-day, and then four-month, service was converted into indefinite service in coast defense and other home duties.

Russia's involuntary entry into the war in June, 1941, coupled with Churchill's instant alliance, made the Quebec situation more difficult because of anti-Communism there, but King took the occasion once more to affirm his government's pledge against conscription for overseas. The death of Lapointe late in 1941 was an irreparable loss to King, for that great statesman was, in Mason Wade's words, Quebec's "only leader in the federal government who thoroughly understood his province, who enjoyed its confidence, and who was a Canadian first and a French Canadian second."

It was Pearl Harbor and the Japanese triumph in the Pacific, however, which produced the first crisis since Duplessis's ill-timed appeal to the voters in October, 1939. On the one hand, no one could maintain any longer that this was merely a "British" war, but on the other, the measure of the ensuing worldwide disasters to the anti-Axis powers could mean nothing but even greater effort from Canada. While voluntary enlistments were still more than adequate for the three rapidly expanding armed services, no one knew what the future would demand. The Conservative party, chiefly its Ontario members, had been demanding outright conscription and a coalition government, and, ominously for Quebec, Meighen had resigned from the Senate in November, 1941, to become the Conservative leader.

In January, 1942, therefore, King announced that his government would "seek, from the people, by means of a plebiscite, release from any obligation arising out of any past commitments restricting the methods of raising men for military service." The result of the voting on April 27 was a 64 to 36 affirmative vote for Canada as a whole, a 4-to-1 affirmative vote in the provinces other than Quebec, but a 72 to 28 negative vote in the French province. Two weeks later, King introduced House Bill Number 80 to repeal the clause of the 1940 Act prohibiting conscription for overseas service.

P. J. A. Cardin, the senior *Canadien* member of the Cabinet, resigned, but King continued to temporize in terms of his stand—"not necessarily conscription but conscription if necessary." Conscription for Home Defense was expanded, however, and by order in council the conscripts were sent to Alaska, Newfoundland, and Labrador in September, 1942, to Jamaica in March, 1943, and to Bermuda, the Bahamas, and British Guiana in August, 1943. One of the regiments launched against Kiska was *Canadien*. Not only did they thus release other troops for combat overseas, but from 1942 onwards a considerable proportion of the Home Defense troops were themselves persuaded to volunteer for overseas duty.

The heroism of *Les Fusiliers de Mont-Royal* at Dieppe in August,

1942, stirred Quebec's pride, but Act Number 80 had furnished a focus for the hitherto scattered forms of Quebec particularism, and extremist *Canadiens* began rapidly to raise a Chinese Wall around themselves. In October, 1942, the antiwar *Ligue pour la Défense du Canada* blossomed into an ethnic political party, *Le Bloc Populaire,* which quickly became the receptacle for all kinds of soreness—over industrialization, alien economic overlordship, urbanization, social disorder, mobilization, "centralized" controls, conscription, women in the services and in industry, and so on. The Montreal industrial region where half the province's population lived, often in squalor, provided most of the tinder for extremists and for demagogic politicians. Things were different down the river, for the reply to German submarines there had been the organization of a defense region at Gaspé manned by *Canadiens.*

It was notable and almost unprecedented that at this time three high-minded leaders, two of them priests, who tried to stem the tide of prejudice and separatism were allowed by their compatriots to be vilified and defamed by the extremists in outrageous fashion—Abbé Armand Sabourin, a heroic chaplain at Dieppe; Abbé Arthur Maheux, an objective historian; and Senator T. D. Bouchard, who characterized in authoritative detail and denounced the conspiratorial and terroristic activities of the extremists' secret Order of Jacques Cartier. The frenzied explosion of opinion following Bouchard's revelations, and his very courageous attempt to assert larger views, rivaled the Guibord Affair of the seventies.

Actually, however, the *Bloc* was not a bloc. Not only was it opposed by the archbishops and higher clergy, although welcomed by many of the lower clergy (notably rural) and some of the religious orders, but it was rent down the middle between demagogic allies of big business on the one hand and sincere corporativists or radical "trust-busters" on the other. In fact it might be argued that the important issue in Quebec at this time was not conscription, but the serious woes of urban industrial labor, whose standards of wages, hours of work, housing, social services, and other amenities were much lower than in Ontario.

This issue was naturally and artificially obscured, not only by various other aspects of separatism but by bitter warfare between international trade unionism and the Catholic syndicates. The internationals were trying to prevent Quebec from becoming an asylum for industries which would threaten the general Canadian, indeed North American, standard of labor by lower wages, longer hours, and inferior conditions generally. The mainspring of the syndicates' motivation was dislike and distrust of "foreigners," particularly when they seemed to be working hand-inglove with the "centralizers" at Ottawa. These alien forces were believed to have destroyed a fine old way of life, paternalistic and mutually accommodating. The classic contest occurred in the aluminum industry in 1942, but the great offensive by the syndicates against the internationals took place in 1944, the year when for the rest of Canada everything was eclipsed by the conscription issue.

The *Canadiens,* popular belief to the contrary, have always been intensely individualistic in the realm of opinion among themselves. It seems likely that they have never been as violently divided over such matters as during 1944.

Logically, Adélard Godbout, the moderate leader of the Liberal government, should have been the choice of the characteristically moderate majority of the *Canadiens,* but in one way and another the radicals of Right and Left made him the scapegoat of Quebec's social distresses and sense of betrayal by Ottawa. This afforded Duplessis an opportunity that he was well able to exploit. In effect, he offered a middle and an allegedly separatist way between almost revolutionary radicals, notably the Order of Jacques Cartier, and the Liberals who persisted in cooperating with Ottawa in spite of conscription. Duplessis was for "provincial rights."

In a wildly confused provincial election in the autumn of 1944 the Liberals received 37 per cent of the vote and 37 seats, Duplessis's *Union Nationale* 36 per cent and 45 seats, and *Le Bloc Populaire* 15 per cent and 4 seats. In Quebec, as in many of the American states, the vote of the countryside outbalances that of the cities. In general, the Liberals won the cities and *Union Nationale* the countryside, but the "new Parties" (*Bloc,* C.C.F., Social Credit, Communist, and Independent) won two-thirds as many votes as the *Union Nationale.* Domestically this was a turbulent Quebec, torn and racked by the intensified industrialization of the war; in terms of the larger Canada it was a reproof to King and to Louis Stephen St. Laurent, the Quebec lawyer whom King had brought to Ottawa in December, 1941, to succeed Lapointe in spite of his inexperience in politics. Because of St. Laurent's Irish mother and his contacts with big business as a corporation lawyer, the extremists were able to represent him as hopelessly anglicized.

It was St. Laurent who saved the situation for King, his government, and party during the final conscription crisis of the autumn of 1944. That ruthlessly expedient affair reflected little honor on any of its leading actors except St. Laurent, J. L. Ralston, the Minister of Defense, and his loyal friend, C. G. Power, the Air Minister from Quebec. With his power, his party, and his basic policy threatened and Canada apparently about to repeat the Great Schism of 1917, King subordinated everything to political success. Broken men and tarnished principles accompanied his victory, but he judged it worth the price.

No adequate account of the crisis can be given until many secret records are revealed. All that can be done here is to sketch what are believed to have been the main outlines during three months of the most tortuous politics in which King ever engaged.

The basic trouble was gross miscalculation, chiefly by the Canadian General Staff, of the need for Army reinforcements following the invasion of France. Some time in August the very bases for King's confidence that voluntary enlistments for service overseas precluded conscription began to be destroyed. When Ralston suspected this, he flew to the Italian and Western fronts, discovered the facts, and came home in mid-October determined to have overseas conscription or resign. King, in response, managed to keep his Cabinet arguing for two weeks over how otherwise to satisfy the Army's need for 15,100 men at once and some 5,300 men a month, at a time when in addition to the normal, but now inadequate, flow of volunteers tens of thousands of trained Home Defense troops could be dispatched overseas by order in council if the government would go back on its pledges to Quebec.

Having secured General McNaughton's pledge to persuade enough men to volunteer without conscription, King struck down Ralston without warning by telling him at a Cabinet meeting that he would use the resignation that Ralston had put in his hands in 1942. Ralston, meanwhile, had had King's worthless promise to introduce conscription if necessary. McNaughton then utterly failed to persuade Home Service men to volunteer as reinforcements. With his Cabinet now hopelessly split and his whole world tottering, King received word from St. Laurent, first that he was willing to accept some conscription if volunteering manifestly failed, and then agreement on immediate action. The prime minister promptly presented his Cabinet with an order in council to draft 16,000 Home Defense troops immediately and went to meet the House of Commons.

He had surrendered the fortress he had held since 1917, he had betrayed Ralston (and Power), and he now exposed McNaughton to humiliation in the political field for which he had no aptitude, and yet these three men spared him from defeat in Parliament by refraining from any suggestion that King's government should be replaced by a coalition under Ralston that could so easily have been formed. Patriotism has many guises, but it is difficult to escape the impression that King's was contaminated by a belief that he himself was indispensable. What really won the day for him was the voice of a new Quebec in St. Laurent. He had told his constituents that he would not pledge himself against conscription for overseas because if it became necessary he would not help to split Canada. Now that he judged it necessary for Canada as a whole, he would accept the consequences. This realistic, if regretful, decision was a monumental turning point for French Canada and for the nation in which it was still a misunderstood minority.

Once more King had, by yielding suddenly at the last possible moment, made his eagerly pressing opponents fall flat before they could recover themselves. Parliament thereupon conducted a long, representative, generally sober, but baffling discussion of the conscription problem. Having acted decisively, King could now afford to be vague. A master parliamentarian, he could help his opponents into difficulties and cross-purposes in their many attempted amendments to the government's motion (of confidence).

Many such amendments were ruled out of order, and it was so impossible for the various groups of King's opponents to get together that a series of proper amendments were voted down by such votes as 168 to 43, 170 to 44, and 165 to 33. A much-amended and vague C.C.F. amendment was accepted, 141 to 70. Then the government's motion was carried, 143 to 70 (including 32 *Canadiens*), for the support of the C.C.F. and Social Credit offset the most obdurate Conservatives and the Quebec defections.

After this consummate exercise in the techniques of parliamentary power, the prime minister who had seemed about to be brought down by Quebec separatists and Ontario Conservatives was able confidently to adjourn Parliament until the end of January. There was some arson, window-breaking, and flag-burning in Quebec, but no bloodshed. Sober opinion there sided with King's compromise as better than a new government and revengeful action. Yet it was notable that the recent loss of confidence in the old political parties was intensified; in fact, political disillusion moved up beside anticlericalism as Quebec struggled to discover new orientations for the democracy and the Catholicism to which it remained essentially devoted. Meanwhile the new common enemy, particularly after the desertion of Poland at Yalta, was "Communism."

When the overseas conscription was set in motion, it became apparent that the resisters came from all three divisions of the Canadian people—French-speaking, English-speaking, and New Canadians. At first a wave of desertions took place, but by the end of March the situation was settling down, particularly since over 10,000 Home Defense troops "went active," that is, volunteered instead of being commandeered. In all, about 13,000 conscripts were sent overseas to fill the deficiencies in volunteering when casualties in the Antwerp sector and the Rhine battles mounted. It is conceivable that Canada might have pulled through on volunteering alone, for the Army in Europe was over 99 per cent voluntary, and Air Force and Navy were entirely so.

Quebec comes out of its shell.—Historically the important consideration seemed to be, not this stand by Quebec against conscription, but a real surge forward in acceptance of world citizenship and the responsibilities associated with it, and in awareness that industrialization and its problems had come to stay and could not be banished by old incantations. Quebec's voluntary co-operation in the war's burdens was far greater than twenty-five years before and her people, now two-thirds urban, were stirring in a new kind of democracy, a new and critical Catholicism, and a new and intense social consciousness. No part of the world had contained more varieties of protest and affirmation, more true radicalism and true conservatism of all complexions during the past quarter century, but no extremist or even purely ethnic party had upset the determination of the majority to walk along the middle of the road.

It seemed highly symptomatic that when, in 1946, King at last had Parliament separate the offices of prime minister and Secretary of State for External Affairs, it was the *Canadien,* St. Laurent, who assumed the new office. It was also striking that two new *Canadien* literary voices of instant and broad appeal, not only in French Canada but in English-speaking North America as well, Roger Lemelin and Gabrielle Roy, wrote movingly and yet somehow gaily about the desperate lives of the urban workers in Quebec and Montreal. And equally symbolically, Gratien Gélinas (*"Fridolin"*) began to emerge as a remarkable tragi-comic portrayer of the little man (*"petit gars"*) in the monologues and plays which he wrote, directed, and acted throughout Canada and the United States. It seemed as if French Canada was taking down, little by little, the Chinese Wall that had failed to quarantine or differentiate her from the outside world.

The provincial problem.—When King, with the end of the European war in sight, called a federal election for June, 1945, his majority was diminished, but with 119 seats his Liberals were still the only national party, for although the Conservatives increased their strength from 40 to 66, only 19 of these seats were outside Ontario. Quebec, having punished King by choosing Duplessis to lead the province, punished the Conservatives by backing the Liberals for the nation.

In federal matters King could still count on even formally independent Quebec members, and a much divided West offered no effective opposition. Social Credit still held Alberta, the C.C.F. captured Saskatchewan, and Liberal-Conservative coalitions held off the C.C.F. elsewhere. The Maritimes remained preponderantly Liberal. Provincial separatism was thus still strong in Canada, but when it came to national government, there was no visible alternative to the party that King had reconstructed after Laurier's death and had nursed along for a quarter of a century.

Following the failure of the dominion-provincial conference on the recommendations of the Rowell-Sirois Report in January, 1941, the crucial problem of finance remained unsettled because of the refusal of Quebec, Ontario, and British Columbia to consider some scheme whereby the richer parts of Canada might ease the burden on the poorer. The response of J. L. Ilsley, Minister of Finance, was to point out that if the dominion used its full taxing powers and if wartime restrictions narrowed the provinces' recent sources of revenue, the latter might find themselves in grave difficulties. Then, in his budget of April, Ilsley not only greatly increased direct and indirect taxes, but invaded what had hitherto been provincial fields of taxation by imposing federal inheritance and gasoline taxes.

At the same time he proposed his ingenious methods of getting round the failure of January. Each province was offered separately, in return for its surrender during the war of personal income and corporation taxes, either an amount equal to that received by the province and its municipalities from these sources during the preceding year, or the cost of the debt service paid during that year less the amount received from inheritance taxes. The weaker provinces obviously had little choice save to accept, and in subsequent years the positions of the stronger ones were considerably altered by federal assumption (after constitutional amendment) of responsibility for unemployment insurance and by other schemes of subsidization.

The situation was clearly an unsatisfactory one for times of peace. The varied levels of well-being in the different parts of Canada seemed to demand central maintenance of equity. Now, thanks to the imperative demands of war, substantial progress had been made beyond the impasse of January, 1941, and presumably ingenuity at Ottawa could discover ways by which to make still more. Yet Canada was still far from solving for peacetime the problems created by the distribution of powers in her federal constitution. Resolute negotiations in 1946 and 1947 still failed to win Quebec and Ontario to a five-year trial period during which the provinces would relinquish income, corporation, and inheritance taxes and receive broader aid in social services in return for federal grants on a per capita basis. Regrettably the bargains made with the other provinces were not uniform, but reflected their bargaining strength.

The Japanese Canadians.—Canada's treatment of her Canadian-born, naturalized, and alien Japanese inhabitants on the Pacific coast during and after the war was plainly discreditable. After sketching the sad story, the Canadian historians C. C. Lingard and R. G. Trotter concluded: "The Canadian people generally and their government were apathetic in their concern for the maintenance of Canadian civil and political liberties and rights of citizenship at home while putting forth a tremendous war effort against the enemies of democracy abroad." Forrest E. La Violette, whose *The Canadian Japanese and World War II* (1948) is an exhaustive study of the available evidence, demonstrates irrefutably the complex interplay of opinion and action that supports that conclusion.

Actually the problem had been foreseen as early as 1940, when a Special Committee on Orientals investigated the British Columbian situation and recommended over a year before Pearl Harbor that Canadians of Japanese race should not be called up for military service, that the Japanese population be carefully re-registered under the supervision of the R.C.M. Police, and that a small standing committee be maintained in British Columbia so as to keep the government informed. All these recommendations were carried out with the eager co-operation of the Japanese themselves, and, when Japan began war, only a few moderate precautionary measures were considered necessary by Ottawa and the R.C.M.P.

At that point an urgent, vociferous layer of British Columbian public opinion and politics blew up, demanding removal of all persons of Japanese stock to "east of the Rockies." The federal government's efforts during January and February, 1942, to maintain calm and pursue moderate courses simply infuriated the British Columbian extremists, who were able to inundate Parliament with a flood of representations from all manner of political and other associations in which panic, and a certain amount of cupidity towards the property which evicted Japanese-Canadians would have to give up, blanketed cooler and juster counsel.

Old resentments against the Japanese for their "lower standard of living," "unfair competition," and "bargain-breaking" also played their parts. On February 26, the government unaccountably surrendered practically completely to the extremists. All persons of Japanese race, irrespective of citizenship, were ordered to be evacuated to the interior. Of these 21,000 victims, 76 per cent were Canadian-born and 15 per cent naturalized Canadians. Their possessions—boats, fishing equipment, dwellings, furniture, and so forth—were lost to them with little or no compensation. They were sent to road camps, beet farms, and the ghost towns of the Kootenay.

In a large sense, much of this could be put down to a traditional local resentment against Orientals and their competition, to obscure emotions about the "inscrutable" Japanese, and to the mood of angry and frightened despair that accompanied Japan's triumph and revengeful cruelties in the Pacific. Even after the tide was turned at Guadalcanal and Midway, the federal government had some excuse for its do-nothing policy in the light of the earlier *fait accompli*.

The indelible blot on Canada's escutcheon, however, occurred long after, in fact after the war was over. In spite of the fact that King had been able to tell Parliament in August, 1944, that "no person of the Japanese race has been charged with any act of sabotage or disloyalty," his government deported to Japan 3926 persons, of whom 2053 were Canadian-born and 626 were naturalized Canadians. The remainder, about 20,000 in all, were dispersed in eastern British Columbia, on the plains, and in eastern Canada.

Yet, as a whole, the Canadian war record had been remarkably strong and praiseworthy. An immense, sparsely and unevenly populated country, racked by depression and by both ethnic and economic sectionalisms, had pulled itself together to develop and exert energies in war and production whose proportions no one would have dared to predict. The enormous agglomeration of Quebec's past history and persisting circumstances into an "instinctive" rejection of foreign war and compulsory military service had been corroded by a broadening relinquishment of isolationism. Some French Canadians became truly aware that other North Americans, in Canada and in the United States, were willing and anxious to understand and accommodate French Canada. Meanwhile, even in a war dominated by immensely greater Powers than Canada, she had earned recognition and influence as a Middle Power. Her odd, uneasy, sometimes negligible and sometimes disproportionately great international role demands attention.

CHAPTER XXX

A Middle Power (1950)

By 1950, Canada was generally regarded as a Middle Power, like Argentina, Australia, Belgium, Brazil, India, Mexico, the Netherlands, and Poland, though closer to the Great Powers than the Small. Like the United States and Russia, she combined large natural resources with advanced and comprehensive industrialization. Her strategic position on the globe was advantageous, protected by a strong rind made up of three oceans and the United States, not to speak of mountain barriers on east and west and formidable obstacles in the barren lands and the clogged arctic archipelago on the north. In her geographical relation to the United States and Russia, the territory of Canada was a vital intervening area, in terms both of global aviation and of North Atlantic and North Pacific navigation, coupled with overland transportation routes.

Clearly circumstances placed Canada in the orbit of the United States. The decline in British power induced greater Canadian reliance on the United States, and strategic considerations forced the Americans to look to Canada. At the same time, everything she could contribute to the success of the United Nations seemed calculated to diminish mere subservience to the United States.

⚜ THE TENTH PROVINCE

At midnight, March 31, 1949, Newfoundland had joined Canada as the tenth province, thus establishing, except for American rights in that island and except for Alaska, a single sovereignty across northern North America. Great Britain, disinclined to contemplate responsibility for Newfoundland's future well-being, had announced in December, 1945, the election of a convention of Newfoundlanders "to make recommendations to His Majesty's Government as to possible forms of future government to be put before the people at a national referendum."

The convention was elected in June, 1946, and its forty-five members met in September. In May, 1947, it sent a delegation to London to learn what its financial position would be under a continued or a revised Commission of Government or under a responsible government of its own. This group learned that the price of self-government must be full financial responsibility. In June, 1947, a delegation was sent to Ottawa, where discussions extended into September. (A proposal to send a delegation to Washington had been substantially rejected.) The Canadian government made a statement of its terms at the end of October. After long, vigorous debate in and out of the convention, that body voted 29 to 16 against federation with Canada, and on January 29, 1948, recommended to the British government that only two choices be offered in the popular referendum—the continued commission form of government or restored responsible government.

This decision was embarrassing to Great Britain and Canada, both of which rather obviously wanted the Newfoundlanders to enter Canada. The Canadians had moved very circumspectly and in full knowledge of past history, present circumstances, and Newfoundlanders' sensibilities. In effect they were offering, in return for incorporation of the great strategic bastion and its human and natural resources, to provide what Newfoundland had been, and apparently would be, unable to provide —a "floor" of social services by way of family allowances, unemployment insurance, pensions for the aged and the blind, and other aids which would assure Newfoundlanders the same minimal standard of living as Canadians possessed.

In the circumstances, therefore, Canada refrained from any expression of opinion. It was the British government that could and did take the bull by the horns; by its own decision Britain added federation with Canada as a third choice in the referendum, with the proviso of a second referendum if necessary to secure an absolute majority.

An aroused Newfoundland sent 88 per cent of its registered voters to the polls on June 3, 1948. Responsible government received 64,900 votes, federation with Canada 64,100 and continuation of commission government 23,300. At the second referendum seven weeks later, 85 per cent of the voters divided, 78,323 for federation with Canada and 71,334 for separate responsible government, with 18 of the 25 electoral districts showing majorities for federation. Eight days later, Mackenzie King welcomed the decision and invited authorized negotiators to Ottawa. After two months' labors, the terms of union were agreed upon and signed by the new Canadian prime minister (St. Laurent), the Acting Secretary of State for External Affairs (Brooke Claxton), and six of the seven Newfoundland delegates. The Canadian Parliament passed the act of approval February 18, 1949, and, after the Commission of Government had announced its approval on February 21, the British Parliament passed the enabling act on March 23.

It had been a deliberate, thoroughly debated procedure. In effect the mercantile, small industrial, and financial community in and around St. John's had been outvoted by the underprivileged majority in the outports when Britain could no longer carry the load and when Canada was willing to undertake it. No one ignored the difficulties—the ancient dislikes and grievances; the shift of a fish-export economy from the sterling to the dollar area; the deficit-breeding railway and car ferry to Sydney; the patronage and denominational problems (particularly in education); the friction-producing anomaly of the great American bases at St. John's, Argentia, and Stephenville; the uncertain effects of free emigration to other parts of Canada; and, enduringly, the problems of provincial finance.

The terms of union incorporated both the federal assumption of Newfoundland's debt and public services and the grant of perpetual annual subsidies, on the one hand, and a complicated twelve-year tax-bargain, on the other, whereby Newfoundland retained its $30,000,000 surplus and was to receive additional diminishing transitional grants, subject to review after eight years, so that Newfoundlanders could maintain their public services without heavier tax burdens than Maritimers. For 1949–50, for instance, current expenditures were expected to be $21,100,000 and current revenues $21,400,000, of which $15,500,000 would be federal grants.

🍁 CANADA IN 1950

Thus the Canada of 1950, in size second only to the U.S.S.R., was larger than Brazil, China, or the United States, yet Canada had a population of not quite 14,000,000 persons, approximately that of New York State. Statistically that meant not quite four persons to each of Canada's 3,845,000 square miles, or, if the Yukon, the Northwest Territories, and Labrador were excluded, about six to the square mile. In terms of actual residence, however, nearly all the Canadians lived within two hundred miles of the international boundary; in fact, three quarters of them lived south of the forty-ninth parallel, and 62 per cent of the population was concentrated along the edges of the deep wedge made by Ontario and Quebec into the United States. Even for the country as a whole, 61 per cent of the population was urban.

Thus, Canada was an industrialized nation whose power and weight came from her immense mechanical productivity rather than from her mere manpower. Indeed Canada had insufficient manpower and was

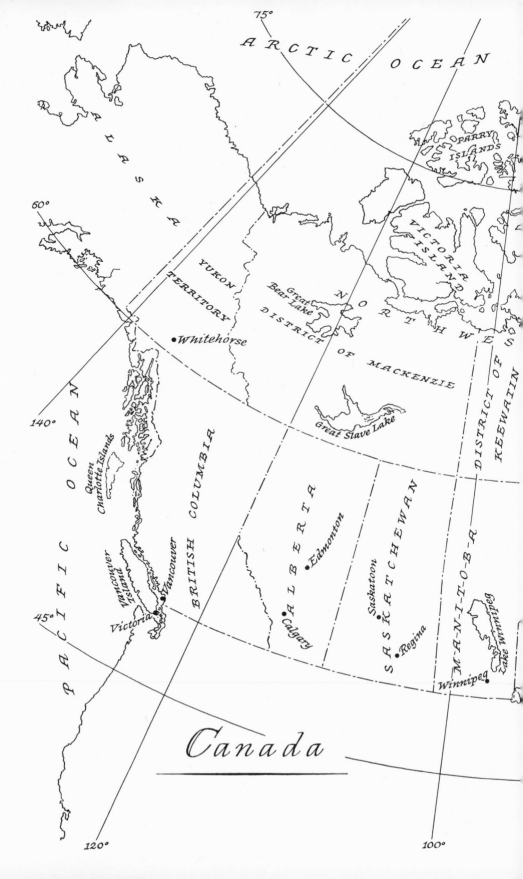

Canada

striving to increase it by generously assisted immigration, in marked contrast to the purposeful exclusions of the thirties. By lavish mechanization and production of power (notably hydroelectrical), Canada carried on the extraction and much of the processing of her natural resources of forests, mines, farms, and fisheries in sparsely peopled regions with a small labor force.

By using national revenues to build up and maintain the costly transportation services that her huge area demanded, she brought these products to Canadian and American centers of consumption or of advanced manufacture, or to the ports from which they went out to the world. Her great industrial region, like that of the United States, lay close to their greatest common possession, the waterway of the Great Lakes and the St. Lawrence. It is not commonly known that in terms of the net tons registered of vessels entered at the principal Canadian ports Ontario (31,550,000 in 1947) stood first, followed by British Columbia (31,538,000), and Quebec (14,125,000). Vancouver (13,516,000) far exceeded Montreal (6,797,000), which was also exceeded by Port Arthur–Fort William (6,979,000). Toronto (3,173,000) exceeded Halifax (3,135,000). More than half as much freight passes through the ports in the Great Lakes as through all the other Canadian ports combined, in spite of the ease and cheapness with which goods can be transported between West and East through the Panama Canal. On a continent where industry sought to operate as near as possible to its largest markets, southern Ontario and Quebec formed an integrated part of a continental concentration of people and production in the middle of the eastern third of North America.

Thus it was that less than fourteen million people, with a labor force of about five million, turned out a gross national product worth $17,-700,000,000 in 1950, as compared with one of $5,600,000,000 in 1939. The national income was $14,000,000,000, or about $1000 per capita, as compared with $4,300,000,000 in 1939. As late as 1947, few Canadians imagined that such a performance was possible. Recalling past history, they had expected World War II to be followed by an enormous shrinkage in their export trade, particularly with an impoverished Great Britain. They also expected that their imbalance in goods and payments with the United States would force them to ration themselves in American goods for want of American dollars.

Both of these expectations were realized to some degree, but were overshadowed by the fruition of long-term developments in the United States which Canadians had been observing for perhaps twenty-five years but had feared would not be reflected in enduring national policy. After about 1934, however, the interdependence of the American with the world economy began to be incorporated in such systematic procedures as the Reciprocal Trade Treaties Act, lend-lease, the United Nations Relief and Rehabilitation Administration, the great loans to Great Britain and other nations, and the remarkable and gigantic devices for international economic recovery and co-operation under the Marshall Plan. This was the twentieth-century analogy to Britain's free trade, export of capital, and free gold market of the nineteenth century, little as anyone would have expected it from American behavior as late as 1932.

Canadians, somewhat incredulously, found themselves pursuing quite similar policies, making huge gifts and loans to impoverished customers, lowering tariffs and removing administrative obstacles to imports, and taking on more and more of the character of what was probably the second most favored economy in the world. In the period 1939–46, Canadian assistance to impoverished customers was on a larger scale in proportion to national income than that of the United States. The Canadian position was complicated by perfectly justified past habits of thought, particularly concerning the behavior of the United States, and by the fact that of the two interlocked North American economies, the smaller Canadian one could be rocked and jarred inadvertently by relatively minor fluctuations or changes of direction in the American.

But Ottawa and Washington now understood each other, their economic interplay, and their relations with the world economy better than ever before. It had become "good" American economic nationalism to help and not, as in the past, to hinder Canada's economic well-being and to co-operate with Canada in forwarding the well-being of other nations. The economic trend of the past half-century, then, might be summed up by saying that, although Canada's interdependence with the United States had increased and that with Great Britain had diminished, even more significant was her own increase in maturity and in the capacity to stand on her own feet.

The situation was neatly reflected in Canada's trading and balance-of-payments position during the relatively normal year, 1949. Of Canada's total exports, worth $2,993,000,000, more than half went to the United States and less than a quarter to Great Britain, whereas ten years before the United States took 41 per cent and Great Britain 35 per cent. During the same year, of Canada's total imports, worth $2,761,000,000, 71 per cent came from the United States and 11 per cent from Great Britain, but the important consideration was that Canada's characteristic negative trade balance with the United States was being reduced to negligible proportions.

This trend towards a healthier balance between the Canadian and

American economies was borne out in Canada's current balance-of-payments. These current balances with all countries had been consistently positive since 1934 and had risen to great heights during World War II, but, while positive in relation to Great Britain and most other countries, had normally been negative in relation to the United States. During 1947 the latter negative balance became so huge that controls had to be set up to protect Canada's reserves of gold and U.S. dollars.

By 1950, however, these had been withdrawn and it appeared that the long-run trend since 1934 towards a practically even current balance had been resumed. For one thing the increase of American investment in Canada was accelerated by the expanding development of pulp, paper, power, and aluminum on the Pacific coast and in Ontario and Quebec; of oil and natural gas in Alberta, "the new Texas"; of iron in Ontario, Quebec, and Labrador; and of the world's largest titanium deposit in Quebec. The figures of long-term investment in Canada in 1950 were: American $6.6 billions, British $1.7 billions, other $.4 billions. Canadian long-term investment abroad was $4.0 billions. The nonresident ownership of Canadian industry declined from 38 per cent in 1939 to 31 per cent in 1950. Twenty-three per cent of Canadian industry was American-owned in 1950.

Large as the American investment was, it was naturally exceeded by the Canadian. Indeed the most striking single aspect of the Canadian economy was the unparalleled and constantly expanding annual capital investment, which rose from about $1,600,000,000 in 1939 to about $3,600,000,000 in 1950 and from 14 per cent of the gross national product in 1946 to 22 per cent of it in 1950. It might be added that in 1949 Canadians were spending and saving, even in terms of 1939 dollars, a total of about 75 per cent more than a decade before, or, putting it another way, each person was consuming about 50 per cent more in goods and services.

Many efforts have been made to compare the Canadian with the American standard of living, but none of the results have been very reliable since purely statistical comparisons become dubious, for instance, in such a matter as the differential nature and cost of housing and heat related to climate. It appears, however, that the American standard fluctuates between an eighth and a third higher than the Canadian, climbing faster during booms and falling faster during depressions.

The fears that the Canadian standard might progressively suffer by comparison (because after 1928 the safety valve of emigration to the United States could be so nearly closed) seemed to be answered by Canada's perceptible shortages of manpower after 1940. Economic depression, industrialization, urbanization, and their attendant influences had cut the rate of natural increase in half after 1921 and the recovery during war and prosperity was only partial.

🍁 CANADA IN WORLD AFFAIRS

It was understandable that Canada should proceed cautiously in world affairs. Many observers expected her to try to establish a bloc of Middle Powers in the United Nations, as Australia apparently attempted unsuccessfully at the San Francisco Conference of 1945. This view overlooked a great deal of past history and present circumstance. In particular, it was one thing for Canada to have acted so resolutely in response to the imperatives of war, but quite another for her to choose among real or imaginary alternatives when war ceased.

Indeed, Canada's transition, say, between 1940 and 1950, was so complex an affair that it cannot yet be explained confidently. Obviously the evidence is incomplete, perspective is lacking, and the dominant characteristics of emergent Canadian policy have not necessarily hardened into a coherent pattern. About all that can be said generally is that Canada abandoned the negativism and isolationism that had characterized her between 1918 and 1939 in favor of positive efforts, alone and in a great variety of international organizations, to promote the kind of international society she wanted, and to do so as much as possible on her own terms rather than in mere acceptance of the mandates of "the cold war" between Russia and the United States.

Mackenzie King had personified secretive caution in foreign affairs, as well he might considering his view of Canadian development during his lifetime. He apparently enjoyed, and perhaps magnified, his recognizable role as intermediary for Churchill and Roosevelt before Pearl Harbor. Yet Churchill's inability to think in terms of free Canadian action must have troubled King greatly. Roosevelt, because the United States was so strong, could nonchalantly go along with Churchill's grand vision of June 4, 1940:

. . . and even if, which I do not for a moment believe, this Island or a large part of it were subjugated and starving, then our Empire beyond the seas, armed and guarded by the British Fleet, would carry on the struggle, until, in God's good time, the New World, with all its power and might, steps forth to the rescue and the liberation of the old.

Two years later, the preponderant voice in the war against the Axis Powers was clearly passing to the United States. No matter how skillfully Churchill and Roosevelt lubricated that transition, there could be no presumption that the former could direct the latter. Canada, being much weaker and, in spite of her refusals of 1912 and 1921 to do as Churchill wanted, still embraced in his stubbornly old-fashioned conception of Empire (he repudiated Commonwealth), was in the much more awkward position of being willing and anxious to do whatever seemed best to win the war (and peace) and yet being bound to reject any presumption that she would automatically do what she was told by any other state. In the circumstances, it proved easier for Roosevelt than for Churchill to be convincingly magnanimous towards Canada.

Down to the end of 1943 the difficulties had not been great, except during 1940–41 when Canada was ignored in the cession of the American bases at Newfoundland. Once Canada's sense of frustration, of having done her utmost for three years to little effect, was ended by the turn in the war's tide during October and November, 1942, the past seemed justified and the future moderately assured.

The spring of 1943 may be said to have marked the beginning in Canada of systematic assessment of foreign policy. In March, the (American) Foreign Policy Association published a serious symposium on the subject by five leading Canadian journalists from British Columbia, Manitoba, Ontario, Quebec, and Nova Scotia. In April, Anthony Eden, the British Foreign Secretary, held discussions with the Cabinet at Ottawa and addressed the Houses of Parliament. In July, Canadian forces invaded Sicily, and by then there were unmistakable stirrings of a sense of positive responsibility for the future.

King responded on July 9 by his first significant pronouncement on the broad issues of foreign policy since 1938, and won Parliament to his new "functional" conception of Canada's role in international organization.

Representation should be determined on a functional basis which will admit to full membership those countries, large or small, which have the greatest contribution to make to the particular object in question. . . . Some compromise must be found between the theoretical equality of states and the practical necessity of limiting representation on international bodies to a workable number. That compromise can be discovered, especially in economic matters, by the adoption of the functional principle of representation.

The one strong dissident note during the ensuing debate came from H. C. Green, a Conservative Member from Vancouver, who declared that "the British family of nations should speak with one voice in foreign affairs." He was answered by Brooke Claxton, President of the Council, who stressed Canada's emergence from colonial status.

The first Quebec Conference.—In August, 1943, Quebec was the meeting place of Churchill, Roosevelt, and King with their staffs for discussions of war and peace, notably, as we now know, for agreement on the well-advanced development of atomic fission. The meetings were rather oddly scattered. Churchill, for instance, spent three days at Hyde Park with Roosevelt after he and Sir John Anderson had spent a day with the Canadian War Committee at Quebec, and after the central Quebec meetings Roosevelt visited Ottawa and addressed the Senate, the Commons, and the general public on Parliament Hill, while Churchill went fishing (and brooding over a broadcast) in the Laurentians.

Quebec was very much in the center of things for about two weeks, little as it knew of the business transacted (the invasion of France, the status of the Gaullist Committee of National Liberation, the use of the Azores, the shape of the war in the Pacific and Southeast Asia, the Four Power substructure of the United Nations, the merging of American lend-lease and British and Canadian Mutual Aid, and the triangular "secret" of atomic research).

Brooke Claxton, President of the Council, was chosen to reveal in general terms where Canada stood after the Conference, and did so in an address to the Canadian Institute of Public Affairs on August 27. He listed seven Canadian objectives: (1) winning the war; (2) promoting the friendship of Great Britain and the United States and their association with Russia and China in leading the United Nations; (3) establishing the organization of the United Nations; (4) allocating representation on the joint administrative boards on a functional basis; (5) supporting the organization of force against aggression; (6) "Even if there is no general system for the organization of defense, Canada should join in the defense of this continent and if necessary of Great Britain as part of the defense of Canada"; and (7) joining in measures to promote trade by removing restrictions, and promoting maximum employment and production at fair prices.

The U.N. specialized agencies.—King's "functional" conception, already broadly founded upon the collaborative boards and other authorities which had characterized the North Atlantic Triangle since the Ogdensburg and destroyers-bases agreements of 1940, enabled Canada to take an appropriate and influential part in the Food and Agriculture Conference of May-June, 1943, out of which grew the U.N.'s Food and Agriculture Organization and its Relief and Rehabilitation Administration; in the Bretton Woods Conference of July, 1944, which led to the International Bank for Reconstruction and Development and the International Monetary Fund; and in the Chicago Air Conference of November, 1944, out of which, after many tribulations, came the International Civil Aviation Organization whose headquarters were established in Montreal.

The substantial merits of a number of Canadian civil servants and officials, permanent or temporary, earned general recognition during these negotiations, and it became apparent that Canada would be called upon in the future to fill some important offices in the agencies of the United Nations. It was also recognized that both at Bretton Woods and at Chicago the Canadians had arranged compromises of opposed British and American positions. These successes were a little ominous, for their continuance might develop into habitual saddling of the Middle Powers with burdens of disagreement among the Great Powers.

Perhaps characteristically, Canada played a relatively inconspicuous part in the creation of the United Nations Educational, Scientific, and Cultural Organization and entered the World Health Organization in a notably uncontroversial and matter-of-fact way. By 1947, Canada was one of six of the fifty-five members of the United Nations which was a member of all eight of its specialized agencies. She was especially active in the International Refugee Organization and the International Trade Organization, but less effective, for various reasons, in the International Labor Organization.

"The Halifax Affair."—The confidence and competence shown in these "practical" fields was at first hardly paralleled in the more purely political arena, for King was convinced that "functionally" Canada should not try to compete with the forces exercisable by the Great Powers. Moreover, shortly after the Moscow Declaration of November 1, 1943, in which China, the Union of Soviet Socialist Republics, the United Kingdom, and the United States announced the necessity of setting up a general international organization, Canada had to absorb an unexpected shock from within the British Commonwealth.

This took the form of a cumulative revival of the "Chamberlainism" of fifty years earlier, the alluring, but often rejected, design of a unified British Commonwealth and Empire. Clearly reflecting the apprehension that Britain and her associates would be overshadowed by the United States, Russia, and China, the movement began with two little-noticed speeches of August and September, 1943, by John Curtin, Labor prime minister of Australia. He caught attention by a more sharply accented speech of December 14, in which he advocated a consultative Empire Council meeting at regular intervals in London, Canberra, Wellington, Pretoria, and Ottawa, and equipped with a permanent, expert secretariat.

Undoubtedly Curtin was listened to outside Australia on this occasion because meanwhile, on November 25, 1943, Jan Smuts, prime minister of South Africa, speaking in London, had advocated two remedies for Britain's weakened position: "working closely together with those smaller democracies in Western Europe which . . . are entirely with us in their outlook and their way of life, and in all their ideals"; and substituting for a centralized colonial Empire regional groupings of the colonies around the dominions, which themselves were already in a consultative grouping around London. These proposals seemed highly dubious, indeed unwelcome, both to countries like the Netherlands and to Britons whose policy of trusteeship for African native races hardly harmonized with South Africa's policies towards them.

Then, on January 24, 1944, presumably after some degree of consultation with the Churchill government, Lord Halifax, British ambassador to the United States, made a speech in Toronto advocating a reintegrated Commonwealth and Empire. His obliviousness to the opinions of most Canadians provoked an explosion that undid the whole adventure.

If, in the future, Britain is to play her part [in a world of three "Titans"] without assuming burdens greater than she can support, she must have with her in peace the same strength that has sustained her in this war. Not Great Britain only, but the British Commonwealth and Empire must be the fourth power in that group upon which, under Providence, the peace of the world will henceforth depend.

The surprisingly violent response to this speech from one end of Canada to the other was admittedly shocking to Canadians themselves. A few Conservative imperialists defended it quite ardently, but for the most part the country was depressed and angered by it. Coming as it did just after Canadians had shed their sense of frustration, after reiteration of the Atlantic Charter, and on the eve of the creation of a general collective security system, this apparent appeal to simple power politics of an outmoded pattern was too much to be borne.

From Halifax to Vancouver men realized that they were Canadians first and that they saw their best chance of remaining so as supporters of the United Nations. Indeed the Commonwealth and Empire themselves would be better off, would act more naturally and effectively, as parts of a world system than in what must in the circumstances be an artificial union of some highly differentiated parts of it. Distinct echoes were heard of Canada's distaste for Britain's foreign policy of the thirties and for the men, including Halifax, who had been associated with it.

King waited a week before dealing with the ideas of Smuts and Halifax in a considerate but decisive speech. "With what is implied in the argument of both these eminent public men, I am unable to agree . . . We look forward . . . to close collaboration in the interests of peace not only inside the British Commonwealth, but also with all friendly nations, small as well as great . . . Our commitments on these great issues must be part of a general scheme, whether they be on a world basis or regional in nature."

Since the Conservatives were in the midst of an embarrassing transition of leaders at the time, the C.C.F. explicitly anti-Halifax, and Social Credit not very certain of its views, public discussion added little more. The Canadian who reported the outcome of the matter in *The Round Table* summed it up accurately by saying: "The Commonwealth cannot in the long run be maintained without an effective internationalism: an effective internationalism cannot be achieved unless the Commonwealth contributes to it."

The subsequent Conference of Commonwealth prime ministers in London, May 1–16, corroborated that view. King was chosen to report it to the British Houses of Parliament and, as he said, "before the entire world." He did so in pre-Halifax terms, in terms of the long tradition from Macdonald and Blake of "free association," "continuing conference of the Cabinets of the Commonwealth," and avoidance of any appearance of "a separate bloc." He hoped that "the peoples of the British Commonwealth and the United States will continue to march at each other's side, united more closely than ever . . . that they will march in a larger company, in which all the nations united today in defense of freedom will remain united in the service of mankind." The Canadian Parliament applauded him ten days later with notable unanimity.

The Great Powers take over.—King's prescience as to Canada's inferior political role in international affairs was bluntly corroborated when his country was not invited to Dumbarton Oaks to share in framing the postwar United Nations. In fact he accepted the monopoly of the Great Powers as "a correct application of the functional idea of international organization," while suggesting the future roles of "other states of lesser power."

The moot point during the Canadian discussions of the Dumbarton Oaks proposals during the autumn and winter, 1944–45, was the obvious intention of the Great Powers to reserve the powerful, executive Security Council (and veto in it) to themselves, and to relegate to the other Powers mere discussions in the Assembly. The Yalta Agreement of February, 1945, emphatically underlined that state of affairs.

When Parliament was asked to approve Canada's acceptance of an invitation to the San Francisco Conference and of the Dumbarton Oaks proposals as "a satisfactory basis for a discussion of the charter of the proposed international organization," it engaged in the most thorough and protracted debate on foreign policy in Canadian history, almost completely on nonpartisan terms. The debate produced no nostrum for increasing Canada's modest political powers, no expectation of checking the Great Powers, but something closely approaching unanimous resolution to work for enlargement of the scope of the Middle and Smaller Powers.

King responded by appointing a delegation composed of Liberals, Conservatives, and C.C.F.-ers (Social Credit was left out on grounds of its provincial particularism). He offered no great hopes of change, but advocated that states that were not represented on the Security Council and had not determined the policies to be enforced be freed from responsibility for serious enforcement.

An American observer at San Francisco, Professor Clyde Eagleton, reported of the Canadians: ". . . the attitude . . . seems to have been to accept reluctantly the inevitable dominance of the great powers without howling about it, to make such adjustments as were possible to improve the system laid down at Dumbarton Oaks, and to take no active part in matters in which Canada had no direct concern such as trusteeships and regionalism."

The Canadian government had been operating systematically on the proposals at the diplomatic level with many countries for almost a year; now its delegation worked purposefully in committees, meanwhile discouraging any assumption that it wanted to lead the Middle and Smaller Powers. The Canadians' principal success was in amending the Security Council. The rules for the election of its six nonpermanent members were drawn so as to permit the choice of states which could contribute substantially to its work. The Canadians also secured temporary representation in the Council for consultation, although not voting power, for affected states. They also contributed more substantially than any other state to the definition and expansion of the hitherto vaguely conceived Economic and Social Council and to clarification of the relationships between that council and the U.N. specialized agencies in whose progenitors Canada had been so active.

In general, the Canadians were less conspicuous and independent than the Australians, who fought vainly against the veto in the Council, or the South Africans and New Zealanders with their special causes. Parliament rather quietly and uneasily approved their work and Canada's entry into the new world organizations in October. Since San Francisco, two atomic bombs had bankrupted many conventional patterns of thought, including the vestiges of isolationism and of other forms of wishful thinking.

The Cold War.—Possibly the First Quebec Conference of August, 1943, by its withholding from Russia of what was being done in atomic research, marked the beginning of "the Cold War" that subsequently divided a good deal of the globe into two hostile camps. At any rate, when, on September 5, 1945, Igor Gouzenko of the U.S.S.R. Embassy at

Ottawa began his revelations of Russia's efforts to discover the secret, it became apparent that the Soviet agents had started their work in Canada practically simultaneously with the arrival of the United Kingdom research group in September, 1942, and the commencement of activity in the new buildings of the University of Montreal.

The Russians had learned a great deal, thanks to their ability to persuade a number of informed Canadians, Americans, and Britons that they owed the information to their allies and to "the higher cause" of Communism. The long Canadian, American, and British investigation of Russian espionage (September, 1945–June, 1946), which coincided with deadlock between the Great Powers, profoundly shocked a friendly and unsuspecting Canada. The international situation began to project Canada into the acceptance of political as well as economic and social responsibilities in the United Nations.

When the United Nations began to function in London in January, 1946, the Assembly's votes revealed the outside world's estimate of Canada's international position. Trygve Lie of Norway was, after serious negotiations, chosen Secretary General over Lester B. Pearson of Canada. J. E. Read of Canada was elected to the International Court of Justice. Canada failed of election to the Security Council, but succeeded in the Economic and Social Council.

The Atomic Energy Commission grew out of the joint declaration (November 15, 1945) on atomic energy, made at Washington by the United States, the United Kingdom, and Canada. As an inevitable permanent member of the Commission, Canada received a stern education in Great Power politics and a strong push towards the creation of a powerful world government. Indeed when King on December 17, 1945, told the Commons something of Canada's share in atomic research, he perhaps marked the turning point in Canadian foreign policy by saying: "The more one ponders the problems with which our world is confronted in the light . . . of the implications of the development of atomic energy, the harder it is to see a solution in anything short of some surrender of national sovereignty." General McNaughton served his country and the world well until the exhausting, vain wrangles of the A.E.C. came to their natural end with the revelation that Russia too had made and used an atomic bomb.

🍁 KING'S RETIREMENT

During 1946 and 1947 King was preparing to lay down his scepter after the longest tenure as prime minister in the history of any Commonwealth country. (His tenure finally totaled over twenty-one years, and he led his party for exactly twenty-nine years.) His retirement was a curious process, for it had to be done while Canada was busy at reconstruction, redistributing parliamentary constituencies, and changing her international course.

There were several middle-aged aspirants to succeed King, but he was, as usual, secretive. He had, however, come increasingly to rely on St. Laurent to act for him as prime minister or as Secretary of State for External Affairs, and the first straw in the wind was the separation of the two offices and St. Laurent's appointment to the latter September 4, 1946. St. Laurent made his presence felt quite distinctly within Canada and abroad. He was elected by a Liberal convention at Ottawa on August 7, 1948, to succeed King as Liberal leader. King handed over the prime ministership to him on November 15, 1948, having persuaded Lester B. Pearson of the Department of External Affairs, who had made a brilliant record for himself in Canada, Great Britain, the United States, and in international bodies during the preceding twenty years, to leave the Civil Service and succeed St. Laurent. Yet King remained a member of Parliament until the dissolution of April 30, 1949.

Once Newfoundland had entered Canada, the new prime minister called a general election in June, 1949, and, as it were, laid before King in his retirement the laurels of an unprecedented nationwide approval of his work—Liberals, 192; Conservatives, 41; C.C.F., 13; Social Credit, 10; others, 6. King died, after a very brief illness, July 22, 1950, but a few months earlier he had drafted a remarkable will which left practically all of his large fortune to the promotion of Canadian scholarship in history, international relations, and industrial relations.

CANADA'S NEW INTERNATIONAL COURSE

If, in December, 1945, King had marked the turning point towards Canada's willingness to surrender some national sovereignty for the creation of an international one, it was the *Canadien,* St. Laurent, and Pearson, as Under-Secretary, who guided Canada's first steps along that road. Much of the story undoubtedly remains to be revealed, but it might be summarized by saying that the North Atlantic Triangle of Great Britain, the United States, and Canada, which had been formulated at Washington in 1871 and had survived seventy-five years of often grave vicissitudes, was enlarged to become the North Atlantic Treaty Organization.

Once he became responsible for foreign policy, St. Laurent began to enunciate it with increasing clarity and Pearson to act it out, particularly in the United Nations. The manifest hostility and aggressiveness of Russia over the Marshall Plan, Roman Catholicism, Czechoslovakia, Berlin, Palestine, Finland, indeed almost every aspiration of the West, made it easier than ever before for French Canadians to fall in behind the second *Canadien* Prime Minister of Canada as he led the way out of political isolationism.

The immediate climax came in 1948 and 1949. First, Western Europe drew together in the mutual guarantees of the Treaty of Brussels, on March 17, 1948. Three months later, the American Senate endorsed the Vandenburg Resolution, which marked the first willingness of the United States to authorize, in advance, positive commitments to other nations in the interest of national security. Multiple negotiations followed, as affecting Scandinavia, for instance, in which it was often hard to tell whether an American, a Briton, or a Canadian, was "carrying the ball" for the North Atlantic team. The outcome was the North Atlantic Treaty of March, 1949, which the Canadian House of Commons accepted with only two opposed votes and which Canada was the first to ratify and deposit at Washington.

Since then Canada has not only been actively committed to maintenance of security in the North Atlantic area, but also to economic and social co-operation within it. She has not thought it necessary to adhere to the South Atlantic Pact of Rio de Janeiro. Regarding the North Atlantic Treaty Organization as a regional buttress for the United Nations, Canada has contributed training facilities, arms, supplies, and men to the defense of the West.

And then, before the end of 1950, she had also to look to the Pacific and share in the defense of South Korea. In addition she had committed herself to the plans devised at Colombo in Ceylon for assisting Southeast Asia in the material improvement of life there. In 1924, Senator Dandurand of Canada said to the nations assembled at Geneva: "We live in a fireproof house, far from inflammable materials." In 1950, Canadians were unmistakably supporting a government which was living out its belief that Canada must co-operate in doing what lay within her powers to defend and to extend the benefits of the free and adaptable Western tradition to which her peoples belonged.

CHAPTER XXXI

Nationality in Diversity

John Stuart Mill once defined nationality as follows:

A portion of mankind may be said to constitute a nationality if they are united among themselves by common sympathies which do not exist between them and any others—which makes them co-operate with each other more willingly than with other people, desire to be under the same government, and desire that it should be government by themselves or a portion of themselves exclusively.

That is, nationality is largely a political thing. It may exist in social and cultural diversity. In fact, the enduring federations of the United States and Canada have been precise responses to the need for political unity felt by diverse peoples. It seems significant, also, that the most persistent designs for a world society have been cast in federal form. In times like the middle of the twentieth century, when political aims find only too much expression in parallel demands for social and cultural uniformity, Canada stands out as an assertion that such monolithic ambitions are needless, undesirable, and futile.

Moreover, "common sympathies" need not be merely political and may co-exist with clashes of tradition and aspiration. Canada's history since 1759, perhaps even since 1710 in the case of the Acadians, seems to show that, once rooted in North America, men and women respond to the spirit of an environment with an intensity that transcends many other considerations. Lorne Pierce has complained of the lack of a single "kindling flame" that would fuse Canada into a great nation, yet ever since the British conquest Canada has risen to her responsibilities, whether of war or of other adversities, with more than adequate gallantry and endurance in spite of manifest divisions. Each time the forced draft of crisis has been applied, the national boiler has provided the needed steam.

🍁 DIVERSITY

Diverse environments.—The subtitle of the geographer Griffith Taylor's *Canada* (1947) is: "a study of cool continental environments and their effect on British and French settlement." That statistical "coolness" is about all that is environmentally common to all Canada, and practically every part of the country except the northernmost Arctic islands contradicts it with blazing heat in summer. Few countries contain greater variety than is afforded by the Maritime region, the St. Lawrence Valley, the Great Lakes Basin, the Shield from its wooded southern margin to its northern tundras, the plains, and the cordilleran region with its lofty mountains, dry inner plateau, and rain-drenched coastal fiords and islands. A third of the Canadians are utterly contained by one or other of these several unique environments, which saturate their senses and exercise the *genius loci* that makes a man say "This is where I belong."

Even the remaining two-thirds, the city dwellers, cannot escape from the grander aspects of their natural setting. St. John's and Halifax look out from rocky inlets on the uninterrupted expanse of the North Atlantic. Charlottetown enjoys a more benign southward vista across intensely blue waters to the mauve highlands of the Isthmus of Chignecto. Saint John is at the ocean's mouth and Fredericton on the lovely upper reaches of a great river flowing between wooded highlands. Not even the most citified Quebeckers and Montrealers can escape the majesty of the St. Lawrence as it carries the waters of a quarter of the continent down the broad trough between the Appalachians and the Laurentians. Ottawa is perched on a plateau above the junction of three rivers, two of them flowing from deep in the Laurentians which form the northern horizon.

The people of Toronto and the other Great Lakes cities not only have the inland seas, connecting rivers, rapids, and waterfalls at their front doors, but close behind them lies the endlessly varied filigree of smaller lakes and waterways in the forested wilderness of the Canadian Shield. Between the Shield and the Rockies, Winnipeg and Regina raise their buildings and their cherished tree plantations to interrupt flat plains extending as far as the eye can view in all directions; Saskatoon and Edmonton bridge the deep, broad coulees which the south and north branches of the Saskatchewan have cut through the steppe; and Calgary, beside its jade-colored mountain river, has the abrupt, glistening face of the Rockies as a backdrop seen through the clear air sixty miles away. On the Pacific coast, Vancouver and Victoria sprawl irregularly outward within the confines of jagged, wooded mountains, broad ocean channels, and twisting narrow fiords.

The automobile merely facilitated, did not create, the common practice among Canadian city-dwellers of having summer cottages in the
wilderness or on the shore. And the cult among them of "roughing it,"
of acquiring the skills of the fisherman, hunter, farmer, canoeist, horse-
man, or mountaineer, reflects romantic longings for the frontier traditions upon which Canada was founded and which some Canadians still
purposefully pursue, disdainful of those who merely imitate them. With
the northern regions yearly yielding greater rewards to the enterprising,
the frontier tradition promises to persist.

Diverse stocks and traditions.—The peoples who live in Canada's
eight or ten insulated sections stem from diverse stocks and traditions.
Newfoundland, for instance, quite apart from the special circumstances
in which her people have lived for centuries, is too newly Canadian, too
aware of past grievances against Canada, and too keyed to foreign
markets to have learned to look inward to North America instead of
outward to the world's seas. Nova Scotia and New Brunswick inherit a
sense of difference from central Canada and feel that they have declined
in importance and weight since, and because of, federation with it. In
both of these provinces the proportion of French stock is increasing, so
much so that New Brunswick contemplates its predominance within a
generation.

The withdrawn rural society and economy of Prince Edward Island
are paralleled elsewhere in Canada only by the society and economy of
rural Quebec, whose total society in turn, by its French North American tradition, is peculiar to itself. "Anti-American" Ontario is probably
the most thoroughly Americanized part of Canada, for the plains
provinces balance their American stock and folkways against cohesive
groups of *Canadiens* and New Canadians and basic to them all is
British stock from the older settled parts of Canada.

Beyond the Rockies, Vancouver and Seattle are likely to understand
each other better than Vancouver and Ottawa, and Vancouver Island,
like Prince Edward Island, stands perceptibly aloof from the rest of
North America. The frontiersmen of the northern regions of Canada
vacillate between an aggrieved sense of being misunderstood and neglected and a liking for occasional descents upon the "bright lights,"
whether of San Francisco or Seattle or Vancouver, Chicago or Winnipeg
or Edmonton, New York or Toronto or Montreal, Boston or Halifax.

While it is true that outside Quebec most of the Canadian stock is a
blend of variegated older ethnic strains—English, Scottish, Irish,
Huguenot, Teutonic, Scandinavian, Slavic, and Mediterranean—assimilation into one Canadianism has been slower than assimilation in
the United States, largely because it threatened to make Canada more

vulnerable to Americanism. Defensiveness against the United States encouraged "colonialism" in Canadians because they felt the need of outside enhancements to their strength and of grounds for differentiation from their overpowering neighbors.

While this was not so true of recent Continental European immigrants, most of whom, even the Polish or Ukrainian Roman Catholics of the West and the Italians of Quebec, tended to merge with the English-speaking rather than the French-speaking portion of the Canadian people, they nevertheless tended to cling to the warmth and color of their own traditions as defenses against gray anonymity in the general mass. In Winnipeg newspapers were issued in twenty-three languages and the publishing of foreign-language books, particularly in Ukrainian and Icelandic, was a substantial business.

The great ethnic antithesis, of course, was that between the *Canadiens* and other Canadians or, in larger terms, between French Canada and the rest of North America. Its history and character have been rehearsed in preceding pages and its persistence as a mutually exasperating problem for both parties seems scarcely open to doubt. No clash could evoke and provoke more prejudice, false history, and overpowering emotion.

The Ontario Orangeman could shut his mind to the fact that the greatest allies of his symbolical Protestant hero, William III, were Catholic sovereigns, including even the pope. Moreover, the Battle of the Boyne in which William's army defeated James II's forces did not take place on July 12th, the Orangemen's anniversary celebration, and Marshall Schomberg, the Jacobite commander who was killed in that battle, had been expelled from the French service as a Huguenot. But myths can be stronger than history. The *Canadien* nationalist could deny that one of the best friends of his people was their first British governor, General James Murray. Religion, language, law, indeed two patterns of life, were in contrast and conflict, and bigots and extremists existed in both camps. Even the great bodies of moderates and the enlightened elite on both sides were seldom instinctively fair in their attitudes and behavior towards each other.

In a novel significantly entitled *Two Solitudes* (1945), Hugh MacLennan has dramatized the clash, with his characters acting it out almost in the categories of the professional sociologist. The amplitude of a novel permits subtleties, gradations, and interplay, but it might be advantageous here to set up the antitheses in their harshest, most extreme forms, while insisting at the same time that there are few extremists on either side.

Men of moderation and good will have prevented Canada from suffering any true equivalent of the English and American civil wars, although superficially the provocation might seem to have been greater. It should never be forgotten that it required two parties to the bargains under which the lost North American colonists of France have preserved their identity for two hundred years.

On the one side, there is the tradition of benevolent despotism, of paternalism, that makes authoritarianism, even on occasion ultramontanism, acceptable; on the other, the tradition of liberty and democracy that, in the case of some Progressives, could border on anarchy. *"Notre maître le passé"* confronts "Trust in the future." Deep concern with stability and with achieved status, as in religion, the professions, and politics, contradicts endless experimentation, love of change, and determination to rise in the world, usually materially.

It would be superfluous to particularize further the familiar characteristics of English-speaking Canadians, even in their often subtle small differentiations within the prevailing North American modes, but it would be well, especially for the English-speaking majority in North America, to bear in mind the particular traditions that two centuries of being in the minority have ingrained in the *Canadiens.* The *Canadien* thinks first in terms of the family, rather than of the individual, and places the maintenance of ethnic purity in marriage far higher than personal choice. His loyalty to his socio-religious community of parish and even of diocese usually quite overshadows any similar feelings towards any political unit except his province as a whole.

His religion subordinates personal well-being, indeed everything else, to salvation, for the "social gospel" and concern over standards of living of the Protestants have only begun to make inroads on his otherworldliness. The education of the *Canadien* faithful, even of the backsliders, belongs to the Church; in its upper levels it is confined to a small elite; and it is much more devoted to philosophical and aesthetic discipline and exercise than the rest of Canadian education, broadly shared and for the most part nonsectarian and focused on things and techniques.

Education in Quebec produces the regular and secular clergy, writers, and lawyers in far greater abundance than engineers, business administrators, and financiers. The medieval dislike and distrust of businessmen and money changers persists strongly, and socially they are still relegated to an inferior station. The arts, both in production and in enjoyment, are generally esteemed.

Economically, the *Canadien* emphasizes capital accumulation rather than the use of credit for the exploitation of resources whose more gradual consumption he tends to contemplate in terms of "inheritance" —a natural growth of population. He characteristically thinks of production for domestic use, not export. Commerce seems "natural" and tolerable only in small units. Handicapped both by his own lack of training for big industry, high finance, and big business, and by the insuperable head start of his British, Anglo-Canadian, and American economic masters in production, capital, and credit, he sees a great wrong to be righted.

Canadien capitalism has hitherto been largely religious; the accumulations of this society meet the eye everywhere in the possessions of the Church, the gratefully acknowledged custodian of the value beyond all other values. Now, in an industrial age, there has grown up alongside it a marked tendency to put large industrial resources under the state, not federal, but provincial. In a society so nearly theocratic, the provincial government can, it is felt, be entrusted with such tasks as taking over private power developments and mediating between great enterprises and *"le petit gars."* Finally, it might be said that the *Canadien* is thoroughly skeptical about the belief of his fellow-Canadians in a progress towards the creation of a heaven on earth.

Minorityism.—Impressive as that array of contrasts is, its sum is less important than the single circumstance that the *Canadiens* are a sensitive, minority people in Canada, and still more in North America, threatened, they believe, by what nearly all men dread, loss of identity. With their old way of life dislocated and destroyed by the industrial revolution of the past fifty years, they are at the same time inundated by the seductive products of that process, not only articles of consumption and use, but news services, periodicals, books, plays, moving pictures, radio, and television.

One of the most homogeneous societies on earth sees its homogeneity assailed in countless ways. A people, which has endured the countless, incommunicable sufferings and slights of having been conquered and abandoned thereafter by its mother country, thinks that it sees a continuance of that conquered and abandoned status in another form. It is this sense of being considered a backward or a second-rate people to be condescended to, exploited, and, presumably, "acculturated" and assimilated, that drives the *Canadiens* in upon themselves as it did the Irish. *Soyons nous-mêmes* means almost the same thing as *Sinn Fein:* "Let us be ourselves" and "Ourselves alone."

To an outsider there seems no reasonable likelihood of the *Canadiens* being assimilated to the rest of Canada or of North America within the foreseeable future. On the other hand, even if "Laurentie" were permitted to become another Eire, it could not withdraw from the world. The problem must be consigned to time. Meanwhile there are two favorable omens. Neither the rest of Canada nor the United States has been showing any substantial intention of trying to dragoon French Canada; and French Canada itself is progressively corroding its own defensiveness by simply, and to the best of its ability, being itself, both within its own confines and through its distinguished sons and daughters elsewhere in Canada, in the United States, and the world at large.

E PLURIBUS UNUM?

General Canadian characteristics.—An Asiatic, an Australasian, or an African finds all kinds of Canadians more alike than different, and it seems reasonable to believe that as a whole society they have developed certain strong common qualities during ten or more generations of life in North America. It is not, of course, a question of characteristics unique in Canadians, but of the noticeable pattern brought out by the Canadians' particular combinations of normal human traits.

One such bundle might be described as frontier virtues. Canada has been a difficult country to master and to maintain during adversity. It enjoyed no such swift and sustained success as the United States. To enterprise and resourcefulness, therefore, Canadians have characteristically had to add determination and endurance, thereby compounding a mixture which might be described as alert dependability.

A second bundle of traits would be political virtues, as exemplified in the successful insistence on responsible government, an infectious new note in modern imperialism; in making federalism embrace manifold diversities for almost a century without secession or civil war; and in a submission to law and order perhaps unequaled by any other country of expansive frontiers.

This law-abiding quality borders upon the most commonly discussed characteristic of Canadians—a cautious distrust of impulsiveness that can approach inertia, or, more generally, a pervasive canniness. It has been said, for instance, that Canada has a weak revolutionary or radical strain, and a strong counterrevolutionary or conservative one. As the English poet, Rupert Brooke, once put it, "Canada is a live country, live, but not, like the States, kicking." The Canadian historian, Edgar McInnis, has described the attribute as an "inescapable sense of limitations," internal and external, "ambition tempered by realism," and "a shrewd sense of the possible."

One has only to recall Canada's past and present vulnerabilities to unearth the roots of these related traits. Menaced by overt force from its southern neighbors at intervals from its founding until 1871, neglected even to the point of abandonment by both France and Britain at various times, easily damaged by American obliviousness and by general economic fluctuations, and struggling constantly against sectionalism at home, Canadians have had wariness ground into them for three hundred and fifty years.

Hence the defensive strength of the loyalist myth with its connotations of aristocracy and privilege; of the Roman Catholic and the national churches; of hierarchical stratification in society; of conventional morality; of respect for law and order; and of the conservative Liberal party since 1921. From one end of Canada to the other, in one form or another, the ideas and institutions making for stability have been the receptacles of conscious and subconscious support which makes radicalisms of all sorts difficult of initial success and short-lived at best.

The search for a national culture.—Every country is the victim, to some extent, of condescension from foreigners, and Canadians have had to put up with a great deal of it, particularly from the Frenchmen, Britons, and Americans whom they have expected to be more instinctively understanding. The natural response, since Durham's day at least, has been a great variety of efforts to discover first regional and then national culture. The discrepancy in size and weight between Canada and the countries whose representatives have principally patronized her has intensified Canadian sensitivity, but the subtle products of that inflamed tenderness have, of course, had infinitely more effect within Canada than on her usually unconscious tormentors. In Canada, as earlier in the United States, the achievement of free and unself-conscious culture, capable of borrowing without guilt and giving without boast, has been slow, complex, and difficult.

One impulse was to enhance native strength by emphasizing identity with something recognizably greater. The *Canadiens,* feeling abandoned by royalist France and repelled by many attributes of republican France, naturally sought to draw strength from the Vatican, sometimes, as has been seen, with an ultramontanism so passionate as to presume to correct the pope. In recent times there have been strong efforts at identification with a Catholic, corporativist pattern of society, economy, and polity of an Italian, Spanish, Vichyist, or Portuguese cast or with the Latinism of the southern American republics.

Anglo-Canadians tended to stress their Britonism, in which Welsh, Scottish, northern and southern Irish affiliations could be submerged, or their membership in the variegated Empire or Commonwealth. In spite of systematic encouragement from Italy, Nazi Germany, and Russia, the Canadian responses have not been great, and a variety of circumstances, chiefly Canadian apprehensiveness towards the United States and resistance to assimilation, have practically precluded any resort to avowed Americanism as an adjunct of strength. For at least a generation now, Canadians of all sorts have been aware of past tendencies to seek greatness in a larger whole and it has become the practice to dismiss them as "colonialism."

Another natural impulse was the effort to keep up to date, to be "cosmopolitan," or, in its involuntary form, the unconscious adoption of foreign cultural fashions. This was a particularly complex area of behavior, for, on the one hand, the pervasive Canadian conservatism and caution operated so as to create a noticeable time-lag, and, on the other, the native cultures were inundated by all kinds of emanations from France, Great Britain, and the United States. A great deal of this foreign influence represented the healthful evolution of rich traditions already in Canadian life, but it was at the same time discouraging to Canadians who wanted desperately to have something purely their own.

The problem was acute in literature. Among them, France, Britain, and the United States consciously and unconsciously intensified the difficulties of book and periodical publication in Canada. Frederick Philip Grove, a dedicated, effective, and uncompromising Canadian writer, used to tell of meeting a fellow Oxonian who was also working for his bread in a canning factory. "How did you get here?" "Drink." "And you?" "Literature."

American editors, once cordial to Canadian writers as such, made obvious their disbelief in a Canadian literature distinct from American. The situation in the theater, moving pictures, broadcasting, music, dance, painting, sculpture, and architecture has been analogous, and it has been far commoner for Canadians especially gifted in these matters to emigrate than to stay at home. Because the *Canadiens* were always more interested than other Canadians in intellectual and aesthetic pursuits, but were cut off from France by their long separation and from the English-speaking world by their language, they were distinctly more successful in maintaining and developing a native culture.

If up-to-dateness and cosmopolitanism were lures which had induced Canadians to support foreign intellectual and aesthetic enterprises more generously than their own, the prescription for a healthier future was to focus attention on what capacities lay within Canadians themselves and to build upon that sure and, in the long run, attractive foundation. The exhortations of the Canada First group of the seventies and of similar groups after 1914 to subordinate other considerations to Canadian setting and to Canadian content had proved to be dangerously shallow advice. Furthermore, resignation to such a description of themselves as A. R. M. Lower's "steady, reliable and sensible but not conspicuously endowed with the gift divine, creative imagination," did not commend itself.

During the thirties and forties, therefore, a mood of stringent self-examination, analysis, and fruitful controversy began to characterize many critics and commentators in education and scholarship and in the creative arts. Canadians were bent upon discovering what they had to build upon, what standards of their own they might use to measure both native achievement and what was poured upon them from abroad.

It is impracticable here to recite the details of the subsequent notable growth in Canadian book publishing; the increase in both serious and popular native periodicals; the expansion in painting, sculpture, etc., and in the purchase of artistic products; the characteristic compromise by which the nationalized Canadian Broadcasting Corporation, with its three networks (one French) and its international short-wave system, co-existed and intermingled with Canadian and American privately owned broadcasting; the nationwide activity in theatricals, music, and dance; the swift winning of international recognition by the National Film Board's documentary films; and the widespread effects upon imaginative, creative Canadians of the encouragement given them by the C.B.C., the N.F.B., the National Gallery, the Dominion Drama Festival, and the musical conservatories of Toronto and Montreal.

The original, creative content in so general an outburst of intellectual and aesthetic pursuits and enjoyment was relatively modest, but the movement was native, unapologetic, and infectious, and it took place in spheres of activity which a "practical" people had been thought to ignore or in which they had too often submitted to their alleged betters.

Poetry as criterion.—It was fairly generally agreed that poetry provided the surest single touchstone of Canadian qualities. Admittedly, however, the traditional idiosyncrasies and the clerical censorship of French Canada conditioned its poetry so severely that it was almost impossible to judge what weight should be given to the few fresh and independent voices, such as those of Robert Choquette, Louis Danton, and Alfred Deroches. Much poetry was being written by the *Canadiens,* particularly religious poetry of great poignancy and intensity, but outsiders usually found it ingrown and particular rather than outgoing and universal.

The critics of Canadian poetry in English had a greatly increased volume to deal with and they had to clear away an overburden before they could assay the ore. The worst obstruction, inevitably, was no longer "applied Canadianism," but derivative, imitative manners and ideas. The characteristic Canadian time-lag exposed these mercilessly, for a knowledgeable critic could easily demonstrate rather belated Canadian responses to changes in the British and American climates of opinion and tone.

John Sutherland, for instance, could document and date the preponderance of religious problems (T. S. Eliot) and of imagism (concerned chiefly with man and nature) during the thirties, the impact of Auden's and Spender's Marxism towards the end of that decade, and the outburst of urban, industrial, class-conscious, political poetry at the beginning of the forties. He felt that the break with Russia destroyed much of the underlying political faith and explained the soul-searching and the religious quests in the poetry of the middle of the century.

Other critics, notably E. K. Brown, Northrop Frye, Ralph Gustafson, and A. J. M. Smith, tried to disregard the overburden of manner and fashion and get at the qualities of the underlying Canadianism. Frye, for instance, found that "there is a recognizable Canadian accent" in Canadian poetry; that a persistent "colonialism" bred "prudery . . . the instinct to seek a conventional or commonplace expression of an idea"; that Canadians were disinclined to admit either the maturity of their country in terms of industrial capitalism or the erudition and research that lay back of some of their best poetry; and that, instead of "Tarzanism" in the approach to nature, there was rather "an intent and closely focused vision."

He (and certain other critics) held that "the outstanding achievement of Canadian poetry is in the evocation of stark terror. Not a coward's terror, of course; but a controlled vision of the causes of cowardice. The immediate source of this is obviously the frightening loneliness of a huge and thinly settled country." Or again: "Nature is seen by the poet, first as unconsciousness, then as a kind of existence which is cruel and meaningless, then as the source of the cruelty and subconscious stampedings within the human mind."

The counterbalance was found to be in the combination of the qualities which have been mentioned earlier in other connections: resourcefulness, energy, fortitude, discipline, endurance, and caution, qualities which might be summed up in the word "poise." Gustafson, after drawing attention to "a quiet pervasive humor, the kind that is cognizant of the follies and foibles of human beings and can be affectionate about them," sums this up by saying: "There is little in Canadian writing that is bitter or sullen or introverted. To put it in a negative way, Canadians, if Canadian writing is a valid reflection, aren't sorry for themselves."

The literary critics have thus carried us full circle back to the historian's diagnosis: "a shrewd sense of the possible." It has been the custom of Canadian self-critics to deplore this because it seems to preclude "passion," "color," and "intensity" in Canadianism as a whole, but these are luxuries which usually come after the attainment of such cultural sustenance as the Canadians now seem to have won for themselves.

🍁 THE MERITS OF DIVERSITY

It could be said, then, that by 1950 Canada had proved eminently capable of creating, maintaining, and asserting national unity in the political and economic spheres, and that she had discovered her substratum of common cultural characteristics. This was nationality, nationality in diversity. Political, economic, and cultural particularisms were obvious, sometimes flamboyant, but they did not disintegrate the whole. In fact, in each of these spheres some Canadians were acquiring enough detachment from their previously passionate concern with unity to acclaim the merits of variety.

The liberal tradition, which accepted diversity, had been considerably debauched by perversion and misuse, but its core was freedom. Domestically its potential uses were many. As long ago as 1877, Laurier had begun to persuade his people that it was quite compatible with their tradition. It had been present in the Anglo-American tradition since the founding of English colonies in North America and had been nurtured (among *Canadiens* as well as among the others) by the conditions of pioneer life. Politically it could be a shield against authoritarianism in federal, provincial, and municipal governments and in their civil services. Economically it could guard against monopoly, whether privately or publicly exercised. Culturally it could set its dancing variety of color, tone, and texture against the neutral gray of uniformity.

Externally the liberal tradition of freedom in diversity could be similarly useful. Economically it could combat autarchy, as in the forwarding of multilateral trade and investment. Politically it could work with other states to temper the polarization of the globe between the United States and Russia, could resist in behalf of Canada an "imperial," "colonial" relationship with the United States, and could expand "functional" international co-operation of many sorts. Culturally, it could encourage many kinds of Canadians to be themselves, for instance in UNESCO, unself-consciously borrowing from others who, in turn, had already shown themselves eager to select from the variety that Canada had to offer.

In all, it is not too much to believe that diversity within Canada will in the future, as in the past, contribute both to her own domestic richness of life and to the society of nations.

CHAPTER XXXII

Canada in the 1950's

Developments after 1950 were in large measure the extension of trends which had already emerged. True to its role as a Middle Power, Canada continued to play an active part in the field of international relations. After a long campaign to secure an enlarged St. Lawrence Seaway, construction was begun in 1954 and completed in 1959, under the joint sponsorship of Canada and the United States. Important developments occurred in the domestic field. The federal government displayed an increased awareness of its social responsibilities. New welfare legislation was passed and the government also adopted policies for the deliberate encouragement of a native Canadian culture. The Canadian economy continued to expand.

CONTINUING PROSPERITY

During the years between 1950 and 1957 Canada maintained a high level of prosperity. In almost every year Canada's foreign trade reached or approached record levels and domestic activity continued to expand. The gross national product, which had been $12 billion in 1946, rose to $24 billion in 1954 and $29.9 billion in 1956. Total Canadian exports, which had averaged $1.2 billion in 1926–29, were $3.9 billion in 1954 and $4.8 billion in 1956. Total imports which averaged $1.0 billion in 1926–29, were $4.0 billion in 1954 and $5.7 billion in 1956— a serious recession occurred in 1957–58, but by the spring of 1959 recovery was well under way.

Considerable change had occurred since the boom period of 1926–29 in the structure of Canadian foreign trade. In 1926–29 more than half of Canada's exports had been of farm origin. By 1951–54 Canada's forest and mineral industries had risen to first and second places, ahead of agriculture as sources of exports.

During the years 1951–54 newsprint paper accounted for 15 per cent of Canadian exports, while lumber and wood pulp accounted for 7 per cent each. The wide use of wood pulp in the textile and chemical industries as well as in the paper industry accounted for the very sharp gain in the exports of the commodity. The international postwar building boom raised exports of lumber to unprecedented heights.

The expansion of exports of mineral origin reflected the discovery of more mineral deposits in Canada. Discoveries of western oil and of iron ore in Quebec and Labrador were the most spectacular examples. There was an increased tendency to refine or further manufacture Canadian metals before export. Aluminum, a very important part of Canada's mineral exports, was entirely produced from non-Canadian ores.

The relative position of wheat and flour was considerably altered. Wheat had accounted for 28 per cent and flour for an additional 5 per cent of Canadian exports in 1926–29. In 1951–54 exports of wheat and flour, while higher in value than in the previous period, had fallen to 12 and 3 per cent of total Canadian exports.

Changes in the industrial origin of imports were less pronounced, but noteworthy. Here too the significance of imports of farm origin had

| | Exports | | |
Origin	1926–29	1951–54	1956
Farm	712.7	1,143.6	1,088.3
Wild Life	22.7	25.3	27.8
Marine	36.9	121.5	132.7
Forest	284.2	1,360.0	1,514.6
Mineral	194.8	1,202.8	1,758.1
Mixed	25.0	200.3	268.2
Total *	1,276.3	4,053.6	4,789.7

| | Imports | | |
Origin	1926–29	1951–54	1956
Farm	439.7	922.7	1,057.9
Wild Life	12.7	11.4	13.4
Marine	3.5	10.7	19.1
Forest	51.9	153.3	233.1
Mineral	483.2	2,449.6	3,581.0
Mixed	92.3	600.1	800.9
Total *	1,083.2	4,147.8	5,705.4

* Detail does not add up to total because of rounding.

been sharply reduced. The most important relative gains occurred in manufactured goods of the mineral origin and mixed origin categories. These reflected the great importance of capital goods and consumer durables in Canadian expenditure in the postwar period and also the use of the chemical industries and the parallel substitution of synthetics for many natural materials.

The preceding tables of annual averages will illustrate the new structure of Canadian trade. The returns for 1926–29 are for years ending on March 31; the 1951–54 and 1956 returns are for calendar years. The returns are in millions of dollars.

A striking description of Canadian economic progress in the postwar years was provided by the Royal Commission on Canada's Economic Prospects under the chairmanship of W. L. Gordon, a distinguished Canadian accountant and economist. The Preliminary Report of the Gordon Commission was printed in December, 1956, and the Final Report in November, 1957. The Gordon Commission made a detailed analysis of the Canadian economy and estimated that by 1980 Canada would have a population of about 27 million and a Gross National Product of 76 billion dollars.

The oil and gas industry.—In the decade between 1947 and 1957 there was a remarkable increase in Canadian oil production. The great turning point in the oil industry in Western Canada came on February 13, 1947, when Imperial Leduc No. 1 blew in on the Alberta prairie. The well opened up an immense oil-producing region. By 1957 Canada was producing 170 million barrels daily, about 70 per cent of domestic oil requirements. In 1954 the Imperial Oil Company made its first important oil shipment overseas, a cargo of gasoline for Japan.

These developments were accompanied by the construction of a network of pipelines to transport oil and gas from Western Canada to distant markets in Canada and the United States.

Two great pipeline systems were completed for the delivery of prairie crude oil to Ontario and the Pacific coast. In 1950 the Interprovincial Pipeline Company constructed the first eastbound pipeline, from Edmonton to Superior, Wisconsin. Three years later the line was extended to Sarnia, Ontario. The pipeline from Edmonton to Sarnia, 1,765 miles in length, was said to be the longest in the world. By the middle of 1955 the system was receiving 250,000 barrels daily and deliveries were being made either directly or by spur lines to refineries at Saskatoon, Moose Jaw, Regina, Brandon, Winnipeg, Wrenshall (Minnesota), Superior (Wisconsin), and Sarnia. From Sarnia crude oil was moving by tanker to refineries at Toronto and Port Credit. In addition Saskatchewan crude oil from the Swift Current area commenced to move to St. Paul, Minnesota, via the interprovincial pipeline and two other lines.

Prairie oil fields were also linked with the Pacific coast. Trans Mountain Pipe Line Company completed a 718-mile line between Edmonton and Vancouver in 1953. During 1954 a twenty-four-mile spur line was constructed from Sumas, British Columbia, across the international boundary to Ferndale, Washington, where General Petroleum Corporation completed a new refinery in October of that year. In 1955 the line was extended thirty-six miles southwest to the new Shell Oil Company refinery at Anacortes. Six major feeder lines supplied the Trans Mountain system with Alberta Crude Oil at Edmonton. Oil was delivered to one refinery at Kamloops, three near Vancouver, and two in the state of Washington.

Construction work continued on secondary lines in the three prairie provinces to supply the large cross-country systems. Important secondary lines were built by the Pembina Pipe Line Company, the Gulf Pipe Line Company, and the South Saskatchewan Pipe Line Company.

Progress was much slower in the construction of pipelines to carry western gas. Trans-Canada Pipe Lines was incorporated in 1951. It was a subsidiary of Canadian Delhi Oil which was controlled by American interests. In 1954, Trans-Canada and a Canadian company, Western Pipe Lines, were merged under the name Trans-Canada Pipe Lines. In the same year the company received a permit from the Alberta government to export gas at a maximum rate of 540,000 thousand cubic feet per day, up to a total of 4,350,000,000 thousand cubic feet over a twenty-seven-year period. In 1954, Trans-Canada also secured a permit from the federal government to move Alberta natural gas across Canada to eastern markets. The federal government approved a substantial export of gas into the United States, at Emerson, Manitoba, with the proviso that Ontario and Quebec were to be served as nearly as possible concurrently with any such export. In February, 1956, control of Trans-Canada passed to new American interests. Of the existing ownership, 51 per cent was taken over by Tennessee Gas Transmission Company, Gulf Oil Corporation (through Canadian Gulf Oil Company), and Continental Oil Company, through Hudson's Bay Oil and Gas Company. Canadian Delhi and the Western Pipelines group retained the remaining 49 per cent interest.

Westcoast Transmission Company received Canadian approval in 1952 to construct a pipeline for delivery of Peace River natural gas to Vancouver and United States markets. Late in 1954 Westcoast signed an agreement with an American company, Pacific Northwest Pipeline

Corporation, which had been given the market franchise for the Pacific Northwest states. The agreement provided for initial deliveries of 300,-000,000 cubic feet of Peace River area gas to the American company's facilities at the international boundary. In addition, Westcoast planned to make initial daily deliveries of up to 50,000,000 cubic feet to Vancouver and nearby Fraser Valley communities. During 1955 United States approval of this agreement was being sought and Westcoast was also continuing with preparations for its 650-mile main line and its 223-mile gathering systems. By the end of 1956, Westcoast Transmission had completed about 70 per cent of the 650 miles of 30-inch main line from Taylor in northeastern British Columbia to Vancouver and the United States border near Huntingdon, B.C.

In 1956 the federal government determined to take a more active part in the completion of the system of pipelines which was to carry Alberta gas eastward. An agreement was negotiated with Trans-Canada Pipe Lines and legislation was introduced in Parliament for its implementation. The government set up the Northern Ontario Pipe Line Crown Corporation, which was to build the Northern Ontario section of the pipe line (from the Manitoba-Ontario boundary to Kapuskasing) and to lease it to Trans-Canada Pipe Lines. The government was empowered to make loans to the Northern Ontario Pipe Line Crown Corporation up to $130,000,000. In order to assist in the construction of the western section of line, from the Alberta-Saskatchewan boundary to Winnipeg, the corporation was empowered to make loans to Trans-Canada. These were not to exceed 90 per cent of the cost of the construction of the line or $80 million. If Trans-Canada defaulted on these loans the government was empowered to take over its assets and to conduct its business. Trans-Canada not only proposed to carry gas to eastern Canada but also to export it to the United States. The company had worked out an agreement with the Tennessee Gas Transmission Company providing for the export of Canadian gas at Emerson, Manitoba, and eventually at Niagara Falls.

The efforts of the Liberal administration to secure the passage of the pipeline bill resulted in a bitter controversy with the Conservative and C.C.F. groups in the House of Commons. The government set a very tight schedule for the passage of the bill. Although its first reading in the House of Commons was on May 15, 1956, it had to secure the governor general's signature by June 7 if the government's undertakings were to be fulfilled. In order to adhere to this schedule, the government resorted to the repeated use of closure in the House of Commons. The opposition objected to the large measure of American participation in Trans-Canada, but they particularly resented the allegedly strong-arm methods employed by the government to secure passage of the bill. Debates in the House of Commons were characterized by stormy scenes. On May 25, when the House was in committee, a prominent Conservative member was expelled for the remainder òf the day for refusing to take his seat when ordered by the chairman to do so. After tremendous exertions the government secured passage of the bill in the House of Commons on June 5. It secured the governor general's signature on June 7. Construction of the system of pipelines was able to begin in the summer of 1956.

However, Trans-Canada failed to secure entry of its gas to the United States. In November, 1958, the United States Federal Power Commission rejected the application of Midwestern Gas Transmission, a subsidiary of Tennessee Gas Transmission, to import Trans-Canada gas. The FPC asserted that the Canadian company's proven reserves were insufficient to meet its expanding Canadian requirements and also those of Midwestern. A Canadian Royal Commission under the chairmanship of Henry Borden had already recommended that the Canadian government should deny Trans-Canada permission to export to the United States.

Inflow of capital.—To a large extent the Canadian economic expansion of the postwar years has been financed by the inflow of nonresident capital. After 1948 there was a sharp rise in the amount of nonresident capital invested in Canada and Canada's balance of international indebtedness had risen by 1955 to a new peak of $7.5 billion. The earlier peak of international indebtedness, occurring in 1930, was $6.5 billion. Foreign investments in Canada reached a new height by the end of 1955, rising well over $13 billion from $12.469 billion at the end of 1954. The growth of investments owned in the United Kingdom and Western Europe reached significant proportions. British investments by 1954 reached a new postwar height of $2.143 billion. United States investments, which reached $9.622 billion at the end of 1954, constituted more than three-quarters of total nonresident capital invested.

A very large share of the capital inflow took the form of direct investments. Between 1950 and mid-1956 this amounted to over $2.300 billion or about two-thirds of the net long-term inflow. The other main channel of capital investment in Canada was the purchase by nonresidents of Canadian securities. Most of the new issues sold by Canadians abroad were provincial and municipal securities, although a number of large new corporation issues were sold in outside markets. Nonresidents in Canada also increased their holdings of common and preferred stock in Canadian corporations. A very large two-way trade in outstanding Canadian securities resulted in a net capital inflow between 1950 and mid-1956 of over $500 million, excluding the trade in Government of Canada securities. An increasing number of Canadian equities were listed on stock exchanges outside Canada.

An analysis of investment in Canada indicates that nonresident investment was concentrated in the resources and manufacturing industries. A number of industries were dominated by a few companies controlled by non-Canadians. These included oil and gas; some sections of the mining, smelting, and refining industries, particularly nickel, iron ore, aluminum and asbestos; some sections of the chemical industry and three important secondary manufactures, automobiles, electrical apparatus and supplies, and rubber products. In the pulp and paper industry slightly over half of the total capital was controlled by non-residents. Foreign capital was of less significance in the primary iron and steel, food processing, textile, transportation, public utility, and construction industries. Nonresident investment in agriculture was negligible while more than four-fifths of capital in the chartered banks was Canadian. In other financial institutions (insurance companies, loan and finance companies) foreign ownership and control was considerable but not dominant.

While appreciating the benefits of foreign investment in their country, Canadians were becoming alarmed at the extent to which Canadian industry was owned by nonresidents. In the 1950's the picture came to be regarded as less satisfactory than that described in Chapter XXX. "No other nation so highly industrialized as Canada has such a large proportion of industry controlled by nonresident companies," declared two Canadian economists in a paper delivered to the Canadian Political Science Association in 1957. Canadians resented the fact that they were unable to acquire any appreciable interest in many of their country's resources which were held by the subsidiaries of foreign companies.

Grain surplus.—In the years after 1953 the accumulation of a large grain surplus, particularly of wheat, in Western Canada became a major problem of the producer and of the Canadian government. At the end of the crop year 1953–54 (July 31, 1954) record farm stocks of wheat, barley, rye and next-to-record stocks of oats and flaxseed provided an unprecedented carry-over of old crop grains. The Canadian surplus occurred in a period in which United States production and world production rose sharply. On August 1, 1954, the record Canadian carry-over of 602 million and the United States surplus of 900 million, added to the surpluses of Argentina and Australia, totaled just under 2 billion bushels.

The difficulties of the Canadian Wheat Board were increased by the unusually tight storage position in Canada. In this situation, the Board tried to ensure all producers an opportunity of delivering grain in as equitable a manner as possible. Marketing arrangements of wheat, oats, and barley continued under a system of crop-year pools administered by the Board. Other grains in Western Canada and all grains in Eastern Canada continued to be sold in the open market. At the beginning of the 1954–55 year the Board established an initial delivery quota of 100 units, each unit the equivalent of three bushels of wheat, or eight of oats, or five of barley, or five of rye. General delivery quotas were gradually increased as space became available.

Perplexed by this marketing problem Canadians were gravely concerned with the wheat policies of the United States government. American concern over the wheat surplus prompted a series of measures calculated to effect its disposal. During the period 1953–55 a series of agricultural surplus disposal acts and programs involving the lavish use of export subsidies caused mounting concern in Canada and other wheat-exporting countries. The Eisenhower administration co-operated vigorously with Congress in this program. Sales for foreign currencies, barter deals, three-cornered arrangements and "give-aways" of various kinds provided for shipments of United States wheat and other grains to Germany, Japan, India, and a number of Asian, European, and Latin-American countries.

Canadian apprehensions in regard to the give-away programs of the United States appeared to be confirmed by returns for the crop year 1954–55, in which the total of Canadian wheat exports showed a decline of 3.3 million bushels compared with 1953–54, while United States exports of wheat increased by 65.1 million bushels. A prominent Canadian economist attributed this to the fact that a number of Canada's smaller markets had been captured by United States give-away programs. There were vigorous protests from that section of the Canadian press which was particularly sympathetic to the wheat producer. In a characteristic editorial the *Winnipeg Free Press* asserted on September 23, 1955:

> The threat to our wheat exports, arising from United States give-aways and subsidies, has been visibly mounting for some time. Far too little has been said about it; Americans, however great their good will, cannot be expected to see with our eyes, to feel our experiences. This is one of the cases where the right course, the only possible way to be heard and understood, is to make a noise. We are not doing it.

Other Canadian newspapers, while to some extent critical of United States policy, attributed the problem of Canadian wheat surpluses largely to the price policies of the Canadian Wheat Board. They advocated open marketing "under the old and long tested law of supply and demand" and criticized the Wheat Board for preventing farmers from selling in world markets at competitive prices.

❧ THE ST. LAWRENCE SEAWAY

Of epochal importance was the achievement of a plan for Canadian-American co-operation in the construction of the St. Lawrence Seaway. The settlement of this question in 1954 removed from the arena of politics an issue which had long aggravated the relations between the two countries.

There were two phases to the St. Lawrence project: development of hydroelectric power and construction of the seaway. The International Joint Commission in 1952 approved the joint development of power in the International Rapids Section of the river by the Ontario Hydroelectric Commission and New York State Power Authority. The American Federal Power Commission on July 15, 1953, granted a license to the New York State Power Authority to construct the United States part of the power project. On November 12, 1953, the Canadian and the United States governments exchanged notes establishing the St. Lawrence River Joint Board of Engineers to review, co-ordinate, and approve plans and specifications for the hydroelectric power project. Meanwhile the International Joint Commission completed arrangements for establishing the International St. Lawrence Board of Control to supervise operation of the works.

Progress in regard to the seaway was slower. In 1952 Canada agreed to construct the seaway without United States assistance. In a joint exchange of notes on June 30, 1952, the Canadian government undertook, when all arrangements had been made to ensure completion of the power project, to construct locks and canals on the Canadian side of the international boundary to provide for an uninterrupted navigation channel twenty-seven feet deep between Lake Erie and the port of Montreal.

However, a movement developed in Congress in 1953 to secure United States co-operation in the seaway project. The movement culminated in the passage of the Wily-Dondero Bill which was signed by President Eisenhower on May 13, 1954. The bill provided for construction by the United States of a forty-six-mile seaway between Lake Ontario and Cornwall at a cost of $105,000,000.

On the whole Canadians were pleased with the bill, although some regretted that Canada was not to "go it alone" in the construction of the seaway. There was some dissatisfaction in Canada at the American stipulation that the canal in the international section was all to be built on the United States side. In August, citizens of Cornwall organized the Citizens' Joint Action Committee for the All-Canadian Seaway. To quiet the protests the Canadian government, on August 17, 1954, gave notice to the United States government of its intention to construct a canal and lock at Iroquois on the Canadian side of the river. The Canadian government reserved the right to complete a twenty-seven-foot navigation channel on the Canadian side of the International Rapids section, when it considered that parallel facilities were required.

The Canadian government emerged from the negotiations with some credit. It had paid considerable regard to the demands of Canadian pride and local interest while availing itself of the solid advantages of United States participation in the seaway and power projects. Preliminary work on the seaway began before the close of the 1954 construction season. The seaway was formally opened by Queen Elizabeth and President Eisenhower on June 26, 1959 at a ceremony at St. Lambert, Quebec.

THE MASSEY REPORT

A significant development in the postwar period was the establishment of the principle that the federal government should play a more positive role in the development of Canadian culture. Recognition of this principle was largely the achievement of the Royal Commission on National Development in the Arts, Letters and Sciences which was set up in 1949 under the chairmanship of the Right Honorable Vincent Massey. The other members of the commission were Arthur Surveyor, a Montreal civil engineer; N. A. M. Mackenzie, president of the University of British Columbia; the Most Reverend Georges-Henri Lévesque, Dean of the Faculty of Social Sciences of Laval University; and Miss Hilda Neatby, Professor of History in the University of Saskatchewan. The anticipated nature of their work was indicated by the Commission of Appointment in which it was asserted, "It is desirable that the Canadian people should know as much as possible about their country, its history and traditions; and about their natural life and common achievements," and "It is in the national interest to give encouragement to institutions which express national feeling, promote common understanding and add to the variety and richness of Canadian life, rural as well as urban."

The Massey Commission held public hearings in each of the Canadian provinces and received a large number of briefs from associations and groups interested in various aspects of Canadian culture. The Massey Report was presented in May, 1951. It was one of the great state papers of Canadian history, ranking in stature with Durham's Report and the Sirois Report. The commission recommended that the existing institutions for the preservation and encouragement of Canadian culture such as the Canadian Broadcasting Corporation, the National Film Board, the National Gallery, the National Museum, and the Public Archives of Canada should be maintained and in some cases reorganized and expanded. It also recommended that a National Library should be established without delay.

The commission also recommended new and positive measures for the support of education and the encouragement of the arts. It recommended that the federal government should make annual contributions to support the work of the universities. These grants were to be allocated on the basis of population in each province and were to be sufficient to ensure that the work of Canadian universities should be carried on in accordance with the needs of the nation. It was proposed that the federal government should grant funds for the establishment and maintenance of an adequate number of scholarships, studentships and bursaries for postgraduate students of Canadian universities in the humanities, social sciences, and law. The commission urged that a system of fellowships, known as the Canada Fellowships, should be established for the encouragement of mature and advanced work in the humanities, social sciences, and law. The most striking recommendation of the Massey Commission was the creation of a body known as "the Canada Council for the Encouragement of the Arts, Letters, Humanities and Social Sciences" to stimulate and help voluntary organizations in these fields, to foster Canada's cultural relations abroad, and to devise and administer the system of scholarships proposed in the report.

The Massey Report was followed by several important measures on the part of the federal government. In 1952, a system of federal grants to universities in all the provinces was inaugurated in accordance with the recommendations of the report. Except for the year 1951–52, Premier Maurice Duplessis and his Quebec government prevented the Quebec universities from accepting the federal grants offered to them. After an interval of six years the Canada Council was established in the spring of 1957. The Canada Council Act, which received the royal assent on March 28, 1957, provided for the appointment of a Council consisting of the chairman, vice-chairman, and not more than nineteen other members. Its object was declared to be "to foster and promote the study and enjoyment of, and the production of works in, the arts, humanities and social sciences." It was to provide grants, scholarships, and loans to persons in Canada for study in these fields and was also to make grants to the universities by way of capital assistance for building projects. The Minister of Finance was empowered to pay the Council $50,000,000 for the University Capital Grants Fund, $50,000,000 for an Endowment Fund, and to advance to the Council $100,000 on terms approved by the governor in council in regard to interest and repayment. Expenditures for purposes other than the capital grants to universities were to be paid from returns on investments made out of the Endowment Fund, the advance of $100,000 and money, and security or property received by the Council by gift, bequest or otherwise. The council was organized and began to function in 1957. The Honorable Brooke Claxton was appointed chairman and the Most Reverend Georges-Henri Lévesque, vice-chairman. A. W. Trueman, a distinguished educationist, was appointed director of the council.

POLITICAL DEVELOPMENTS

The Liberals remained in office at Ottawa until 1957. They were returned to power in 1953 with 173 seats in a House of 265 members. They continued to occupy the position of a moderate, middle-of-the-road type of party. They balanced moderate protection for industry with price supports for agricultural commodities, particularly wheat. They continued to favor policies of social amelioration. They had secured passage of the Unemployment Insurance Act in 1940 and the Family Allowances Act of 1944. They now passed the Old Age Security Act of 1951. In the sphere of dominion-provincial relations, they continued to press for taxation agreements which would redress the balance between "have" and "have-not" provinces. The appointment of the Right Honorable Vincent Massey as governor general in January, 1952, was a significant step in Canada's progress toward nationhood. Mr. Massey was the first Canadian to hold this office.

In spite of the conspicuous contribution of the Liberals to the economic, social, and cultural development of Canada, the long period of Liberal rule came to an end in June, 1957.

In the election on June 10, the Liberals secured only 104 seats while the Conservatives secured 109. The C.C.F. elected 25 members and the Social Credit Party 19. The St. Laurent ministry resigned and was succeeded by the Conservatives under John G. Diefenbaker. The Liberal defeat was the result of a number of factors including resentment against the use of closure in the debates on the Pipe Line Bill and dissatisfaction with the "tight money" policy of the government and the Bank of Canada. Western farmers were dissatisfied with the government's wheat policy. Maritimers objected to the suggestion in the preliminary report of the Gordon Commission that people might be encouraged to emigrate from the Maritime Provinces. Probably many electors were influenced by the cry so often directed against governments in office, "It's time for a change."

The Conservatives under John G. Diefenbaker took office on June 21, 1957. During the subsequent session of Parliament (October 14, 1957–February 1, 1958) the administration secured the passage of legislation providing for increases in old-age pensions, cash advances on farm-stored wheat, and financial assistance to support power developments in the Maritime Provinces. On October 16, 1957, a Royal Commission was appointed under Mr. Henry Borden to make recommendations as to the most effective use of Canada's sources of energy, such as oil, natural gas, coal, water, and uranium. Mr. St. Laurent announced on September 16, 1957, that he would resign as Liberal leader as soon as the party named a successor. The Honorable Lester B. Pearson was elected as Liberal leader on January 16, 1958, at the convention in Ottawa. Anxious to strengthen the position of his administration in the House of Commons, Mr. Diefenbaker announced the dissolution of Parliament on February 1, 1958. Despite national unemployment which had reached serious proportions by December, 1957, the Conservatives won a tremendous victory in the election of March 31, 1958. The Conservatives secured 209 seats while the Liberals held only 48 and the C.C.F. 8. The Conservatives won 50 seats out of 75 in Quebec, and every seat but one in the prairie provinces.

EXTERNAL AFFAIRS

In the field of international relations Canada continued to play a creditable role and made a distinct contribution to the maintenance of world peace. In the Korean War the Canadian infantry brigade served in the Commonwealth Division from 1950 until the conclusion of hostilities in 1953. The withdrawal of Canadian troops began in 1954 and was virtually complete by April of 1955, except for a small token force. The Canadians had suffered 1,642 casualties, of which 309 were killed in action or died of wounds and 91 died from nonbattle causes.

Just as Canadian involvement in Korea was coming to an end, Canada assumed new responsibilities in 1954 in the supervision of the armistice in Indochina. In Indochina the French had been fighting the communist Viet Minh for seven long years. Early in 1954 the Viet Minh had made alarming progress in Vietnam in the direction of the Red River Delta and Hanoi. At the Geneva Conference which sat from April to July, 1954, negotiations for a cease-fire were carried on by Great Britain, France, Russia, the Peoples' Republic of China, and the Indochinese Associated States. A cease-fire was finally arranged on July 20. The settlement consisted of three agreements for Vietnam, Laos, and Cambodia respectively. Vietnam was to be partitioned, roughly along the seventeenth parallel, between Northern Vietnam which was given to the Communist Viet Minh, and Southern Vietnam. In Laos and Cambodia the existent regimes were recognized by the Communists; the Viet Minh troops were to be withdrawn.

The Canadian government, which had taken little interest in the settlement, suddenly became involved on July 21 when Canada was invited by Eden and Molotov, the co-chairmen of the Geneva Conference, to serve on the three international commissions which were being set up to supervise the execution of the armistice agreement. India and Poland were also invited to participate. While the invitation posed grave problems for Canada, the Canadian government eventually decided to accept. The reasons were indicated by L. B. Pearson, the Secretary of State for External Affairs, on July 28:

Canada is geographically remote from Indochina and her collective security responsibilities in Southeast Asia are limited to those that arise from membership in the United Nations. We know from experience, however, that just as local conflicts can become general war, so conditions of security and stability in any part of the world serve the cause of peace everywhere. If, therefore, by participating in the work of these Indochinese Commissions, Canada can assist in establishing such security and stability in Southeast Asia, we will be serving our own country, as well as the cause of peace.

The actual execution of the cease-fire agreements was the work of the two sides directly concerned, the French and the Viet Minh, functioning through Joint Commissions. The functions of the international commissions were supervisory, judicial, and mediatory. They carried on those supervisory activities through the use of inspection teams, some of them mobile and some operating at fixed points. The international commissions functioned fairly smoothly in spite of some obstruction by the Poles and by the local authorities in Vietnam. In the 300 days ending on May 18, 1955, over 800,000 persons moved from North to South Vietnam and some 2500 from South Vietnam to North Vietnam. The record of the Canadians on the commissions was one of tact and discretion and of courageous adherence to the cause of justice, in the face of grave difficulties.

During the 1950's Canada and the United States worked together even more closely than before in the development of measures for the defense of North America. The two countries cooperated in the construction of two chains of radar stations, Pine Tree Line and Distant Early Warning Line (Dew Line), to provide warning of the approach of enemy aircraft from the north. Canada also built a third, the Mid-Canada Line, or McGill Fence. In 1957, a joint air defense command [NORAD] was provisionally set up with Canada as the junior member and with headquarters at Colorado Springs. The supreme commander was an American, General Earle Partridge; the deputy commander was a Canadian, Air Marshal Roy Slemon. The joint command was formally established by an exchange of notes between the Canadian and United States governments on May 12, 1958.

Canada continued to play an active part in the deliberations of the United Nations. Canada served on the Disarmament Commission of the United Nations and on the subcommittee of the Disarmament Commission which was set up on April 19, 1954. The Canadian resolution on disarmament at the ninth session of the U.N. General Assembly received Russian support and was passed on November 4, 1954. It referred the question of disarmament back to the Disarmament Commission and gave directions as to the types of disarmament which the Commission should consider. Although the resolution produced no very positive result it possessed one distinction. It was the first time since 1946 that the U.S.S.R. had joined the Western powers in sponsoring a disarmament resolution.

Canada gained considerable honor from the passage of the so-called package deal which effected the entry of sixteen nations to the United Nations at the end of 1955. This achievement was largely the result of a vigorous campaign by the Honorable Paul Martin, the chairman of the Canadian delegation to the Assembly. When the tenth Assembly was convened in the autumn of 1955, Canada circulated a draft resolution informally among the members of the United Nations. The resolution provided for the admission of all the current applicants with the exception of Korea and Vietnam. The response indicated that this resolution would have strong support in the Assembly. In December, 1955, Canada and twenty-seven other nations introduced a resolution calling on the Security Council to consider the application of eighteen countries for admission. The resolution was approved by the Assembly on December 8 by 52 to 2, with 5 abstentions. When the question was considered by the Security Council on December 13, Nationalist China appeared to have wrecked the scheme by vetoing the admission of Outer Mongolia. Russia then vetoed the admission of thirteen non-Communist countries. Just when all seemed lost, Russia proposed a compromise measure providing for the admission of sixteen of the eighteen applicants. Outer Mongolia and Japan were to be excluded. This measure was passed by the Security Council on December 14 and shortly afterwards by the General Assembly. Canadians felt some regret that Russia had the honor of proposing the successful resolution; but Canada derived added prestige from her part in the negotiations.

Canada's most notable contribution to world peace came after the outbreak of hostilities in the Middle East in October, 1956. The Israeli invasion of Egypt had been followed by the commencement of British and French occupation of the Suez Canal area. The Canadian government regretted Israeli and also British and French intervention. Mr. St. Laurent, the prime minister, declared on November 4, 1956:

> Though we recognize the vital importance of the Canal to the economic life and international responsibilities of the United Kingdom and France, we could not but regret also that, at a time when the United Nations Security Council was seized of the matter, the United Kingdom and France felt it necessary to intervene with force on their own responsibility.

In spite of this attitude, Canada abstained from supporting the United States resolution which was passed in the Assembly of the United Nations on November 2. The resolution called for the prompt withdrawal of forces from Egyptian territory and the end of military shipments to the area. In explaining the Canadian abstention, Mr. Pearson expressed regret that the Assembly had not, before taking the vote, devoted more attention to the best means of effecting a cease-fire. On November 3, Mr. Pearson introduced his notable resolution requesting the Secretary General to submit within forty-eight hours a plan for the dispatch of a United Nations force to the Middle East to secure and supervise the cease-fire arrangements. He intimated that the Canadian government would be willing to recommend Canadian participation in the force. Mr. Pearson's resolution passed the Assembly early in the morning of November 4 without a single dissenting vote. The resultant dispatch of the United Nations Emergency Force was an important contribution to the re-establishment of peace in the Suez area. The Nobel Peace Prize was awarded to Mr. Pearson in 1957 in recognition of his personal services to the cause of world peace. It was also a recognition of the increased stature of Canada.

CHAPTER XXXIII

Canada in the 1960's

The story of Canada in the 1960's is one of solid economic and social achievement, accompanied by the challenge of many perplexing problems. The challenge of Quebec separatism, the protests of Canadians from the Prairies and from the Atlantic provinces inveighing against regional economic disparities, and the discontent of Canada's native people, Indians and Eskimos, continued to perplex Canadian administrators and to make the future uncertain. Student unrest, both in schools and universities, perturbed school administrators and governments.

The economic progress of the country was sufficiently obvious. The gross national product, which had been $12 billion in 1946 and $24 billion in 1954, rose to $35 billion in 1960 and $57.7 billion in 1966. Total exports which had averaged $1.2 billion in 1926–29 and which had been $3.6 billion in 1954, rose to $5.3 billion in 1960 and $10.3 billion in 1966.

The growth of population kept pace with Canada's economic expansion. Canada's population which had been 10,377,000 in 1931 rose to 18,238,247 in 1961 and to 20,015,000 in 1966. These people consisted of persons of British descent, French Canadians, and Europeans in the approximate proportion of nine, six, and five. The last group consisted mainly of Scandinavians, Germans, Italians, Netherlanders, Poles, and Ukrainians. The native peoples of Canada comprised some 225,000 Indians and 13,000 Eskimos.

Trade union membership kept pace with the expansion of business, although membership did not rise very sharply in the 1960's. Total union membership reached 1,446,000 by 1960 and exceeded 1,500,000 in 1966. In 1966 of trade union members 85 percent were in one or other of the great labor federations, the Canadian Labor Congress (CLC) or the Confederation of National Trade Unions (CNTU).

The decade of the 1960's was characterized by great progress in the field of social legislation. The passage of the Canada Pensions Act in 1965, the Medical Care Insurance Act in 1966, and the vast increase in federal assistance to schools and universities were cases in point. Yet Canadians seemed more impressed by their problems than by their legislative achievements.

🍁 THE QUEBEC CHALLENGE

Problems posed by French Canada were a dominating factor of Canadian politics from 1960 on. At the end of the 1950's relations between French-speaking and English-speaking Canadians appeared to be comparatively amicable. As late as March 1961 a federal cabinet minister, J. W. Pickersgill, was able to congratulate the country on the placidity of the Quebec situation. Speaking at Bishop's University on March 17, 1961, Mr. Pickersgill said that Canada's greatest accomplishment in the 1950's was the establishment of a "bicultural, biracial and-to-some-extent-bilingual society." There was much evidence to support this judgment in 1961, but developments in the ensuing decade were to indicate profound French-Canadian dissatisfaction not only with the position of French culture in Canada as a whole, but also with the situation in Quebec itself.

As early as 1960 a movement had emerged in Quebec provincial politics stemming from the discontent of French Canadians with the state of their own province, and particularly with alleged English dominance in Quebec. The movement became politically effective with the election to office of the Liberals under Jean Lesage on June 22, 1960.

Under Lesage the Quebec government entered upon the "Quiet Revolution." Lesage headed a cabinet composed of young, able ministers who began a program calculated to realize the potential of French Canada and to ensure the principle of *"maîtres chez nous."* The program was particularly inspired by René Lévesque, minister of natural resources 1960–65, and minister of welfare 1965–66, and Paul Gérin-Lajoie, minister of education.

The policy of the Quebec Liberals was different from that of their predecessors in office, the Union Nationale. Duplessis, the great leader of the Union Nationale until his death in 1959, had been a great champion of French culture and French provincial rights, but he had always cultivated good relations with English-Canadian, British, and American business interests and had opposed the idea of government control of industry. Unlike Duplessis, the Lesage administration favored government participation in the economic affairs of the province. On November 14, 1962, Lesage won a second election in which the principal issue was his proposal to nationalize the Quebec hydroelectric companies. The result was the nationalization of eleven power companies and the formation of Quebec Hydro.

Inspiring the policy of the Lesage government was a strong nationalist element which was determined not only that French-Canadians should have more control over the Quebec economy but also that the French language should secure more recognition in the business life of the province. The great spokesman of this aspect of government policy was René Lévesque who asserted in 1966:

Our long-range and not-so-long-range objective is to take over the economic life of Montreal as of the rest of the province on the basis of something comparable to what we represent in the province because people are more important than businesses, and as people we are 80 percent. And no self-respecting people in the world would ever accept to be something like a servant in his own homeland.

The educational reforms of the Lesage government stemmed not from a reaction against English control, but from general discontent with the state of education in Quebec. This discontent was expressed in witty form in a volume which appeared in 1960 called *The Impertinences of Brother Anonymous*. The author, a Catholic teacher, Brother Jean-Paul Désbiens, had made an effective and searching critique of the educational system of Quebec.

The Lesage administration stood for greater governmental participation in education. A large-scale policy of school development and reorganization was heralded by a Royal Commission under Monseigneur A. M. Parent. The commission presented reports in 1963, 1964, and 1966 recommending a thorough revision of the Quebec system of education, including the appointment of a minister of education to coordinate and to promote educational services at all levels. Under Gérin-Lajoie the provincial department of education was reorganized and unified. In secondary education school districts were reorganized, and a policy of building centralized schools at the collegiate level was developed. Government control over the universities was also extended.

The policy of the Lesage government was moderate in the sense that its exponents proposed to improve the position of the French within the framework of Confederation; but a more extreme, separatist movement, favoring the independence of Quebec, made its appearance in 1961.

The most substantial advocate of separatism was Dr. Marcel Chaput, a federal civil servant, who resigned from his post to press the cause of Quebec separatism. He concluded the fifth section of his book, *Why I Am a Separatist* (1961) by rejecting the invitation of other

Canadians to the separatists to remain in Confederation. He said: "The whole of Quebec would reply in chorus: No, thank you. We like you fine as a neighbour, but we prefer to govern ourselves. We do not wish to become a minority."

An extremist organization, the Front de libération québecois, or the F.L.Q., became active in the spring of 1963 and caused a number of bomb explosions. After 1963 the bomb outrages abated temporarily, but the ferment of discussion continued. The visit of Queen Elizabeth to Quebec City in October 1964 was attended by separatist demonstrations.

In the election of June 5, 1966, the Lesage administration was defeated by the Union Nationale led by Daniel Johnson. Under the Johnson administration the "quiet revolution" was continued, although its progress was less spectacular than under Lesage.

FEDERAL POLITICS:
THE DIEFENBAKER ADMINISTRATION

The administration of John G. Diefenbaker (1957–63) was less obviously concerned with the problem of French Canada than was its successor, the Pearson administration. Indeed, failure to maintain support in Quebec eventually helped to bring about Mr. Diefenbaker's defeat, but the administration had other achievements to its credit.

The administration was largely dominated by the prime minister. Diefenbaker, a colorful and dynamic personality, was a superb political campaigner and perhaps the most effective debater in the Canadian House of Commons in modern times.

Diefenbaker's career in office was marked by the passage of a Bill of Rights which received the Royal Assent on August 10, 1960. Although its operation was limited to the area within the jurisdiction of the federal government, the Bill of Rights was a notable statement of the rights guaranteed to Canadians: liberty, security of the person, enjoyment of property, and freedom of religion, speech, assembly, and association. Diefenbaker's tenure of office was also marked by important steps in the development of the Canadian North and by a significant change of policy in the field of dominion-provincial relations. The administration increased blind disability and war veterans' pensions and twice increased old-age pensions. The government's "roads to resources" policy of improving access to Canada's natural resources made some appeal to Canadians.

In foreign policy the Diefenbaker government effected a considerable change. Canadian foreign policy became more vigorously nationalist.

In 1961–62 Diefenbaker was extremely critical of Britain's proposed entry into the European Common Market on the ground that it would have serious economic repercussions in Canada. He made a scathing denunciation of the projected British entry, at the Prime Ministers' Conference of September 1962. The policy of the administration toward the United States was characterized by a certain nationalist independence. Although the administration had negotiated the establishment of the North American Defense Command (Norad) in 1957–58, it also carried out policies unacceptable to the United States. Canada's policy of business as usual, pursued with Castro's Cuba, after the application of an American embargo in 1960, and Canada's large wheat sales to Communist China beginning in January 1961, both ran counter to United States policy. Reluctance to accept nuclear warheads for Bomarc missiles in Canada involved Diefenbaker in controversy with elements in his own party as well as with the Liberals and, to some extent, with the Kennedy administration in the United States. The controversy over warheads was a factor in the defeat of the Diefenbaker administration in the House of Commons on February 5, 1963.

FEDERAL POLITICS: THE PEARSON ADMINISTRATION

The administration headed by Lester B. Pearson, who took office on April 22, 1963, was competent in spite of some major errors in tactics, such as the handling of the budget in 1963.

One of Pearson's major achievements was the adoption of a Canadian flag. The Prime Minister's announcement on May 17, 1964, that the government favored a flag with a maple leaf design touched off a vigorous discussion in Parliament and in the country. Many Canadians were reluctant to adopt a flag which did not contain the Union Jack. Finally, on the night of December 11–12 the motion in favor of a flag with a single maple leaf design passed the House of Commons. The debate had taken thirty-seven days of the 1964 session.

The Pearson administration had an impressive record in the social welfare field. The Canada Pension Plan, passed in 1965, was coordinated with the Quebec Pension Plan to provide one nationwide system of contributory pensions. In 1966 the government won consent for the Canada Assistance Plan, a consolidation and extension of programs to provide public allowances to underpaid groups. The Medical Care Insurance Act, passed in December 1966, provided large-scale federal assistance to the provinces on condition that they introduced medical care schemes which fulfilled certain requirements laid down by the federal government. Many of the provinces made objections and when the scheme came into effect on July 1, 1968, only Saskatchewan and British Columbia participated; but by the end of the decade most of the provinces accepted the plan.

During the first three months of 1966 the debate in the House of Commons centered around national security and especially as it concerned the cases of George Victor Spencer and Gerda Munsinger. Spencer, a postal clerk in British Columbia, had been discharged for providing information to a foreign power in order to assist in the establishment of an espionage network. Gerda Munsinger, a German woman who had been in Canada in 1955–61 was suspected of espionage activities in Europe prior to her arrival. Having been associated with a federal cabinet minister during her stay in Canada, she was regarded as a security risk. The Liberals and the Conservatives accused each other of laxity in regard to questions of security in these two cases. The debates in the House of Commons were bitter and time-consuming and showed the House at its worst. Two Royal Commissions respectively upheld the government and censured the Conservative opposition.

Pearson made a determined effort to alleviate French-Canadian grievances in regard to alleged unfair treatment under Confederation. With this end in view the government in July 1963 appointed the Royal Commission on Bilingualism and Biculturalism, under the co-chairmanship of André Laurendeau of Montreal, an editor of *Le Devoir,* and Davidson Dunton, president of Carleton University in Ottawa. The commission was instructed "to inquire into and report upon the existing state of bilingualism and biculturalism in Canada and to recommend what steps should be taken to develop the Canadian Confederation on the basis of an equal partnership between the two founding races." Account was to be taken of the contribution made by other ethnic groups to the cultural enrichment of Canada.

In October 1967 the commission presented its first report, recommending "that English and French be formally declared the official languages of the Parliament of Canada, of the federal courts, of the federal government, and of the federal administration." The report also recommended that Ontario and New Brunswick, which had large French-speaking minorities, should recognize English and French as official languages. It was also recommended that any province whose "official" (i.e., English or French) minority had reached 10 percent of the population should recognize both languages as "official." In a second report issued in December 1968 the commission set forth the right of all Canadians to have their children educated in the "official" language of their choice and made recommendations in regard to the schools and universities necessary to make this possible.

Pearson's final step in the direction of good relations between the English and the French in Canada was the Dominion-Provincial Conference, which was held in Ottawa from February 5 to 7, 1968, shortly before he vacated office. Discussion at the conference in regard to the position of Quebec in Confederation was vigorous. Premier Daniel Johnson demanded much greater powers for Quebec in the fields of international affairs, social welfare, and broadcasting. These demands were opposed by Minister of Justice Pierre Elliott Trudeau. Premier Ernest Manning of Alberta asserted that his province was not prepared to accept fundamental constitutional changes without precise knowledge of the extent of Quebec's demands. The conference ended by endorsing the findings of the Royal Commission on Bilingualism and Biculturalism and asserted that "French-speaking Canadians outside Quebec should have the same rights as English-speaking Canadians in Quebec."

Under the Liberals, Canadian-American relations entered a more placid phase than had existed under Diefenbaker. Canada accepted nuclear arms when negotiations with the government of the United States were completed on August 16, 1963. Canada was to secure from the United States nuclear weapons for the Bomarc B, and also in Europe for the Voodoo interceptor, the Honest John artillery rocket, and the CF-104 Starfighter strike-reconnaissance aircraft. Relations with the United States, however, were not entirely amicable. In April 1965 Pearson incurred the obvious displeasure of President Lyndon Johnson by suggesting in a speech the advisability of a temporary halt to American bombing in Viet Nam.

The Pearson administration extended Canada's peace-keeping role. In 1964 Canada gave strong assistance to U Thant, the secretary general of the United Nations in organizing a peace-keeping force in Cyprus to contain hostilities between Cypriot Greeks and Turks. Out of a force of about 6200 men, Canada contributed some 1150.

THIRD PARTIES

While the Liberals and Conservatives held the center of the stage in federal politics, the C.C.F. and Social Credit parties went through a process of reorganization. Both were more successful in provincial than in federal politics.

In the summer of 1961 the C.C.F. was reorganized as the New Democratic Party (N.D.P.), and developed a closer liaison with the trade unions. Its program still laid great emphasis upon policies of social amelioration, including full employment through economic planning, subsidized job training, and expansion of public and cooperative ownership of utilities. T. C. Douglas, who had been premier of Saskatchewan since 1944, succeeded M. J. Coldwell as leader. In his speech to the delegates at the Ottawa Convention following his election as leader August 3, 1961, Douglas made a vigorous attack on the free enterprise system and asserted: "What Canada needs, says the New Democratic Party, is a planned economy which will stimulate economic growth and make available to the people of this land the goods and services which technological advancement now makes possible."

Under Douglas' leadership, the N.D.P. preserved a respectable position in the House of Commons, securing nineteen seats in 1962, seventeen seats in 1963, twenty-one in 1965, and twenty-two in 1968.

In Saskatchewan, where the N.D.P. (under the name C.C.F.) had been in power for sixteen years, Woodrow Lloyd succeeded Douglas as premier in 1961. Under Lloyd the administration became involved in a bitter controversy over its scheme of medical care. Passage of the Saskatchewan Medical Care Insurance Act in 1961 produced vigorous opposition from Saskatchewan doctors. The opponents of the act organized groups such as the Keep Our Doctors Committee, which conducted vigorous agitation. When the bill went into effect on July 1, 1962, many doctors closed their offices, although essential medical services were maintained in the hospitals. Eventually, Lord Stephen Taylor, a British physician, negotiated an agreement on July 23, 1962, between the Saskatchewan government and the Saskatchewan Council of the College of Physicians and Surgeons. Two years later, on April 22, 1964, the Lloyd administration was defeated by the Liberals under Ross Thatcher, a former member of the C.C.F. The Liberals secured thirty-three seats to twenty-two for the N.D.P.

However, the N.D.P. captured power in Manitoba in 1969. E. R. Schreyer, who had been head of the N.D.P. only since June 7, 1969, led the party to an upset victory over the Conservative government of Premier Walter Weir on June 25, 1969. Schreyer's party elected one less than a majority in the Manitoba legislature, but was joined shortly after the election by the Independent member for Churchill, Manitoba.

The Social Credit Party suffered from the friction between Quebec and the rest of Canada. Owing to the division between its Quebec and western wings, the party, in federal politics, was split in two. The Social Credit Party secured thirty seats in the election of 1962, but twenty-six of these were in Quebec. The leader of the Quebec group in federal politics, Réal Caouette, emerged as a dynamic and colorful personality who made an especial appeal to the unskilled workers and farmers in the province. After 1962 the federal Social Credit Party declined in power in Western Canada, but continued to prosper in Quebec. Relations between Robert Thompson, the leader of the party, and Caouette, were far from cordial after the 1962 election. In September 1963 Caouette and twelve Quebec supporters left the Social Credit Party and assumed the designation Le Ralliement des Créditistes. Thompson remained as leader of the Social Credit Party, which became a western group with eleven seats in the House of Commons. In 1965 Thompson secured five seats in the House of Commons and Caouette, nine. In 1968 the western Social Credit group failed to elect any members to the House of Commons, as Thompson had been elected as a Progressive-Conservative. Caouette and Le Ralliement des Créditistes elected fourteen members.

Meanwhile, the provincial Social Credit governments continued in power under W. A. C. Bennett in British Columbia and Ernest Manning in Alberta. In December 1968 Manning was succeeded by Harry E. Strom as leader of the provincial party and premier of Alberta.

EDUCATION

Reference has been made to the educational reforms in Quebec, but indeed there were important developments in education throughout Canada. The prevailing tone of education in Canadian primary and secondary schools continued to be progressive. In spite of determined and often enlightened opposition from educational conservatives, Canadian primary and secondary education continued to be widely influenced by the ideas of the American pragmatist John Dewey and by the school of progressive educators who reflected his thought.

In 1968 a provincial committee on education in Ontario, headed by Mr. Justice E. M. Hall and L. A. Dennis published a significant report. The Hall-Dennis report reflected, as its title *Living and Learning* indicated, the progressive trend in Canadian education. The report was characterized by the traditional emphasis of the Progressive on a child-centered school in which the teacher maintains a democratic relationship and "guides" but does not "indoctrinate." The report denigrated the grade system and the concept of failing or passing and insisted: "One of the fundamental issues facing Ontario schools is the shift of focus from structured content to the child, or young person, as an individual learner" (p. 169).

Canadian universities continued to expand in size and numbers during the 1960's. University enrollment, which totaled 65,000 in 1955, reached 114,000 in 1960 and 232,000 in 1967. In 1966–67 there were nearly four hundred institutions of higher learning in Canada, of which about fifty, exclusive of twenty theological schools, had degree granting powers. A number of new universities were established, either as new organizations or as coordinating existent colleges. Laurentian University was established in 1960 at Sudbury, Ontario, by federating l'Université de Sudbury and Huntingdon College, a United Church institution. Laurentian represented an interesting venture in bilingualism. In 1959–60 complicated negotiations among the educational institutions in the Kitchener-Waterloo area culminated in the emergence of two universities, Waterloo Lutheran University and the University of Waterloo. Other foundations followed, including the University of Guelph, established in 1964 by the union of the Ontario Agricultural College, Ontario Veterinary College, Macdonald Institute, and a new arts college, Wellington College.

In the period after 1945 governments increased their financial support of universities and also gradually increased their control of them. In 1948–49 eight principal Canadian universities derived 56 percent of their income from fees, 32 percent from provincial governments, and 10 percent from the federal government in the form of veterans' allowances. In 1952 the federal government began to give large, regular subsidies to the universities. In general, however, the role of the provinces was greater than that of the federal government in financing the universities. Thus, in 1963–64, out of a total operating university income of $276.8 million, the provinces contributed $110.8 million and the federal government $50.6 million. In the same year the provinces contributed 60.7 percent of the capital funds of the universities compared to 7.7 percent from the federal government. Increasing financial assistance was accompanied by increasing control by provincial governments of budgets, building programs, and other features of university policy. In 1964 the Ontario government established the Department of University Affairs, an indication of the size and importance of the government's relations with fourteen Ontario universities.

The universities themselves accomplished a great deal in organizing interuniversity associations. The Association of Universities and Colleges of Canada (A.U.C.C.), originally organized in 1911 as the National Conference of Canadian Universities (N.C.C.U.), operated for "the promotion of higher education in all its forms in Canada." The Association became a quasi-accrediting body, since admission to its membership constituted a form of official recognition. The Canadian Association of University Teachers (C.A.U.T.) was organized in 1950 as a body working in the interests of the professional members in the universities. Meetings of the "Learned Societies" annually, at one or other of the university centers, in Canada became an important element in the development of a university community in Canada. Originally begun by the Royal Society of Canada and the Canadian Historical Association, the meetings came to include a large number of learned societies concerned with particular disciplines.

Regional associations among Canadian universities also began to be formed in the 1960's, such as the Committee of Presidents of the Universities of Ontario, formed in 1962 to represent the universities in dealings with the provincial government. The committee made important progress in coordinating work among the universities, particularly at the graduate level. There was some regional cooperation in other parts of Canada also. The western universities combined to open a veterinary college at Saskatoon in 1969.

While university administrators moved toward consolidation there were demands in the universities for more control by staff and students. These demands were given impetus in 1966 by the Duff-Berdahl Report, *University Government in Canada.* The report was the work of a commission sponsored by the Canadian Association of University Teachers and the Association of Universities and Colleges of Canada. In this intellectual climate suggesting more control by staff and students in the universities, Canadian students began to demand more student participation in university administration at every level of university organization. Their demands met with considerable success. A report in *University Affairs* published by the A.U.C.C. in July 1969 gave an account of student progress in university administration. Out of forty-four institutions reporting, students had representation on the senate or an equivalent body in eighteen, and representation on the board of governors or an equivalent body in nine. The students were also represented on important committees, such as those to choose new presidents at the University of British Columbia and the Regina Campus of the University of Saskatchewan. For the most part Canadian universities escaped demonstrations similar to those which had partly disrupted the universities of the United States in 1968–69. One important exception was the serious situation arising out of the demonstration at Sir George Williams University in Montreal on February 11, 1969.

The Canadian Union of Students (C.U.S.), which emerged in 1963 after a reorganization of the older National Federation of Canadian University Students, provided an important mouthpiece for student reformers. Although it was weakened somewhat by the secession of the Quebec universities, Laval, Montreal, and Sherbrooke in 1964, C.U.S. conducted a vigorous campaign in 1965 for free tuition in the universities. C.U.S. was divided between the advocates of purely university reform and those desiring the advocacy of social and political reform beyond the limits of the university. Thus, the annual convention at Port Arthur, Ontario, in September 1969 was sharply divided between "radical leftist groups" who demanded uncompromising revolutionary stands and those who wished to concentrate upon the problems of the universities.

✵ FEDERAL POLITICS AT THE END OF THE DECADE, 1967-70

In the final stages of the period Canadian affairs were still largely dominated by the grievances of Quebec; but there were other grievances, too, in Canada, and to some extent they stemmed from what was regarded as the preferred role being given to Quebec. Western protests were largely the result of a desire for better fiscal treatment at the hands of the federal government. Manitoba resented the proposal of Air Canada to shift its overhaul base from Stevenson's Field, Winnipeg, to Dorval, Quebec. When the transfer was first announced in 1962, the Manitoba government began a determined struggle to prevent it. A federal commission was set up in 1965 to consider the issue, and though the controversy continued for some years it appeared more and more unlikely that Manitoba would be able to prevent the transfer, which was finally effected in 1969. The Maritime Provinces, like the West, resented the extent of federal help to Quebec and demanded more assistance from Ottawa.

Canada's Indians and Eskimos promoted a movement toward the reestablishment of their distinctive cultures and a throwing off of governmental controls. The Indians were anxious to retain their reserves but to secure complete autonomy. They were not satisfied with such measures as the federal Indian Act of 1951, which gave a degree of self-government to the Indians.

To cope with these continuing problems, the major political parties elected new leaders in this period. The Conservatives replaced Diefenbaker on September 9, 1967, with Robert L. Stanfield, the premier of Nova Scotia. Diefenbaker had become unpopular with a considerable section of the party, particularly in the urban parts of eastern Canada, where his predilection for grass-roots agrarianism had always been suspect. The Quebec issue was much in the foreground at the convention which elected Stanfield. The Conservatives had held a study conference at Montmorenci, Quebec, on August 6-10, 1967, and had endorsed the so-called two-nations principle, based upon the idea of one federal political system containing a country in which there were two "nations," that is, cultural and linguistic groups. Diefenbaker roundly condemned the two-nations principle. In an interview in Ottawa, reported in the Toronto *Globe and Mail* on September 2, 1967, Diefenbaker asserted:

I say at once that insofar as the problem of national unity is concerned, the expression of the viewpoint, the acceptance of the concept of two nations, is contrary to every principle that this party has stood for for 100 years and more.

Diefenbaker took the same stand at the Conservative Convention, but his eloquent speech did not prevent Stanfield's election as leader.

The Quebec question was a dominant issue at the Liberal Convention in April 1968 when Pierre Elliott Trudeau was elected leader in succession to L. B. Pearson. Trudeau's election as leader was partly a result of his charismatic charm and his ability to enlist the personal support of delegates, particularly the younger ones. While he was minister of justice in the Pearson administration, Trudeau had attracted national attention by opposing the claims for special status for Quebec in Confederation, which Prime Minister Daniel Johnson, the Quebec premier, put forward at the Dominion-Provincial Conference on February 6, 1968. Trudeau was widely regarded as an opponent of the two-nation theory as expounded by the Conservatives. He was also identified with the cause of social reform.

The federal election in June 1968 was fought largely on the merits of the two-nation theory, with Marcel Faribault, an able Montreal business executive, running in Quebec as a leading Conservative exponent of the theory. Trudeau opposed the two-nation theory but identified himself with the slogan "the just society." He asserted in a Liberal campaign pamphlet published in 1968:

I believe in progress. I believe in change—I believe we must experiment with our times and risk some solutions which may not be comfortable but are necessary to put us into the world of tomorrow instead of staying with the world of yesterday.

The election on June 25, 1968, resulted in a decisive Liberal victory. The Liberals won 155 seats, the Conservatives 72, the N.D.P. 22, and the Créditistes 14. For the first time since their accession to office in 1963 the Liberals constituted a majority government.

After the 1968 election the Trudeau administration continued its concern for domestic issues, particularly the problems posed by the desire for bilingualism and biculturalism in Canada and the demands of the Western and the Atlantic provinces for a better fiscal position. The Dominion-Provincial Conference of February 1969 indicated the difficulties and desires of the federal government. Before the conference the prime ministers of the three prairie provinces dispatched telegrams to Ottawa demanding that the discussion of fiscal matters be placed on the agenda. Discussion at the conference indicated Trudeau's concern for the problem of bilingualism and the insistence of the Western provinces for a greater degree of tax-sharing between Ottawa and the provincial governments. The Atlantic provinces also shared in the demand for an improved financial position, insisting upon the principle of regional economic equality.

The conclusions reached by the conference were less significant than the problems it considered. For the most part the prime ministers merely provided for further discussion. It was resolved to reconvene the federal-provincial tax-structure committee to reconsider the problem of tax-sharing. The conference also resolved to establish committees of ministers to consider regional economic disparities and another committee of ministers to consider the recommendations of the Royal Commission on Bilingualism and Biculturalism.

On July 9, 1969, however, the Royal Assent was given to Trudeau's Official Languages Act, securing the language rights of English or French minorities in relation to the federal administration in bilingual districts across Canada.

The preoccupation of the Trudeau administration with domestic policy involved some change in Canadian foreign policy. Since 1945 Canadian policy had been characterized by strong support of NATO and extensive participation in peace-keeping activities, notably in Germany, Korea, Egypt, the Congo, and Cyprus. Shortly after his assumption of office, Trudeau began to canvass the possibility of Canada withdrawing troops from the NATO force in Europe. After considerable delay in proclaiming a clear-cut policy, Trudeau gave an interview on April 3, 1969, in which he asserted that his government had decided on continuing Canadian membership in NATO, but in a phased reduction of Canadian European commitments. The prime minister asserted that Canada needed forces in Canada "in order to carry out a wide range of activities involving the defense of the country." He said further, "The Canadian Government intends on consultation with Canada's allies, to take early steps to bring about a planned and phased reduction of the size of the Canadian forces in Europe." On April 23 Trudeau asserted that Canada would soon end its nuclear role in Europe and put more money in foreign aid.

The policy of disengagement was unacceptable to Canada's NATO allies. Thus, two British cabinet ministers, Denis Healey and Michael Stewart, warned in Ottawa in March 1969 that any reduction in Canada's commitment to NATO could have far-reaching and even dangerous results. After the Canadian announcement of phased reductions at the meeting of the NATO Council in Washington in April 1969, the Council's communiqué administered a rebuke which was not the less significant because it was couched in diplomatic language. The Council asserted that "the allies participating in the NATO integrated defense program agreed it was extremely important that during an era of negotiations the defense posture of the alliance should not be relaxed and that premature expectation of solutions to outstanding questions should not be generated."

In Canada there was much soul-searching in regard to Trudeau's modification of traditional Canadian foreign policy. The Commons Committee on External Affairs on March 26, 1969, presented a report insisting upon the continuation of the Canadian military role in NATO, presumably without any reduction, until the mid-1970's. The committee asserted "that the military strength of the Warsaw Pact is greater today than ever before, and that NATO continues to offer the most effective means of providing for the security of Western Europe." On April 14 the Leader of the Opposition, Robert L. Stanfield, opposed the government proposals, insisting in the House of Commons that the decision to reduce troop commitments in NATO had weakened chances of negotiating an East-West détente. Within the government party itself there was a sharp division of opinion. One of its results was the resignation on April 7 of Senator John Black Aird, a prominent Liberal and former treasurer of the party, from the chairmanship of the Canadian NATO Parliamentary Association.

In spite of this opposition the government proceeded with its policy of disengagement in Europe and on September 19, 1969, announced that Canada's land and air forces in Europe would be reduced from 9800 to 5000 by the fall of 1970.

Proposed Canadian withdrawal in Europe was not accompanied by any increase in Canadian participation in the politics of the Western Hemisphere. Canada still remained outside the Organization of American States, in spite of strong appeals from President John F. Kennedy during his visit to Ottawa, May 16–18, 1961, that Canada should join. The reasons for Canada's nonparticipation were convincingly set forth by a Canadian political scientist, Eugene Forsey, in a letter to the Toronto *Globe and Mail* on March 17, 1969:

If we went into the OAS, wouldn't the United States always expect us to line up on its side of any controversy, and wouldn't the Latin-Americans always expect us to line up on their side? If we supported either, we should incur the wrath of the other; if we merely abstained, we should incur the wrath of both. And what would we accomplish?

🍁 FRENCH-ENGLISH RELATIONS AT THE END OF THE DECADE

The problem of relations between English-speaking and French-speaking Canadians continued to perplex the country to the end of the decade. In spite of the attempts of the Bilingualism and Biculturalism Commission at conciliation, many developments in 1967–68 aggravated relations between Quebec and the rest of Canada. The visit of President Charles de Gaulle to Quebec and his utterance at Montreal on July 24, 1967, "Vive le Québec libre," excited great enthusiasm in the province and comparable dismay in Ottawa. On October 14, 1967, René Lévesque, the most dynamic of the Quebec Liberals, broke with the Quebec Liberal Party and declared himself in favor of separatism. Lévesque then formed a separatist party, the Mouvement Souveraineté Association, which in August 1968 merged with another separatist group, the Ralliement National led by Gilles Grégoire.

Protests about grievances on the part of French Canadians had their effect on English-speaking and moderate French-Canadian opinion. Prime Minister Manning of Alberta wrote to the joint chairmen of the Bilingualism and Biculturalism Commission asserting that any extension of the French language in areas beyond those in which it was guaranteed official status at the time of Confederation would impair Canadian unity. The Quebec Federation of Protestant Home and School Associations in 1965 took firm ground against the expression of French Canadian grievances, asserting that "French Canadian isolation, insecurity and insularity spring from certain factors which French Canada chose as being necessary or desirable for its own particular development or its way of life." Moderate French Canadian opinion favored greater privileges for Quebec and the French language, while opposing separatism. In accordance with this policy the Quebec Liberal Party on October 14, 1967, at its provincial convention, strongly repudiated separatism.

Indications that many French Canadians did not want a bilingual Quebec but a unilingual one with French as the dominant language created resentment and fear among the English in the province. They were particularly alarmed by the developments in St. Léonard in 1968–69. St. Léonard, a suburb of Montreal had a large population of Roman Catholic Italian immigrants who were anxious that their children become English-speaking. On June 10, 1968, representatives of a French nationalist organization, Le Mouvement pour l'Integration Scolaire won control of the St. Léonard Catholic school board. The object of the group was to promote the education in French of all Quebec children not of English, Irish, or Scottish descent. The St. Léonard Catholic school board began the policy of abolishing instruction in the English language, in stages, beginning with grade one in the autumn of 1968. In spite of vigorous protests from the Italian minority the board adhered to its policy. Mr. Jean-Guy Cardinal, the minister of education, failed to interfere. There were moves against the English minority in other districts, particularly in La Prairie and Hull. Jean-Jacques Bertrand, who succeeded Daniel Johnson as prime minister of Quebec in September 1968, attempted to safeguard the language of English-speaking groups by introducing a language rights bill in the Quebec legislature on December 9, 1968. The bill would have given statutory guarantees to the English minority by allowing parents the right to have their children taught in either French or English; but, in the face of vigorous opposition outside and within his party, Bertrand withdrew the bill on March 19, 1969.

CONCLUSION

In 1967 Canadians celebrated the one-hundredth anniversary of Canada as a united country in a great series of centennial projects. The most notable of these was the World Exposition, commonly called Expo '67, which was held in Montreal. The conspicuous impressiveness of Expo stimulated the national pride of Canadians and increased Canada's stature in the minds of many foreign peoples.

After this year of rejoicing Canadians took stock of their situation. They faced the future with some concern. The decade of the 1960's had been less placid than the 1950's. The chapter in this volume on the 1950's is mainly an account of solid economic progress; but this was not the distinctive note of the 1960's. The dominant theme of this decade had been protest and controversy.

Yet many Canadians were proud of Canada's solid achievements since 1867 and during the last decade. They were confident that the Canadian federation, put together in 1867 and extended and consolidated over the years, would survive the challenge of centrifugal forces. While some Canadians were speaking in divisive terms, many others were convinced that the Canadian experiment in nationhood would in the end prevail. They were determined that the country would remain, in the language of the British North America Act, "one Dominion under the name of Canada."

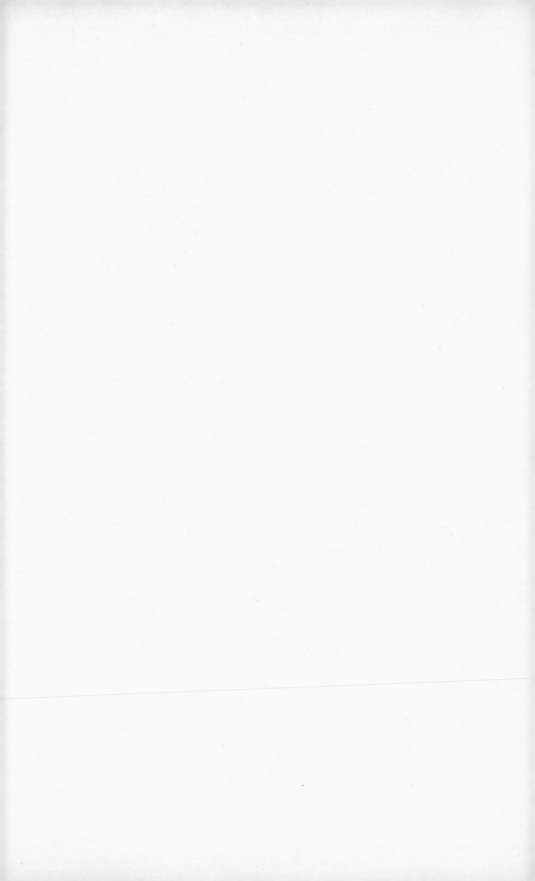

SUGGESTED READINGS

Readers who would like to investigate other views or special subjects may be guided by the following bibliographical notes. They are necessarily selective, are confined largely to recent works in English, and include few of the hundreds of articles in which original research has been recorded, but many of them provide guidance to that underlying scholarship. For convenience, general works are followed by special works, introduced under the first chapter to which each is applicable.

GENERAL WORKS

The principal works of reference are: *Canada Year Book* (Ottawa), an annual statistical abstract of remarkable coverage and timely special articles; W. S. Wallace (ed.), *Encyclopedia of Canada* (7 vols.; Toronto, 1935–49) and *Dictionary of Canadian Biography* (2 vols.; Toronto, 1945); John E. Robbins (ed.), *Encyclopedia Canadiana* (10 vols.; Ottawa, 1957–58); and the articles, reviews, and cumulative bibliographies of history, social studies, and literature provided by *Canadian Historical Review, Canadian Journal of Economics and Political Science,* and *University of Toronto Quarterly,* each published quarterly by the University of Toronto Press.

Among the more recent single-volume histories of Canada are *Canada and Newfoundland (Cambridge History of the British Empire,* vol. VI, Cambridge, Eng., 1930); Carl F. Wittke, *History of Canada* (New York, 1941); A. L. Burt, *Short History of Canada for Americans* (Minneapolis, Minn., 1944); D. G. Creighton, *Dominion of the North* (Boston, 1944); A. R. M. Lower, *Colony to Nation* (Toronto, 1946); Edgar McInnis, *Canada* (New York, 1947); and Jean Bruchési, *History of Canada* (Toronto, 1950). A useful topical, but rather slightly historical, examination of modern Canada by a large group of specialists and containing a critical bibliography is G. W. Brown (ed.), *Canada* (Berkeley, 1950). André Siegfried, *Canada* (New York, 1949) is also chiefly contemporary analysis.

Special aspects of Canadian history as a whole are dealt with in: W. L. Grant (ed.), *Makers of Canada* (rev. ed., 12 vols.; Toronto, 1926); Mason Wade, *The French Canadians, 1760–1945* (Toronto, 1956); R. Blanchard, *L'est du Canada français* (Montreal, 1935) and *Le centre du Canada français* (Montreal, 1947); M. Giraud, *Le Métis Canadien* (Paris, 1945); A. M. Tory (ed.), *History of Science in Canada* (Toronto, 1939); National Gallery of Canada, *Development of Painting in Canada, 1665–1945* (Toronto, 1945); V. C. Fowke, *Canadian Agricultural Policy* (Toronto, 1946); A. H. Gosselin, *L'église du Canada* (4 vols.; Quebec, 1911–17); W. T. Easterbrook and H. G. J. Aitken, *Canadian Economic History* (Toronto, 1956); S. D. Clark, *The Social Development of Canada* (Toronto, 1942) and *Church and Sect in Canada* (Toronto, 1948); D. C.

Harvey, *The Colonization of Canada* (Toronto, 1936); M. L. Hansen and J. B. Brebner, *The Mingling of the Canadian and American Peoples* (New Haven, 1940); W. P. M. Kennedy, *The Constitution of Canada* (Oxford, 1938); H. L. Brittain, *Local Government in Canada* (Toronto, 1951); H. A. Innis, *The Cod Fisheries* (Toronto, 1954); C. W. Jefferys, *Picture Gallery of Canadian History* (3 vols.; Toronto, 1942–50); G. P. de T. Glazebrook, *History of Transportation in Canada* (Toronto, 1938) and *History of Canadian External Relations* (Toronto, 1950); J. B. Brebner, *North Atlantic Triangle: The Interplay of Canada, the United States, and Great Britain* (New Haven, 1945); and Gustave Lanctot and others, *Les Canadiens français et leurs voisins du sud* (Montreal, 1941). A. R. M. Lower, *Canadians in the Making* (Toronto, 1958) is a pioneer work in Canadian social history.

CHAPTER I. LAND AND ABORIGINES

New national atlases of Canada and the United States which will, by overlapping and other devices, be accommodated to each other, are now in preparation. Since the old ones are outdated, use must be made of maps in current official publications such as the *Canada Year Book* and *Canada: Descriptive Atlas* (Ottawa, 1951); Henri Baulig, *Généralités—Canada* (*Amérique septentrionale,* vol. I, Paris, 1935); Griffith Taylor, *Canada* (London, 1947); D. F. Putnam *et al., Canadian Regions* (Toronto, 1952); A. W. Currie, *Economic Geography of Canada* (Toronto, 1945); Geological Survey of Canada, *Geology and Minerals of Canada* (Ottawa, 1947); and Diamond Jenness, *The Indians of Canada* (Ottawa, 1932).

CHAPTER II. EUROPE REPELLED

J. B. Brebner, *The Explorers of North America, 1492–1806* (New York, 1955).

CHAPTER III. EUROPE STRIKES ROOTS

H. A. Innis, *The Fur Trade in Canada* (Toronto, 1956); Morris Bishop, *Champlain* (New York, 1948); J. B. Brebner, *New England's Outpost: Acadia before the Conquest of Canada* (New York, 1927); T. H. McGrail, *Sir William Alexander* (Edinburgh, 1940); and M. H. Long, *New France* (*History of the Canadian People,* vol. I, Toronto, 1943). E. E. Rich, general editor of the Hudson's Bay Record Society, will shortly publish a systematic history of the Hudson's Bay Company. See also Douglas Mackay under Chapter IX.

CHAPTER IV. FRENCH NORTH AMERICA

G. L. Nute, *Caesars of the Wilderness* (New York, 1943); and Benoît Brouillette, *La pénétration du continent américain par les Canadiens français* (Montreal, 1939). There is no adequate biography of La Salle, but Jean Delanglez indicates the recent scholarship concerning him in *Life and Voyages of Louis Jolliet* (Chicago, 1948).

CHAPTER V. GREAT BRITAIN CLOSES IN

L. H. Gipson, *The British Empire before the American Revolution* (9 vols.; New York, 1936–56); Guy Frégault, *La civilisation de la Nouvelle-France* (Montreal, 1944); G. S. Graham, *Empire of the North Atlantic* (Toronto, 1950); a systematic study of Samuel Vetch by G. M. Waller will soon be published; meanwhile see *Dictionary of American Biography*, XIX, pp. 260–62. Alan Gowans, *Church Architecture in New France* (Toronto, 1955).

CHAPTER VI. BRITISH NORTH AMERICA

A. L. Burt, *The Old Province of Quebec* (Minneapolis, 1933); J. B. Brebner, *The Neutral Yankees of Nova Scotia* (New York, 1937); D. G. Creighton, *The Commercial Empire of the St. Lawrence, 1760–1850* (Toronto, 1937); L. B. Namier, *England in the Age of the American Revolution* (London, 1930); H. H. Peckham, *Pontiac and the Indian Rising* (Princeton, N.J., 1947).

CHAPTER VII. PARTITION AGAIN

G. M. Wrong, *Canada and the American Revolution* (New York, 1935); A. L. Burt, *The United States, Great Britain and British North America* (New Haven, Conn., 1940); G. S. Graham, *British Policy and Canada, 1774–1791* (London, 1930); Chilton Williamson, *Vermont in Quandary* (Montpelier, Vermont, 1949).

CHAPTER VIII. THE PARTITION CONFIRMED

G. S. Graham, *Sea Power and British North America, 1783–1820* (Cambridge, Mass., 1941); F. Landon, *Western Ontario and the American Frontier* (Toronto, 1941); J. W. Pratt, *The Expansionists of 1812* (New York, 1925); R. A. MacKay (ed.), *Newfoundland* (Toronto, 1946).

CHAPTER IX. PARTITION IN THE WEST

A. S. Morton, *History of the Canadian West to 1870–71* (London, *c.* 1938) and *Sir George Simpson* (Toronto, 1944); K. W. Porter, *John Jacob Astor* (2 vols.; Cambridge, Mass., 1931); Douglas Mackay, *The Honourable Company* (Indianapolis, Ind., 1936); J. P. Pritchett, *The Red River Valley, 1811–1849* (New Haven, 1942); Frederick Merk (ed.), *Fur Trade and Empire* (Cambridge, Mass., 1931).

CHAPTER X. EMPIRE AND NEIGHBORHOOD

R. L. Schuyler, *The Fall of the Old Colonial System* (New York, 1945); D. C. Masters, *The Reciprocity Treaty of 1854* (London, 1937); A. K. Weinberg, *Manifest Destiny* (Baltimore, Md., 1935); A. B. Corey, *The Crisis of 1830–1842 in Canadian-American Relations* (New Haven, Conn., 1941); J. B. Brebner, "Patronage and Parliamentary Government," *Report of the Canadian Historical Association* (Toronto, 1938); H. T. Manning, "The Colonial Policy of the Whig Ministers, 1830–37" *Canadian Historical Review* (Sept. and Dec., 1952).

CHAPTER XI. NEWFOUNDLAND

Väinö Tanner, *Newfoundland-Labrador* (2 vols.; Cambridge, Eng., 1947); A. H. McLintock, *The Establishment of Constitutional Government in Newfoundland, 1783–1832* (London, 1941).

CHAPTER XII. NOVA SCOTIA

The bulletins, publications, and reports of the Public Archives of Nova Scotia (Halifax, since 1933) contain much new basic scholarship, for instance, that of D. C. Harvey, J. S. Martell, C. B. Fergusson, Margaret Ells, and Mrs. R. G. Flewelling used in this chapter, but this and other new knowledge and interpretation for the period since 1783 has not yet been systematically drawn together in a general history.

V. L. O. Chittick, *Thomas Chandler Haliburton* (New York, 1924); W. L. Grant, *The Tribune of Nova Scotia* (Toronto, 1926); S. A. Saunders, *Studies in the Economy of the Maritime Provinces* (Toronto, 1939); T. H. Raddall, *Halifax* (Toronto, 1948); F. W. Wallace, *Wooden Ships and Iron Men* (London, 1924) and *In the Wake of the Wind Ships* (Toronto, 1927).

CHAPTER XIII. PRINCE EDWARD ISLAND

A. B. Warburton, *History of Prince Edward Island* [to 1831] (Saint John, 1923); D. Campbell, *History of Prince Edward Island* (Charlottetown, 1875); and F. MacKinnon, *The Government of Prince Edward Island* (Toronto, 1951).

CHAPTER XIV. NEW BRUNSWICK

Miss K. F. C. MacNaughton's *Education in New Brunswick, 1784–1900* (Fredericton, 1947) transcends its title, particularly before 1865, by providing critical and well-informed general history. J. Hannay, *History of New Brunswick* (2 vols.; Saint John, 1909); E. C. Wright, *The Miramichi* (Sackville, N.B., 1945), *The Petitcodiac* (Sackville, N.B., 1946), *The St. John* (Toronto, 1950), *The Loyalists of New Brunswick* (Ottawa, 1955); H. W. Davis, *The St. Croix* (Orono, Me., 1950); W. H. Davidson, *William Davidson* (Saint John, 1947); D. G. G. Kerr, *Sir Edmund Head* (Toronto, 1954).

CHAPTER XV. LOWER CANADA

Thomas Chapais, *Cours d'histoire du Canada* (8 vols.; Quebec, 1919–34); G. Filteau, *Histoire des patriotes* (3 vols.; Montreal, 1938–42); C. P. Lucas (ed.), *Lord Durham's Report on the Affairs of British North America* (3 vols.; Oxford, 1912); C. W. New, *Lord Durham* (Oxford, 1929); A. R. M. Lower, *The North American Assault on the Canadian Forest* (Toronto, 1938); A. Faucher, "The Decline of Shipbuilding at Quebec in the Nineteenth Century," *Canadian Journal of Economics and Political Science*, May, 1957.

CHAPTER XVI. UPPER CANADA

Aileen Dunham, *Political Unrest in Upper Canada, 1815–36* (London, 1927); William Smith, *Political Leaders in Upper Canada* (Toronto, 1931); E. C. Guillet, *The Great Migration* (Toronto, 1937) and *The Lives and Times of the Patriots* (Toronto, 1938); C. B. Sissons, *Egerton Ryerson* (2 vols.; Toronto, 1937, 1947); A. R. M. Lower, *Settlement and the Forest Frontier in Eastern Canada* (Toronto, 1936); H. G. J. Aitken, *The Welland Canal Company* (Cambridge, Mass., 1954).

CHAPTER XVII. THE WEST

F. W. Howay, H. F. Angus, and W. N. Sage, *British Columbia and the United States* (Toronto, 1942); W. N. Sage, *Sir James Douglas and British Columbia* (Toronto, 1930); F. G. Roe, *The North American Buffalo* (Toronto, 1951).

CHAPTER XVIII. THE CANADIAN KEYSTONE

G. N. Tucker, *The Canadian Commercial Revolution, 1845–51* (New Haven, 1936); A. J. M. Smith, *The Book of Canadian Poetry* (Chicago, 1943); E. D. Adams, *Great Britain and the American Civil War* (2 vols.; London, 1925); D. G. Creighton, *John A. Macdonald* (2 vols.; Toronto, 1952, 1955).

CHAPTER XIX. A MARI USQUE AD MARE

W. M. Whitelaw, *The Maritimes and Canada before Confederation* (Toronto, 1934); D. G. Creighton, *British North America at Confederation* (Ottawa, 1939); R. G. Trotter, *Canadian Federation* (Toronto, 1924); C. P. Stacey, *Canada and the British Army, 1846–71* (London, 1936); L. H. Jenks, *The Migration of British Capital to 1875* (New York, 1927); O. D. Skelton, *The Life and Times of Sir A. T. Galt* (Toronto, 1920); G. F. G. Stanley, *The Birth of Western Canada* (London, 1936); L. B. Shippee, *Canadian-American Relations, 1849–74* (New Haven, Conn., 1939); Allan Nevins, *Hamilton Fish* (New York, 1937); Chester Martin, *Foundations of Canadian Nationhood* (Toronto, 1955). One of the best brief accounts of Canadian politico-economic development, 1867–1939, is contained in volumes I and II of the *Report of the Royal Commission on Dominion-Provincial Relations* (Ottawa, 1939).

CHAPTER XX. INTEGRATION VS. DISINTEGRATION

L. J. Burpee, *Sandford Fleming* (London, 1915); G. M. Grant, *Ocean to Ocean* (Toronto, 1873); H. A. Innis, *History of the Canadian Pacific Railway* (Toronto, 1923); A. S. Morton, *History of Prairie Settlement* (Toronto, 1938); P. F. Sharp, *Whoop-Up Country* (Minneapolis, Minn., 1955).

CHAPTER XXI. EMERGENCE OF A NEW SYMBOL

Fred Landon, "The Canadian Scene, 1880–1890," *Report of the Canadian Historical Association* (Toronto, 1942); D. C. Masters,

The Rise of Toronto, 1850–1890 (Toronto, 1947); J. E. Tyler, *The Struggle for Imperial Unity, 1868–1895* (London, 1938); B. H. Brown, *The Tariff Reform Movement in Great Britain, 1881–1895* (New York, 1943); C. M. MacInnes, *In the Shadow of the Rockies* (London, 1930); O. D. Skelton, *Life and Letters of Sir Wilfrid Laurier* (2 vols.; Toronto, 1921); W. J. Wilgus, *The Railway Interrelations of the United States and Canada* (New Haven, Conn., 1937).

CHAPTER XXII. A PROFITABLE NATIONAL ECONOMY

H. A. Innis, *Settlement and the Mining Frontier* (Toronto, 1936); D. A. MacGibbon, *The Canadian Grain Trade* (Toronto, 1932); R. F. Grant, *The Canadian Atlantic Fishery* (Toronto, 1934); W. A. Carrothers, *The British Columbia Fisheries* (Toronto, 1941); "The Growth of Population in Canada," *Seventh Census of Canada* (1931), vol. I (Ottawa, 1936); G. A. Cuthbertson, *Freshwater* (Toronto, 1931); W. Havighurst, *The Long Ships Passing* (New York, 1942); E. S. Moore, *American Influence in Canadian Mining* (Toronto, 1941); W. R. Plewman, *Adam Beck and the Ontario Hydro* (Toronto, 1947).

CHAPTER XXIII. THE CANADIAN PEOPLES

A. Siegfried, *The Race Question in Canada* (London, 1907); A. R. M. Lower, "Two Ways of Life," *Report of the Canadian Historical Association* (Toronto, 1943); W. A. Mackintosh and W. L. G. Joerg (eds.), *Canadian Frontiers of Settlement* (8 vols.; Toronto, 1934–38) deals chiefly with the plains, and volumes IV (W. A. Mackintosh), V (R. W. Murchie), VI (C. A. Dawson and R. W. Murchie), VII (C. A. Dawson), and VIII (C. A. Dawson and E. R. Younge) are especially concerned with settlement in its relatively recent economic and social aspects; F. P. Grove, *Over Prairie Trails* (Toronto, 1929) and *Fruits of the Earth* (Toronto, 1933); H. A. Logan, *Trade Unions in Canada* (Toronto, 1948).

CHAPTER XXIV. POTENTIAL INDEPENDENCE

John Buchan, *Lord Minto* (London, 1924); R. M. Dawson, *The Development of Dominion Status, 1900–1936* (Oxford, 1937); J. M. V. Foster, "Reciprocity and the Joint High Commission, 1898–99," *Report of the Canadian Historical Association* (Toronto, 1939); R. A. Mackay and E. B. Rogers, *Canada Looks Abroad* (Toronto, 1938); J. W. Dafoe, *Clifford Sifton* (Toronto, 1931); L. E. Ellis, *Reciprocity, 1911* (New Haven, Conn., 1939); H. Borden (ed.), *Robert Laird Borden: His Memoirs* (2 vols.; Toronto, 1938); C. J. Chacko, *The International Joint Commission* (New York, 1932); V. K. Johnston, "Canada's Title to the Arctic Islands," *Canadian Historical Review*, March, 1933; R. M. Dawson, *The Civil Service of Canada* (Toronto, 1939).

CHAPTER XXV. THE TESTS OF WAR

Sir Charles Lucas (ed.), *The Empire at War* especially vol. II by F. H. Underhill (5 vols.; London, 1921–26); C. P. Stacey, *The Military Problems of Canada* (Toronto, 1940); G. N. Tucker, *The Naval Service of Canada* (2 vols.; Ottawa, 1952); E. H. Armstrong, *The Crisis of Quebec, 1914–18* (New York, 1937); G. M. Weir, *The Separate School Question in Canada* (Toronto, 1934); R. L. Borden, *Canadian Constitutional Studies* (Toronto, 1922) and *Canada in the Commonwealth* (Oxford, 1929); D. Carnegie, *History of Munitions Supply in Canada, 1914–19* (London, 1925); J. J. Deutsch, "War Finance and the Canadian Economy, 1914–21," *Canadian Journal of Economics and Political Science,* Nov. 1940; J. A. Corry, *The Growth of Government Activities since Confederation* (Ottawa, 1939); H. Marshall, F. A. Southard, and K. W. Taylor, *Canadian-American Industry* (New Haven, Conn., 1936); C. D. Blyth, *The Canadian Balance of International Payments* (Ottawa, 1949); C. L. Cleverdon, *The Woman Suffrage Movement in Canada* (Toronto, 1950).

CHAPTER XXVI. FIRST STEPS

Thorough biographies of Borden and Meighen are as yet lacking. The first volume of what will be for some time the standard life of King has been published:—R. M. Dawson, *William Lyon Mackenzie King, A Political Biography 1874–1923* (Toronto, 1958). See also Bruce Hutchison, *The Incredible Canadian* [King] (London, 1952); H. S. Ferns and B. Ostry, *The Age of Mackenzie King* [to 1919] (London, 1955); A. Meighen, *Unrevised and Unrepented* (Toronto, 1949); J. B. Brebner, "Canada, the Anglo-Japanese Alliance, and the Washington Conference," *Political Science Quarterly,* March, 1935; G. M. Carter, *The British Commonwealth and International Security, 1919–39* (Toronto, 1947); A. R. M. Lower, *Canada and the Far East* (New York, 1940); C. J. Woodsworth, *Canada and the Orient* (Toronto, 1941).

CHAPTER XXVII. VULNERABLE STRENGTH

D. C. Masters, *The Winnipeg General Strike* (Toronto, 1950); H. S. Patton, *Grain Growers' Cooperation in Western Canada* (Cambridge, Mass., 1928); W. L. Morton, *The Progressive Party in Canada* (Toronto, 1950); W. K. Rolph, *Henry Wise Wood* (Toronto, 1950); S. M. Lipset, *Agrarian Socialism* (Berkeley, 1950); G. E. Britnell, *The Wheat Economy* (Toronto, 1939); the succinct contrast provided by A. Maheux, *Canadian Unity: What Keeps Us Apart?* (Quebec, 1944) and L. A. Groulx, *Why We Are Divided* (Montreal, 1944); F. B. Housser, *A Canadian Art Movement* (Toronto, 1926); M. K. Strong, *Public Welfare Administration in Canada* (Chicago, 1930); C. Mc-Naught, *Canada Gets the News* (Toronto, 1940); M. E. Nichols, *CP —The Story of the Canadian Press* (Toronto, 1948); H. G. Skilling, *Canadian Representation Abroad* (Toronto, 1945).

CHAPTER XXVIII. DEPRESSION AND SECTIONALISM

H. A. Innis and A. F. W. Plumptre (eds.), *The Canadian Economy and Its Problems* (Toronto, 1934); H. M. Cassidy, *Social Security and Reconstruction in Canada* (Toronto, 1943) and *Public Health and Welfare Organization* (Toronto, 1945); L. Gérin, *Le type économique et social des Canadiens* (Montreal, 1938); E. Minville, *Labour Legislation and Social Services in the Province of Quebec* (Ottawa, 1939); J. M. Jones, *Tariff Retaliation* (Philadelphia, 1934); W. K. Hancock, *Problems of Economic Policy, 1918–39* (vol. II of *Survey of British Commonwealth Affairs,* London, 1940); *Report of the Royal Commission on Dominion-Provincial Relations* (3 vols. and appendices; Ottawa, 1939–40); *Newfoundland Royal Commission, 1933, Report* (London, 1933); F. H. Soward and A. M. Macaulay, *Canada and the Pan-American System* (Toronto, 1948); F. H. Soward *et al., The Pre-war Years* (vol. I of *Canada in World Affairs,* Toronto, 1941); W. A. Riddell, *World Security by Conference* (Toronto, 1947); C. B. Macpherson, *Democracy in Alberta* (Toronto, 1953).

CHAPTER XXIX. THE FORCING-FRAME OF WAR

E. C. Hughes, *French Canada in Transition* (Chicago, 1943); The following volumes in *Canada in World Affairs* (Toronto, 1943–50): vol. II, *Two Years of War, 1939–1941,* by R. M. Dawson; vol. III, *September, 1941, to May, 1944,* by C. C. Lingard and R. G. Trotter; vol. IV, *From Normandy to Paris, 1944–1946,* by F. H. Soward; C. P. Stacey, *The Canadian Army, 1939–45* (Ottawa, 1948) which is a brief preliminary to the *Official History of the Canadian Army in the Second World War* (in progress; I, 1955, II, 1956); Joseph Schull, *The Far Distant Ships* (Ottawa, 1950); *The R.C.A.F. Overseas* (3 vols.; Toronto, 1944–49); T. Sheard, "The B.C.A.T.P. and Defence Policy," *International Journal,* Winter, 1946–47; W. Eggleston, *Scientists at War* (Toronto, 1950); R. W. James, *War-time Economic Cooperation* (Toronto, 1949); C. A. Dawson (ed.), *The New North-West* (Toronto, 1947); F. E. La Violette, *The Canadian Japanese and World War II* (Toronto, 1948).

CHAPTER XXX. A MIDDLE POWER

The Canadian Institute of International Affairs, Toronto, not only produces the current series, *Canada in World Affairs,* noted under XXVIII and XXIX, but publishes a quarterly, *International Journal.* See also F. H. Soward and E. W. McInnis, *Canada and the United Nations* (New York, 1956); and H. F. Angus, *Canada and the Far East, 1940–53* (Toronto, 1953). The Department of External Affairs, Ottawa, issues a monthly, *External Affairs.* R. M. Dawson, *The Government of Canada* (Toronto, 1947); M. Lamontagne, *Le fédéralisme canadien* (Quebec, 1954).

CHAPTER XXXI. NATIONALITY IN DIVERSITY

Historical and critical writings about Canadian culture have been somewhat unsatisfactory because of the ethnic divisions, self-consciousness, and timidity until relatively recent times. *French-Canadian Backgrounds* (Toronto, 1940) by O. Maurault, *et al.*, and also J. C. Falardeau (ed.), *Essais sur le Québec contemporain* (Quebec, 1953) afford significant contrasts. Bruce Hutchison, *The Unknown Country* (Toronto, 1948) stresses the diversity; Vincent Massey, *On Being Canadian* (Toronto, 1948) underestimates it; and L. A. Pierce, *A Canadian People* (Toronto, 1945) laments it. E. K. Brown, *On Canadian Poetry* (Toronto, 1944) is illuminating. The serious periodicals, *Dalhousie Review* (Halifax), *Revue de l'Université Laval* (Quebec), *Culture* (Quebec), *Relations* (Montreal), *Revue de l'Université d'Ottawa*, *Queen's Quarterly* (Kingston), and *University of Toronto Quarterly* publish little that is experimental in arts and letters, but *Canadian Forum* (Toronto), *Northern Review* (Montreal), *Canadian Review of Music and Art* (Toronto), and *Here and Now* (Toronto) are all alert to the contemporary. *Canadian Geographical Journal* (Ottawa) and *Beaver* (Winnipeg) are unusually good illustrated magazines. D. W. Buchanan (ed.), *From Paul Kane to the Group of Seven* (vol. I of *Canadian Painters*, Oxford, 1945) contains excellent reproductions and it is to be hoped that the series will be continued. W. Kirkconnell and A. S. P. Woodhouse, *The Humanities in Canada* (Ottawa, 1947); J. B. Brebner, *Scholarship for Canada* (Ottawa, 1945). *Report: Royal Commission on National Development in the Arts, Letters and Sciences, 1949–1951* and its supplement, *Royal Commission Studies* (both Ottawa, 1951), constitute the most systematic and comprehensive account yet given, together with urgent recommendations for change.

CHAPTER XXXII. CANADA IN THE 1950'S

Canada Year Books; Royal Commission on Canada's Economic Prospects (Ottawa, Preliminary Report, 1956; Final Report, 1957); *Canada in World Affairs*, vol. VII, *September, 1951 to October, 1953*, by B. S. Kierstead (Toronto, 1956), vol. VIII, *1953 to 1955*, by Donald C. Masters (Toronto, 1959); Lester B. Pearson, *Democracy in World Politics* (Princeton and Toronto, 1955). The Department of External Affairs, Ottawa, issues a number of publications, including the annual *Canada and the United Nations;* the annual *Report of the Department of the External Affairs; External Affairs*, a monthly bulletin; and *Canadian Weekly Bulletin*. The Department releases *Statements and Speeches* periodically in multigraphed form.

CHAPTER XXXIII. CANADA IN THE 1960'S

J. M. Beck, *Pendulum of Power, Canada's Federal Elections* (Scarborough, 1968); *Canada Year Books*, 1960–1968 (Ottawa); *Canadian*

Annual Review, John T. Saywell ed. (Toronto, 1961–68); *Canadian News Facts,* 3 vols. (Toronto, 1967–69); Ramsay Cook, *Canada and the French-Canadian Question* (Toronto, 1966); Dominion Bureau of Statistics, *Canada 1867–1967* (Ottawa, 1967); James Eayrs, *The Art of the Possible: Government and Foreign Policy in Canada* (Toronto, 1961); Richard Jones, *Community in Crisis: French-Canadian Nationalism in Perspective* (Toronto, 1967); *Living and Learning, The Report of the Provincial Commission on the Aims and Objectives of Education in the Schools of Ontario* (Toronto, 1968) [Hall-Dennis Report]; Arthur R. M. Lower, *Colony to Nation, A History of Canada* (Toronto, 1964); Peyton V. Lyon, *The Policy Question* (Toronto, 1963); D. C. Masters, *Protestant Church Colleges in Canada, A History* (Toronto, 1966); Jon B. McLin, *Canada's Changing Defense Policy* (Toronto, 1967); W. L. Morton, *The Kingdom of Canada* (Toronto, 1969); Peter C. Newman, *Distemper of Our Times* (Toronto, 1968); Peter C. Newman, *Renegade in Power* (Toronto, 1963); Patrick Nicholson, *Vision and Indecision* (Toronto, 1968) [for Diefenbaker and Pearson]; Richard A. Preston, *Canada in World Affairs: 1959 to 1961* (Toronto, 1965); Peter Russell, *Nationalism in Canada* (Toronto, 1966); *University Affairs,* bulletin published nine times a year by the Association of Universities and Colleges of Canada.

INDEX